Ferenczi's Influence on Contemporary Psychoanalytic Traditions

This collection covers the great variety topics relevant for understanding the importance of Sándor Ferenczi and his influence on contemporary psychoanalysis. Pre-eminent Ferenczi scholars were solicited to contribute succinct reviews of their fields of expertise.

The book is divided in five sections. 'The historico-biographical' describes Ferenczi's childhood and student days, his marriage, brief analyses with Freud, his correspondences and contributions to the daily press in Budapest, exploration of his patients' true identities, and a paper about his untimely death. 'The development of Ferenczi's ideas' reviews his ideas before his first encounter with psychoanalysis, his relationship with peers, friendship with Groddeck, emancipation from Freud, and review of the importance of his *Clinical Diary*. The third section reviews Ferenczi's clinical concepts and work: trauma, unwelcome child, wise baby, identification with aggressor, mutual analysis, and many others. In 'Echoes', we follow traces of Ferenczi's influence on virtually all traditions in contemporary psychoanalysis: interpersonal, independent, Kleinian, Lacanian, relational, etc. Finally, there are seven 'application' chapters about Ferenczi's ideas and the issues of politics, gender and development.

Aleksandar Dimitrijević, PhD, is interim professor of psychoanalysis and clinical psychology at the International Psychoanalytic University, Berlin, Germany. He is a member of the Belgrade Psychoanalytical Society (IPA) and Faculty at the Serbian Association of Psychoanalytic Psychotherapists (EFPP), and the editor or co-editor of ten books or special journal issues, as well as author of many conceptual and empirical papers, about attachment theory and research, psychoanalytic education, psychoanalysis and the arts.

Gabriele Cassullo is a psychologist, psychotherapist, doctor in research in human sciences and interim professor in psychology at the Department of Psychology, University of Turin. He researches and publishes on the history, theory, and technique of psychoanalysis.

Jay Frankel is an adjunct clinical associate professor and clinical consultant in the New York University postdoctoral program in psychotherapy and psychoanalysis; faculty at the Institute for Psychoanalytic Training and Research, and at the trauma studies program at the Manhattan Institute for Psychoanalysis, both in New York; associate editor, and previously executive editor, of *Psychoanalytic Dialogues;* co-author of *Relational Child Psychotherapy*; and author of over two dozen journal articles and book chapters, and numerous conference presentations, on topics including the work of Sándor Ferenczi, trauma, identification with the aggressor, authoritarianism, the analytic relationship, play, child psychotherapy, relational psychoanalysis, and others.

"This extraordinarily comprehensive volume, with contributions by a galaxy of leading scholars and clinicians, will become an indispensable resource for all future work on Ferenczi, the most important, influential, and inspiring forerunner of contemporary self psychology, relational psychoanalysis, and trauma theory."

– Peter L. Rudnytsky, University of Florida & Chicago Institute for Psychoanalysis

Lines of Development

Evolution of Theory and Practice over the Decades

Series Editors: Norka T. Malberg and Joan Raphael-Leff

Other titles in the series:

The Klein Tradition: Lines of Development—Evolution of Theory and Practice over the Decades
edited by Kay Long and Penelope Garvey

The Lacan Tradition: Lines of Development—Evolution of Theory and Practice over the Decades
edited by Lionel Bailly, David Lichtenstein and Sharmini Bailly

The Anna Freud Tradition: Lines of Development—Evolution of Theory and Practice over the Decades
edited by Norka T. Malberg and Joan Raphael-Leff

Fairbairn and the Object Relations Tradition
edited by Graham S. Clarke and David E. Scharff

The Winnicott Tradition: Lines of Development—Evolution of Theory and Practice over the Decades
edited by Margaret Boyle Spelman and Frances Thomson-Salo

The W. R. Bion Tradition: Lines of Development—Evolution of Theory and Practice over the Decades
edited by Howard B. Levine and Giuseppe Civitarese

Ferenczi's Influence on Contemporary Psychoanalytic Traditions

Lines of Development—Evolution of Theory and Practice over the Decades

Edited by Aleksandar Dimitrijević, Gabriele Cassullo, and Jay Frankel

Routledge
Taylor & Francis Group
LONDON AND NEW YORK

First published 2018
by Routledge
2 Park Square, Milton Park, Abingdon, Oxon OX14 4RN

and by Routledge
711 Third Avenue, New York, NY 10017

Routledge is an imprint of the Taylor & Francis Group, an informa business

British Library Cataloguing-in-Publication Data
A catalogue record for this book is available from the British Library

Library of Congress Cataloging-in-Publication Data
A catalog record has been requested for this book

ISBN: 978-1-78220-652-1 (pbk)
ISBN: 978-0-4294-4126-4 (ebk)

Typeset in Times New Roman
by Apex CoVantage, LLC

For ease of reading, "he" is used throughout for general reference to the infant, the patient, or the individual, and "she" for general reference to the analyst, or the student, but at any point the opposite gender can be substituted.

Contents

List of Editors xi
List of Contributors xii
Abbreviations xx
Series editors' Introduction xxii
Editors' Introduction xxiv
Prologue xxviii
FRANCO BORGOGNO

PART I
Biographical-Historical 1

Introduction 3

1 Amidst hills, creeks and books Sándor Ferenczi's childhood in Miskolc 6
KRISZTIÁN KAPUSI

2 Ferenczi's Budapest 12
TOM KEVE

3 Ferenczi before Freud 18
GABRIELE CASSULLO

4 Ferenczi and Freud: Subservient disciple to independent thinker 25
LOUIS BREGER

5 Ferenczi's analyses with Freud 30
CARLO BONOMI

6 A fateful quadrangle: Sándor Ferenczi, Sigmund Freud, Gizella Palos-Ferenczi, and Elma Palos-Laurvik 38
EMANUEL BERMAN

7 Ferenczi in and out of correspondence 48
ERNST FALZEDER

8 Ferenczi and the foundation of the international and Hungarian psychoanalytical societies 53
JANOS HARMATTA

9 Ferenczi in early psychoanalytic circles 59
ANNA BENTINCK VAN SCHOONHETEN

10 Ferenczi's work on war neuroses and its historical context 65
ANDREAS HAMBURGER

11 The figure of Sándor Ferenczi in representative organs of the Hungarian press between 1910 and 1933 72
MELINDA FRIEDRICH

12 Georg Groddeck's influential friendship with Sándor Ferenczi 78
CHRISTOPHER FORTUNE

13 Ferenczi's patients and their contribution to his legacy 85
B. WILLIAM BRENNAN

14 Some things you may want to know before reading Sándor Ferenczi's *Clinical Diary* 98
ÉVA BRABANT-GERŐ AND JUDITH DUPONT

15 Ferenczi's untimely death 105
PETER HOFFER

PART II
Clinical 111

Introduction 113

16 Ferenczi's paradigm shift in trauma theory 115
JUDIT MÉSZÁROS

17 Ferenczi's concept of "the unwelcome child" 122
JOSÉ JIMÉNEZ AVELLO

18 Ferenczi's concept of the "wise baby" 129
LUIS MARTÍN CABRÉ

19 Psychological enslavement through identification with the aggressor 134
JAY FRANKEL

20 Splitting, fragmentation, and psychic agony 140
THIERRY BOKANOWSKI

21 Regressing to reality: Finding and listening to the inner world of the traumatised child 147
ELIZABETH HOWELL

22 Ferenczi's experiments with technique 153
ENDRE KORITAR

23 Ferenczi's dialogue of unconsciouses, mutual analysis, and the analyst's use of self in the shaping of contemporary relational technique 159
ANTHONY BASS

24 Countertransference and the person of the therapist 165
IRWIN HIRSCH

PART III
Echoes 169

Introduction 171

25 The Ferenczi—Balint filiation 173
MICHELLE MOREAU RICAUD

26 Ferenczi and the Independents—Bowlby, Fairbairn, and Winnicott: Towards a third way in British psychoanalysis 180
GRAHAM S. CLARKE

27 Melanie Klein's development of, and divergence from, Sándor Ferenczi's ideas 190
LUIS MINUCHIN

28 Sándor Ferenczi and Jacques Lacan: Between orthodoxy and dissidence 196
YVES LUGRIN

29 Mind your tongue! On Ferenczi's confusion of tongues, Laplanche's general theory of seduction, and other "misunderstandings" 201
TIMO STORCK

30 The influence of Ferenczi on Interpersonal Psychoanalysis 206
ROBERT PRINCE

31 Psychoanalysis and psychosis: Ferenczi's influence at Chestnut Lodge 213
ANN-LOUISE SILVER

32 Echoes of Ferenczi in psychoanalytic self psychology: Ancestor and bridge 220
DONNA M. ORANGE

33 Ferenczi's contributions to relational psychoanalysis: The pursuit of mutuality 227
MADELEINE MILLER-BOTTOME AND JEREMY D. SAFRAN

34 The influence of Ferenczi's thinking on child psychoanalysis 232
PATRIZIA ARFELLI AND MASSIMO VIGNA-TAGLIANTI

PART IV
Applications and Extensions 239

Introduction 241

35 "Eat, bird, or die!" The contribution of Sándor Ferenczi's ideas to the critique of authoritarianism 243
ESZTER SALGÓ

36 Against violence: Ferenczi and liberal socialism 248
FERENC ERŐS

37 From individual to massive social trauma 255
CLARA MUCCI

38 Hello Baby. In the footprints of Sándor Ferenczi: Welcoming a child into a contemporary family 262
JULIANNA VAMOS

39 Sándor Ferenczi's impact on clinical social work and education 268
STEVEN KUCHUCK

40 Gender, sexuality, and the maternal 276
JOSETTE GARON

41 "Confusion of tongues" as a source of verifiable hypotheses 282
ALEKSANDAR DIMITRIJEVIĆ

Epilogue: closing thoughts 291
ANDRÉ E. HAYNAL

Index 298

Editors

Aleksandar Dimitrijević, PhD in clinical psychology, is interim professor of psychoanalysis and clinical psychology at the International Psychoanalytic University, Berlin, Germany; member of the Belgrade Psychoanalytical Society (IPA); and faculty at the Serbian Association of Psychoanalytic Psychotherapists (EFPP). He is editor or co-editor of ten books or special journal issues as well as author of many conceptual and empirical papers about attachment theory and research, psychoanalytic education, and psychoanalysis and the arts.

Gabriele Cassullo is a psychologist, psychotherapist, doctor in research in human sciences, and interim professor in psychology in the department of psychology, University of Turin. He researches and publishes on the history, theory, and technique of psychoanalysis.

Jay Frankel is an adjunct clinical associate professor, and clinical consultant, in the New York University postdoctoral programme in psychotherapy and psychoanalysis; faculty at the Institute for Psychoanalytic Training and Research, and at the trauma studies programme at the Manhattan Institute for Psychoanalysis, both in New York; associate editor, and previously executive editor, of *Psychoanalytic Dialogues*; co-author of *Relational Child Psychotherapy*; and author of over two dozen journal articles and book chapters, and numerous conference presentations, on topics including the work of Sándor Ferenczi, trauma, identification with the aggressor, authoritarianism, the analytic relationship, play, child psychotherapy, relational psychoanalysis, and others.

Contributors

Patrizia Arfelli, MD, is a child neuropsychiatrist, and a Tavistock-trained adolescent and child psychoanalytical psychotherapist. She worked as a chief in the inpatient adolescent division of the child neuropsychiatry division of Turin University, where she received extensive experience working with suicidal patients. She was also a court consultant in cases of abused children, and is currently a lecturer at the postgraduate school of clinical psychology at Turin University. She translated into Italian Eric Rayner's *The Independent Mind in British Psychoanalysis* and *The Inner World and Joan Riviere* edited by Athol Hughes. She works in private practice with children, adolescents, and parents, and is particularly interested in traumatised and deprived patients and in adoptive children and families.

José Jiménez-Avello, PhD, is a psychiatrist, psychoanalyst, full member of the International Federation of Psychoanalytic Societies (IFPS). He is the author of *Para leer a Ferenczi* [Reading Ferenczi] (Madrid, Biblioteca Nueva, 1998) and *La isla de sueños de Sándor Ferenczi* [Sándor Ferenczi's Island of Dreams], appearing in French as *L'île des rêves de Sándor Ferenczi* (Campagne Prèmiere, 2013), and articles about Ferenczi published in Spanish, French, English, and German. He is a member of the scientific committee of the International Ferenczi Conferences in Madrid, Torino, Buenos Aires, Budapest, and Toronto, and works in private practice.

Anthony Bass, PhD, is on the faculty of several different institutes and training programmes, including the NYU postdoctoral programme in psychoanalysis, the Columbia University Center for Psychoanalytic Training and Research, the National Institute for the Psychotherapies national training programme, the Institute for Relational Psychoanalysis of Philadelphia, and the Stephen Mitchell Center for Relational Studies, which he co-founded and for which he serves as president. He is an editor in chief of *Psychoanalytic Dialogues, the International Journal of Relational Perspectives*, and a founding director of the International Association for Relational Psychoanalysis and Psychotherapy.

Anna Bentinck van Schoonheten, Phd, is a psychoanalyst in private practice in Amsterdam, member of the Dutch Psychoanalytic Society and the IPA, and president of the board of the *Dutch Journal of Psychoanalysis*. She specialises in the early history of psychoanalysis, with a special focus on Freud and the secret committee. Her latest publication (2016) is *Karl Abraham: Life and Work, a Biography* (London: Karnac).

Emanuel Berman, PhD, is professor emeritus of psychology at the University of Haifa; training and supervising analyst at the Israel Psychoanalytic Society; chief international editor of *Psychoanalytic Dialogues*; editor of Hebrew translations of Freud, Ferenczi,

Balint, Winnicott, Bowlby, Ogden, Aron, Britton and others; recipient of the Sigourney Award; author of *Impossible Training: A Relational View of Psychoanalytic Education* (2004); and editor of *Essential Papers on Literature and Psychoanalysis* (1993). His discussions of Ferenczi's work appeared in journals and books in English, Hebrew, French, Italian, German, Polish, Turkish, and Hungarian.

Thierry Bokanowski is a psychiatrist and psychoanalyst; he is a training and supervising analyst at the Paris Psychoanalytical Society (SPP). He is the author of a large number of articles published in different journals including the *IJP.* He has participated in the publication of numerous collective publications in French and in English. He is the author of several books, *Sándor Ferenczi* (PUF, 1997, third edition); *De la pratique analytique* (PUF, 1998), (*The Practice of Psychoanalysis*, Karnac, 2006); *Le Processus analytique, voies et parcours* (PUF, 2015), (this book, *The Analytical Process: Journeys and Routes* will be published by the IPA (Karnac, 2017).

Carlo Bonomi, PhD, is a training analyst of the Società Italiana di Psicoanalisi e Psicoterapia Sándor Ferenczi (SIP-SF), and a faculty member of the Postgraduate Erich Fromm School of Psychotherapy in Prato, Italy. He is president of the International Sándor Ferenczi Network. He has taught history of psychology and dynamic psychology at the State University of Florence and is a former president of the Centre for Historical Studies of Psychoanalysis and Psychiatry. He is author of *The Cut and the Building of Psychoanalysis, Vol. I, Sigmund Freud and Emma Eckstein* (Routledge, 2015) and *Vol. II Sigmund Freud and Sándor Ferenczi* (Routledge, 2018), (Relational Perspectives Book Series).

Franco Borgogno, is a training and supervising psychoanalyst (SPI/IPA), and a full professor of clinical psychology, teaching at Turin University on grounds of "distinguished renown". He is the author of *Psychoanalysis as a Journey* (1999); *The Vancouver Interview* (2007); *The Girl Who Committed Hara-Kiri and Other Clinical and Historical Essays* (2011); and editor, with P. Bion Talamo and S. A. Merciai, of *W. R. Bion: Between Past and Future* (1999), and, with A. Luchetti and L. Marino Coe, of *Reading Italian Psychoanalysis* (2016). His papers on Ferenczi appeared in journals and books in many languages. He is chair of the IPA committee "Psychoanalysis and the university", and recipient of the Mary Sigourney Award in 2010.

Éva Brabant-Gerő is a psychoanalyst of Hungarian origin, living in France; training analyst at Association de Psychanalyse et d'Anthropologie – Recherche, transmission, échange (Aparté), author of *Ferenczi et l'école hongroise de psychanalyse* (Paris, L'Harmattan, 1993); co-editor of *Sigmund Freud, Sándor Ferenczi, Correspondance* (Paris, Callman-Lévy, 1992, 1996, 2000 – published also in English, German, Spanish, and Hungarian); author of biographical notes about members of the Hungarian school of psychoanalysis in *Dictionnaire International de la Psychanalyse,* under the direction of Alain de Mijolla (Paris, Calmann-Lévy, 2002), including Sándor Ferenczi (Vol. I, pp. 602–604) and Géza Róheim (Vol. II, pp. 1500–1501); editor in chief of the review *Le Coq-Héron*; and author of several papers published in this review.

Louis Breger (born 1935) is an American psychologist, psychotherapist, and scholar. He is emeritus professor of psychoanalytic studies at the California Institute of Technology. He is the author of (among others): *Freud's Unfinished Journey: Conventional and Critical Perspectives in Psychoanalytic Theory* (Routledge & Kegan Paul, 1981); *Feodor*

Dostoevsky: The Author as Psychoanalyst (New York University Press, 1989, reissued by Transaction Publishers, 2009); *Freud: Darkness in the Midst of Vision* (John Wiley & Sons, 2000); *A Dream of Undying Fame: How Freud Betrayed His Mentor and Invented Psychoanalysis* (Basic Books, 2009).

B. William Brennan ThM, MA, LMHC, is a psychoanalyst and psychoanalytic historian in Providence, Rhode Island, USA. He is the co-chair of the History of Psychoanalysis committee of the International Forum for Psychoanalytic Education. His historical research and writing has focused on Ferenczi's American pupils Izette de Forest, Clara Thompson, and the patients in Ferenczi's *Clinical Diary*.

Graham S. Clarke, MA, Tavistock, PhD, University of Essex, visiting fellow at the Centre for Psychoanalytic Studies, University of Essex, UK, is the author of *Personal Relations Theory: Fairbairn, Macmurray, Suttie* (Routledge, 2006), currently being translated into German for publication by Psychosozial-Verlag. He is lead editor of *Fairbairn and the Object Relations Tradition* (Karnac, 2014) in the Lines of Development series. His new book, *Thinking Through Fairbairn*, is due to be published by Karnac Books at the end of 2017.

Judith Dupont-Dormandi, born in 1925 in Budapest (Hungary), living in Paris since 1938, is a doctor in medicine; psychoanalyst member of L'Association psychanalytique de France; literary representative of Sándor Ferenczi; translator of works of Ferenczi, Balint, and several papers by various authors from Hungarian, German, English; author of *Manuel à l'usage des enfants qui ont des parents difficiles* (Le Seuil), translated into several languages, and *Au fil du temps ... Un itinéraire psychanalytique* (Edit. Campagne Première, 2016).

Ferenc Erős studied psychology and literature at the ELTE University in Budapest, and graduated in 1969. He obtained his PhD in 1986, and bears the title "Doctor of the Hungarian Academy of Sciences" (2002). He is professor emeritus at the faculty of humanities of the University of Pécs where he directs a doctoral programme in psychoanalytic studies. The focus of his research includes the social and cultural history of psychoanalysis in Central Europe, and psychoanalytic theory and its application to social issues. He is the author of several scientific books and articles in English, Hungarian, German, and French. He edited the Hungarian translation of the Freud-Ferenczi correspondence, and (with Judit Szekacs-Weisz) *Sándor Ferenczi – Ernest Jones: Letters 1911–1933* (London, Karnac, 2013).

Ernst Falzeder, (born 1955) PhD in psychology (University of Salzburg), is a senior research scholar at University College London. He has more than 200 publications: among them: main editor of the Freud/Ferenczi correspondence (3 vols., Harvard University Press), editor of the Freud/Abraham correspondence (Karnac), translator of Jung's seminars on children's dreams (Princeton), co-editor, with John Beebe, of Jung's correspondence with Hans Schmid-Guisan (Princeton), and author of *Psychoanalytic Filiations* (Karnac).

Christopher Fortune is a historian of psychoanalysis who focuses on Sándor Ferenczi. He has lectured and published internationally in scholarly journals including *Psyche, British Journal of Psychotherapy, Psychoanalysis and History, American Journal of Psychoanalysis*, and *Journal of Analytical Psychology*, and popular journals including *Psychology Today* and *The Village Voice*. He is editor of the *Sándor Ferenczi-Georg Groddeck*

Correspondence: 1921–1933. His original research establishing the identity and background of Elizabeth Severn ("RN") was published in *The Legacy of Sándor Ferenczi: Ferenczi's Turn in Psychoanalysis*, and *100 Years of Psychoanalysis*. He is an associate of the Institute for the Humanities, Simon Fraser University, Vancouver.

Melinda Friedrich, PhD student at the University of Pécs (PhD programme for psychology, theoretical psychoanalysis). Her main research field is the presentation and representation of psychoanalysis in the press and the wider socio-cultural environment in the period before World War Two.

Josette Garon studied philosophy and, after a psychoanalytic training in Paris, now works as a psychoanalyst, psychotherapist, and supervisor. She is a member of the SPM and the IPM (CPS, CIP); director of the IPM and of the CIP; associate editor of the *Canadian Journal of Psychoanalysis;* and has presented papers at many conferences nationally and internationally, especially at the International Ferenczi Conferences. She was co-chair of the International Ferenczi Conference, Toronto, May 2015, and has published many articles in different languages, amongst those in English: "Skeletons in the closet" (*International Forum of Psychoanalysis*, 2004), and "From disavowal and murder to liberty" (*The American Journal of Psychoanalysis*, 2012).

Andreas Hamburger, psychoanalyst (DPG); professor of clinical psychology, International Psychoanalytic University, Berlin; training analyst (DGPT); and supervisor, Akademie für Psychoanalyse und Psychotherapie, Munich, Germany. Current research: Scenic narrative microanalysis, social trauma, psychoanalytic supervision, and film analysis. Recent international books: editor of *La Belle et la Bête – Women and Images of Men in Cinema* (London, Karnac, 2015); editor, with D. Laub, of *Psychoanalysis, Social Trauma and Testimony: Unwanted Memory and the Holocaust* (London, New York, Routledge, 2017); and editor of *Trauma, Trust, and Memory* (London, Karnac, 2017).

János Harmatta, MD, PhD, is associate professor at the Semmelweis University, Budapest; member of the Hungarian Psychoanalytical Society; co-founder and member of the staff of the Sándor Ferenczi Society; honorary president of the Hungarian Psychiatric Society; and head of department for psychosomatics and psychotherapy in the National Institute for Medical Rehabilitation. He is the author of several papers on the history of Hungarian psychoanalysis.

André E. Haynal, MD, philosopher, professor of psychiatry (University of Geneva), psychoanalyst (IPA, Swiss S.), author of more than a dozen books and hundreds of publications, the responsible scientific editor of the Freud/Ferenczi Correspondence (1992–2000). Recipient of the Sigourney Award for his life work. Latest publications: *Disappearing and Reviving* (Karnac, London); and an autobiographic text: *Encounters with the Irrational. My Story* (IPBooks, NYC/US, 2017).

Irwin Hirsch, PhD, is distinguished visiting faculty, William Alanson White Institute; faculty, supervisor, and former director, Manhattan Institute for Psychoanalysis; and adjunct clinical professor of psychology and supervisor, Postdoctoral Program in Psychotherapy and Psychoanalysis, New York University. He is the author of over eighty psychoanalytic articles and book chapters; the 2008 Goethe Award-winning book, *Coasting in the Countertransference: Conflicts of Self-Interest between Analyst and Patient* (Routledge); and *The Interpersonal Tradition: The Origins of Psychoanalytic Subjectivity* (Routledge,

2015). With Donnel Stern he is co-editor of volume one of a two-volume series, *The Interpersonal Perspective in Psychoanalysis, 1960s–1990s: Rethinking Transference and Countertransference* (Routledge, 2017) and the forthcoming *Volume 2: The Interpersonal Perspective in Psychoanalysis, 1980s–2010s: Emerging Interest in the Analyst's Subjectivity* (Routledge, 2018).

Peter T. Hoffer, PhD, is emeritus professor of German at the University of the Sciences in Philadelphia, a fellowship associate member of the Psychoanalytic Center of Philadelphia, and an educator associate of the American Psychoanalytic Association. He is co-translator (with Axel Hoffer) of Sigmund Freud's *A Phylogenetic Fantasy: Overview of the Transference Neuroses* and translator of the three-volume *Correspondence of Sigmund Freud and Sándor Ferenczi* and Richard Sterba's *Handwörterbuch der Psychoanalyse* (Dictionary of Psychoanalysis). He is also the author of several published papers on the history of psychoanalysis.

Elizabeth Howell is on the editorial board of the *Journal of Trauma and Dissociation*, faculty for the New York University postdoctoral programme in psychotherapy and psychoanalysis, and faculty and supervisor, trauma programme, Manhattan Institute for Psychoanalysis. Her award-winning books include: *The Dissociative Mind*; *Understanding and Treating Dissociative Identity Disorder: A Relational Approach*; and (edited, with Sheldon Itzkowitz), *The Dissociative Mind in Psychoanalysis: Understanding and Working with Trauma*. She has written over thirty articles on trauma and dissociation.

Krisztián Kapusi, MA, is a historian-archivist in Miskolc, Hungary. Articles in English: "Books and mud" (about the Ferenczi family in Miskolc); "Mama Róza" (Sándor Ferenczi's mother) (*Sándor Ferenczi Returns Home* (2008, Miskolc)); "Toward a biography of Sándor Ferenczi: Footnotes from Miskolc" (*American Imago,* Vol. 66).

Tom Keve has a PhD in crystallography from Imperial College, London and is a fellow of the Institute of Physics. Since retiring from an active career in scientific research and industry, he has become an author, with a special interest in the history of science and the history of psychoanalysis. His book *Triad: the Physicists, the Analysts, the Kabbalists* (in its French translation, *Trois explications du monde*) was shortlisted for the 2010 European Book Prize. Together with Judit Szekacs-Weisz, he co-edited *Ferenczi and his World* as well as *Ferenczi for our Time*, both published by Karnac, London, in 2012.

Endre Koritar is a training and supervising analyst in the Vancouver Institute of Psychoanalysis, a member of the Canadian Psychoanalytic Society, a founding member of the International Sándor Ferenczi Network, and clinical assistant professor of the University of British Columbia. He actively trains candidates in psychoanalytic theory and technique, and psychiatry residents in dynamic psychotherapy. He helps to organise conferences, teaches, and publishes on various themes inspired by Sándor Ferenczi's writings on theory and technique.

Steven Kuchuck, LCSW, is editor-in-chief of *Psychoanalytic Perspectives*; associate editor, Routledge Relational Perspectives Book Series; board member, supervisor, faculty, and co-director of curriculum for the psychoanalytic training programme, National Institute for the Psychotherapies (NIP), and faculty/supervisor at the NIP National Training Program, Stephen Mitchell Relational Study Center, and other institutes. He is president-elect of the International Association for Relational Psychoanalysis and Psychotherapy. His writing focuses primarily on the analyst's subjectivity and, in 2015 and 2016, he won the Gradiva Award for best psychoanalytic books: *Clinical Implications of the Psychoanalyst's Life Experience: When the Personal Becomes Professional* and *The Legacy of Sándor Ferenczi* (co-edited with Adrienne Harris).

Yves Lugrin, PhD, is a clinical psychologist, psychoanalyst, and a member of the Society of Freudian Psychoanalysis (SPF). He has presented papers at many national conferences and is the author of *Impardonnable Ferenczi, malaise dans la transmission* (2012) and *Ferenczi, entre Freud et Lacan* (2017).

Luis Jorge Martín Cabré (Madrid), is a full member and training and supervising analyst of the Psychoanalytic Association of Madrid (APM); training and supervising analyst in child and adolescent psychoanalysis; member of the Institute for the Study of Psychosomatic Medicine; founding member of the International Sándor Ferenczi Foundation; member of the European editorial board of the *IJP*; member of the editorial board of the *American Journal of Psychoanalysis*; member of the training committee of the APM from 1995 to 1997 and from 2002 to 2003; from 2009 to 2013, president of the Psychoanalytic Association of Madrid (APM); and Eurorepresentative member of the board of the IPA from 2014.

Judit Mészáros, PhD, is honorary professor at the Eötvös Loránd University, Budapest; training and supervising analyst at the Hungarian Psychoanalytical Society, and member of the training committee; co-founder and president of the Sándor Ferenczi Society and the International Ferenczi Foundation; author of several books, the latest being *Ferenczi and Beyond: Exile of the Budapest School and Solidarity in the Psychoanalytic Movement during the Nazi Years* (Karnac, 2014). Together with Carlo Bonomi she managed the fundraising for the Ferenczi House and purchased the former office of Ferenczi's original villa, which now serves as the Ferenczi Centre and Archives. She is a psychoanalyst in private practice.

Madeleine Miller-Bottome, MA, is a doctoral candidate at the New School for Social Research. Madeleine has published several peer-reviewed articles on the topic of attachment and psychotherapy and helped to develop the Patient Attachment Coding System (PACS), the first validated session transcript-based measure of patients' attachment. She is the recipient of the Prize Fellowship at the New School for Social Research.

Luis Mario Minuchin, is a full member, and a training and supervising analyst of the Psychoanalytic Association of Buenos Aires (ApdeBA); training and supervising analyst in children and adolescents; member and professor of the IUSAM (University Institute of Mental Health – ApdeBA); member and professor of the Argentine Association of Psychotherapy Universidad de la Matanza, Buenos Aires; chair of psychoanalytic studies, Panamá, IPA; professor of ILAP, Latin-American Institute of Psychoanalysis; author, with Dr Horacio Etchegoyen, of *Melanie Klein Seminars: Introduction to her Work* (Editorial Biebel, Buenos Aires). Author of several psychoanalytic papers published in psychoanalytic journals all over the world.

Michelle Moreau Ricaud is professor of psychology; associate researcher at University Paris Diderot; psychoanalyst member of Quatrième Groupe; and member of the International Balint Federation and leader of the Balint Group. She is author of: *Cure d'ennui: Ecrivains Hongrois autour de Sándor Ferenczi* (Paris, Gallimard, 1992); *Michael Balint: Le renouveau* *de l'Ecole de Budapest* (Toulouse, Erès, 2007); *Michael Balint: El nuevo comienzo de la Escuela de Budapest* (Madrid, Sintesis, 2003); "Michael Balint: An introduction (*The American Journal of Psychoanalysis, 2002*); "Healing boredom: Ferenczi and his circle of literary friends (*Ferenczi and his world: Rekindling the Spirit of the Budapest School*, Karnac, London); and "The founding of the Budapest School (*Ferenczi's Turn in Psychoanalysis*, New York and London Press, 1993). She is editor, with Judith Dupont, of three special issues on "The life and work of Michael Balint of *The American Journal of Psychoanalysis*.

Clara Mucci, PhD, psychoanalytic psychotherapist, is full professor of clinical psychology at the University of Chieti, Italy. She received her PhD from Emory University, Atlanta, USA, where she studied English literature and psychoanalysis. The author of several books on Shakespeare, literary theory, women's narrative, and psychoanalysis, she has focused most recently on trauma theory, personality disorders, massive trauma, and the Shoah. Among her most recent publications is *Beyond Individual and Collective Trauma: Intergenerational Transmission, Psychoanalytic Theory, and the Dynamics of Forgiveness* (Karnac, 2013) and, with G. Craparo, she edited the collection *Unrepressed Unconscious, Implicit Memory, and Clinical Work* (Karnac, 2016).

Donna Orange, educated in philosophy, clinical psychology, and psychoanalysis, PhD, PsyD, teaches at NYU Postdoc (New York); IPSS (Institute for the Psychoanalytic Study of Subjectivity, New York); and in private study groups. She also offers clinical consultation/supervision in these institutes and beyond. Recent books are *Thinking for Clinicians: Philosophical Resources for Contemporary Psychoanalysis and the Humanistic Psychotherapies* (2010); *The Suffering Stranger: Hermeneutics for Everyday Clinical Practice* (2011); *Nourishing the Inner Life of Clinicians and Humanitarians: The Ethical Turn in Psychoanalysis* (2015); and *Climate Crisis, Psychoanalysis, and Radical Ethics* (2016).

Robert Prince, PhD, ABPP, is clinical associate professor, New York University postdoctoral programme in psychotherapy & psychoanalysis, where he is also past co-chair of the Interpersonal Track. He is past-president of psychologist-psychoanalyst clinicians and an associate editor of *The American Journal of Psychoanalysis*. He is author of over thirty-five other articles and chapters. His books include *The Legacy of the Holocaust* and *The Death of Psychoanalysis*.

Jeremy D. Safran, PhD, is professor of psychology at the New School for Social Research, and faculty at The New York University postdoctoral programme in psychotherapy & psychoanalysis. Dr Safran is co-founder and co-chair (along with Lewis Aron and Adrienne Harris) of The Sandor Ferenczi Center at the New School for Social Research and past-president of The International Association for Relational Psychoanalysis & Psychotherapy. He has published several books including: *Negotiating the Therapeutic Alliance: A Relational Treatment Guide* (2000), *Psychoanalysis & Buddhism: An Unfolding Dialogue* (2003), and *Psychoanalysis and Psychoanalytic Therapies* (2012), for which he received The Gradiva Award.

Eszter Salgó, PhD, teaches at the department of political science and international affairs at the John Cabot University in Rome. Her previous book, *Psychoanalytic Reflections on Politics: Fatherlands in Mothers' Hands* (Routledge, 2014), portrays nostalgia for paradise as a yearning intrinsic in human nature and politics as a realm where people's desire to experience transcendence is played out. Her latest book, *Images from Paradise:*

The Visual Communication of the European Union's Federalist Utopia (Berghahn Books, 2017) explores the symbolic order that the European Union has been propagating since 2008 in an attempt to legitimate itself.

Ann-Louise Silver, MD, was a medical staff member and director of education for twenty-five years at Chestnut Lodge. She is on the faculties of the Washington Center for Psychoanalysis and the Washington School of Psychiatry, was the founding president of ISPS-US (the international society for the psychological treatments of schizophrenia, the US chapter), and was a past president of the American Academy of Psychoanalysis and Dynamic Psychiatry. She edited and contributed to four books and many articles on the psychodynamic treatment of psychosis. She now works from an office at home.

Timo Storck is professor for clinical psychology and psychotherapy at Psychologische Hochschule Berlin and works as a psychotherapist and psychoanalyst in Heidelberg. Scientifically, he works within the fields of psychoanalytical hermeneutics, psychosomatics, inpatient analytical treatment, psychoanalysis and art (especially film and television shows), and basic concepts in psychoanalysis.

Julianna Vamos, PhD, is a clinical psychologist and psychoanalyst; member of the Paris Psychoanalytical Society (SPP); perinatalist in a progressive maternity clinic, "Les Bluets", Paris; founding member and training analyst of Pikler Loczy Association, France; and member of the editorial board of the Journal *Spiral*.

Massimo Vigna-Taglianti, MD, is a child neuropsychiatrist, full member of the Italian Psychoanalytical Society and the IPA, and a training and supervising analyst, and scientific chair, of the Italian Psychoanalytic Society. He is an adjunct professor of child and adult psychiatry at Aosta University, and also works as a psychoanalyst with children, adolescents, and adults in private practice. He writes about transference/countertransference dynamics with a special focus on role-reversal phenomena, as well as the meaning of action and play in psychoanalysis.

Abbreviations

IPA International Psychoanalytical Association
IJP *International Journal of Psychoanalysis*

Correspondence is shown in the form: "Fer/Fr" (Ferenczi to Freud)

Abr Abraham
Fer Ferenczi
Fr Freud
Grod Groddeck
Jo Jones
Ju Jung

Reference to correspondence

Falzeder, E. & Brabant, E. (Eds.) (1993, 1996, 2000). *The Correspondence of Sigmund Freud and Sándor Ferenczi*. 3 Vols. Cambridge, MA/London: Belknap.

Fortune, C. (Ed.) (2002). *The Sándor Ferenczi-George Groddeck Correspondence 1921–1933*. London: Open Gate.

McGuire, W. (Ed.) (1974). *The Freud/Jung Letters. The Correspondence between Sigmund Freud and C. G. Jung*. London: Routledge and Hogarth.

Paskauskas, R.A. (Ed.) (1993). *The Complete Correspondence of Sigmund Freud and Ernest Jones*. Cambridge, MA/London: Belknap.

Where not differently stated, reference to the most quoted works of Ferenczi is abbreviated as:

Edu–Ferenczi, S. (1908). Psychoanalysis and education. In: *Final Contributions to the Problems and Methods of Psycho-Analysis* (pp. 280–290). London: Karnac, 1994.

Adapt–Ferenczi, S. (1927). The adaptation of the family to the child. In: *Final Contributions to the Problems and Methods of Psycho-Analysis* (pp. 61–76). London: Karnac 1994.

Elast–Ferenczi, S. (1928). The elasticity of psychoanalytic technique. In: *Final Contributions to the Problems and Methods of Psycho-Analysis* (pp. 87–101). London: Karnac, 1994.

Unwel–Ferenczi, S. (1929). The unwelcome child and his death instinct. In: *Final Contributions to the Problems and Methods of Psycho-Analysis* (pp. 102–107). London: Karnac, 1994.

Relax–Ferenczi, S. (1930). The principles of relaxation and neocatharsis. In: *Final Contributions to the Problems and Methods of Psycho-Analysis* (pp. 108–125). London: Karnac, 1994.

ChildAn–Ferenczi, S. (1931). Child Analysis in the Analysis of Adults. In *Final Contributions to the Problems and Methods of Psycho-Analysis*. London: Karnac, 1994 (pp. 126–142).

Conf–Ferenczi, S. (1932). Confusion of tongues between adults and the child. In *Final Contributions to the Problems and Methods of Psycho-Analysis* (pp. 156–167). London: Karnac, 1994.

Diary–Ferenczi, S. (1932). *The Clinical Diary of Sándor Ferenczi. January–October 1932*. Ed. J. Dupont. Cambridge, MA: Harvard University Press, 1995.

Frag–Ferenczi, S. (1920–32). Notes and fragments. In *Final Contributions to the Problems and Methods of Psycho-Analysis* (pp. 216–279). London: Karnac, 1994.

Series editors' Introduction

In February 2017 a most successful four-day conference took place in Washington DC. Entitled "Lines of Development" it celebrated the four published volumes in this series to date, and three books in proof stage, including this one on Ferenczi. The conference revisited historically controversial issues with lively dialogues between representatives of different schools of thought – Ferenczi-Freud; Klein-Fairbairn; Klein-Anna Freud; and Winnicott-Bion.

Coincidentally, Washington had also featured large in Ferenczi's own American experience, as in 1925 he delivered five lectures there under the auspices of the Washington Psychoanalytic Association, founded by Clara Thompson (who later travelled to Budapest to become his analysand until his death, and was instrumental in keeping his posthumous influence alive in the USA).

While in Washington, one of us joined the three co-editors of this Ferenczi volume on one of their exploratory jaunts to the famous Library of Congress, to mine the Freud Archives for the unexpected.

We fancy that Ferenczi would have approved that our journey to this source of hidden knowledge was preceded by a sumptuous meal in a Serbian restaurant nearby, accompanied by far-reaching transcultural discussions. And indeed, at the library, several interesting documents and passionate *cris de cœur* emerged from the archive's ordinary-looking office box-files, to enrich this book.

Apart from their shared excitement in psychoanalytic scholarship and meticulous attention to detail, what struck us most about this lively threesome was their caring camaraderie, humour, and all-roundedness – qualities that make for productive co-editing. You the reader, will enjoy the bountiful fruits of this fertile collaboration.

For this book is a treasure trove of revelations. As the story unfolds against the backdrop of a Budapest heady with new hopes and poignant spoilage, we come to know a complex man riven by contradictory needs to provoke and be loved.

Early chapters in this volume explore his origins as eighth child in a large family growing up above the eighteenth-century Baroque-style bookstore on the main street of Miskolc, run by their father, and later, their widowed mother – which served as a hub for the Budapest intelligentsia of famous writers, poets, artists, and middle class radicals. We see how the bereaved award-winning adolescent's admixture of intellect and flesh prefigured the adult's intricate personality: adventurous yet compliant; fiercely loyal and kind yet provocative and vengeful; gregarious yet intensely private.

Throughout the following chapters we come to realise that despite exceptional qualities that rendered him so uniquely imaginative with patients and inspiring to his students, he was hampered by the antagonism he aroused among envious peers regarding his status as "crown prince" to Freud. Notwithstanding his professional standing and one hundred pre-Freudian publications, and despite his significant organisational efficiency and prescience in founding an international body with standardised training requirements (including a personal analysis), as a psychoanalyst Ferenczi was under-appreciated in his own time. Indeed, positive recognition of his exquisitely fine-tuned clinical skills in work with traumatised, borderline and extremely difficult patients was stalled for decades during his lifetime, both by conservative forces and his own ambivalence, and after his death by malicious gossip and political undercurrents that denied him publication.

The psychoanalytic movement as a whole was deprived by writing this most creative member out of its history. His radical understanding of countertransference and theories regarding the crucial role of the preoedipal mother and pernicious long-lasting after-effects of early trauma are pertinent today. His discovery of the defence mechanisms involved (e.g., splitting, dissociation, fragmentation (atomisation), denial, and projection) are often ascribed to his analysand Melanie Klein, while introjection, internalisation of split identifications, and identification with the aggressor are still attributed to Abraham and Torok, Fairbairn, and Anna Freud respectively.

To redress this deficit the three co-editors commissioned the topmost Ferenczi scholars in the field all over the world to contribute to this book by retracing the evolution and eventual acceptance and dissemination of Ferenczi's controversial ideas, way beyond their Hungarian origins – especially regarding the reality of early trauma and the potency of emotional regression/re-living in therapy.

These chapters describe how, although impaled on the barbed conventions and prejudice of his era and the prevailing rivalries between Vienna and Zürich, political rifts, and ugly Christian/Jewish schisms within psychoanalysis, Ferenczi's ideas managed to survive. We see their enormous influence on theory and technique in contemporary psychoanalytic traditions – amongst the British Independents, the French schools of Lacan and Laplanche, the American interpersonal theorists, intersubjectivists, self-psychologists, and relational schools, as well as within social science and the humanities, across disciplines such as social psychiatry, ethnography, psychotherapy, gender studies, social work, pedagogy, attachment theory, and infant mental health.

In our multifaceted twenty-first century, almost 150 years after Sándor Ferenczi's birth, we have finally stopped denying the widespread reality of childhood sexual abuse. His explanatory system of intergenerational transmission of trauma remains apposite, delineating the dynamic confusion between the child's desire for tenderness and imposed adult eroticism, inducing the victim's assumption of guilt. Likewise, Ferenczi's modifications of technique have primed our own expectations of therapeutic authenticity and the importance of sincerity in the reparative acknowledgment of mistakes.

Although we shall not know his like again he can be glimpsed between the covers of this fine book.

Editors' Introduction

The *Lines of Development* series opened with a volume examining the contributions of Anna Freud. The following books in the series were devoted to other pioneers of psychoanalysis: W. R. D. Fairbairn, Donald Winnicott, W. R. Bion, Melanie Klein, Jacques Lacan. Direct your gaze to the psychoanalytic skies and these will certainly be the brightest objects you see; a couple more psychoanalytic stars and the skies might be pretty well mapped.

Why, then, continue the series with a volume on Sándor Ferenczi? Does his work, scientific or clinical, make him important enough in the world of contemporary psychoanalysis to be granted a place among the psychoanalytic stars? As editors of this book, we are grateful to the series editors, Norka Malberg and Joan Raphael-Leff, as well as Oliver Rathbone of Karnac Books, for providing us with this extraordinary opportunity to show, with a "little" help from our friends in the "Ferenczi community", why the answer is a resounding "Yes!". Ferenczi's place in the psychoanalytic firmament, then, as well as now, is so fundamental that without him psychoanalysis would not be what it is. If it were possible, for the sake of argument, to eschew his contributions to theoretical and clinical psychoanalysis, the edifice would crumble and be unrecognisable. We are grateful that the generous contributions of our more than forty Ferenczi experts demonstrates that this is so, making possible what we believe is a comprehensive overview of Ferenczi's life, work, and legacy.

To name only a handful of points demonstrating Ferenczi's pivotal place in the development of psychoanalysis, for any sceptics, it was Ferenczi—hailed by all, Freud included, as the best clinical psychoanalyst of his time—who came up with the idea of an international society of those devoted to Freud and psychoanalysis, and became one of its early presidents; who developed a radical new understanding of psychological trauma, introducing new conceptions of identification, splitting, regression, traumatic progression, and others, that remains cutting-edge; who was far ahead of his time in his efforts to extend the reach of psychoanalytic treatment, and whose experiments in technique were the first, pioneering forays of some of today's most influential clinical psychoanalytic approaches; and who analysed the founders of what would turn out to be the object-relations and interpersonal traditions in contemporary psychoanalysis.

And if Nietzsche's idea that each theory is half drawn from autobiography was ever an understatement, Ferenczi is a case in point. To a significant extent, Ferenczi's psychoanalytic ideas grew out of his endless efforts to overcome the emotional wounds of his childhood and his profound disappointment in his three brief periods of analysis with Freud. This prototype of a wounded healer gave his best, and more, to providing his patients what he himself had not received—either from his harsh mother or from his analyst, who was also his intimate friend with whom he travelled, exchanged family secrets and love troubles, and shared professional endeavours as well as gossip and personal intrigues. Barely anything significant happened in the world of psychoanalysis between 1908 and 1933, the year of his death, without Ferenczi's involvement and, often, his personal initiative.

Towards the end of his life, Ferenczi himself became the source of profound—and it turns out, enduring—controversy. It should come as no surprise that a central figure as controversial as Ferenczi was "disappeared" from the history of psychoanalysis for several decades. A search of PEP-Web shows that between the end of the Second World War and 1985 there were only forty-eight papers with the name "Ferenczi" in the title. The contributions of Ferenczi's final years were long dismissed not just as different from Freud's, a legitimate scientific difference, but as a consequence of Ferenczi's mental deterioration. Specifically, it was the efforts of Ernest Jones that led the psychoanalytic world to believe that Ferenczi had grown psychotic and that his last papers were worthless (Bonomi, 1998). Ostracism and censorship are, unfortunately, not unfamiliar to the world of psychoanalysis (and Ferenczi himself was actively involved in enforcing a few such campaigns, for instance, against his friend and collaborator Otto Rank). But, as psychoanalysts know better than anyone, repressed contents start appearing everywhere, in thin disguises. Indeed, Ferenczi became an inspiration to the next generation of dissidents, like Sullivan, Bowlby, and Lacan, as well as a silent presence in the work of everyone who treated traumatised patients or paid special attention to countertransference.

Truth be told, many were not aware of Ferenczi's ideas, and he could have ended up as a footnote to psychoanalytic history were it not for two flame keepers. In January, 1939, Bálint Mihaly emigrated to Manchester, and Ferenczi's widow Gizela asked him to bring Ferenczi's manuscripts with him to safety. As soon as Balint become Michael, he translated into English Ferenczi's *Clinical Diary* and several papers written by Ferenczi after 1928. While the papers were published, though only in the late 1940s and during the 1950s, the *Diary* was considered unpublishable—Jones, Anna Freud, and Alexander and Margarete Mitscherlich all believed it would only reinforce the belief that Ferenczi had been mad (Dupont, 2015). With Balint's death, in 1970, Ferenczi's stepdaughters gave the role of Ferenczi's literary executor to Judith Dupont, a Hungarian-born psychoanalyst, living, since her youth, in Paris, who as a child played in Ferenczi's garden while her grandmother, Vilma Kovacs, and her aunt Alice, later to become Mrs Balint, discussed serious topics (Dupont, 2016). It was through the efforts of Mme Dupont that the *Diary* was published in French, in 1985, and three years later in English, followed by the translations of the complete correspondence between Freud and Ferenczi in the following decade.

Despite earlier predictions, the book received a unanimously positive reception and triggered what Emanuel Berman would soon term the Ferenczi Renaissance (1996). The number of scholarly papers about Ferenczi increased greatly after the 1980s; since the late 1980s, international conferences focused on Ferenczi have been held roughly every three years somewhere in the world; many books and special journal issues have been devoted to Ferenczi in English, French, Hungarian, Italian, and Spanish. Ferenczi came to be recognised as a predecessor of all those who searched for more comprehensive clinical perspectives and more effective clinical approaches, and who dared to look outside conservative psychoanalytic doctrine to find these. His ideas, sometimes jotted down at the end of a long workday as mere diary notes, were rediscovered, their value newly appreciated, and they were tested out in the consulting room: for instance, the importance of tenderness and of honesty, in the family and in the analytic relationship; the reality of trauma, in such forms as rejection, sexual abuse, what Ferenczi termed the "terrorism of suffering" and hypocrisy; the reappearance of often-disavowed trauma in the analytic relationship; and traumatic consequences, including dissociation, regression, traumatic progression, and identification with the aggressor.

This book is the culmination of a great effort made by a community of scholars—our authors—with the most diverse psychoanalytic trainings. Unsatisfied with the power of many psychoanalytic theories to explain their observations in daily analytic practice, these scholars converged on Ferenczi—an early guide whose contributions continue to light the way for those who attempt to heal others' psychological suffering. Part I of the book traces Ferenczi's life from his childhood in Miskolc and his medical studies in Vienna to his untimely death at the age of fifty-nine, via the major turning-points of his life—his pre-psychoanalytic papers, his analyses with Freud, the complicated dynamics of a love life that became enmeshed with his relationship with Freud, collaboration and competition with his analytic colleagues, his role in the public life of Budapest and in the international and local psychoanalytic communities, along with detailed descriptions of many of his patients, even those whose identity had been hidden. Equally encompassing is the presentation, in Part II, of Ferenczi's clinical contributions, by authors who have devoted years to studying them: his conceptions of trauma, dissociation, regression, the "unwelcome child", the "wise baby", identification with the aggressor, mutuality, countertransference... Succinct presentation of all Ferenczi's major ideas can now be found in one place. Following this, in Part III, the focus turns to Ferenczi's influences on contemporary psychoanalytic traditions. (Un)surprisingly, most analytic traditions are, in some way, descendants of Ferenczi: the Independents and Klein, Lacan and Laplanche, the interpersonalists, self psychology, and relational psychoanalysts. Indeed, there are contemporary schools that consider Ferenczi, rather than Freud, their true originator; and more and more psychoanalysts understand their patients in ways that derive more from Ferenczi than from Freud. Finally, Part IV shows how Ferenczi's ideas can be applied beyond the analytic consulting room. There we meet Ferenczi the political thinker, and we see how his ideas have been enlisted to deconstruct authoritarianism and illuminate the treatment of mass social trauma. We find out how Ferenczi's ideas have been put to use in helping new parents become better attuned to their infants. We learn about Ferenczi's thinking regarding the nature of sexuality, the feminine, and the maternal. And we discover how Ferenczi influenced the development of the field of clinical social work.

In editing this book, we took special efforts to avoid romanticising Ferenczi, to avoid setting him up as the new unquestioned saint of psychoanalysis, much the way Freud has often been treated, or to position him one-dimensionally as the good psychoanalyst, as opposed to Freud, the bad one. We strove for a balanced, appreciative but appropriately critical, view of the man and the oeuvre, where weaknesses of character and mistakes in his work are not hidden. We hope our comprehensive, systematic, grounded approach to our subject can become a foundation for close reading (and re-reading) of Ferenczi, and for future research that extracts what is most valuable in his work for our understanding of people's psychological struggles and how to help people who suffer from them.

What do we think is most essential in Ferenczi's legacy? Ferenczi was a model clinician in important ways: highly motivated to find better cures for his patients; audacious enough to learn from his own experience, to experiment and to take risks, despite conformist pressures; and scrupulously, rigorously critical towards his own new ideas and techniques. And this approach led him to a radical new understanding of the psychoanalytic process. He was the first to realise that psychoanalytic treatments inevitably include the unconscious of the analyst in an unconscious dialogue with the patient, and he worked on countertransference deeply and openly, and decades before anyone else. The result was that the comfortable position of the anonymous and detached analyst gave way to a new, more mutual approach, characterised by the analyst's openness and honesty. And, through his new way of working, which welcomed aspects of the patient that may remain unobserved in a more classical approach, he reached a more profound understanding of trauma and its consequences than any of his contemporaries; in the opinion of some, he was even able to help some patients seen as hopeless.

Careful reading, especially of the *Diary*, suggests that there is still more to be digested. Drafted, almost in passing, are gems that clinicians and researchers of today have yet to hone and polish; for instance, the idea that the perpetrator of sexual abuse is not looking for satisfaction, but to "steal" the last moments of the child's innocence.

We leave this endeavour to new teams, feeling our current mission has been accomplished.

References

Berman, E. (1996). The Ferenczi Renaissance: *Sándor Ferenczi: Reconsidering Active Interventions*, by Martin Stanton (Northvale, NJ: Aronson, 1991, xv + 226 pp.) *The Legacy of Sándor Ferenczi*, edited by Lewis Aron and Adrienne Harris (Hillsdale, NJ: The Analytic Press, 1993, xxiii + 294 pp.) *The Correspondence of Sigmund Freud and Sándor Ferenczi*, Vol. 1, 1908–1914, edited by Eva Brabant, Ernst Falzeder, and Patrizia Giampieri-Deutch under the supervision of André Haynal; translated by Peter T. Hoffer (Cambridge, MA: Belknap Press of Harvard University Press, 1993, xxxv + 584 pp.). *Psychoanalytic Dialogues*, *6*: 391–411.

Bonomi, C. (1998). Jones's allegation of Ferenczi's mental deterioration: A reassessment. *International Forum Psychoanalysis*, *7*: 201–206.

Dupont, J. (2015). *Au fil du temps... Un itinéraire analytique*. Paris: Editions Campagne Première.

Dupont, J. (2016). A multifaceted legacy: Sándor Ferenczi's clinical diary. In A. W. Rachman (Ed.), *The Budapest School of Psychoanalysis: The Origin of a Two-person Psychology and Emphatic Perspective* (pp. 15–25). Abingdon: Routledge.

Prologue

The need for Ferenczi's voice in psychoanalysis

Franco Borgogno for Judith Dupont

The need for a volume that traces the tradition originated by a psychoanalyst emerges as we identify the presence of a noteworthy body of thought or knowledge, with its own set of ideas and concepts, and a terminology that arises from it. In our own field—in addition to the many studies of this kind dedicated to Freud—Jung, Klein, Winnicott, Bion, Lacan, and others have been deemed to merit such volumes; Adler and Sullivan would surely also be more than worthy candidates on the basis of their role in advancing psychoanalysis in Europe and North America. Anna Freud is another who developed a specific body of thought and knowledge that changes her father's psychoanalysis in small but also in major ways—a fact that is often not grasped (see Malberg & Raphael-Leff, 2011). Moving across the Atlantic to North America, we should also doubtless consider ego psychologists like Hartmann, Kris, Loewenstein, and Rapaport, as well as those from different traditions: Horney, Thompson (a pupil of Ferenczi), and Fromm. Moving a little forward in time, we might think of Erikson and (still later) Kohut's self-psychology and Kernberg's antagonistic response thereto.

When it comes to placing Ferenczi's contribution within such an articulated historical, geographical, and theoretical development of psychoanalysis, I should immediately state my opinion that he too is clearly a worthy subject for such a study. Ferenczi's thought and knowledge are in no way less significant than that of the aforementioned authors; and even though it was not to Ferenczi's liking to present his concepts and ideas within a systematic structure (indeed, these were often mere flash-images, associations, sensations, impressions, intuitions, or analogies), his unique and vibrant expressive style, and the extraordinary freshness of his themes for psychoanalysis itself, are unparalleled in our field ("He was always able to look at … things and … phenomena, without bias and as naively as if he were seeing them for the first time" (Balint, 1949, p. 216)).

In Ferenczi's case, moreover, Freud himself has justified our taking such a line. His obituary of Ferenczi describes the latter not just as a pupil but as a master—and not only to all other psychoanalysts, but also to Freud himself (Freud, 1933). Freud reserved this kind of recognition for very few—perhaps for no other. Ferenczi had a uniquely intimate place in Freud's professional and personal life—they shared "an intimate community of life, feelings and interests" (Fr/Fer, 11 January 1933, p. 446).

But I can still hear some critics wondering: Why is it so clear-cut that Ferenczi should be included in the pantheon of great psychoanalytic authors who might be deemed entitled to such a study?

I would first reply that this is because Ferenczi's oeuvre is no less rich and complex than those of the other authors cited thus far. Unlike the work of many of these authors, however, the richness and complexity of Ferenczi's writings lies not in the degree of homogeneity and coherence attained, but rather in the experiential journey that he has undergone within himself and within psychoanalysis. This is what makes Ferenczi's oeuvre unique, as summed up so brilliantly by Granoff (1958) when he wrote that if Freud invented psychoanalysis, then it was Ferenczi who put it into practice, becoming its incarnation and testing ground.

Having said this, if we dwell a moment longer on the principal characteristics of Ferenczi's works, we should specify that, if he gradually builds up his oeuvre after his meeting with Freud and on the basis of his clinical experience, the writer and author Ferenczi can already be traced in his "pre-analytic writings" (Cassullo, Chapter Three), written before his first contact with psychoanalysis (Lorin, 1983; Mészáros, 1991; Sabourin, 1985).

Even then, his curious and indomitable explorer's spirit is, *de facto*, clearly evident—that spirit which, never satisfied with ideological abstractions and easy solutions, would lead him to become a "present-day doubting Thomas", wanting to feel for himself the veracity of Freud's proposals and to address himself to the reformulation of the nascent discipline of psychoanalysis in a direction more consonant with its basic spirit (Borgogno, 1999).

In this regard, we need only consider the fact that the leitmotif that recurs right across his oeuvre is his focus on the distinctive traits of the personality and the suffering of each individual patient and on the limitations, shortcomings, and difficulties of those who care for them (be they doctors or psychoanalysts) in a professional context—on what he defines in *The Clinical Diary* as the "sins" of psychoanalysts (insufficient listening-and-attention to our patients and to the analyst's own verbal and non-verbal communications), including himself first of all (Diary, pp. 199–202, 209–210).

We might add at this point that Ferenczi never dreamt of creating a psychoanalysis alternative to that of Freud, and never declared himself a dissident intending to establish a new school. Proof of this can be found in the fact that, having attained to a position of rather painful independence from Freud in his final works, *The Clinical Diary* and *Notes and Fragments*, Ferenczi nonetheless continued to eulogise Freud's influence on medicine (1933b), showing himself to be a "classical" psychoanalyst.

The second question on which I wish to reflect is whether Ferenczi developed "his own voice", and when and how did he acquire it?

To answer the question, *in primis* we should reflect on Ferenczi's autonomy from, but also dependence on, Freud, and his consequent (surely, in part, neurotic) ambivalence as a disciple towards his master. This ground, incisively explored by Haynal (2002, pp. 101–109), is covered in the current book by Louis Breger, Carlo Bonomi, and others.

Before introducing my ideas on the issue, however, I would highlight that, even when Ferenczi responded to Freud's request that he become President of the IPA by saying that the only presidency he could assume in that period was over his own thoughts—the only children he was still able to produce (Fr/Fer, 12 May 1932 to 11 January 1933)—he nonetheless continued to evince a (not necessarily neurotic) yearning that he might reconcile Freud's distant and antithetical approach with the psychoanalytic trend he himself had launched, since Freud remained for him the cornerstone for psychoanalysis.

Coming now more directly to the question to which I referred above, I would at once underline here that Ferenczi, right from the beginning, had a particular propensity to pay heed to "the voice of the other" before his own (Vida, 1997), since for Ferenczi it is always the patient who knows most about his own condition—more than even the most enlightened, well-equipped mind specialist (the case of Rosa K; Cassullo, Chapter Three). This was in fact the very goal that Ferenczi pursued through his analyses, in which he sought, as he recalls, "to loosen" the patient's "tongue" (Conf, p. 166) and to defend his "capacity for producing his own material" (ChildAn, p. 134). These are, as we know, often difficult to bring into motion and articulate, either because of inadequacies in nurturing marked by projective, intrusive and extrajective, pressures, which do not correspond to the real children's needs or, more generally, because of the educative mandates imposed by the (authoritarian and hypocritical, if we think of the time in which Ferenczi himself grew up) hegemonic culture (Gaburri & Ambrosiano, 2003).

Ferenczi had, himself, struggled with such disturbances resulting from his own nurturing and education. He sought to free himself from the chains imposed by his family and also by the psychoanalytic community within which he was developing—restrictions that, incidentally, taking advantage of the need that children and pupils have to be loved and approved of, had encouraged him to relinquish his own voice, rather than to emancipate it.

Two other points are relevant here. The first is the fact that it usually takes a long time for someone to attain to his own voice and language, along the road to adulthood and also in the scientific-professional domain. In both of these situations, one must inevitably first master the language of others by learning from and imitating their voices before coming to possess a language and a voice of one's own.

The second point is that Ferenczi was a creative soul who was ahead of his time. As is often the case with such individuals, he was inexorably alone in pursuing his idiosyncratic research and did not receive the support that would have enabled him to recognise the merit and soundness of that which he was expressing. At the end of his life, therefore, Ferenczi eventually sought from his patients, such as Elizabeth Severn, affirmation of the merit and soundness of his own approach—affirmation of an understanding of psychic processes and events far beyond the grasp of his colleagues and especially of Freud himself.

Consequently, Ferenczi's slowness in appropriating a voice felt to be his own and worthy of respect could be due not exclusively to an affective immaturity, but rather to his (self-)critical character as a scholar.

Ferenczi, *inter alia*, also died prematurely, and precisely when all that he had intuited and pursued from the outset of his career was on the point of condensing and coalescing into a more solid form of expression, able to foreground his original vision.

Although we obviously cannot know what would have happened had Ferenczi lived longer, if we examine his career we cannot but conclude that he would very probably have continued to ask himself questions and to review his own clinical-theoretical theses. It does not belittle the emotive turbulence of *The Clinical Diary* and the late *Notes and Fragments* to suggest that his constant making and unmaking of his thought might have gradually attenuated, facilitating a surer, more balanced conceptualisation that would have allowed him to continue to doubt whilst finding a greater degree of reconciliation with himself and his mentor.

A further question is: What do we mean when we refer to Ferenczi's specific voice, and how can we profitably identify it and bring it into focus?

To answer this, we should immediately state, as we have already implied between the lines of the present reflection, that Ferenczi's contribution to psychoanalysis should not only be understood as the new theorisation at which he arrived towards the end of his life, when he began to propose a metapsychology and a cure for trauma that diverged significantly from those proposed by Freud.

Indeed, many other concepts that arose directly from or in connection with Freud, with common sense, with the medicine and the psychiatry of the time, or with other sciences and fields such as biology, horticulture/agriculture, zoology, botany, religion, mythology, mathematics, social psychology, geology, chemistry-mineralogy, ethology, esotericism, sexology, physics, and so on, can also be connected to Ferenczi. Some of these concepts can be considered to have become Ferenczian as a result of the singular way in which he applied them and of the peculiar mental and emotional attitude with which he inflected them, modifying their usual application without, often, being himself aware of the conspicuous shifting or alteration in meaning that he was producing and promoting.

We might then broadly say that Ferenczi proceeded by grafting his own specific intuitions on to the originary psychoanalytic plant, on to other areas of human knowledge, or even on to the current usage of the language. These graftings can doubtless be attributed to his own inclination towards a theoretical-technical amphimixis (Antonelli, 1997), or convergence, or else to his poetic soul, which frequently sought recourse to linguistic nuances, analogies, metaphors, sensory similarities, or other processes of figurability (Botella & Botella, 2001; Galdi, 2016; Gondar, 2011).

Many of these conceptualisations, furthermore, frequently fall short of a theoretically-clinically articulate fullness and often remain in a nascent state, perhaps emerging and re-emerging on numerous occasions across his work before locating themselves in a more wide-reaching vision recognisable as his own. Herein, incidentally—in the fact that Ferenczi does not always sign off on and acknowledge his own contributions—lies the reason why it has been so easy (and this remains the case today) to plunder Ferenczi's works without the theft being recognised and without the stolen ideas being traced back to their owner.

All of which leads to the conclusion that a volume on Ferenczi's tradition should by no means limit itself to listing and providing clear definitions of the theories and concepts that he introduced into psychoanalysis (introjection, identification with the aggressor, traumatic ego progression, etc.), discussing their relevance for our contemporary, everyday practice. It should, instead, show the developments that, although often masked by a nominal continuity, can be seen in his works to express a radical change in his way of thinking and working, which he himself did not fully perceive at the moment of their emergence. And it should link them to the history of Ferenczi's involvement in psychoanalysis, of his relationship with Freud and the other pioneers, and of the legacy they left to so many later, seminal authors, as well as to us.

References

Antonelli, G. (1997). *Il mare di Ferenczi* [The sea of Ferenczi]. Roma: Di Renzo.

Balint, M. (1949). Sándor Ferenczi, Obit 1933. *International Journal of Psychoanalysis*, *30*: 215–219.

Borgogno, F. (1999). *Psychoanalysis as a Journey*. London: Open Gate, 2007.

Botella, C., & Botella S. (2001), *La figurabilité psychique*. Lausanne: Delachaux et Niestlé [Engl. Transl. *The Work of Psychic Figurability: Mental States without Representation*. London: Routledge, 2004].

Ferenczi, S. (1933b). Freud's influence on medicine. In: S. Ferenczi (1955), *Final Contributions to the Problems and Methods of Psycho-Analysis* (pp. 143–155). London: Karnac.

Freud, S. (1933). Sándor Ferenczi. *S. E.*, *12*: 225–229. London: Hogarth.

Gaburri, E., & Ambrosiano, L. (2003). *Ululare con i lupi. Conformismo e reverie* [Howling with the wolves. Conformism and reverie]. Torino: Bollati Boringhieri.

Galdi, G. (2016). Private communication.

Gondar, J. (2011). Things in words: Ferenczi and language. *American Journal of Psychoanalysis, 71*: 329–337.

Granoff, V. (1958). Ferenczi: faux problème ou vrai malentendu [Ferenczi: False problem or real misunderstanding]. *La Psychanalyse, 6*: 255–282, 1961.

Haynal, A. E. (2002). *Disappearing and Reviving: Sándor Ferenczi in the History of Psychoanalysis*. London: Karnac.

Lorin, C. (1983). *Le jeune Ferenczi. Premiers écrits 1899–1906* [The young Ferenczi. First writings 1899–1906]. Paris: Aubier Montaigne.

Malberg, N.T., & Raphael-Leff, J. (2011). *The Anna Freud Tradition*. London: Karnac.

Mészáros, J. (1991). Sándor Ferenczi debuttante [Sándor Ferenczi as a beginner]. In: J. Mészáros & M. Casonato (Eds.), *La mia amicizia con Miksa Schächter. Scritti preanalitici, 1899–1908* (pp. xii–xix) [My friendship with Miksa Schächter. Preanalytic writings, 1899–1908]. Turin: Bollati Boringhieri, 1992.

Sabourin, P. (1985). *Ferenczi, paladin et grand vizir secret*. Paris: Éditions Universitaires.

Vida, J. E. (1997). The voice of Ferenczi: Echoes from the past. *Psychoanalytic Inquiry, 17*: 404–415.

Part I

Biographical-Historical

Introduction

Part I provides a biographical-historical foundation for understanding Ferenczi's psychoanalytic contributions most fully. In this section, we get an overview of Ferenczi's personal and professional life, from its beginnings to its end, and trace the evolution of Ferenczi's thinking within this context. We see the places and meet some of the important people—family, friends, colleagues, patients—that shaped him as a person and contributed to the development of his ideas. We learn of his role in developing the institutions of organised psychoanalysis, and read of his presence in the Hungarian popular press.

Krisztián Kapusi starts us off with a guided tour of the Miskolc that Sándor Ferenczi grew up in—the "Middle-European middle-town" of the late nineteenth century, behind its current-day incarnation. Kapusi recreates for us the sights and sounds of the family bookstore and the street where Sándor lived, invites us along on Sándor's daily morning walk to the high school from which he graduated in 1890 (as well as on some detours), introduces us to Sándor's parents, and reconstructs various notable moments in the life of his family and hometown.

Next, we follow Tom Keve to the Budapest Ferenczi discovered after moving there on completing his medical training in Vienna—a vibrant boomtown, modeled after Paris and about to celebrate the Hungarian Millennium, which had not long before become the second capital of an empire. He draws back the curtain on the thriving cultural, artistic, and intellectual life that became Ferenczi's world during the years that spanned the *fin-de-siècle*, the tragic consequences of the rapid-fire political revolutions and antisemitism that followed the end of the Great War, and the city's partial recovery despite political threats at home and beyond Hungary's borders.

Gabriele Cassullo then surveys Ferenczi's "pre-psychoanalytic" writings, showing how many of Ferenczi's later psychoanalytic interests were already present in this early work: the mind-body connection; unconscious interpersonal communication and mutual influence in the therapy relationship; appreciation of the essential role of the physician's honesty, sincerity, and humility, and of trust, in healing; the role of omnipotent fantasies, and their disillusionment, in psychic life and development; and a social-reformist zeal.

Louis Breger tracks the development of the Freud-Ferenczi relationship, emphasising Ferenczi's painful struggle, especially toward the end of his life, to pursue his own clinical discoveries, and the theoretical ideas to which they led him, against the strong tide of Freud's authoritarian control.

Carlo Bonomi explores Ferenczi's *analyses*—plural—with Freud. He traces these through Ferenczi's self-analysis, the correspondence and overall relationship between these two men, as well as the formally designated analysis of Ferenczi by Freud—all analytic, and interrelated in complex ways. Bonomi emphasises the unresolved emotional conflicts, ambivalences, projections, and disavowals in Freud, not just in Ferenczi, that shaped their relationship; the distorting influence of Freud's intrusive entanglements with important people in Ferenczi's life, and of Freud's agenda regarding Ferenczi's role in the psychoanalytic movement; and Ferenczi's sacrificial responsiveness even to Freud's unacknowledged pressure.

Emanuel Berman provides a wealth of primary-sourced information, and a thoughtful, compassionate meditation, on the knotty and inauspicious web of relationships between Ferenczi and his future wife Gizella; her daughter Elma, who Ferenczi took on as a patient and also fell in love with; and Freud, who, for a while, took over Elma's treatment, though with discretion and neutrality notably absent. We hear directly from the participants about their struggles during this painful episode. Berman concludes by discussing ethical issues that can arise from the unavoidable impact of the analyst's subjectivity on the patient, and from analysts' approach to power relations and boundaries within the analytic relationship.

Ernst Falzeder explores Ferenczi's personal correspondence with colleagues, noting that the Ferenczi who emerges from his letters, to Freud and to others, often defies "the various pigeonholes into which he has so often been stuck." Ferenczi strove for a high level of mutual understanding, honesty, and openness in his correspondence, yet he could also be withdrawn and aloof. He struggled between orthodoxy and dissidence. For Falzeder, as for many of us, it's easy to see Ferenczi's humanity in his letters, and to like him.

Janos Harmatta takes us through the twists, turns, and political minefields that had to be navigated in the founding and early evolution of the International Psychoanalytical Association (IPA). He also describes the early history of the Hungarian Psychoanalytical Society. While Ferenczi had a founding role in the history of both organisations, and was elected president of the IPA at the end of the First World War, he held this role only briefly, due to communication difficulties created by the collapse of the Empire. Perhaps ironically, he turned down Freud's offer of the IPA presidency late in his life, largely in order to preserve his freedom to pursue interests that diverged from what was acceptable to Freud and the psychoanalytic mainstream.

Anna Bentinck van Schoonheten traces out Ferenczi's place in the social and professional world of early psychoanalysis, from the lead-up (with Jung as intermediary) to Ferenczi's first meeting with Freud, and their fast-blossoming, intimate, and increasingly conflictual relationship; through Ferenczi's clumsy efforts to establish the International Psychoanalytical Association, and his later disappointments as he pursued its presidency; his idea to establish the "secret committee" that successfully pushed Jung out of psychoanalysis; and his relationships with the committee's other members, most notably his complicated, increasingly sour connection with Jones, and his political struggles with Eitingon.

Next, Ferenczi's studies of war neurosis, based upon his experience treating war-traumatised soldiers during the First World War, are examined by Andreas Hamburger. Hamburger explores the historical context of these studies on several different levels—the circumstances surrounding Ferenczi's attention to war neurosis, the psychoanalytic-political situation at the end of the war and the reception Ferenczi's war-neurosis work received within psychoanalysis, the place of Ferenczi's discoveries in the development of his trauma theory, and the relationship of the contemporary interest in trauma studies to our current zeitgeist. Hamburger also describes Ferenczi's clinical discoveries about war neuroses—most notably, that they result from psychological causes, specifically from narcissistic injury.

Melinda Friedrich unearths Ferenczi's writings in the popular press. Based upon her research into a trove of information largely unknown to contemporary Ferenczi scholars,

Friedrich informs us that Ferenczi was an active presence in Budapest's popular press. His lectures were advertised and reported in detail, and he presented his opinions on issues of the day, about psychology and related medical and scientific matters but also political questions, in publications across the political spectrum. Friedrich offers fascinating morsels of what Ferenczi had to say in his press interviews.

Christopher Fortune describes Ferenczi's relationship with Georg Groddeck, a most intimate friend, personal physician, and in various senses an analyst to Ferenczi, during the last dozen years of Ferenczi's life. Groddeck was a unique figure in the psychoanalytic movement, marginal yet important—a free-thinking self-described "wild analyst" who explored mind-body connections, the psychological treatment of organic disorders, and the importance of early trauma and the mother: all interests he shared with Ferenczi. Perhaps most important, he played a key role in helping Ferenczi develop his own autonomous voice within psychoanalysis.

B. William Brennan gives a detailed overview of Ferenczi's patients, especially those Ferenczi wrote about in his *Clinical Diary*. Brennan, based on his own groundbreaking research, identifies the real people whom Ferenczi disguised by code letters in the *Diary*, giving us brief sketches of their lives, and describing the often-intimate interrelationships among the members of what was essentially a group of expatriate Americans who had come to Budapest to be analysed by Ferenczi. Brennan also tells us about many of the other patients Ferenczi worked with over the years, locating them socially and, for his many patients who were also analysts, professionally.

Éva Brabant-Gerö and Judith Dupont-Dormandi tell us some things we may want to know before reading Ferenczi's *Clinical Diary*. Brabant prepares us for how we may feel as we witness, through the *Diary*'s pages, Ferenczi's intimate struggles with his own traumas and with Freud's painful inability or refusal to understand Ferenczi's radically new, intersubjective, trauma-based view of psychoanalysis—a perspective that has become foundational for twenty-first-century psychoanalysis. Then Dupont, editor of the *Diary* and Ferenczi's former literary executor, takes us through the difficult history of its half-century delay in publication, and the personal engagement necessary if a reader is to take in most fully the human and clinical insights it offers.

Lastly, Peter Hoffer offers a detailed account of Ferenczi's final illness and death against the background of an emotionally strained, increasingly tense relationship with Freud. And Hoffer lays out a dispassionate examination of the still-controversial question of Ferenczi's mental deterioration during the final stages of his illness.

With the biographical-historical foundation of this first section of the book in place, we will be well positioned to approach Ferenczi's clinical and theoretical contributions, the topic of the book's second section.

Chapter 1

Amidst hills, creeks and books Sándor Ferenczi's childhood in Miskolc

Krisztián Kapusi

Middle-European middle-town. It would be irremediably average, even with its eclecticism, if it had a main square, if it still had its uniform architecture, if its firewalls didn't stick out left and right over the neighbouring rooftops, and it weren't irreparably wrinkled and broken. An old church with ringing bells, a theatre portico, clanking tram. The main street rises from the east, its dual curvature resembling a human spine: at its lower vertebrae, the city's skeleton, that is, the eastern portion bends in a careful arch; at the top, however, from the Sötétkapu (Dark Gate), it turns sharply toward its head, the town hall. From the summits of the Bükk Mountains, ridges, opening like compasses, accompany the Szinva stream's Miskolc valley to the Great Hungarian Plain. From the south, the foot of the Avas hill closes off the double folding screen of viticulture at the foot of the mountain. From the north, in turn, Tetemvár is the final element of the ridge reaching the lowlands. These noticeable slopes indicate downtown Miskolc to the traveller on the highway. Instead of the scions of bourgeois guild families, it is almost always others who inhabit it, therefore there are no tarnished signs, legendary stores, and dynasties, like those of the Austrians or the Czechs. Instead, rows of banks and telephone stores, all sorts of cheap Chinese clothing, Balkan bakeries, Arab kebabs. Nowadays, you have to explain where Miskolc's first bookstore stood, operated by the Ferenczi family.

Days, weeks, months: between 7 July 1873 and September 1890, a Miskolc kid grows up. He roves the central streets; climbs the neighbouring hills; breathes the air of households, stores, squares; knows the lights and shadows of the alternating seasons. Lives the city, with memories tied to each and every nook and cranny.

On Miskolc's main street, (Széchenyi Street, numbers 11–13), in place of a modern multistory brick building, stood the Ferenczi bookstore. It was built sometime in the second half of the eighteenth century by Greek merchants in the Baroque style. Ferdinánd János Groszman opened Miskolc's first bookshop in this greenish-yellow house built from heavy sandstone, in 1835. Groszman went bankrupt, so in 1847, Mihály Heilprin, the learned poet of the war of independence, the secretary of the ministry of the interior, re-established the bookstore. Due to his past as a revolutionary, he left for America in the years of neoabsolutism. In 1856 the store was taken over by Bernát Fraenkel (his brother in law's brother, specifically the younger brother of his little sister's husband), who later, in 1879, Magyarised his name to Ferenczi. Locally, in Miskolc, his store became a legend. Worldwide, his eighth child, Sándor Ferenczi became famous. He made their family name, was known as Sigmund Freud's disciple, and revolutionised Hungarian psychotherapy.

The estate, opening on to the main street, was fairly narrow, ten to fifteen metres wide, but its length, which extended to the Pece stream, was nearly one hundred metres. Made

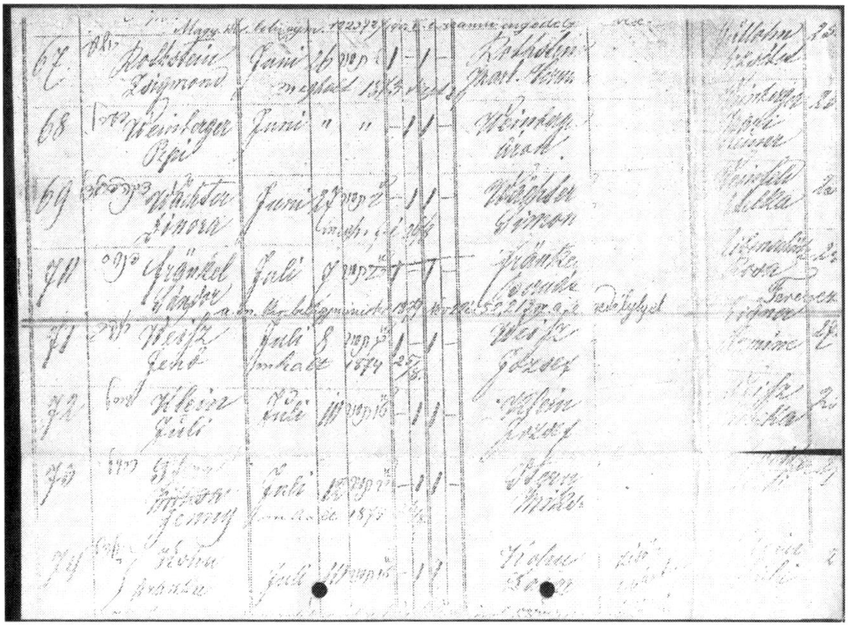

Miskolc birth registry from 1873, with entry "Fraenkel, Sandor"
courtesy Judit Meszaros

up of 315 squares, its area was about 1130 square metres. Its front, looking on to the promenade, completely filled the building. Next to the bookstore, spanning the ground floor, on the eastern side of the facade, a driveway through a wrought iron gate led into the courtyard. The stairwell leading to the living quarters was to the left, under the driveway. There were three windows on the top floor, above the bookstore's display and sign-board ("B. Ferenczi bookshop, Founded 1835"), then two more on the level of the driveway, so altogether five windows looked on to the Sötétkapu across the way. Behind the bookshop and the living quarters, there was plenty of usable area; tenants lived in the buildings in the yard and various businesses were operated there (in 1911, for example, a laundry, a carpenter, and a locksmith).

The iron door creaks. Teenaged Sándor Ferenczi steps out on to the main street, on the way to school. Across from their house, the Dark Gate swallows him; he still turns around and sees that the neighbouring "Pharmacy to the Hungarian Crown" (Széchenyi Street, number 11), is getting ready to open. It's time. He has to pick up his pace.

He speeds up on Püspök (today, Rákóczi) Street, clanging across the Szinva Bridge. He turns to the right, that is, to the west. Another sixty to eighty metres and he reaches the Reformed Church high school's building (today, Papszer Street, number 1). He attends a sombre, several-hundred-year-old school, which is not old-fashioned, in spite of its patina.

Due to the damages of the great Miskolc flood (30 August 1878), the building is renovated a few years before Sándor's enrolment. The main front faces the Avas hillside. After all, it is separated from downtown by the Szinva stream's course, which today is covered.

The adolescent Ferenczi has no reason to stress. Several of his brothers study in the upper grades, and his father is a respected patron of the institution.

Bernát Ferenczi. What's most important: Sándor is a superb student; in his free time he writes competition essays and wins awards for his translations, historical essays, and solutions of geometry problems. He has trouble with gym class only. With regards to his other subjects: Hungarian, history, geography, and mathematics went equally well, as did Latin, German, Greek, Jewish religious studies, and preliminary studies in philosophy. As a prospective physician, he had the highest marks in natural history and science. Still, languages and history interested him the most.

The school's Ferenc Kazinczy Literary Society announced competitions. Ferenczi won prizes for Latin ("A song of Anacreon in translation"), German (from the Paraenesis of Kölcsey, from Hungarian to German), and Greek (Herodotus' account of the Battle of Plataea, from Greek to Hungarian) translations, historical essays ("Causes and effect of the Wallachian Hora-Kloska revolt", "The establishment of the Hungarian kingdom, with its causes and effect"), and solutions to algebraic and geometric problems.

He was an officer and the treasurer of the society; he received special commendations for expert criticisms of entries. He graduated with ease between 27 and 31 May 1890, with excellent marks.

Meanwhile, his behaviour didn't fit his amazing scholarly achievements by any means, amusing himself with obscene Latin poems with his accomplices in the breaks between classes, and the closeness of the Avas hills and the host of streetwalkers using the abandoned cellars there as workplaces exciting his fantasy perhaps more than it should have.

The diary of the psychoanalyst approaching the end of his life captured bizarre childhood moments, for example: "one of the maids let me play with her breast, and then pressed my head between her legs."

In his letters to his friend Georg Groddeck, Ferenczi confessed his adolescent self being a "secret onanist" and visiting "prostitutes on stolen money". He considered his mother to be too strict, and also unfair, even later in life.

In his quoted diary, he referred to the angry and demeaning proclamations of his mother, Róza Eibenschütz, several times: "You murder me,"; "You are a murderer." The situation's unexpected amelioration was hinted at in one of Ferenczi's letters to Freud, in which he wrote as follows: "until the death of my father, my mother was strict, and according to my feelings then, and probably also according to my assessment today, unfair".

According to the diary, the cold atmosphere lasted until Bernát Ferenczi's death on 25 November 1889. Sándor was sixteen when he lost his father. He began his university studies in Vienna the following September.

The death took a serious toll on the whole family. Decades later, Mother Róza had this text carved on to her own tomb: "My children, do not cry! Here, at your dear father's side, I find the consolation and rest that I searched for on Earth in vain since his death."

The friendly, unreserved relationship of his parents is suggested by Ferenczi's—for that matter, not particularly cheery—memory: "at the age of 14, I was very shaken, when I heard that my father, unaware of my presence, told my mother that so and so married a whore."

Mother Róza didn't remain alone, although several of her children had grown up; the youngest, Zsófia, (born 18 July 1883), was only six years old when the father died. The widow inherited the bookshop, and mother Róza ran the shop on a day-to-day basis as well.

The usual Ferenczi oomph was unchanged: the issued postcards immediately reflected the cityscape's development at the turn of the century, showing, for example Lajos Kossuth's statue, the steam bath, and the new building of the Reformed Church high school.

In the millennium years, the widowed Mrs Ferenczi rebuilt the bookshop's display, lived through the First World War, the Soviet Republic, and Trianon. Her mental freshness hardly withered. Ferenczi took pride in the mental health of his mother.

Mother Róza had herself treated in Marienbad during the summer of 1913. This was when she was able to meet with Professor Freud, resting there, through her son's intervention. She made a good impression on the father of psychoanalysis, who wrote in a letter to his friend that his mother is a "remarkably bright-eyed, refined woman".

This all pleased Ferenczi, and in his answer he noted in agreement that indeed mother Róza, "compared to her age, is remarkably alert mentally". Maybe the spirit can defy biological age, the body less so.

Approaching her eightieth year, mother Róza needed constant supervision. A woman's care was required, so after the war, she moved to her eldest daughter, Ilona, in Nyíregyháza. Her children visited her, or at least on 11 December 1920, all her living sons and daughters congratulate her on her eightieth birthday. (Nyíregyháza was a family location for a while at that point: in the 1870s, the Ferenczi bookshop already had a local branch there; after the founding father's death, Miksa, then József, became the manager of the store, highly regarded by notable writer Gyula Krúdy.)

Sándor is there too. In a letter, he writes to Freud that in Nyíregyháza "I found my elderly mother surprisingly alert mentally, and also in a rather good physical state." The professor's telegraph of greetings is delivered on time. Mother Róza is happy to receive well wishes from Vienna, but she is of course even happier about her children and grandchildren arriving from Berlin, Budapest, and Miskolc.

The moments of the last birthday of the woman who had lived through a lot: her heart failure cannot be helped much longer. On 16 July 1921, Ferenczi goes to Nyíregyháza again, the "mischievous child" spends her days of agony with her, tries to ease her suffering with morphine. He informs Freud in a letter about the details, so we know that mother Róza has "intense pain between doses, but mentally is perfectly clear".

On Thursday morning, 20 July 1921, mother Róza dies. Only Sándor is in his mother's room, surveying the dying woman seated in an armchair also as a doctor, but he can't help her anymore. Finally he lays the corpse on to the bed, ties up her chin, and says goodbye.

Among mother Róza's last wishes was for her final resting place to be by her father's side, in the Avas Jewish cemetery in Miskolc. Sándor was against the complicated transport, but his opinion lost out against his siblings' sense of resolve.

The corpse had to be transported to Miskolc in a metal coffin, but nevertheless, on the day after her death, Friday afternoon, she could be buried. At that time, the cemetery on the hilltop could most easily be reached from downtown, from the northwest side of the Avas.

It was hot outside. For the horse's sake, the heavy metal coffin was placed on a smaller cart, but it did not lay stably so had to be placed back on the bigger, heavier cart. The procession moved slowly. The gravediggers prepared the grave assuming a traditional wooden coffin.

The anomaly was discovered during the descent, and the coffin stood up, a veritable horror, as the foot end of the coffin reached the bottom of the pit, while the side towards the head was caught! Re-digging took an hour. Mother Róza's corpse reached the grave in the Avas cemetery's first plot, number 57/3 under unique circumstances …

The side of the Avas hill is also an important location from a lighter, happier point of view. At the time, on the southeast slope, named Szentgyörgy, lay Bernát Ferenczi's vineyard. Allegedly, Sándor is the favourite child, who he often takes out with him to the mountain.

The path is known until the Szinva bridge, but during the school break, instead of leaving the high school on the right, father and son probably head east, through the Mélyvölgy, or climb the Kálvária hill covered, since 1864, by a chapel and stations of the Cross, to reach the vineyard of Avas.

During harvest, they fight their way up with a host of carts. Throughout this time, the populous family, along with friends and servants, spend days living in the vineyard. Successful work is usually concluded with fireworks. As we have already said: the Avas has also, of course, a less cheerful face.

The Jewish cemetery, referred to as "Jewish sorrow", lies on the northwest side. There lie Sándor Ferenczi's siblings who passed away in their childhoods. At the head of a mass funeral procession, at the age of sixteen, he accompanies his beloved father on his last trip up the Avas (Bernát Ferenczi was buried on 26 November 1889).

Sándor lives through the death of his favourite older brother Henrik (9 February 1912), who had been ailing for a long time; and we see that he was at the farewell ceremony of his mother Róza Eibenschütz Ferenczi in the Miskolc Jewish cemetery (July 1921).

Nowadays, under the Avas, at the southeast foot of the hill, is the Sándor Ferenczi Medical Vocational School /Mihály Szigethy Street 8. A relief sculpture in the aula (Ágnes Máger's work, 1994), calls to mind the eminent Miskolc-born psychoanalyst.

In connection to his Jewish heritage, terrible emotions split the Miskolc community in 1871, the schism occurring after decades of lead-up. The main divisive factor may have been the interior layout of the Kazinczy Street synagogue, consecrated in 1863.

The new synagogue was built to be Neolog, so the Torah-reading podium stood not in the centre, but in front of the eastern wall. A choir and a built-in organ accompanied the prayers. All this triggered the rage of the local Jews who conservatively stuck to tradition.

Defying their cursing, the reformists declared, in writing, that they insisted on the liturgical arrangement permitted by the authorities. Among those to sign the statement dated May 1866 was Sándor Ferenczi's father, Bernát Fraenkel (who only Magyarised his family name in 1879).

The viewpoints didn't become closer, so, due to the separation of the dissatisfied Orthodox, two communities existed in Miskolc between 1871 and 1875: the Fraenkel—Ferenczi family belonged to the Neolog organisation. With their bourgeois mentality they visited the Neolog synagogue on Kazinczy Street—at least during the more important holidays—instead of the old synagogue on Palóczy Street.

(The bookshop on the main street, with its baroque features, disappears without a trace in 1963. The iron door, its bars, its gates are placed in a museum after the building is torn down. Nowadays, the two iron doors of the former Ferenczi house are visible a few metres from the Déryné Street entrance of the synagogue, in the driveway of the Museum of the History of Drama and Acting, Déryné Street 2.)

The rowdy Italian postmodern journalist Massimiliano Parente states that "great men's biographies start when they are already great. Before that, we have the biographies of normal people reinterpreted in retrospect, and they are always very boring. When I read a biography, I immediately flip to the important part, right away to the moment when the great person became great. Before that, it bores me. I skip over pages, and look for the point where greatness began."

When and where did Sándor Ferenczi's greatness start? When he broke away from Freud's classical methods? Or already, when as a young physician, he picked up *The Interpretation of Dreams*?

Or when, as a beginner from Miskolc, he published a scientific study about the psychology of being a tourist? Or when he was browsing for hours in his father's bookshop? …

Chapter 2

Ferenczi's Budapest

Tom Keve

The Millennium

In 1896, Budapest, and indeed the whole of the Kingdom of Hungary, celebrated the one thousandth anniversary of the Magyar tribes' conquest of the Pannonia basin. The extensive and resplendent festivities, attended by the Imperial family and dignitaries from overseas, were not only intended to mark the Magyar Millennium, they also proclaimed to the world Hungary's arrival as a full-fledged, modern European nation and celebrated the emergence of Budapest as a metropolis on the West-European, but especially the Parisian, model.

Two factors in the immediate past combined to forge the Budapest of 1896. The first was the Reconciliation of 1867, which laid to rest the ghosts of the failed 1848 Hungarian revolution against Austrian rule. The Reconciliation recognised the Kingdom of Hungary as partner to the Austrian Empire, within the Austro-Hungarian Monarchy, and served as the starter's gun to a frenzied race to revive the economy of the country. The other factor was the unification of the three neighbouring towns of Buda, Obuda, and Pest into the city of Budapest, second capital of Austria-Hungary, and undisputed hub of Hungary's political life, its economic heart and cultural centre.

The ink on his medical diploma from Vienna was barely dry when Ferenczi took up residence in Budapest. He arrived just before the Millennium celebrations in what can only be called a boom town. In the decade of 1890 to 1900, the population of Budapest increased by fifty per cent. While the growth-rate was highest in that particular decade, the boom lasted forty years, from 1870 to the First World War, with the city's population more than trebling in that period (KSH, 2011, Table 1.1.1.1).

The city was blessed with a natural beauty, bisected by the broad river, connected by the beautiful Chain Bridge (1849) and the more prosaic Margaret Bridge (1876). The hills of Buda on the western side were dominated by the hilltop Royal Palace. The flat expanse of Pest, on the other bank, had been laid out with grand Parisian avenues and boulevards.

On his arrival Ferenczi would have witnessed a hive of activity. The Grand Boulevard (Nagykőrút), built over the preceding ten years, was (practically) completed by the Millennium celebrations. Along it ran the first electric tram in the country. The third great bridge over the Danube, named after Emperor Franz-Joseph, was opened by him in 1896. In the inner city, speculators built grand apartment houses with ornate decorations, while the city fathers ensured that only the noblest of public edifices were erected. The grandiose, neo-Renaissance, Hungarian State Opera House was opened in 1884, just ten tears after the Salle des Capucines (later the Palais Garnier) in Paris. The baroque, architecturally over-adorned Comedy Theatre (Vigszinház) was built in just one year on what had been marshland and opened its doors to the public in 1896. Some distance along the boulevard, the luxurious Grand Hotel Royal, which was to play a part in Ferenczi's life, was inaugurated that same year. The opulent New York coffee house, yet further along the boulevard, had already been open for two years, and had become the hub of the literary and theatrical life of the city. Andrássy út, the Champs Élysées of Budapest, was built in the 1870s and 80s, with the last empty lot built on in 1885. A straight, broad avenue, it runs from the city centre, crossing the boulevard and ending in the City Park, lined with new apartment blocks on the city end and opulent villas on the park end. Underneath the avenue ran the first underground railway on the continent of Europe, inaugurated in 1896 for the Millennium celebrations. On the bank of the Danube, the iconic Parlament Building, unashamedly modelled on Westminster, was being built throughout the 1890s. Although not yet finished, the first sitting of parliament was held there in 1896, again, to commemorate the millennium. The St Stephen Bazilika building was also finished about this time, although it was only consecrated in 1905. A half kilometre away, the Synagogue at Dohány utca had been functioning for three decades. When it was built, it was the largest in the world, (soon to be overtaken by Temple Emmanu-El in New York City). Elizabeth Bridge spanned the Danube in 1902; at the time it was the longest single-span bridge in the world. Opened in 1905, the new stock exchange building and its trading floor were the largest in Europe. In addition, hundreds of apartment houses, numerous coffee houses, theatres, and other public buildings were completed in this period. The Budapest that we still see today was created in the last fifteen years of the nineteenth century.

Intellectual and cultural life

The thriving intellectual life of Budapest in the early twentieth century was undoubtedly led by the literary giants of the period, of which there were an unusually large number. It is difficult for non-Hungarians to appreciate the quality and quantity of the output of the authors, poets, and playwrights, or the esteem in which they were held by the general public. Only a few of them broke out of the straight jacket of Hungarian, which was a strange language that sat like an island in the ocean of polyglot Europe. They held court in the opulent coffeehouses of Budapest and often did most of their writing there as well. It is well known that Ferenczi, who frequented the Royal Coffee House, across the road from his consulting rooms on the Boulevard, was very close to these literary circles. The writer Ignotus, editor of the influential literary journal *Nyugat*, was a founder member of Ferenczi's Budapest Psychoanalytical Association. Dezső Kosztolányi was an analysand, who, under the pseudonym of Dr Moviszter, included Ferenczi in his bestselling novel *Édes Anna* (English translation: Kosztolányi, 1991). The most famous and prolific satirist of the time, Frigyes Karinthy, was also a crony of Ferenczi's, although they conducted a heated exchange in print on the merits of psychoanalysis. The much younger Sándor Márai, pre-eminent author of the first half of the twentieth century, several of whose novels and plays have appeared in English, was also a close friend. All three men wrote moving obituaries on Ferenczi's death in 1933 (see Baczoni's translation in Szekacs-Weisz & Keve, 2012).

Even more than the novelists, Budapest's poets were stuck on their linguistic island. The likes of Endre Ady and Attila József were regarded as the spokesmen of the nation, their words repeated and treasured, yet remained unknowns in the wider world. But music knows no boundaries and the works of Bartók and Kodály quickly spread across Europe and further. Others, like Dohnányi took a little longer. Ferenc Lehár and Imre Kálmán, composers of the most popular operettas, were able to conquer the world from their Budapest base. Music had been an essential element of the city. The glittering opera house was sold out every night. Attending concerts was de rigueur for the bourgeoisie. Everyone hummed the lighter music of the Operetta Theatre, there were gypsy bands in restaurants and tea dances in outdoor cafes on Margaret Island, and youngsters were taught piano or violin. The Music Academy was filled with students, a number of whom would be world famous in later years. This vibrant musical vitality was not only for the elite, it was an essential element of Budapest life.

Academia was also not isolated. While many of the intelligentsia went abroad to study, to Berlin, or, like Ferenczi, to Vienna, the Budapest high schools and universities were of a good standard. Mathematics especially turned out to be a Hungarian speciality. And again, these elements were not isolated but part and parcel of the Budapest milieu. It was not a large city. The middle classes frequented the same coffee houses and theatres and they were often linked by family ties. One of the greatest mathematicians of the twentieth century, John von Neumann, was, for instance, the nephew of Ferenczi's brother-in-law, Alajos Alcsuti.

As elsewhere, debate and argument was the life-blood of the intellectual youth. The Galilei Circle of left-leaning free-thinking students was founded in 1908, with Károly Polányi, later a world famous economist and social historian, as president, and Mátyás Rákosi, post-Second World War communist dictator, as future secretary. Psychoanalysts Imre Hermann and Lilly Hajdu were members in their student days. Several other members, like György Lukács, the Marxist philosopher, and Michael Polányi, chemist and philosopher, as well as mathematician György Pólya, subsequently became world-renowned, each in their own field. In the years before the Great War the circle thrived and became politically influential. The new and groundbreaking field of Freudian psychoanalysis was one of the areas that fascinated the group. Sándor Ferenczi was invited to address them on more than one occasion. He even mentioned this in his correspondence with Freud (Fer/Fr, p. 88).

Jewish Budapest

In the nineteenth century Magyars were a minority in their country, the largest one but still less than fifty per cent of the population. To increase their numbers, and as a matter of genuine liberalism, they encouraged Jews to consider themselves Magyars. The Magyar cause was taken up with enthusiasm by many Jews, and as part of the historic 1867 Reconciliation with Austria, Jews were granted full civil rights in Hungary. They were free to enter universities, the professions, and to live wherever they wished. Many chose to move to the booming capital. In fact, throughout the population boom, the Jewish population of Budapest grew as the city grew, remaining fairly constant as a percentage at just over twenty per cent. The clustering of Jews in certain parts of Pest resulted in districts such as Lipótváros, Terézváros, and Erzsébetváros having up to forty per cent of their population identifying themselves as Jewish (Ujvári, 1929, p. 153).

It would not be an exaggeration to say that Jews dominated the middle classes of the city. Budapest had become industrialised by the turn of the century, so there was a large working class population, mainly in the outer districts, where the industry was also located. The civil service was dominated by the minor gentry, and of course the aristocracy were above the professions except perhaps for leading political positions. This left the Jews, who in 1910 provided more than half the doctors, lawyers, journalists, and veterinarians, one third of all actors and pharmacists, and one fifth of all school teachers in Budapest. While a large proportion were employed in small business activities, such as shopkeepers and clerks, tradesmen or bank tellers, a rather small, but important fraction provided the financial elite of the country. These were Jewish families, many ennobled by Franz Joseph, who had grown wealthy as industrialists, merchants, or bankers (ibid.).

There were numerous synagogues, and religious education was compulsory under Franz Joseph (that is to say, for Jewish schoolchildren instruction in Judaism was mandatory), but the majority of Budapest Jews took the practice of their religion fairly lightly. They defined themselves as Jews primarily by culture and later, as the objects of anti-Semitism, rather than religion.

The success of the Jews in professions and industry in just a generation or two awakened resentment, which easily transmuted into anti-Semitism. It was the nationalist, and populist, mayor of Vienna who first called the city Judapest. Clearly meant to be derogatory, the term is now used as the name of a major Jewish cultural festival in Budapest. But the term did signal a perceived split between the nationalist, conservative, agricultural, Magyar countryside and the progressive, liberal, industrial, western-oriented, Jewish capital. So while anti-Semitism was smouldering in the country, in Budapest it was more or less restrained, only a minor inconvenience.

Ferenczi was part and parcel of Jewish Budapest. He moved to the city from Miskolc (via Vienna) as part of the 1890s wave from the provinces to the capital. He lived on the newly built Boulevard (at 54 Erzsébet kőrút, opposite the Grand Hotel Royal and its coffee house) in one of the middle class, Jewish areas. Many of his colleagues at the Rokus hospital were Jewish, as were his psychoanalytical patients and, presumably, the majority of his friends. While the shared background and shared problems of Jews formed a natural social bond, there was also simply the weight of numbers. Since Ferenczi lived and worked in an area where forty per cent of the population were Jewish, he was bound to have a great number of Jewish contacts.

The Great War and its immediate aftermath

Budapest life, the glittering, good life, later referred to nostalgically as *békebeli béke* or "the peacetime peace", continued up to the First World War. In fact the war itself had a relatively minor effect on Budapest life, considerably less than it did some other European cities. The men were conscripted of course, but life continued more or less as ever. Formally, food was rationed but never in short supply and the fighting was always far, far away, both physically and psychologically. At the start of the war Ferenczi was conscripted as an army doctor and sent to the town of Pápa, about an hour from Budapest, but by 1916 he was posted back to the capital and took up residence in the Grand Hotel Royal. As can be seen from his letters to Freud, his life returned pretty much to normal for the remainder of the war.

In September of 1918, while the final, great battles of the Western Front were raging, Budapest hosted the Fifth International Psychoanalytic Congress. The grand edifice of the Academy of Sciences on the riverbank at the Pest foot of the Chain Bridge was deemed appropriate to welcome Sigmund Freud and his followers from within the Central Powers. It was also the venue where Sándor Ferenczi was elected president of the IPA.

But while the war itself was not very turbulent for Budapest, the same could not be said of the months and years following. By the end of October 1918 soldiers returning from the front were demonstrating in the city. To show their peaceful intention, they placed flowers, mainly asters, in their gun-barrels. What became known as the Aster Revolution resulted in Hungary being declared an independent republic, with a liberal-democratic government. At the same time, the Spanish flu epidemic was ravaging Budapest. Ferenczi wrote to Freud, both of his "mourning" for the old Hungary and the relentless advance of the influenza in the same letter, dated 22 October 1918 (Fer/Fr, p. 302).

The next few months were characterised by political turmoil, until in March of 1919 the "bourgeois" government resigned and the Hungarian Democratic Republic was replaced by the Hungarian Council Republic, modelled on the Soviet Government of Lenin, itself only a few months old. Led by Hungarian communists returning from Moscow and the "old" guard of the Galilei Circle socialist youth, this government lasted less than five months. In that brief period numerous Bolshevik measures were introduced, such as land reform, nationalisation, and educational measures. What became known as the "red terror" was unleashed to silence or eliminate any opposition. In that period, the communist government also fought and lost a war. It was this government that appointed Ferenczi to the world's first chair of psychoanalysis, although the matter had already been under consideration by the previous regime. Ferenczi's appointment was signed by the People's Commissar for Education, György Lukács, previously of the Galilei Circle, and countersigned by the Deputy People's Commissar, Theodor von Kármán, much later founder and director of the Jet Propulsion Laboratory in Pasadena, California (Keve 2000, p 194; original in Ferenczi archives, Freud Museum, London).

By the summer, a counter-revolution had begun, which, although it did not take hold in Budapest, was supported in the south of the country by the invading Romanian forces, who were backed by the French. By August 1919, Romanian troops had occupied Budapest and the Council Republic passed into history.

This change was followed by the "white terror", an ultra-nationalist campaign of murder and pillaging, with a view to avenging the victims of the "red terror" and eliminating any political opposition. Many of the leaders of the Council Republic government were Jewish and the "white terror" became a pogrom against not only political enemies but the Jewish population in general. Life in Budapest was uncertain and insecure. Gangs roamed the streets and Jews feared for their lives. George Hevesy, another professorial appointee of the Council Republic, later winner of the Nobel Prize for chemistry, wrote in November 1918 to his friend Niels Bohr of the "material and moral decay" of the country and of his colleagues being dismissed from the university simply for being Jewish (Keve, 2000, p. 201). Similarly, Ferenczi reported to Freud that "[t]he blackest reaction prevails at the university. All Jewish assistants were fired, the Jewish students were thrown out and beaten" (Fer/Fr, p. 366).

Civil order was restored only at the end of the year, when Admiral Horthy took power as regent of a reconstituted, sovereign-less Kingdom of Hungary.

The 1920s

The Trianon Treaty of 1920 resulted in Hungary being reduced in size by two thirds. It was also transformed from a multinational country to a nation-state with a small minority of non-Magyars. Budapest, having been one of the twin capitals of Austria-Hungary, became the capital of a small Central European country, a role for which it was possibly over-qualified.

One of the first acts of the new government, the fifth in a twelve-month period, was to declare all university appointments of the communist regime invalid. Among a number of others, Ferenczi's professorship was cancelled. He was also dismissed from the Hungarian Medical Association.

Civil order was restored during 1920, but anti-Semitism did not end; it became official. In July, the *Numerus Clausus* Law was passed by the Hungarian Parliament, restricting the number of Jews in higher education. This resulted in Jewish university professors taking positions as high school teachers, while undergraduates like Eugene Wigner, Edward Teller, and John von Neumann left Budapest to continue their studies abroad, particularly in Germany. Ferenczi had no future in academia, but his work did not require him to be attached to a university. During the 1920s he was kept busy with his private patients and was prolific in his published work. He considered emigrating, but did not actually take the step. Instead, he travelled to Germany, Austria, the United States, and elsewhere as one of the major figures of the international psychoanalytic community. It was not until 1928 that he held public lectures in Budapest again.

Gradually, especially once the post-war hyperinflation had been brought under control, normality and uneasy prosperity returned to Budapest. Jews in trade and the professions were not molested and as the economy improved, they thrived. The middle classes prospered; the cafes were overflowing, intellectual life flourished, the old literary flame flared up again. Glamour returned to the capital. Ladies in furs with their men in evening wear rode to the opera in polished motor cars with long bonnets. Sunday afternoon tea-dances were frequented by the bourgeoisie. In winter they skated on the frozen lake in the City Park. New luxury hotels sprang up to accommodate distinguished visitors, who flocked to Budapest to admire its beautiful setting on the two banks of the Danube and to enjoy its racy nightlife.

Towards the end

In order to escape the busy, noisy metropolis that was Pest, the upper middle classes created a verdant refuge in certain quarters of the Buda hills. Lovely villas with large gardens nestled on tree-lined streets. Ferenczi achieved his dream of owning such a home when in 1930 he acquired Lisznyai utca 11, on Naphegy, just west of Castle Hill and the Royal Palace. He spent his last years there, immersed in his work, and, judging by his correspondence, largely unaware of the storm clouds that were gathering on the horizon.

The Great Depression had its effect on Hungary. Grain exports slumped, industrial production declined, businesses went bankrupt, and the economy was in the doldrums. A period of austerity ensued. By 1933 unemployment in Hungary reached thirty-five per cent. In Budapest twenty per cent of the population were below the poverty line. The middle classes also felt the squeeze. Although Budapest still wore its party clothes, all was not well. The politics of the country shifted further to the right, a portent of what was to come. It was in this atmosphere of unease that, on 22 May 1933, the capital learned of the loss of one of its great citizens, the psychoanalyst, Sándor Ferenczi.

References

Keve, T. (2000). *Triad: The Physicists, the Analysts, the Kabbalists*. London: Rosenberger & Krausz.

Kosztolányi, D. (1991). *Anna Édes*. New York: New Directions.

KSH (2011). *Népszámlálás 2011* [Census 2011]. Budapest: Központi Statisztikai Hivatal [Budapest: Central Bureau of Statistics]. www.ksh.hu/nepszamlalas/tablak_teruleti_01

Szekacs-Weisz, J., & Keve, T. (2012). *Ferenczi and his World: Rekindling the Spirit of the Budapest School*. London: Karnac.

Ujvári, P. (1929). *Magyar Zsidó Lexikon* [Hungarian Jewish lexicon]. Budapest: Zsidó Lexikon Kiadása.

Chapter 3

Ferenczi before Freud

Gabriele Cassullo

In the book *Disappearing and Reviving* Haynal (2002) raises the issue whether "everything in Ferenczi's career *before* he met Freud in 1908 was *pre*-psychoanalytic, and everything that came after was ... psychoanalytic." In fact, "three months after the first conversation between the two men, Ferenczi was addressing the Salzburg Congress. Had he become a psychoanalyst in three months? That would be a record even for Ferenczi! The truth is plainly more complex" (p. 1). Additionally, in 1909 Ferenczi published a contribution that has become a cornerstone of psychoanalytic theory and technique, "Introjection and transference", showing an in-depth knowledge of the discipline. Where had that knowledge come from?

In order to answer the question we need to focus on Ferenczi's works before his meeting with Freud. These include forty-seven journal articles, book reviews, and translations, written between 1899 and 1908, which have been collected and studied by Mészáros and Casonato (1992), and were first published in 1992 in Italian. Some of those writings had already been summarised in French by Lorin (1983). As Casonato remarks: "There is no doubt about the importance of those pre-analytic writings: the first mention, or even the first detailed presentations, of the themes that would resurface in the whole of Ferenczi's oeuvre … can really be found in those writings" (Casonato, 1992, p. xxii).

Most of the journal articles appeared in *Gyógyászat* [Therapy], a progressive medical journal edited by Miksa Schächter. According to Haynal, "Schächter was a kind of paternal friend: here Ferenczi can already be seen seeking an idealized father as an interlocutor for his self-analysis, the same role that he later expected Freud to fulfill" (Haynal, 2002, p. 4). Mészáros echoes Haynal, by arguing that: "Ferenczi was bound to Schächter by filial love, which is revealed by the choice of the subjects for his juvenile writings" (Mészáros, 1992, p. xiv). When Schächter died, in 1917, Ferenczi devoted a heartfelt *in memoriam* to the figure of his first mentor: a single, powerful, and protective man, in his words (Ferenczi, 1917, p. 430), whom he tried to emulate to the point of being nicknamed "Schächter junior" (p. 431).

By the time he returned to Budapest, after completing his medical training in Vienna, in 1899, Ferenczi was a twenty-six-year-old ambitious physician who could only find employment on the venereal diseases ward of a city hospital. For more than a year he mainly worked with prostitutes; but as time passed, he grew less and less satisfied with the occupation, because his aspiration was to treat mental diseases. Being familiar with Janet's groundbreaking research on hypnosis, hysteria, and the subconscious mind, he started experimenting with automatic writing for producing a "doubling" of his personality:

> As I had no chance to perform psychological experiments, I had begun to experiment on myself. I had tried to explore the so-called "occult" phenomena ... It happened once

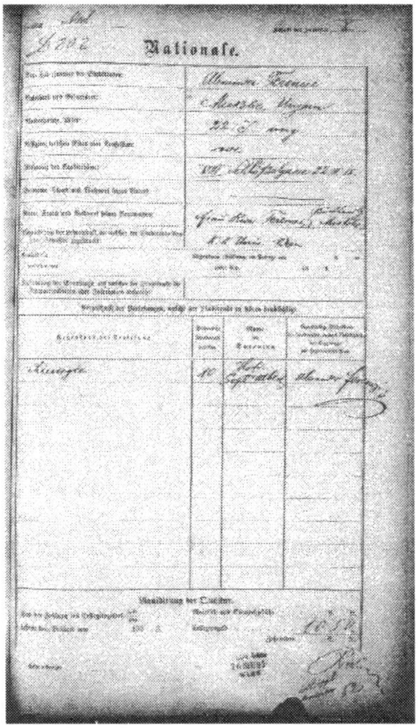
Nationale.

Ferenczi's student record

courtesy Ferenc Eros and the University of Vienna Archives

> that, following a dinner with friends, I walked through the permanently locked gates of the "Little Rokus" [Hospital] well after midnight. I went to the junior physicians' room and engaged in "automatic writing" ... It occurred to me that it was already very late; I was tired and somewhat aroused emotionally. All these circumstances favoured the exploration. So I picked up a pencil and, holding it loosely in my hand, I pressed it against a piece of blank paper. I decided to let the pencil move "on its own", letting it write whatever it wished. Senseless scribbles came first, then letters, words (some of them strange to me), and finally whole sentences.
>
> (Ferenczi, 1917, p. 430)

In a short period of time he could begin to have a "dialogue" with his pencil, which suggested to him to write a paper for Miksa Schächter, the editor of *Gyógyászat* (Ferenczi, 1917, p. 430). The paper was written, accepted, and published in the same year, under the title of "Spiritism". It dealt with "the big questions" of the meaning of life, the limits of human knowledge, transcendence, and so on. In this paper Ferenczi makes an argument against the dominant ideology of scientific materialism, and he describes spiritism, spiritualism, medianism, animism as different manifestations of the return to metaphysics. In particular, he rejects atomistic materialism when applied to the study of the human mind and wishes for science to overcome the idea that "consciousness is but a secretion of cerebral matter" (Ferenczi, 1899, p. 6). In other words, it seems that at this early stage Ferenczi is already yearning for a kind of metaphysics of the soul: that is, a conceptual framework that could bridge body and mind, which he would eventually find in Freud's metapsychology.

Incidentally, a particular interest in spiritism, telepathy, and the so-called "occult phenomena" was not uncommon among the psychologists and physicians of the time (to name just one, William James; see Ellenberger, 1970), many of the pioneers of psychoanalysis included[1]—so much so that some scholars remarked on the continuity between that area of investigation and later research on intrapsychic and interpersonal unconscious communications, transference-countertransference dynamics, etc. (e.g., Gyimesi, 2009, 2016; Massicotte, 2014). As an example, Helene Deutsch's classical work on the distinction between concordant and complementary identifications—which in the 1950s was to be taken up by H. Racker (1968) in his work on countertransference—was titled "Occult processes occurring during psychoanalysis" (1926), and was published in George Devereux's book *Psychoanalysis and the Occult*. With the purpose of linking occult phenomena and transference-countertransference dynamics, it is telling that that very book also includes "On the role of transference and countertransference in psychoanalysis", an early study on the intertwinement of transference and countertransference in psychoanalytic cure, which was first presented in Budapest on the occasion of the death of Ferenczi (in 1933) by Hann-Kende (1933), an Hungarian pupil of Ferenczi's and analysand of Deutsch's. Hann-Kende would later expatriate, join the New York Psychoanalytic Society, and thus become one of the numerous "bearers on the field" of Ferenczi's way of thinking and working in psychoanalysis.

Ferenczi's second early writing takes us from the dazes of the spiritual to the more terrestrial field of psychotherapy. It is a review of Ranschburg and Décsi's book *Spiritual Therapeutic Methods (Psychotherapy)*, where Ferenczi draws the following conclusions: "Spiritual curative methods are to be considered useful devices – and sometimes even the only possible device – for the physician who wants to treat organic patients and, as Ziehen states, 'psychotherapy is necessary for any kind of hospitalization; without the aid of psychological therapies you may be cutting shoes or grafting plants, but you cannot cure sensitive and thinking beings'" (Ferenczi, 1900a, p. 13).

Here we can trace a second leitmotif of Ferenczi's. That is, the curative implications of the psychological qualities of the physician. In many writings Ferenczi emphasises the importance of suggestion and psychological influence, which can take the patient to trust the physician but only when accompanied by honesty, sincerity, responsibility, trust in one's own healing possibilities and in the curative process, willingness to admit one's own limits, a warm attitude (Ferenczi, 1900b, 1902c, 1902d, 1903a, 1903b, 1904a, 1904b, 1906b).

A third point is made in the fundamental writing "Consciousness and evolution", where Ferenczi depicts the human mind as an apparatus that is not only made of a series of mechanical functions but is somehow more than the totality of its parts (Ferenczi, 1900b, p. 15). This is about twenty-five years before Jan C. Smuts' book *Holism and Evolution*, and thirty-five years before the rise of Gestalt psychology as well as of any "systemic" approach to the human mind. Moreover, according to Ferenczi, consciousness is not just created by the inter-connectedness between psychological elements that are to be found within the individual mind, but it goes beyond personal boundaries: it emerges "between subjects that exert

1 For instance, Jung had been interested in these kinds of phenomena since his doctoral dissertation, which is dated 1902 and titled "On the psychology and pathology of so-called occult phenomena".

reciprocal effects on one another" (Ferenczi, 1900b, p. 15). Here one can see the seeds of Ferenczi's intersubjective inclination.

Towards the end of the paper, Ferenczi touches on the "proto-psychoanalytic" issue of the fall of omnipotence, infantile illusions, idealisation, and any kind of naive faith (Ferenczi, 1900b, p. 19). He recognises that it takes a long path, and many disappointments, for the subject to become conscious of his own limits—provided that "the subject can never know oneself completely" (p. 14).

> Blood and tears have been poured out in order for us to get here. Eventually – at the price of disappointments maybe – every man, just like humankind, understands that any kind of knowledge bears its own limits, which cannot be overlooked; we then interrupt any clear-cut denial or statement about anything ..., having become aware of our weakness.
>
> (p. 19)

The affective implications of that disillusional process are described in "Love in science" (1901a), where Ferenczi proposes his brilliant and seminal analysis of the sentiment of love.

> Love can make the man with the most steady nerves a subject of illusions, and maybe even delusions: "The whole world is now colorful for him"; when he is happy, everything is lively, smiling, sparkling; when he is unhappy, the sky gets obscured, the earth becomes a desert and even trees start crying. The person who is in love judges his love object to possess the greatest perfection, being blinded to any real physical, spiritual or moral deficiency.
>
> (p. 49)

One is tempted to reproduce the whole of Ferenczi's paper. But what is striking are his early hints—most likely with autobiographical resonance—at a (hypo) manic state of mind, the process of splitting of the object, and the following depressive working-through, all the somatic repercussions included: "What poets call disillusion, boredom, oblivion" (Ferenczi, 1901a, p. 51).

Then we come to the first clinical case study. "On the coordinated and the assimilated mental diseases" (1901b) reports on what today we would call a dual diagnosis, and which Ferenczi calls "a coordination of two diseases" (p. 55). In discussing the paranoid symptoms of his patient (Antal H), Ferenczi borrows something of Janet's conceptual horizon, such as the idea of "psychical weakness" (*faiblesse psychologique*), and leans on degeneration theory (Pick, 1989). In those years, that theory was the main controversial point between Janet and Freud, and the reason why the latter developed his drive/defence etiological model (Cassullo, 2014).

The theory of degeneration is also applied to the next case studies by Ferenczi: "Feminine homosexuality" (1902a) and "Paranoid dementia" (1902b). "Feminine homosexuality" elicited the interest of contemporary scholars for Ferenczi's sensitive description of the subjective experience of a patient with gender issues (Borgogno, 1999; Haynal, 2002; Lorin, 1983; Rachman, 1993).[2] To be sure, in all his early clinical cases Ferenczi shows a particular respect

2 Four years later Ferenczi returned to the topic of sexuality in the paper "The sexual states of transition" (Ferenczi, 1906a), showing that it was a subject of interest for him well before his encounter with Freud and psychoanalysis.

for the subjective point of view of the patient (Ferenczi, 1908). Furthermore, "Paranoid dementia" explores the "peculiar sensations" and modifications in the "colour" of the state of mind that foreshadow any delusional ideation (Ferenczi, 1902b, p. 82). In fact, according to Ferenczi, delusional ideas are not primary in kind, on the contrary they follow an underlying bodily-affective process and in a way represent the subject's attempt at interpreting such a process. Some ten years later, Freud discussed Schreber's delusions, explaining them as his personal attempt to make sense of and recover from the psychotic breakdown, reconstructing his inner world on the stones left by the catastrophe (Freud, 1911c, p. 71). This approach would become typical of British Independent analysts' work with psychotic patients (Cassullo, 2015).

In conclusion, I cannot but agree with Mészáros and Casonato (1992) who saw in Ferenczi's early writings the embryo of some of the ideas he continued to shape and develop all his life long. Moreover, we can appreciate Ferenczi's attitude to the cure of the human soul, his social reformism,[3] as well as some of his distinctive features: such as enthusiasm, intuitiveness, and sensitivity. At the same time, we can already recognise his "idealizing tendency" (Haynal, 2002), and a sort of "missionary zeal": some years later he will take that very same attitude towards Freud and psychoanalysis.

References

Borgogno, F. (1999). *Psychoanalysis as a Journey*. London: Open Gate.

Casonato, M. (1992). Il periodo preanalitico di Ferenczi (1899–1908) [Ferenczi's preanalytic period (1899–1908)]. In: J. Mészáros & M. Casonato (Eds.), *La mia amicizia con Miksa Schächter. Scritti preanalitici, 1899–1908* [My friendship with Miksa Schächter. Pre-analytic writings, 1899–1908] (pp. xx–xxvi). Turin: Bollati Boringhieri, 1992.

Cassullo, G. (2014). Splitting in the history of psychoanalysis: From Janet and Freud to Fairbairn, passing through Ferenczi and Suttie. In: G. Clarke & D. E. Scharff (Eds.), *Fairbairn and the Object Relations Tradition* (pp. 49–58). London: Karnac.

Cassullo, G. (2015). *L'uomo dietro al lettino. Charles Rycroft e la psicoanalisi Indipendente britannica* [The man behind the couch. Charles Rycroft and British Independent psychoanalysis]. Lecce: Frenis Zero.

Deutsch, H. (1926). Occult processes occurring during psychoanalysis. In: G. Devereux (Ed.), *Psychoanalysis and the Occult* (pp. 133–146). New York: International Universities Press, 1953.

Ellenberger, H. F. (1970). *The Discovery of the Unconscious*. New York: Basic Books.

Ferenczi, S. (1899). Spiritism. *Psychoanalytic Review, 50A*: 139–144, 1963.

Ferenczi, S. (1900a). Recensione a *Metodi terapeutici spirituali (Psicoterapia)* di P. Ranschburg e K. Décsi [Review of *Spiritual Therapeutic Methods (Psychotherapy)* by P. Ranschburg and K. Décsi]. In: J. Mészáros & M. Casonato (Eds.), *La mia amicizia con Miksa Schächter. Scritti preanalitici, 1899–1908* [My friendship with Miksa Schächter. Pre-analytic writings, 1899–1908] (pp. 11–13). Turin: Bollati Boringhieri, 1992.

Ferenczi, S. (1900b). Coscienza ed evoluzione [Consciousness and evolution]. In: J. Mészáros & M. Casonato (Eds.), *La mia amicizia con Miksa Schächter. Scritti preanalitici, 1899–1908* [My

3 In this chapter I have focused on topics that reflect Ferenczi's later psychoanalytic interests. His early writings also deal extensively with public-health issues like alcoholism, palliative care, nutrition, pharmaceuticals, health conditions of the lower-class, medical insurance, deceiving "diagnostic trends" in psychiatry, asylums, and the economic status of young physicians.

friendship with Miksa Schächter. Pre-analytic writings, 1899–1908] (pp. 14–19). Turin: Bollati Boringhieri, 1992.

Ferenczi, S. (1901a). L'amore nella scienza [Love in science]. In: J. Mészáros & M. Casonato (Eds.), *La mia amicizia con Miksa Schächter. Scritti preanalitici, 1899–1908* [My friendship with Miksa Schächter. Pre-analytic writings, 1899–1908] (pp. 47–52). Turin: Bollati Boringhieri, 1992.

Ferenczi, S. (1901b). Sulle malattie mentali coordinate e assimilate [On the coordinated and assimilated mental diseases]. In: J. Mészáros & M. Casonato (Eds.), *La mia amicizia con Miksa Schächter. Scritti preanalitici, 1899–1908* [My friendship with Miksa Schächter. Pre-analytic writings, 1899–1908] (pp. 53–63). Turin: Bollati Boringhieri, 1992.

Ferenczi, S. (1902a). L'omosessualità femminile [Female homosexuality]. In: J. Mészáros & M. Casonato (Eds.), *La mia amicizia con Miksa Schächter. Scritti preanalitici, 1899–1908* [My friendship with Miksa Schächter. Pre-analytic writings, 1899–1908] (pp. 73–76). Turin: Bollati Boringhieri, 1992.

Ferenczi, S. (1902b). Dementia paranoides [Paranoid dementia]. In: J. Mészáros & M. Casonato (Eds.), *La mia amicizia con Miksa Schächter. Scritti preanalitici, 1899–1908* [My friendship with Miksa Schächter. Pre-analytic writings, 1899–1908] (pp. 77–83). Turin: Bollati Boringhieri, 1992.

Ferenczi, S. (1902c). Recensione a *Confessioni di un medico pratico* di W. Weressajew [Review of *Confession of a Practical Physician* by W. Weressajew]. In: J. Mészáros & M. Casonato (Eds.), *La mia amicizia con Miksa Schächter. Scritti preanalitici, 1899–1908* [My friendship with Miksa Schächter. Pre-analytic writings, 1899–1908] (pp. 84–85). Turin: Bollati Boringhieri, 1992.

Ferenczi, S. (1902d). Il credo del medico [On the belief of the physician]. In: J. Mészáros & M. Casonato (Eds.), *La mia amicizia con Miksa Schächter. Scritti preanalitici, 1899–1908* [My friendship with Miksa Schächter. Pre-analytic writings, 1899–1908] (p. 107). Turin: Bollati Boringhieri, 1992.

Ferenczi, S. (1903a). Recensione a *La terapia delle melattie nervose* di E. E. Moravcsik [Review of *Therapy of Nervous Diseases* by E. E. Moravcsik]. In: J. Mészáros & M. Casonato (Eds.), *La mia amicizia con Miksa Schächter. Scritti preanalitici, 1899–1908* [My friendship with Miksa Schächter. Pre-analytic writings, 1899–1908] (pp. 138–139). Turin: Bollati Boringhieri, 1992.

Ferenczi, S. (1903b). Quando la cronaca tace ("where memory sleeps"). [When the news fall silent ("where memory sleeps")]. In: J. Mészáros & M. Casonato (Eds.), *La mia amicizia con Miksa Schächter. Scritti preanalitici, 1899–1908* [My friendship with Miksa Schächter. Pre-analytic writings, 1899–1908] (pp. 140–146). Turin: Bollati Boringhieri, 1992.

Ferenczi, S. (1904a). Traduzione da *Il ruolo della fede nella terapia* di P. C. Kalloc [Translation of *The Role of Faith in Therapy* by P. C. Kalloc]. In: J. Mészáros & M. Casonato (Eds.), *La mia amicizia con Miksa Schächter. Scritti preanalitici, 1899–1908* [My friendship with Miksa Schächter. Pre-analytic writings, 1899–1908] (pp. 149–151). Turin: Bollati Boringhieri, 1992.

Ferenczi, S. (1904b). Sul valore terapeutico dell'ipnosi [On the therapeutic value of hypnosis]. In: J. Mészáros & M. Casonato (Eds.), *La mia amicizia con Miksa Schächter. Scritti preanalitici, 1899–1908* [My friendship with Miksa Schächter. Pre-analytic writings, 1899–1908] (pp. 156–162). Turin: Bollati Boringhieri, 1992.

Ferenczi, S. (1906a). Sugli stati sessuali di transizione [On the sexual states of transition]. In: J. Mészáros & M. Casonato (Eds.), *La mia amicizia con Miksa Schächter. Scritti preanalitici, 1899–1908* [My friendship with Miksa Schächter. Pre-analytic writings, 1899–1908] (pp. 195–206). Turin: Bollati Boringhieri, 1992.

Ferenczi, S. (1906b). Cura con suggestione ipnotica [Healing through hypnotic suggestion]. In: J. Mészáros & M. Casonato (Eds.), *La mia amicizia con Miksa Schächter. Scritti preanalitici, 1899–1908* [My friendship with Miksa Schächter. Pre-analytic writings, 1899–1908] (pp. 207–211). Turin: Bollati Boringhieri, 1992.

Ferenczi, S. (1908). Il disturbo mentale maniaco-depressivo in una prospettiva soggettiva [Manic-depressive mental disorder in a subjective perspective]. In: J. Mészáros & M. Casonato (Eds.), *La mia amicizia con Miksa Schächter. Scritti preanalitici, 1899–1908* [My friendship with Miksa Schächter. Pre-analytic writings, 1899–1908] (pp. 241–251). Turin: Bollati Boringhieri, 1992.

Ferenczi, S. (1917). My friendship with Miksa Schächter. *British Journal of Psychotherapy*, 9: 430–433.

Freud, S. (1911c). Psychoanalytic notes upon an autobiographical account of a case of paranoia (Dementia paranoides). *S. E., 12*: 1–82. London: Hogarth.

Gyimesi, J. (2009). The problem of demarcation: Psychoanalysis and the occult. *American Imago, 66*: 457–470.

Gyimesi, J. (2016). Why spiritism? *International Journal of Psychoanalysis, 97*: 357–383.

Hann-Kende, F. (1933). On the role of transference and countertransference in psychoanalysis. In: G. Devereux (Ed.), *Psychoanalysis and the Occult* (pp. 158–167). New York: International Universities Press, 1953.

Haynal, A. E. (2002). *Disappearing and Reviving: Sándor Ferenczi in the History of Psychoanalysis*. London: Karnac.

Lorin, C. (1983). *Le jeune Ferenczi. Premiers écrits, 1899–1906* [The young Ferenczi. The early writings, 1899–1906]. Paris: Aubier.

Massicotte, C. (2014). Psychical transmissions: Freud, spiritualism, and the occult. *Psychoanalytic Dialogues, 24*:1, 88–102.

Mészáros, J. (1992). Sándor Ferenczi debuttante [Sándor Ferenczi as a beginner]. In: J. Mészáros & M. Casonato (Eds.), *La mia amicizia con Miksa Schächter. Scritti preanalitici, 1899–1908* [My friendship with Miksa Schächter. Pre-analytic writings, 1899–1908] (pp. xii–xix). Turin: Bollati Boringhieri, 1992.

Mészáros, J., & Casonato, M. (Eds.) (1992). *La mia amicizia con Miksa Schächter. Scritti preanalitici, 1899–1908* [My friendship with Miksa Schächter. Pre-analytic writings, 1899–1908]. Turin: Bollati Boringhieri.

Pick, D. (1989). *Faces of Degeneration*. Cambridge: Cambridge University Press.

Rachman, A. W. (1993). Ferenczi and sexuality. In: L. Aron & A. Harris (Eds.), *The Legacy of Sándor Ferenczi* (pp. 81–100). Hillsdale, NJ: Analytic Press.

Racker, H. (1968). *Transference and Counter-transference*. New York: International Universities Press.

Chapter 4

Ferenczi and Freud: Subservient disciple to independent thinker

Louis Breger

The relationship between Freud and Ferenczi follows the trajectory of other early followers who were initially taken with Freud but later expelled from the movement when they challenged him. Their connection was special in many ways and has continued to elicit both clinical and historical commentary. For twenty-five years they were friends and companions, shared ideas and projects, worked together in the psychoanalytic movement, and discussed their personal affairs. Freud hoped that Ferenczi might marry his eldest daughter Mathilda and, at a later time, was therapist and adviser to his Hungarian colleague, his mistress Gizella Palos, and her daughter Elma. He wrote more letters to Ferenczi than to any other correspondent. As was the case with C. G. Jung and Otto Rank, their closeness required that Ferenczi remain a dutiful, admiring, son-disciple, a role for which his own background made him ideally suited. He was the eighth of twelve children whose father, to whom he was close, died when he was fifteen. This left him with an over-burdened mother who he described as a harsh and severe disciplinarian. He emerged from this background with a great need to be loved, and Freud became the paramount authority in his life—in some ways his therapist—and psychoanalysis his calling and belief system. At the same time he was a man of originality and creativity who searched for better ways to understand both himself and his patients. During the final years of his life he was engaged in experiments with psychoanalytic technique that took him far from Freud's orthodox position. His late papers, along with the *Diary* he wrote in 1932, contained new ideas and methods that anticipate significant contemporary developments in the field, as found in self-psychology, relational psychoanalysis, intersubjectivity, and control mastery theory. These set him on a collision course with "The Professor", as Freud was called by his loyal followers.

Many people described Ferenczi as warm, affectionate, enthusiastic, hopeful, empathic, and, above all, accepting and understanding of others. He could also be boyish, with an endearing playfulness and naïveté. For many years he struggled to become independent from Freud but, at times, was slavishly obedient.

Ferenczi was seventeen years younger than Freud, a similar age difference to that between The Professor and Jung and, like Jung, he was an established psychiatrist with some years of clinical work and several publications to his credit when they first met. Like the others in the early group, he found both Freud the man and psychoanalysis enormously appealing. In contrast to the descriptive psychiatry of the time, which offered little, here was a treasure trove of new ideas and treatment methods. In addition, almost all the early psychoanalysts wished to understand themselves and The Professor held out the promise of not only being their leader and guide but also their therapist. This was particularly true of Ferenczi.

Freud, for his part, was instantly taken with his new convert from Budapest. At their first meeting he suggested that Ferenczi present a paper at the next psychoanalytic meeting and also invited him to join the family on their summer vacation. Such vacations were repeated over the years, including joining him and Jung on the trip to the United States for the Clark lectures in 1909. Ferenczi became another in the line of intimate male friends of Freud's adult years—Wilhelm Fliess being the most intense—as he promised a desired closeness that was simultaneously threatening to the older man. Ferenczi was unique, since he was the ideal mirror for Freud's drive for fame. He was able to sense and anticipate The Professor's needs and respond to them. Freud was drawn to the openly emotional Ferenczi and then pulled back, branding the younger man's wish for honesty and intimacy, "infantile" and "homosexual" (Breger, 2000, p. 343).

Ferenczi's early work displayed the breadth of his clinical interests, yet remained clearly within the framework of established psychoanalysis. In 1910, following Freud's suggestion, he helped found the IPA, with Jung as president, provoking conflicts with the Viennese analysts and, in 1911, went along with the expulsion of Adler and his supporters. In 1912 he met with Ernest Jones to form The Committee—a secret group meant to protect Freud from challenges to his authority—in reaction to the split with Adler and in anticipation of conflicts with Jung. At this time he was a loyal member of the palace guard and, as proof of his fealty, published a highly critical review of *Symbols of Transformation*, Jung's book central to his differences with Freud. Twelve years later, when the conflict between Freud and Rank came to a head, Ferenczi, who had worked closely with Rank—co-authoring a book, *The Development of Psychoanalysis*—and considered him a valued friend, attempted to mediate, but, in the end, was not able to stand up against Freud and went along with the expulsion of his comrade.

For many years, Ferenczi struggled, with much vacillation and difficulty, to break free from the position of dutiful son, to become independent and express his own views. In his son role, he could sound like the doctrinaire Karl Abraham or follow Freud into the murky waters of theoretical speculation. At the same time, he was driven to find more effective ways of working with his patients and continually pushed the limits of the classical approach. He was not satisfied with attributing stalemates or treatment failures to resistance; he tried to see things from the patient's point of view, how they experienced his silence, abstinence, neutrality, and interpretations. And he was never comfortable playing the role of analyst-as-all-knowing-authority. In his last years, he experimented with more active forms of therapy and settled on what he termed "the principle of relaxation" and "neocatharsis" (Koritar, Chapter Twenty-two). These methods involved the creation of a safe environment in which patients would feel comfortable expressing as much of their experience as possible, including traumatic material and any and all reactions to the analyst.

The essential features of Ferenczi's innovations were developed in a series of papers that he published between 1928 and his death in 1933, papers that give a clear picture of his evolution as a psychoanalyst. He came to recognise the importance of tact and empathy and the centrality of the analyst-patient relationship as a curative force in itself, unlike Freud's view of it as a resistance. As he put it, "One must never be ashamed to unreservedly confess one's own mistakes" (ChildAn, p. 138). What is more, the analyst must be "indulgent;" he should not frustrate the patient, an idea in direct contradiction to Freud's rules of "neutrality" and "abstinence". Ferenczi's understanding of the cause of neuroses stressed the importance of actual traumas—as opposed to fantasies and drives—and a variety of parental abuses, along with the way these are covered up and distorted in families. As he put it, "one gets the impression that children get over even severe shocks without amnesia or neurotic consequences, if the mother is at hand with understanding and tenderness and – what is most rare – with complete sincerity" (ibid.).

Ferenczi's final paper, *Confusion of Tongues*, is perhaps his best known. In his work up to this point he had attempted to reconcile the irreconcilable: to fit his ideas within the orthodox psychoanalytic framework. He finally abandoned this impossible task. The "confusion of tongues" of the title refers to the different meanings of love and physical contact for children and adults. Because children look for tenderness in physical and emotional forms he argued that trauma results when parents or others interpret these overtures as adult-like sexuality and then impose their "passion" on the child, what would, today, be called child abuse.

This was Ferenczi's solution to the oft-debated seduction versus fantasy question. He makes clear that people do not become disturbed because of their drives or fantasies, but the traumas and abuse children suffer take a variety of forms, from subtle to gross. He was aware of the different mental capacities of children who are only too ready to comply and accept parental definitions of reality. He also called attention to the damage that results when parents cover up their abusive treatment with half-truths and lies.

Ferenczi was finally able to leave orthodox psychoanalysis behind. It was only when he opened himself to his patient's experience, created a safe atmosphere, and took their criticisms to heart that he was able to move beyond the dance of authoritative-analyst and compliant-patient. "I started to listen to my patients when, in their attacks, they called me insensitive, cold, even hard and cruel, when they reproached me with being selfish, heartless, conceited" (Conf, p. 157). These insights were his most radical and threatening challenges to Freud for they showed how psychoanalysis, practiced in the classical manner, was a retraumatisation of the patient. Where Freud thought of himself as a strong and firm father figure, many patients experienced such treatment as harmful.

It was at this time that Ferenczi was able to break free on the personal level from Freud's authority. He wrote his strongest criticisms in the privacy of his *Diary*: "The analytic situation, but specifically its rigid technical rules, mostly produce in the patient unalleviated suffering and in the analyst an unjustifiable sense of superiority accompanied by a certain contempt for the patient ... Analysis offers to a person who is otherwise somewhat incapacitated and whose self-confidence and potency is disturbed an opportunity to feel like a sultan, thus compensating him for his defective ability to love" (Diary, p. 194).

Ferenczi came to his new approach to psychoanalysis because of his great capacity for empathy, his ability to see things from the patient's point of view. His continually evolving work made him the most scientific of the early psychoanalysts, his ideas grounded in observable material and open to change when new evidence emerged, though Freud and the loyalists always characterized him as a mere therapist—a man driven by his need to help and cure—while promoting themselves as the real scientists. This can be seen in a brief obituary that Freud wrote after Ferenczi's death in which he praised his former colleague's most fanciful theoretical flights—as in his 1924 book, *Thalassa*—while simultaneously derogating his clinical contributions.

> After this summit of achievement, it came about that our friend slowly drifted away from us. ... The need to cure and to help had become paramount in him. He had probably set himself aims which, with our therapeutic means are altogether out of reach today. From unexhausted springs of emotion the conviction was borne in upon him that one could effect far more with one's patients if one gave them enough of the love which

> they had longed for as children … Signs were slowly revealed in him of a grave organic destructive process which had probably overshadowed his life for many years already. Shortly before completing his sixtieth year he succumbed to pernicious anemia. It is impossible to believe that our science will ever forget him.
>
> (Freud, 1933, p. 229)

This is Freud the propagandist: subtle yet insidious. The "need to cure" is presented as an unrealistic—by implication wishful and childish—hope while the "unexhausted springs of emotion" suggest the irrationality of Ferenczi's therapeutic efforts. Freud always interpreted the ideas of those who disagreed with him as emotional—driven by blind feeling—in contrast to his calm rationality. Finally, there is the comment that an "organic destructive process overshadowed his life for many years" (ibid.), a deliberate distortion, since Freud knew that Ferenczi's anemia only appeared in his last year.

While Freud presented this distorted account in a journal article, Ferenczi's own picture of The Professor was confined to his private diary, only discovered and published many years later. Here, he voiced his feelings about the man he loved, revered, and followed for many years:

> Freud no longer loves his patients. He has returned to the love of his well-ordered and cultivated superego – further proof of this being his antipathy toward and deprecating remarks about psychotics, perverts, and everything in general that is "too abnormal" … he still remains attached to analysis intellectually, but not emotionally … his therapeutic method, like his theory is becoming more and more influenced by his interest in order, character, the replacement of a bad superego by a better one; he is becoming pedagogical … He must have felt very comfortable in this role; he could indulge in his theoretical fantasies undisturbed by any contradiction and use the enthusiastic agreement of his blinded pupil to boost his own self-esteem. In reality, his brilliant ideas were usually based on only a single case, like illuminations as it were which dazzled and amazed, for example me … the advantages of following blindly were: 1) membership in a distinguished group guaranteed by the king, indeed with the rank of field marshal for myself—crown prince fantasy – 2) one learned from him and his kind of technique various things that made one's life and work more comfortable: the calm, unemotional reserve; the unruffled assurance that one knew better; the theories; and the seeking and finding of the causes of failure in the patient instead of partly in ourselves.
>
> (Diary, pp. 184–185)

Ferenczi visited Freud a final time in 1932 to read his *Confusion of Tongues* paper, hoping that his colleague would listen and try to understand the clinical innovations in which he had invested so much of himself. But Freud had already turned on his disciple, branding him a heretic in comments to the loyal Max Eitingon and his daughter Anna. At the end of this final meeting, Ferenczi held out his hand for an affectionate goodbye but Freud turned his back and walked out of the room.

Ferenczi thus suffered the fate of a number of predecessors—Adler, Stekel, Jung, Rank, and others—when they did not comply with Freud's orthodoxy: all were expelled from the movement as heretics, lied about, and slandered. All of this reveals that for all the claims that psychoanalysis was a science, in fact, it had more in common with a religious cult.

After the final encounter with Freud, Ferenczi was permitted to read the *Confusion of Tongues* paper at the Psychoanalytic Congress in 1932, and it was published in German in the

Internationale Zeitschrift. But Ernest Jones blocked its publication in the English language *IJP* which he edited. This crucial act of censorship kept Ferenczi's ideas hidden for many years because, with the rise of Hitler, psychoanalysis was banned in Germany and Austria and, until the war ended in 1945, new psychoanalytic publications were only available in English. With Ferenczi's death and the censorship of his work in English publications it was easy to misrepresent his contributions and slander him personally. This was done by Jones, in his officially approved biography, who spoke of: "Mental deterioration ... latent psychotic trends ... a final delusional state ... Freud's supposed hostility ... violent paranoiac and even homicidal outbursts" (Breger, 2000, p. 354). This account was perpetuated by Peter Gay in his 1988 biography. A number of people, such as Michael Balint, had contact with Ferenczi in his final months and they all reported that there was absolutely no truth to the accounts of Jones and others. To picture the gentle and loving Ferenczi as a "violent paranoiac" given to "homicidal outbursts" is absurd. In fact, he was such a sensitive soul that Freud's harsh rejection, after their many years of friendship, probably hastened, if it did not actually cause, his death.

References

Breger, L. (2000). *Freud: Darkness in the Midst of Vision*. New York: John Wiley.
Freud, S. (1933). Sándor Ferenczi. *S. E.*, *12*: 225–229. London: Hogarth.

Chapter 5

Ferenczi's analyses with Freud

Carlo Bonomi

> "Contrary to all the rules of technique that he established himself, he [Freud] adopted Dr. F[erenczi] almost like his son. As he himself told me, he regarded him as the most perfect heir of his ideas. Thereby he became the proclaimed crown prince ..."
>
> (Diary, 4 August 1932, p. 184)

Chronicle

Ferenczi's analysis with Freud occurred in a period when self-analysis was the method recommended by Freud for budding psychoanalysts (Freud, 1914d, p. 20); it cannot be clearly separated from Ferenczi's self-analysis, nor from Ferenczi's personal and intellectual relationship with the founder of psychoanalysis. The rare intensity of this relationship is amply reflected in their rich correspondence, which contains also a great quantity of "self-analytic" material. Since Ferenczi's self-analysis took shape by writing to Freud, this material has a hybrid character. Ferenczi himself compared it to a "gratis analysis".

One of the main catalysers of Ferenczi's "self-analysis with Freud" was the famous 1909 trip to America, in which Freud and Jung engaged in a mutual analysis. Indeed, Ferenczi's deeper desire was to engage Freud in a mutual analysis. Ferenczi's hope for a relationship of perfect reciprocity encountered serious obstacles, such as the Palermo incident. Freud and Ferenczi decided to vacation in Italy together in September of 1910 with Freud proposing that they join forces and work on an interpretation of President Schreber's memoires. Freud, however, proceeded to dictate rather than to engage Ferenczi in dialogue during their working vacation. When Ferenczi suddenly "rebelled" and objected, Freud responded by accusing him of behaving neurotically. Freud then proceeded to work on Schreber on his own. Recalling the episode in a letter to Groddeck years later, at Christmas of 1921, Ferenczi wrote: "I was left out in the cold [by Freud] – bitter feelings constricted my throat". That incident featured a primal fight scene and disagreement between Ferenczi and Freud, which both "foreshadowed and shaped Ferenczi's [future] personal analysis with Freud as well as their theoretical and technical divergences" (Aron & Starr, 2015, p. 153).

Freud was at that time deeply upset by the abrupt end of Emma Eckstein's second analysis with him in the Spring of 1910 (Bonomi, 2015, 2018), and experienced dreams that featured Wilhelm Fliess, his former friend from Berlin. It seems that Freud was attempting to master his feelings then by analysing Schreber's delusional system, perhaps in an effort to help dissolve his old transference to Fliess. Shortly after the Palermo incident, Freud wrote to Ferenczi to say:

> I no longer have any need for that full opening of my personality, but you have also understood it and correctly returned to its traumatic cause. Why did you thus make a point of it? This need has been extinguished in me since Fliess's case, with the overcoming of which you just saw me occupied. A piece of homosexual investment has been withdrawn and utilized for the enlargement of my own ego. I have succeeded where the paranoiac fails ... My dreams at the time were, as I indicated to you, entirely concerned with the Fliess matter.
>
> (Fr/Fer, 6 October 1910, p. 221)

Only when Ferenczi's hope in a relationship characterised by mutuality had to be definitively put aside, Ferenczi asked Freud to initiate an analysis with him. This demand was first formulated in a long self-analytic letter dated 26 December 1912, to which I will come back later. The beginning of the analysis was continuously postponed by Ferenczi, however. Freud, in his turn, expressed his reluctance in committing to a process that, he sensed, might "expose one of my indispensable helpers to the danger of personal estrangement brought about by the analysis" (Fr/Fer, 4 May 1913, p. 482). Ferenczi immediately replied: "I am convinced that my analysis will only better the relationship between us" (Fer/Fr, 12 May 1913, p. 485). Still, he did not find a suitable time to begin the analysis. The main reason for Ferenczi's fear of Freud was his own "stubborn tendency to get back with Elma" (Fer/Fr, 16 October, 1913, p. 514).

Ferenczi's triangle with Gizella and Elma Pàlos, and quadrangle with Freud, has been described in detail by Emanuel Berman in this volume (Chapter Six). In 1911 Ferenczi had fallen in love with Elma Pàlos, while he was treating her. Elma was the difficult daughter of Gizella Pàlos, a married woman, eight years Ferenczi's senior, with whom he had a relatively stable liaison. Scared of hurting Gizella, and unable to make a choice between the two women, Ferenczi turned to Freud for help. On 14 November, while feeling upset and torn by his situation, he wrote to Freud to confess: "I wanted to commit a terrible act of violence. Dissatisfied with both parents [i.e. Frau Gizella and Professor Freud], I wanted to make myself independent!" In a postscript to his letter, he decided to incorporate and share two poetic lines with Freud: "I remain a 'son'. Have religion!" (p. 312).

"Dear son"—Freud responded on 20 November of 1911—"your struggle for liberation doesn't need to take place in such alternation of rebellion and subjugation" (p. 314). At this point Ferenczi got trapped in a labyrinth from which he could no longer get out.

In the ensuing months, Elma pursued her analysis with Freud, who became convinced that she was dangerous for Ferenczi. Freud also began to regularly express his deep admiration for Gizella's spiritual qualities in his letters to him. Following Freud's advice, Ferenczi repeatedly tried to convince himself that Gizella was the good choice, but was unable to suppress his fantasies of marriage, progeny, and happiness with Elma. Thereafter, for several years, a great part of Ferenczi's self-analysis with Freud concerned his being torn between his loyalty to Gizella and his passionate desire for Elma (cf. Fer/Fr, 14 November 1911; 18 January, 18 February, 17, 23, and 25 April, 10 June, 12 and 18 July, 26 December 1912; 16 October 1913; 17 and 23 October; 18 November 1916).

Under "Freud's unrelenting pressure" (Berman, Chapter Six), Ferenczi finally wed Gizella in 1919 and this choice later arrived to feed his bitter accusations against Freud (Haynal,

1988, p. 44). In fact, a year later, Ferenczi wrote Freud to say: "Since the moment in which you advised me against Elma, I have had a resistance toward your own person" (23 May 1919, p. 356). Three years later, he wrote a letter to Groddeck where he reflected more deeply on the entire situation: "Prof. Freud … persists in his original view that the crux of the matter is my hatred for him, because he stopped me ... from marrying the younger woman (now my step-daughter). Hence my murderous intentions toward him which express themselves in nightly death scenes (drop in body temperature; gasping for breath)" (27 February 1922, p. 19).

Circling back to Ferenczi's resistance at initiating his analysis with Freud, it is easy to trace it to Freud's attitude towards Ferenczi's sentimental life and choices. A not less important reason was Ferenczi's difficulty in asserting himself in front of Freud. As Ferenczi put it in a letter he wrote on 18 April 1914: "My position with respect to you, specifically, is still not completely natural, ... your presence arouses inhibitions of various kinds in me that influence, and at time almost paralyze, my actions and even my thinking" (p. 549). Only when Freud told Ferenczi that he wanted to remain alone during his summer vacation, adding "I also don't work easily together with you in particular. You grasp things differently and for that reason often put a strain on me" (22 July 1914, p. 6), did Ferenczi renew his request of being analysed as a means to correct his deficiencies. "My reason," he wrote on 23 July, "tells me that the manner in which you grasp things is the correct one; still, I can't prevent my fantasy from going its own way (perhaps astray). ... If I had the courage simply to write down my ideas and observations without regard for your method and direction of work, I would be a productive writer ... I hope you will make it possible for me to deal with these things psychoanalytically" (p. 8). In the same letter Ferenczi felt the need to assure Freud of his loyalty. He was frightened by his unconscious identification with Jung, but also certain of the fact that he would not "deviate even one step from the firm ground of psychoanalysis. The most that my 'complexes' could achieve," he added, "is work inhibition; they will never bring about something positive (rebellion …)" (p. 7). Ferenczi was simply terrorised by the idea of being abandoned by Freud. Analysis with him was openly envisaged as a way to better cling to the master and his ideas.

At the end of July 1914 the First World War broke out, and only at this point did the two men take the decision to start the continually postponed analysis. As noted by Judith Dupont (1994), the situation served well "Ferenczi's ambivalence toward his plan to be analysed: Freud asks him to come, but Ferenczi is in a position to be mobilised [into military service] any day" (p. 304). But again Ferenczi kept on postponing the first session, showing now "his ambivalence toward the one whom he has chosen as his analyst" (ibid.). Ferenczi's analysis finally began in October 1914: he arrived late to the train station and missed his first session!

Ferenczi's analysis lasted a total of eight and a half weeks; the total number of hours was 131 (May, 2007). Two intensive weeks of analysis (two sessions a day) were interrupted because Ferenczi had to report for military duty. The second period of analysis (two sessions of one and a half hours a day) extended from 14 June to 5 July 1916. This time Ferenczi learned a lot about the role of repetition, but remained sceptical with reference to the question that bothered him the most, his sentimental life (Dupont, 2015, p. 157). The third period lasted between 25 September and 9 October 1916, when Freud decided that the analysis was finished. Ferenczi was then deeply troubled by an ending that he was not ready to accept. Indeed, he tried to extend the cure by letter, and Freud had to repeat several times that the analysis was finished but not terminated (24 October 1916, p. 149), "broken off because of unfavorable circumstances" (16 November 1916, p. 153).

Ferenc and Freud in Papa, during the second (iteration of) the analysis

Ferenczi was desperate and unable to accept the premature ending of his analysis because he had not yet found the courage to disclose himself. Only when he realised that Freud was immovable, some of the things that he had omitted to report began to surface in his letters, such as his sexual enactments, the worsening of his relationship with his mother, and his hostility to Freud. On 18 November 1916, he explained that he was taking out on his mother what he was sparing Gizella, "thereby returning to the original source of [his] hatred of women" (p. 155). "But what is my fate?" he added, "Must I dissociate myself from every woman—like a Flying Dutchman (or, like him, kill the woman and myself)?" (ibid.). Then, in his letter of 27 November, he noted that he was sacrificing all women for his "father's sake" (p. 164). One day later, while describing his hostility to "the father", he wrote: "I know only too well that it is here a matter of the repetition of the defiant rebellion in Palermo" (p. 165).

Ferenczi, who had been too scared to lose the love of Freud, would begin to express and work through his feeling of hostility in the context of his relationship with George Groddeck. After an occasional session with Freud in 1922, he wrote to Groddeck: "I must admit it did me good to talk for once to this dearly loved father about my hate feelings" (p. 19). In 1930, reflecting on the conflictual character of his relationship with Freud, Ferenczi wrote to Freud, on 17 January:

> First you were my revered teacher and unattainable model ... Then you became my analyst, but the unfavorable conditions did not permit carrying out my analysis to completion. I was especially sorry that you did not comprehend and bring to abreaction in the analysis the partly only [Reading uncertain. It could also be "in me"] transferred, negative feelings and fantasies. As is well known, no analysand can do that without help. (p. 383)

In "Analysis terminable and interminable" Freud (1937c) would defend himself from Ferenczi's reproach that he failed to analyse Ferenczi's negative transference by saying that the latter "was not currently active ... at the time" (p. 222). It is not easy to understand this statement by Freud, since expressions of Ferenczi's "defiant rebellion" can be found throughout the entire correspondence. Of course, it is misleading to speak of a negative transference generated by the analytic situation, since Ferenczi's ambivalence was a specific trait of his relationship with Freud, already long before the beginning of his formal analysis (Dupont, 2015, p. 158). In his *Clinical Diary* Ferenczi spoke, in this regard, of a "mutually castration-directed aggressivity", overlaid by a "harmonious father-son relationship" (Diary, p. 185).

Ferenczi's "crown prince" fantasy

Ferenczi's ambivalence was so outspoken that one wonders how it is possible that Freud could ignore Ferenczi's behaviour and preverbal messages to such an extent. In the *Clinical Diary* Ferenczi suggested that a large share of what is described as transference is provoked by the analyst (Diary, p. 93). Following this suggestion, I will integrate the chronicle of Ferenczi's analyses with Freud with a few comments.

Ferenczi wanted, of course, to be loved by Freud, and this made him especially sensitive and responsive to Freud's desire to find in Ferenczi a "most perfect heir of his ideas" (Diary, p. 184). To Ferenczi, Freud was not a "blank screen", but an open book. By making large pieces of his self-analysis public through *The Interpretation of Dreams* and other works, Freud managed to create a public space where unresolved traumas were deposited for future generations. As symbol of his great self-analytic effort, Freud offered his dream of his self-dissection of the pelvis, a shocking and puzzling dream that helped in transforming the space in question into a place of transmission. In this dream the idea in fact surfaced that "children may perhaps achieve what their father has failed to [achieve]" (Freud, 1900a, p. 452) and, further, that Freud should have to leave it to his children "to reach the goal of [his] difficult journey" (p. 477).

The child initially appointed by Freud as his "successor and crown prince" was Jung (Fr/Ju, 17 January and 16 April 1909; Ju/Fer, 6 December 1909; Adler, 1973, p. 12), but in 1912 the relationship between the two men had become more and more difficult. Already at the beginning of the year Freud wrote to Ferenczi to say that he was working to reconcile himself "to the idea that one also has to leave this child [Jung] to *Ananke*" (p. 340).[1] Then, at the end of 1912, the situation came to a head. After Freud's second fainting spell, Jung found himself no longer able to tolerate Freud's neurosis, and this led to a final and definitive break between them.

Freud's second fainting spell occurred on 28 November 1912, during a scientific meeting. This time he was heard muttering "How sweet it must be to die" as he regained consciousness (Jones, 1953, p. 147). Anzieu (1986, p. 427) interpreted Freud's fainting spells as a repetition of the death anxiety at the heart of his dream of self-dissection. The ceremonial aspects of Freud's attempt to control his *Todesangst* (death anxiety) were described and discussed in detail by Max Schur (1972). The fact that Ferenczi predicted Freud's second fainting spell (see his letter to Freud of 28 November 1912) suggests that he had come to fully internalise Freud's funeral and death fantasies.

Jung and Ferenczi were each shocked by the intensity of Freud's death fantasies. They were disappointed by his vulnerability and sceptical about self-analysis and its capacity to

1 In Greek mythology *Ananke* (*Necessitas* in Roman mythology) involved a compulsion that was more powerful than the gods. She was mother of the Moirae—the three goddesses of fate, who personified the inescapable destiny of man and sang in unison "the things that were, the things that are, and the things that are to be" (Plato, *Republic 617c*).

cure and resolve symptoms. Jung, moreover, could no longer tolerate the contradictions between Freud's spectacular requests for assistance and help and his refusal of being helped through analysis. Instead of becoming angry (as Jung did) at Freud's unwillingness to be analysed by another person, or confronting him on these topics, Ferenczi instead responded by offering himself to Freud as a sick person in need of analysis.

In his letter to Freud of 26 December 1912, Ferenczi admitted that he himself had gone through a period of rebellion. He also added that he had finally realised that mutual analysis was "nonsense" and that Freud, in spite of his severe neurotic symptoms, was the only one who could permit himself to do without an analyst. Ferenczi's demand to be taken in analysis was therefore his way of assuring Freud of his loyalty, a self-sacrifice, attested to also by a dream he had dreamt that night: it featured a "somewhat small and frail but firmly erect penis" which had been "cut-off" and brought in on a saucer (*Tasse*). Since this totemic meal was modeled on the very symbol of Freud's self-analysis (his dream of his self-dissection of the pelvis), it also spoke of Ferenczi's desire to become the most perfect heir of Freud's ideas.

In the dream of Ferenczi the *corpora cavernosa* (cavernous bodies) of the penis were laid bare. This detail reminds me of Freud's self-dissection dream, since peering down to his eviscerated pelvis, the founder of psychoanalysis saw the cavernous bodies of the rectus (hemorrhoids) laid bare. The same detail also serves to remind us of Fliess's controversial theories regarding the connection between "nose and genitalia", and of Freud's masochistic enactments and homosexual submissions to Fliess: Freud was operated on the nose by Fliess in February 1895, when also Emma Eckstein was operated on, and in September 1895, after his Irma dream. Freud himself advanced the hypothesis that the nasal *corpora cavernosa* functioned as a "sense organ" for internal stimuli, as he wrote in the letter to Fliess of 1 January 1896.

In November 1912 Ferenczi also began experiencing nasal symptoms. This led Ferenczi to entertain the idea of submitting himself to a rhinological intervention in Vienna, during his upcoming visit to Freud at Christmas. We can consider this plan an expression of Ferenczi's unconscious identification with Freud. Ferenczi's nasal symptoms in fact decreased as soon as he produced a remarkable theory about fantasies, which featured castigation and punishment (Fer/Fr, 7 December 1912), indeed the first version of his theory of the "identification with the aggressor" (Frankel, Chapter Nineteen). At Christmas 1912 Ferenczi was not operated on the nose, and had his dream instead. Ferenczi (1919) himself later suggested that "congestion of the turbinate represented unconscious libidinal phantasies", adding that the connection "between the nose and sexuality was discovered by Fliess" (p. 101). Ferenczi had his nose operated on in the spring of 1912 and, again, on Christmas Day of 1913. A number of nasal symptoms resurfaced as his analysis with Freud progressed during the next few years. In March 1916 Freud interpreted Ferenczi's nasal symptoms and desire to travel to Berlin to consult with a nose specialist (Fliess?) as a product of his resistance to analysis, indeed as an expression of his fear of the "father".

Finally, the detail of the laid bare *corpora cavernosa* in the penis turns the latter into a feminine symbol (a concave penis), thus anticipating Ferenczi's dream of the occlusive pessary, the initial dream of his analysis with Freud. In a reading that I have developed elsewhere (Bonomi, 1996, 2018), I have suggested that Ferenczi was resuming the mystical journey in the unconscious at the precise point where it had been discontinued by the father of psychoanalysis.

The pessary child

After many postponements, in the summer of 1914 Freud and Ferenczi decided to begin the analysis in September 1914. On 8 September, Ferenczi sent Freud in advance a detailed self-analysis of a dream, which was however presented as a patient's dream in a manuscript written for publication. It was the famous dream of the occlusive pessary (Ferenczi, 1915): "I stuff an occlusive pessary into my urethra. I am alarmed as I do so lest it might slip into the bladder from which it could only be removed by shedding blood" (p. 304).

In the manuscript the analysis of this dream was restructured in the form of a dialogue between doctor and patient. The subject of the dialogue was not the beginning of an analysis, but its termination: the doctor informs the patient that the analysis is terminated and that, from now on, he can rely on his self-analysis and do it alone. This initial dream was a clear expression of Ferenczi's fear of being abandoned by Freud. Ferenczi's interpretation of his dream also contained a harsh criticism of self-analysis, which was of no help in overcoming his impasse—again his indecision between Gizella and Elma. In September 1914, Elma got married and showed up as a bride the day before the dream of the occlusive pessary. This reactivated Ferenczi's conflict, which, in the associations, is presented as an incapacity to make a choice between two women (p. 309). Apparently, Ferenczi's complaints about the inconclusiveness of his self-analysis also represent a criticism of Freud's trust in his own self-analysis. "Mockery and scorn", the doctor says in the fictive dialogue, "are concealed behind such nonsense dreams" (ibid.).

Since it was a manuscript written for publication, Ferenczi presented himself as the doctor. At the same time, in the letter to Freud accompanying the manuscript, he presented himself as the patient, while identifying the figure of the doctor with Freud. Thus, as remarked by Falzeder (1996), the article resulted in a "masterpiece of ambivalence, meta-discourse and hidden messages" (p. 7). The very subject of this hall of mirrors seems to be again the symbol of Freud's self-analysis: the dream of the self-dissection of the pelvis: in both dreams "there is an operation, performed by the dreamer on the lower part of his own body, in both cases the associations link this operation with self-analysis" (p. 9).

Commenting on the meaning of the "occlusion", Falzeder (1996) suggested that "the representative of [Freud] in Ferenczi remained to be a hardly digested 'introject'" (p. 269). In other works (Bonomi, 1996, 2018), I have suggested that the occlusive pessary represents Freud's heritage of non-abreacted emotion that, after having been incorporated by Ferenczi, was felt as an obstruction by him. Ferenczi had forced Freud to take him as patient, but at the moment when he had to entrust himself and placed himself in Freud's hands, it was his analyst's personality he was most afraid of. Remarking on the failure in object choice, in Ferenczi's self-interpretation the doctor says: "Therefore in the dream *you make yourself into the pessary child* ... In our technology this is called a 'regression'" (Ferenczi, 1915, p. 309, italics in original). This theme and the psychic dimension neglected by Freud would be explored in depth by Ferenczi and his pupils, especially Michael Balint (1968). At the same time, the pessary child brings into representation a role reversal. Thus the dream, and the way Ferenczi deals with it, also anticipates Ferenczi's idea of the "wise baby" (Martín Cabré, Chapter Eighteen), namely the theory of the patient who is forced to become his own analyst's analyst.

References

Adler, G. (Ed.) (1973). *G.C. Jung Letters. Volume I (1906–1950)*. London: Routledge.
Anzieu, D. (1986). *Freud's Self-Analysis*. New York: International Universities Press.
Aron, L., & Starr, K. (2015). Freud & Ferenczi: Wandering Jews in Palermo. In: A. Harris & S. Kuchuck, *The Legacy of Sándor Ferenczi* (pp. 150–1676). London: Routledge.
Balint, M. (1968). *The Basic Fault*. London: Tavistock.
Bonomi, C. (1996). Mute Correspondence. *International Forum of Psychoanalysis*, *5/3*: 165–189.
Bonomi, C. (2015). *The Cut and the Building of Psychoanalysis. Volume 1. Sigmund Freud and Emma Eckstein*. London: Routledge.
Bonomi, C. (2018). *The Cut and the Building of Psychoanalysis. Volume 2. Sigmund Freud and Sándor Ferenczi*. London: Routledge.
Dupont, J. (1994). Freud's analysis of Ferenczi as revealed by their correspondence. *International Journal of Psychoanalysis*, *75*: 301–320.
Dupont, J. (2015). *Au fil du temps… Un itinéraire analytique*. Paris: Campaigne Première.
Falzeder, E. (1996). Dreaming of Freud: Ferenczi, Freud, and an analysis without end. *International Forum of Psychoanalysis*, *5*: 265–270.
Ferenczi, S. (1915). The dream of the occlusive pessary. In: *Further Contributions to the Theory and Technique of Psycho-Analysis* (pp. 304–311). London: Hogarth, 1950.
Ferenczi, S. (1919). The phenomena of hysterical materialization. Thoughts on the Conception of hysterical conversion and symbolism. In: *Further Contributions to the Theory and Technique of Psycho-Analysis* (pp. 89–104). London: Hogarth, 1950.
Freud, S. (1900a). *The Interpretation of Dreams. S. E., 4–5*. London: Hogarth.
Freud, S. (1914d). On the history of the psycho-analytic movement. *S. E.*, *14*: 1–66. London: Hogarth.
Freud, S. (1937c). Analysis terminable and interminable. *S. E.*, *23*: 216–254. London: Hogarth.
Haynal, A. (1988). *The Technique at Issue*. London: Karnac.
Jones, E. (1953). *The Life and Work of Sigmund Freud*. New York: Basic Books.
May, U. (2007). Freud's patient calendars: 17 analysts in analysis with Freud (1910–1920). *Psychoanalysis and History*, *9*: 153–200.
Schur, M. (1972). *Freud: Living and Dying*. New York: International Universities Press.

Chapter 6

A fateful quadrangle: Sándor Ferenczi, Sigmund Freud, Gizella Palos-Ferenczi, and Elma Palos-Laurvik

Emanuel Berman

The theoretical differences between Freud and Ferenczi did not first develop during Ferenczi's later years as Freud (1937c) claimed, but have their roots early in their relationship. The personal and professional levels in their dialogue were intertwined all along the way. Two major aspects of this admixture were the quadrangle between Freud, Ferenczi, Gizella—Ferenczi's lover and eventually his wife—and her daughter Elma; and Ferenczi's analysis with Freud, which was an outgrowth of that quadrangle (Dupont, 1994).

Ferenczi's original insights into the underlying mutuality of the analytic relationship first developed in the context of his yearning for a greater mutuality in his personal relationships—with Freud, with Gizella, and then with Elma; while Freud consistently expressed his scepticism in all these situations (Aron, 1998). Later on, Ferenczi's painful dilemma, in choosing between mother and daughter, made him dependent on Freud's advice and help, and gradually more prone to accept Freud's hierarchical world view. Freud encouraged Ferenczi to accept Gizella and himself as transferential parents. Ferenczi's stormy ambivalent feelings made him defiantly cling to Elma at one point; but later brought him closer to Freud, including the wish to be analysed by him and the willingness to marry Gizella. Eventually, however, the unresolved conflict re-aroused his antagonism to Freud, and inflamed the dormant theoretical disagreement as well (Berman, 2004a, 2004b; Bonomi, Chapter Five).

To study this quadrangle more fully we must supplement the Freud-Ferenczi correspondence (Falzeder, Chapter Seven) with other documentary sources (now accessible at the Freud Museum in London) that enable us to better portray the two "silent" partners in the drama, Gizella and Elma. Only by allowing the women in the story to regain their missing voices can we hope to complete the puzzle.

Publishing the correspondence, including its intimate personal parts, was an issue debated for years by Gizella, Elma, Anna Freud, and Michael Balint, Ferenczi's literary executor. The passage of time, changing norms as to what can be openly disclosed, and the courage of Judith Dupont who replaced Balint in his role eventually allowed for the full publication.

Sándor first alludes to Gizella in 1909, a year after the beginning of his enthusiastic friendship and correspondence with Freud. (Sándor's and Gizella's first union took place in 1900; Fer/Fr, 17 October 1916, p. 141). In 1909 Sándor was single, thirty-six years old; Gizella was married, aged forty-four, the mother of two daughters: Elma (almost twenty-two) and Magda (twenty).

Gizella Altschul was born on 29 October 1866 in Miskolcz. The Ferenczis (formerly Fraenkels) and the Altschuls were neighbours, two Jewish families that were well acquainted. Gizella's father Simon was a grain merchant, originally from Prague. He and his wife Sophie (who died when Gizella was about six) had three sons and four daughters. After their

Gizella with her daughters
courtesy Emanuel Berman

mother's death the children were brought up by Aunt Titi (Ernestine), a well-educated but domineering French governess, who was reputed to have also been the father's mistress.

Gizella, always a powerful and sophisticated woman, married Dr Geza Palos, a weak and passive man, who gradually became deaf. She apparently never loved him. Elma was born on 28 December 1887, Magda on 28 April 1889. Their temperaments were different; even in

Elma Palos

courtesy Emanuel Berman

early photos Elma often appears to be serious, introverted, complicated, and Magda tends to be smiling and easygoing. Magda married Lajos, Sandor's younger brother (who was a bank executive), in 1909. They lived together till he died—apparently of a heart attack—towards the end of the Second World War. Elma's relationships with men were more tormented.

Sandor writes to Freud about Gizella: "The difficult and painful operation of producing complete candor in me and in my relationship with her is proceeding rapidly" (26

October 1909, p. 87); "the confession that I made to her… and the truth which is possible between us makes it seem perhaps less possible for me to tie myself to another woman *in the long run,* even though I admitted to her and to myself having sexual desires towards other women. … Evidently I have *too much* in her: lover, friend, mother, and, in scientific matters, a pupil, i.e., the child" (p. 88).

Freud has his doubts: "It belongs to the ABC of our worldview that the sexual life of a man can be something different from that of a woman, and it is only a sign of respect when one does not conceal this from a woman. Whether the requirement of absolute truthfulness does not sin against the postulate of expediency and against the intentions of love I would not like to respond to in the negative without qualification, and I urge caution. Truth is only the absolute goal of science, but love is a goal of life" (10 January 1910, p. 122). Ferenczi, planning a trip to Vienna with Gizella and Elma, asks Freud to advise them about Elma's stormy romantic life (3 January 1911, p. 248). Freud surprises him after the visit by diagnosing Elma as a mild case of *dementia praecox*, schizophrenia (7 February 1911, p. 253). Freud adds: "Frau G.'s visit was very nice; her conversation is particularly charming. Her daughter [Elma] is made of a coarser material, participated little, and for the most part had a blank expression on her face" (8 February 1911, p. 254).

***

Half a year later, Ferenczi reports taking Elma into psychoanalytic treatment: "The effect is favorable" (14 September 1911, p. 296). Freud wishes him success, but warns: "I fear that it will go well up to a certain point and then not at all. While you're at it, don't *sacrifice* too many of your secrets out of an excess of kindness" (20 September 1911, p. 296).

Elma's analysis suffers a setback when a man she was involved with romantically shoots himself on her account. Ferenczi realises: "I wanted to commit a terrible act of violence. Dissatisfied with both parents, I wanted to make myself independent! [of Freud and of Gizella]" (14 November 1911, p. 312). He then relates this rebellion to his fantasies of marrying Elma, indicating these appeared prior to the analysis.

"I was not able to maintain the cool detachment of the analyst with regard to Elma, and I laid myself bare, which then led to a kind of closeness which I can no longer put forth as the benevolence of the physician or of the fatherly friend", Ferenczi now reports (3 December 1911, p. 318). He told Gizella, who is "unstintingly kind and loving" (was it a masochistic submission?) and he thinks of his wish for a family, complicated by Gizella's age (ibid.). Freud responds immediately: "First break off treatment, come to Vienna for a few days ... don't decide anything yet" (5 December 1911, pp. 318–319).

Two weeks later, Freud sends Ferenczi a letter for Gizella, where he interprets Ferenczi: "His homosexuality imperiously demands a child and ... he carries within him revenge against his mother" (17 December 1911, p. 320). He raises many doubts regarding Elma's character, the pace of the process, and the complication of marrying her mother's former lover. A day later Ferenczi writes: "Marriage with Elma seems to be decided. What is still missing is the fatherly blessing." Freud succumbs: "I will congratulate you wholeheartedly when you let me know that the time has come" (18 December 1911, p. 322).

After two more weeks, "doubts crept into *Elma's* mind"; "the scales fell from my eyes ... I had to recognize that the issue here should be one not of marriage but of the treatment of an illness ... she consented to go to Vienna and enter treatment with you" (1 January 1912, p. 324). Ferenczi accepts Freud's view of Elma, and turns her over to him. Freud ambivalently agrees.

The following stage in the correspondence involves Freud's detailed (and by today's standards highly unethical) reports to his friend about Elma's analysis. Emotionally, Freud fluctuates. At times he is attempting to "prepare" Elma for Sándor (13 January 1912, p. 327). At other moments he is more pessimistic, warning Ferenczi "that masochistic impulses very frequently take their course in an unfavorable marital choice", while utilising negation: "I am in no way taking sides against Elma" (13 February 1912, p. 345).

Ferenczi is becoming more and more sceptical. He now says: "I would find sufficient compensation for the loss of family happiness in the understanding and loving company of Frau G. and in scientific intercourse with you" (18 January 1912, p. 328). He visits Freud in Vienna, and then writes: "You were right when, on my first trip to Vienna where I revealed to you my intention to marry, you called attention to the fact that you noticed the same defiant expression on my face when I refused to work with you [refused to take dictations of the Schreber case; Bonomi, Chapter Five] in Palermo" (8 March 1912, pp. 352–353).

Elma is back in Budapest. Gizella encourages Sandor to marry her daughter after all, promising to remain his friend. "I made it clear to her that the possibility ... depended on two conditions: Elma's suitability – and the fact that she becomes agreeable to *me*. (And on Elma's inclination as well, naturally)" (17 April 1912, p. 365). The last sentence appears to be an afterthought; his wishes are more crucial than hers.

Elma's suitability will be examined through a renewed analysis with Ferenczi, who also demands of her to "speak with me freely and uninhibitedly, to admit all her resistances. If she doesn't do that, then I am firmly resolved to give her up" (23 April 1912, p. 369). Freud follows the process with encouraging interest. The two friends appear to have now a joint Pygmalion fantasy, but also enact their common misogyny (Bonomi, 1997, p. 156). They view woman—a view typical in their cultural milieu—as a dangerous seductress, motivated by "the animal side of her self" (Freud, 1915a, p. 163), who must be tamed. "I am very glad that you have remained consistently firm against Elma and have thwarted her tricks", Freud writes (20 July 1912, p. 395).

Ferenczi appears to have given up, for a while, all his egalitarian and feminist ideals. The intense countertransference of both Ferenczi and Freud must have blinded them to the cruelty of the experiment, and to the hopeless double bind created by making analytic openness the precondition for marriage with the analyst.

But the suffering of both Gizella and Elma grows. "In today's hour Elma was quite ill; she didn't say a word; I think she is struggling inwardly but doesn't have the courage to make a decision" (10 June 1912, p. 381). "Frau G. … has difficulty bearing her daughter's suffering" (14 June 1912, p. 381).

Ferenczi extensively quotes a letter from Elma, now allowing her a voice: "I know quite certainly that you will not come to get me. And yet I have such a terrible anxiety about it … I feel almost as if everything will freeze inside me. … I told you how terribly impatient I am, how I burn with desire. It is a very, very good thing for me to be with you; I don't think there could be anything better. … I also feel really a little like your child, so much do I wish to be led by you. Only if we had our child could I feel as if I were your wife. … Talk about yourself, for once; up to now you have been talking only about me! … Write to me once, one single time, honestly, the way one speaks to an adult, and tell me what you really feel" (date unknown, volume I, pp. 383–385).

Naturally, the whole experiment fails: "I have given up Elma's analysis and in so doing severed the last thread of the connection between us" (8 August 1912, p. 402). Towards the end, Ferenczi writes: "Giving up my (almost realized) fantasy with Elma and the analytic executioner's work with which I had to put this fantasy to death by myself still gives me considerable pain" (26 July 1912, p. 396). Subsequently, Elma gets married and leaves for the US; Sandor returns to Gizella, and eventually marries her on 1 March 1919, under Freud's unrelenting pressure during and after Sandor's analysis with him.

Gizella left Geza Palos—who had been very hurt by her affair—in late 1917. The day Gizella and Sandor got married, Geza died. Whereas we cannot be certain if it was a coincidental heart attack, as Ferenczi said, or a suicide (Roazen, 1998), this event must have added an additional burden to "the marriage, sealed under such unusually tragic circumstances" (Fer/Fr, 23 May 1919, p. 356).

Although their marriage was successful in many ways, Sandor's conflict was never fully resolved. On 23 May 1919 he wrote to Freud: "Since the moment in which you advised me against Elma, I have had a resistance toward your own person" (p. 356). Later, on 27 February 1922, he wrote to Groddeck: "Prof. Freud ... persists in his original view that the crux of the matter is my hatred for *him*, because he stopped me ... from marrying the younger woman (now my stepdaughter). Hence my murderous intentions toward him" (p. 19). These quotes highlight the defensive nature of Freud's claim, in "Analysis terminable and interminable", that Ferenczi's analysis "had a completely successful result. He married the woman he loved" (Freud, 1937c, p. 221)—a simplification aimed at presenting Ferenczi's later antagonism as coming "out of the blue".

Ferenczi was afraid of Elma's revenge, dreaming "that she was tearing up my papers like a mad dog" (26 December 1912, p. 451).We never hear from him of regret or guilt about his tantalising attitude towards Elma. Freud, while oblivious of his active role, does tell Ferenczi: "You, because of your infidelity to Elma, have inflicted a deep wound on her and have confused the possible future with demonic dexterity" (6 July 1917, p. 226).

A few months after separating from Elma, Ferenczi writes to Freud: "Mutual analysis is nonsense, almost an impossibility" (26 December 1912, p. 449). This is the occasion he asks Freud to take him into analysis, abandoning the fantasy he expressed two years earlier, when still striving for greater equality with Freud, that he could help Freud as "an unimpeachable therapist" to be more open with him (p. 224). As we know, his eventual disappointment with the analysis with Freud coincided with his renewed belief in mutuality, in the value of speaking "honestly, the way one speaks to an adult". In the work described in the *Diary*—especially in his attempted mutual analysis—Ferenczi finally meets Elma's frustrated challenge, after a long detour.

***

Elma married John Laurvik, an American who was initially a sailor, and later a journalist and an art merchant. They met in 1913 and got married in 1914. Their relationship was stormy, with many separations. In a document signed in 1957 she wrote: "I returned to San Francisco some time during 1920. However, because of Mr. Laurvik's unstable character and because of differences in our point of view, I decided to return again to Budapest, Hungary, some time during 1924. We never divorced legally because he always assured me that he wanted me to come back to him and promised that he would change and we could start a new life together again. He never kept his promises and so I never returned to him ..."

"As he never sent me any support I had to start to work for my living and I joined the American Foreign Service in 1925. I was appointed to the American Legation in Budapest ... I worked there from 1925 until World War II. Then the American Legation had to close its offices and I was sent to Bern, Switzerland ... I never divorced Mr. Laurvik. He passed away in 1953."

Elma and her husband Laurvik

courtesy Emanuel Berman

Gizella always cared deeply for Elma. Sandor wrote, "She, too, loves her problem child most" (19 January 1919, p. 327). In spite of their complex past, Elma became part of Sándor's family, as his stepdaughter.

Sandor's premature death on 22 May 1933 was painful for Gizella. Elma lived during the Second World War in Lisbon, then in Bern. Gizella, Magda, and Lajos stayed in Budapest during the war years and the Nazi occupation of 1944–1945. They were all protected by the Swedish diplomat Raul Wallenberg. In 1946, Elma invited Gizella and Magda (now also a widow) to join her in Bern. Gizella died in Bern on 21 March 1949, aged eighty-two. Elma and Magda stayed there, moving to New York City in 1955 (into Laurvik's former apartment, which Elma inherited). Elma died on 4 December 1971 after suffering from Alzheimer's disease; Magda died on 11 May 1972 of a heart attack.

***

A major source of insight into Elma's later years, into her personality and into her view of Sándor, is her rich correspondence during the 1950s and 1960s with Michael Balint, Ferenczi's most prominent disciple (Berman, 2004b).

On 28 April 1966 Balint reports his agreement with Anna Freud to publish a selection from the Freud-Ferenczi correspondence, accompanied by a historical account of their relationship, written by him. He adds: "This now raises a very tricky problem, which is your relationship with Sandor … So may I ask you to reflect on this very intimate and touchy problem, and in due course let me know what your feelings are about it."

Elma's answer on 7 May 1966 indicates the emotional intensity of the challenge. She speaks of herself bitterly: "In spirit I was immature, self-conscious and desirous of love … I was a young girl with a fiery spirit… I was an evil seducer, I was only thinking about myself and did not care about my victims. But perhaps I was not evil at all, only the slave of nature!"

Older Elma

courtesy Emanuel Berman

"All in all after a few sessions Sandor got up from his chair behind me, sat on the sofa next to me and, considerably moved, kissed me all over and passionately told me how much he loved me and asked if I could love him too. Whether or not it was true I cannot tell, but I answered 'yes' and – I hope – I believed so."

"We were cruel when telling it to Mum, who was astonished, but with her presence of mind she said that if the two people whom she loved most in the world were going to get married she could only be happy about it. She was glad that Sandor would have children after all."

Elma goes on to describe her growing realisation that she does not love Sandor that much. "The transitory nature of feelings was the greatest disappointment of my life. The one I could love was my husband, but he was a Peer Gynt and our life dissolved ... When I got back to Budapest Sandor and Mum were already man and wife. When I first saw him again we were both somewhat embarrassed but later on the situation became natural. Sometimes when we were two he would whisper some kind words to me, once in a while he even approached me, but fortunately I remained impassive. My evil nature had disappeared by that time". Elma closes her letter saying: "It was not easy to put all these memories into words".

***

Our expanded understanding of the Freud-Ferenczi relationship enables us to better explore how insights gained from the emerging picture can illuminate major issues regarding the nature of the psychoanalytic encounter, sources of transference and countertransference, the place of reality and fantasy, the role of boundaries, and the relationship between men and women.

The picture emerging here points to the utopian nature of Freud's belief in an objective, impartial, impersonal psychoanalytic technique. The place of subjectivity and of countertransference is ubiquitous.

Freud drew conclusions from the Elma affair (as well as from the Jung-Spielrein affair) in his paper on transference-love (Freud, 1915a), but barely touches countertransference. He perpetuates the image of man's struggle against woman's seduction. But is countertransference-love any less important than transference-love?

Ferenczi's seductive behaviour was influenced by his stormy personality and by his limited analytic experience at the time. But its impact was great.

Ethical issues are crucial. The loose mixture of personal and professional relationships, characteristic of that period, appears to us now as dangerous. The need for boundaries and for confidentiality as defining a sharply delineated asymmetrical analytic field is clear, also in relational and intersubjective analytic models. Denial of the power relations inherent in any therapy may enhance the abuse of power that characterised the analyses of Elma with both Ferenczi and Freud.

And whose perception was sharper? Freud's view of Elma as a limited, disturbed person? Or Ferenczi's initial respect and love for her? Elma's own account of the drama was suppressed by her for decades. She was a very discrete person, deeply loyal to both Freud and Ferenczi; she protected Ferenczi's reputation all her life. She treated Freud and Ferenczi with greater loyalty than they invested in her during that crucial period.

I experience her as an outstanding person: wise, tactful, serious, and—contrary to her self-image—very reliable. Ferenczi's initial "countertransference-love", rather than clouding his perception, may have connected him with Elma's deeper potential. Freud may have mistaken her youthful turmoil for more profound psychopathology, which did not characterise her life.

Can Elma's living alone (or with her sister) most of her life be attributed to the post-traumatic effect of her "confusion of tongues" with both Ferenczi and Freud? Undoubtedly, she did suffer a deep wound.

References

Aron, L. (1998). "Yours, thirsty for honesty, Ferenczi": Some background to Sandor Ferenczi's pursuit of mutuality. *American Journal of Psychoanalysis*, *58*: 5–20.

Berman, E. (2004a). *Impossible Training: A Relational View of Psychoanalytic Education*. Northvale, NJ: Analytic Press (Routledge).

Berman, E. (2004b). Sandor, Gizella, Elma: A biographical journey. *International Journal of Psychoanalysis*, *85*: 489–520.

Bonomi, C. (1997). Mute correspondence. In: P. Mahony, C. Bonomi & J. Stensson (Eds.), *Behind the Scenes: Freud in Correspondence* (pp. 155–202). Oslo: Scandinavian University Press.

Dupont, J. (1994). Freud's analysis of Ferenczi as revealed by their correspondence. *International Journal of Psychoanalysis*, *75*: 301–320.

Freud, S. (1915a). Observations on transference-love. *S. E.*, *12*: 157–171. London: Hogarth.

Freud, S. (1937c). Analysis terminable and interminable. *S. E.*, *23*: 209–254. London: Hogarth.

Roazen, P. (1998). Elma Laurvik, Ferenczi's stepdaughter. *American Journal of Psychoanalysis*, *58*: 271–286.

Chapter 7

Ferenczi in and out of correspondence

Ernst Falzeder

How to give a comprehensive and balanced overview of Ferenczi as a correspondent within the scope of such a short article, even if limiting it to a discussion of the 707 letters he wrote to Freud, fifty-two to Georg Groddeck,[1] thirty-nine to Ernest Jones (Ferenczi & Jones, 2013), and his ninety-three letters to the Committee (in Wittenberger & Tögel, 1999, 2001, 2003, 2006)?[2] Those nearly nine hundred letters were written over a quarter century in very different moods, to very different people, in the most various phases of fluctuating relationships, and in different contexts. They treat the most diverse topics, from the most intimate and personal to the mundane, from family to theoretical, business and institutional matters, and so on. They also bear witness to the profound personal and professional development Ferenczi underwent during that period. He was a very complex personality who does not easily fit into all the various pigeonholes into which he has so often been stuck. It is indeed instructive to note that his personality and development have elicited the most diverging, even mutually exclusive, assessments. There is hardly another psychoanalyst about whom opinions have been so divided for a very long time.[3]

The most famous example is probably his alleged mental illness or even psychosis during his last years (cf. Jones, 1957), against the protestations of those near him who claimed that "mentally he was always clear" (Balint, 1958, p. 68). I have always been puzzled by the fact that extremely competent and experienced psychoanalysts, such as Ernest Jones and Michael Balint (but also others), could not come to an agreement whether one of their teachers and colleagues had a perfectly clear mind or was psychotic. Opinions also differ as to whether he was basically an open-minded and very tolerant spirit, or rather someone who showed "a masterful or even domineering attitude" (Jones, 1955, pp. 157–158).

1 A first edition appeared in French in 1982 (German 1986; both edited by Judith Dupont). A corrected and expanded edition was published in 2000, edited by Christopher Fortune. Michael Giefer's German edition of 2006 can be considered the authoritative one. It includes updated editorial footnotes, but above all fourteen additional letters by Ferenczi (and several by his wife Gizella and her daughter Elma), as well as numerous postscripts omitted in previous editions. Some reading errors and inadvertent omissions in earlier editions were silently corrected (cf. Falzeder, 2007).

2 Copies of four letters Ferenczi wrote to Rank in 1924 are at the Library of Congress, and have also been kindly made available to me by Judith Dupont and his daughter, the late Hélène Rank Veltfort. They are also quoted, among others, in the Rank biographies by Lieberman (1985) and Taft (1958).

3 I am excluding here the cases of those who left the psychoanalytic movement altogether and founded their own schools, and where the differences in opinion were institutionalised, as it were.

In his letters with other psychoanalysts—above all in those with Freud, Groddeck, and Rank, less so in those with Jones, and in his letters to the Committee—Ferenczi often tried for a deep level of mutual understanding and of great honesty. He continuously attempted to be "in synch", or "in correspondence", with the other, often by trying to seduce him through a disclosure of his own innermost feelings and thoughts. Ferenczi is often described as someone who spoke and wrote in an unusually frank and open way, as someone who did not hold back his feelings and thoughts, noting them down as they came to him, "right from the spigot" (Fer/Fr, p. 21). His letters to Freud abound indeed with "confessions" of the most intimate nature, in an attempt at complete honesty: "Just think what it would mean if one *could tell everyone the truth*, one's father, teacher, neighbor, and even the king. … The eradication of lies from private and public life would necessarily *have to* bring about better conditions" (Fer/Fr, p. 130). This he tried to do with Freud, with his friends, with his lovers, and also, sometimes to an extreme extent, with his patients, as in his experiments with "mutual analysis".

On the other hand, he could also be withdrawn and reticent. Lou Andreas-Salomé noted already in 1913 that Ferenczi seemed to live on "his dearest ideas … in his rather profound solitude", but that at the same time he called these ideas "his 'folly', his 'pathological curiosity', and his burning 'desire to know everything'" (1958, p. 137; trans. mod.). He began an extremely candid letter to his close friend (and also occasional physician/analyst) Georg Groddeck with the avowal that: "For a very, very long time now, I have indulged in a kind of proud aloofness, and have hidden my feelings, often also from those nearest to me. … I have never been so open with another man, not even with … Freud", and not even in the tranches of analysis he had had with him: "I could never be completely free and open with him" (Fer/Grod, pp. 7–8). After the last painful meeting with Freud before the Wiesbaden Congress in 1932, when Freud did not even shake his hand in farewell, it took Ferenczi nearly a month to write again: "You can measure by the length of the reaction time the depth of the shock", not without adding: "even though I also have to concede that more courage and more open talk on my part … would have been advantageous to me" (Fer/Fr, pp. 443–444).

These different sides manifested themselves also in other areas, as in his vacillations between "orthodoxy" and "dissidence" (cf. Falzeder, 2010). While he is often, and justifiably so, seen as an innovator and restless experimenter, his very first circular letter to the so-called Secret Committee claimed, on the contrary, that its goal should be to preserve Freud's work "as unmodified as possible", and with a "kind of dogmatism [sic]" (Wittenberger & Tögel, 1999, p. 45).[4] The "secret rebel" (Thompson, 1944) could indeed also be very authoritarian, as in the statutes he proposed ("in correspondence" with Freud) for the IPA at its founding congress, as well as in his disregard of those very statutes: the Committee should be the "*highest* authority" in the psychoanalytic movement, he wrote, disregarding "parliamentary formalities" (Wittenberger & Tögel, 2001, p. 109). "In science," he claimed, one can only be "either brother or enemy. We must not accept compromises" (Wittenberger & Tögel, 2006, p. 364). In this spirit, he wrote programmatic, "orthodox" criticisms of, for example, Jung (1913), Bleuler (1914), Adler (1917), and of Rank (1927). One could say that at times he could play either the role of the "enfant terrible" (ChildAn, p. 127[5]), or that of the "wise baby" (Martín Cabré, Chapter Eighteen).

4 Whereas Freud wrote, still in 1926: "we have not yet earned the right to dogmatic rigidity" (Freud & Andreas-Salomé, 1996, p. 163).

5 Although, as Judith Dupont comments, "[h]e was hurt by [this] nickname" (in Fer/Grod, p. xxii).

The letters with Freud surely constitute the by far most important correspondence, both in quantity and quality. The *average* frequency is about one letter per week, and this for a quarter of a century. Of course, there are fluctuations in frequency: interruptions when they spent time together, fewer letters during illnesses or times of overwork, but also in times of conflict, most notably during the growing estrangement in Ferenczi's last years. There are peaks, on the other hand, when there were serious conflicts with third persons (Jung, members of the Committee), or in special situations, as in the imbroglio around Ferenczi, Gizella, Géza and Elma Palós, in which Freud repeatedly intervened.

Much has been written about this exchange, and it is impossible to do justice to its complexity and many-sidedness in this context, but I sometimes wonder how many people have really read and studied the whole correspondence in depth. I would suggest that it offers a unique insight into *both* men, contrary to Jones's opinion that its main themes would be "of more interest to a student of Ferenczi's personality than of Freud's" (1955, p. 155). For instance, for both of them the letters are like a parallel oeuvre to the published works. Both throw light on each other. Many plans, articles, books are discussed and commented upon in them.

Of course, both of them also wrote about very personal matters, which for some makes them equally open to personal criticism. Jones dismisses Ferenczi's letters as "most painful reading … displaying a thoroughly unstable und suffering personality", not without adding, somewhat mischievously: "whom I personally had always loved" (letter to Dr Magoun, 31 October 1957; Erich Fromm Archives). Yes, Ferenczi was indeed unstable and suffering at times, but let us not forget that so are we all, and so was Freud. Not only was Freud a very insecure, severely neurotic man as a young adult, prone to periods of depression and extreme mood swings, phobic symptoms, fits of jealousy, etc., indeed suffering "from a very considerable psychoneurosis" (Jones, 1953, p. 304), as is amply documented in the unabridged betrothal letters (Freud & Bernays, 2011, 2013, 2015), it is also simply an illusion that through his so-called self-analysis he then emerged as a kind of superman, free of any vestiges of neurosis, "the serene and benign Freud, henceforth free to pursue his work in imperturbable composure" (Jones, 1953, p. 352). See that charming slip of the pen when Freud wrote about his "weakness" and added: "I am also that ψα superman whom we have constructed", forgetting the "not" after "also" (Fr/Fer, p. 221).[6]

But it is precisely from those personal crises that both Freud and Ferenczi sometimes rose to great heights and developed ideas that would be fruitful and highly influential for decades to come. In fact, it is exactly those instances of sometimes great vulnerability and insecurity, crucially combined with their ability to cope with them and to deal with them on a theoretical level, that makes them men of flesh and blood as well as great psychologists—rather than screens on which we could project either our unqualified idolising or pathologising.

The correspondence with Groddeck is a testament of a close friendship and also of an analytic relationship, perhaps the closest and longest friendship he developed with another psychoanalyst. When they got to know each other, Ferenczi was already a prominent and established proponent of the Freudian cause, who originally was very sceptical of Groddeck's unconventional ideas, whereas Freud warmly welcomed Groddeck to the "wild horde" (Freud & Groddeck, 2008, p. 59). To the extent that Freud's enthusiasm for Groddeck

6 Unfortunately, in the English edition the "not" was silently inserted without any reference to Freud's oversight in the original.

waned, however, and also the other members of the Committee increasingly criticised him, the friendship between those two became closer. Ferenczi opened his heart to Groddeck, also with reference to his relationship with Freud, and spent many months as a patient and guest in Groddeck's sanatorium. There were also misunderstandings and priority disputes, although at the time (1929) Ferenczi saw "no reason for breaking off our friendly relationship" (Fer/Grod, p. 90). In the end, however, Groddeck distanced himself from Ferenczi's late theoretical and technical ideas and experiments. After Ferenczi's death, he wrote to his widow, Gizella: "All those past years I couldn't think about Sándor's life but with a heavy heart. … One could help Sándor as little as one could stop a torrential river with one's bare hand. … He was … already so far away from me in his flight to the stars [*Sternenflug*], in which I could not and would not join him" (in ibid., pp. 112–114; trans. mod.).

The few extant letters with Rank were written at the height of the conflicts within the Committee, and show how they were forging a close alliance against the heavy criticisms raised by other members, and increasingly also by Freud. They immediately informed each other of what Freud had written or said to either of them, and discussed counter-measures. After their break, however, when Ferenczi was in New York and they met by chance in Penn Station, he ignored Rank. "He was my best friend," complained Rank bitterly afterwards, "and he refused to speak to me" (Taft, 1958, p. xvi).

Tragically, all these relationships ended, to a greater or lesser extent, on a sour note and in mutual misunderstandings: the estrangement with Freud, the break with Rank, the growing distance from and the severe conflicts with Jones and other Committee members, and even the alienation between him and Georg Groddeck. Ferenczi instead immersed himself in his work with his patients, to whom he devoted extraordinarily much time and affection. He took up to seven patients with him in the holidays with his wife (Ferenczi & Groddeck, 2006, p. 166), and he spent up to five hours per day with Elizabeth Severn, whom he called "her ladyship, the Countess", or even "the Queen" (ibid., pp. 105, 96).

As the controversy between Balint and Jones shows, one can arrive at diametrically opposed conclusions on the basis of the same material, such as the Freud/Ferenczi correspondence. Ferenczi's letters are so rich and multi-faceted that they lend themselves to the most diverse projections. I confess I find it hard not to sympathise with Ferenczi and to like him in these letters, and hard not to feel sorry for him in his blunders and failures. "Somehow, something always went wrong with him," sighed Michael Balint (1949, p. 215). This may be so, but yet: "One is continually amazed by the courage of the man" (Peter Lomas).[7]

References

Andreas-Salomé, L. (1958). *The Freud Journal of Lou Andreas-Salomé*. New York: Basic Books, 1964.

Balint, M. (1949). Sándor Ferenczi, obit 1933. *International Journal of Psychoanalysis*, *30*: 215–219.

Balint, M. (1958). Letter to the editor (Sándor Ferenczi's last years). *International Journal of Psychoanalysis*, *39*: 68.

Falzeder, E. (2007). Sándor Ferenczi und Georg Groddeck, Briefwechsel. Hg. von Michael Giefer. *Luzifer-Amor, Zeitschrift zur Geschichte der Psychoanalyse*, *20*: 165–167.

Falzeder, E. (2010). Sándor Ferenczi between orthodoxy and dissidence. *American Imago*, *66*: 395–404.

7 Endorsement on the back cover of Ferenczi's *Clinical Diary*.

Ferenczi, S. (1913). Kritik der Jungschen "Wandlungen und Symbole der Libido". *Internationale Zeitschrift für ärztliche Psychoanalyse, 1*: 391–403.

Ferenczi, S. (1914). Prof. E. Bleuler: Kritik der Freudschen Theorien. *Internationale Zeitschrift für ärztliche Psychoanalyse, 2*: 62–66.

Ferenczi, S. (1917). Adler, A., und Furtmüller, K.: Heilen und Bilden. *Internationale Zeitschrift für ärztliche Psychoanalyse, 4*: 115–119.

Ferenczi, S. (1927). O. Rank: Technik der Psychoanalyse. *Internationale Zeitschrift für Psychoanalyse, 13*: 1–9.

Ferenczi, S., & Groddeck, G. (2006). *Briefwechsel* (Ed. M. Giefer). Frankfurt/Main: Stroemfeld.

Ferenczi, S., & Jones, E. (2013). *Letters 1911–1933* (Eds F. Erős, J. Székács-Weisz, K. Robinson). London: Karnac.

Freud, S., & Andreas-Salomé, L. (1966). *Letters* (Ed. E. Pfeiffer). London: Hogarth, 1972.

Freud, S., & Bernays, M. (2011). *Sei mein, wie ich mir's denke. Juni 1882 – Juli 1883. Die Brautbriefe, Band 1.* Frankfurt am Main: S. Fischer.

Freud, S., & Bernays, M. (2013). *Unser "Roman in Fortsetzungen". Juli 1883 – Dezember 1883. Die Brautbriefe, Band 2.* Frankfurt am Main: S. Fischer.

Freud, S., & Bernays, M. (2015). *Warten in Ruhe und Ergebung, Warten in Kampf und Erregung. January 1884 – September 1884. Die Brautbriefe, Band 3.* Frankfurt am Main: S. Fischer.

Freud, S., & Groddeck, G. (2008). *Briefwechsel* (Ed. Michael Giefer). Frankfurt am Main: Stroemfeld/Roter Stern.

Jones, E. (1953, 1955, 1957). *The Life and Work of Sigmund Freud* (3 Vols). New York: Basic Books.

Lieberman, J. (1985). *Acts of Will: The Life and Work of Otto Rank.* New York: The Free Press.

Taft, J. (1958). *Otto Rank.* New York: The Julian Press.

Thompson, C. (1944). Ferenczi's contribution to psychoanalysis. *Psychiatry, 7*: 245–252.

Wittenberger, G., & Tögel, C. (Eds.) (1999). *Die Rundbriefe des "Geheimen Komitees". Band 1: 1913–1920.* Tübingen: edition diskord.

Wittenberger, G., & Tögel, C. (Eds.) (2001). *Die Rundbriefe des "Geheimen Komitees". Band 2: 1921.* Tübingen: edition diskord.

Wittenberger, G., & Tögel, C. (Eds.) (2003). *Die Rundbriefe des "Geheimen Komitees". Band 3: 1922.* Tübingen: edition diskord.

Wittenberger, G., & Tögel, C. (Eds.) (2006). *Die Rundbriefe des "Geheimen Komitees". Band 4: 1923–1927.* Tübingen: edition diskord.

Chapter 8

Ferenczi and the foundation of the international and Hungarian psychoanalytical societies

Janos Harmatta

The IPA was founded in March 1910, at the Second Congress of Psychoanalysis, known as the Nuremberg Congress. The initiative for this had come from Ferenczi. On 27 December 1909 he had written to Freud about such an organisation: "It would be appropriate to determine the program in advance ... Besides the psychological and pathological problems, someone would have to treat the practical experiences to date and the most expedient methods of *propaganda* for our psychological movement" (Fer/Fr, 27 Dec 1909, p. 117, italics in the original). Freud's acceptance arrived on 1 January 1910.

They discussed the idea during a meeting in late January, and some weeks later Ferenczi notified Freud of having written to Jung, giving him the title of his speech "about the motives and methods of an organisation of Freudian adherents" (Fer/Fr, 16 Feb 1910, p. 141).[1]

Ferenczi wrote to Freud two weeks before the Congress: "I have already written down the Nuremberg lecture, i.e., the motivation for rallying, as well as the preliminary draft of statutes. The latter still has to be talked through precisely" (Fer/Fr, 15 Mar 1910, p. 151). Freud and Ferenczi travelled together to Nuremberg; the definitive address was presumably shaped on the way. Meanwhile, since Jung had to go to America, the final organisational work was done by his wife. Jung arrived at Nuremberg on the first morning of the conference.

Yet why was there a need to found an international organisation? Psychoanalysis as a young discipline was coping with problems of legitimacy and recognition. Nuremberg and the foundation of the IPA was a crucial passage for circumscribing, standardising, and governing psychoanalysis by means of training, theoretical, and technical standards (Makari, 2008, pp. 239–292).

Since 1902 Freud had been meeting regularly with some Viennese physicians and men of culture who had gathered around him. This was the so-called Wednesday Psychological Society. However, some of its members had begun to use Freudian theories to assert the urgency of a sexual revolution in society. The debate concentrated on the person of Fritz Wittels (Makari, 2008, p. 168*f*, p. 233) and threatened the public image of psychoanalysis. For the first time, Freud "tossed a follower overboard" (p. 234) in 1909.

This was the precursor of a number of splits that would mark the development not only of the movement but also of the theory and technique of psychoanalysis. In that regard, Nuremberg was a divide, because from then on the Freudians tried to defend the good name of

1 The final title was "Report on the necessity of a closer amalgamation of the adherents to Freudian doctrine and suggestions for founding a permanent international organisation".

psychoanalysis by circumscribing the field of those who could be considered psychoanalysts. As Ferenczi declared to the attendees to the Congress:

> We cannot take responsibility for all the nonsense that is served up under the name of psychoanalysis, and we therefore need, in addition to our own publications, an association, membership of which would offer some guarantee that Freud's own psychoanalytic methods were being used, and not methods cooked up for the practitioner's own purposes. One of the special tasks of the association would be to unmask the scientific looting to which psycho-analysis is subjected to-day.
>
> (Ferenczi, 1911, pp. 305–306)

The call for standardisation, however, increased the dissent and marginalisation of some of Freud's followers, starting with the old guard of Viennese analysts led by Stekel and Adler (Falzeder & Handlbauer, 1992). It did not take long for them to leave the Freudian vessel.

In the years preceding the Nuremberg Congress Freud had been absorbed by his relation with the Burghölzli, the psychiatric clinic based in Zurich and directed by Eugen Bleuler, that had first granted an academic-scientific legitimation and recognition to his theories (Falzeder, 1997). Through the Burghölzli, a whole generation of psychiatrists would make contact with Freudian theories and access the psychoanalytic movement: people such as Carl Gustav Jung, Karl Abraham, Ernest Jones, A. A. Brill, Max Eitingon, Ludwig Binswanger, and Sabine Spielrein. And this was the door through which Ferenczi entered psychoanalysis in 1908.

A further and relevant source of scientific recognition came from G. Stanley Hall. In 1909 he invited Freud and Jung to lecture at Clark University, in Massachusetts, and Freud wanted Ferenczi to accompany them.

By that time, Ferenczi had taken the role of a kind of faithful "standard bearer" of Freudian thinking, so it was natural for him to become the main promoter of the formation of an association of psychoanalysts (Kröll, 2011).

In his Nuremberg speech, Ferenczi (1911) depicted a scientific organisation fostering the exchange of ideas, organising education, sponsoring its own conferences and journal, and legitimising psychoanalysis as a science. At the same time, it would have to be a professional organisation, which enabled its members to practice (like a guild or a chamber). Members had to have publications and later to graduate from psychoanalytic training. Those who did not become members had no right to call themselves psychoanalysts. This went far beyond the concept of scientific organisations of the time. But Ferenczi suggested that, as psychoanalysts, the members of this "professional family" would have been better suited than those in other organisations to work collaboratively, due to their capacity for self-reflection.

On the other hand, Ferenczi also envisaged the possible "excrescences" of associative life: that is, "childish megalomania, vanity, admiration of empty formalities, blind obedience, or personal egoism prevail instead of quiet, honest work in the general interest" (Ferenczi, 1911, p. 302). And, many years before Freud's *Group Psychology and the Analysis of the Ego*, Ferenczi analysed these excrescences in the light of psychoanalytic wisdom:

> The characteristics of family life are repeated in the structure and the very nature of all organizations. The president is the father, whose pronouncements and authority are incontrovertible and sacrosanct; the other officials are the older children, who treat their juniors with superiority and flatter the father-figure, but wish at the earliest suitable moment to push him from his throne in order to reign in his stead. The great mass of members, in so far as they do not follow their leader with no will of their own, listen now

> to one agitator, now to another, follow the success of their seniors with hatred and envy, and would like to oust them from the father-figure's favour. Organizations are the field in which sublimated homosexuality can live itself out in the form of admiration and hatred. Thus it seems that man can never rid himself of his family habits, and that he really is the gregarious animal ... described by the Greek philosopher.
>
> (Ferenczi, 1911, pp. 302–303)

On practical grounds, the sharing of authority between Freud and the president was the most difficult problem. In fact, according to Freud's instructions, Jung would be the President and Zurich, rather than Vienna, would become the centre. The Viennese group protested: they could not accept Jung for president, nor could they accept the idea that the centre would move to Zurich. Voting had to be postponed and Freud attended a special meeting in the evening with the Viennese only. As Breger discusses:

> The largest group in the IPA and Freud's first supporters, they had been chafing as he ignored them in favour of Jung and the Swiss. When Stekel called a meeting of the Vienna group to discuss their opposition, Freud appeared and made an emotional plea: "Most of you are Jews, and therefore you are incompetent to win friends for the new teaching. Jews must be content with the modest role of preparing the ground. It is absolutely essential that I should form ties in the world of general science."
>
> (Breger, 2000, p. 191)

Compromise was possible only after the Viennese leadership was split. Freud left the leadership of the group to Adler and asked Stekel to become the editor of the new journal (*Zentralblatt für Psychoanalyse*). Such division of power and decentralisation seemed a good idea for the time being. Yet, to get the final positive vote, the term of the presidency had to be reduced to two years. While the IPA president would govern and organise the society, it was obvious that the informal power and leadership would remain in Freud's hands.

The IPA opened up new possibilities, but also gave rise to new tensions, which were inherent in the various polarities around which the organisation was built: globalism/familism, scientific/professional, hierarchic/democratic, Jewish/non-Jewish, formal/informal leadership. The person of the incoming president also carried a number of risks: Jung was not accepted by everybody. Immediately upon his return to Vienna, Freud wrote to Ferenczi:

> Your impassioned pleading had the misfortune of unleashing so much opposition that they forgot to thank you for your significant inspiration ... But we are both a little at fault, since we didn't sufficiently take into account the effect this would have on the Viennese... But that is not the essential thing. It is more important that we have accomplished a big piece of work that will have a far-reaching influence on the shape of the future. I am happy to state that we have both found ourselves in clear agreement, and I thank you very much for your decidedly successful support. Events will now continue ... The infancy of our movement has ended with the Nuremberg *Reichstag*;[2] that is my impression. I hope that a rich and beautiful youth is now coming.
>
> (Fr/Fer, 3 Apr 1910, pp. 155–156)

2 In 1356 Karl IV, in Nuremberg, declared the German Golden Bull, which included the order that every newly elected emperor had to hold his first meeting of the Empire in this place.

Concerning the further development of the psychoanalytic movement, we can see that there were some short-term problems stemming from the Congress. It brought radical change in the life of the two local groups: Vienna and Zürich. On the one hand, the problem in Zürich was that only psychoanalysts could be members of the IPA, and this caused a split. In the end, Bleuler did not become a member and turned away from psychoanalysis. Binswanger, the new president in Zürich, did not accept that only psychoanalysts could be members. Jung compromised and let in those who were interested but did not pay the membership fee, which Freud did not like. On the other hand, the Viennese group broke up and a first rival orientation was born from within the movement itself, with the leadership of Stekel and particularly Adler. In retrospect, Freud came to believe that the psychoanalytic organisation had been founded too soon.

Nevertheless, this new chapter heralded a great development (Ermann, 2011, p. 88), as the international model was in many ways successful. The local groups were opening one by one, eight of them in several years' time: the Vienna Psychoanalytic Society in 1908, the Freud Society in Zurich in 1910, the Berlin Psychoanalytic Association in 1910, the Moscow Group in 1911, the New York Psychoanalytic Society in 1911, the American Psychoanalytic Association in the same year in 1911, the Hungarian Psychoanalytical Society in 1913, the London Psychoanalytic Society in 1913. Psychoanalysis became a global movement. Newcomers received a relatively standardised training. It was also possible to find ways for Freud to remain partially in the background, while continuing to participate in the important decisions. The global society was able to unite almost all analysts during the two World Wars.

Although he first proposed founding the association, Ferenczi held no position in it. He suffered from that, and wrote to Freud: "You have kept in reserve for me the expression of your trust (in your latest letter). I can maintain with psychoanalytic honesty that is worth more to me than honors from outside (although I do not disdain the latter)" (5 Apr 1910, pp. 158–159). Ferenczi became the elected President of IPA much later, during the Budapest Congress in 1918. Yet because of the communication difficulties in the collapsed Austro-Hungarian Empire after the First World War Ferenczi passed on his duties in the IPA to Jones in 1919 and the presidency in 1920, Freud writes in his obituary of Ferenczi: "At the Nuremberg Congress of 1910, I arranged that he should propose the organization of analysts into an international—a scheme which we had thought out together" (Freud, 1933c, p. 226).

Ferenczi's ideas and role remained in the background, but he was justifiably proud of his initiative and organisation plans. In fact, he considered the foundation of the IPA as a part of his life achievement. In an interview given in 1928, Ferenczi said: "Of course, I still see as my most enduring creation the IPA to which I gave life, an organisation that by now has constituent groups in nearly every cultural hub throughout the world" (Mészáros, 2015, p. 27).

There is an ironic postscript to the story of Ferenczi and the IPA presidency. In April 1932, in the course of the hardest period of Ferenczi's conflict with Freud and just before the Wiesbaden Congress, Freud asked Ferenczi to sacrifice the comforts of the isolation in which he had retired himself and offered him the presidency of the IPA again, so to rescue him from the "island of dreams" where—according to Freud—Ferenczi was playing with his "fantasy-children" (i.e., developing his radical new theories) and bring him back to the less threatening (to Freud) arena of social-organisational life (Haynal, 2002, p. 122). Ferenczi refused, on the grounds that this time around he had to take care of himself, his health, and his own children-ideas. As Haynal observed, the presidency of the IPA "would probably … demand too much loyalty – beyond the limits of his evolution towards more freedom" (ibid.).

Hungarian psychoanalytic society celebrates Ferenczi's 50th birthday
courtesy Judit Meszaros

While putting the first stones for the foundation of the IPA, Ferenczi also launched the Hungarian Psychoanalytical Society. He wrote to Freud: "I conferred with [Décsi] over the founding of a psychoanalytical society (modelled on Vienna) and made contact with Stein" (Fer/Fr, 5 Feb 1910, p. 131). Freud replied: "Wait until new people come to you" (Fer/Fr, 8 Feb 1910, p. 133).

Both Freud and Jung advised Ferenczi to begin courses and acquire pupils, as the basis for the group. Ferenczi took to the task with gusto: "In the Fall I will found the branch society with the better elements of the course and then, of course, also bring in Stein and Décsi" (Fer/Fr, 27 May 1910, p. 176). The attempt remained an intention. The two did not attend the meeting and excluded themselves from the future of psychoanalysis. Therefore, Ferenczi delayed until he had found more reliable companions. He spent a lot of time with young physicians, giving lectures at the Galileo Circle, which had been "formed by students of medicine and engineering with an expressly bourgeois radical approach for the purpose of putting an end to the anti-culturalism of their semi-feudal country. … Károly Polányi, Mihály Polányi's brother, was its founding president" (Mészáros, 2014, p. 31). Members of the group remained in contact with Hungarian psychoanalysts over the years: in fact, "it was Mihály Polányi who would emigrate and eventually assist Michael Balint and his wife Alice Balint in resettling in the United Kingdom in the late 1930s" (ibid., pp. 31–32).

The final attempt to create the Hungarian Society took place in 1913, when Ferenczi wrote to Freud that he intended to found it before the Munich IPA Congress. Freud replied: "If you can found your local group, then do it right away, and before the Congress, not just because of the votes but also because of the position that it bestows on you" (13 May 1910, p. 486).

The local group was finally organised on 19 May 1913. Founding members were Ferenczi (president), István Hollós, psychiatrist (vice president), Lajos Lévy, internist (treasurer), Sándor Radó, medical student (secretary), and Ignotus, the writer.

The society grew and got stronger fast. In 1918 they took on another eleven members and the membership grew to nineteen. Among them was Ernest Jones, too. Melanie Klein became a member of the society in 1919. Ferenczi's popularising activity and the quality of his analytic work ensured the supply of new members and the maturation of the group as a whole. Not having been plagued by the splits that had characterised Vienna and Zurich, an unbroken growth began that eventually brought Ferenczi to the presidency of the IPA in 1918, and made Budapest one of the capitals of psychoanalysis. The rise of the group, however, was traumatically interrupted when dramatic socio-political changes occurred, both in Europe and, especially, in Hungary; which made "the potential for Budapest to remain a hub for the psychoanalytic movement" suddenly disappear (Mészáros, 2014, p. 51), but the Budapest School of Psychoanalysis developed and enriched the heritage of modern psychoanalysis.

References

Breger, L (2000). *Freud: Darkness in the Midst of Vision.* New York: Wiley.

Ermann, M. (2011). Über die Notwendigkeit (und die NOT) einer ständigen Internationalen Organisation. Sándor Ferenczi und der Institutionskonflikt der Psychoanalyse. In: E. Metzner & M. Schimkus (Eds.) (2011), *Die Gründung der Internationalen Psychoanalytischen Vereinigung durch Freud und Jung* (pp. 75–90). Grießen: Psychosozial Verlag.

Falzeder E., & Handlbauer B. (1992). Freud, Adler et d'autres psychanalystes. Des débuts de la psychanalyse organisée à la fondation de l'Association Psychanalytique Internationale [Freud, Adler, and the other psychoanalysts. From the beginning of organised psychoanalysis to the foundation of the International Psychoanalytical Association]. *Psychothérapies, 12*: 219–232.

Falzeder E. (1997). The story of an ambivalent relationship: Sigmund Freud and Eugen Bleuler. In: *Psychoanalytic Filiations: Mapping the Psychoanalytic Movement* (pp. 177–196). London: Karnac, 2015.

Ferenczi S. (1911). On the organization of the psycho-analytical movement. In: *Final Contributions to the Problems and Methods of Psycho-Analysis* (pp. 299–307). London: Karnac.

Freud, S. (1933c). Sándor Ferenczi. *S. E., 22*: 225–230. London: Hogarth.

Haynal A. (2002), *Disappearing and Reviving.* London: Karnac.

Kröll, F. (2011). Mitglied oder Anhänger? Organisationsprobleme der Psychoanalyse. In: E. Metzner & M. Schimkus (Eds.), *Die Gründung der Internationalen Psychoanalytischen Vereinigung durch Freud und Jung* (pp. 57–74). Psychosozial Verlag.

Makari, G. (2008). *Revolution in Mind: The Creation of Psychoanalysis.* New York: Harper Collins.

Mészáros, J. (2014). *Ferenczi and Beyond: Exile of the Budapest School and Solidarity in the Psychoanalytic Movement during the Nazi Years.* London: Karnac.

Mészáros J. (2015). Ferenczi in our contemporary world. In A. Harris & S. Kuchuck (Eds.), *The Legacy of Sándor Ferenczi* (pp. 19–32). New York: Routledge.

Chapter 9

Ferenczi in early psychoanalytic circles

Anna Bentinck van Schoonheten

In the early days of psychoanalysis, Ferenczi was much-liked and valued by his colleagues, but at the same time he was criticised and underrated as well. His need to be loved made it difficult for him to really assert himself.

It was not until fairly late in life, when he was over fifty, that Freud made a name for himself, and even then it was not for some years that he became truly famous. One of the colleagues who made powerful contributions to Freud's growing fame was a contemporary, Eugen Bleuler (1857–1939), director of the Burghölzli clinic in Zurich and one of the most eminent and well known psychiatrists of his day. Bleuler became interested in psychoanalysis and asked a young doctor's assistant who worked with him, Carl Gustav Jung, to read and comment on Freud's *The Interpretation of Dreams*. Jung was less than impressed at first, but gradually he grew fascinated by the work and became an enthusiastic champion of both psychoanalysis and Freud.

Through Bleuler, Jung, and the Burghölzli, a number of young doctors came into contact with psychoanalysis and, by working in cooperation with Freud, gave it a huge boost. Among them were Sándor Ferenczi from Budapest, Karl Abraham from Berlin, and Ernest Jones from London. Later on, from 1912 onwards, they would form, together with Hanns Sachs and Otto Rank from Vienna, the "secret committee" that, along with Freud, would shape the development of the psychoanalytic movement for fourteen years (Bentinck van Schoonheten, 2016, p. xxii).

Accompanied by his wife Emma and his young colleague Ludwig Binswanger, Jung visited Freud for the first time in Vienna on 3 March 1907. It was to become an historic encounter. From Vienna, Jung and his wife travelled to Budapest, where they visited Fülop Stein who introduced them to Ferenczi (Fr/Ju, p. 24; Harmat, 1988, p. 21). When Stein in turn visited Jung at the Burghölzli, he brought along his friend and colleague Ferenczi, during which visit Jung was deeply impressed with Ferenczi's keen interest in psychoanalysis. He arranged a meeting with Freud (Fr/Ju, 28 June 1907) for Ferenczi and Stein, which took place on 2 February 1908. This visit was very quickly followed by an intensive exchange of ideas as well as a developing friendship between Freud and Ferenczi. Only two months later, at the first psychoanalytic conference in Salzburg on 27 April 1908, Freud invited Ferenczi to spend his vacation in Berchtesgaden where Freud would be with his family for the summer and, in addition, to then accompany him on a trip. Ferenczi accepted both invitations and found himself plunged into the centre of the psychoanalytic world (Fr/Fer, p. 59*n*, p. 62). In 1909, at the invitation of Stanley Hall, Freud went with Jung to America, where each was to give lectures at Clark University in Worchester, Massachusetts. Freud had asked Ferenczi to join them and, having gathered together the money for the crossing, the latter helped Freud every morning during their walks to prepare the lecture of the afternoon. In America, they had their most significant encounter with the sixty-three-year old James Putnam, a physician and professor of neurology at Harvard, who was to become a great advocate of psychoanalysis in the United States and in 1911 established the American Psychoanalytic Association. There is an extensive correspondence between Freud and Putnam, while Ferenczi, too, corresponded with him for a few years (Hale, 1971).

In these early years of psychoanalysis, it seems that Ferenczi mainly followed and assisted Freud theoretically and practically. He published a great deal. Well-liked because of his geniality and original contributions on the one hand, he was also criticised and at times extremely critical on the other.

At the conference in Nuremberg in 1910, Ferenczi presented a jumbled plea for Freud's idea of establishing an international organisation. That international society, the IPA, was indeed founded. However, during his speech Ferenczi interspersed his presentation with taunts at not only the enemies of psychoanalysis but also at Freud's Viennese group, to which he rather tactlessly referred as being inferior to the Zurich group. The intention was for Zurich to have a central position, with Jung as the president of the IPA. The entire affair caused such a riot that with the greatest effort Freud was only barely able to calm the ruffled feathers and was forced to make Adler and Stekel editors of the new, yet to be established, *Zentrallblatt für Psychoanalyse* (Clark, 1980, pp. 295–299).

Two years later Ferenczi criticised Putnam's article on the importance of philosophy for the development of psychoanalysis. He objected to the fact that Putnam was a supporter of the idea that psychoanalysis should fit in with, and be submissive to, philosophy (Ferenczi, 1912). Putnam reacted courteously, but it heralded the end of their correspondence. The question is whether Ferenczi, who had taken a rather scathing tone, was expressing his own opinion or that of Freud. Freud could not afford to have a difference of opinion with Putnam, who was far too important for psychoanalysis in the United States. It is possible that in this case Ferenczi did the job for Freud, just as he had already done in Nuremberg. The opinions about Ferenczi were noteworthy. It was as if Ferenczi's colleagues felt he still needed to come out of his role of younger, irresponsible son, a role he inhabited in spite of his position and contributions.

Lou Andreas-Salomé was impressed with Ferenczi but, as she wrote in her diary in 1913, thought that his time was yet to come. She saw him as the one who would complete Freud's work (1983, p. 147).

Bleuler was exceedingly critical of Ferenczi. He found that his lecture at the conference in Weimar in 1911 on homosexuality and the accompanying ideas on alcoholism gave evidence of the prototype of a Freudian student who tends to speculate while lacking a sufficiently empirical basis, thereby doing psychoanalysis more harm than good (Schröter, 2012, p. 173). Ferenczi took offence at Bleuler's criticism (1911, pp. 853–857).

When Binswanger heard that, after the break with Stekel and Adler in 1912, Freud wanted to make Ferenczi editor-in-chief of the *Zeitschrift*, he asked Freud whether he himself could not become editor-in-chief. Ferenczi presumably did not have the scientific and critical perspective that an editor-in-chief would need (Fichtner, 2003, p.105).

The secret committee

The secret committee was an idea that came to Ferenczi's mind in July 1912 in Vienna when he, Rank, and Jones discussed the political problems within psychoanalysis—problems that had begun because Jung was putting forward his own version of psychoanalysis where early childhood sexuality barely played a role anymore. He had started to extricate himself from Freud and, in view of Jung's charisma and popularity, this was a serious threat. The idea was to form a small group of faithful followers around Freud who would represent the true psychoanalysis, to whom others would direct themselves to learn the profession (Brome, 1968; Grosskurth 1991; Schröter, 1995; Wittenberger & Tögel, 1999). Jones informed Freud, who instantly implemented the idea, turned it into a "secret committee", and nominated the members who should be added, notably Abraham and Sachs (Fr/Jo, 1 August 1912). The committee's first action was a harsh one. Jung was bombarded with negative critiques from the committee members, and subsequently withdrew as president of the IPA. That had, in fact, been precisely the intention.

The secret committee turned into an extremely creative, hardworking group whose members stimulated one another immensely. Great friendships were born and great conflicts arose, but in the early stages, when psychoanalytic technique was still in its infancy, the mutual relationships were far too complicated, mostly because of the lack of confidentiality and boundaries. So it happened that, at Jones' request, his partner Loe Kann went into analysis with Freud in the summer of 1912. Kann left Jones at the end of March 1913. Her analysis came up for extensive discussion in the correspondence between Freud and Jones, while Kann let Freud read Jones' letters to her (Fr/Jo, 28 October 1912). Jones in turn would write to Freud to report on what Kann had written him about the analysis (Fr/Jo, 13 November 1912). At Ferenczi's request, his patient with whom he was in love (who also loved him), Elma Palos, the daughter of Ferenczi's partner Gizella Palos, also went into analysis with Freud from January to April 1912. This relationship, too, was discussed extensively in the correspondence between Freud and Ferenczi. Subsequently, that relationship was also broken off on the advice of Freud (Berman, Chapter Six).

In addition, in June 1913, Jones went to Budapest for two months for an intensive analysis of two hours a day with Ferenczi. Jones was afraid that Ferenczi would write about this to Freud, which he actually did, albeit secretly (Fr/Fer, 17 June 1913). Of course, the whole situation produced an inextricable tangle of transferences and anger on the part of Jones and Ferenczi over the loss of their loved ones. It must have seriously influenced their subsequent entanglements.

Jones and Ferenczi

Ferenczi liked Jones a great deal better than he had expected and wrote to Freud: "Jones is very pleasant as a friend and colleague" (Fr/Fer, 17 June 1913, p. 493), adding that scientifically he turned out to be far more valuable than Ferenczi had estimated. The analysis must have been a solace to Jones as well, providing an opportunity to express his rage since the loss of Loe Kann had been a great blow to him (Fr/Jo, 3 June 1913). Ferenczi and Jones developed a friendship during Jones' analysis and their ensuing correspondence was warm (Erős et al., 2013). Ferenczi even suggested and arranged with Jones that he would not spend the summer vacation of 1914 anywhere near Freud, as he had been doing for years, but visit Jones in London, proposing they would then take a trip together. However, the First World War broke out and Jones suddenly belonged to the enemy power and epistolary contact was no longer really possible. There is one last letter of 15 May 1915 in which Ferenczi thanks Jones for translating his articles.

After Jung's resignation

After Jung's resignation the leadership of the psychoanalytic movement fell to Freud and the "secret committee", whose members succeeded one another as presidents of the IPA. Abraham followed Jung and became interim president in 1914. Ferenczi was elected as president in 1918 during the first conference near the end of the First World War. His presidency did not last long. The arrival of the Horthy regime in 1919 brought with it a wave of serious anti-Semitism in Hungary, so that Ferenczi lost his position at the university and even his membership at the Budapest Royal Medical Society, while psychoanalysis was driven entirely into a corner. At Freud's urging, and most likely encouraged by Jones, Ferenczi handed over the IPA presidency to Jones until the next conference. Mészáros believes that this is where Jones' strong rivalry with Ferenczi already emerged (Mészáros, 2014, p. 55). Such was undoubtedly the case, but the vehemence of the later explosions of Jones and Ferenczi toward each other does raise the question whether there wasn't more to it than that. What was the influence of the complications in 1912 and 1913? A third party was involved and that was Freud. Did Jones and Ferenczi project their ire over their lost loves on to each other instead of on Freud? What had happened to their friendship?

Ferenczi's revenge

Ferenczi was not elected to be the president at the subsequent conference. Jones continued as chair at the conference in The Hague in 1920 and was re-elected in 1922 in Berlin, but did not have an easy position after the First World War. He was less accessible, while the other committee members lived near one another. He was in England where after the First World War strong anti-German sentiments were the rule (Buruma, 2016, p. 93). That is why he constantly tried to delete the Germanisms from the translations for the *IJP*, since they instantly provoked resistance in England—something for which Rank as the director of the Psychoanalytic Publishing House had no patience (Brome, 1968, p. 170*ff*). Furthermore, there was a smear campaign going on against psychoanalysis in the newspapers in England, while Jones tried with all his might to defend psychoanalysis (Maddox, 2006, p. 168). There were also continuous conflicts over money and the journals between Rank and Jones and in 1923, to top it all off, Freud fell seriously ill. He had cancer.

It had become a tradition that in a year when no international conference was being held the committee would come together for a few days. In 1923, they would gather in San Cristoforo near Freud's vacation home in Lavarone, but this time without Freud, who was too ill and in deep mourning, besides; his favourite grandchild Heinerle, the small son of his deceased daughter Sophie, had died. In San Cristoforo, the committee members heard from Felix Deutsch that Freud was suffering from cancer. It had a huge impact on the group and the tension could be cut with a knife.

Much has been written about the meeting in San Cristoforo (Brome, 1968; Grosskurth, 1991). A day was spent on the conflict between Rank and Jones in which Abraham played a mediating role. Jones was especially blamed, they called him neurotic, and Ferenczi thought that he should enter into one more analysis. The affair escalated when Ferenczi found out from Brill that Jones had supposedly written that Rank was a "swindling Jew". Ferenczi was furious and Rank immediately wanted Jones to be ousted from the committee. Jones apologised to Rank for having unintentionally wounded him. However, it seems that he barely defended himself against the accusation of being anti-Semitic. It was characteristic of the extremely tense relationships of that moment that no one wondered if what Brill had said was true, while it was common knowledge that Brill tended to handle facts with a rich imagination. It was months before Brill, who had returned to the USA shortly after his pronouncement, would admit that Jones had written something substantially different. He had complained that Rank's "general way of conducting business was distinctly oriental". Even months later it made no difference to the irate Ferenczi, it was a matter of intent not of words. It is hardly surprising that Jones felt ostracised, specifically by Ferenczi, his former analyst. That years later Jones in turn ostracised Ferenczi again by declaring him to be a madman has been elaborately described (Bonomi, 1999).

Eitingon supersedes Ferenczi

Much too little has been written about Max Eitingon, a member of the "secret committee" from 1919 onwards. From 1926 on, he was the most powerful man in the world of psychoanalysis, but even that is barely known. It was his generous financial contributions that enabled the founding of the Berlin Policlinic and kept the publishing house going.

One of the most curious events at this time was the fact that Eitingon superseded Ferenczi for the presidency of the IPA, which occurred in late 1925.

Abraham, who became president of the IPA in 1924, died in 1925 at the age of forty-eight. Eitingon was in Italy during the last months of Abraham's illness, but came back post-haste after Abraham died and demanded that the interim presidency be his. That this demand should be agreed to was not at all obvious, as Eitingon did not publish and barely practiced analysis, in contrast to Ferenczi, who was the most qualified and also wanted to be president. Nevertheless, Eitingon apparently managed to browbeat Ferenczi by mentioning that he would lose face if he weren't to become President. It would give the impression that he was unfit for the presidency. Due to Eitingon's intervention, the chairmanship of the Berlin Society also did not go to Ferenczi but to Simmel. Some of the most important members of the Berlin Society had asked Ferenczi to become their president and Ferenczi seriously considered this proposition. Berlin was the centre of psychoanalysis at that moment even more than Vienna (Fr/Fer, 30 December 1925; 18 January 1926).

After these events of 1925–26 and the committee's collapse, Ferenczi became isolated and he and Freud drifted farther and farther apart. At the same time, it was the period in which Ferenczi's originality came to full bloom.

References

Andreas-Salomé, L. (1983). *Tagebuch eines Jahres (1912/1913).* Berlin: Ullstein.

Bentinck van Schoonheten, A. (2016). *Karl Abraham, Life and Work: A Biography.* London: Karnac.

Bonomi, C. (1999). Flight into sanity: Jones's allegation of Ferenczi's mental deterioration reconsidered. *International Journal of Psychoanalysis, 80*: 507–542.

Buruma, I. (2016). *Their Promised Land.* London: Atlantic.

Brome, V. (1968). *Freud and his Early Circle.* New York: William Morrow.

Brome, V. (1982). *Ernest Jones: Freud's Alter Ego.* Pittsburgh: Caliban.

Clark, R. W. (1980). *Freud, the Man and the Cause.* New York: Random House.

Erős F., Szekacs-Weisz J., & Robinson. K. (Eds.) (2013). *Ferenczi - Jones Letters 1911–1933.* London: Karnac.

Ferenczi, S. (1911). Alkohol und Neurosen: (Antwort auf die Kritik des Herrn Prof. Dr. E. Bleuler). *Jahrbuch für psychoanalytische und psychopathologische Forschung, 3*: 853–857.

Ferenczi, S. (1912). Philosophie und Psychoanalyse. *Imago, 1*: 519–526.

Fichtner, G. (Ed.) (2003). *The Sigmund Freud-Ludwig Binswanger Correspondence, 1908–1938*. London: Open Gate.

Grosskurth, P. (1991). *The Secret Ring: Freud's Inner Circle and the Politics of Psychoanalysis*. New York: Addison Wesley.

Hale, G. (1971). *James Jackson Putnam and Psychoanalysis*. Cambridge: Harvard University Press.

Harmat, P. (1988). *Freud, Ferenczi und die ungarische Psychoanalyse*. Tübingen: diskord.

Maddox, B. (2006). *Freud's Wizard: The Enigma of Ernest Jones*. London: John Murray.

Mészáros, J. (2014). *Ferenczi and Beyond*. London: Karnac.

Schröter, M (1995). Freuds Komitee 1912–1914. Ein Beitrag zum Verständnis psychoanalytischer Gruppenbildung. *Psyche, 49*: 513–563.

Schröter M. (Ed.). (2012). *Sigmund Freud – Eugen Bleuler. Ich bin zuversichtlich, wir erobern bald die Psychiatrie. Briefwechsel 1904–1937*. Basel: Schwabe.

Wittenberger G., & Tögel, C. (Eds.) (1999, 2001, 2002, 2006). *Die Rundbriefe des "Geheimen Komitees"*. Vol. 1: 1913–1920. Vol. 2: 1921. Vol. 3: 1922. Vol. 4: 1923–1927. Tübingen: diskord.

Chapter 10

Ferenczi's work on war neuroses and its historical context

Andreas Hamburger

The historical context

When Ferenczi started to think about war, he already had combat experience. Not only in what Freud used to call his "inner warsite", the ménage à trois with Gizella and Elma, a ménage à quatre, including Freud (Berman, Chapter Six), but also serving in the latter's *wildem Heer14*[1] as his new ally. And he was in the midst of his unresolved transference to Freud, having completed only three and a half weeks of his long-delayed analysis, fourteen hours per week, before he joined the army (Bonomi, Chapter Five).

Initially, he had direct contact neither with combat, nor with prisoners of war from the nearby large POW camp, the *k.u.k. Kriegsgefangenenlager* Csót.[2] This changed when on 26 June 1915, Ferenczi learned that, in combat, the penis of a young cadet from his regiment had been cut off and put it in his mouth. His comment, however, sounds aloof: "I think to myself: this strange and very widespread act of vengeance can be traced to ambivalence. Consciousness is only filled with hate, but repressed sympathy expresses itself in the means of punishment" (Fer/Fr, p. 60). Also, his plan to design an institution for traumatised soldiers in Budapest served mainly as a way to achieve a transfer to the capital (Fer/Fr, 24 September 1915, p. 71). When the war got fiercer, however, the tone in the correspondence changed. Freud was concerned about his sons in the field, and Ferenczi, who was eventually appointed director of a new department for war-traumatised veterans at the Maria Valeria Hospital in Budapest, mentions his traumatised patients only occasionally:

> I analyzed (allowed to free-associate) a sufferer from war trauma for an hour. Unfortunately, it turned out that the year before the shock of the war he had lost a father, two brothers (through the war), and a wife through unfaithfulness. When such a man then has to lie for twenty-four hours underneath a corpse, it is difficult to say how much of his neurosis is due to war trauma. (He trembles and speaks in a mumble.)
>
> (Fer/Fr, 24 January 1916, p. 107*f*)

Freud encouraged a publication (Ferenczi, 1916), though advising Ferenczi to "keep your nice theoretical points of view there to yourself" (Fer/Fr, 24 January 1916, p. 115). That is,

1 Freud referred to the psychoanalytic movement as a "wild hunt" in a letter to Georg Groddeck (Groddeck, 1977, p. 36).

2 A huge camp, which had even issued a series of its own banknotes since 1 August 1916 (Navona Numismatics, undated). The mental state of its prisoners was described by one of them, the psychologist Dalla Volta (1919).

the connection to the "Lamarckian project", for example, the interpretation of post-traumatic trembling as a "phylogenetic regression" (ibid.), should not be mentioned.

Things started to move when the Fifth International Psycho-analytical Congress came to Budapest, and Ferenczi (1919) gave a keynote lecture on war neuroses, discussed in a panel by Karl Abraham (1921 [1919]) and Ernst Simmel (1921).

Ferenczi's Papers on War Neurosis

In his first paper on war neurosis, based on a clinical lecture, Ferenczi (1916) describes the confusing impression of the group of 200 patients under his observation at the clinic and discusses neurophysiological *vs.* psychodynamic aspects. Presenting some cases more closely, he concludes that the observed symptoms can be explained by mental processes rather than by neural lesions. He distinguishes monosymptomatic war neuroses from general traumatic abasia-astasia. The first category shows symptoms that mirror the innervation patterns at the moment of the trauma, and Ferenczi parallels it to conversion hysteria. The latter is explained as an anxiety hysteria: ambulatory disorders of the patients who had previously been highly ambitious persons were explained as avoidance reactions against the damage to their exaggerated self-confidence as a result of being overwhelmed in battle. Following Freud's advice, Ferenczi resorts to allusions when it comes to theory: "I can only mention here that the root of every neurotic dread is a sexual one (Freud)"; but also, he refers to repetition compulsion and a damage of narcissistic ego-cathexis. His own phylogenetic theory is touched only parenthetically: "The stage to which these two neurotics regressed seems to be the infantile stage of the first year of life, a time when they could not yet either walk or stand properly. We know that this stage has a phylogenetic model; the upright gait being after all a fairly late achievement of our ancestors among the mammalia" (Ferenczi, 1926, p. 137).

A second presentation of Ferenczi's ideas about war neuroses came in his lecture at the Fifth International Congress in Budapest, in 1918, where traumatic war neurosis occupied centre stage (Giefer, 2007). The congress panel with Ferenczi, Abraham, and Simmel appeared in a booklet, together with Jones' lecture and an introduction by Freud (Ferenczi et al., 1919). In 1921, it was translated into English.[3] Ferenczi argues that the literature on war neuroses mostly takes a purely mechanistic stance, only few authors acknowledging mental aspects—this latter section of the literature, however, is suspected of piracy: "introduction of psycho-analysis into modern neurology, an introduction which has been effected to some small extent openly, but for the most part with hesitation and under false colours" (ibid., p. 6). After this opening discussion, Ferenczi briefly adds some of the central theses of his 1916 paper, including the distinction between conversion and anxiety hysteria and some allusions to atavistic prototypes of regression. To the print version he adds a parallel to the Moro reflex, a "little shock (or traumatic) neurosis", which can be seen in newborns and infants of monkeys, too, where the infant clasps its "fingers to the mother's fur while she climbs about the trees. We would say: Atavistic reversion of the method of reaction in sudden terror" (Ferenczi, 1921, p. 21).

3 In the translation, however, Abraham's and Simmel's contributions were no longer marked as discussions ("Korreferat") of Ferenczi's paper.

Reception

Ferenczi's first war neuroses paper (1916) has never become well known, although the author included it in his collection *Hysterie und Pathoneurosen* (Ferenczi, 1919). In contrast, his second paper was soon published, together with the other congress contributions on the topic and with a foreword by Freud (Ferenczi et al., 1919) and translated (1921). Interestingly, Freud (1919d) hardly mentioned Ferenczi's paper in his introduction. Was it the difference between Ferenczi's engagement and Freud's aloofness (Kilborne, 2008) that led Freud to ignore his closest companion? Or was it a discomfort with Ferenczi's autonomous biological speculation, which was more prominent in the congress paper than in 1916? Despite his belated—and ambivalent—praise in his obituary of Ferenczi (Freud, 1933c), Freud was sceptical about Ferenczi's speculations about phylogenetic heritage. Or should we think on a deeper, transferential level? Was Freud so sure of Ferenczi that newer followers occupied more of his attention—for instance, Simmel, whose book (1918) Freud had taken as a proof "that German war medicine has taken the bait" (Fr/Fer, 17 February 1918, p. 264)? War neuroses, for Freud, were essentially a "bait" to attract public and scholarly attention to the principles of psychoanalysis. The volume was praised in an anonymous review in the *IJP* (B.D., 1922) as the breakthrough of narcissism theory on the subject of war neuroses. Ferenczi's originality on the topic, however, was rarely noted. French (1941) mentioned the paper in his review in the *Bausteine* as one of Ferenczi's strongest. It was, however, only in the mid-1980s, with the recent experience of the American war in Vietnam, as well as the metapsychological wars at the dusk of ego psychology (Gedo, 1985; Kolb, 1983), that Ferenczi was read as a precursor of modern object-relations theory. One could say that Ferenczi's 1919 paper on war neuroses hibernated in an "inner crypt" before being excavated by such readers as Nicolas Abraham and Maria Torok (Yassa, 2002), who understood it as a groundbreaking text of a philosophical traumatology of the "psychic phantom" (Abraham, 1994). On the other hand, this late revival might also be understood as a part of the construction of a Ferenczi myth (Erös, 2004), as will be discussed below.

Organisational significance: War neuroses and the rise of the IPA

The decision to transfer the Fifth International Congress from Wroclaw (then Breslau) to Budapest was taken on an extremely short notice of only eighteen days—and Ferenczi managed to arrange for a grand venue (the Hungarian Academy of Science), an opening address by the Mayor of Budapest, the first-class hotel Gellért, and even a hired Danube vessel for the guests. The programme, too, appears to have been designed in a hurry—there is no evidence that the panel on war neuroses had been planned very far in advance.[4] However, it was this very topic that was considered decisive in bringing psychoanalysis into public view in the very last days of the war. The presence of high-ranked military physicians, carefully arranged by the organisers, was understood as a promise of social acknowledgement; even the establishment of psychoanalytic centres was envisaged (Freud, 1919d, p. 207). War trauma was the great white hope for the future of psychoanalysis. In the short term, the dream seemed to come true: Ferenczi was elected president of the IPA, became the first professor

4 A circular announcing the adjournment of the congress mentions neither the panel nor Simmel.

of psychoanalysis, and was offered a psychoanalytic hospital by the Hungarian Army (Fer/Fr, 8 October 1918, p. 298).

In the course of a few months, due to changing political circumstances, all these dreams faded away. Yet by that time the contributions of psychoanalysis to understanding war neuroses had been semi-officially acknowledged by military psychiatry, to the extent that Freud was called in 1927 as an expert witness to the trial before the Military Commission on Duty Violations against Prof Wagner-Jauregg, because of his forced electrotherapy with war neurotics (Freud, 1956; Gunther & Trosman, 1974)—an alliance, that Cremerius (1990) adds to the "shameful history" of organising psychoanalysis like a church, breaking "most drastically the basic principle of psychoanalysis: the carrying out of its task in opposition to society" (p. 115). Less critical, Elisabeth Ann Danto (2016) connects the war neurosis discussion as well as Freud's testifying in the Wagner-Jauregg trial to his turn towards a socially activist role after the end of the First World War, accusing military psychiatrists of being "machine guns behind the front" (p. 1).

Freud surely saw war neuroses as a selling point for psychoanalysis, and commented on the fading of this hope self-ironically with a Christian metaphor: "No sooner does it [psychoanalysis] begin to interest the world on account of the war neuroses than the war ends … But hard luck is one of the constants of life. Our kingdom is indeed not of this world" (Fr/Fer, p. 311).

Theoretical significance: Narcissism

Ferenczi's papers contributed to a theoretical paradigm shift. As White (1921) stated, the emergence of war neuroses in WWI "revivified the old problem of the traumatic neuroses" (as inconsistent with Freud's libido theory of neurosis) and created pressure for a revision of theory—which, in fact, had been inaugurated by Freud's paper on narcissism (1914c) and Ferenczi's (1913) paper on the development of the sense of reality. Consequently, Ferenczi explained war neuroses as a lesion of the narcissistic ego libido. However, his own contribution touched upon a peculiar topic, his "Lamarckian project": the view that neurotic symptoms do not root just in libidinal economy, but in atavistic, phylogenetic reflexes and body memories. This was a line of thought Freud had inaugurated in *Totem and Taboo* (1912–13), in sharp distinction to Jung's proposal of a cultural definition of the libido concept (Jung, 1911, see Hamburger, 2005). Therefore, Freud might not have appreciated the eagerness with which Ferenczi was willing to construct a general phylogenetic libido theory. Eventually, Ferenczi will publish it alone (1924). And it will differ widely from Freud's (1985 [1915] phylogenetic fantasy as well as from *Beyond the Pleasure Principle* (1920g).

Possibly, narcissism played an additional role on the level of personal relations and the familiar problem of priority. On 27 October, after the Congress, Freud wrote to Ferenczi about a new idea: that "traumatic war neurosis … has to do with a conflict over two ego ideals, the one that one is accustomed to and the one forced upon one by the war. The latter rests totally on fresh object relations (superiors, comrades). … on the basis of a libidinal object cathexis, a *new ego* is developed, which is supposed to be overthrown by the former ego; a struggle in the ego, instead of between ego and libido, but basically the same thing" (Fr/Fer, p. 305). Only a few days later, he insisted: "I am very eager to know what you will say to my theory of war neuroses which I suggested recently, and whether anything will come of your ward" (p. 306). Of course, this suggestion can be regarded as a turn in trauma theory, since it supposes the co-existence of two ego formations (May, 2013), and Freud even uses the term "object cathexis" in this context. But it is curious that Freud does not mention Ferenczi's theory of narcissistic trauma and reparative repetition compulsion, which was formulated two years earlier, and limits the latter's contribution (as in the Palermo episode; Bonomi, Chapter Six) to the receptive part, assigning him the role of providing case material to confirm Freud's theory. Ferenczi's answer sounds, in comparison to his usual enthusiasm, quite dry: "The interpretation of the traumatic neurosis would have to be tested in a case" (Fer/Fr, p. 309).

In the end, Freud will explain the repetition compulsion inherent in post-traumatic neurosis by a biological death instinct (1920g), while Ferenczi (1934) ascribes it to "catastrophes of phylogenetic development accumulated in the germplasm. Thenceforward these act in the same manner as does, according to Freud, the unresolved precipitating trauma in the case of the traumatic neurosis: that is to say, they compel one to a perpetual repetition of the painful situation" (p. 23). This theory, as Rudnytsky (1996) states, is "scientific rubbish with little or no relevance to the contemporary practice of psychoanalysis" (p. 5); it is, rather, an evolutionary phantasy, suggesting a phylogenetically engraved history that parallels ontogenetic evolution. Thus, it prefigures Ferenczi's later object-relational trauma theory. Even the appropriation of the Moro reflex in his early 1919 paper can be read as allusion to the baby's striving for close relatedness (Mészáros, 2009).

Clinical significance

Ferenczi's clinical description of war trauma is partly compatible with modern definitions of post-traumatic stress disorder, for example, when he observes dissociation (Van der Kolk & Van der Hart, 1991), narcissistic self-diminution (Hirsch, 2004), and regression to psychotic and primitive states (Harris, 2011). What is more important, however, is that Ferenczi insisted on a thorough anamnesis of the patient. His clinical attitude and his empathic descriptions make him an early precursor of modern trauma therapy, even more than his theoretical constructs. Furthermore, he expressed confidence in the self-repairing function of trauma repetition or re-enactment (Frankel, 1998). Ferenczi's significance for trauma therapy is not a result of his metapsychological speculations in the backwash of Freud (and in the context of their unanalysed transference relation), but of the way he allowed his clinical experience to sprout in his mind. His later writings, where infantile trauma gained central significance, can be regarded as a late container, an après-coup, for an earlier experience with war neuroses that despite his efforts he could not express in terms of classical metapsychology.

But a reading of the war trauma papers simply as a precursor of Ferenczi's later writings on trauma would fall short of a full appreciation of Ferenczi's main heritage, the interpersonal perspective. Thinking analytically in this lineage, we should reflect on our motives to construct Ferenczi as an ancestor of modern trauma theory. The present-day emphasis on trauma theory and therapy is a social phenomenon (Alexander et al., 2004), and unearthing Ferenczi's early efforts to understand war trauma is a statement. Interest in (social) trauma depends on preoccupations and concerns prevailing in society (Hamburger, 2017). In our time, a well-developed sensitivity to trauma is a counterpart, and counterweight, to the structural and colonial violence inherent in modern Western civilisation, notably in its current embodiment as globalisation. Thus, the après-coup is not just a matter of Ferenczi's later conceptualisation of an earlier experience. It is also an après-coup in the history of psychoanalytic thought; searching for a link to an ancestor amidst the evolving destructiveness of the contemporary world.

References

Abraham, K. (1921) Symposium on psychoanalysis and the war neurosis held at the fifth international psycho-analytical congress Budapest, September 1918. In: S. Ferenczi, K. Abraham, E. Simmel, E. Jones & S. Freud, *Psycho-Analysis and the War Neuroses*. London, Vienna, New York: The International Psycho-Analytical Press, 1919.

Abraham, N., & Torok, M. (1994). *The Shell and the Kernel*. Chicago: University of Chicago Press.

Alexander, J.C., Eyerman, R., Giesen, B., Smelser, N. J. & Sztompka, P. (Eds) (2004). *Cultural Trauma and Collective Identity*. Berkeley: University Of California Press.

Aron, L., and Harris, A. (2010). Sándor Ferenczi: Discovery and rediscovery. *Psychoanalytic Perspectives*, *7*: 5–42

Cremerius, J. (1990). Training analysis and power. *Free Associations*, 1U: 114–138.

Dalla Volta A. (1919). *Studi sulla psicologia e psichiatria della prigionia di guerra* [Essays on psychological and psychiatric aspects of war imprisonment]. Firenze: Ricci.

Danto, E. A. (2016). Trauma and the state with Sigmund Freud as witness. *International Journal of Law and Psychiatry*, *48*: 50–56.

Erös, F. (2004). The Ferenczi cult: Its historical and political roots. *International Forum of Psychoanalysis*, *13*: 121–128.

Ferenczi, S. (1913). Stages in the development of the sense of reality. In: *First Contributions to Psycho-analysis* (pp. 213–239). London: Karnac, 1994.

Ferenczi, S. (1916). Über zwei Typen der Kriegsneurose. *Internationale Zeitschrift für Psychoanalyse*, 4: 131–145.

Ferenczi, S. (1919). Die Psychoanalyse der Kriegsneurosen. In: S. Ferenczi, K. Abraham, E. Simmel & E. Jones, *Zur Psychoanalyse der Kriegsneurosen* (Mit einer Einleitung von Sigmund Freud) (pp. 9–30). Leipzig, Wien: Internationaler Psychoanalytischer Verlag.

Ferenczi, S. (1919). *Hysterie und Pathoneurosen*. Leipzig: Internationale Psychoanalytischer Verlag.

Ferenczi, S. (1921). Symposium on psychoanalysis and the war neurosis held at the fifth international psycho-analytical congress Budapest, September 1918. In: Ferenczi, S. et al., *Psycho-Analysis and the War Neuroses* (pp. 5–21). London, Vienna, New York: The International Psycho-Analytical Press.

Ferenczi, S. (1926). *Further Contributions to the Theory and Technique of Psycho-Analysis*. New York: Brunner/Mazel.

Ferenczi, S. (1934). Thalassa: A Theory of Genitality. *Psychoanalytic Quarterly*, *2*: 361–364; 3: 1–29; 3: 200–222.

Ferenczi, S., Abraham, K., Simmel, E., & Jones, E. (1921). *Psycho-Analysis and the War Neuroses. With an Introduction by Prof. Sigm. Freud*. London, Vienna, New York: The International Psycho-Analytical Press.

Frankel, J. B. (1998). Ferenczi's trauma theory. *American Journal of Psychoanalysis*, 58: 41–61.

French, T. M. (1941). Review of *Bausteine zur Psychoanalyse* (The Fundamentals of Psychoanalysis) Four Volumes. *Psychoanalytic Quarterly*, *10*: 657–657.

Freud, S. (1914c). On narcissism: An introduction. *S. E.*, *14*: 73–1-4. London: Hogarth.

Freud, S. (1919d). Introduction to Psycho-Analysis and the War Neuroses. *S. E.*, *17*: 205–216. London: Hogarth.

Freud, S. (1912–13). Totem and taboo. *S. E.*, *13*: 1–164. London: Hogarth.

Freud, S. (1920g). Beyond the Pleasure Principle. *S. E.*, *18*: 1–64. London: Hogarth.

Freud, S. (1933c). Sándor Ferenczi. *S. E.*, *17*: 225–230. London: Hogarth.

Freud, S. (1956). Memorandum on the electrical treatment of war neurotics (1920). *International Journal of Psychoanalysis*, *37*: 16–18.

Freud, S. (1985 [1915]) *A Phylogenetic Fantasy* (Ed. I. Grubrich-Simitis). Cambridge: Harvard University Press, 1987.

Gedo, J. E. (1985). On the dawn of experience: The past recaptured. *Psychoanalytic Inquiry*, *5*: 601–620.

Giefer, M. (Ed.) (2007). *Korrespondenzblatt der Internationalen Psychoanalytischen Vereinigung 1910–1941*. CD-ROM. Privately published. Available at: http://www.luzifer-amor.de/fileadmin/bilder/Downloads/korrespondenzblatt_1910-1941.pdf

Groddeck, G. (1977). Correspondence with Sigmund Freud (1917–1934). In: *The Meaning of Illness. Selected Psychoanalytic Writings* (pp. 31–108). London: Maresfield.

Gunther, M. S., & Trosman, H. (1974). Freud as expert witness; Wagner-Jauregg and the problem of the war neuroses. *Annual of Psychoanalysis*, *2*: 3–23.

Hamburger, A. (2005). Das Motiv der Urhorde. Ererbte oder erlebte Erfahrung in Freuds *Totem und Tabu*. In: W. Mauser & J. Pfeiffer (Eds.), *Kulturtheorie* (pp. 45–86). Würzburg: Königshausen & Neumann.

Hamburger, A. (2017). Genocidal trauma. Individual and social consequences of the assault on the mental and physical life of a group. In: D. Laub & A. Hamburger (Eds.), *Psychoanalysis and Holocaust Testimony: Unwanted Memories of Social Trauma* (pp. 66–91). London: Routledge.

Harris, A. (2011). Ferenczi's work on war neuroses. *Psychoanalytic Perspectives*, *7*: 183–190.

Hirsch, M. (2004). *Psychoanalytische Traumatologie – Das Trauma in der Familie: psychoanalytische Theorie und Therapie schwerer Persönlichkeitsstörungen*. Stuttgart: Schattauer.

Kilborne, B. (2008). Human foibles and psychoanalytic technique: Freud, Ferenczi, and Gizella Palos. *American Journal of Psychoanalysis*, *68*: 1–23.

Kolb, L. C. (1983). Return of the repressed. *Journal of the American Academy of Psychoanalysis and Dynamic Psychiatry*, *11*: 531–545.

May, U. (2013). Freud's "Beyond the pleasure principle": The end of psychoanalysis or its new beginning? *International Forum of Psychoanalysis*, *22*: 208–216.

Mészáros, J. (2009). Contribution of Hungarian psychoanalysts to psychoanalytic psychosomatics. *American Journal of Psychoanalysis*, *69*: 207–220.

Navona Numismatics (without year) http://navonanumis.blogspot.de/2016/05/csot-austria-hungary-habsburg-pow-camp.html (accessed 12. 9. 2016).

Rudnytsky, P. L., Bokay, A., & Giampieri-Deutsch, P. (Eds.) (1996). *Ferneczi's Turn in Psychoanalysis*. New York: New York University Press.

Simmel, E. (1918). *Kriegs-Neurosen und 'psychisches Trauma': Ihre gegenseitigen Beziehungen, dargestellt auf Grund psychoanalytischer, hypnotischer Studien*. München: O. Nemnich.

Simmel, E. (1921). In: S. Ferenczi, K. Abraham, E. Simmel, E. Jones & S. Freud, *Psycho-Analysis and the War Neuroses* (pp. 42–60). London, Vienna, New York: The International Psycho-Analytical Press, 1919.

Van der Kolk, B. A., & Van der Hart, O. (1991). The intrusive past: The flexibility of memory and the engraving of trauma. *American Imago*, *48*: 425–454.

White, W. A. (1921). Psychoanalysis and the war neuroses. *Psychoanalytic Review*, *8*: 448–449.

Yassa, M. (2002). Nicolas Abraham and Maria Torok — the "inner crypt". *Scandinavian Psychoanalytic Review*, *25*: 82–91.

Chapter 11

The figure of Sándor Ferenczi in representative organs of the Hungarian press between 1910 and 1933

Melinda Friedrich

For many years, Ferenczi was actively present in the Hungarian daily press. Journals advertised and reported Ferenczi's open lectures held in various organisations, like the Galilei Circle and the Free School of Social Sciences (U.A., 1926b, 1928b). Ferenczi also publicly presented his opinions on several current issues.

Ferenczi was most intensively present in the press in the 1920s, because he joined the common effort of the time to popularise psychoanalysis. As R. Urbantschitsch formulated it for the journal *Pesti Napló* in 1925: "It is high time to show what psychoanalysis actually is, what can be reached with it" (Ráskay, 1925, p. 6). The strengthening of the rival psychoanalytic schools in Hungary led Ferenczi to draw a similar conclusion in a letter to Freud of the same year: "We must now unfold somewhat more propaganda to the public here and have already been deliberating about the modalities. (Open lectures, publications, etc.)" (Fer/Fr, 25 October 1925, p. 235).

Ferenczi's presence in the different organs is fostered by personal and political factors, such as his personal contacts, as well as the positive attitude towards psychoanalysis of the given newspapers. With his activity and personality, Ferenczi made "an impression on the best forces in [his] homeland" (Freud/Ferenczi, 28 May 1911, p. 285), and among those "best forces" there were several writers/journalists gathered around the prominent literary journal *Nyugat*.

Yet *Pesti Napló* [Pest Daily], an old and influential liberal journal, had the largest circulation among the examined papers (Lengyel, 2006). *Budapesti Hírlap* [Budapest Newspaper] is the only conservative paper among the examined ones. *Népszava* [Voice of the People] was a socialist periodical of the Hungarian Social Democratic Party. *Színházi Élet* [Theater Life] was a politically neutral illustrated journal of arts and theater. Ferenczi was interviewed by *Pesti Napló* sixteen times between 1922 and 1933, once by *Népszava* in 1912, once by *Budapesti Hírlap* in 1930.

Nevertheless, the opinion of a psychoanalyst was seldom allowed to appear in organs like *Budapesti Hírlap*, so it is remarkable that we can find there a reportage where Ferenczi was addressed. In 1930 a urologist, a psychiatrist, and Ferenczi, as a psychoanalyst, were asked about sleeping and insomnia (Büky., 1930, p. 10). Ferenczi offered a viewpoint different from that of his contemporaries: he insists that sleeping is an instinct. Furthermore, he considers it extremely important that "the child could have psychic peace before sleeping" (ibid.). Then he stressed the role of the soul as much more relevant than any technique, and discussed how in his clinical experience most cases of insomnia resulted from a restlessness of the soul (ibid.).

Also in *Népszava* we can find only one interview with Ferenczi. In 1912 he expressed his views on the animal experiments of von Osten and Krall with "clever horses", which had drawn worldwide attention for their ability to count, talk, and reason: "There is no doubt the

Osten-Krall experiments mean a big step forward in animal psychology and psychology in general. This is the first serious proof that the human soul is not some unique entity without precedent, but it is only a higher level of development of psychological abilities that exist in animals as well (and which, as the example shows, can be developed). Psychoanalysis has revealed the primitive (if you like, animal) mechanisms hidden deep within the human soul; the experiments of Krall have shown that these primitive mechanisms can reach … a level in animals the possibility of which had been hypothesized only in humans so far" (U. A., 1912, p. 9).

In *Színházi Élet*, a major weekly journal of arts and theatre, Ferenczi's name shows up on several occasions, such as in a couplet (U. A., 1918), in a horoscope (U. A., 1926d), or in an interview with "the famous dancer Margaret Severn[1] from New York", who "sometimes visits doctor Ferenczy [sic!], who conducts psychoanalytic experiments on her" (U. A., 1926c, p. 28). *Színházi Élet* presented, among other prominent people of the time, the daily routine of Ferenczi (U. A., 1929). Yet one would look in vain for any interview with Ferenczi in that journal, and its absence can be explained by the dominance of a rival psychoanalytic school, the Hungarian Stekelian Group, which presented psychoanalysis in its own popular form (Szinetár, 1932, pp. 137–140).

Conversely, a letter of Ferenczi allows us to assume a relatively regular contact between him and the editor of *Pesti Napló*, Sándor Mester (1875–1958).

The editor of one of the better Hungarian daily newspapers (*Pesti Napló*), who is not inimically disposed toward psychoanalysis and has already been of some service to us, called me up yesterday and asked me if he … might publish a few pages of your new book in Hungarian translation (Fer/Fr, 5 January 1930, p. 379).

This explains why, of all the investigated organs, Ferenczi is most actively present in *Pesti Napló*. He published there some of his writings (Ferenczi, 1927, 1928), his lectures were advertised, and most of them were also reported in detail. Ferenczi's name was mentioned in several writings of various genres, and *Pesti Napló* turned to him for expert advice on various issues.

For instance, he was asked an opinion—together with a police officer, a criminologist, the wife of a metalworker, and a private servant—about how the psyche of man and the whole society changed after the First World War. Ferenczi's answer may seem to be a paradox, but he holds that "human nature has actually not changed under the influence of the war … For the past thirty years … psychoanalysis has been saying that those who believe that … mankind had indeed reached some higher level of development, and thus a return to barbarity must no longer be a concern, indulge in false idealism" (U.A., 1922, p. 6).

In the next year, *Pesti Napló* turned to Ferenczi with a similar issue. They asked him how the nerves of Budapest were affected by historical events. "Pest is not nervous, at least not much more nervous than once, in blissful, real peace … Its health statistics are not at all alarming … Anyway, it is an interesting observation of ours that this alleged peace was able to heal something: the feeling of peace … deleted ninety-five percent of the nervous shocks of the war. Only half of the remaining five percent is hopeless; the other half, simply, unconsciously does not want to heal, and maybe would take it unkindly if he/she was healed, his/her illness being a source of bread-winning" (U.A., 1923, p. 6). Ferenczi regretfully added that "the wire fence illness" of returned prisoners of war "is still flourishing" (ibid.). And

1 Margaret Severn was the daughter of Ferenczi's patient Elisabeth Severn.

then he shared his ideas about the factors that influenced people's spirit: "It is interesting that the Commune[2] affected people's spirit much more intensively than the war and the revolution. Maybe the risk of loss of material goods is more troubling than that of life? Money may have here a remarkable symbolic value. *Blut ist ein besonderer Saft* [Blood is a juice of very special kind], said Goethe. I could say: *Geld ist ein besonderer Stoff* [Money is a substance of very special kind]." He, furthermore, tells that he rarely finds pathogens of a financial nature in neuroses, nor can he perceive any difference between the proportion of men and women among patients; though, he admits, he has many unmarried female patients, in whom the roots of the disease pattern can ultimately be traced back to financial factors.

"Dangerous ideals. Sándor Ferenczi on the psychic bankruptcy of today's Europe" is the title of a 1923 interview with Ferenczi in which he attributed a much greater importance to the influence of the current political and financial situation on the nervous life of people than he had a few years earlier: "Today's harsh financial and political conditions absolutely have a great impact on mental life, especially of those who are inclined to mental problems. Two things attract our particular attention. One of them is the escape into suicide, the other into religious fanaticism. During the Bolshevism [the Hungarian Soviet Republic] many people committed suicide because their wealth had been taken away. Today, impoverishment and its consequences rush a certain percentage of people into voluntary death" (U. A., 1925, p. 9). Ferenczi offered the same explanation for both phenomena: people regarded their property as a crucial part of their ego. And he went on to talk about the disappointment in the socialist idea: "One mistake of the socialists was that they had not taken notice of mental needs … Socialist teachings came to us Hungarians from Germany, transmitted by Austrians. And German socialism was perfectly permeated with German Idealism. It took the idea of freedom, equality, and fraternity literally … Exaggerated idealism takes revenge. Its two extremes today are roughly the strong militarist chauvinism and communism. If we Hungarians get the socialist doctrine from England, the picture of our financial and social situation would undoubtedly be quite different today" (ibid.). At last, Ferenczi was asked what he thought of the near future. "Of the near future, nothing," he answered with a serious face, "but in the distant future, I think, science in a deeper sense will have a role in the government of nations. Thus the people who govern will know the true nature of mankind" (ibid.).

In March 1926 Ferenczi was asked about the background of the epidemic spread of quackery and superstition in Budapest, of the phenomenon that people's trust in institutions was shaken and changed by mysticism. Ferenczi showed no sign of surprise: "People became disappointed in what they had rationally trusted" (U. A., 1926a, p. 9). "People blindly trusted in their homeland, which represented a father, but war changed everything, and traditions seem to be collapsing" (p. 10). "The labile mass turns to the other extreme. What is reasonable seems to be … hopeless. … This is why they turned to those who heal by irrational elements, so to speak wonders … The saddest part about it is that trust in the old, fundamental truth seems to have ceased completely" (ibid.). Ferenczi sums up: "Souls became childishly impatient. What they need needs to be provided immediately. The desire for rapid success has the psychic result of people turning away from reason to magic" (ibid.).

An interview with Ferenczi apropos of the charge of quackery against Theodor Reik was published in 1926 (Ráskay, 1926, p. 4). Ferenczi outlines here his well-known position on

2 The Commune was established in 1919. It was also called the Hungarian Soviet Republic or the Republic of Councils.

lay analysis, concluding that psychoanalysis, which extends to all human sciences, must not be degraded to being the privilege of the medical profession (ibid.).

In the same year, *Pesti Napló*'s New York correspondent visited Ferenczi in Hotel St. Andrew, during his American stay, and interviewed him on "the soul of America and the new results of psychoanalysis" (Fodor, 1926, p. 9). Ferenczi praised Americans' open minds towards psychoanalysis and spoke about their "fashion of understanding everything" (ibid.). As for analytical differences between Europe and America, he claimed that "neuroses are different according to nations" (ibid.), and at the same time, in England and the United States he found hardly any difference between Christians and Jews. Finally, Ferenczi's opinion about the soul of Americans is the following: "*The conflict between the aggression of the pioneer character and social conventions is slightly stronger* than in Europe. My impression is that under the influence of this conflict the number of neurotics … is greater. As the naive ways of acting out are made difficult exactly due to this conflict, the interest of the whole society shifts to a *neutral field*, which is *making money*" (ibid., italics in the original).

The spread of girls' suicide was another motive for *Pesti Napló* to turn to Ferenczi for enlightenment. The suicide of juveniles, as Ferenczi explains, is "a heavy psychopathological problem, as the problem of suicide itself has by far not been cleared. Suicide itself is not only a psychological, but also a biological problem" (U. A., 1927, p. 4). As for the solution of the issue, Ferenczi takes as an example an institution conceived by an American university, where university lecturers advise students with psychological problems. Yet he warns that "as long as the experts themselves are not aware of the nature of the problem, an arrangement like this does not help much" (ibid.).

"The ultimate secrets of love" is the title of an interview with Ferenczi "on the archaic beginnings of human and animal life and their development up to their present forms," from 1928 (U. A., 1928c, p. 53). Ferenczi presented his theories from *Thalassa*. He proudly showed the interviewer the list of his collected works at the end of one of his books, which contained "173 items" at the time. This made him think: "'Am I justified to call my writings creative work?' Ferenczi wonders, standing in front of his bookshelf. "Creative work is a serious, great word … if there is one of my writings I can regard as a creative work, it is my book [*Thalassa*]" (ibid.).

"If we once remove the faults of human character …" (Csánk, 1928, p. 38) is the title of an interview made in Ferenczi's house on Buda's Marton Hill. Ferenczi spoke—with his dog Kuki laying by his feet—about the present and future of psychoanalysis, and the "blank areas" on the soul's map, which were not blank anymore (ibid.). Ferenczi depicted the colorful "field" of analysis, calling Freud "the least orthodox Freudian of the world" (ibid.). He then claimed that "the psychoanalytic transformation of character has entered the gate of possibilities", and stated that "psychoanalysis will sooner or later – rather later than sooner – gain ground and triumph" (ibid.).

Mademoiselle X was the name of a twenty-three-year-old needlewoman, a murderess in prison. She had loved a woman and killed her. Suspected motive: jealousy. Her name was Erzsébet Molnár, but the case was so mysterious and full of secrets that she was only called Mademoiselle X. A criminologist and Ferenczi were interviewed by *Pesti Napló*'s journalist Szirmai about the case (1930, p. 13). Ferenczi seemed to be definite in his answer: "No, no, I do not answer this. This question – what I see in Erzsébet Molnár, what I see in her crime, behind her crime, before her act, after her act, what the standpoint or assumption or suspicion of the psychoanalytic criminology is – no, I do not answer this. I think – and I am convinced – that if a psychoanalyst dares to answer such a question about this case, that cannot be a professional psychoanalyst. That may not be honorable. Because the most recent results of psychoanalysis do not afford an answer to these questions. Psychoanalytic criminology has not evolved at all" (Szirmai, 1930, p. 13). Ferenczi's scepticism about using psychoanalysis in this field makes it clear that he saw limits to psychoanalysis. Therefore, if there was a criminal case to comment on, *Pesti Napló* frequently turned to Ferenczi's opponent, the Stekelian Sándor Feldmann.

Ferenczi was interviewed by *Pesti Napló* for the last time in 1933, a few months before his death. An abbot, a gynaecologist, a lawyer, a prosecutor, a psychiatrist, and Ferenczi were invited to give their opinion on the cynicism of "today's man" (Bozzay, 1933, p. 14). Ferenczi discussed the various forms of cynicism: personal disappointment, blasphemy, sexual disappointment, and social and political cynicism. His last statement is impossible to read without considering its political content. "Generally, it can be said that in cynicism, the negative emotional color of personal experience extends to institutions; however, it is also true that the behavior and actions of the leading men of some ages can shake plenty of people's trust in wonderful and noble ideas" (ibid.).

To conclude, the questions asked of Ferenczi, as well as the answers given, reveal a lot about the interests of his times; but they also show the person of Sándor Ferenczi, his wisdom and open-mindedness, from a contemporary perspective.

References

Büky, Gy. (1930). Tanuljunk meg aludni. Mit mond az orvostudomány az alvásról? [Let us learn to sleep. What does Medicine say about sleeping?]. *Budapesti Hírlap, 191*: 10.

Bozzay, M. (1933). Cinikus... nem cinikus [Cynic... not cynic]. *Pesti Napló, 18*: 14.

Csánk, E. (1928). Ha majd eltüntetjük az emberi jellem hibáit .... Beszélgetés Ferenczi Sándorral a pszichoanalízis jelenéről és jövőjéről s a lélek térképének "fehér foltjairól", amelyek nem fehér foltok többé [If we once remove the faults of human character... A conversation with Sándor Ferenczi about the present and future of psychoanalysis and about "blank areas" on the soul's map, which were no blank areas any more]. *Pesti Napló, 153*: 38.

Ferenczi, S. (1927). A szívfájdalomról [On the pain of the heart]. *Pesti Napló, 293*: 46.

Ferenczi, S. (1928). Pszichoterápiai jelszavak [Psychotherapeutic keywords]. *Pesti Napló, 120*: 46. Republished: *Thalassa, 12*: 144–145, 2001.

Fodor (1926). A dollárláz: az amerikai lélek menekülése a belső konfliktusok elől. Dr. Ferenczi Sándor Amerika lelkéről és a pszichoanalízis új eredményeiről [The dollar-fever: the escape of the American soul from inner conflicts. Dr. Sándor Ferenczi on the soul of America and the recent results of psychoanalysis]. *Pesti Napló, 262*: p. 9.

Lengyel, A. (2006). Hatvany Lajos Pesti Naplója (1917–1919). *Magyar Könyvszemle, 4*: 444–463.

Ráskay, L. (1925). Beszélgetés Urbanschich Rudolffal, a pszichoanalitikai nevelésről [A conversation with Rudolf Urbanschich (sic)]. *Pesti Napló, 68*: 6.

Ráskay, L. (1926). Kuruzslás-e a pszichoanalízis, ha nem orvos alkalmazza? [Is psychoanalysis a quackery if applied by a non-physicians?]. *Pesti Napló, 157*: 4.

Szinetár, E. (1932). Pszichoanalitikus iskola [Psychoanalytic School]. *Színházi Élet, 52*: 137–140.

Szirmai, R. (1930). Mademoiselle X. A kriminológia, az orvostudomány és a pszichoanalízis fantasztikus rejtélye [Mademoiselle X. The fantastic mystery of criminology, medicine, and psychoanalysis]. *Pesti Napló, 95*: 13.

Unknown Author (1912). A tudomány világából. Az okos lovak [From the world of science. Clever horses]. *Népszava, 278*: 8–9.

U. A. (1918). Dr. Huszár. *Színházi Élet, 19*: 38.

U. A. (1922). A háború után felfordult világ új embere társadalomtudományi, rendőri, lélekelemzési és asszonyi megvilágításban [The new man of the world turned upside down after the war from the perspective of social sciences, policemen, psychoanalysis, and women]. *Pesti Napló, 88*: 6.

U. A. (1923). Nem is olyan ideges ez a Pest [Pest is not so nervous]. *Pesti Napló, 39*: 3.

U. A. (1925). Veszélyes ideálok. Dr. Ferenczi Sándor a mai Európa lelki csődjéről [Dangerous ideals. Sándor Ferenczi on the psychic bankruptcy of today's Europe]. *Pesti Napló, 116*: 9.

U. A. (1926a). Az intézményekbe vetett hit indokolatlanul megrendült, helyébe jött a miszticizmus. A lélekelemzés a mai lélek válságairól [The unwarranted collapse of trust in institutions, replaced by mysticism. Psychoanalysis on the crises of today's psyche]. *Pesti Napló, 66*: 9–10.

U. A. (1926b). Freud-ünnepély. *Pesti Napló*, p. 13.

U. A. (1926c). Miss Margaret Severn, egy híres New York-i táncosnő Budapesten keres partnert magának [Miss Margaret Severn, the famous dancer from New York is looking for a partner in Budapest]. *Színházi Élet, 31*: 28–29.

U. A. (1926d) A Színházi Élet horoszkópja [The horoscope of Színházi Élet]. *Színházi Élet, 10*: 20.

U. A. (1927). Leányöngyilkosságok. Dr. Ferenczi Sándor a fiatalkorúak szaporodó öngyilkosságairól [Girl suicides]. *Pesti Napló, 236*: 4.

U. A. (1928a). Ha a lélek beteg ... Ferenczi Sándor előadása a pszichoanalízisről [If the soul is ill... Sándor Ferenczi's lecture on psychoanalysis]. *Pesti Napló, 43*: 4.

U. A. (1928b). Népszerű előadások a pszichoanalízis köréből [Popular lectures on psychoanalysis]. *Pesti Napló, 31*: 9.

U. A. (1928c). A szerelem végső titkai. Beszélgetés dr. Ferenczi Sándorral az emberi és állati élet ősi kezdeteiről és fejlődéséről a mai formákig [The ultimate secrets of love. A conversation with Dr. Sándor Ferenczi on the archaic beginnings of human and animal life and their development up to their present forms]. *Pesti Napló, 292*: 53. Republished: *Thalassa, 17*: 203–206, 2006.

U. A. (1929). Nagy emberek 24 órája [24 hours of great people]. *Színházi Élet, 12*: 22.

Chapter 12

Georg Groddeck's influential friendship with Sándor Ferenczi

Christopher Fortune

Georg Groddeck (1866–1934), a German physician drawn to Freud and psychoanalysis in 1917, is much less known to English-speaking audiences than his good friend, Sándor Ferenczi. Groddeck produced a prolific body of writing, most untranslated into English. An early explorer of the relationship between physical and mental illness, Groddeck established a sanatorium in Baden-Baden in 1900. He believed that illness is a symbolic psychic expression and, as body and mind are inseparable, the treatment must be both psychological and physical. He has often been championed as the "father of psychosomatic medicine" (Groddeck, 1977, p. 9). In the years before meeting Freud, Groddeck rejected the "Freudian school", later admitting he had been jealous of Freud. He then taught himself psychoanalysis (p. 32). While most of the psychoanalytic world was suspicious of Groddeck, Freud declared that he had to "claim" Groddeck because "the discovery that transference and resistance are the most important aspects of treatment turns a person irretrievably into a member of the wild army [of psychoanalysis]" (p. 36). In his first letter to Groddeck, Freud connected him with Ferenczi by mentioning Ferenczi's recent paper, "Disease- or patho-neuroses" (1916/17) (p. 36). Later, Freud assured Groddeck's renown, acknowledging in his book, *The Ego and the Id*, that he had borrowed the term "Id" (*Das Es*) from Groddeck.

Groddeck's best known work, *The Book of the It* (1923), is a psychoanalytic classic in which he spiritedly presents his ideas on illness and the inseparability of the body and mind. Groddeck also wrote fiction and authored the first psychoanalytical novel, *The Soul-Seekers* (1921a). In addition, *The Meaning of Illness* (1977) consists of a collection of Groddeck's essays, autobiographical notes, and his correspondence with Freud from 1917 to 1934.

In 1920, at the Sixth IPA Congress, in The Hague, Groddeck presented his paper, "On psychoanalyzing the organic in human beings" (1921b). Not yet widely known within psychoanalysis, Groddeck caused a stir by defiantly proclaiming himself to Freud, Ferenczi, and the assembled analysts as a "wild analyst" (Groddeck, 1977, p. 7). Thus, Ferenczi had been introduced to his future physician, analyst, friend, and correspondent. Ferenczi positively reviewed Groddeck's 1917 paper, "Psychic conditioning and the psychoanalytic treatment of organic disorders," stating: "Dr. Groddeck … is the first to make the courageous attempt to apply the results of Freud's discoveries to organic medicine" (1917, pp. 342–343).

In 1921, Ferenczi wrote to Groddeck, inquiring about staying at his sanatorium to study Groddeck's use of psychoanalysis in treating organic illnesses (Fer/Grod, p. 4). Beginning that summer, Ferenczi and his wife, Gizella, visited the sanatorium for "therapeutic holidays" almost every year for more than ten years. A close friendship—the primary friendship of the last decade of Ferenczi's life—developed between the two men and their wives, and lasted until Ferenczi's death in May, 1933. Groddeck died just one year later, in June, 1934.

Ferenczi's confidence and independence grew over those years. His successful 1926–1927 trip to America led to an influx of patients, more money, and boosted his reputation. His international renown for treating the most difficult patients flourished. It was between 1927 and 1933 that Ferenczi published his most daring and challenging papers.

In addition to their common interest in the mind-body relationship, Groddeck also shared and supported a number of Ferenczi's crucial ideas, including championing the experience of the child, the significance of early trauma, and the developmental role of the mother, which led to object-relations theory. In 1923, Ferenczi wrote to Groddeck: "I consider to be the particular merit of your approach: namely that you have never ceased emphasizing, along with the role of the father, the exorbitant importance of the *mother*" (Fer/Grod, 9 June 1923, p. 49).

Furthermore, the idea of "mother" informed key relationships for both Ferenczi and Groddeck. Grosskurth (1991) argued that Ferenczi and Groddeck wanted Freud to be their mother, but Freud ultimately refused them both. So Ferenczi, according to Grosskurth, looked to Groddeck to "replace Freud as the mother Ferenczi always wanted" (p. 200). Certainly, Groddeck seems to have been a "good enough" mother for Ferenczi. Later, Ferenczi also addressed his own mother transference in his mutual analysis with Elizabeth Severn (Fortune, 1993, 1994, 1996).

As far as the historical record shows, Groddeck's great contribution to Ferenczi lay less in specific ideas that may have influenced him, and more in Groddeck's role in "mothering" Ferenczi. As Ferenczi's friend, Groddeck was an informal but essential "analytic" presence who fostered Ferenczi's courage to follow his creative intuitions despite the controversy they were sure to arouse. Groddeck was a free-thinking spirit with the courage to go his own way, and this surely emboldened Ferenczi to free himself from his own submissiveness to Freud.

A more "real" "analyst" than Freud, Groddeck's generative analytic approach was also more accepting, and served to open Ferenczi up, encouraging his "exploratory" attitude, and acted as a counterpoint to Ferenczi's analysis and relationship with Freud, which had reinforced Ferenczi's "clinging" attitude. Furthermore, Groddeck's friendship helped spark Ferenczi to find his own voice, and to articulate and stand up for his ideas. It also helped Ferenczi develop the courage to challenge Freud, the master, and eventually propelled him into his radical technical experiments and writings of the later 1920s and early 1930s.

Based on the perspectives outlined in this chapter, I would argue that without Georg Groddeck's support and influence, the later phase of Ferenczi's career, which was characterised by his challenge to Freud and his expansion of the frontiers of psychoanalysis, would not have taken place.

The Ferenczi-Groddeck correspondence clearly illustrates the importance of their relationship during the crucial period of the mid-1920s until the early 1930s, and provides important new insights into Ferenczi's professional and personal life.

Ferenczi's letters, particularly the critical Christmas 1921 letter, illuminate the personal roots of his professional drive and suggest the origins of his radical clinical and theoretical experiments, as well as his reconsideration of the importance of early trauma. This letter reveals the effects of Ferenczi's own childhood traumas—specifically his perception of his mother as critical and unloving. Using Groddeck as a sounding-board and analyst, Ferenczi attempted to work through his early traumas, and integrate them into his evolving ideas on theory and practice. He writes: "I can declare myself totally vanquished by your unpretentious manner, your natural kindness and friendliness. I have never been so open with another man, not even with 'Siegmund'" (Fer/Grod, 25 December 1921, p. 8). In contrast to his letters to Freud, whom he clearly saw as a father figure, Ferenczi pursued a more open friendship with Groddeck, as though he were a favourite older brother.

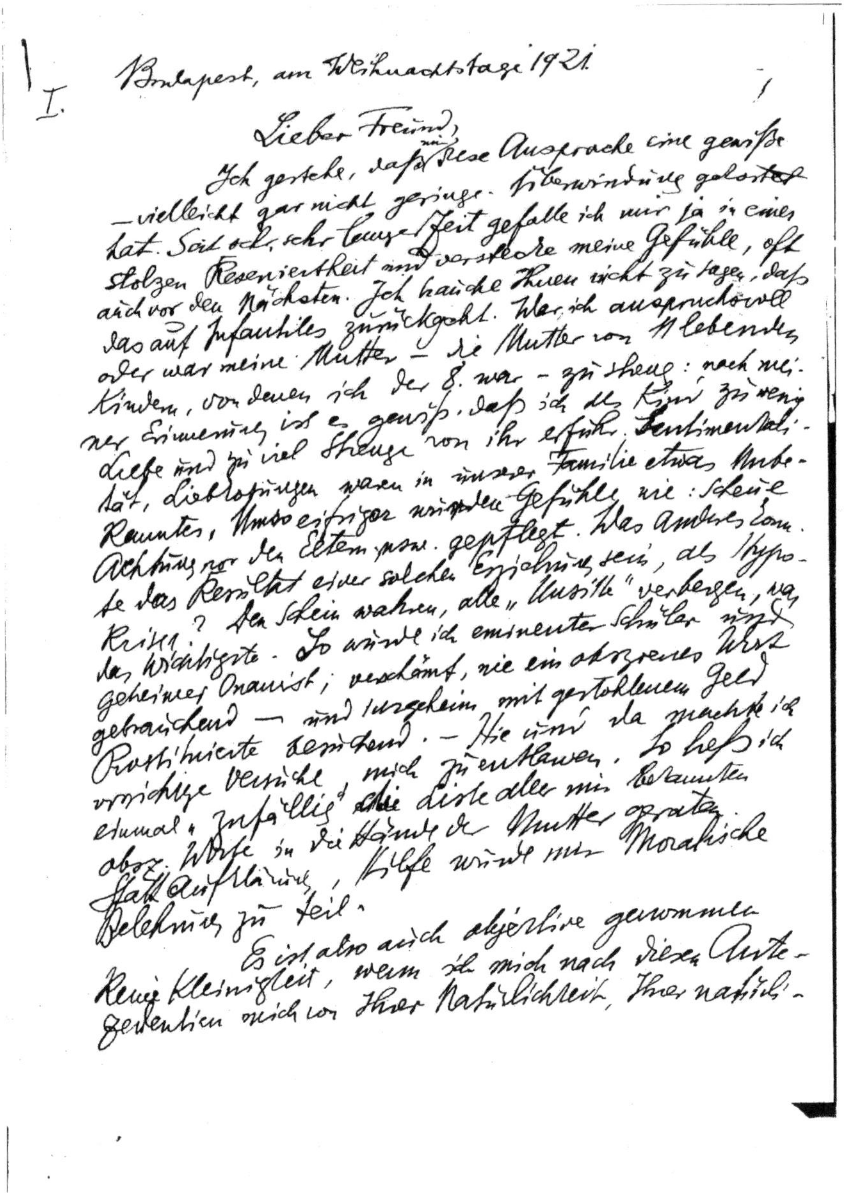
I.

Budapest, am Weihnachtstage 1921.

Lieber Freund,

Ich gestehe, dass mir diese Aussprache eine gewisse – vielleicht gar nicht geringe – Überwindung gekostet hat. Seit ach, sehr langer Zeit gefalle ich mir ja in einer stolzen Reserviertheit und verstecke meine Gefühle, oft auch vor den Nächsten. Ich brauche Ihnen nicht zu sagen, dass das auf Infantiles zurückgeht. War ich anspruchsvoll oder war meine Mutter – die Mutter von 11 lebenden Kindern, von denen ich der 8. war – zu streng: nach meiner Erinnerung ist es gewiss, dass ich als Kind zu wenig Liebe und zu viel Strenge von ihr erfuhr. Sentimentalität, Liebkosungen waren in unserer Familie etwas Unbekanntes, umso eifriger wurden Gefühle wie: scheue Achtung vor den Eltern usw. gepflegt. Was anderes kann das Resultat einer solchen Erziehung sein, als Hypokrisie? Den Schein wahren, alle „Unsitte" verbergen, war das Wichtigste. So wurde ich eminenter Schüler und [illegible] geheimer Onanist; verschämt, wie ein [illegible] [illegible] gebrauchend – und insgeheim mit gestohlenem Geld [illegible] Prostituierte besuchend. – Hie und da machte ich vorsichtige Versuche, mich zu entlarven. So ließ ich einmal „zufällig" die Liste aller mir Bekannten [illegible] in die Hände der Mutter geraten. Moralische Aufklärung, Hilfe wurde mir statt Belehrung zu Teil.

Es ist also auch objektive genommen keine Kleinigkeit, wenn ich mich nach diesen Antezedentien mich vor Ihrer Natürlichkeit, Ihrer natürli-

Ferenczi's "Christmas 1921 letter" to Groddeck

courtesy Cristopher Fortune

Groddeck encouraged Ferenczi to speak more authentically and honestly to Gizella in addressing the complex emotional triangle involving his wife and step-daughter, Elma (Berman, Chapter Six). In the Christmas 1921 letter Ferenczi writes:

> Your letter spurred me on to greater efforts; it helped me remove my mask in front of my wife, too – albeit partially. I spoke to her again about my sexual frustration, about my suppressed love for her daughter (who should have been my wife; indeed who in effect was my bride until a somewhat disparaging remark of Freud's prompted me to fight this love tooth and nail – literally to push the girl away from me).
>
> (p. 9)

Prefiguring the surprising positive analytical outcomes of his negative transference disclosures ten years later during mutual analysis with his patient, Elizabeth Severn, Ferenczi continues: "Oddly enough, with us these confessions usually end with me drawing closer to her [Gizella] again" (pp. 9–10).

Ferenczi pursued a much more open professional friendship with Groddeck, who was also his physician, which challenged the traditional limits of the doctor-patient and analyst-analysand relationships. During Ferenczi's yearly therapeutic holidays to Groddeck's sanatorium, the two men engaged in an open dialogue—frequently a vigorous debate of shared interests. For example, besides the body-mind relationship, they wrestled with the question of whether psychoanalysis could be a science, as well as issues such as self-analysis and mutual analysis—which they tried for a brief time.

In his 1926 letter on Groddeck's sixtieth birthday, Ferenczi commented on the history of their friendship, and Groddeck's contributions to psychoanalysis:

> There are decided differences between us with regard to the scientific method we employ; yet we always managed to bridge these outward differences with a bit of goodwill on both our parts and essentially to harmonize our views ... I have learned a lot from the carefree courage with which you 'come to grips' with the psychomorphology of the organic.
>
> (Fer/Grod, p. 78)

Did Ferenczi also look to Groddeck as an experienced writer to inspire him to overcome his writer's block? In his Christmas 1921 letter, he confides in Groddeck: "I hadn't the courage to do it. Time and again I've let myself be drawn into writing small *ad hoc* pieces instead of this quintessential work" (pp. 10–11). He continues, writing of his "inhibition about work", and his difficulty in completing *Thalassa,* which he linked to a myriad of chronic somatic symptoms and to criticisms he suffered in childhood. Comparing himself to Groddeck, Ferenczi writes:

> Am I trying to behave like a fish, or to enact my genital theory of fishes [*Thalassa*, 1924], which I won't write down? ... If I was as talented a writer as you I would continue in this vein and discharge my physical and mental pain on paper.
>
> (p. 15)

Ferenczi's deeply felt palette of physical symptoms is also evoked in *Thalassa.* The symptoms he describes to Groddeck could be seen as mirroring the metaphors of the evolutionary movement from sea to land that he outlines in his thesis, and specifically relate to his *not* writing the book. These symptoms included difficulty in breathing, acute sensitivity to heat and cold, sleep disturbances, and blood problems (Hoffer, Chapter Fifteen). While Ferenczi does not go into greater detail about his "blood problems", one might speculate that these symptoms could have been an early indication of his pernicious anemia, the disease that would ultimately be responsible for his death.

In *Thalassa*, Ferenczi speaks of a desire throughout life to return—particularly to "return to the mother", and to the womb. This notion, and his championing of the child, suggests that Ferenczi was pulled back to the innocence of childhood. Groddeck not only supported Ferenczi's childlike qualities, but shared and celebrated them as a rebellion. He wrote to Ferenczi: "The pompous aura surrounding the grown-up's godforsaken head, to ensure that nothing goes in or comes out, is in the eyes of us children no more than a game, thank God, only play" (Grod/Fer, p. 36).

Through Groddeck, Ferenczi finally found his writer's backbone, overcame his block, and completed his biological magnum opus, *Thalassa*, which encompassed a bold leap of imagination linking trauma, sexuality, gender, psychology, biology, and evolution.

Given Groddeck's empowering influence, and the timing of Ferenczi's completing a work that had been stalled for many years, it seems likely that Ferenczi was inspired to finish *Thalassa* thanks to Groddeck's own highly original, even daring, writings of the period. These included his semi-autobiographical psychoanalytic novel, *The Soul-Seekers* (1921a) and *The Book of the It* (1923), a unique collection of "letters to a woman friend" on the theme of Groddeck's concept of Das Es, translated as the "It"—the "wondrous force" that directs man—"both what he himself does, and what happens to him" (Groddeck, 1923, p. 2).

In his Christmas 1921 letter, again evoking Groddeck's mothering, Ferenczi wrote: "I notice that I'm imitating *your* 'Letters to a Woman Friend' in peppering this letter with these entertaining morsels. Are *you* by any chance this female friend for me, or am I using your friendship in a homosexual way to replace her?" (p. 11).

Ultimately, Ferenczi had a breakthrough year in 1923. He was able to complete two original writing projects on which he had procrastinated, including *Thalassa* (1924) and his collaboration with Rank, *The Development of Psycho-Analysis* (Ferenczi & Rank, 1924). Subsequently, having gained strength and independence through overcoming his writing block, Ferenczi's work mood improved.

Ferenczi's dialogue with Groddeck about the relationship of body and mind—which is not really found in their correspondence, but was most likely carried out during their time together in Baden-Baden—was a discourse not found in psychoanalysis until that time. Groddeck's positive and inclusive view of the body/mind—his instinctual "It"—spoke to Ferenczi, particularly with respect to his own psychosomatic symptoms, and also influenced his clinical desire to better understand the deeper layers of the psyche. Through his use of water therapy, diet, exercise, and deep massage, Groddeck brought to Ferenczi (and psychoanalysis) the bodily side of the equation that had been neglected during Ferenczi's long association with Freud.

As close as their friendship was, in the final years, Groddeck could not follow Ferenczi's irrepressible spirit of scientific investigation, and he saw Ferenczi's passionate thirst for psychological knowledge as self-destructive. After Ferenczi's death, Groddeck wrote to Gizella suggesting that Ferenczi had gone too far, abandoning his advice, and refusing to acknowledge his own physical, mental, and emotional limitations: "All these years I could only think about Sándor's life with a heavy heart. He became a victim of his own spirit of inquiry" (Fer-Grod, p. 112). He continues, explaining how he came to view Ferenczi's demise:

> Being such a close friend of Sándor's … I was … horrified to see him proceed to investigate this human cosmos scientifically … He became completely consumed by this endeavour. He expressed it thus to me: I atomise the soul [deconstruct]. Such atomisation, though, if pursued seriously, can only end in the dissolution of the self, for another

Sándor and Gizella in Baden-Baden
courtesy Judit Meszaros

> human being is, and always will remain hidden to us. We can only atomise our own soul, and that will destroy us.
>
> (p. 113)

In his last words about Ferenczi, Groddeck wrote: "External events only acquired meaning in the life of this rare human being as he belonged to the givers, to those who give again and again" (p. 114). Gizella responded to Groddeck's tragic and unsettling view of Ferenczi's end:

> The last years showed me that nobody – not even you – could help him. A gradual transformation in him not only began to destroy his body, but also had an enormous influence on his mental life. His 'ascent to the stars,' as you put it so beautifully, took him such immense distances that he himself lost sight of the final goal. This desperate brooding, his struggle with knowledge and conscience, his constant questioning of the results of his research – all this served to undermine his health.
>
> (p. 115)

Affirming the importance of Groddeck's friendship to Ferenczi, Gizella continued:

> If there was anyone who did him good in his battle … it was you. You yourself know how rejuvenated he always was when he left you, how he loved being with you – and nobody had such a continuous influence on him as you …. Not only that you always attended to Sándor as his physician, but that you, as no other, loved, appreciated and honoured him.
>
> (p. 115)

While Ferenczi may have refused to acknowledge his limits at the expense of his own well-being, he (yet again) opened new horizons that ultimately had the effect of enriching all of psychoanalysis (Fortune, 1993, 1994, 1996). In his clinical work of the late 1920s, Ferenczi's attention to the body in analysis was a critical component in his return to a theory of trauma. Ferenczi's last papers, most of which also took the view from the perspective of the child, and challenged Freud's rejection of these ideas, made great contributions to psychoanalytic theory and practice. However, it must be said, "it was both a hero's and a fool's journey. Sándor Ferenczi caught therapeutic fire, and tragically it ultimately consumed him" (Fortune, 1996, p. 184).

Georg Groddeck, through his free-thinking spirit, made a great contribution to the development of psychoanalysis by "remothering" Ferenczi and inspiring him to follow his creative instincts. Without Groddeck's support and influence in their very important friendship, as well as in their relationship as physician and analyst, the later crucial phase of Ferenczi's career, which was characterised by his challenge to Freud and the development of new and critical ideas, would not have taken place.

References

Ferenczi, S. (1917). Review of psychic conditioning and the psychoanalytic treatment of organic disorders. In: *Final Contributions to the Problems and Methods of Psycho-analysis* (pp. 342–343). London: Karnac, 1994.

Ferenczi, S. (1924). *Thalassa: A Theory of Genitality.* London: Karnac, 1984.

Ferenczi, S., & Rank, O. (1924). *The Development of Psycho-Analysis*. New York/Washington: Nervous and Mental Disease Publishing Company, 1925.

Fortune, C. (1993). The case of RN: Sándor Ferenczi's radical experiment in psychoanalysis. In: L. Aron & A. Harris (Eds), *The Legacy of Sándor Ferenczi* (pp. 101–120). Hillsdale, NJ: Analytic Press.

Fortune, C. (1994). A difficult ending: Ferenczi, "R.N.", and the experiment in mutual analysis. In: A. Haynal & E. Falzeder (Eds), *100 Years of Psychoanalysis* (pp. 217–223). Geneva: Universitaires de Psychiatrie de Geneve.

Fortune, C. (1996). Mutual analysis: A logical outcome of Sándor Ferenczi's experiments in psychoanalysis. In: P. Rudnytsky, A. Bokay & P. Giampieri-Deutsch (Eds), *Ferenczi's Turn in Psychoanalysis* (pp. 170–186). New York: New York University Press.

Groddeck, G. (1921a). *Der Seelensucher: Ein Psychoanalytischer Roman* [The soulseeker: A psychoanalytic novel]. Vienna/Leipzig: Internationaler Psychoanalytischer Verlag.

Groddeck, G. (1921b). On psychoanalyzing the organic in human beings. *Internationale Zeitschrift fur Psychoanalyse*, *7*.

Groddeck, G. (1923). *The Book of the It*. London: Vision Press, 1950.

Groddeck, G. (1977). *The Meaning of Illness: Selected Psychoanalytic Writings Including his Correspondence with Sigmund Freud* (Selected with introduction by L. Schacht). London: Hogarth.

Grosskurth, P. (1991). *The Secret Ring: Freud's Inner Circle and the Politics of Psycho-Analysis*. Reading, MA: Addison-Wesley.

Chapter 13

Ferenczi's patients and their contribution to his legacy

B. William Brennan

Balint wrote that "Ferenczi never forgot that psychoanalysis was really discovered by a patient" (1957, p. 238), and this chapter turns to the patients, who, lying on Ferenczi's couch in Budapest, helped him discover and advance new ideas in theory and technique. Ferenczi's various experiments and pioneering work were always a response to his patients, and often to particular impasses in treatment. Sandor Lorand quotes him as saying that he took the "dried-up difficult cases whom no one else wanted to work with" (in Alexander et al., 1966, p. 22). This chapter gives an overview of Ferenczi's patients, some who have occupied centre-stage in contemporary discussions of Ferenczi's ideas of trauma or mutual analysis, and others who have remained only footnotes, initials, or even nameless. My research has focused on his American pupils and the identities of the eight patients who appear in *The Clinical Diary* and *Notes and Fragments*, many who were previously only known by initials that concealed their identities (Brennan, 2015a).

Nestled a block from the bustling Rákóczi út on the Pest side of Budapest, Ferenczi saw his analytic patients in the office in his apartment on Nagydiófa Utca 3. Patients from abroad would often stay at the Hotel Hungaria, the Gellért Hotel, or the Ritz Duna Polata. In 1930 Ferenczi moved to the villa at Lisznyai Utca 11, in the Buda hills where he would write his *Diary* and live his last days. Aside from analytic patients seen in his own office, he worked in other settings during his career. From 1898 to 1900, Ferenczi interned at the Szent Rókus Kórház, where he treated patients with venereal diseases, many of whom were prostitutes. From 1900 to 1903, Ferenczi worked as a neurologist at the Erzsébet Szegényház Kórháza (1900–1903) where he also provided care to the impoverished (Haynal, 2002; Mészáros, 2014). Ferenczi's outpatient work flourished when he worked (1904–1910) on the neurology outpatient ward of the General Workers' Sick-Benefits Society, where his patients were members of the lower working class. By the time he met Freud, Ferenczi had also been appointed as a forensic psychiatric specialist for the Royal Court of Budapest (1905–1918). In 1914, during wartime, he was the chief physician to the Seventh Militia (Honvéd) Hussar-Regiment in Pápa, and then worked at the Mária Valéria Military barracks on Üllői útan where he treated many shell-shocked patients (Harris, 2015). During his time in Pápa, he analysed his commandant while on horseback, demonstrating that psychoanalysis was not limited to the consulting room, and that regardless of the context he could apply the psychoanalytic method. In 1926, he lectured at the New School for Social Research in New York City, influencing many within American psychiatry and championing the cause of lay analysts. Given Ferenczi's diverse work settings, and the shifting socio-political scene within Hungary, his patients ran the gamut, with every socio-economic class represented, from the underbelly of society to members of the Royal Court, from soldiers to artists and members of the literati. Some patients sought him for a second analysis, others because of his experience treating psychotic states. Many of his patients were themselves analysts in training, becoming future leaders in the field, such as Ernest Jones, John Rickman, Melanie Klein, and Michael Balint. It should be noted that with analysts in training there can be some confusion whether the pupil was in analysis with Ferenczi or was in supervision (control analysis), and whether they were seeking a didactic analysis (training analysis) or a therapeutic analysis. Ferenczi saw no difference between the latter two, believing the "best analyst is a patient who has been cured" and that "other pupils must first be made ill, then cured and made aware" (Diary, p. 115). Moreover, in the early days of psychoanalysis a training analysis could last as little as several months. (For more in-depth commentaries on Ferenczi's patients see Brennan, 2015a; Falzeder, 2015; Mészáros, 2014.)

Patients from Ferenczi's case studies

Perhaps the first patient of note is Rosa K, who appears in Ferenczi's early writings before he met Freud (Cassullo, Chapter Three; Ferenczi, 1902; Mészáros, 1999). Rosa K was a forty-year-old lesbian woman, who called herself Robert, and today would be considered gender queer or transgendered. She dressed as a man and was attracted to women, and at one time worked as a waiter in a restaurant. Ferenczi had Robert write his autobiography and sensitively explored how his gender and sexuality collided with societal norms, leading to mockery, misunderstandings, and legal trouble with the police. The account not only captures the patient's subjectivity, but also includes Ferenczi's own countertransference feelings. Ferenczi included a photograph of the patient, in which he unmistakably looked like a man. Perhaps what is most moving about this case is Ferenczi's question of where a person like Robert/Rosa can exist and find a place of freedom to be himself, to be able to live and work free from insults and mockery, and not be "shuffled between the poorhouse, the prison and the psychiatric hospital" (p. 20).

In 1913, Ferenczi published his case of "The little rooster man," which in many ways mirrors Freud's treatment of Little Hans. The case documents his analysis of five-year-old Árpád, who during the summer of 1910, at the age of three and a half, had developed an identification with chickens, and consequently acted like one, only answering with sounds of clucks and crowing. Returning to Budapest from an Austrian spa where the family had spent the previous summer, little Árpád resumed speaking normally, but his thoughts and play remained rather poultry, obsessed with cocks, hens, and chickens. The little boy's play repeatedly enacted selling live poultry and he relished the final scenes of cutting their necks as they cried out in agony. At the same time, Árpád remained afraid of live cocks. In his case study, Ferenczi applied his psychoanalytic understanding of "fowl play" and traced how little Árpád had encountered a trauma a year earlier, when at the age of two and a half he was urinating at the chicken coop and one of the birds pecked his penis. Layered into his experience were masturbatory prohibitions against playing with his own genitals; Ferenczi interprets the different iterations of his play as reflecting the secrets of the family dynamics and his castration anxiety.

Another of Ferenczi's colourful case studies was the Croatian musician who experienced stage fright and blushing when she was playing and performing finger exercises in front of an audience (1921). Utilising his active technique, Ferenczi had the woman sing for him in sessions, and in another session had her act out being the conductor of the orchestra to overcome her modesty and uncover her unconscious desires, which included her exhibitionism, penis envy, and her masturbatory fantasies. In his work with patients Ferenczi paid close attention to gesture, to how the unconscious spoke through the ventriloquism of the body (Stanton, 1991), and he linked play with unconscious fantasy; therefore it is not surprising that some of his patients went on to be important figures in the psychoanalysis of children—Melanie Klein, Ada Schott, and Alice Balint (Arfelli & Vigna-Taglianti, Chapter Thirty-four).

The Clinical Diary

In Ferenczi's *Diary*, which he wrote in 1932, he recorded his work with eight patients, all referred to by code letters. I have previously written (2015a) about decoding the identities of these patients. In this section, I will present an overview of them.

Izette de Forest (1887–1965)—patient Ett. Although de Forest only appears briefly in the *Diary*, she is an important patient, particularly in regard to her relationship with patient B of the *Diary*. De Forest was in analysis with Ferenczi beginning in February 1925, around the same time that Elizabeth Severn started treatment, during the end of his active technique phase and when he began to transition to his "relaxation therapy" (Brennan, 2009, 2011a). De Forest was a lay analyst and the first to write about her understanding of Ferenczi's technique in the *IJP* (1942), garnering a response from Clara Thompson. Her book *The Leaven of Love* (1954) elucidated her understanding of Ferenczi's contribution to technique, highlighting some of the subtle differences from the orthodox Freudianism of her day, especially in regard to the analyst's love for the patient, the handling of countertransference, and emphasising emotional engagement rather than intellectual understanding. Her husband Alfred de Forest, who was a cousin of Dorothy Burlingham, was also in analysis with Ferenczi in the summer of 1925. Izette maintained a correspondence with Clara Thompson and they both sought out Erich Fromm for further analysis. De Forest had a practice in New York for a short time before moving to Cambridge, Massachusetts, and New Hampshire, where she continued to see patients as well as teach. De Forest had an intimate relationship with Alice Lowell, who she then referred to Ferenczi, and Lowell appears prominently in the *Diary* as patient B.

Alice Lowell (1906–1982)—patient B.—started working with Ferenczi in mid-February 1930 and remained in analysis until 12 March 1933. She was from one branch of the Lowell family, Boston aristocracy—cultured, musical, and known for her commanding style. Growing up she would spend the summers in Cotuit, Massachusetts, where James Jackson Putnam, eminent neurologist and contributor to psychoanalysis, was a neighbour. Her brother Fred joined her in Budapest and was in analysis with Clara Thompson. Lowell seemed to be one of Ferenczi's favourite patients. After her analysis, she was in a study group in New York along with de Forest, Thompson, and the Menakers, who had returned from being analysed in Vienna (Menaker, 1989). Initially, Lowell wanted to become a psychoanalyst, but her medical studies took her career in a different direction. She became one of the leading woman physicians in the Boston area, becoming medical director and chief of medicine at the New England Hospital in Boston. She continued to have romantic relationships with women, and was partner to Annella Brown, Boston's first female surgeon.

Clara M. Thompson (1893–1953)—patient Dm.—is often remembered as the patient who got Ferenczi in trouble with Freud when he learned through his analysand Edith Banfield Jackson that Ferenczi let Thompson kiss him.[1] Thompson is an important figure in American

1 For more on Clara Thompson see Brennan 2015b, Green 1964, and Shapiro, 1993.

psychoanalysis, a founding mother of the Baltimore-Washington Psychoanalytic Society and the William Alanson White Institute, the home of interpersonal psychoanalysis, as well as the analyst of Harry Stack Sullivan. Thompson grew up in Providence, Rhode Island, in a working-class family and, after graduating from Brown University's Pembroke Women's College, she pursued a medical education and psychiatry training at John Hopkins University, studying under Adolf Meyer at the Phipps Clinic in Baltimore, Maryland. Thompson's first analyst Joseph Cheesman Thompson (same last name—no relation) complicated her tenure at Phipps as Meyer disapproved of him and created tension between her work in the clinic and in her private practice, finally culminating in her resignation (Edmunds & Small, 2012). Thompson first met Ferenczi when he was lecturing in the United States in 1926, and wanted to go into analysis with him, but his hours were fully booked. Financial constraints caused Thompson to wait until the summer of 1928 to begin her analysis. She moved to Budapest in 1931 and remained there until Ferenczi died in 1933. In her interview with Kurt Eissler for the Freud Archives (Thompson, 1952), she described the analysis as helping her overcome her schizoid detachment, but at the same time she felt that character defences prevented his therapeutic love from being metabolised (Brennan, 2011b, 2015b). Thompson never married. However, in 1948 she had a relationship with the Hungarian painter Henry Major, and they summered together in Provincetown, Massachusetts, a place so important to them that they are buried there next to each other. Thompson has been critiqued for not fully embracing Ferenczi's ideas about trauma (Shapiro, 1993) and for privileging the here-and-now of the analytic experience over regression. Where de Forest exuded warm enthusiasm for Ferenczi's ideas, Thompson was more reserved. During her time in analysis with Ferenczi, she had an affair with another American patient, the New York businessman Teddy Miller, who had a questionable character and was known for being a philanderer. Thompson had a strong aversion for Severn, and envied Lowell. Ferenczi struggled with his countertransference towards Thompson because of her body odour and at times her vulgarity, both a response to her strict upbringing with a very religious Puritanical mother, who often would not wash Thompson's undergarments.

Elizabeth Severn (1879–1959)—patient R.N.—is best known as the patient with whom Ferenczi in his "grand experiment" entered into a mutual analysis.[2] Born Leota Loretta Brown, and growing up in the "middle West", her father Marcus M. Brown, a lawyer and real estate developer in Illinois, abandoned her and her mother when she was eleven years old. As a sickly child, four years later, she dropped out of a private girls' school. In 1898, she married Charles K. Heywood and moved to Birmingham, Alabama, giving birth to her daughter Margaret in 1901. The details of the following eight years are somewhat hazy, but Severn was hospitalised for a mental breakdown and her daughter sent to her paternal grandparents. During this time she also had an oophorectomy (Brennan, 2015c) without her consent; this procedure was often used to cure hysteria at the time. In 1909, she reclaimed her daughter, moved to San Antonio, divorced her husband, and, starting a new chapter, reinvented herself as Elizabeth Severn. Severn sold encyclopaedias door to door, but her interest in theosophy led her to establish herself as a healer, teacher, psychotherapist, writer, and public speaker. Severn had taken some classes at the Armour Institute in Chicago, but it is unclear if she even earned a PhD, although she called herself "Dr" intermittently. Severn considered herself a psychic and had the ability to go into trance states. She was a member of the Society

2 For more on Severn see Fortune 1993, 1994, 1996, Rachman, 2015, and Smith 1988, 1989.

for Psychical Research in London, and honorary vice president of the Alchemical Society. She was also a close friend and metaphysician to Arthur E. Waite, and joined his Independent and Rectified Rite of the Golden Dawn in 1913 (Gilbert, 1987). Severn was interested in psychoanalysis early in her career and had been in analysis with Smith Ely Jeliffe, Joseph Jefferson Asch, and Otto Rank, before coming to Ferenczi in 1925. She was the author of three books, including *The Discovery of the Self* (1933), which she wrote during her last year in the analysis. When Severn started analysis with Ferenczi she recalled paying him $15 and later $20 a session (Severn, 1952). Severn suffered from violent headaches, deep depressions, and was often suicidal. Two years into the analysis she discovered that behind her childhood amnesia were memories of being drugged and horrific sexual abuse at the hands of her father. The *Diary* records the splits in her psyche, including one she called Orpha, the organising intelligence or life instinct, a maternal guardian angel, who first appeared when she was five years old. Severn's recollection of her trauma did not improve her symptoms and her dreams pointed to Ferenczi's Jecountertransference feelings as the cause of the impasse, and Ferenczi reluctantly agreed to the experiment in mutual analysis. Reflecting on the analysis Severn told Eissler that together they discovered two foundational principles, that the analyst needs to be sensitive to patients' needs (which Ferenczi framed in terms of the analyst's love for the patient), and the necessity of the analyst to be analysed in order to overcome any countertransference that could interfere with the treatment. Ferenczi credits Severn in two of his papers. In "The principle of relaxation and neocatharsis", he credits her with the idea that there is a psychotic splitting of the personality as a consequence of trauma, which is then expressed in neurotic symptoms. In "Child-analysis in the analysis of adults", he gives her credit for the idea that a patient's phantasy-productions are better furthered with simple questions rather than statements or interpretations from the analyst. After her analysis Severn returned to London and then to New York where she continued to maintain her private practice as a lay analyst and lived with her daughter Margaret. Margaret was a dancer, famous for her dances wearing masks; she also saw Ferenczi for a number of sessions, as well as Ruth Gates who had studied with Ferenczi.[3]

Natalie Rogers (1902–1949)—patient O.S.—was a wealthy American socialite, heir to the Schiff and Warburg banking fortune. As a medical student at Cornell University, in 1924, along with her first husband Oscar de Lima Mayer, and her college friend Ora Ford, she was one of the first white women to explore the Bolivian Amazon. For a period of time she had unofficially adopted Kyra Nijinsky, daughter of Vaslav Nijinsky. Rogers was bisexual and during her time in Budapest was involved with Roberta "Robbie" Nederhoed, who was an aspiring writer.

Roberta "Robbie" Nederhoed (1891–1947)—N.D./N.H.D.—was born in Melbourne, Australia, to English parents and travelled to the United States in 1916 with her husband, William Nederhoed, who was of Dutch decent, along with their daughter Anke/Ann. As an up-and-coming writer Robbie wrote for the *Woman's Home Journal*, *Town and Country*, as well as *Harper's Bazaar*, including a piece on "Eating in Budapest" (1931). According to Margaret Severn's autobiography, her mother had considered writing a book with Nederhoed, but this never came to fruition. After Ferenczi's death, Nederhoed checked into a sanatorium outside Vienna, and she parted ways with her companion Miss Rogers. Nederhoed eventually settled

3 Margaret's unpublished autobiography, "Spotlight: Letters to my mother", contains the many letters she wrote in response to her mother's letters.

in Hertfordshire, England. Her daughter Anke Weihs' autobiography (1989) *Whither From Aulis?* sheds some light on her life, which ended in her dying alone from alcoholism.

Countess Harriot (Hattie) Sigray (1884–1950)—Case S.I.—was the youngest daughter of Marcus Daly, an Irish immigrant who became one of the wealthiest men in America, after founding a copper mine in Butte, Montana (Powell, 1989). In 1910 Harriot's fortune was estimated to be seven million dollars. In 1908, attending the wedding of Gladys Vanderbilt and Count Széchenyi, the twenty-four-year-old Hattie met her future husband Count Anton Sigray, also a member of the Hungarian House of Lords. They married on March 29 1910, and their only child Margit was born ten months later. In his *Diary*, Ferenczi is very fond of Sigray, he prefers the moments of mutual analysis he has with her. After Ferenczi's death, Sigray continued to support the psychoanalytic clinic in Budapest. During the war, Count Sigray survived his imprisonment in the Mauthausen concentration camp, while his wife and daughter aided the resistance.

Theodore "Teddy" Miller (1902–?)—patient U.—was originally born in Brest-Litovsk, Poland, before emigrating to the United States in 1914. He was an American businessman and passenger records reveal that he sailed to Europe in 1929 with Sándor Lorand, and in 1931 he was living in Budapest and listed Clara Thompson as his closest relative. From the *Diary* we learn he was having an affair with Thompson. In a letter to her friend Ilona Vass, Thompson describes how when Ferenczi died, "I clung to Teddie and he to me, but gradually it became apparent that one of us must get free because we were in a way holding each other down" (Shapiro, 1993, p. 168).

Anjelika Bijur Frink (1884–1969)—Mrs. G.—was born into the wealthy Wertheim family, which had made their fortune in the cigar industry. During her childhood, her mother had eloped with a French Count, a scandal at the time, leaving her in the position of lady of the house. Around 1900, her father remarried, and seven years later Angie married the wealthy financier Abraham Bijur, and they adopted two daughters. Although Anjelika plays a minor role within the *Diary*, she plays an important role in the history of psychoanalysis, as she was in treatment with, and then, in 1922, married Horace Frink, an American psychiatrist and psychoanalyst, who was Freud's analysand. Freud saw Frink as a potential future leader of psychoanalysis in the United States. After the marriage, Horace continued to suffer from severe mood swings, at times violent and suicidal, and Angelika was upset that Freud had given his blessing to the marriage despite knowing Frink's unstable mental state (Edmunds, 1988; Warner, 1994). Moreover, she felt that this was all a grand scheme so that she could bankroll the psychoanalytic establishment. However, in the same month Freud had actively dissuaded the even wealthier Guggenheim from becoming a patient, which raises doubt about the financial-motives hypothesis. By 1924, Anjelika was pursuing a divorce, which was complicated by Frink's suicide attempt and several hospitalisations. Her half-sister Viola Wertheim Bernard became an analyst, continuing Anjelika's link to the psychoanalytic establishment.

An interesting aspect is that all the patients in the *Diary* can be linked to each other, and the geometry of their relationships intersected in ways that can only have complicated their analyses. In his *Diary*, Ferenczi even comments that it is not dissimilar from a group analysis (Berman, 2015). Izette de Forest was having a relationship with Alice Lowell. Countess Sigray had previously been a patient of Elizabeth Severn, and she helped relieve the debt of some of the money Severn owed Ferenczi for the analysis. Natalie Rogers had adopted Kyra Nijinsky, who was in analysis with Izette de Forest. Elizabeth's Severn's daughter knew and socialised with both Natalie Rogers and her partner Robbie Nederhoed. Izette de Forest's daughter Judy stayed with her aunt Dorothy Burlingham, attended Anna Freud's Heitzig School and was in analysis with Miss Freud. Kyra Nijinsky and Roberta Nederhoed's daughter Anke/Ann also attended the school. Countess Sigray's sister and brother in-law James Gerard, the American ambassador to Germany, socialised with Elizabeth Severn and her daughter Margaret. Both of Izette de Forest's children were in analysis with Clara Thompson. Clara Thompson was having an affair with Teddy Miller. Severn's daughter Margaret was in analysis for a brief period with Ruth Gates, who was also an analysand and pupil of Ferenczi. Also, given the small number of Americans in Budapest (Thompson recalled around thirty-five in the 1930s), there was inevitable social contact outside of the analytic setting.

Some noteworthy lesser-known patients

Eugénie Sokolnicka (1884–1934), born in Warsaw, began her training with Jung at the Burghölzli, followed by a three-month analysis with Freud in 1914, then in 1920 spent a year in Budapest with Ferenczi. Sokolnicka had a reputation for having a difficult personality and Freud did not hold back in disclosing his dislike of her to Ferenczi in his letter of 17 June 1920, calling her "repugnant" and "basically disgusting" (p. 29). We have a unique window into her analysis with Ferenczi, as he discussed her case in some detail in his letters to Freud. The smooth beginning to the analysis was short-lived, after two and a half months Ferenczi writes on 4 June 1920, "thick clouds gathered between us" (p. 26), a response to Ferenczi's "active technique" and his instructing her to give up masturbation as a way of accessing her early infantile neurosis. Another intervention, which was met with a better outcome, was having her give a lecture to the local psychoanalytic society in order to overcome her shyness. Ferenczi also records how at times she started analysing him and he found some of her insights helpful. Despite her being a very difficult patient, Ferenczi did not want to give up on her, fearful of her suicidal impulses, and in the midst of describing the various impasses that he encountered he would write to Freud in the same 4 June letter: "She is a very valuable personality" (p. 26). Returning to Paris in 1921, she helped establish the psychoanalytic movement in France. Although Ferenczi did not consider her cured, he did feel she had made significant progress. Sokolnicka was a founding member and vice president of the Société Psychanalytique de Paris, and after her death by suicide in 1934 was remembered as the first person to practice psychoanalysis in France (Groth, 2015). Sokolnicka is also important because of the uncanny parallels she shares with Elizabeth Severn (Rudnytsky, 2002)—both had difficult personalities, insisted on analysing Ferenczi, exhibited grandiosity, had a history of suicidal impulses, couldn't tolerate separation, and wanted to go on vacation with Ferenczi and continue the work, counted out Ferenczi's "analytic sins", had financial difficulties that interfered with the analysis, coerced Ferenczi into gratifying particular demands, and activated Ferenczi's negative countertransference feelings related to his own mother.

Elvin Morton Jellinek (1885–1968) was a patient of Ferenczi's. Despite his illustrious career, periods of his life have been an enigma for many biographers, and his status as a patient of Ferenczi is often missed. Jellinek (1960) is best known for his work *The Disease Concept of Alcoholism*, which has shaped the field of alcohol research worldwide. Jellinek was born in New York City, to Austro-Hungarian parents, his mother a famous opera singer. They returned to Hungary to take over the family transportation business. Jellinek is first mentioned in the Freud/Ferenczi correspondence in October 1916 as a friend of Roheim, and in June 1917 Ferenczi refers to him as a patient finishing his doctorate. Ferenczi relates to

Freud a dream Jellinek had told him about a signet ring, as well as a story of an Australian tribal ritual of sealing friendships with dried ends of an umbilical cord. Jellinek gave a paper entitled "On friendship" discussing blood-brother rites at the Fifth International Congress of Psychoanalysis in Budapest in 1918. In 1919, Jellinek delivered a "ring of the Nibelung" from Freud to Ferenczi, as a gift to Ferenczi's wife, and also seems to have been involved in helping Freud with some financial and banking situation. Parts of Jellinek's story have been shrouded in mystery and controversy. He was very close to Róheim, they were studying in Leipzig together, although current biographers have not been able to verify whether he ever finished his PhD. He worked for a time as a biometrician at the Government School for Nervous Children in Budapest. In 1920, Jellinek was a ministerial secretary and on 29 June 1920 a warrant was put out for his arrest for fraud, embezzlement, and smuggling; he was purportedly involved in a money-laundering scheme. He was last seen taking a train to Szeged and, lacking documentation to cross the Tisza Bridge, he got into a small boat and disappeared. On 12 June 1920 Ferenczi submitted a report to the investigation, which stated "Mr. Morton Jellinek, ministerial secretary, who has been in treatment with me since January 1917, with some interruptions, has suffered since childhood from high-grade psychoneurosis. Symptoms: various forced thoughts, frequent forced acts, restlessness, impatience and attention deficit. Unable to concentrate on one place for a long time. At the current time, unsuitable for any mental work" (Roizen, 2009). Supposedly, after his disappearing act Jellinek continued his work in biometrics in Sierra Leone and Honduras, often working under a pseudonym. He would reappear in 1931 and was appointed the chief statistician at Worcester State Hospital, in Massachusetts, and later, in 1938, was instrumental in bringing Róheim there. Jellinek continued his career at the laboratory of applied psychology at Yale University, establishing the field of alcohol research. He also worked at the University of Toronto, Stanford University, and for the World Health Organization. While always having a head for numbers and statistical research, it has been noted that his background in anthropology and psychoanalysis continued to inform his thinking, as can be evidenced by his 1977 article "The symbolism of drinking: a culture-historical approach".

William Blumenthal (1878–?) was present in the Freud/Ferenczi correspondence, where Freud mentioned a patient by the name of Blumenthal whom he had referred to Ferenczi. Freud parted with the patient, refusing Blumenthal's demand to let him dictate a letter of recommendation for him to Ferenczi. Blumenthal was afraid that Freud would not write favourably about him, and he was correct about Freud's negative countertransference, as Freud referred to him as the "pension animal". In his letter of 7 February 1929, Freud warned Ferenczi that although he might be well behaved at first, he was dishonest and arrogant. In a subsequent letter on 11 January 1930, Freud remarked that he had chased him away out of boredom. At the same time, Freud is eager to know if Ferenczi is making headway with him or with Rickman, whom he had also referred. Ferenczi replied a week later that he was working with both of them, but didn't give any further details regarding either case. My research has identified Blumenthal as Joseph Ferdinand William Blumenthal, born in New York City on 15 February 1878. William Blumenthal was a linguist, earning degrees from Yale and Oxford. He was an attaché in the American Diplomatic Service, appointed secretary of the legation at Lisbon, May 27th 1904, third secretary of the embassy at Paris, March 10th 1905, second secretary of the embassy at Constantinople, November 27th 1908 and retired on 19 April 909. Blumenthal was with Freud for three years. According to one of his physicians he had a phobia of doctors—as a child he witnessed the obstetrician leaving his mother's bedroom, and he was told not to enter—he concluded it therefore had to have been contaminated by the doctor. In the 1950s, his physician (Johannsen, 1953) reported that he spent his later years living in large New York hotels, where he maintained a living room with another room adjoining, where he would see his physician. All furniture in the room was covered in white sheets. He would wear specially designed white pyjamas and socks. He would use fifty to sixty towels a day to wash his hands, and often all the cupboards would be filled with dirty laundry. He was unkempt, he never bathed, and his hair and beard were matted. When the situation would become untenable he would move to another hotel. He also had a phobia of the number thirteen and would not make telephone calls if the numbers on his watch added up to thirteen at the time he was placing the call. He would not commence anything new on a Friday, or a death day, or burial day of one of his relatives. He also would not open letters. Blumenthal had a number of health problems including diabetes and in 1951 was in hospital for two and a half years.

Eleanor Morris Burnet (1885–1967), who wrote under the pseudonym Mrs F. H. (1952, 1954), was twenty-five years old when she started receiving psychiatric treatment. Burnet was afraid of sunlight and retreated to a life confined to a darkened room. Burnet had spent time in one psychiatric clinic, two sanitariums, and underwent psychoanalysis in England, before she finally sought out Ferenczi, and was in treatment with him for six months when he was at the New School for Social Research. Writing about her experience, Burnet noted this marked a turning point in her life—she experienced a therapeutic relationship and a psychoanalytic method that she would continue to use in her own self-analysis. Burnet notes that Ferenczi was not a "superdetective" but a "kind latitudinarian". Describing Ferenczi's personality Burnet stresses his humanitarianism, his "Puckish humor", his gentleness, his patience. "One felt safe, safer with him than with any other man or woman" (1954, p. 2). Burnet describes how Ferenczi invited her from the very beginning not just to say whatever came to her mind, but also insisted that she "speak out anything about himself" (1954, p. 2). When they reached an impasse Ferenczi utilised his "active technique", urging Burnet to face her fears of being outside in daylight. Demonstrating the elasticity of technique, he initiated a peripatetic analysis as they ventured out together into the hustle and bustle of Broadway and walked the avenues of Manhattan. Moreover, from Burnet's description it is evident that Ferenczi wanted her to introject him as a good object, and it was this introjection that enabled Burnet to continue her own self-analysis when she could not complete the analysis and follow him back to Budapest. Burnet's description of her experience as "redemption by love" (1952, p. 177) inspired the title of de Forest's book *The Leaven of Love*.

Conclusion: Overlapping and intersecting circles

Ferenczi's patients can be seen as belonging to different circles, often overlapping and intersecting. There was the creative and artistic circle with Ferenc Hatvany, Lajos Hatvany, Hugó Ignotus, Dezső Kosztolányi, Frigyes Karthiny, Sándor Kovács, Géza Szilágyi, and Sándor Brody. Another circle of patients were members of the Hungarian Psychoanalytic Society: Vilma Kovács, Géza Róheim, Lajos Lévy, Kata Lévy, Mrs Felszeghy, Aurél Kolnai, Erzsébet Révész-Rado, Margit Dubovitz, Géza Dukes, Lászlo Révész, and Zsigmond Pfeifer. (For a detailed study of the Budapest school see Mészáros, 2014.) There were also analysts in analysis with Ferenczi who were affiliated with another institute outside of Budapest, or who later emigrated, such as Barbara Lantos, Therese Benedek, Ada Schott, and Sándor Lorand.

Another psychoanalytic circle were members of the British Psychoanalytical Society, whom I list with the approximate time period they were in analysis with Ferenczi:

Ernest Jones (1879–1958) had sessions twice a day in June and July 1913
Melanie Klein (1882–1960) was in analysis intermittently between 1914 and 1920
David Eder (1865–1936) in analysis in 1923
Estelle Maud Cole in analysis in 1922 and 1925
Marjorie E. Franklin (1877–1975) in analysis between 1924 and 1926
William S. Inman (1876–1968) went to Budapest in 1924
John Rickman (1891–1951) was in analysis from 1928 to 1931
Ethilda Budgett Meakin-Herford (1872–1956) was in training analysis in 1922 to 1923
Col. Claud Dangar Daly (1884–1950), three and a half months in 1925 and then again in 1926
Michael (1896–1970) and Alice Balint (1898–1939) worked with him between 1924 and 1926.

On his return from his year lecturing at the New School of Social Research in New York City, Ferenczi stopped off in England in June 1927 and all his pupils were eager to spend time with him, squabbling amongst themselves to secure time in his itinerary. It is worth noting that Jones seems to have been biased against Ferenczi's analysands when they were seeking full membership in the British society.

Another circle were Ferenczi's American patients, which can be divided up into the medically trained analysts, and the group of lay analysts. Edward Kempf, and his wife were his analysands, as well as George S. Amsden, who spent three summers with Ferenczi from 1927–1929, and sought him out specifically, because he wanted help in working with persons with psychoses. Joseph J. Asch also worked with Ferenczi when he was at the New School for Social Research, and Lewis B. Hill saw him for supervision in Budapest when he was in analysis with Clara Thompson. The group of lay analysts, whom Jelliffe in a letter to Ernest Jones caricatured as the "Greenwich Village bunch" led by the "Bolshevik Free Love Feminists" (Burnham, 1983, p. 226), consisted of Ruth Gates, who often held seminars at her house, Izette de Forest, Caroline Newton, Rosetta Hurwitz, Elizabeth Severn, Grace Potter, and Adam Empie and his wife Margery.[4] Ruth Gates (1884–1943) had spent two months in 1922 in Vienna and also from April to December 1923 was in Vienna working with Reik, and in January 1924 went to Budapest to work with Ferenczi.

The other patient who features prominently in Ferenczi's writing is himself. Ferenczi's autobiographical writing is not only found in his *Diary* and his correspondences with Freud and Groddeck, but is also disguised in his short papers "The dream of the occlusive pessary" (1915)[5] and "The dream of the 'clever baby'" (1923). Ferenczi's consideration of himself as part of the equation gives his writing a contemporary feel, making his own subjectivity accessible and no less a part of the analytic inquiry. In his papers, Ferenczi would often mention how much he owes to his patients for his discoveries and revisions, wanting to honour their contributions to his thinking. While this chapter is not an exhaustive study, I hope it

4 This list of names comes from the letters of Izette de Forest (family private collection).

5 See Falzeder's (2015) chapter "Dreaming of Freud: Ferenczi, Freud, and an analysis without end", and Bonomi, Chapter Five.

pays tribute to the many men and women who found their voice on a couch in Budapest and contributed to what Ferenczi called the "dialogues of the unconscious".

Note

1 For scholarship on Jellinek see Roizen (2011), Roizen and Ward (2013), Ward (2014, 2016).

References

Alexander, F., Eisenstein, S., & Grotjahn, M. (Eds.) (1966). *Psychoanalytic Pioneers*. New York: Basic Books.

Balint, M. (1957). *Problems of Human Pleasure and Behavior.* London: Maresfield.

Berman, E. (2015). On "Polygamous analysis". *The American Journal of Psychoanalysis*, *75*: 29–36.

Brennan, B. W. (2009). Ferenczi's forgotten messenger: The life and work of Izette de Forest. *American Imago*, *66*: 427–455.

Brennan, B. W. (2011a). Se necesitan dos para bailar tango—las vicisitudes de la transferencia en el análisis de Izette de Forest hecho por Ferenczi [It takes two to tango—the vicissitudes of the transference in Ferenczi's analysis of Izette de Forest]. In: Pedro J. Boschan (Ed.), *Sándor Ferenczi y el Psicoanalisis del Siglo XXI* [Sándor Ferenczi and psychoanalysis of the 21st century] (pp. 41–52). Buenos Aires: Letra Viva.

Brennan, B. W. (2011b). On Ferenczi: A response—From elasticity to the confusion of tongues and the technical dimensions of Ferenczi's approach. *Psychoanalytic Perspectives*, *8*: 1–21.

Brennan, B. W. (2015a). Decoding Ferenczi's *Clinical Diary*: Biographical notes. *The American Journal of Psychoanalysis*, *75*: 5–18.

Brennan. B. W. (2015b). Out of the archive/unto the couch. Clara Thompson's analysis with Ferenczi. In: A. Harris & S. Kuchuck (Eds.), *The Legacy of Sándor Ferenczi* (pp. 77–95). New York: Routledge.

Brennan, B. W. (2015c). The medium is the message—Turning tables with Elizabeth Severn. Paper presented at the International Sándor Ferenczi Conference, May 7–10 2015, Toronto, Canada.

Burnet, E. M. (1952). Recovery from a long neurosis. *Psychiatry*, *15*: 161–177.

Burnet, E. M. (1954). Ferenczi. *Psychiatric Quarterly Supplement*, *28*: 10–14.

Burnham, J. (1983). *Jelliffe: American Psychoanalyst and Physician and his Correspondence with Sigmund Freud and C. G. Jung* (Ed. William McGuire). Chicago: University of Chicago Press.

de Forest, I. (1942). The therapeutic technique of Sándor Ferenczi. *International Journal of Psychoanalysis*, *23*: 120–139.

de Forest, I. (1954). *The Leaven of Love: A Development of the Psychoanalytic Theory and Technique of Sándor Ferenczi.* New York: Harper.

Edmunds, L. (1988). His master's choice. *Johns Hopkins Magazine*, *40*: 40–49.

Edmunds, L., & Small, L. (2012). The 90-year divide. *Johns Hopkins Magazine*, *64*: 50–56.

Falzeder, E. (2015). *Psychoanalytic Filiations: Mapping the Psychoanalytic Movement.* London: Karnac.

Ferenczi, S. (1902). Female homosexuality. In: J. Borossa (Ed.), *Selected Writings*. London: Penguin, 1999.

Ferenczi, S. (1913). The little rooster man. In: J. Borossa (Ed.), *Selected Writings*. London: Penguin, 1999.

Ferenczi, S. (1915). The dream of the occlusive pessary. In: J. Borossa (Ed.), *Selected Writings.* London: Penguin, 1999.

Ferenczi. S. (1921). The further development of the "active technique" in psychoanalysis. In: J. Borossa (Ed.), *Selected Writings.* London: Penguin, 1999.

Ferenczi, S. (1923). The dream of the "clever baby". In: J. Rickman (Ed.), *Further Contributions to the Theory and Technique of Psychoanalysis* (pp. 349–350). New York: Basic Books, 1955.

Fortune, C. (1993). The case of "R. N.": Sándor Ferenczi's radical experiment in psychoanalysis. In: L. Aron & A. Harris (Eds.), *The Legacy of Sándor Ferenczi* (pp. 96–110). Hillsdale, NJ: The Analytic Press.

Fortune, C. (1994). A difficult ending: Ferenczi, "R. N.," and the experiment in mutual analysis. In: A. Haynal & E. Falzeder (Eds.), *100 years of psychoanalysis* (pp. 217–223). Geneva: Cahiers Psychiatriques Genevois.

Fortune, C. (1996). Mutual analysis: A logical outcome of Sándor Ferenczi's experiments in psychoanalysis. In: P. L. Rudnytsky, A. Bókay & P. Giampieri-Deutsch (Eds.), *Ferenczi's Turn in Psychoanalysis* (pp. 170–186). New York: New York University Press.

Gilbert, R. A. (1987). *A. E. Waite: Magician of Many Parts.* Wellingborough: Aquarian Press.

Green, M. (Ed.) (1964). *Interpersonal Psychoanalysis: The Selected Papers of Clara M. Thompson.* New York: Basic Books.

Groth, J. (2015). Eugenia Sokolnicka–A contribution to the history of psychoanalysis in Poland and France. *Psychoanalysis and History, 17*: 59–86.

Harris, A. (2015). Ferenczi's work on war neurosis. In: A. Harris & S. Kuchuck (Eds), *The Legacy of Sándor Ferenczi* (pp. 127–133). New York: Routledge.

Haynal, A. (2002). *Disappearing and Reviving.* London: Karnac.

Jellinek, E. M. (1960). *The Disease Concept of Alcoholism.* New Haven, CT: Hillhouse Press.

Jellinek, E. M. (1977). The symbolism of drinking: A culture-historical approach. *Journal of Studies on Alcohol, 38*: 852–866.

Johannsen, M. W. (1953). *Interviews and Recollections, Set A., 1914–1998 with K. R. Eissler/Interviewer.* Sigmund Freud Papers, (Box 114). Manuscripts Division, Library of Congress, Washington, DC.

Menaker, E. (1989). *Appointment in Vienna: An American Psychoanalyst Recalls her Student Days in Pre-War Austria.* New York: St. Martin's Press.

Mészáros, J. (Ed.) (1999). *Ferenczi Sandor: A pszichoanalizis felé. Fiatalkori irások 1897–1908* [Towards Psychoanalysis: Early Papers 1897–1908]. Budapest: Osiris.

Mészáros, J. (2014). *Ferenczi and Beyond: Exile of the Budapest School and Solidarity in the Psychoanalytic Movement During the Nazi Years.* London: Karnac.

Nederhoed, R. (1931). Eating in Budapest. *Harper's Bazaar.* May, p. 165.

Powell, A. (1989). *The Dalys of the Bitter Root.* Montana: A. Powell.

Rachman, A. W. (2015). Elizabeth Severn: Sándor Ferenczi's analysand and collaborator in the study and treatment of trauma. In: A. Harris, & S. Kuchuck (Eds.), *The Legacy of Sándor Ferenczi.* New York: Routledge.

Roizen, R. (2009). E. M. Jellinek's departure from Budapest in 1920, part one. *Ranes Report Blog.* Posted on 26 December 2009. Retrieved from http://www.roizen.com/ron/rr17.htm

Roizen, R. (2011). E. M. Jellinek's departure from Budapest in 1920, part two. *Points: The Blog of the Alcohol and Drugs History Society.* Posted on August 11 2011. Retrieved from https://pointsadhsblog.wordpress.com/2011/08/05/e-m-jellineks-departure-from-budapest-in-1920-part-two/

Roizen, R., & Ward, J. (2013). On E. M. Jellinek's trail. *Points: The Blog of the Alcohol and Drugs History Society.* Posted on April 25, 2013. Retrieved from http://pointsadhsblog.wordpress.com/2013/04/25/on-e-m-jellineks-trail

Rudnytsky, P.L. (2002). *Reading Psychoanalysis: Freud, Rank, Ferenczi, Groddeck.* Ithaca, NY: Cornell University Press.

Shapiro, S. (1993). Clara Thompson: Ferenczi's messenger with half a message. In: L. Aron & A. Harris (Eds.), *The Legacy of Sándor Ferenczi* (pp. 159–174). Hillsdale, NJ: The Analytic Press.

Severn, E. (1952). *Interviews and Recollections, Set B, 1952–1960 with K. R. Eissler/Interviewer.* Sigmund Freud Papers, (Box 126). Manuscripts Division, Library of Congress, Washington, DC.

Smith, N. A. (1998). Orpha reviving: Toward an honorable recognition of Elizabeth Severn. *International Forum of Psychoanalysis*, *7*: 241–246.

Smith, N. A. (1999). From Oedipus to Orpha: Revisiting Ferenczi and Severn's landmark case. *The American Journal of Psychoanalysis*, *59*: 345–366.

Stanton, M. (1991). *Sándor Ferenczi: Reconsidering Active Intervention.* Northvale, NJ: Jason Aronson.

Thompson, C (1952). *Interviews and Recollections, Set A., 1914–1998 with K. R. Eissler/Interviewer.* Sigmund Freud Papers (Box 119). Manuscripts Division, Library of Congress, Washington, DC.

Ward, J. H. (2014). E. M. Jellinek: The Hungarian connection. *Substance Abuse Library and Information Studies: Proceedings of the 36th Annual SALIS Conference*, 1, 42–54. Retrieved from http://library.alcoholstudies.rutgers.edu/sites/library.alcoholstudies.rutgers.edu/files/documents/SALISJOURNAL/5WardSALISjn2014.pdf

Ward, J. H. (2016). Re-introducing Bunky at 125: E. M. Jellinek's life and contributions to alcohol studies. *Journal Studies Alcohol and Drugs, 77*: 375–383.

Warner, S. L. (1994). Freud's analysis of Horace Frink, M.D.: A previously unexplained therapeutic disaster. *Journal of the American Academy of Psychoanalysis*, *22*: 137–152.

Weihs, A. (1989). *Whither from Aulis? A Childhood Autobiography.* Great Britain: Floris.

Chapter 14

Some things you may want to know before reading Sándor Ferenczi's *Clinical Diary*

Éva Brabant-Gerő and Judith Dupont

The context of the *Diary* (Éva Brabant-Gerő)

The *Diary* of Ferenczi, written in 1932 and published in French for the first time in 1985, remains unknown by a large number of psychoanalysts. Its presence for several decades on the "black list" of a "politically correct" psychoanalysis is probably not the only reason for this seeming lack of interest. The reader of this work without equal in psychoanalytic literature can't avoid the impression of committing an act of indiscretion, of looking through a keyhole watching a man undressing, becoming an intruder on privacy, a voyeur. An analyst may find it an easier task to listen to a patient talking about his sexual life than to look at one of the founding fathers of his discipline in the nude.

As an attentive reading of Ferenczi's correspondence with Freud reveals, some of his ideas and questions developed later in his *Diary* were germinating from the beginning of their relationship. The wish to expose his feelings without shame or guilt is already present in his letter of 3 October 1910, written after their journey to Sicily. Ferenczi, trying to reduce their conflict to a simple misunderstanding, proposed to clear it away by a frank expression of their feelings:

> I strive for absolute mutual openness and … I believed that this apparently cruel, but in the end only useful, clear-as-day openness, which conceals nothing, could be possible in the relations between two P.a. minded people who can really understand everything and, instead of making value judgements, can seek the determinants of their (psy) impulses. (Fer/Fr, p. 217)

But Freud did not share with Ferenczi this wish for total sincerity. As he wrote in his answer of 6 October 1910, ever since the rupture with his friend Fliess, "I no *longer* have any need for that full opening of my personality" (Fr/Fer, p. 221). Apparently, Ferenczi's proposal for a perfectly transparent relationship plunged Freud into the past and opened wounds not entirely healed. And Ferenczi, besides having to face the refusal of his idealised father figure, was also forced to accept the fact that Freud had been able to put his trust, at another time, in another. However, in his Christmas-day 1921 letter to Groddeck, (Fer/Grod, pp. 7–18), recounting the history of his relation to Freud, Ferenczi did not allude to this painful experience. Talking about his inhibition about expressing himself freely to the master, he preferred to attribute it to an excessive admiration.

One can see Ferenczi's proposal for a relationship founded on complete sincerity as a way to formulate a demand for recognition. As he wrote to Groddeck in the same letter, rather than playing the part of a secretary simply taking notes, he wanted to participate in the elaboration of the "famous paranoia text (Schreber)" (p. 8). Undeniably, behind this proposal appears the wish of the child to pry into the secrets of the father. But at the same time, this demand is the expression of a desperate need to put into words never-formulated experiences of childhood. Ferenczi, assuming his role of "wise baby" (Martín Cabré, Chapter Eighteen), was trying to approach his hidden traumas and to transform them, by the intervention of another person willing and capable of listening, into a story. Thus Freud's refusal can be considered as the starting point for Ferenczi's reflections about the analyst's relationship with the patient. These reflections became a cornerstone of the construction of his theories. By 1929 he abandoned his active, pedagogic approach for a more attentive, permissive one and this new technique was founded on the sincerity of the analyst allowing the patient to express his childhood trauma. In his letter of 25 December 1929 to Freud, following his paper "The unwelcome child and his death-instinct", he advances the following reason for contesting Freud's theories on trauma: "In *all* cases in which I penetrated deeply enough, I found the traumatic-hysterical basis for the illness," adding further: "psychoanalysis engages much too one-sidedly in obsessional neurosis and character analysis, i.e., ego psychology, neglecting the organic-hysterical basis for the analysis; the cause lies in the overestimation of fantasy – and the underestimation of traumatic reality in pathogenesis" (Fer/Fr, p. 376).

Freud, who refused to enter into a dialogue about these questions, was placing their debates on personal ground and blaming Ferenczi for the decline of their friendship. But according to Ferenczi, as he pointed out in his letter to Freud of 17 January 1930 (Fer/Fr, p. 382), their estrangement had already begun during his analysis of 1916: "[You] did not comprehend and bring to abreaction in the analysis the partly only transferred, negative feelings and fantasies ... I do not, e.g., share your view that the process of healing is an unimportant procedure, or one that should be neglected" (ibid., pp. 382–383).

In his conference paper, "Child-analysis in the analysis of adults", delivered in Vienna in 1931 on the occasion of Freud's birthday, Ferenczi evoked the reputation of the " 'orthodoxy' of our master ... his 'Old Testament' severity" (ChildAn, p. 126), attributing these negative opinions to "people". This criticism, denied as soon as pronounced, seems to indicate that after exposing his new ideas in vain for several years, he finally gave up the hope to create a dialogue with Freud.

A year and a half later he took the decision to create a dialogue with himself in order to grapple with the questions on his mind. On 7 January 1932 he started noting in a diary (which became *The Clinical Diary*) his thoughts and feelings about Freud, his preoccupations about his patients, and his ideas about psychoanalysis. These problems, closely linked and stemming from the same roots, led him to a critical view about the psychoanalysis of his time. Refusing the idea that the clinic should be a mere support for the theory, he took the measure of the analyst's preoccupations about the patient as an essential part of his activity.

Parting from these reflexions, Ferenczi opened the way for a psychoanalysis differing in many points from the one created by Freud. His theories, constructed in search of sincerity, revealed new aspects of the human psyche. But these constructions did not allow him to overcome his own traumas: as he amply expressed in the *Diary*, he never ceased to suffer from Freud's lack of comprehension.

As their correspondence clearly reveals, the master, ageing and ill, turned a deaf ear to his disciple's interrogations. Ferenczi's ideas appeared to him probably as nebulous, leading to slippery ground, representing a danger for the future of psychoanalysis. However, as some of his letters reveal, his reactions to Ferenczi's way of thinking and the change they implied

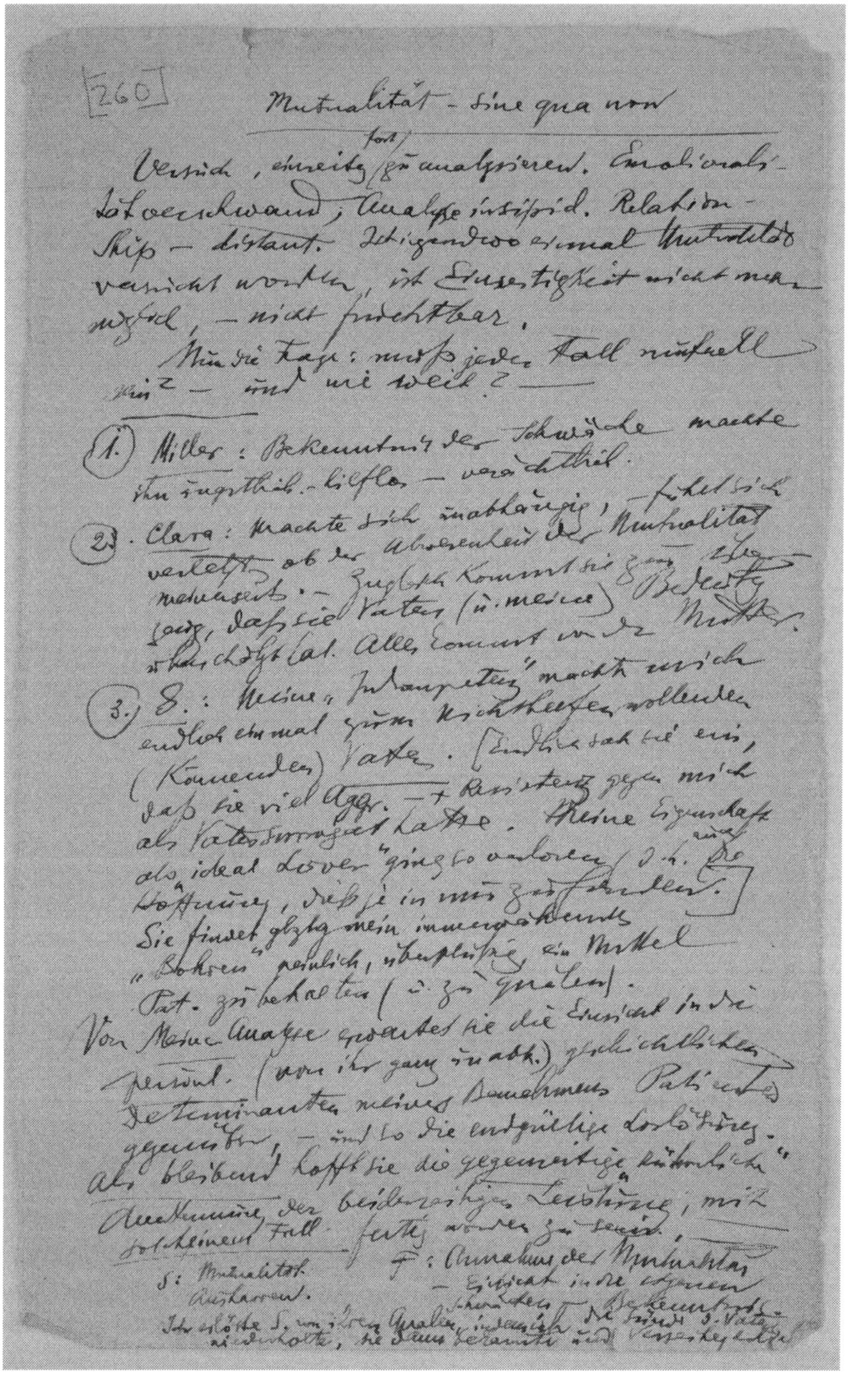

Clinical Diary

courtesy Freud Museum London

for psychoanalysis would hardly have been different one or two decades earlier. Once his friends and disciples, from Fliess to Ferenczi, criticised his ideas and distanced themselves from him he considered them paranoiac. In his letter to Ferenczi of 10 January 1910, talking about the personal background of Fliess's motivation for the medical profession, he makes the following remark: "This piece of analysis, unwanted by him, was the inner cause of our break, which he effected in such a pathological (paranoid) manner" (Fr/Fer, p. 122). In his letter to Jung on 3 December 1910, he writes, making reference to Adler: "[he] awakens the memory of Fliess but an octave lower", and then adds: "The same paranoia" (Fr/Ju, p. 376). And there is his memorable letter to Jones of 29 May 1933, written after Ferenczi's death, where the expression of his feelings of sorrow at the loss of his friend is followed by the description of his "mental degeneration in the form of paranoia developed with uncanny logical consistency" (Fr/Jo, p. 721).

Being firmly convinced about the scientific character of psychoanalysis, Freud considered his oedipal theories to reveal the truth. He did not see psychoanalytic theory as a creation but as a discovery, and that discovery was to make him an equal to Copernicus and Darwin (Freud, 1917a). Ferenczi, on the other hand, became the analyst of all analysts, without ever striving to found a school. He did not aspire to become a master, aiming only to reach his patients through his self-analysis. This may be the principal reason for Freud's refusal to enter in a dialogue with Ferenczi during the last years. The disciple opened a door to a domain the master never dared to penetrate. In considering psychoanalysis as a science, Freud defended himself against the frightening idea that we are not only inhabited by our own drives and feelings but also by the drives and feelings of others, thus creating, inside our little person, a whole world, past and present.

The controversies between these great men during the last years of Ferenczi's life originated from the difference of their aims and preoccupations. While Freud was concentrating on the construction of his theories, Ferenczi was more and more absorbed in his clinical researches. He carried these researches as far as engaging in mutual analysis with some of his patients, but, as some of his notes in the *Diary* reveal, having understood its dangers, he greatly restricted its application. This appears clearly in his note of 3 June 1932: "Mutual analysis: only a last resort! Proper analysis by a stranger, without any obligation, would be better" (Diary, p. 115).

According to general agreement, *The Interpretation of Dreams,* by Freud, published in 1899, is the fundamental text of psychoanalysis. In contrast, Ferenczi's *Diary*, written thirty-two years later, essentially for himself, was seen for several decades as an excessively personal, pathological, and therefore unpublishable document. However, one can detect in it the source of the psychoanalytic development of the twenty-first century. Today's analysts no longer attribute the problems of their patients exclusively to oedipal factors but take into consideration their traumas, thereby drawing from Ferenczi's reservoir. As Balint noted in 1949, "The central idea, to which Ferenczi returned time and again, is the essential disproportion between the child's limited capacity for dealing with excitation and the adults' unconscious and consequently uncontrolled, passionate and simultaneously guilt-laden, over- or under-stimulating of the child" (Balint, 1949, pp. 218–219). Ferenczi challenged himself by subjecting his theories to constant revision, thus treating his doubts as part of his knowledge. His challenges are at the root of a radical transformation of the analytic process which is considered, from then on, as a dialogue between the unconsciouses of two participants (see Bass, Twenty-three). As André Haynal pointed out, Ferenczi, underlining the importance of experience, departed from the Freudian notion of insight (Haynal, 1988, p. 29). The analyst no longer aspires to be a mirror; he is conscious of the mutual communication between transference and countertransference. And countertransference shifted from being an attitude to eliminate, to an indispensable instrument (Vida, 1994). As shown by Balint, Ferenczi's vision of problems of regression and trauma brought important modifications not only to analytic practice but also to theory (Balint, 1968).

The work of analysis entails a large number of risks and dangers. In order to embark on an analysis—this journey through a strangely familiar landscape—everyone needs a person who serves alternately as a partner and as a guide. As his *Diary* reveals, Ferenczi had to explore this landscape alone. As disturbing a reading as this book may be, it should enable current-day analysts to grasp the obstacles on the analytic journey, and better confront them.

The history of the publication of *The Clinical Diary* (Judith Dupont)

Sándor Ferenczi's *Diary*, written in 1932, is an exceptional text, unique in psychoanalytic literature. Although it is a true "diary", written up each day and highly personal in tone, it was probably intended, at least in part, for publication, as most of it was dictated to a secretary and typed up. A much smaller section was handwritten, on separate pages, and this deals primarily with the relationship between Ferenczi and Freud, as well as being an attempt to understand certain elements of Freud's character. This section includes disappointment and criticism toward Freud and was almost certainly not intended to be disseminated.

When Michael Balint left Hungary in 1939, Ferenczi's widow, Gizella, put the *Diary* in his care. He had been a student and a close friend of her husband's, and she hoped thus to preserve it from possible destruction by the Nazis and to ensure its publication, when the time was right.

Right from the beginning, Balint had intended to publish the *Diary*—originally written in German and roughly translated into English by Balint himself—at the same time as the Freud-Ferenczi letters, believing that each text would shed light on the other. This, however, proved to be impossible. Anna Freud resisted the release of the correspondence with her father because it would reveal the full history of her family—something she found difficult to face. The correspondence also allows the reader to see all the weaknesses of both men, their hesitations, their misunderstandings, their contradictions. Anna Freud could not accept revealing her father in this light. When Balint died in 1970, he had just begun to collect material for a biography of Ferenczi, but death did not leave him time to do it. Therefore, the project was still not realised; and after his death the management of Ferenczi's literary legacy passed to me, with Enid Balint retaining the right of oversight for the correspondence and the *Diary*. Enid had reservations about publication of the *Diary*, as she feared that it might reinforce Jones' claim that Ferenczi was mentally ill. We therefore agreed to ask two renowned German analysts, Alexander and Margarete Mitscherlich, to examine the text. Both experts concluded that publication would be impossible, as the *Diary* was much too personal and also very neurotic.

Despite this, the French translation group,[1] which had just completed volume four of Ferenczi's *Oeuvres complètes* (Complete Works), decided to start translation of the *Diary*, and

1 The translation group was mostly composed by the team of the review *Le Coq-Héron*. Its members were: Suzanne Achache-Wiznitzer, Judith Dupont, Susanne Hommel, Georges Kassaï, Pierre Sabourin, Françoise Samson, Bernard This.

examine at a later date the issue of when and how to make this available to the psychoanalytic public. It was a lengthy task and, in the meantime, Ferenczi's writings had appeared in various languages, and the view of his mental state was changing. The translation group therefore decided that the time had finally come to publish the *Diary*. When it appeared in French for the first time, in 1985, it was met not with the expected scandal, but with respect and admiration.

The spirit of *The Clinical Diary* (Judith Dupont)

This text captures and communicates genuine human experience. It demands a reading that goes far beyond an intellectual scrutiny of its range of ideas and insights and requires sensitivity, empathy, imagination, and free association with the thoughts, intuitions, and feelings in the text. It requires, in fact, something close to Ferenczi's "dialogue of the unconsciouses".

There is much to consider here. Ferenczi takes us through a range of practice to find ways of reaching and mobilising the wounded areas, the psychotic zones of all those who came to him for help; how to harness regression rather than prevent it; attempts at mutual analysis; the rejection of the death instinct; and many other issues of theory and practice. He takes us through his daily work with a number of seriously ill patients, discussing his perception of them but also taking account of his own reactions and inner experiences. He tries to understand the interplay between their emotions and his own, in order to create a tool that could allow the patient to rebuild himself. In reading this, the psychoanalyst has to put his own methods and abilities in question: is he capable of examining himself so intensely? Does he even wish to do so? How prepared is he to invest in such an endeavour?

The reader must draw on all his own sensitivity and empathy to accompany the author through his suffering and to the riches that he draws from it. It is a profoundly emotional

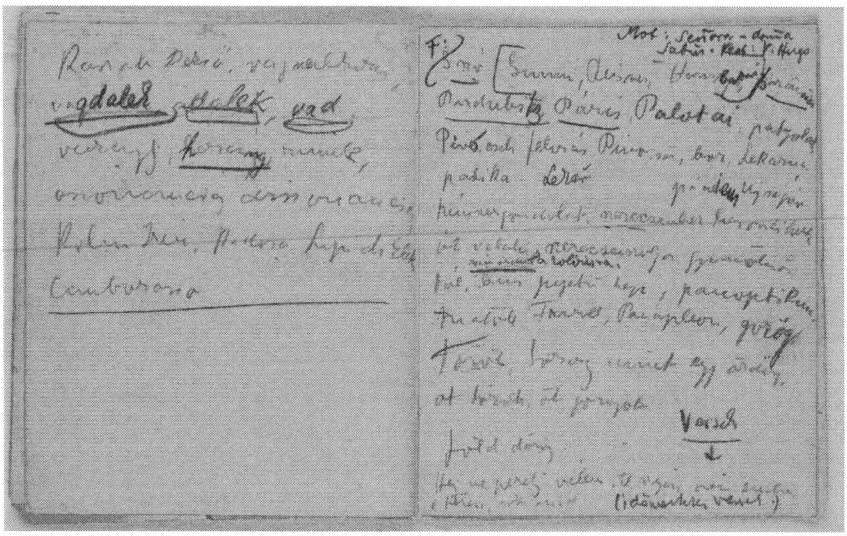

"small diary" written with Robert Bereny

courtesy Freud Museum London

experience, sometimes painfully so. When Ferenczi faces the possibility of pursuing his work without the support of Freud, he feels this is killing him, as if his path in life has been blocked. In that sense, one can talk of Ferenczi's "mad" sense of duty, even of his "mad" ambition to come to the aid of all suffering, whatever the cost—with "madness" here thought of as response to a kind of excessive, somehow impossible, demand on the analyst.

References

Balint, M. (1949). Sándor Ferenczi, Obit 1933. *International Journal of Psychoanalysis*, *30*: 215–219.

Balint, M. (1968). *The Basic Fault: Therapeutic Aspects of Regression*. London: Tavistock.

Freud, S. (1917a). A difficulty in the path of psycho-analysis. *S. E.*, *17*: 135–144.

Haynal, A. (1988). *The Technique at Issue: Controversies in Psychoanalysis from Freud and Ferenczi to Michael Balint*. London: Karnac.

Vida, J. E. (1994). Sándor Ferenczi: Amalgamating with the existing body of knowledge. In: A. Haynal & E. Falzeder (Eds.), *100 Years of Psychoanalysis* (pp. 257–263). London: Karnac.

Chapter 15

Ferenczi's untimely death

Peter Hoffer

In a letter to Freud on 6 November 1929, Ferenczi reveals the second of two thoughts [*Einfälle*] that came to his mind as he was writing:

> The other (purely personal) thought is the evidently shocking impression that your statement, which was made in passing, to the effect that my appearance was an indication of *premature senility,* made on me. ... In the meantime I feel (physically) not significantly better; my sleep is being disturbed by the well-known symptoms; but my daily work (despite seven-eight-nine hours) is of undiminished, often enthusiastic interest. I am learning more every day.
>
> (Fer/Fr, p. 372)

In his terse reply of 13 December, more than a month later, Freud asks the following questions:

> I am supposed to have said that you are looking prematurely senile? Really, I don't remember. To you yourself? Or to someone else who reported it to you? And to whom? At most I could have said that you look older than I did at your time of life. But as always—if it had the result of having rekindled your activity and even had the further result [of having rekindled] your desire for correspondence with me, then I am glad if I said it.
>
> (p. 373)

This exchange, containing the ebb and flow of sentiments characteristic of a relationship that had endured for more than twenty years, reflects a heightening of tension between the two principals not heretofore evident to such a degree in their earlier communications. Freud, for his part, was troubled by his perception that "you have doubtless outwardly distanced yourself from me in the last two years" (ibid.); Ferenczi, in turn, was sensitive to the fact that his evolving ideas about psychoanalytic theory and technique were negatively impacting both his personal relations with Freud and his physical condition, which had been the subject of his and Freud's analytical scrutiny from the start of their relationship. Following another exchange of letters, the content of which had the effect of temporarily easing the tension between them, Ferenczi writes to Freud in a letter of 14 February 1930, in which he encloses a fair copy of the lecture he had delivered at the Eleventh International Psychoanalytic Congress in Oxford in August 1929, which would be revised and published in the following year as "The principles of relaxation and neocatharsis":

> [M]y self-analysis led me to the insight that the childish sensitivity toward your facetious allusion to my getting old was actually the expression of a deep inner unease about my bodily ailments. My nightly rest disturbances (respiratory disturbance and spells of headache) have been returning almost uninterruptedly for more than a year and make me fear premature aging. Also at this moment I am writing early, at five o'clock in the morning, frightened by the symptoms that I have often related to you ... This hypochondriacal, but in part also justified, anxiety may, incidentally, also be one of the reasons that urge and have urged me to publish ideas that have been held back.
>
> (Fer/Fr, pp. 387–388)

I have cited the foregoing exchange of views and sentiments as a preface to the construction of a narrative that seeks to shed some light on the circumstances, events, and motivations, internal and external, that led up to and influenced Ferenczi's fatal illness and untimely death on 22 May 1933. In the space allotted to me I will attempt to provide a balanced account in the narrative, without, to the extent possible, drawing conclusions as to causation and placing undue emphasis on any one of the motivating factors. As in any narrative, however, subjective considerations on the part of the narrator inevitably play a role in the selection of content, both in its inclusion and omission.

In the weeks and months following these exchanges, the personal relations between Freud and Ferenczi remained in a state of relatively stable equilibrium, as the tenor of their correspondence indicates, punctuated by continuing exchanges about Ferenczi's technical innovations, reports about their respective states of health—Freud had been undergoing numerous painful and debilitating surgical procedures for treatment of his oral cancer—, and their mutual concerns regarding the politics of the IPA, for whose presidency Ferenczi had become the presumptive candidate.

At the end of October 1931, Ferenczi spent three days with Freud in Vienna to discuss their differences in what would be their penultimate face-to-face meeting and prove to be a watershed event in their further declining personal relations. The details of the meeting and its immediate vicissitudes have been discussed elsewhere (Hoffer, 2010; Jones, 1957, p. 163). Suffice it to say, it led to increased consternation on Freud's part over what he had learned about Ferenczi's continuing technical experiments, "which to me seem to lead to no desirable end" (Fr/Fer, p. 418) and Ferenczi's concomitant distress over Freud's perceived intolerance toward them. In material terms, it led to Freud's writing the well-known letter admonishing Ferenczi for his "kissing technique" (pp. 421–422) and Ferenczi's decision to begin writing what would become his *Clinical Diary*, with the words "Insensitivity of the Analyst" (Diary, p. 1).

The spring and summer of 1932 passed relatively uneventfully, despite some hesitancy on Ferenczi's part to take on the presidency of the IPA on account of the concern that might be engendered among his colleagues over his technical deviations, "from which, at some time or other ... definitely, something not worthless will come" (Fer/Fr, 1 May 1932, p. 432), to which Freud responded in a firm tone, "I am sorry that you are so easily able to renounce the presidency; I would like to insist on it for you ... the presidency should have the effect on you of a drastic measure [*Gewaltkur*], to move you again to convivial participation and to the acceptance of the role of leader to which you are entitled" (p. 433). Ferenczi's response, in a letter of 19 May, written in a tone of restrained resentment over Freud's suggestion that the presidency would serve as a kind of occupational therapy, or even shock treatment, which would restore his mental and emotional equilibrium, reads: "I can't conceive of the presidency as a drastic measure against an illness which I don't actually recognize as such. So, I don't think I am doing useless work if I continue in my present manner of working for a time. If you believe that this can be brought into harmony with the expectations which one has for the president of an association ..., I will consider it an honor also to stand for once as president of the society on the founding of which I collaborated and in the activity of which I actively participated for a long time (p. 435).

Over the summer months the correspondence between Freud and Ferenczi is punctuated by numerous lapses in frequency, and what there is of it is devoted largely to matters concerning the politics and administration of the IPA, with occasional reference to preparations for the forthcoming International Congress scheduled for 4 to 7 September in Wiesbaden, Germany, including Ferenczi's planned plenary address. Then, in a letter of 21 August, Ferenczi announces to Freud:

> After long and anguished hesitation, I have decided to renounce my candidacy for the presidency ... in the course of the exertion to structure my analyses more deeply and more effectively, I have gotten into decidedly critical and self-critical waters, which seem to necessitate in some respects not only extensions but also corrections of our practical and, in part, also our theoretical views.
>
> (p. 441)

The controversy surrounding Ferenczi's abrupt decision to renounce the presidency of the IPA and the presentation of his lecture on the "Confusion of tongues" and its vicissitudes has been discussed and debated by numerous commentators (Blum, 1994; Hoffer, A., 1991; Hoffer, P., 2010; Masson, 1984; Rachman, 1997, among others). It is not my intention here to add anything of substance to this discussion or to revive the debate; my main purpose in citing it here is to provide a contextual basis for my ongoing narrative.

In a letter to Eitingon of 29 August 1932, in the midst of the turmoil that occurred within the leadership of the IPA as a result of Ferenczi's surprising announcement, Freud writes:

> Brill and Radó were with me yesterday, back from Budapest. They reported sad things that coincide with one another. Ferenczi is said to look miserable. White as chalk, profoundly depressed. Radó, whose perspicacity is razor-sharp, thinks he is in a state of advanced sclerotic degeneration. I would like to place much of the impression on the conflict that is shaking him, breaking away is obviously very difficult for him.
>
> (Schröter, 2004, p. 825; my translation)

Almost uncannily, these observations resonate on at least one level with what Ferenczi writes in the last entry of his *Diary* of 2 October 1932, a month after his fateful last meeting with Freud in Vienna and shortly after receiving the diagnosis of pernicious anemia, the illness that would eventually end his life:

> In my case the blood-crisis arose when I realized that not only can I not rely on a "higher power" but *on the contrary* I shall be trampled under foot by this indifferent power as soon as I go my own way and not his ... Is it worth it always to live the life (will) of another person—is such a life not almost death?
>
> (Diary, p. 212)

The common denominator in each of these utterances, expressed on different occasions and under different circumstances, is contained in the respective meanings of the words "breaking away" and "go my own way". For Freud they are a reflection of his fear that, like Otto Rank, almost a decade earlier, Ferenczi was on the verge of "founding a new variety of analysis" (Fr/Fer, p. 442) and abandoning the cause that they had both so passionately defended for a quarter of a century; for Ferenczi they emanate from something much more profound: the dread of having to renounce his " 'identification' with the higher power ... the support that once preserved [him] from final disintegration" (Diary, p. 212), a feeling that had been with him for some time and was now being intensified by the prospect of the reality of the final disintegration, of his soul, and now of his body as well.

Much has been written in recent years about Ferenczi's fatal illness in the context of Jones' (1957, p, 178) allegation that Ferenczi was mentally ill during the last months and weeks of his life (Balint, 1958; Bonomi, 1998; Dupont, 1988; Gay, 1988; Hoffer & Hoffer, 1999; Lorand, 1966, among others). As I continue to describe the last phase of Ferenczi's life I will not attempt to arrive at a definitive conclusion as to the validity of Jones's allegation, but rather I will seek to integrate the views of the various commentators, many of whom were Ferenczi's friends and contemporaries, into a coherent narrative that takes as much of the available evidence as possible into account.

Shortly after he made the diagnosis of pernicious anemia, Lajos Lévy, Ferenczi's friend and personal physician, initiated treatments with Campolon, the German trade name for an injectable liver extract, which improved Ferenczi's condition to the extent that he could resume his work (Lévy, 1998, p. 25). On 14 December, Ferenczi was able to report to Freud: "The anemia and its consequences have disappeared for the time being, the signs of fatigue, etc., are over, number and shape of the cellular blood components is normal again" (p. 445). The weeks and months that followed, however, saw a progressive worsening of the state of his health. On 29 March, Ferenczi writes:

> Perhaps you have heard from Dr. Lévy that, in the last few weeks, I experienced a relapse in the symptoms of my illness (anemia perniciosa)—but this time less in the worsening of the condition of my blood than in a kind of nervous breakdown, from which I am only slowly recovering.
>
> (p. 447)

Ferenczi's cursory, but candid, characterisation of his current physical and emotional state as a "nervous breakdown" lends some credence to Jones' assertion that Ferenczi's illness "exacerbated his latent psychotic trends" (Jones, 1957, p. 176), although it does not rise to the level of substantiating his allegation that Ferenczi harboured "delusions about Freud's supposed hostility" (p. 178) and that his last writings demonstrate that he "was insane during the last three years of his life" (Dupont, 1988, p. 250).

In a letter to Robert Waelder of 18 October 1958, Lévy gives the following assessment of Ferenczi's condition three months before his death:

> In spite of a nearly normal blood count, in the beginning of March [19]33 there appeared symptoms of a funicular myelopathy, which spread rapidly. Disturbances in walking, ataxia of the upper extremities, disturbances in vision, bladder and bowel incontinence set in, and very soon manifestations of relational and persecutory delusion, which then

also degenerated into aggressions against his wife ... As one who has seen quite a number of cases of pernicious anemia, I must explain that one can and may not view the psychically pronounced paranoid manifestations that one can quite often observe in severely anemic patients as a genuine paranoia. In the course of the Second World War and also afterwards, one could see patients with a laboratory result of pernicious anemia who presented with a hallucinatory psychosis or paranoid manifestations ... Such consequences of malnutrition and solitary confinement are today well known and should be sharply distinguished from a genuine paranoia. ... One can muster up much as characteristic for Ferenczi's psychic constitution, but nothing than could speak in favor of a paranoid disposition.

(Lévy, 1998 [1958], p. 25; my translation)

The foregoing is congruent with Balint's (1958, p. 68) and Hermann's (1974, p. 116) assessment of Ferenczi's condition, both of whom spoke with him during the last phase of his illness. Although, as in Balint's words, "despite his progressive physical weakness, mentally he was always clear" (1958, p. 68), it is evident that he suffered greatly and was subject to episodes of confusion and disorientation in his daily activities. In an interview with Kurt Eissler on 4 June 1952, Clara Thompson, who remained in analysis with Ferenczi during the last few months of his life, notes: "His mind was definitely affected ... He had combined sclerosis symptoms, I mean he staggered and was not sure of his walking" (in Brennan, 2015, p. 88). Brennan notes that "Thompson realized that Ferenczi was 'mentally disturbed' the morning he uncharacteristically showed up to her hour thirty minutes late", but that "[she]

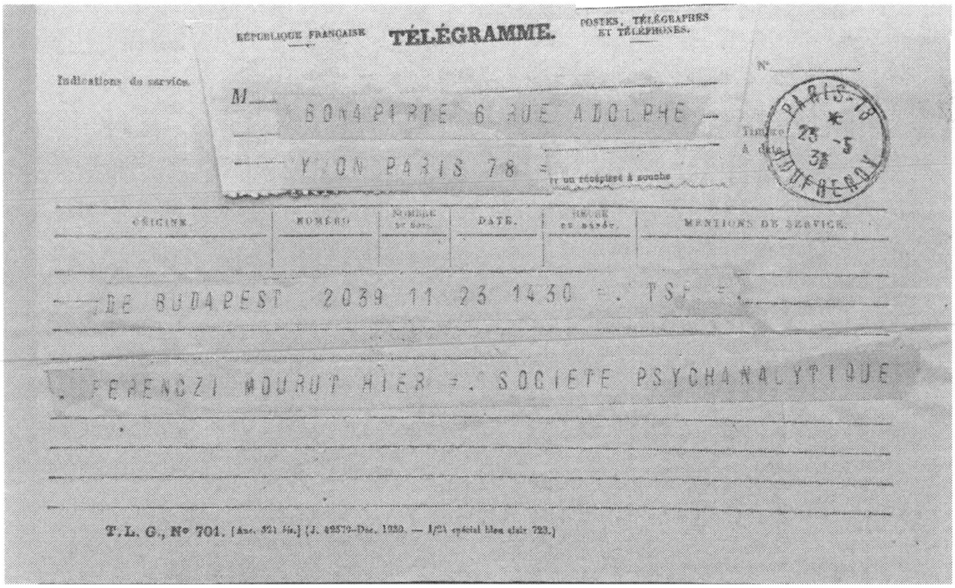
RÉPUBLIQUE FRANÇAISE TÉLÉGRAMME. POSTES, TÉLÉGRAPHES ET TÉLÉPHONES.

Indications de service. M BONAPARTE 6 RUE ADOLPHE — YVON PARIS 78 =

DE BUDAPEST 2039 11 23 1430 = . TSF =

FERENCZI MOURUT HIER = . SOCIETE PSYCHANALYTIQUE

T.L.G., N° 701.

Telegram from Hungarian psychoanalytic society to Marie Bonaparte, sent on May 23, 1933, now in the Library of Congress, Washington, DC

courtesy Hungarian psychoanalytic society

does not state that he was delusional or paranoid. Gizella, his wife, had also told Thompson that during his last illness he was often reading the newspaper upside down" (ibid.).

Ferenczi died suddenly of respiratory failure on 22 May 1933.

I would like to close this narrative with a general observation: although the intellectual and emotional tensions that had existed between Freud and Ferenczi to some degree during the entire course of their relationship reached their height in the personal and political turmoil that pervaded the analytic community shortly before the diagnosis of Ferenczi's fatal illness was made, the bond of friendship that continued between them until the end was never broken, thanks in large measure to Ferenczi's unstinting loyalty and devotion to and love for his revered analyst, mentor, colleague, and companion.

References

Balint, M. (1958). Sandor Ferenczi's last years. *International Journal of Psychoanalysis, 39*: 68.

Blum, H. (1994). The confusion of tongues and psychic trauma. *International Journal of Psychoanalysis, 71*: 871–882.

Bonomi, C. (1998). Jones's allegation of Ferenczi's mental deterioration: a reassessment. *International Forum of Psychoanalysis, 7*: 201–206.

Brennan, B. W. (2015) Out of the archive/unto the couch. In: *The Legacy of Sándor Ferenczi*. London: Routledge.

Dupont, J. (1988). Ferenczi's "madness". *Contemporary Psychoanalysis, 24*: 250–261.

Gay, P. (1988). *Freud: A Life for Our Time*. New York: Norton.

Hermann, I. (1974). Die Objektivität in Jones' Diagnose über Ferenczis Krankheit. *Jahrbuch der Psychoanalyse, 7*: 115–116.

Hoffer, A. 1991. The Freud-Ferenczi controversy—a living legacy. *International Review of Psychoanalysis, 18*: 465–472.

Hoffer, P. (2010). From elasticity to the confusion of tongues: A historical commentary on the technical dimension of the Freud/Ferenczi controversy. *Psychoanalytic Perspectives, 7*: 90–103.

Hoffer, P., & Hoffer, A. (1999). Ferenczi's fatal illness in historical context. *Journal of the American Psychoanalytic Association, 47*: 1259–1268.

Jones, E. (1957). *The Life and Work of Sigmund Freud, Vol. 3: The Last Phase 1919–1939*. New York: Basic Books.

Lévy, L. (1998) [1958]. Trois lettres sur la maladie de Sándor Ferenczi. *Le Coq-Héron, 149*: 23–26.

Lorand, S. (1966). Sándor Ferenczi 1873–1933. Pioneer of pioneers. In: F. Alexander, S. Eisenstein & M. Grotjahn, (Eds.), *Psychoanalytic Pioneers* (pp. 14–35). New York: Basic Books.

Masson, J. (1984). *The Assault on Truth: Freud's Suppression of the Seduction Theory*. New York: Farrar, Straus & Giroux.

Rachman, A. (1997). The suppression and censorship of Ferenczi's Confusion of Tongues paper. *Psychoanalytic Inquiry, 17*: 459–485.

Schröter, M. (Ed.) (2004). *Sigmund Freud, Max Eitingon: Briefwechsel,* Vol. 2. Tübingen: Edition diskord.

Part II

Clinical

Introduction

The clinical section of this book is, naturally, its centrepiece. Although psychoanalysts may contribute to our understanding of developmental issues, or apply their findings to phenomena that are usually the focus of other disciplines, and Ferenczi was indeed active on both of these fronts, clinical problems preoccupy most psychoanalysts who are trying, day in and day out, to help people overcome emotional constraints or mental disorders. And it is precisely the originality of Ferenczi's clinical contributions that makes him still relevant and that has made him, as we saw in the previous section, controversial and, one might say, revolutionary. He understood psychopathology in a unique way and introduced new forms of psychoanalytic treatment.

We believe that all Ferenczi's most important clinical contributions are charted in the nine chapters of this section. As editors, we were very happy to receive contributions from leading scholars in the field, all of whom have devoted decades to studying Ferenczi's work and testing it in their clinical practices, and are renowned for their contributions to the topics they have kindly summarised for this collection.

The section opens with an overview of Ferenczi's trauma theory, written by Judit Mészáros, which adequately positions Ferenczi as the originator of a psychoanalytic model substantially different from Freud's. Close reading of Ferenczi's late papers and manuscripts, those written after 1928, enables Mészáros to portray her compatriot's work as the source of a range of contemporary theories and treatments of trauma-related disorders.

One of these original contributions, introduced by Ferenczi in 1929, was the notion of the suffering of "unwelcome children", those who, most probably like the author himself, are neither wished for nor eagerly awaited by caring and emotionally available parents. In his chapter on the topic, Jose Jiménez Avello reviews Ferenczi's *cri de cœur* to parents (maybe also to psychoanalysts) that children without the experience of being loved grow up to be uncreative, feeble, prone to illness and mental disorders; or, in other words, that actual interpersonal relationships are just as important as the inner unconscious constellations. Making his contribution even richer, Avello provides inspiring clinical material.

Another of Ferenczi's central concepts is discussed by Luis Martín Cabré: the "wise baby" phenomenon. Traumatised children, Ferenczi was led to believe both by his clinical experience and his self-analysis, may develop an uncanny capacity for understanding others' mental states, alongside a splitting off, or "amputation", of their own emotional life. This idea is further connected to Ferenczian notions of "traumatic progression" and "Orpha", as well as his own suffering following what he experienced as Freud's cold rejection.

The heart of the matter may be the mechanism of identification with the aggressor. Jay Frankel succinctly weaves together almost all of Ferenczi's basic innovations (such as "terrorism of suffering", hypocrisy in families and in psychoanalysis as a profession) to focus on what may be the most basic element of all: "the child must introject the aggressor—create an internal model with which she can identify, to know his feelings and intentions from the inside"; Frankel then reviews the behavioural, mental, and moral dimensions of identification with the aggressor.

Thierry Bokanowski turns to the concepts, widely used these days, of splitting and dissociation. These mechanisms were first elaborated by Pierre Janet at the end of the nineteenth century and then, in the early 1930s, integrated by Ferenczi with the Freudian conception of infantile sexuality. The chapter is additionally valuable because it offers a close reading of some of the *Clinical Diary*'s incompletely explored treasures.

In a similar vein, the next chapter, by Elizabeth Howell, addresses the concept of regression and its relation to dissociation. Howell explains how Ferenczi enabled his patients to make contact with their dissociated states, which, once re-experienced, became possible to analyse and integrate into the self.

With Endre Koritar we move to the other group of clinical papers, those focused on therapeutic action. "Diagnosed" by Freud as suffering from *furor sanandi*—the rage to cure—Ferenczi certainly spent a lot of time trying not only to understand how psychoanalysis helps patients, but also to improve its effectiveness. This chapter reviews many of Ferenczi's papers in order to explicate his clinical experiments and innovations.

Anthony Bass focuses on what may be one of Ferenczi's most widely recognised contributions to contemporary psychoanalysis, that of mutuality or, as it is also known, two-person psychology. It was highly controversial in Ferenczi's day to bring the "dialogue of the unconsciouses" between patient and analyst into the explicit communication between patient and analyst. In this chapter we get not only a review of theory about the ubiquitous mutual psychological influence between patient and analyst, but also a very telling example from the author's clinical practice.

Directly connected to this, the last chapter in this section, by Irwin Hirsch, addresses countertransference. In his writings, Ferenczi emphasised that treatments cannot progress without the analyst's awareness of his/her resistances toward a patient and communicating those openly and honestly. These ideas, which predated Winnicott, Heimann, and the early interpersonal explorations in this area, are the foundation of all interpersonal/relational approaches in psychoanalysis.

The nine chapters of the clinical part thus tell the elaborate story of Ferenczi the clinician, famous for being the great early clinical pioneer of psychoanalysis and, at the same time, controversial for his originality and the level of his devotion to his patients—Ferenczi, we dare say, whose clinical lead is now followed by more psychoanalysts than even Freud's, and whose intuitions have been distilled and transformed into guidelines for the students of today.

Chapter 16

Ferenczi's paradigm shift in trauma theory

Judit Mészáros

Freud's trauma theories

Freud developed three trauma theories between 1895 and 1917.

The first was the seduction theory. He writes in the "Aetiology of hysteria" that "at the bottom of every case of hysteria there are *one or more occurrences of premature sexual experience*" (Freud, 1896c, p. 203, italics in original). Every neurotic is damaged and the fundamental damage is in the domain of sexuality. Early infantile sexual traumas are driven out of consciousness/memory as a result of repression, and become unconscious.

Freud soon revised that theory. His patients' memories of sexual abuse seemed improbably frequent. In his second theory he then saw his patients' traumas as caused by pathological fantasies of what had happened to them. It was not even necessary, he thought, for real external events to be in the background.

Finally, Freud introduced the so-called economic model. In this third theory he paid attention to frustration. Trauma can be caused by the lack of satisfaction. Freud also added to this his concept of the helpless ego: one becomes neurotic when one somehow loses the ability to regulate the libido. The individual becomes helpless because she is left alone or is overstimulated (Freud, 1916–1917).

Towards a new trauma paradigm

Ferenczi's research into the mechanisms of trauma stood at the centre of his clinical-theoretical work during the final years of his life. Relying upon both his clinical observations and his self-reflective capacity, Ferenczi developed new perspectives on trauma that were radical and profound enough to be deservedly called a *paradigm shift* in trauma theory (Mészáros, 2004) and attracted a lot of attention (Bonomi, 2004; Borgogno, 2007; Dupont, 1998; Frankel, 1998; Mészáros, 2010; Vida, 2005).

Before a more detailed discussion of the elements of Ferenczi's new trauma construction, the heart of this paradigm shift can be stated succinctly. While returning to Freud's first trauma theory by asserting that it was *not* pathological fantasies but external reality, *real events*, that cause trauma, he understood the core traumatising element of these events in a completely new way—it was not only the sexual trauma itself but *hypocrisy*: the very people upon whom the abused child is most dependent, and to whom she turns for comfort and understanding after the assault, who emotionally abandon her by lying about what was done to her.

The reality of trauma and the pathogenic role of adults' hypocrisy

Ferenczi saw trauma as a real event. It is not fantasy that masquerades as real events; it is not fantasy that causes trauma. Decades earlier, Freud had asked how there could be such a major divergence between the events of childhood and the later memories of adults. Ferenczi ultimately rejected the premise of that question, proposing instead that the real question was about people's failure to remember trauma, or their compulsion to doubt the truth of their traumatic memories.

Ferenczi's answer focused on what he saw as hypocrisy by parents/teachers/adults in regard to the abuse: "Almost always the perpetrator behaves as though nothing had happened", and the molested child's attempts to gain comfort and understanding from the second parent "are refused by her as nonsensical" (Conf, pp. 162–163). It is this emotional abandonment that causes her to abandon her own authentic experience, resulting in lasting damage to her personality: she doubts her own perceptions, withdraws from reality, splits off of her experience, her personality is fragmented, and she identifies with the aggressor. In all these ways, the child's subjective experience is enduringly altered (Bokanowski, Chapter Twenty, Frankel, Chapter Nineteen).

Therapeutic implications of Ferenczi's understanding of pathogenesis

The therapeutic implications of adults' hypocrisy are profound, and quite different from the interpretive approach suggested by Freud's theory of traumatic memories as fantasies. The analyst must accept the patient's subjective truth, not question whether it is "right" or "wrong", "true" or "false". In this way, the analyst accepts the patient's subjective experience as the parents, traumatically, had not. The patient's experience is not denied, and the patient is not left alone with it; rather, she is emotionally accompanied. Michael Balint (1968), following up on Ferenczi's ideas, suggested that interpretation was experienced by such patients as a kind of "interference, cruelty, unwarranted demand or unfair impingement, as a hostile act …" (p. 175)—in other words, as the opposite of the emotional accompaniment that the patient needs.

Further, patients who have suffered from parental hypocrisy are likely to be very sensitive to even subtle dishonesty or "*professional hypocrisy*" (Conf p. 158, italics in original) in their analysts. "I cannot see any other way out than to make the source of the disturbance in us fully conscious and to discuss it with the patient, admitting it perhaps not only as a possibility but as a fact" (p. 159), Ferenczi says. "The analyst must be an authority that for the first time admits its faults, especially hypocrisy" (Diary, p. 120). His experience had taught him that such "frank discussion freed, so to speak, the tongue-tied patient … produced confidence in his patient" (Conf, p. 159)—opposite to the effect of professional hypocrisy, which repeats patients' early trauma and retraumatises them. "The setting free of [the patient's] critical feelings, the willingness on our part to admit our mistakes and the honest endeavour to avoid them in future, all these go to create in the patient a confidence in the analyst. *It is this confidence that establishes the contrast between the present and the unbearable traumatogenic past* … the past no longer as hallucinatory reproduction but as objective memory" (p. 160, italics in original). Interpretation—focusing on patients' fantasies at such moments of crisis—is likely to be felt by patients as self-serving defensiveness by the analyst.

Closely related to the issue of hypocrisy, Ferenczi's early study "Psycho-analysis and education" (1908) discusses the pathogenic effect on children of the behaviour of adults who invest themselves with the myth of infallibility, and notes the frequent occurrence of this phenomenon in a wider context of superordinate–subordinate social relations.

Lastly, Ferenczi understood that healing traumatic experience required repeating the experience of trauma—which he understood to be inevitable in the analytic situation (Conf, p. 159)—though under more favourable conditions. In *The Development of Psycho-Analysis* (1925), Ferenczi and Rank placed *experience* (*Erlebnis*) at the core of psychoanalytic therapy. This echoes Ferenczi's notion of "subjective truth" from his earliest work, "Spiritism", published in 1899 (Cassullo, Chapter Three). Ferenczi and Rank realised that the effectiveness of psychoanalytic treatment was not achieved by remembering and an intellectual focus on interpretation within a context of an emotionally one-way, transference-based communication, but by re-living traumatic experiences and subsequently working them through on an emotional level. The necessity of creating a two-way relationship characterised by authentic communication, honesty of the analyst, and a consequent mutual trust and confidence (Elast; Hoffer, 1996) had emerged—see also Ferenczi's (1919) earlier suggestion of integrating countertransference into the healing process (Hirsch, Chapter Twenty-four).

Trauma in the light of interpersonal–intrapsychic dimensions

Ferenczi understood traumatic experience to take place within an interpersonal and intrapsychic sequence of processes, opening a new perspective that pushed understanding the process of traumatisation into the sphere of object relations—both actual intersubjective relations and their internalisation by the child. This sequence starts with the early mother-infant/child, and hypothetically even before it, in the prenatal relationship, as can be found in Ferenczi's paper "The unwelcome child and his death instinct" (Jiménez Avello, Chapter Seventeen). "Children who are received in a harsh and unloving way die easily and willingly" (Unwel, p. 105). A patient of mine, whose childhood could be described in such terms, said that "the best child is a dead child"—it would have been better if she had not been born, or if she at least had not been a girl. Her response to her mother's wish was that she become seriously ill, develop a boyish identity, and have an accident so that she too could enter the realm of those worthy of love. Similar phenomena can be observed in cases of depression, psychosomatic disorders, and replacement children. According to Ferenczi, the baby reacts to the mother's conscious and unconscious wishes, especially her lack of love and acceptance, by developing symptoms or disturbances in development. Ferenczi's proposal was the earliest statement of what has become the "dominant biosocial view of emotional development [which] holds that mother and infant form an affective communication system from the beginning of life" (Gergely & Watson, 1996, pp. 1186–1187).

Ferenczi's ideas about the central role of the infant's emotional helplessness can be seen to clearly resonate with Freud's ideas of helplessness/lonely ego from his third trauma theory.

Ferenczi described the ego-defence mechanisms (though this term was yet to be coined) with which children/victims cope with an assault and its aftermath; and the very different defences used by perpetrators. Ferenczi described the child facing an attack as simply wanting tenderness, as being unsuspecting when the assault comes, and defenceless and paralysed during it (Frag, pp. 239–240, 253). She tries to protect herself, during and after the assault, through splitting, dissociation, and fragmentation, as well as identification with the aggressor. All of these help to understand how vulnerable humans protect themselves from unbearable pain in a traumatic situation. While Ferenczi writes about fragmentation and splitting as "psychic advantages" for surviving the trauma (Diary, p. 38), these and the other defences carry great costs for the integrity and functioning of the personality in survivors.

In one case, for example, a young girl had, for years, been sexually abused by her uncle. As an adult in analytic psychotherapy, when she was finally able to bring herself to face what had happened, one image came to her mind. She was lying on a bed, her uncle on top of her, playing with the medal hanging from his neck, batting it back and forth, back and forth ... This phenomenon has been described as the experience that facilitates survival: that of "watching a film" in a traumatic situation; the dissociative trance serves as a survival strategy. Emotionally she is not there, what is going on is not happening to her: "A body progressively divested of its soul, whose disintegration is not perceived at all or is regarded as an event happening to another person, being watched from the outside" (Diary, p. 9).

When Ferenczi describes defences on the aggressor's side, he opens a new window to understanding how they can reject their responsibilities while avoiding intrapsychic conflict after their actions. He offers vivid descriptions of the aggressor's defences after the assault: "Father having seduced her [R.N., i.e., Elizabeth Severn] ... punishes and reviles her" (Diary, p. 119), or "the perpetrator behaves as though nothing had happened" (Conf, pp. 162–163). It is not difficult to recognise denial (nothing has happened), projection (the aggression was only a reaction to a provocation by the victim), or minimisation and dehumanisation ("Oh, it is only a child, he does not know anything") (p. 163) as defence mechanisms widely used by perpetrators of child abuse and of other kinds of trauma.

Identification with the aggressor

Ferenczi's concept of identification with the aggressor, coined in 1932 (Frankel, Chapter Nineteen), has a central place in his theory of how children cope with sexual abuse and violence, but it goes beyond this—it helps explain, more generally, how people emotionally survive defencelessness in the face of a variety of aggressions or long-term captivity.[1] Identification with the aggressor involves losing one's own perceptions and desires, and rather than rebelling against the aggressor, becoming the object the aggressor requires. Ferenczi emphasised that this mechanism allows the child to be able to maintain the illusion of being loved. But this brings about a paradoxical situation: it ensures survival, but at the price of perpetuating the traumatic situation. This phenomenon became well-known as the Stockholm syndrome.[2] The aim of this unconscious process is to tame the aggressor. This ego-defence mechanism is a general capacity of human beings, seen also in moral agreement with the aim of the perpetrators at an individual or societal level with regard to authoritarian/dictatorial figures/leaders (Casoni & Brunet, 2007; Šebek, 1996).

1 Anna Freud adopted this concept and discussed it in her monograph on ego-defence mechanisms (1936). Dupont makes a distinction between Ferenczi's and Anna Freud's identification with the aggressor by pointing out that Anna Freud, in contrast to Ferenczi, talked about children "who anticipate a dreaded aggression ... preventively becoming aggressors themselves"; or that it "implies minor or fantasized aggression" rather than, as for Ferenczi, real danger (Dupont, 1998, p. 236).

2 It was named when bank employees in Stockholm were held hostage during a robbery in 1973, and the victims developed positive feelings, even love, toward their captors.

Ferenczi emphasised one aspect of identification with the aggressor as particularly damaging to the child: the "introjection of the guilt feelings of adult" (Conf, p. 162)—which results in a persisting feeling of "badness" (Frankel, 2015), low self-esteem, and shame in children (and in victims in a wider sense). The child introjects the guilt, and also the fear and anxiety, of the perpetrators, which are then experienced as her own feelings.

Ferenczi also noted another kind of child abuse, which he named "terrorism of suffering" (Conf, p. 166). When weak parents use their children for purposes of regulating themselves, "children have the compulsion to put to rights all disorders in the family ... in order to be able to enjoy again the lost rest and the care and attention accompanying it. A mother complaining of her constant miseries can create a nurse for life out of her child ... neglecting the true interest of the child" (ibid.). Here the child identifies herself with the adult's needs.[3] As Ferenczi observed: "I identify myself (to understand everything = to forgive everything), I cannot hate" (Diary, p. 170). The "*Posttraumatic effect*: identifications (superegos) instead of one's own life" (p. 171). Ferenczi thus expanded the understanding of the process of identification to extend beyond sexual abuse or other flagrant assault.

Dread and desire—"pleasure principle" in trauma

A special burden for victims of sexual abuse is that they not only suffer but may also experience some form of satisfaction—a pleasure that goes beyond successfully mollifying the aggressor, maintaining the system of necessary family relations, or restoring the previous situation of tenderness (Conf, p. 162). These, of course, are essential aims of identification with the aggressor in families or other small, tightknit groups like schools, sports teams, or religious communities. Fear and pleasure, or, as I have called it, "dread and desire" (Mészáros, 2014a, p. 213), can run together. The shadowy side of this Janus-faced phenomenon is that the pleasure leaves the door open for the child to seek repetition of her abuse. In clinical work, the psychotherapist has to take into account the patient's strong feeling of shame or guilt due to the pleasure they felt during their abuse, and their resistance to facing their unconscious ambivalence about their traumatic experience.

Post-traumatic conditions that facilitate healing

For Ferenczi the presence, or lack, of a trusted person in the post-traumatic situation, to whom the victim can turn, is key in determining the later fate of the traumatised individual. This holds true not only for children, but also for someone who meets trauma later in life. Permanent personality damage from the trauma is far less likely if, following the trauma itself, the victim has an opportunity to tell what happened, and have the other accept the traumatised person's experience. Solidarity, emotional and intellectual aid from a trusted person or people, all provide a chance to process, symbolise, and integrate the traumatic experience, rather than dissociate it, along with aspects of one's aliveness. In the immediate moment, such help can facilitate the rapid decrease of anxiety, guilt, shame, and feelings of helplessness and defencelessness. In the presence of a trusted and empathic other, trauma

3 This happened en masse to children of Holocaust survivors. Wardi (1992) writes that survivor-parents often designated certain children as "memorial candles" to fill an emotional void. Many children identified with the unconscious wish of the parents, giving up the development of their own selves.

sufferers are not further traumatised by isolation. The traumatic event does not become a secret and then a taboo, and the process of transgenerational trauma is not initiated. Talking to the trusted person and sharing the traumatic experience represent the first, important step in working through the trauma.

"Traumatic progression" and the "wise baby" syndrome

Ferenczi was the first to call attention to children who show different behaviour as an outcome of trauma, comparing them with others who do not. "One is justified – as opposed to the familiar regression [in response to trauma] – to speak of a traumatic progression, of a precocious maturity ... Not only emotionally but also intellectually, can the trauma bring to maturity a part of the person" (Conf, pp. 164–165). Ferenczi called this the "wise baby" syndrome (Martín Cabré, Chapter Eighteen).

Environmental help in coping with trauma

Notably, Ferenczi's discovery of an environmental factor that is crucial in enabling a child to cope with trauma (Mészáros, 2014b)—the opportunity to turn to a trusted person and have one's experience heard and accepted—has received subsequent systematic empirical confirmation (Dimitrijević, Chapter Forty-one). Resilience studies have underlined that competent parenting and warm relationships with at least one primary caregiver are key positive factors developing resilience in children (Fonagy et al., 1994). These factors allow one to maintain one's integrity, to facilitate psychic resources needed for survival, and "even to extract some amount of human warmth and loving kindness in the direst of circumstances" (Apfel and Simon, 1996, p. 9). Ferenczi, Balint, and Winnicott, who emphasised the importance of quality in the early mother–infant relationship, would not have been surprised at this result.

The chapters that follow in this part of the book will elaborate these elements of Ferenczi's conception of the child's response to trauma.

References

Apfel, R. J., & Simon, B. (1996). Introduction. In: R. Apfel & B. Simon (Eds.), *Minefields in their Hearts. The Mental Health of Children in War and Communal Violence* (pp. 1–17). New Haven, CT: Yale University Press.

Balint, M. (1968). *The Basic Fault: Therapeutic Aspects of Regression*. Hove: Routledge, 1986.

Bonomi, C. (2004). Trauma and the symbolic function of the mind. *International Forum of Psychoanalysis, 13*: 45–50.

Borgogno, F. (2007). Ferenczi's clinical and theoretical conception of trauma: A brief introduction. *American Journal of Psychoanalysis, 67*: 141–149.

Casoni, D., & Brunet, L. (2007). The psychodynamics that lead to violence: Part 2: The case of "ordinary" people involved in mass violence. *Canadian Journal of Psychoanalysis, 15*: 261–280.

Dupont, J. (1998). The concept of trauma according to Ferenczi and its effects on subsequent psychoanalytical research. *International Forum of Psychoanalysis, 7*: 235–240.

Ferenczi, S. (1908). Psycho-analysis and education. In: M. Balint (Ed.), *Final Contributions to the Problems and Methods of Psycho-analysis* (pp. 280–290). London: Karnac, 1994.

Ferenczi, S. (1919). On the technique of psycho-analysis. In: M. Balint (Ed.), *Further Contributions to the Theory and Technique of Psycho-Analysis* (pp. 177–189). London: Maresfield Reprints, 1980.

Ferenczi, S., & Rank, O. (1925). *The Development of Psycho-Analysis*. Madison, CT: International Universities Press, 1986.

Fonagy, P., Steele, M., Steele, H., Higgitt, A., & Target, M. (1994). The Emanuel Miller Memorial Lecture 1992. The theory and practice of resilience. *Journal of Child Psychology and Psychiatry, 35*: 231–257.

Frankel, J. B. (1998). Ferenczi's trauma theory. *American Journal of Psychoanalysis, 58*: 41–61.

Frankel, J. B. (2015). The persistent sense of being bad: The moral dimension of identification with the aggressor. In: A. Harris & S. Kuchuck (Eds.), *The Legacy of Sándor Ferenczi* (pp. 205–222). London, New York: Routledge.

Freud, A. (1936). *The Ego and the Mechanisms of Defence.* London: Karnac, 1993.

Freud, S. (1896c). The aetiology of hysteria. *S. E., 3*: 187–221. London: Hogarth.

Freud, S. (1916–1917). *Introductory Lectures on Psycho-Analysis. S. E., 15–16.* London: Hogarth.

Gergely, G., & Watson, J. S. (1996). The Social Biofeedback Theory of Parental Affect-Mirroring. *International Journal of Psychoanalysis, 77*: 1181–1212.

Hoffer, A. (1996). Asymmetry and mutuality in the analytic relationship: contemporary lessons from the Freud–Ferenczi dialogue. In: P. L. Rudnytsky, A. Bókay & P. Giampieri-Deutsch (Eds.), *Ferenczi's Turn in Psychoanalysis* (pp. 107–119). New York: New York University Press.

Mészáros, J. (2004). Psychoanalysis is a two-way street. *International Forum of Psychoanalysis, 13*: 105–113.

Mészáros, J. (2010). Building blocks toward contemporary trauma theory: Ferenczi's paradigm shift. *American Journal of Psychoanalysis, 70*: 328–340.

Mészáros, J. (2014a). *Ferenczi and Beyond: Exile of the Budapest School and Solidarity in the Psychoanalytic Movement during the Nazi Years*. London: Karnac.

Mészáros, J. (2014b). Ferenczi's "wise baby" phenomenon and resilience. *International Forum of Psychoanalysis, 23*: 3–10.

Šebek, M. (1996). The fate of the totalitarian object. *International Forum of Psychoanalysis, 5*: 289–294.

Vida, J. E. (2005). Treating the "wise baby". *The American Journal of Psychoanalysis, 65:* 3–12.

Wardi, D. (1992). *Memorial Candles: Children of the Holocaust.* London, New York: Tavistock-Routledge.

Chapter 17

Ferenczi's concept of "the unwelcome child"

José Jiménez Avello

The unwelcome child

A terminological reflection, arising from the Spanish translation ("El niño mal recibido"), comes to my mind about the existing standard translations for "Das Unwillkommenne Kind". Ferenczi's notion seems to have more to do with the Spanish verb "acoger", to take in, with its connotations of taking care of, as Ferenczi is not focusing just on the initial moment of the "reception", but his idea encompasses from that point to some (undefined) later moment. Standard translations in Portuguese, French, and to some extent the English one ("criança indesejada", "l'enfant mal accueilli", "unwelcome child") put the effective starting point neatly at the moment of birth (disregarding "bad previous expectations" often implied by them). In contrast, the semantic field of the Spanish "acoger" or the English "take in" and other non-standard equivalents in other languages do include that reception (birth) moment plus a later period, as we can see in the expressions "casa (o centro) de acogida" or "shelter/foster house", which are places where the, let's say, orphan child is not just "received" but also cared for and educated afterwards. In fact, among the standard translations known by me, and even adding to them the German original, I think that only the Italian translation ("mal accolto") would take up fully the notion, more encompassing, that underlies Ferenczi's thinking. Because it certainly may happen that the initial reception is good, but later circumstances such as the death of someone significant, financial hardships, etc., eventually turn it into a bad acceptance or "taking in".

The unwelcome child and his death instinct

"The unwelcome child and his death instinct", in fact, deals with patients who came into the world as "unwelcome guests of the family":

> [Who] had observed the conscious and unconscious signs of the aversion or impatience of the mother, and ... their desire to live had been broken by this. In later life relatively slight occasions were then sufficient motivation for a desire to die, even if this was resisted by a strong effort of will. … One could also note ill-disguised longing for (passive) tenderness, repugnance to work, incapacity for prolonged effort, and thus a certain degree of emotional forced character-strengthening.
>
> (Unwel, pp. 126–127)

A few lines later, we come to the core hypothesis of the paper, which really is an astonishing anticipation of Spitz's research on children's early institutionalisation and the development of "anaclitic depression" (1945):

> I only wish to point to the probability that children who are received in a harsh and disagreeable way die easily and willingly. Either they use one of the many proffered organic possibilities for a quick exit, or if they escape this fate, they keep a streak of pessimism and of aversion to life.
>
> (Unwel, p. 127)

Lastly, Ferenczi concludes his short paper with an observation regarding the treatment of this kind of patient:

> I found myself gradually compelled ... to relax my demands for active efforts ... as the treatment went on. Finally, a situation became apparent which could only be described as one in which the patient had to be allowed for a time to have his way like a child, not unlike the 'pre-treatment' which Anna Freud considers necessary in the case of real children. Through this indulgence the patient is permitted, properly speaking for the first time, to enjoy the irresponsibility of childhood, which is equivalent to the introduction of positive life-impulses and motives for his subsequent existence. Only later can one proceed cautiously to those demands for privation which characterize our analyses generally. However, such an analysis must of course end ... with adaptation to a reality full of frustrations, but supplemented, one hopes, by the ability to enjoy good fortune where it is really granted.
>
> (Unwel, pp. 128–129)

I find it a wise choice on the part of the editors that the heading of this chapter only includes the first part of the title of Ferenczi's paper, as after this paper the problem of the unwelcome child is not going to remain bound any more in his thinking to the death instinct, nor does the introduction of the second drives theory appear to concern him much. The unwelcome child as a driving force/idea in Ferenczi's whole work shows up as an embryo already in 1908, when he is just a newcomer to psychoanalysis, in "Psycho-analysis and education", resurfaces again in 1913, in "Stages in the development of the sense of reality", and eventually hatches in Ferenczi's last works, such as "The adaptation of the family to the child" and the *Diary*.

The 1929 paper constitutes the hinge between Ferenczi taking into account the notion of the death instinct and his later work, in which he basically ignores it. Even the title is already foreshadowing the imminence of his neglecting of the death instinct, as the emphasis is put on the quality of that "welcoming". Should it be deficient, without "counter-pressure" (Diary, p. 127), then the death instinct comes to the forefront; if, on the contrary, the child is (and remains) truly welcome, love will prevail. Oddly, the death instinct is only named as such at the beginning, but then Ferenczi focuses on the child's desire to die. He finds this concept useful to reflect on the epileptic seizure, which he views as an instinctual defusion, and about cases in his clinical practice as an army physician where this desire to die appeared as a consequence of the patient being an unwelcome guest of the family. Additionally, cases of alcoholism, the tendency to cosmogonic speculations, certain thermoregulation disorders, and, in general, any pathology in the infantile development of the ability to live are linked by him with the patients' condition of having been unwelcome guests.

Avoiding a frontal clash with Freud by means of presenting these cases as if they were different ones, he asserts that "in all our cases the innateness of the sickly tendency is [simulated][1] and not genuine, owing to the early incident of the trauma" (Unwel, p. 128).

The unwelcome child after (or without) his death instinct

A year after this paper Ferenczi starts his dated annotations, written between 1930–1932 and for the most part collected in "Notes and fragments" and *The Clinical Diary*. In the very first date of the preserved annotations (10 August 1930) he wonders: "(death instinct?)". And answers himself: "It would be better to choose a word that would express the absolute passivity of this process" (Frag, p. 220). A few days later (24 August 1930) he would dethrone the death instinct, promoting instead "the instinct of tranquillity" to the status of "principal instinct, to which the life (egotistic) and death (altruistic) instincts are subjected" (Frag, p. 225).

That way, just by using two parentheses, Freudian theory on instincts gets superseded by an alternative dualism that thinks in terms of egoistic and altruistic instincts, both striving to achieve "tranquillity". Ferenczi will also call the former ones "drives for self-assertion", and the later, "drives for conciliation" (Diary, p. 41).

Building on the newest aspects of this reformulation—the drives for conciliation and their preponderance over the self-assertion ones—Ferenczi will start to fit together, metapsychologically, his own trauma theory, his own explication about the obnoxious consequences of a bad welcoming for the child, so deep and destructive as to get easily confused with an "innateness tendency" (which they are, in Freud's thinking).

This primacy of the drives for conciliation occurs naturally in the newborn. Ferenczi appeals to the developmental stages of the sense of reality as described in 1913, but extends them by adding a new one: the neonatal. He introduces it with these words (Diary, pp. 147–148): "The hallucinatory period, therefore, is preceded by a purely mimetic period", which is nothing but a re-assessment of the notion of primary identification: "identification as a stage preceding object relation", in one "psychic process the importance of which has perhaps been insufficiently appreciated, even by Freud himself."

And what perhaps was not appreciated enough by Freud is the malleability of the psyche in this stage. The most characteristic term Ferenczi will use to allude to this "semifluid" (Diary, p. 176) or "half-dissolved" state (p. 81), is "mimicry" (p. 150), as in the "protective mimicry" shown by certain species, such as the chameleon's changes in colour in order to blend into its surroundings, protecting itself from the environment by becoming diluted, "conciliated" with it.

During this "purely mimetic period", the "self-assertive" tendencies are very weak, according to Ferenczi. An excessive pressure opposing its fulfilment will make the pleasure principle tilt and procure such fulfilment through this "protective mimicry": "mimicry

1 The Karnac edition contains an error that alters the meaning of the paragraph. The translation reads "deceptive" where it should read "simulated". French and Spanish editions carry over the mistake when they talk respectively about "simulé" and "simulado" (personal communication from Judith Dupont).

reaction [..] is more primary than the self-assertive or self-important reaction [..] (more childish)" (Diary, p. 150).

The child needs "counterlove": "Without such a counter-pressure, let us say, counterlove, the individual tends to explode, to dissolve itself in the universe, perhaps to die" (Diary, p. 129). If the acceptance of the child is amorous, if it does not run against the tendency to self-assertion, it will support the crystallisation, as it were, of this "semifluid" psyche: the individuation.

On the contrary, facing an unwelcoming environment, "the unpleasure also comes to an end at last, though not by changing the external world but by.. an immediate resignation and adaptation of the self to the environment" (Diary, p. 148).

This surrendering of the self to the environment enables the profound pathogenic presence of the aggressor adult within the assaulted subject: "Adults forcibly inject their will, particularly psychic contents of an unpleasable nature, into de childish personality. These split-off, alien transplants vegetate in the other person during the whole of life" (Diary, p. 81).

The expression "alien transplants" evokes grafts coming from some other plant and becoming a part of the new one. The sharpness of the differentiating barrier between the subject and the other gets lost. The (Freudian) confusion between what stems from the outside and what is constitutional finds a possible explanation here.

These mechanisms, as conceived by Ferenczi, are the concretion of a class of defences that he calls autoplastic, that is, those seeking to change the subject herself, in contrast with the alloplastic ones, which seek to influence the external world. Among these autoplastic defences, we should also include what he first called "autotomy", which is the ability of some animals to lose a part of the body in order to save themselves, that is, the lizard losing its trapped tail. Later, he will translate these ideas into strictly psychological terms: "fragmentation", "narcissistic self-splitting", etc.[2] This is one of the great contributions of Ferenczi to the trauma theory and to metapsychology in general: cleavage, the splitting in fragments when someone undergoes a traumatic situation.

"Drives for conciliation", "purely mimetic period", "mimicry", "alien transplants", "autotomy," etc., are the notions Ferenczi introduces in order to explain the damage produced by a bad reception, without having to invoke any "mystical" death instinct. I will add to that list his deep examination of the notion of "passion".

The term is abundantly used in his late writings without further detail, but for what seems like a brief, almost cryptic allusion to Descartes in the final appendix to "Confusion of tongues between adults and the child". But such an allusion is related to an annotation prior to the September 1932 Wiesbaden lecture at which Ferenczi presented the draft for "Confusion of tongues" with the title "The Passion of adults and their influence of the sexual and character development of children" (Diary, p. 150). The annotation is dated about two months earlier, with a title that is virtually identical: "Projection of our own passions or passionate tendencies onto children" (p. 155).

The day of that annotation, Ferenczi looked up several items in the *Encyclopaedia Britannica* (Passion, Cartesianism) and read about Descartes' *Treatise on Passions*.

If I use a Spanish dictionary (RAE, 2014) in trying to replicate Ferenczi's search in the *Encyclopaedia*, under the entry for Passion I would pick these two meanings: "1. The action

2 For reference and further description of all those concepts see Bokanowski, Chapter Twenty and Martín Cabré, Chapter Eighteen.

of suffering/enduring" and "7. Vehement appetite or inclination towards something". Both of them match quite well Ferenczi's idea, especially in regards to the "vehement" nature of these inclinations as opposed to the "tender" ones. From the *Encyclopaedia*, Ferenczi quotes that: "The modern use generally restricts the term to strong and uncontrolled emotions" (Diary, p. 150). Weaving together both sources, we may have it that passions refer to a suffering because of vehement, strong, and uncontrolled, appetites and inclinations.

For the rationalistic thinker, passion never originates from within the soul (in the constitution, we could say), but is introduced in the *res cogitans* as a consequence of man being at the same time *res extensa*. It would be a response of the *res cogitans* to the suffering of the body—caused in turn by the "depraving" environment, in the Ferenczian view.

If Descartes credited the pineal gland with being the pivot point between the soul and the world, we can think with Ferenczi that the Freudian theory leads to a confusion between what is a "passion" inserted in the subject's pineal gland by the world's events, and an alleged death instinct emanating from the "soul", from the *res cogitans*.

In previous works (e.g., Jiménez Avello, 1998) I have called this auto-destructive imprint that the victim receives from his aggressor, "death passion". This is a term that I find useful in order to draw a contrast with the Freudian notion of death instinct. I understand it as the inoculation in the child, in the manner of an "alien transplant", of a deep imprint of suffering that disrupts his vital balance to an extent so vast as to easily be confused with something else that seems to arise from the constitution.

Thus, even if in 1929 Ferenczi's own words were "The unwelcome child and his death instinct", his later contributions may lead us to think rather of "the unwelcome child and his death passion".

An unwelcome child

Eloísa "being beside herself"

Some aspects from the treatment of Eloísa, known by me in my role as supervisor, may help us to articulate at the clinical level these Ferenczian neo-concepts. Eloísa is little more than thirteen years old when she comes in for consultation, accompanied by her mother, because of increasingly serious academic blocks and a psychological unrest that is also growing more intense.

The hardships she and her mother have lived through are prominent in her ideation. They are the only two members of a family in which the father has been absent for several years, since the mother decided to escape from an unhappy economic and marital situation and emigrated with the child.

As an immigrant in Spain, the mother has been through every kind of deprivation and effort, resulting in meagre returns: many hours of exhausting jobs that have little interest or none at all.

The painful nature of this situation is shared between mother and daughter. The similarity between their two narratives, both in tone and in content, is remarkable. I also had a few interviews with the mother, in which we additionally learnt that Eloísa was born from a "casual" pregnancy, which she was content with because she wanted to have children. But by the time the baby was born the couple's relationship had started to deteriorate. Around the second or third year in Eloísa's life the mother was suffering abuse as well as affective and material abandonment: "I began to learn how hard it is to have a child." Eloísa knows in detail about this unfortunate story: in part because of her own memories, in part through her mother's recounts.

Eloísa has plenty of feelings of impotence and envy: she and her mother are both "outcasts" and they will never be able to change that. There are guilty feelings as well, as she is making her mother's hard life even harder (poor student, girl with difficulties..). And now she needs psychotherapy too.

The course of the treatment makes increasingly clear Eloísa's guilt, a guilt coming not from her own destructiveness, but induced by a narrative that places Eloísa as the prime culprit of the fateful maternal story.

As Eloísa is a good-looking girl, properly groomed, goes to school, speaks correct Spanish (unlike her mother), and has leisure time; at least at the present time one would not describe her life as unfortunate as her mother's.

Therefore, in our eyes, Eloísa qualifies as an "unwelcome child". Not accepted by her father from the start, indeed, but also not well accepted by a mother who, even having a "welcoming" attitude at first and being devoted to her afterwards, at some point in time also started to blame her daughter as the main cause of her own misfortune.

Both the therapist in charge and myself were feeling the looming threat of a psychotic break:

- During brief moments, each around one minute at most, Eloisa looks totally absent, "being beside [her]self", "being gone" (Diary, pp. 32). The psychiatry handbooks label this as "mental fading", formally similar to epileptic absences and regarded as distinctive phenomena for the early diagnosis of schizophrenic psychosis.
- She entertain fantasies that are as attractive as they are frightening to her "because of they are too real". When she tries to speak about them, her gestures become distressed. The therapist is doubtful as to whether this is the construction of an illusory phantasy or if it is a delusional or hallucinatory content imposing itself on her so forcefully that she barely succeeds in blocking it.
- She often recounts, with a nostalgic expression, fantasies, "even pleasant", in which she is a stone, a tree, or some other element of nature. In one of the silences following one of these occasions, the therapist finds himself thinking about the suicidal risk of this girl. After the silence Eloísa effectively talks about suicidal ideas, but making it clear that she has never attempted it.

This is the clinical information deemed necessary for the illustrative purposes of this vignette. The story of Eloísa condenses a significant part of Ferenczi's neo-concepts: lack of "counterlove" on the part of her father and insertion of "psychic contents of an unpleasurable nature" in having Eloísa witnessing his abuse of her mother, plus making Eloísa herself the object of his contempt. These "alien transplants" are compounded with the ones inserted by a difficult life.

The "fading" moments in which she is "beside herself" can be seen as moments of renunciation to self-assertion, because her environment barely exerts any "counter-pressure". Thus, the tendency towards a fusion with the environment.

We may understand the para-suicidal ideas as an attempt to achieve an immediate and brutal resolution to her death passion, an "alien transplant" grafted on to her "drives for conciliation" with the father's sadistic hate and with the (almost) unnoticed blame game of the mother. Such autolytic ideas gain power also from a yearning to return (to nature, to the universe..), at the service of which comes the "protective mimicry" leading her to yearn to be a stone or a tree: a satisfaction (not the same thing as a fulfilment) of the "instinct of tranquillity".

And where do we find the death instinct among all this conceptualisations? Nowhere. As it is written in a note in a notebook unearthed from the ruins of Ferenczi's house, in the manner of a message in a bottle found on a deserted beach: "Nothing but life instinct. Death instinct is a mistake (pessimistic)" (Dupont, 1998, p. 69).

References

Dupont, J. (1998). "Les notes brèves inédites de Sándor Ferenczi". *Le Coq-Héron, 149*: 69–83.

Real Academia Española (RAE) (2014). *Diccionario de la Lengua Española* [Dictionary of the Spanish language]. Madrid: R.A.E.

Spitz, R. A. (1945). Hospitalism—An inquiry into the genesis of psychiatric conditions in early childhood. *Psychoanalytic Study of the Child, 1*: 53–74.

Jiménez Avello, J. (1998). Metapsychology in Ferenczi. Death instinct or death passion? *International Forum of Psychoanalysis, 7*: 229–235.

Chapter 18

Ferenczi's concept of the "wise baby"

Luis Martín Cabré

The notion of "wise baby" first appeared in 1923, in a brief note of about twenty-five lines with the title "The dream of the 'clever baby'"[1] (1923). Ferenczi describes a typical dream or fantasy related by many patients, in which "the newly born, quite young children, or babies in the cradle, appear, who are able to talk or write fluently, treat one to deep sayings, carry on intelligent conversations, deliver harangues, give learned explanations and so on" (p. 349). In his view, the manifest content of this dream would point, by means of irony, to a repressed wish of an oedipal nature that aims to overcome and defeat the "grown-ups", thus reversing the condition in which the child is in relation with the adult.

The analysis of this dream opened up, even then, many thought-provoking interpretations about the difficulties that children run into in their relation with the adults, but it would acquire its maximum relevance in Ferenczi's contributions on the psychoanalytic theory of trauma. Eight years later, in "Child analysis in the analysis of adults", he refers again to the "dream of the wise baby", but in this text his approach is a new and radically different formulation, related to the clinical situation of the traumatised child.

> We all know that children who have suffered much morally or physically take on the appearance and mien of age and sagacity. They are prone to "mother" others also; obviously they thus extend to others the knowledge painfully acquired in coping with their own sufferings, and they become kind and helpful. It is, of course, not every such child who gets so far in mastering his own pain: many remain arrested in self-observation and hypochondria.
>
> (ChildAn, p. 136)

If we consider carefully this reflection of Ferenczi, we see that rather than a defence mechanism, the concept of "wise baby" refers to a survival mechanism, entirely different from that of repression, and that it is a direct consequence of a self-splitting that brutally transforms the object relationship into a narcissistic one (narcissistic self-splitting). The intelligence of the child behaves, in the fantasies of the analysis, as "another" person (a split part) that comes forward to help a mortally wounded child. But the "wise baby" not only has the ability to read her own unconscious, but also that of the adults, and innocently believes that they will appreciate this information.

1 Although in the first English edition of Ferenczi's works "gelehrten Säugling" is translated as "clever baby", in the present book we preferred to follow more recent publications that translate it as "wise baby", as we think it is more fitting to Ferenczi's thought.

This key notion of narcissistic self-splitting implies that a part of the self develops a protective ability towards another infantile and unprotected part. Yet, at the same time, self-splitting involves the internalisation of a bad primary object that hinders the constitution of a healthy narcissism and of the ability to regulate the excitations provoked by internal and external stimuli, with a consequent shortcoming in the domain of mental representation. All this results in the subject feeling a persistent sense of loneliness, helplessness, even despair for the possibility to receive help and support from the environment, a state that may become irreversible and lead the person to trust only himself.

In this sense, trauma translates the absence of a suitable response on the part of the object in the face of a situation of fragility that fragments and cripples forever the child's self, maintaining a permanent traumatic state and a feeling of primary helplessness (Freud's *Hilflosigkeit*; see Bokanowski, Chapter Twenty) that is triggered by almost any circumstance, over the whole lifetime and even in the analytic situation itself. Perhaps this is the reason why patients who are severely traumatised show markedly poor symbolisation capacity and have difficulty using the analyst's interpretations.

In "Confusion of the tongues" Ferenczi returns to the idea of the "wise baby" when he asserts that, under the pressure of a traumatic experience, the child on the one hand remains in an embryonic emotional state, but on the other hand may manifest all the various emotions that we would ascribe to a mature adult or a reflective philosopher, but with a decoupling between words and affects.

This would be Ferenczi's thesis. An adult who uses the language of passion unconsciously manoeuvres the eroticism of both love and hate and clashes violently with the child's language of tenderness. The adult refuses the vulnerable child—who had deposited all her trust in the adult—the acknowledgment of her thoughts and feelings that she needs. This provokes not only fear, disappointment, and pain but, and above all else, inevitably leads to a splitting. In contrast to the splitting in Freud, according to which a part of the ego accepts reality while others disavows it, in Ferenczi's conception a part dies and the other lives on, but devoid of affects, anaesthetised, remaining excluded from its own existence as if someone else, a "wise baby", is living its life.

In addition to splitting, infantile trauma may generate fragmentation, atomisation, and autotomy. This notion of "autotomy", coined by Ferenczi (1921), well describes the amputation of a part of the self. Therefore, as I said before, from a Ferenczian point of view a part of the subject "dies" through splitting. It does not feel pain because it does not exist anymore. Even more: "He is no longer worried about breathing or about the preservation of his life in general. Moreover, he regards being destroyed or mutilated with interest, as if it is no longer his own self but another person who is undergoing these torments" (Diary, p. 6). The psyche defends itself by means of its own self-destruction and by destroying whomever offers help or affect. We could say that a sort of "superior intelligence" is at work.

If we transfer these views to the domain of the analytic relationship, we may ask ourselves how this narcissistic self-splitting caused by the impact of the traumatic experience can be revived and activated in the transference. As we know, the elaboration of mental suffering constitutes a key axis in the development of any analytical process, but at the same time it brings to the fore the mental pain of the analyst too, who must elaborate on his part the suffering projected by the patient and has to be able to tolerate and contain the rage, attacks, and seductions without becoming paralysed in his own thinking. Every analyst can find patients who live with the impossibility of experiencing pain and who use very primitive mechanisms in order to avoid suffering. They become silent, motionless, sarcastic, insensitive, and eradicate any trace of emotivism from their discourse. A consequence of this is the impoverishment of their mental life and their analytic relationship, but also the need to enact these frozen sentiments in the form of self-destructive acts, especially on the occasion of separations or when interrupting the sessions. How is the analyst able to become a wise baby for the patient, allowing her to reduce the necessity of resorting to self-splitting and facilitating, instead, an integrative process? In order to achieve this, to empower the patient to access the innermost kernels of her inner world, and, above all else, to promote a psychic change that enables the patient to alleviate her own suffering and despair, the analyst cannot rely only on the tool of interpretation. Apparently, regarding this task, Ferenczi places the analyst in the position of hearing the impossible, and not only against the edges of the psychic and somatic domains, but even of what is thinkable.

The "wise baby" phenomenon is a major clinical indicator of what is known as "traumatic progression" (Conf, p. 165). This is a precocious maturity, acquired at the expense of an intense emotional suffering, manifested through intellectual abilities that sometimes are very stunning. However, these abilities—often inappropriately valued and reinforced by society—conceal the necessity that these patients have of being heard, understood, and contained in their "buried alive" pain, in order for them to be able to elaborate and overcome it.

Let us review briefly the proximity of the "wise baby" notion with that of Orpha, which allows for interesting suggestions.[2] In the *Diary* (p. 8) Ferenczi defines Orpha, a concept suggested to him by his patient Elizabeth Severn during her analysis with him, as "organizing life instincts", which "in place of death allow insanity to intervene": that is, an unconscious factor that awakens in the instant of trauma. Its function is that of playing a role as a "guardian angel", trying to stay alive at any cost, and "it produces wish-fulfilling hallucinations, consolation fantasies; it anesthetizes the consciousness and sensitivity against sensations as they become unbearable". Orpha is able, therefore, to create a kind of "artificial" or "wise baby" psyche in order to keep the body alive, to save it from death, but at the cost of putting together a fragmented individual, composed of different parts.

Already in "Notes and fragments", 21 September 1930, Ferenczi had referred to a "certainly quite unconscious internal force, as yet unrecognized in its essence, which estimates with mathematical accuracy both the severity of the trauma and the available ability for defence, produces with automatic certainty and according to the pattern of a complicated calculating machine the only practical and correct psychological and physical behaviour in a given situation" (Frag, p. 230).

And in several passages of the *Diary* Ferenczi would return again and again to this concept (17 January, 1 May, and 12 June), but it is above all in the notes dated 10 May where he describes his concept in an exemplary manner. "At moments of dire need a guardian angel emerges within us, as it were, who is able to make use of our physical strength to a far greater extent than we would be able to under normal circumstances". It is a "guardian angel ... shaped from parts of one's own psychic personality, probably consisting of parts of the affect of self-preservation", and takes the place of a non-existent exterior help.

2 Besides being linked to Orpha, the concept of "wise baby" also anticipates Winnicott's intuition of a "false self", which develops as a mental process with the purpose of interacting with the exterior and preserving the life of the "true self," and that of "mind-object", which refers to a typical dissociation between the mind and the body. Furthermore, Ferenczi's "wise baby" also anticipate Searles' idea of "The patient as therapist to his analyst" (1975), and Bion's "reversible perspective" (1963).

Lastly, I would like to emphasise the way in which the whole concept of the "wise baby" was implicit in the mental functioning and the affective situation of Ferenczi himself. He had succeeded for many years in containing internally the unavoidable disappointment in his analysis and his relationship with Freud—caused by the impossibility of working through his infantile mourning, derived in turn from the libidinal decathexis from his mother, which had become reactivated at the transferential level—by means of his heavy dependence on his mentor. Moreover, not having the possibility to receive the help of an analyst able to treat him, Ferenczi fell back on himself, to "a part of his own self", which in the manner of a "wise baby" would enable him to elaborate his impossible suffering. It would not suffice.

When he felt abandoned by that "higher power" that Freud represented at both the intellectual and affective levels, every exit seemed to become sealed off. In fact, one still remained open: to concentrate on his work with his patients and, in the theoretical dimension, to reclaim the role of trauma in psychoanalytical theory.

Ferenczi himself, in several dramatic passages of the *Diary*, described a few ideas that, on the one hand, relate to his work with patients but, on the other, also seem to portray his personal condition at the time: his own narcissistic self-splitting and the role of "his own inner wise baby" as a therapist for his illness. Thus, on 10 January 1932 he comments:

> In moments of great need, when the psychic system proves to be incapable of an adequate response, or when these specific organs or functions (nervous and psychic) have been violently destroyed, then the primordial psychic powers are aroused and it will be these forces that will seek to overcome the disruption. In such moments, when the psychic system fails, the organism begins to think.
>
> (Diary, p. 6)

But there is no doubt that he writes the most telling, and moving, passage on 2 October, where he establishes an intimate connection between what is psychic and what is somatic, that is, between his illness and the emotional aspects related to it. The hematic crisis (pernicious anaemia) was, in the words of Ferenczi, aroused "when I realised that not only can I not rely on the protection of a 'higher power' but on the contrary I shall be trampled underfoot by this indifferent power as soon as I go my own way and not his" (Diary, p. 257). He hints at the idea that what had preserved him from disintegration up to that moment was the "identification" with a "higher power" (Freud), a paternal surrogate, and the conviction of being able to count on the protection of his thinking in every type of adverse circumstance. Here he asks himself some questions: "And now, just as I must build new red corpuscles, must I (if I can) create a new basis for my personality, if I have to abandon as false and untrustworthy the one I have had up to now? Is the choice here one between dying and 'rearranging myself' – and this at the age of fifty-nine?" (Diary, p. 212). And he seems eager to suggest even more questions: "On the other hand, is it worth it always to live the life (will) of another person – is such a life not almost death? Do I lose too much if I risk this life? *Chi lo sa*? [Who knows?]" (ibid.).

Unfortunately, the pernicious anaemia that ended his life exposed the fact that the defensive reaction triggered by him against the danger of a perceived external threat ended up incorporating the threat itself and owning it, thus generating a self-destructive process that eventually dismantled his own identity. And in such a way, not only the *enfant terrible* but also the wise baby of psychoanalysis, left a marvellous legacy for all of us psychoanalysts, the legacy of a man who not only distinguished himself because of his intelligence and honesty but also, as Groddeck wrote to Gizella (Berman, Chapter Six) in his last letter, as one of those rare human beings who belong to the givers, "to those who give again and again" (in Fer-Grod, 19 February 1934, p. 114): the ones that always die for the ideas of someone else, but live instead thanks to their own.

References

Bion, W. R (1963). *Elements of Psycho-Analysis*. London: Heinemann.

Ferenczi, S. (1921). On epileptic fits. Observations and reflections. In: *Final Contributions to the Problems and Methods of Psycho-Analysis* (pp. 197–205). London: Hogarth.

Ferenczi, S. (1923). The dream of the "clever baby". In: *Further Contributions to the Theory and Technique of Psycho-Analysis*. London: Hogarth.

Searles, H. F. (1975). The patient as a therapist of his analyst. In: P. L. Giovacchini (Ed.), *Tactics and Techniques in Psychoanalytical Therapy. Vol. II*. New York: Jason Aronson.

Chapter 19

Psychological enslavement through identification with the aggressor

Jay Frankel

From the late 1910s through to the early 1930s, Ferenczi experimented with ways to revive stalled treatments of his narcissistically disturbed patients—patients who, he discovered, generally had been severely abused as children. His technical experiments tracked his deepening understanding of psychological trauma. Ultimately, he placed his discovery of identification with the aggressor (IWA) at the heart of the traumatic response, and shaped his method of treating the sequelae of childhood trauma around it.

While many of Ferenczi's patients had suffered extreme sexual abuse or violence in childhood, less blatant but still exploitative parental acts also appeared traumatic: disguised aggression, disguised coercive sexuality (Unwel, Relax, ChildAn, Conf, Diary); "terrorism of suffering" (Conf, p. 166), where a parent displays "her constant miseries" (ibid.) to her helpless child; narcissistically disturbed parents requiring "superperformance[s]" (Diary, pp. 89, 99, 80)—precocious or forced emotional responses—to buoy the parent's mood (cf. Miller, 1997, Faimberg, 2005). Ferenczi saw not being loved (Unwel) and the withdrawal of love (ChildAn, p. 138; Diary, p. 190)—implicit in most or all forms of intra-family trauma—as perhaps the most basic trauma.

Ferenczi also observed, in his patients' descriptions of their childhood abuse, parents' hypocrisy about the assault itself. Ferenczi believed that "children get over even severe shocks without amnesia or neurotic consequences, if the mother is at hand with understanding and tenderness and (what is most rare) with complete sincerity" (ChildAn, p. 138). But "[a]lmost always the perpetrator behaves as though nothing had happened" (Conf, pp. 162–163), though he may also blame the child for the abuse (ibid.). The child's efforts to find help "are refused as nonsensical" (ibid.). "Probably the worst way of dealing with such situations is to deny their existence, to assert that nothing has happened and that nothing is hurting the child … These are the kinds of treatment which make the trauma pathogenic" (ChildAn, p. 138; and see Diary, p. 193). More recent research confirms the destructive "conspiracy of silence" that surrounds child sexual abuse (Butler, 1996).

Ferenczi's view that parents' hypocrisy was decisive in causing his patients' pathology was supported by their traumatic response to a similar, defensive "*professional hypocrisy*" (Conf, p. 158) in him, their analyst.

Hypocrisy, whether explicit or implied by not responding to a child's pain, strong-arms her into repudiating her own experience and going along with the adult's message. Parental hypocrisy is such a damaging form of emotional abandonment and narcissistic exploitation because it erodes a child's trust in other people (Frag, p. 270) and even in her own perceptions (Conf, p. 162).

Identification with the aggressor

How do children respond to abuse? While Ferenczi had much to say on the subject (see Frankel, 1998), he saw IWA as being the core of children's traumatic response:

> One would expect the first impulse to be that of rejection, hatred, disgust and energetic refusal. "No, no, I do not want it, it is much too violent for me, it hurts, leave me alone", this or something similar would be the immediate reaction if it would not be paralyzed by enormous anxiety. These children feel physically and morally helpless, their personalities are not sufficiently consolidated in order to be able to protest, even if only in thought, for the overpowering force and authority of the adult makes them dumb and can rob them of their senses. *The same anxiety, however, if it reaches a certain maximum, compels them to subordinate themselves like automata to the will of the aggressor, to divine each one of his desires and to gratify these; completely oblivious of themselves they identify themselves with the aggressor.*
>
> (Conf, p. 227, original italics)

Terrified and overwhelmed, "the child becomes hypnotically transfixed on the aggressor's wishes" (Howell, 2014, p. 50) and completely subordinated to his will, moulded to his image of who she must be.[1] Subordination is a survival response when real danger threatens, and also a tactic to ensure continued belonging in the family when rejection looms.

In order to adapt most precisely, the child must introject the aggressor—create an internal model with which she can identify, to know his feelings and intentions from the inside. This includes introjecting the aggressor's image of who she must become. The introjection process requires that the child's own experiential reality be "vacated [to be] filled by the will of what has terrified her" (Diary, p. 48).

Ferenczi also wrote about how splitting, dissociation, and introjection combine to minimise the child's fear and psychic pain by creating a soothing, false reality alongside her frightened, urgent focus on the real aggressor. The suffering part of the person is "repressed" (Diary, p. 9), leaving an emotionless "guardian angel" (ibid.) to cope with impinging reality while anaesthetizing the feeling part of the personality with "consolation fantasies" (ibid.) and hallucinations: "Through the identification, or let us say, introjection of the aggressor, he disappears as part of the external reality, and becomes intra- instead of extra-psychic; the intra-psychic is then subjected, in a dream-like state as is the traumatic trance, to the primary process ... it can be modified or changed by the use of positive or negative hallucinations. In any case the attack as a rigid external reality ceases to exist ..." (Conf, p. 162). Anaesthetising the child's feelings may even require "squeezing the entire psychic life out of the inhumanly suffering body" (ibid.).

Given their complex interrelationships and high degree of coordination, submission, splitting, dissociation, introjection, identification, and compliance can be understood as different facets of a single operation—as aspects of IWA.

1 Ferenczi was the first to use the term "identification with the aggressor" (Conf). His use is related to, but differs from, Anna Freud's (1936) later, better-known conceptualisation of it as a mechanism of defence in which a victim of aggression copes with her helplessness by *becoming* an aggressor toward a third party.

Dimensions of IWA

We can think of IWA as including behavioural, mental, and moral dimensions, with the latter two supporting behavioural accommodation in its crucial task of managing, placating, satisfying, soothing, or otherwise neutralising the aggressor.

Mental accommodation includes, first, dissociation. In addition to evacuating her own experiential reality so she can bear the assault and focus completely on and identify with the abuser, the child also dissociates particular perceptions, thoughts, and feelings that could interfere with playing her role well. Ferenczi said, "In order to ensure silence, also *internal silence*: forgetting, repression" (Diary, p. 118). The child, terrified of exclusion, faces the dilemma succinctly articulated by Marx (Groucho): "Who you gonna believe, me or your own lying eyes?"—and chooses the former. Dissociation can range from doubting one's perceptions or the validity of one's feelings, to blocking particular feelings or memories, to being completely unable to think or feel, or—most extreme—even to remain conscious (Diary, p. 130). Jettisoning one's own direct experience removes the foundation for the senses of authenticity and agency.

Mental accommodation also requires creating necessary inner experiences. In addition to generating fantasies and hallucinations that numb her own inner agony, a child develops precocious capacities designed to manage the real aggressor—what Ferenczi called "*traumatic progression*" (Conf, p. 165; and see Gurevich's, 2015, discussion of "Orpha"). These include receptive abilities: hypersensitivities and superintelligences (e.g., Frag, p. 262; Diary, pp. 81, 203, 214) that gauge the environment and calculate the best way to survive. Ferenczi said about one patient: "she penetrated by her thought-processes [her parents'] psychic mechanisms, motives, even their feelings so thoroughly ... that she could apprehend the hitherto unbearable situation quite clearly—as she herself had ceased to exist as an emotional person. The trauma made her emotionally embryonic, but at the same time wise in intellectual terms" (Diary, p. 203). Traumatic progression also includes precocious responses to the abuser, as the situation requires—for instance, premature sexuality or caregiving. And children can manufacture other feelings and thoughts, if these will calm the adult. One must feel and believe one's role in order to play it most convincingly.

IWA depends on deactivating the capacity to think for oneself. The purpose of the parent's aggression is "helplessly binding a child to an adult" (Conf, p. 165)—control over the child's mind as well as behaviour: a psychological enslavement that ensures that the child serves the adult's needs rather than her own. But independent, critical thinking is inherently an act of psychological separation, and its exercise facilitates separation—it undermines efforts by the child, dreading emotional expulsion, to stifle her own separation and autonomy and fit in.

IWA also entails moral accommodation: the victim blames herself for being abused or abandoned. This includes feeling guilty and shamefully defective—losing a sense of goodness and wholeness (Frankel, 2015a). Ferenczi referred to "*introjection of the guilt feelings of the adult*", which he saw as most damaging (Conf, p. 162). But is it certain that all abusers feel guilty on some level? A decade later, Fairbairn gave similar observations a different explanation and a new name, "the moral defence" (1943, p. 65): the child takes the parent's badness on to herself so she can feel she has good parents—more vital to her sense of security than feeling *herself* as good, according to Fairbairn. The sense of being bad can feel like an essential tie to an emotionally abandoning (outer and internalised) parent, making it very resistant to therapeutic influence.

A child's guilt often reflects her belief that she caused her self-absorbed parent's unhappiness, and has failed to rescue her parent from it—a fantasy often galvanised by the parent's ongoing display of misery: the "terrorism of suffering" (Conf, p. 166). The child's guilt may also express an omnipotent undoing of the traumatic helplessness she feels in this situation. Such a child is likely to become a caregiver to parents and others—a "nurse for life" (ibid.).

Ferenczi also noted the child's sense of shame (Conf, p. 162). Psychoanalyst Heinz Kohut (1972) and affect-researcher Silvan Tomkins (1987) both observed that shame results when someone's expression of feelings is met with indifference or a refusal of affective exchange (and cf. Kilborne, 2002)—Ferenczi's trauma of emotional abandonment, implicit in all intra-familial trauma. The person wonders, "What's wrong with *me*?", believing the other's lack of response reflects some defect in oneself.

Both guilt and the sense of shameful defect enforce submission. A guilty child feels her self-assertion damages her parent, while a sense of shameful defect makes a child doubt her ability to function as an autonomous person.

The behavioural, mental, and moral aspects of IWA work together synergistically. The child feels: I'll be what you want, I'll like it and won't question it, and if I'm unhappy something's wrong with *me.*[2]

Persistence and prevalence of IWA

The tendency to IWA, in its various dimensions, often persists through life, though over time what began as an automatic organismic reaction takes on a purposeful, defensive dimension (Howell, 2014). A persisting IWA tendency is widespread, observable clinically in many patients who have not been victims of gross trauma (Frankel, 2002); in social phenomena like the Stockholm syndrome (de Fabrique et al., 2007), where hostages develop positive feelings toward their captors; and in experiments like Milgram's (1963) simulated-electric-shock studies of obedience, and, especially, in Zimbardo's (Haney et al., 1973) Stanford Prison experiment, where normal subjects, randomly assigned to be guards or inmates in a mock prison, often quickly and completely identified with these roles, sometimes even when this offended their character.

The frequency of the persisting IWA tendency—certainly far greater than the incidence of gross familial child abuse—supports the idea that less obvious acts like symbolic aggression, disguised seduction, emotional abandonment, and narcissistic exploitation (Faimberg, 2005; Miller, 1979) can traumatise children (e.g., Relax).

The pervasiveness of IWA suggests that this response potential, triggered by an inbuilt fear of social exclusion, may have evolved to maintain a necessary degree of social hierarchy, obedience, conformity, and cooperation in a species reliant, as ours is, on a group survival strategy (Frankel, 2015b). Its pervasiveness also suggests that it plays a significant role in sociopolitical life. Indeed, IWA is a useful concept in understanding the prevalent, yet self-defeating, submission and compliance upon which authoritarian political movements depend (Frankel, 2015b; and see Adorno et al., 1950; Fromm, 1941).

2 Ferenczi thought of the loss of self resulting from IWA as "partial death" (Bonomi, 2002, p. 156; and see Gurevich, 2015).

Narcissistic compensation

Ferenczi described how people escape traumatic experience through "positive or negative hallucinations" (Conf, p. 162), soothing regressed trance states (ibid.), and confused defiance (p. 163). Often, people who forfeit their sense of self through IWA cloak this in illusions of bold self-assertiveness—the self doesn't go quietly. These fantasies typically also include a sense of special belonging that denies the feelings of emotional abandonment that drive IWA—denies them by idealising a person, group, or idea with whom one feels a self-enhancing bond. Paranoid and manic splitting amplifies this specialness by projecting all badness on to a person or group seen as evil or contemptible, and injecting an aggressive excitement that hides vulnerability.[3] These omnipotent fantasies actually facilitate continued capitulation, precisely by dulling the despair of losing one's self and one's place.

Some broad clinical implications

Ferenczi's emphasis on emotional abandonment as traumatic suggests that analysts should make themselves palpably present when their patients seem unable to hold on to a vital inner sense of them (cf. Bach, 1994). A traditional abstinent frame may be traumatising in such situations.

Analysts should heed Ferenczi's (Conf, p. 158; Relax, p. 124) warnings about how "proper" technique (i.e., anonymity, abstinence, interpretation) and analytic authority can be used to mask countertransference enactments, and should strive to be as egalitarian as possible, consistent with a patient's other therapeutic needs.

Occasionally, but inevitably, analysts will fail their patients through such "professional hypocrisy" or other forms of emotional abandonment. Patients may respond with a conspicuous "resistance" that is, in fact, a self-protective reaction to what is essentially a subtle assault, or with a hidden resistance in the form of IWA and compliance—for example, avoiding anger at the analyst, compulsively accepting interpretations (Conf, p. 157), or using self-examination as a way to blame themselves instead of criticising the analyst. Analysts should be alert to their own lapses and patients' identificatory reactions, and when these become clear, follow Ferenczi's recommendation of "frank discussion" (p. 159) with patients about the analyst's own mistakes, even disclosing what was going on in their own minds (despite that fact that the analyst cannot fully grasp its meaning). Ferenczi thought this could restore patients' trust and free them to speak more openly (p. 159). Ferenczi's mutual-analysis experiment, near the end of his life, was the radical prototype of this self-disclosing position, which has gained currency, in more limited forms, among analysts of many stripes in recent decades (e.g., Bass, Chapter Twenty-three). Repairing disruptions caused by analytic hypocrisy and, through this, working through the damage caused by earlier parental hypocrisy, is perhaps the key rationale for a more disclosing analytic stance.

Analysts' unavoidable (hopefully only occasional) defensiveness shows that patients can also feel like aggressors to analysts. At such times, analysts, being people, may respond with IWA—for instance, by turning necessary analytic restraint into masochistic self-suppression (cf. Racker, 1968, chap. 7), becoming compulsive caregivers in order (unconsciously) to manage their own distress more than the patient's, or—for intersubjectively focused analysts—dwelling on their own contributions to impasses while overlooking those of the patient.

3 Narcissistic compensation can be flagrant or subtle.

References

Adorno, T. W., Frenkel-Brunswick, E., Levinson, D. J., & Sanford, R. N. (1950). *The Authoritarian Personality*. New York: Harper & Row.

Bach, S. (1994). *The Language of Perversion and the Language of Love*. Northvale, NJ: Aronson.

Bonomi, C. (2002). Identification with the aggressor: An interactive tactic or an intrapsychic tomb? *Psychoanalytic Dialogues, 12*: 153–158.

Butler, S. (1996). *Conspiracy of Silence: The Trauma of Incest*. Volcano, CA: Volcano Press.

de Fabrique, N., Romano, S.J., Vecchi, G.M., & van Hasselt, V.B. (2007). Understanding Stockholm syndrome. *FBI Law Enforcement Bulletin*, 76: 10–15. https://leb.fbi.gov/2007-pdfs/leb-july-2007

Faimberg, H. (2005). *The Telescoping of Generations*. New York: Routledge.

Fairbairn, W. R. D. (1943). The repression and return of bad objects. In: *Psychoanalytic Studies of the Personality* (pp. 59–81). London: Routledge & Kegan Paul, 1952.

Frankel, J. (1998). Ferenczi's trauma theory. *American Journal of Psychoanalysis, 58*: 41–61.

Frankel, J. (2002). Exploring Ferenczi's concept of identification with the aggressor: Its role in trauma, everyday life, and the therapeutic relationship. *Psychoanalytic Dialogues, 12*: 101–139.

Frankel, J. (2015a). The persistent sense of being bad: The moral dimension of identification with the aggressor. In: A. Harris & S. Kuchuck (Eds.), *The Legacy of Sandor Ferenczi* (pp. 204–222). New York: Routledge.

Frankel, J. (2015b). The traumatic basis for the resurgence of right-wing politics among working Americans. *Psychoanalysis, Culture and Society, 20*: 359–378.

Freud, A. (1936). *The Ego and the Mechanisms of Defense*. New York: International Universities Press.

Fromm, E. (1941). *Escape from Freedom*. Austin: Holt, Rinehart & Winston.

Gurevich, H. (2015). The language of absence and the language of tenderness: Therapeutic transformation of early psychic trauma and dissociation as resolution of the "identification with the aggressor". *Fort Da, 21*: 45–65.

Haney, C., Banks, W. C., & Zimbardo, P. G. (1973). A study of prisoners and guards in a simulated prison. *Naval Research Review*, 30: 4–17.

Howell, E. F. (2014). Ferenczi's concept of identification with the aggressor: Understanding dissociative structure with interacting victim and abuser self-states. *American Journal of Psychoanalysis, 74*: 48–59.

Kilborne, B. (2002). *Disappearing Persons: Shame and Appearance*. Albany, NY: SUNY Press.

Kohut, H. (1972). Thoughts on narcissism and narcissistic rage. *Psychoanalytic Study of the Child, 27*: 360–400.

Milgram, S. (1963). Behavioral study of obedience. *Journal of Abnormal and Social Psychology, 67*: 371–378.

Miller, A. (1997). *The Drama of the Gifted Child*. New York: Basic Books.

Racker, H. (1968). *Transference and Countertransference*. New York: International Universities Press.

Tomkins, S. S. (1987). Shame. In: D. L. Nathanson (Ed.), *The Many Faces of Shame* (pp. 133–161). New York: Guilford.

Chapter 20

Splitting, fragmentation, and psychic agony

Thierry Bokanowski

All of Ferenczi's conceptual advances today form part of the theoretical and clinical tools available to the analyst today for his reflections and daily work. They were established in the light of his experience doing treatment because he was trying to identify as closely as possible the most appropriate countertransference responses and techniques for overcoming the transference impasses encountered in the treatments of difficult situations regarded as being "at the limits" of the analysable or of what is treatable in psychoanalysis.

Theoretical perspectives in *The Clinical Diary*

This is the essential axis of *The Clinical Diary*. It is linked to Ferenczi's wish to set down, stone by stone, his latest theoretical hypotheses concerning trauma. At the same time as he was trying to see what they might contribute to the handling of the countertransference when faced with certain types of transferences (passionate, among others); he saw them as a means of approaching, in everyday practice, the trying clinical experience of the "limits".

Having perceived intuitively the economic and metapsychological importance of the pair trauma/splitting, Ferenczi saw it as a leitmotif that would enable him, like an "interpretative grid", to tackle certain complex situations, indeed certain transference/countertransference impasses linked to them. The mutative importance of the concept of trauma, along with that of splitting, remains, throughout this document, at the centre of his questionings and reflections. I shall now endeavour to follow its principal stages.

The clinical notes under the entry 12 January 1932 (the *Diary* begins on the 7th) on the subject of a patient, Elisabeth Severn (R. N.), gave Ferenczi the opportunity of dwelling on the question of splitting and of trying to define its contour at the metapsychological level with regard to the geography of trauma.

This patient had been subjected to three sexual attacks (seductions) during the period extending from her infancy to her pre-adolescence: the first at the age of one and a half; the second at the age of five; and the third, a rape, at the age of eleven. These traumas, registered in the patient's psyche, led to a complete "atomization of her psychic life", a real "dislocation" of her personality, which was "shattered to its very atoms", writes Ferenczi, who sees the organisation of a "sort of artificial psyche for this body forcibly brought back to life" (Diary, p. 10).

On the basis of the clinical elements that appeared during the patient's treatment, Ferenczi drew up a list, in a descriptive manner, of the consequences of the splittings employed during the different traumatic situations encountered by his patient prior to her adolescence:

- the existence, within the adult, of a "seduced child". This adult presents herself as being overwhelmed by her psychic suffering; excited, she can only compensate for her excitations by countercathecting them and by protecting them by means of a somnambulic trance of a hysterical type. The analyst, Ferenczi writes, can only "make contact" with this part, the "pure repressed affect: "This part," he adds, "behaves like a child who has fainted, completely unaware of itself, who can perhaps only groan, who must be shaken awake mentally and also sometimes physically" (Diary, p. 9);
- the different fragmentations create a "soulless" personality, a "soulless body", owing to a devitalisation of the psyche and the loss of the affective and emotional quality of what has been lived and felt;
- these fragmentations can lead to an "atomization" or "pulverization" of psychic life with feelings of agony.

This is evocative today of the "false self" described by Winnicott (1960), and of "as if" personalities (Deutsch, 1942). In my view, the disqualification of feelings and lived experience of which Ferenczi speaks here, is at the origin of a psychic devitalisation.

The effects of splitting

In an attempt to give a general structure to the clinical picture, Ferenczi describes the effects of the different forms of splitting in the following way:

> From now on the "individuum," superficially regarded, consists of the following parts: (a) uppermost, a capable, active human being with a precisely – perhaps a little too precisely – regulated mechanism; (b) behind this, a being that does not wish to have anything more to do with life; (c) behind this murdered ego, the ashes of earlier mental sufferings, which are rekindled every night by the fire of suffering; (d) this suffering itself as a separate mass of affect, without content and unconscious, the remains of the actual person.
>
> (Diary, p. 10)

Thanks to these notes we can see that for Ferenczi, splitting, like fragmentation, short-circuits the mechanisms of repression, which he seeks to illustrate by evoking "the separate mass of affect, without content and unconscious" (Diary, p. 10). Consequently, he conceives of and treats infantile amnesia as the result of splitting, a splitting which is a veritable *Spaltung*, that is, ego splitting, secondary to the shock effect of the trauma. The excluded part of the memory survives in secret: split-off from its possibilities of representation in a neurotic mode, it cannot be translated by words, but manifests itself through the body (hysterical trances).

The same patient led him, not long after, on 24 January 1932, to wonder about the *content* of splits:

> What is the content of the split-off ego? ... The content of the split-off ego is always as follows: natural development and spontaneity, protest against violence and injustice,

> contemptuous, perhaps sarcastic and ironic, obedience displayed by the fact of domination, but inward knowledge that the violence has in fact achieved nothing; it has altered only something objective, the decision-making process but not the ego as such. Contentment with oneself for this accomplishment, a feeling of being bigger and cleverer than the brutal force.
>
> (Diary, p. 19)

What Ferenczi is describing here is a mode of "self-cure" through the development in the subject of a narcissistic split; this allows for the creation of an apparently protective narcissism but it can also become "megalomaniac". As we have seen in connection with the metaphor of the "wise baby", we are now seeing the metapsychological importance and clinical consequences that Ferenczi accords to the concept of narcissistic splitting (see also Martín Cabré, Chapter Eighteen).

Fragmentation

After describing the paralysis of the activity of thinking as a secondary effect of trauma, Ferenczi deals in his notes with the question of denial as a mechanism that reinforces repression. But it is in an important note called "Fragmentation", dated 21 February 1932, that he raises the question of the work of the analyst faced with traumatic situations and with splitting.

> Psychic advantages: the unpleasure that arises when certain connections are made is avoided by the giving up of these connections. The splitting into two personalities, which do not want to know about each other, and which are grouped around different impulses, avoids subjective conflict ... The task of the analyst is to remove this split.
>
> (Diary, pp. 38–39)

What matters here for Ferenczi is to "revive" the "dead" split-off part, which, although it has gone into hibernation, may nevertheless be subject to the "agony of anxiety" and thus actively stimulate thinking by "reviving the 'ghost' that has been given up ... and slowly persuading the dead or split-off fragment that it is not dead" (Diary, p. 39).

In other words, translated into more recent analytic language, the analyst's task consists in offering the patient thoughts and representations that, by means of word-presentations, allow feelings and emotions to rediscover their affective qualities. This allows the analyst to hope, in the long term, for a resymbolisation and repsychisation of the suffering zones (psychic agony). Ferenczi goes on to conclude provisionally that:

> The question remains open whether there are not some cases in which the reunification of the traumatically split-off complexes is so unbearable that it does not fully occur and the patient retains some neurotic characteristics or sinks even deeper into a state of not-being or not-wanting-to-be [*Nichtseinwollen*].
>
> (Diary, p. 40)

Once again, we can appreciate here the extraordinary clinical intuition of Ferenczi who notes the prognostic importance of negative processes (Green, 1993) within the psyche and in analysis.

Likewise, as he indicates in a note dated 25 March 1932, it is thanks to the transference and to the positive feelings that are established with the patient that, in his own words, certain deferred anti-cathexes can be constituted that could not organise themselves when the trauma took place, permitting a significant reduction of splitting:

> In the transference the opportunity would present itself to provide that protection and support which were absent during the trauma ... The positive feelings produce, as it were, a deferred anticathexis that did not occur when the trauma took place ... If a trauma strikes the soul, or the body, unprepared, that is, without countercathexis, then its effect is destructive for the body and mind, that is, it disrupts through fragmentation. The power that would hold the individual fragments and elements together is absent.
>
> (Diary, pp. 68–69)

The "split-off alien transplants"

The concept of the "wise baby" (that is, a child that is intellectually hypermature, but affectively immature) led him, in a note dated 7 April 1932, to evoke the powerful idea of "split-off alien transplants":

> I am indebted to several patients for the idea, recorded elsewhere, that adults forcibly inject their will, particularly psychic contents of an unpleasurable nature, into the childish personality. These split-off, alien transplants vegetate in the other person during the whole of life.
>
> (Diary, p. 81)

For Ferenczi, the "alien transplant" accounts for a process that favours splitting and results in "the implanting of psychic contents into the psyche of the victim, dispensing unpleasure, causing pain and tension" (Diary, p. 77).This implantation brings about in the child an intromission of seductive fantasies, which, owing to their primal and sexualised character, become traumatic (ibid.).

Here, Ferenczi is describing an excited and helpless child (patient), overwhelmed by an excess of libidinal excitation (external, but above all internal), who, as he does not have at his disposal the means of discharge or elaboration, finds himself in a state of complete distress or helplessness (*Hilfslösigkeit*).

The concept of "infantile trauma"

Ferenczi had written the year before in *The Clinical Diary* that what "we here see taking place is the reproduction of the mental and physical agony which follows upon incomprehensible and intolerable woe" (ChildAn, p. 138).

This pain reproduces that which was experienced in early childhood as a result of a trauma, which may have been of a sexual type, but not only sexual; its consequence is the "splitting of the self into a suffering, brutally destroyed part and a part which, as it were, knows everything but feels nothing" (ChildAn, p. 135).

This splitting (auto-narcissistic) leads to an evacuation/expulsion/extrojection of a part of the ego (Bokanowski, 1997); the part of the ego left empty is replaced by an "identification with the aggressor", with its affects of the type "terrorism of suffering"; the expelled/extrojected part of the ego becomes omniscient, omnipotent, and affectless: it then gives rise to a psychic configuration of the type "wise baby".

To sum up: while the trauma may assume derivative forms in relation to sexuality (fantasies of sexual seduction or castration, etc.), it essentially belongs to an experience with the object, not with regard to what has taken place, but with regard to what could *not* take place—that is to say, an absence or series of absences of adequate responses from the object in the face of a situation of distress. This absence mutilates forever the ego, maintains psychic suffering in relation to the internalisation of a "deficient" primary object, and leads to a sensation of primary distress (*Hilflosigkeit 36*[1]), which, throughout life, is reactivated at the slightest occasion.

Thus, not only the narcissism of the *infans*, as well as his potentialities, are seriously damaged but, further, the violent recourse to defence mechanisms (projection and splitting) becomes such that the organisation of the instinctual drive economy, as well as symbolisation and, consequently, the autonomy of the ego, are seriously disturbed.

By extending in this way the question of seduction, Ferenczi, makes a considerable advance by envisaging the traumatic aetiology as the result either of a psychic rape of the child by the adult or of a "confusion of tongues" between them, or, alternatively, of a denial by the adult of the child's despair. This negativising and painful experience results in a "tear in the self" (a split), which brutally transforms object-relations, henceforth impossible, into narcissistic ones.

Dissensions

As can be seen, with such advances, the nature of the trauma is modified considerably by the fact that it calls into question the nature of the object when faced with a situation of distress and, consequently, that of the analyst. That is why, for Ferenczi, the analytic situation can itself reinforce the initial modalities of the organisation of the trauma.

These advances, however innovative, were to make conflict with Freud inevitable because, for him, a real theoretical gap was developing, a gap whose demarcation line was the conception of infantile trauma.

In effect, for Freud, invoking the compulsion to repeat as a repetition of the traumatic situation, making the object responsible for it, boils down to underestimating the resources of the psychic apparatus and its capacity to transform the trauma, as well as the psychic pain that is associated with it: in other words, for Freud, the therapeutic and technical consequences (particularly, neocatharsis, technical elasticity, and especially the so-called technique of mutuality) that Ferenczi derived from the introduction of his clinical discoveries, amounted to a step backwards (a return to a period before 1897) and, as a result, to a theoretical deviation.

1 As Laplanche and Pontalis (1967) remark: "The word '*Hilflosigkeit*' constitutes a permanent reference-point for Freud, and it deserves to be signalled out and translated consistently. … This common word has a specific meaning in Freudian theory, where it is used to denote the state of the human suckling which, being entirely dependent on other people for the satisfaction of its needs (hunger, thirst), proves incapable of carrying out the specific action necessary to put an end to internal tension. For the adult, the state of helplessness is the prototype of the traumatic situation which is responsible for the generation of anxiety" (p. 189).

Freud, a "reader" of Ferenczi

Ferenczi died in 1933. Freud, who had practically not spoken of trauma since *Inhibitions, Symptoms and Anxiety* (Freud, 1926d), evoked this situation once again in a text considered testamentary, *Moses and Monotheism* (Freud, 1939a), in which he takes up again the whole question of trauma from the angle of its links with the genesis of the neuroses, and presents, for the first time, a conception of trauma linked to the problem of narcissism and its constitution.

Freud stresses that the traumatic experiences that are originally constitutive of psychic functioning and its organisation can lead to early injuries to the ego and create injuries of a narcissistic order resulting in a split in the ego: "The experiences in question fall within the period of infantile amnesia", Freud adds, and "relate to impressions of a sexual and aggressive nature, and no doubt also to early injuries to the ego (narcissistic mortifications)" (1939a, p. 74).

We may reasonably suppose, then, that Freud had become not only a latent but a patent "reader" of Ferenczi, perhaps in connection with the painful and conflictual experience of mourning that he must have gone through since the death of his former disciple and patient, friend and confidant.

The "original traumatic scar": the *Ururtraumatisch*

Having recalled all the above points, let us now return to *The Clinical Diary*. It is worth pointing out that, in his note of 10 April 1932, Ferenczi was trying to identify the psychic locus where the trauma was inscribed originally, and the imprints, actual mnemic traces, that it leaves:

> In this connection the question arises whether the primal trauma is not always to be sought in the primal relationship with the mother, and whether the traumata of a somewhat later epoch, already complicated by the appearance of the father, could have had such an effect without the existence of such a pre-primal-trauma [*Ururtraumatischen*] mother-child scar. Being loved, being the center of the universe, is the natural emotional state of the baby, therefore it is not a mania but an actual fact. The first disappointments in love (weaning, regulation of the excretory functions, the first punishments through a harsh tone of voice, threats, even spankings) must have, in every case, a traumatic effect, that is, one that produces psychic paralysis from the first moment. The resulting disintegration makes it possible for new psychic formations to emerge. In particular it may be assumed that a splitting occurs at this stage.
>
> (Diary, p. 83)

Thus, for Ferenczi it was clearly on the side of the deficiencies of the relationship linked to the primary object or the failures of the latter's capacity to serve as a container and protective shield (which would become the "deficiencies of the environment" or the "non-facilitating" environment for Winnicott)—owing to an excess of early seduction that this object has induced, either through excess or through lack—that the *Ururtraumatisch* originates. The latter is the locus of the origin of disorders of symbolisation and thought, the alienation of the I, states of ego-alteration, states of primary violence (manifestations of primary hate and love), disorders of auto-eroticism (auto-erotic weaknesses), all of which will become a breeding ground for the denials and splitting at the origin of passionate transferences, primary and anaclitic depressions, as well as impasses in analysis and patients' negative psychoanalytic reactions.

References

Bokanowski, T. (1997). *Sándor Ferenczi.* Paris: Presses Universitaires de France.

Deutsch, H. (1942). Some forms of emotional disturbance and their relationship to schizophrenia. *Psychoanalytic Quarterly, 11*: 301–321.

Freud, S. (1926d). Inhibitions, Symptoms and Anxiety. *S. E., 20*: 75–174. London: Hogarth.

Freud, S. (1939a). Moses and Monotheism. *S. E., 23*: 7–140. London: Hogarth.

Green, A. (1993). *The Work of the Negative* (A. Weller, Trans.). London: Free Association Books, 1999.

Laplanche J., & Pontalis J.-B. (1967). *The Language of Psychoanalysis.* London: Hogarth, 1972.

Winnicott, D. W. (1960). Ego distortion in terms of true self and false self. In: *The Maturational Process and the Facilitating Environment* (pp. 140–157). New York, NY: International Universities Press, 1965.

Chapter 21

Regressing to reality: Finding and listening to the inner world of the traumatised child

Elizabeth Howell

> "I assumed that one has no right to be satisfied with any analysis until it has led to the actual reproduction of the traumatic occurrences."
>
> (Ferenczi, 1931, p. 472)

By providing a safe and honest treatment milieu that fostered trust, Sándor Ferenczi welcomed normally unwelcome, traumatised states of mind to emerge into the relational space between patient and analyst. By his courage to recognise the reality of his patient's reports, often the reality of sexual or other abuse, Ferenczi helped his patients to regress to the reality of their dissociated traumatic experiences. Sharing and working with these experiences helped the patient to heal from the effects of locked up unbearable affect and truths. But Ferenczi meant something different by regression than did Freud, for whom regression meant moving backwards to an earlier stage of development, as a defence. As Hainer (2016) notes, when Ferenczi "spoke of regression he was describing dissociative states: switches in self-states, trances, and the feeling like he was actually *with* a young child..." (p. 60).

For Ferenczi, regression was not defensive, but was helpful, even necessary for the treatment. Ferenczi worked to create an atmosphere of maternal warmth and trust. As he listened to and learned from his patients, he strove to avoid paternalistic and "superior" attitudes. He learned to avoid intrusive interpretations that interrupted the patient's flow of associations and to emphasise mutuality and "elasticity", a therapeutic creation initially devised by a patient, in which patient and analyst pull upon each other equally, as if each party held one end of a large rubber band. He wanted his patients to feel welcome in the treatment room, which often had not been the case in their families of origin. He listened carefully to the affective aspects of communication. Rather than intellectual recollection and reconstruction, he emphasised indulging patients' wishes in the treatment to enable what he called a neocatharsis. The strong affective content of neocatharsis "had much more feeling of actuality and concreteness about it than heretofore, approximated much more closely to an actual recollection, whereas till then the patients had spoken only of possibilities ... degrees of probability and had yearned in vain for memories" (1930, p. 437). Ferenczi felt that it was not helpful to over-frustrate the patient. Rather, regression occurred in response to the invitation that the analyst (Ferenczi) offered to his patient, via the creation of a real, relaxed, honest, and compassionate therapeutic milieu. At times such regression was also triggered, as associations brought the patient to an earlier traumatic reality that had been dissociated, and therefore never formulated or resolved. But it was not resistance to the treatment. Rather it served the treatment. Only by such regression could the trauma be met and treated. Part of Ferenczi's *furor sandandi*, or rage to cure, involved getting to the trauma:

> So far as my experience goes, however, there comes sooner or later (often, I admit, very late) a collapse of the intellectual superstructure and a breaking through of the fundamental situation, which after all is always primitive and strongly affective in character. Only at this point does the patient begin to repeat and find a fresh solution for the original conflict between the ego and its environment, as it must have taken place in his early childhood.
>
> (1931, p. 480)

Regression and growth

By accepting the emergence of quasi-hallucinatory or trance states, Ferenczi was fostering his patients' ability to access their own experience and produce their own material. Comparing the analyst's to the parent's power, he notes that as analysts "we might fashion that greater power into a means of educating them to greater independence and courage" (1931, p. 475). Ferenczi's "regression" was a regression in service of the treatment. (For me, this anticipated Ernst Kris' (1936) later formulation of "regression in the service of the ego" that involved the use of regression in creativity and art.) Enabling dissociated pieces of experience to become linked within the personality is integrative, and this facilitates creativity.

Ferenczi's "regression", time, and the dissociative unconscious

Although Freud's use of the term "regression" relied on a metaphor of a temporal retreat, that is, it meant moving backwards in linear time to an earlier stage of development, for Ferenczi regression usually referred to the emergence of, or a switch to, a dissociated traumatised state—a non-linear emergence of an encapsulated piece of experience from the patient's internal world. In his 1930 paper on relaxation and neocatharsis he compared the mind of the neurotic "to a double malformation, something like the so-called *teratoma* which harbours in a hidden part of its body fragments of a twin-being which has never developed" (p. 441). It was not so much that Ferenczi was trying to go backwards in time but that he was trying to reach the origin of the patient's illness: "When you consider that, according to our experience hitherto … most pathogenic shocks take place in childhood, you will not be surprised that the patient, in the attempt to uncover the origin of his illness, suddenly lapses into a childish or child-like attitude" (1931, p. 472). The appearance of these traumatised self-states, then, was less of a temporal backwards movement than an entry into a particular encapsulated world in which time had stopped. Such self-states know no future, but only a timeless dissociated present that continuously repeats itself.

Even though he did not call it that, when Ferenczi's patients reached their traumatised self-states, they had reached the dissociated unconscious. Trusting the truth of what he was discovering by listening to his patients—that there was real trauma at the root of their symptoms—he cut his way through the obscurations of orthodoxy, re-illuminating the dissociative unconscious.

Trauma and dissociation

In his late papers Ferenczi continually wrote of dissociative splits resulting from trauma. His statement in his 1933 "Confusion of tongues" essay, that "there is neither shock nor fright without some trace of splitting of the personality" (Conf, p. 229), is consistent with the view that trauma may be understood as "event(s) that cause dissociation" (Howell, 2005, p. ix). Ferenczi noted that as the shocks increase during a child's development, so do the splits. Eventually "it becomes extremely difficult to maintain contact without confusion with all the fragments each of which behaves [as] a separate personality yet does not know of even the existence of others" (Conf, p. 229). Even though he used the diagnostic terms and language of his time, for example, "hysteria" and "neurosis", in this and other papers, notably "Child analysis in the analysis of adults" (1931), it is clear that he was often describing what we now call dissociative identity disorder (DID).

In their treatments, Ferenczi's patients often reached dissociated traumatic experiences and dissociated injured child or adolescent self-states. Ferenczi wrote of hysterical attacks that "actually assumed the character of trances, in which fragments of the past were relived and the physician was the only bridge left between the patients and reality. I was able to question them and received important information about dissociated parts of the personality" (1930, p. 437). Ferenczi often described patients' hallucinatory trances in which traumatic events were re-enacted. In one particular instance a patient lapsed into a child or adolescent self-state. This was a trance-logic world or dream-like state in which contradictory things are possible:

> For example, a patient … resolved, after overcoming strong resistances, and especially his profound mistrust, to revive in his mind incidents from his earliest childhood. Thanks to the light already thrown by analysis on his early life, I was aware that in the scene revived by him, he was identifying me with his grandfather. Suddenly, in the midst of what he was saying, he threw his arm round my neck and whispered in my ear: "I say, Grandpapa, I am afraid I am going to have a baby!" Thereupon I had what seems to me a happy inspiration: I said nothing to him for the moment about transference, etc., but retorted, in a similar whisper: "Well, but why do you think so?"
>
> (1931, p. 471)

Ferenczi's response here was an illustration of what he called "the game", in which he joined with the dissociated self-states in a dialogue about their experiences, as current-day therapists who work with dissociative disorders usually do. Ferenczi (1931) emphasised that what has been learned from these re-enactments and dialogues must then be thoroughly analysed and worked through, but that "You must catch your hare before you can cook him" (p. 473).

"The game", however, can be a delicate business for both therapist and patient. One proviso is that when patients drop their role in the game and "act out infantile reality in terms of adult behavior, it must then be shown to him that it is he who is spoiling the game" (ibid.). Rude behavior of this sort does not call for indulgence; rather "it is better to admit honestly that we find the patient's behavior unpleasant" (op. cit., p. 474).

The caretaker self

However, in the treatments, it was not only injured child self-states that emerged; Ferenczi also found self-states that protected the injured ones. The treatment did not just reach the trauma, but a dissociative structure—because without protectors in external interpersonal reality, the traumatised child must create inner protectors. One particularly important protector self-state that Ferenczi described is the caretaker self, which had various manifestations. He described how one part of the psyche becomes a caretaker for the rest, protecting it, so that "the task of adaptation to reality [is] being shouldered by the fragment of the personality which has been spared" (1930, p. 442). He notes that "under the stress of imminent danger, part of the self splits off and becomes a psychic instance self-observing and desiring to help the [traumatised] self, and that possibly this happens in early—even the earliest—childhood" (1931, p. 474). He wrote that: "One definitely gets the impression that to be left deserted results in a dissociation of personality. Part of the person adopts the role of father or mother in relation to the rest, thereby undoing, as it were, the fact of being left deserted" (1931, p. 476). Ferenczi also wrote of the "wise baby" who does not experience the pain of the trauma, can be precociously helpful to the child, and who teaches wisdom to the entire family (Martín Cabré, Chapter Eighteen).

Ferenczi developed the concept of a caretaker self in different ways, pointing to some of the shared elements of dissociative thought disorder and psychosis. He understood how the traumatic shock of sexual abuse may cause the child to become temporarily psychotic. Not only did he view the splitting off of part of the personality that occurred as a result of shock as psychotic, but he emphasised this psychotic aspect more specifically when he wrote of the "introjection" of the aggressor in 1933, in "Confusion of tongues". In this process the aggressor "disappears as a part of external reality and becomes intra- as opposed to extra-psychic; the intrapsychic is then subjected, in a dream-like state as is the traumatic trance, to the primary process, i.e., according to the pleasure principle it can be modified or changed by the use of positive or negative hallucinations" (p. 228).

Ferenczi eloquently described how an aspect of the process of self-splitting, as a result of the object-relation having become intolerable, moves the psyche into narcissism:

> The man abandoned by all gods escapes completely from reality and creates for himself another world in which he, unimpeded by earthly gravity, can achieve everything he wants. Has he been unloved, even tormented, he now splits off from himself a part which in the form of a helpful, loving, often motherly, minder commiserates with the tormented remainder of the self, nurses him and decides for him; and all this is done with deepest wisdom and most penetrating intelligence. He is intelligence and kindness itself, so to speak a guardian angel. This angel sees the suffering or murdered child from the outside.. He wanders through the whole Universe seeking help, invents fantasies for the child that cannot be saved in any other way, etc.
>
> (Frag, p. 237)

But eventually, this self-parenting strategy usually does not work because by relying on the inner world for organisation and help, the child loses touch with the outer world. Ferenczi wrote that the "first reaction to a shock seems to be always a transitory psychosis, i.e., a turning away from reality." He went on to say: "It seems likely that a psychotic splitting off of a part of the personality occurs under the influence of shock. The dissociated part, however, lives on hidden, ceaselessly endeavoring to make itself felt, without finding any outlet except in neurotic symptoms" (1930, p. 440). One might add that the hallmark of this "psychotic-like" primary process is that dissociative subjectivities are interrelating on the inside.

In his trauma work, Ferenczi not so much uncovered, but welcomed the traumatic past into the analytic space of the dyad. And he welcomed this not only into the dyad but into the intrapersonal system of the patient, thereby allowing the system to reorganise, so that it relies less on protector parts and is more open as a system to care and tenderness from real others.

Closeness and coherence *vs.* emotional distance and dissociation

Ferenczi understood how when a child is forced into an aloneness by trauma, fragmentation may occur.[1] Ferenczi was working to stay close to his patients' experiences, and by doing so, he was helping them to repair fragmentation and to pull their experiences together, thereby assisting them to achieve greater personal coherence.

In sum

By creating an atmosphere of trust, Ferenczi fostered the emergence of dissociated experiences (regression) that lay at the root of the patient's problems. The information and affect revealed and released by these experiences could then be analysed. He described how psychic trauma splits the self, as well as the functions of these different encapsulated subjectivities. The treatment must accept this fractured self, this dissociated mind. A major part of the treatment is lessening or undoing the splits, and this is aided by an atmosphere of relaxation, warmth, and an analyst who strives to listen in a way that is close to the patient's experience.

So many of Ferenczi's discoveries and insights have recently been arrived at again about seventy-five years later, by others in the trauma field, in the dissociation field, and in self-psychology, for starters. As Hainer (2016) notes, Ferenczi's work on dissociation was dissociated in the psychoanalytic field for many years. Ferenczi's works, especially his later works, are a storehouse of wisdom, containing brilliant and passionately conceived insights and theories of regression, trauma, and dissociation. His writings will dramatically enrich the thinking of anyone who has not read them before—or who reads them again.

References

Ferenczi, S. (1930). The principle of relaxation and neocatharsis. *International Journal of Psychoanalysis*, *11*: 428–443.

Ferenczi, S. (1931). Child analysis in the analysis of adults. *International Journal of Psychoanalysis*, *12*: 468–482.

Hainer, M. L. (2016). The Ferenczi paradox: His importance in understanding dissociation and the dissociation of his importance in psychoanalysis. In: E. F. Howell & S. Itzkowitz (Eds.), *The*

1 I suggest that rather than unity and dividedness, a more meaningful juxtaposition is closeness *vs.* dividedness. For various reasons, on which I will only very briefly elaborate here, the concept of unity is problematic. Rather than starting out unified, people start out with behavioural states that need to be connected in time (Putnam, 1997). And there are always sub-units and supra-units. Perhaps the popular juxtaposition of unity *vs.* dividedness of the self has impeded our noticing the important juxtaposition of closeness to experience *vs.* dividedness. From an interpersonal perspective, it makes sense to me that staying close to patients' experiences allows pieces of their lives to cohere in context, to make internal sense. By dividedness, I mean shutting off one set of experience from another, or not connecting these experiences (Howell, 2017).

Dissociative Mind in Psychoanalysis: Understanding and Working with Trauma (pp. 57–69). Abingdon: Routledge.
Howell, E. F. (2005). *The Dissociative Mind.* Hillsdale, NJ: Analytic Press.
Howell, E. F. (2017). Speaking to and validating emotional truth in the jury-built self: On therapeutic action in the psychoanalytic treatment of trauma. In: R. B. Gartner (Ed.), *Trauma and Countertrauma, Resilience and Counterresilience*. Abingdon: Routledge.
Kris, E. (1936). The psychology of caricature. *International Journal of Psychoanalysis, 17*: 285–303.
Putnam, F. W. (1997). *Dissociation in Children and Adolescents*. New York: Guilford Press.

Chapter 22

Ferenczi's experiments with technique

Endre Koritar

Introduction

Ferenczi enthusiastically applied Freud's psychoanalytic methodology (as described in his "Papers on technique" (1911–1914)) in his clinical work with patients. He initially faithfully applied the fundamental rule (free association, abstinence, neutrality) in his technical approach with some success but, inevitably, he treated some patients who did not respond to standard technique. His enthusiasm for the psychoanalytic approach did not waiver however, and he considered the treatment resistance attributable to inadequate technique and not to the intractableness of the patient's condition (ChildAn). He experimented empirically by varying some of the basic technical parameters, reporting his observations on the outcomes of his experimentation in various early papers on active technique (1919, 1921, 1924, 1925b). A closer examination of these papers and "Contra-indications to the active psycho-analytical technique" (1925a) will be useful in understanding how he refuted his early experiments and arrived at the principles of elasticity and relaxation in technique. Ferenczi's innovations, although suppressed for over half a century, were harbingers of contemporary psychoanalytic technique.

Theoretical underpinnings of active therapy

In "Technical difficulties in the analysis of a case of hysteria" (1919), Ferenczi considered stagnation of analyses to be linked with his patients' indulging themselves in "larval forms of onanism" (p. 155) expressed in various forms of behaviour: crossing of legs, stereotypical bodily movements or positions, tics, rubbing of the skin, frequent urination. Thus, having gratified libidinal drive, there was no motivation to change characterological ways of being, which perpetuated psychopathology. In a deviation from the fundamental rule, Ferenczi forbade his patients from indulging in these masturbatory manifestations, which resulted initially in the reporting of repressed early childhood memories and traumatic experiences, and in the longer term, reversal of anorgasmic sexual activity and diminution of behavioural and psychosomatic symptoms. Ferenczi likely derived his active technical approach as an empirical experiment based on Freud's (1915c) reflections on the economic theory of drives.

Briefly formulated: frustration results from accumulation of libidinal or aggressive drive energy. Discharge of drive energy through sexual or aggressive behaviours leads to a sense of satisfaction. Repressed drive energy may be discharged through various behaviours, which are masturbatory equivalents. Theoretically, inhibition of these behaviours could result in a re-channeling of the drive energy into conscious transference reactions and to preconscious or conscious symbolic representation, resulting in retrieval of repressed memories and affects in the analysis, and symptom resolution.

Ferenczi considered his experiments with active technique a success. Actively prohibiting patients from indulging in "larval forms of onanism" resulted in the retrieval of traumatic memories, memories of early infantile sexuality, and transference reactions. Encouraged by these "successes", Ferenczi applied the active approach to other types of resistances.

In "On Forced fantasies" (1924), Ferenczi describes a defence using the principle of free association, which he calls logorrhea, or talking past the point. Such patients may be able to speak freely, but the work remains superficial and absent of affective expression to the material produced due to inhibition of certain lines of associations and fantasies. Ferenczi actively encouraged these patients to produce fantasies of transference reactions, early infantile memories, and masturbatory fantasies. This was contrary to standard technique, which encourages the therapist to be passive and allow the patient to associate freely without influencing the direction of their associations. In pursuing an idea suggested by Rank he set a premature termination date with a patient who had not made any progress in analysis over several months. His rationale was that he would pressure the patient into more effective analytic work. This approach seemed to have a positive outcome, as the patient produced various libidinal and aggressive fantasies from childhood and in the transference. However, he quickly relapsed symptomatically after termination, requiring a recommencement of the analysis. Ferenczi commented that this experiment in premature termination not only caused unnecessary hardship emotionally for his patient but also resulted in a negative therapeutic reaction, which actually prolonged the analysis.

In "Psychoanalysis of sexual habits" (1925b) Ferenczi gave his patients various directives: to delay urination in a patient with frequent urination; to delay bowel movements in a patient during a session who urgently had to evacuate his bowels; and, he instructed a patient not to have sexual relations during treatment. In all these cases, the patient produced repressed memories, infantile recollections, or transference associations. He considered such "breakthroughs" as justification for his active technique while oblivious to the intrusive nature of his instructions and insensitive to the distress he may be causing his patients. In his enthusiasm to apply Freud's metapsychology to the clinical situation, he treated his patients as experimental subjects and not as disturbed, traumatised individuals in whom he might be repeating past traumas, in the analysis.

Glover's critical review (1924) of Ferenczi's active therapy focused on its impact on the transference. He suggested that there is an optimal psychic unfolding of the transference and curtailing it prematurely would complicate the working through process. Second, he speculated that active manipulation of the transference may represent a repetition in the transference, of the trauma experienced by the patient in the original situation. Third, in reference to setting a termination date strategically, he considered that, in the course of an analysis, the analysis of transference and its dissolution is an expected outcome. The choice of a termination date should be contingent upon this process, which varies according to individual dynamics.

Shift to elasticity and relaxation

"Contra-indications to the 'active' psychoanalytical technique" (1925a) represented a partial refutation of the principles of active therapy. He clarified that he had never intended activity in therapy as a primary technical parameter, and that it was only to be used in later phases of analysis once an unequivocal positive transference had been established, but when resistance based on characterological rigidity resulted in stagnation of analysis. On further reflection, however, he came to the realisation that, in his activity, he represented a transference authoritarian object suppressing his patient's self-determination, resulting in a repetition of past conflictual object relations, and in iatrogenic negative transference, which itself was problematic for the analysis, not to mention the distress induced in the patient. Whereas most of the paper is versed in metapsychological discussion of the underlying theory of activity in psychoanalysis, Ferenczi finishes the paper with an interesting perspective: "I personally feel myself to be turned completely to the Freudian positivism, and prefer to see in you who sit there before me and hear my words, not ideas in my ego, be real beings with whom I can identify myself. I cannot put that on a logical basis for you" (1925a, p. 229). In this enigmatic statement one might hear Ferenczi's disenchantment with the positivist metapsychological approach to analysis, preferring instead a relational approach in his analytic work with patients.

Ferenczi's disenchantment with Freudian metapsychology and technique has deeper roots than his disappointment with the results of his experiments with active therapy. In *The Development of Psychoanalysis* (Ferenczi & Rank, 1925c), written in 1923 with Otto Rank, he critically re-evaluated psychoanalytic methodology and concluded that there was too much emphasis on metapsychological interpretation of unconscious material, that is, making the unconscious conscious, whereas the experiential aspect of analysis, that is, analysis of the transference and countertransference relationship between analyst and analysand, was less emphasised. Freud considered repetition-compulsion and acting out unconscious conflicts as problematic in analysis. Through interpretation of unconscious drives underlying the phenomena, symbolic representation, and working through, repressed unconscious conflicts and fantasies could be made conscious, and the drive energy compromised by the repression could be liberated and made available for creative activity (Freud, 1914g). Ferenczi (Ferenczi & Rank, 1925c), on the other hand, believed that repetition of repressed trauma in the transference provided the patient with another opportunity to work through difficult experiences in the analysis, that is, in the here and now, reliving past trauma with the analyst as a benign object, and hopefully having a different outcome in the working through. Ferenczi's vision of the analyst's efficacy and the patient's healing was that it depended on the establishment of an actual object relationship in the analysis, with both analyst and patient experiencing the repetition of repressed trauma in the analytic situation, with a resolution occurring through the symbolic representation of what had been unrepresented but experienced and repressed. From 1925 on, Ferenczi devoted his work and writing to further elaborate on psychoanalytic technique as addressing the actual relationship with the patient in the analysis.

In his later papers—"Elasticity of psychoanalytic technique" (Elast), 1928, "The unwelcome child and his death drive" (1929a), "The principle of relaxation and neocatharsis" (1929b), "Child-analysis in the analysis of adults" (ChildAn), 1931, "Confusion of tongues" (Conf), 1932, and in *The Clinical Diary* (Diary), 1933—Ferenczi emphasises the importance of countertransference analysis and attunement to the patient's expressed or unexpressed needs.

In "Elasticity of psychoanalytic technique" (Elast) he emphasised the centrality of the second fundamental rule—the importance of the analyst's own analysis and his countertransference analysis in the analytic work. Repetition of past traumas in the analysis being unavoidable, he reasons it behooves the analyst to analyse how he has contributed to the current cycle of re-traumatisation and, in honestly acknowledging the patient's experience of the analyst's role as tormentor, create a space for a new type of object relationship, different from the original. He uses the metaphor of an elastic band (as suggested by a patient) to describe the analytic interaction between analyst and analysand. The analysand at one end pulling the elastic in her direction, pulls the analyst at the other end in his direction, while the analyst, offering resistance, pulls the analysand back in the other direction. Thus, in analysis, there is a constant approaching and pulling back by both analysand and analyst, responding to each other's pressure in the opposite direction. This metaphor redefined analytic work into a situation of object relational mutual experiencing and responding where transference and countertransference are constantly in flux. The analyst, at the same time as maintaining an objective, observing position, is a participant in the intersubjective experience and alternately moves towards and away from the patient, from subjective immersion to objective symbolisation. "One gradually becomes aware how immensely complicated the mental work demanded from the analyst is. He has to let his patient's free associations play upon him; simultaneously he lets his own fantasies get to work with the association material.... One might say that his mind swings continuously between empathy, self-observation and making judgments" (Elast, pp. 95–96).

In his last major papers (1929a, 1929b, ChildAn, Conf), Ferenczi distances himself from rigid adherence to standard psychoanalytic technique in favour of a more relational, intersubjective analytic approach, particularly in patients with significant traumatic developmental histories and suffering from characterological problems. He argues that standard analytic technique, in rigidly applying the principles of abstinence and neutrality, precipitates a re-traumatisation of the patient along the lines of the initial actual trauma and results in an outcome in the analysis similar to the initial outcome: identification with the aggressor (Frankel, Chapter Nineteen), this time the analyst, while the patient's self remains stunted. He argues that in analysis, just as in healthy child development, principles of frustration and indulgence are both necessary, in facilitating and stimulating the stunted self to develop and mature along normal lines. This requires of the analyst an attunement to the needs of the patient, much like a parent who strives to be constantly aware of the developing child's needs in her developmental process. In the analysis attempts at understanding and responding to each other in a thoughtful, self-reflective mode, have a salutary therapeutic effect, helping to heal wounds sustained by emotional, physical, and sexual traumas. Adults who are developmentally stuck in an early phase of the maturational process may need to go through a period of indulgence in their childish pursuits and behaviours before more adult demands and frustrations are presented in the analytic process. "Through this indulgence the patient is permitted, properly speaking for the first time, to enjoy the irresponsibility of childhood, which is equivalent to the introduction of positive life impulses and motives for his subsequent existence" (1929a, p. 273). "And long before psychoanalysis came into existence, there were two elements in the training of children and of the masses: Tenderness and love were accorded to them, and at the same time they were required to adapt themselves to painful reality by making hard renunciations" (1929b, p. 282).

Ferenczi was reputed to have success with so-called "hopeless" cases that did not respond to standard technique. He believed that while neurotic patients may respond to this standard approach (where the analyst acted as a blank screen on to which patients projected while subjected to the analyst's abstinence, with their drive frustrated), traumatised patients, or patients with characterological disorders, required a period of indulgence in their analyses, with relaxation of abstinence and neutrality, before they could be become amenable to more standard analytic work. His technical approach with some patients included overt expressions of tenderness (hugging, greeting enthusiastically, caressing, kissing), thus providing unconditional positive regard that they had been deprived of in their childhood (Quinodoz, 2006, p. 116). Other modes of relaxation in analysis included prolonging sessions when patients were distressed, increasing the frequency of sessions up to several sessions per day, allowing patients to take time off in the analysis when sick, continuing to see patients if they could not afford to pay (Ferenczi, 1929b). He reported good success with the combination of indulgence and frustration, achieving a deeper level of analysis with the mobilisation of affects in a "neocatharsis", the experiencing of "hysterical attacks", trance states, and psychosomatic symptoms, which he labelled as "physical memory symbols". Memories of repressed traumatic episodes emerged of "real psychic traumas and conflicts with the environment" (1929b). His use of relaxation technique yielded unexpected insights and progress in formerly stagnated analyses.

Ferenczi was equally enthusiastic in applying methods of relaxation of technique as he had been earlier with active therapy. He tested the limits of technical parameters in moving from extremes of frustration to extremes of relaxation. There were potential hazards of both paths in therapy. In active therapy, repetition of past traumas; in relaxation, potential boundary crossings either in reality or fantasy. In his passion to heal, he experimented empirically with technique to hasten the process of healing in traumatised and damaged patients anguished by their psychopathology and pleading for relief from their suffering. His most radical innovation was his mutual analysis with Elizabeth Severn (Fortune, 1996; and see Bass, Chapter Twenty-three; Brennan, Chapter Thirteen; Dupont & Brabant, Chapter Fourteen). After a prolonged negative therapeutic reaction, at Severn's prompting, Ferenczi agreed to have Severn analyse him in an effort to overcome his negative transference, which she considered to be the resistance impeding the analysis.

While such measures would be considered extreme and unwise by today's standards, Ferenczi enjoyed success in helping patients who currently would likely be diagnosed as borderline, psychotic, bipolar, PTSD, or schizophrenic. Studying his work in order to elicit the essential elements of his technique has been useful for contemporary therapists in developing approaches that can potentially shorten therapy, and for more regressed patients who do not respond well to standard analytic technique. Short-term dynamic psychotherapy, the British middle school, self-psychology, intersubjective and relational schools of analysis, can all be considered to have elaborated some aspect of Ferenczi's early technical experiments and ideas expressed in his later papers. Technical approaches, including active work with the negative transference, setting a termination date in short-term therapies, work with mirroring and idealising transferences, countertransference analysis, role responsiveness, role reversal, learning from the patient, limited self-disclosure, and working with enactments, are examples of contemporary therapeutic techniques that might be considered to have their roots in Ferenczi's early experiments with technique.

But Ferenczi's true legacy for contemporary dynamic clinicians is his example as a clinician motivated to find an effective therapeutic approach suited to working with whatever dynamic situation confronted him. Each therapeutic situation is unique and requires the clinician, usually through trial and error, to find the optimal approach in the analytic work. Being genuine and honest in admitting one's errors, while seeking to learn from one's patients what they require from the therapist in their work, helps to cement an effective working alliance. Being attuned to one's patient also requires that the therapist analyse his countertransference regularly and use insights gleaned from self-analysis to better understand patients' inner worlds and their torments, while commiserating with them despite being helpless in relieving their suffering. Human connectedness, while suffering through the return of the repressed, helps in ultimately working through past traumas, thus leaving past fixations behind and facilitating the healing of a fragmented, stunted self.

This was the internal landscape that Ferenczi explored and the legacy he left future generations of therapists. In doing so, he departed from Freud's positivist recommendations for technique, developing his own relational approach: acknowledging the importance of environmental trauma, and in his clinical work, emphasising introjection and identification with patients, sharing their experience, countertransference analysis, and responding to their expressed or unexpressed needs. Ferenczi may have gone to extremes in his empirical experiments with technique, but his intent was to find more expedient approaches in helping patients heal their damaged selves and relieve them of their suffering. His ideas and his example continue to inspire a new generation of psychodynamic therapists who are searching for an optimal approach in treating patients with significant psychopathology.

References

Ferenczi, S. (1919). Technical difficulties in the analysis of a case of hysteria. In: J. Barossa (Ed.), *Selected Writings* (pp. 151–158). London: Penguin, 1999.

Ferenczi, S. (1921). Further development of the active technique. In: J. Barossa (Ed.), *Selected Writings* (pp. 187–204). London: Penguin, 1999.

Ferenczi, S. (1924). On forced fantasies. In: J. Barossa (Ed.), *Selected Writings* (pp. 222–232). London: Penguin, 1999.

Ferenczi, S. (1925a). Contra-indications to the "active" psychoanalytical technique. In: *Further Contributions to the Theory and Technique of Psychoanalysis* (pp. 217–230). New York: Brunner/Mazel, 1950.

Ferenczi, S. (1925b). Psychoanalysis of sexual habits. In: *Further Contributions to the Theory and Technique of Psychoanalysis* (pp. 259–297). New York: Brunner/Mazel, 1950.

Ferenczi, S., & Rank, O. (1925c). *The Development of Psychoanalysis.* Madison, CT: International Universities Press, 1986.

Ferenczi, S. (1929a). The unwelcome child and his death instinct. In: J. Barossa (Ed.), *Selected Writings* (pp. 269–274). London: Penguin, 1999.

Ferenczi, S. (1929b). The principle of relaxation and neocatharsis. In: J. Barossa (Ed.), *Selected Writings* (pp. 275–292). London: Penguin, 1999.

Fortune, C. (1996). Mutual analysis: A logical outcome of Sándor Ferenczi's experiments in psychoanalysis. In: P. Rudnytsky, A. Bokay & P. Giampieri-Deutsch (Eds.), *Ferenczi's Turn in Psychoanalysis* (pp. 170–186). New York: New York University Press.

Freud, S. (1911–1914). Papers on technique. *S. E.*, *12*: 83–173. London: Hogarth.

Freud, S. (1914g). Remembering, repeating, working through. *S. E.*, *12*: 145–156. London: Hogarth.

Freud, S. (1915c). Instincts and their vicissitudes. *S. E.*, *14*: 117–140. London: Hogarth.

Glover, E. (1924). "Active therapy" and psychoanalysis: A critical review. *International Journal of Psychoanalysis*, *5*: 269–311.

Quinodoz, J-M. (2006). *Reading Freud.* New York: Routledge.

Chapter 23

Ferenczi's dialogue of unconsciouses, mutual analysis, and the analyst's use of self in the shaping of contemporary relational technique

Anthony Bass

Freud, Ferenczi, and psychoanalytic relations

Since the posthumous publication in English of his *Diary* in 1988, there has been a growing appreciation of the ways in which Ferenczi's clinical investigations have had a profound impact on psychoanalytic thought and practice. Developments in the relational theory of technique, especially with regard to our views and uses of countertransference phenomena, bear the unmistakable imprint of Ferenczi's discoveries. His work offered a profound counterpoint in the therapist's uses of the self to approaches associated with classical traditions (Bass, 2015). Ferenczi began his *Diary* with a sharp critique of how analysis was practiced at that time:

> Mannered form of greeting, formal request to "tell everything," so-called free-floating attention, which ultimately amounts to no attention at all, and which is certainly inadequate to the highly emotional character of the analysand's communications ... This has the following effects: (1) the patient is offended by the lack of interest ... (2) since he does not want to think badly of us ... he looks for cause of this lack of reaction in himself ...
>
> (Diary, p. 1)

Ferenczi recognised transference as different from how it was traditionally conceived: an endogenous unfolding of inner psychic contents projected on to a blank-screen analyst able to interpret its unconscious meaning to the patient. He discerned a more complex relationship between transference and countertransference. The patient's experience of the analyst was not an inevitably distorted response to the person of the analyst, which gave the analyst access to the recesses of the patient's unconscious mind via the particulars of his transference constructions. Rather, patients' views usually included accurate perceptions of the analyst, including aspects of the therapist of which the therapist himself remained unaware. This finding called for new forms of therapeutic participation (and conceptualisations of therapeutic action), requiring greater receptivity to the patient's experience of, and observations of, the therapist.

Ferenczi realised that each psychoanalytic journey involves, to varying degrees, a conjoint working through of the intersubjective obstacles to analytic exploration. Each analysis carries the potential for deepening self-awareness and for the working through of new realms of psychic experience for both participants. The therapeutic action of psychoanalysis is like the proverbial "river that flows two ways".

Ferenczi realised that patients' perceptions constitute not only windows into their unconscious transferences, inspiring interpretations to illuminate unconscious sources of their difficulties, but also signals, orienting the therapist through the thickets of countertransference resistances to his own unconscious participation in the therapy. The analyst is far from anonymous—the patient far from oblivious to the person before (or behind) him.

Ferenczi's understanding of the bi-directional, reciprocal nature of communication between therapist and patient introduced a radically different perspective on therapeutic relations from Freud's, setting the stage for many of the changes in the technique of therapy associated with relational schools.

Ferenczi and the dialogue of unconsciouses

The revelation that unconscious dimensions of the mind played a fundamental part in shaping human experience was one of Freud's groundbreaking discoveries. "It is a very remarkable thing," wrote Freud, in 1915, about what was quintessentially psychoanalytic about the kind of conversation that psychoanalytic work entailed, "that the *Ucs.* [unconscious mind] of one human being can react upon that of the other, without passing through the *Cs.* [conscious mind]" (1915e, p. 194). Even earlier, he claimed that the analyst "must turn his own unconscious like a receptive organ towards the transmitting unconscious of the patient. He must adjust himself to the patient as a telephone receiver is adjusted to the transmitting microphone. Just as the receiver converts back into sound waves the electric oscillations in the telephone line which were set up by sound waves, so the doctor's unconscious is able, from the derivatives of the unconscious which are communicated to him, to reconstruct that unconscious, which has determined the patient's free associations" (1912e, pp. 115–116).

The same year that Freud was penning these historic words staking out the unconscious as a central frame of psychoanalytic reference, Ferenczi put forward a conception of the nature of unconscious relations between people that differed in one important respect. For Ferenczi, the connection between one mind and another was conceived as a "dialogue of unconsciouses" (rather than simply a relation between "sender" and "receiver"). "In my opinion," Ferenczi (1915) noted, "we have to do here with one of those numerous cases that I am in the habit of calling *Dialogues of the Unconscious*, where namely, the unconscious of two people completely understand themselves and each other, without the remotest conception of this on the part of the consciousness of either" (p. 109). As the years passed and Ferenczi continued to track the secret, uncanny responsiveness of one unconscious to another, his bi-directional conception of unconscious-to-unconscious relations gave rise to a different perspective on the analytic relationship itself and on therapeutic action. In his *Diary*, Ferenczi described the dialogue with reference to the analytic relationship: "When two people meet for the first time … an exchange takes place not only of conscious but also of unconscious stirrings. Only analysis could determine for both why, quite inexplicably to either of them, sympathy or antipathy has developed in them. Ultimately I meant by this that when two people converse, not only a conscious dialogue takes place but an unconscious one, from both sides" (Diary, p. 84).

Ferenczi's understanding of the reciprocal nature of communication at an unconscious level that shaped the experience of the therapy and of one another, forged a deep divide in the way Ferenczi and Freud viewed the therapeutic process, psychotherapeutic technique, and the nature of the relationship between therapist and patient.

For Ferenczi, the process by which one unconscious understands another "without the remotest conception of this on the part of the consciousness of either" revealed a bi-directional process, in which either analyst or patient might be the first to grasp the unconscious of the other. Freud believed that he could view the unconscious from a kind of blind viewing post, his own unconscious safely out of view. The analyst was believed to assume a kind of cloak of invisibility. In Freud's telephonic metaphor, he had anticipated the mute button by almost a century.

Ferenczi realized that neither participant is privileged when it comes to hearing the sounds of his own unconscious, while both have the advantage when it comes to apprehending the unconscious of another. This insight upended the fundamental bulwark of the analyst's anonymity and neutrality, introducing a new set of problems and opportunities.

Ferenczi and mutual analysis

The reciprocal nature of the ways in which we come to read one another is an aspect of what a dialogue of unconsciouses describes. Ferenczi's efforts to make room for a sufficiently elastic technique and psychoanalytic frame to accommodate this finding, to make fuller use of the unique contribution that each partner can bring to the development of the therapeutic relationship, led to his experiments in mutual analysis.

The inevitable limits of his self-awareness meant that he needed to listen to patients in new ways. Ferenczi's explorations in mutual analysis constituted his effort to explore the implications for psychoanalytic technique of his discovery that in the psychoanalytic situation, no less than in other forms of intimate human relation, unconscious communication takes place on a two-way street.

Ferenczi's *Diary* detailed the evolution of clinical experiments intended to explore the therapeutic possibilities of full mutual engagement between patient and analyst. His experiments in mutual analysis grew out of his efforts to work his way out of stalemated therapies in which it became evident that his patients' transferences, resistances, and anxieties were inextricably linked to his own countertransferences, counter-resistances, and counter-anxieties. In the case of his patient Elizabeth Severn, he describes it this way: "The patient did not have the impression of me that I was completely harmless, that is to say, full of understanding. The patient sensed unconscious resistances and obstacles in me; it was for this reason that mutual analysis was proposed" (Diary, p. 73).

The patient could feel free to risk taking her own analysis further only to the extent that the analyst could feel free to risk taking his own analysis further, with her. Ferenczi discovered that when he was able to tolerate his patient's analysis of his own unconscious negativity and hostility, the patient felt safer and freer to gain access to her own feelings. Ferenczi understood that stalled analyses frequently foundered on the shoals of the analyst's own unconscious resistances. Among the factors that Ferenczi noted in considering how analyses fail was "artificiality in the analyst's behavior" (Diary, p. 11), his feigned friendliness, a posture intended to mask or deny countertransference feelings, and responses at odds with the analyst's preferred self-image. Ferenczi experimented with the full disclosure of his feelings as analyst:

> Any kind of secrecy, whether positive or negative in character, makes the patient distrustful; he detects from little gestures (form of greeting, handshake, tone of voice, degree of animation, etc.) the presence of affects, but cannot gauge their quantity or importance; candid disclosure regarding them enables him to counteract them.
>
> (Diary, p. 11)

For contemporary analysts in the interpersonal, and later the relational, traditions, who had come to see the blank-screen, anonymous, abstinent model of analytic participation as an inadequate, even harmful approach to practice, the discovery of Ferenczi's critique was a breath of fresh air revealing origins of contemporary ways of working in the early days of psychoanalysis.

I believe Ferenczi would be pleased to find a psychoanalytic culture today in which his vision has been substantially realised. The recognition of the ways in which increased personal self-awareness and growth of patient and analyst as integrally linked is widely taken for granted among relationally informed therapists today. Ferenczi found that to reach a patient in the deepest possible way, complementary areas of his own psychic life inevitably became illuminated, resonating like a tuning fork connecting one unconscious to another. He was not the dispassionate observer whose very objectivity constituted the means by which he would come to know his patient. He realised instead that important aspects of himself were exposed to his patients, revealing a subjective, rather than objective, presence, whether he intended such exposure or not. Far from countertransference detritus that called for greater self-control or disciplined bracketing of his own subjectivity, such unbidden, unintended, and often unconscious communications played an important role in the analytic process itself. When the analyst is able to facilitate the patient's fullest possible collaboration in elaborating and exploring the experience of both partners in therapy, a process is engaged through which aspects of the analyst became more accessible to himself, just as the aspects of the patient became more accessible to himself. Such forms of mutual engagement have become part of quotidian therapeutic work today, rather than exceptional radical experiments, as they were in Ferenczi's day.

An example of ordinary mutual analysis today

A patient of mine recently noticed me yawning during a session, and inquired whether I had not had enough sleep. Perhaps I was affected by the overheated atmosphere of the room, or whether he was "making" me sleepy. The question was a genuine inquiry, not rhetorical in form or tone. He was interested in the impact he had on others, believed that he could be boring at times. We were accustomed to using our experiences in therapy as a point of departure for exploration of his inner life and its interpersonal representations. I had yawned without paying much attention to the origins of the psychic state the act might have represented. Rather than starting with a query about his "fantasy" about what my yawn might signify, I thought about his question and told him that the combination of not having had a great night's sleep, and the heat of the room, as he had suggested, probably contributed to my yawning, as far as I could tell.

I acknowledged too that what I "knew" was unlikely to constitute the entire story. I would be interested in learning more about it if we could. Had he entertained other hypotheses about my condition? Was there something he had noticed, in himself or in me, that might shed some light on what my sleepy symptom might represent? My interest was not that of a transference fishing expedition, though I was of course mindful of what my yawn might have meant to him. I knew the meaning of my yawn would be shaped in part by his long-held feelings about himself, how others respond to him, and whether he can hold another's interest. But his query about the source of my yawn directed my attention to aspects of my own experience in the session that I now realised may have been outside my own awareness. I didn't think that the occasional yawn in a session was unusual for me, so I wondered if there might have been something in particular that drew his attention to it this time. Had he picked up something in the session that may have raised a question about my responsiveness to him, my presence, which, together with my yawn, peaked his interest about what it might suggest?

I noticed that with my own curiosity primed, my head had cleared and I felt suddenly as if I had had a much better night's sleep. I had the sensation that a fog had lifted that I hadn't even known was there. I also knew that any further insight into the matter was as likely to come from his associations and introspections as from my own. After a minute of quiet reflection on both our parts, he said it occurred to him that he had had some thoughts about me, before my yawn, that he hadn't bothered to mention. It seemed possible to him that I registered some holding back on his part, which I might have experienced in some subliminal way as soporific. Now that we were thinking about it together, he was able to home in on the thought that had eluded us, and we were able to delve further into considering what might have made the missing thoughts go missing. The conversation came to include his further ideas about how it was that he lost track of what he was thinking before he could tell me (it didn't feel like a conscious choice), as well as his astute sense of why his losing track of the thought might have had the effect of "making" me foggy. His insight into the nature of my response and how it related to what he sensed about me felt accurate. His construction of the moment included observations and speculations about the way I unconsciously respond to information withheld, leading me to new insights about its origins in my own history. As Ferenczi observed, it may be advisable that the patient's analysis of the analyst proceeds "only to the extent that ... the patient's needs require it" (Diary, p. 34). Our discussion of the yawn, its likely origins in both of us, and newly emergent links to other moments in our therapy that we now could consider retrospectively, was helpful to both of us and led each of us to greater awareness about ourselves, each other, and our relationship.

Conclusion

The centrality of psychoanalytic mutuality is, for me, at the heart of what makes psychoanalysis relational, and distinguishes the relational approach to listening and engaging. We see the evidence of a dialogue of unconsciouses shaping therapeutic work in a variety of ways, some of which are taken up directly between patient and therapist, while others operate at a more implicit level. An analysand of mine, a therapist herself, found that as she was beginning to think new kinds of thoughts in her own therapy, her patient began to move into new, parallel areas of his own. The opposite of an "attack on linking", as Bion (1959) has described, the freeing of space within the therapist's mind seems to make new connections possible for the patient too, in a kind of mutual linking process. Apparently the analyst's openness to her own experience provides a link of access for the patient to her own experience. My patient realised that her patient had not been able to risk thinking about certain aspects of her own experience until she (her therapist) could inhabit a place in her own mind where she could receive these thoughts and think about them along with her. She believed that her patient sensed her greater comfort in areas that they had both struggled with, which made it possible for her patient to begin to do new work. It seemed to my patient that her patient had waited until she was ready to take the next step.

A special kind of analytic expertise is born from the experience we gain pursuing the pathways of our inner lives, as well as that of our patients, as these intersect and interpenetrate in the work. Therapeutic work is a process of joint self-discovery, in which each dyad finds unique ways to expand the possibilities for deep and transformative experience, encountering limits, and finding ways of transcending them, as far as any particular psychoanalytic dyad finds that it is able.

References

Bass, A. (2015). The dialogue of unconsciouses, mutual analysis and the uses of the self in contemporary relational psychoanalysis. *Psychoanalytic Dialogues, 25*: 2–17.

Bion, W. R. (1959). Attacks on linking. *International Journal of Psychoanalysis, 40*: 308–315.

Ferenczi, S. (1915). Psychogenic anomalies of voice production. In: *Further Contributions to the Theory and Technique of Psychoanalysis* (pp. 105–109). London: Karnac, 1994.

Freud, S. (1912e). Recommendations to physicians practicing psychoanalysis. *S. E., 12*: 109–120. London: Hogarth.

Freud, S. (1915e). The unconscious. *S. E., 14*: 166–215. London: Hogarth.

Chapter 24

Countertransference and the person of the therapist

Irwin Hirsch

What has been called the postmodern, or relational, turn in psychoanalysis, coming to fruition in the 1980s, has shifted prevailing psychoanalytic thinking away from an earlier view of psychoanalysis as an objective science. Not only does each psychoanalytic tradition have its own views of human development and clinical process—I suggest that each individual clinical psychoanalyst works in ways that reflect his unique personality (Wolstein, 1975), his irreducible subjectivity, at least as much as membership in any school of thought allows.

But the decline of the view that psychoanalysis is a science and, similarly, of the possibility that the analyst is an objective observer, began not with the relational movement in the 1980s but with its forerunners, Sándor Ferenczi in Europe in the 1920s and early 1930s, and Harry Stack Sullivan and interpersonal psychoanalysis in the United States, beginning in the 1940s (Sullivan, 1953; Thompson, 1950); indeed, Sullivan was influenced by Ferenczi's earlier work. While Ferenczi's revolutionary contributions eventually changed the face of psychoanalysis, due to various factors (Hirsch, 2008) it took a long time for his ideas to be recognised, valued, and integrated by the classical psychoanalytic mainstream.

As I see it, Ferenczi's most basic and essential paradigm-shifting idea was that the relationship between analyst and patient had more mutative power than did insight produced by analysts' interpretive interventions alone—an idea that, at the time, was seen as apostasy and a profound threat to a relatively new and still-marginal profession whose practitioners were trying doggedly to market themselves as objective medical scientists.

There are fundamentally two ways to think about the mutative action of psychoanalysis as a function of a new experience with a professional yet subjective other—and Ferenczi (e.g., Ferenczi & Rank, 1924) introduced both. In the first, which originates in Ferenczi's relaxation-technique experiments (approximately 1928–1931), the analyst can be thought of as a replacement object to repair patients' developmental traumas; in the second, deriving from Ferenczi's experiments with mutual analysis (approximately 1931–1932), the analyst is an unwitting co-participant in the repetition of patients' core relational patterns, with the aim that this mutual enactment will evolve into something new and better. The former can be seen as the forerunner of both the British object relations and self psychology approaches, while the latter is the predecessor of the American interpersonal tradition. In each paradigm, analytic success depends on patients' internalisation of an emotionally significant and enriching personal analytic experience. Who the analyst is as a person, and his personal aesthetic, and especially the unique ways each individual analyst tends to interact with other people (Wolstein, 1975), has much to do with which school he chooses to embrace (Hirsch, 2008; 2015, Kuchuck, 2013).

According to Clara Thompson (1950), who had been Ferenczi's patient, and, more recently, to Harris and Kuchuck (2015), Ferenczi's personality had everything to do with his theoretical and clinical emendations—certainly true of all great psychoanalytic thinkers. Ferenczi is often described as an egalitarian and democratic soul with a strong distaste for hierarchy and authoritarian pretense (Thompson, 1950). And, indeed, he rejected traditional doctor-patient hierarchy, and was sceptical about scientific-sounding theories that pigeonholed people into categories with prescribed technical interventions (Ferenczi & Rank, 1924). Ferenczi felt that Freud's theories of mind too often led to patients being seen as less-than-unique individuals and as pawns to validate current theoretical conceptions (Ferenczi & Rank, 1924). He is described as enthusiastic, inexhaustible, and experimental on one hand, and empathic, loving, and warm on the other, engaging with patients more as an equal and a friend than as a distant medical authority. He was critical about the use of psychoanalytic theory to support the abuse of authority by analysts. Ferenczi's democratic professional attitude sensitised him to the facts that who the analyst is as a person will invariably impact the way he engages patients (Kuchuck, 2013), and, even more revolutionary, that the patient is able to perceive who the analyst is as a separate subjectivity (Aron, 1996). The now widely accepted idea that the analytic process consists of an interaction between two subjective co-participants originated with Ferenczi.

Ferenczi had long had an interest in unconscious mutual influence between patient and analyst, evident, for instance, in his conception of the "dialogue of unconsciouses" (1915, p. 109) between patient and analyst, and his even earlier interest in unconscious "thought transference" between people (de Peyer, 2016; Cassullo, Chapter Three). But he came to more fully understand the tremendous impact on the patient of the analyst's countertransference much later, through his troubled analysis of Elizabeth Severn, documented in his *Diary*. For a long time, Ferenczi found himself unable to get beyond his dislike for this haughty, demanding, entitled woman. Yet his relaxation-technique approach pressed him to give in to her ever-intensifying wishes and demands. Ultimately, her relentless demands forced him to limit his indulgence of her; nevertheless, her demands continued (Diary, p. 98).

Additionally, Severn continued to feel that an obstacle to her progress was Ferenczi's hatred of her—a feeling of which Ferenczi was, at the least, not fully aware—and she demanded that she be allowed to analyse those feelings in him (Diary, p. 99). After about a year, he agreed, and discovered through Severn's analysis of him—an experiment he called "mutual analysis"—how she evoked in him a transference to his own mother, whom he both feared and hated. Discovering and expressing his hatred, and understanding its transferential source, led Severn to feel vindicated and become less demanding, which in turn allowed Ferenczi to feel more open and become a better analyst to her and to his other patients.

An implicit though essential element of mutual analysis was the egalitarian attitude—so different from the hierarchical, authoritarian attitude, typical of the psychoanalysis of his day, that Ferenczi was so critical of (Conf, p. 158)—that patients can be as sensitive to analysts' participation and psychic properties as trained analysts are towards their patients. Again, he encouraged his patient, Elizabeth Severn, to share her perceptions of him directly—and he was open to what she had to say.

This case, at the least, reinforced Ferenczi's belief (e.g., Unwel) that the analyst's love for his patient is, in many cases, an essential ingredient for a positive outcome, and that all impediments to analytic loving must be removed—most notably, resistances introduced by the analyst's (counter)transference to the patient. Ferenczi's openness through mutual analysis became his route for mitigating these counter-resistances—the key element of which may have been his verbal admission to the patient of his mistakes. This stands in contrast to the approach of more traditional analysts, perhaps including most contemporary analysts, who are content to be *aware* of countertransference feelings as a way of illuminating something happening in the patient, and who might be more likely to use their own errors as a springboard to explore patients' transferentially influenced perceptions of their analyst.

One can certainly speculate that Ferenczi's own open and loving nature and his strong desire to be loved cannot be separated from his views about what patients need and what analysts must provide. This said, I believe that many of my colleagues would agree with Ferenczi's belief that a successful analytic experience is unlikely if the analyst does not grow to feel a strong intimacy, attachment, and love towards a patient.

Ferenczi abandoned mutual analysis—ambivalently, and perhaps due to his increasing incapacity to tolerate the strains of mutual analysis, as a result of the pernicious anemia that would soon end his life (Diary, pp. 212–214). But mutual analysis left a profound legacy for contemporary analysts, perhaps especially for relational analysts: an appreciation of the inevitable influence that analyst and patient will have upon one another, much of it neither consciously intended nor consciously experienced (see Aron, 1996). The fact of this mutual influence underscores the importance of analysing the transference-countertransference matrix in a robustly two-person way. The patterns of mutually influenced interaction invariably bear similarity to patients' internalised relational configurations (Mitchell, 1988)—the internalised source of the patient's interpersonal difficulties.

Contrary to Ferenczi's belief, at least during the mutual-analysis period, that patient and therapist influence one another and discuss this influence in an equally candid symmetrical way, most contemporary analysts are more reserved than Ferenczi, preferring to address their *patients'* experience of their analyst's influence. I cannot, however, underscore enough the degree to which the respect that Ferenczi held for his patients' abilities to see the flaws and problems of their analyst has changed the essential ethos of contemporary analytic thinking. The offensive (and inaccurate) hierarchy of a model that situates the doctor as an opaque and objective scientist and the patient as a naive and unperceptive subject exists today in only small minority, and no one bears more responsibility for this shift than Ferenczi.

Ferenczi's contemporary influences

Ferenczi's interest in the pervasive impact of countertransference, his humanistic, egalitarian attitudes, and his warm, open, and loving nature later found expression not only in his own relaxation and mutuality experiments, but in two broad psychoanalytic pathways to which these experiments pointed the way—pathways that, by the way, have become some of the most well-trod in psychoanalysis.

Ferenczi's nurturing relaxation technique, built on a model that sees certain psychopathology as resulting from deficiencies in the young child's maternal environment, and the analyst as needing in some ways to compensate for these shortcomings, was in important ways the prototype for the approaches of the British Middle School/Independents (Clarke, Chapter Twenty-six) and self psychology (Orange, Chapter Thirty-two). Indeed, in regard to the former, Michael Balint (Moreau Ricaud, Chapter Twenty-five), Ferenczi's patient and student, emigrated to Britain and became a colleague within that small group, whose best known member, Winnicott, developed ideas that strongly echoed Ferenczi's. Even the openness of Ferenczi's later, mutual-analysis period can be understood to involve a level of symmetry that is felt by patients as very giving.

American interpersonal psychoanalysis is a successor to Ferenczi's mutuality period (see Prince, Chapter Thirty). This school—long the home of more mutual clinical approaches (Bass, Chapter Twenty-three)—emphasises the influence of countertransference and forms a core of the later school of relational psychoanalysis (Miller-Bottome and Safran, Chapter Thirty-three). Interpersonal psychoanalysis began with two figures who were directly influenced by Ferenczi—Clara Thompson, who had been Ferenczi's patient, and Sullivan, who had had some contact with Ferenczi during his time in New York in the mid-1920s, and who subsequently was analysed by Thompson (see Conci, 2010, for more on these events).

Ferenczi had personal courage—to experiment clinically in order to help his disturbed patients, even at the risk of alienating his mentor Freud, whose love and approval he desperately needed; to face the shortcomings of approaches that he himself developed and had become committed to, and start in new directions; to open himself in a personally vulnerable way to very destructive patients. Ferenczi's courage to do what he believed was best for his patients, even at personal and professional risk, presents psychoanalysts of all persuasions with a role model of the highest ethical standards.

References

Aron, L. (1996). *A Meeting of Minds.* Hillsdale, NJ: Analytic Press.

Conci, M. (2010). *Sullivan Revisited–Life and Work.* Trento: Tangram.

de Peyer, J. (2016). Uncanny communication and the porous mind. *Psychoanalytic Dialogues, 26*: 156–174.

Ferenczi, S. (1915). Psychogenic anomalies of voice production. In: *Further Contributions to the Theory and Technique of Psycho-Analysis* (pp. 105–109). London: Karnac, 1994.

Ferenczi, S., & Rank, O. (1924). *The Development of Psycho-Analysis.* New York: Dover, 1956.

Harris, A., & Kuchuck, S. (2015). *The Legacy of Sandor Ferenczi.* New York: Routledge.

Hirsch, I. (2008). *Coasting in the Countertransference: Conflicts of Self-Interest between Analyst and Patient.* New York: Routledge.

Hirsch, I. (2015). *The Interpersonal Tradition: The Origins of Psychoanalytic Subjectivity.* New York: Routledge.

Kuchuck, S. (2013). *Clinical Implications of the Psychoanalyst's Life Experience: When the Personal Becomes Professional.* New York: Routledge.

Mitchell, S. (1988). *Relational Perspectives in Psychoanalysis.* Cambridge, MA: Harvard University Press.

Sullivan, H. S. (1953). *The Interpersonal Theory of Psychiatry.* New York: Norton.

Thompson, C. (1950). *Psychoanalysis: Evolution and Development.* New York: Hermitage.

Wolstein, B. (1975). Countertransference: The psychoanalyst's shared experience and inquiry with his patient. *Journal of the American Academy of Psychoanalysis, 3*: 77–89.

Part III

Echoes

Introduction

The first part of this book was devoted to the development of Ferenczi's thinking and work, explicating along the way the controversial—indeed, almost heretical—position his late work had, both in his time and in the following decades. In the second part, various authors approached Ferenczi's contributions from different angles, elaborating ideas that Ferenczi often expressed in only a condensed or tentative fashion—ideas that are now central to so many contemporary psychoanalytic camps. It is, however, impossible to overlook the incongruity between these two sentences: if Ferenczi's ideas were rejected back then, how have they become so relevant today?

That is exactly the focus of our third part. Titled "Echoes", it follows the paths Ferenczi's legacy traversed between 1932 and 1985: often unacknowledged, sometimes deliberately hidden or even smuggled, all too rarely openly appreciated. For decades, Ferenczi was almost never present in reference lists or name indexes, despite the facts that he had analysed "everyone" and that subject indexes were full of "his" topics. If Freud was the father of psychoanalysis, Ferenczi was like the ghost of Hamlet's father: omnipresent through his resounding absence.

For the fact that we still think about Ferenczi, we should thank Michael Balint, his student, analysand, collaborator, friend, and literary executor. Michelle Moreau Ricaud, Balint's biographer, reveals details of this relationship as well as elaborating Balint's efforts to translate Ferenczi's late works into English and get them published—most importantly Ferenczi's *Clinical Diary* and his correspondence with Freud. Balint did not live to see these books published, but Balint's own work is infused with Ferenczi's contributions.

Balint, of course, became instrumental in the development of the Independent school of British psychoanalysis. How Ferenczi influenced Fairbairn, Bowlby, and Winnicott is the focus of the chapter by Graham Clarke, himself a co-editor of *The Fairbairn Tradition*, previously published in this series. We learn about the key role of the Sutties (the wife being Ferenczi's translator, the husband author of a book on tenderness), Bowlby's unapologetic reference to Imre Hermann's concept of the clinging instinct, the recent discovery of Fairbairn's annotated copy of a book by Ferenczi, and the likelihood that Winnicott may often have "glanced at" Ferenczi's works, perhaps even as frequently as at Freud's.

Luis Mario Minuchin looks at echoes of Ferenczi in the work of one of his many analysands who become influential figures in the history of psychoanalysis—Melanie Klein. Under the heading of "Emotional influence", Minuchin discusses Klein's analysis, divorce, and decision to start analysing children, the last of which was explicitly encouraged by Ferenczi. Although he believes that Ferenczi's intellectual influence was less strong than his generative emotional role in her life, Minuchin traces several of Klein's ideas to the earlier papers of her analyst, in whom she saw a streak of genius.

Ferenczi was present and influential in French psychoanalysis long before the 1985 publication of the *Diary*. Yves Lugrin's contribution focuses on Lacan, who approved of Ferenczi when most did not dare. It turns out, however, that Lacan's reasons were not so much related to conceptual or clinical issues, but to political ones: Lacan felt Ferenczi had been unjustly ostracised—the same fate that awaited Lacan himself.

A more profound presence of Ferenczi's thinking is found in the later work of Jean Laplanche. With the help of Timo Stork, we can see the idea of confusion of tongues—already in the late 1960s, but more fully in the late 1980s, when the Ferenczi renaissance had already begun—as central to Laplanche's "general theory of seduction".

From France we move to various trends in American psychoanalysis. Robert Prince takes us *in medias res* with his depiction of Ferenczi's influence on Clara Thompson, whose analyst Ferenczi was, and Harry Stack Sullivan, but also on subsequent generations of interpersonal psychoanalysts, who consider Ferenczi to be one of the originators of their tradition through his ideas about mutuality, countertransference, trauma, and many others.

The interpersonalists of the William Alanson White Institute exchanged weekly visits with the members of Washington Institute, who, on their part, were associated with the Chestnut Lodge hospital, *the* hospital for psychoanalytic treatment for persons suffering from psychotic disorders. Ann-Louise Silver, who worked there for twenty-five years, writes about regular meetings Ferenczi had in Baden-Baden with Frieda Fromm-Reichmann, the beating heart of the Lodge, what Fromm-Reichmann learned from him, and how she applied that in her clinical practice on a daily basis, despite almost never writing about Ferenczi's influence openly.

Founder of psychoanalytic self psychology, Heinz Kohut, was born and underwent his first analysis in pre-Second World War Vienna. Donna Orange looks for the uncited Ferenczian melodies between the lines of Kohut's papers, but also in the work of second generation self-psychology theorists, and of the interpersonalists, and includes the description of Ferenczi's influence on her own work as well.

Protagonists of the most recent trend in US psychoanalysis, relational psychoanalysis, perceived Ferenczi, much more than Freud, as their predecessor in terms of both clinical work and conceptual foundation. Madeleine Miller-Bottome and Jeremy Safran show us some of the most important reasons for this fascination: the focus relational analysts share with Ferenczi is on actual trauma, countertransference analysis, and mutuality.

The section comes to a close with a chapter on child analysis. Patrizia Arfelli and Massimo Vigna-Taglianti systematise Ferenczi's understanding of children's suffering, and argue that Ferenczi, despite not analysing children himself, turned analysts' attention to pre- and paraverbal modes of communication, and not just its explicit content, making possible innovations like play-analysis and what will later be named transitional objects.

Ferenczi died at the age of fifty-nine, isolated and abandoned, and some of his major works were not available for the next half-century. Yet it takes us ten chapters to follow the echoes of his revolutionary ideas, and it turns out to be almost impossible to find a corner of the psychoanalytic world where they do not now resound. Many questions remain; one of the most important might be: To what use are we going to put these ideas?

Chapter 25

The Ferenczi—Balint filiation

Michelle Moreau Ricaud

Michael Balint (1896–1970) was a British psychoanalyst of Hungarian origin, physician (MD Budapest, 1920), doctor of science (Berlin, 1924), psychiatrist (Budapest, 1930), psychologist (Manchester, 1945), president of the British Psychoanalytical Society (1968–1970). A psychoanalyst of the third generation, he was trained both in Berlin and Budapest. He was an analysand, colleague, and faithful friend of Ferenczi, and also his literary executor and his "successor" in analytic theory and practice. I will trace the legacy Balint received from Ferenczi and developed in his own way (Moreau Ricaud, 2000).

Young Balint

Born Mihály Bergsmann in Budapest, he was the son of Dr Ignac Bergsmann, a general practitioner known for his difficult, authoritarian, impulsive personality, and Margit Berger, a soft, plain, loving, and optimistic mother (Swerdloff, 1965). He had a sister, Emmi, a future mathematician and actuary. Mihály was a very clever pupil with an enormous curiosity. Nevertheless, he could be a scamp and make mischief: one night, with some comrades, he switched the nameplates on the offices of doctors, lawyers, a veterinarian, and a dentist. Was Balint an *enfant terrible*? As an adolescent, he challenged his father regularly. Was his reputation as "revolutionary" started by his father? When he was seventeen, in his last year of secondary school, he changed his family name for a Magyar one, Bálint, and converted from Judaism to Unitarianism (Moreau Ricaud, 2010). In response, his father broke off their relation until Balint's emigration to England, in 1939 (Balint, 2000).

Early encounter with Freudian theory and love

Balint was erudite: before entering university he studied science, arts, and religion. After some hesitation, he chose to pursue the study of medicine. In the second year of his medical studies he "fell in love with chemistry" (Swerdloff, 1965). When the First World War broke out, he was sent to the Russian and Italian fronts. Wounded in his thumb, he returned to Budapest in 1916 and resumed his studies. He earned his living as junior assistant in the Institutes of Physiology and Hygienics. In 1917, he met his first love in a mathematics seminar. Alice Szekely-Kovacs was a student in ethnology and a great reader of Freud. She lent him two books that marked him for the rest of his life: *Totem and Taboo* and *Three Essays on Sexuality*. He had already read *The Interpretation of Dreams*, but did not like it very much. This time he liked it passionately!

Encounter with Ferenczi, professor of psychoanalysis

The Fifth Congress of Psychoanalysis, held in Budapest in autumn, 1918, was highly publicised. Freud was present. It was a great success for the analytic cause, as Freudian therapy was acknowledged by the representative governments of Central Europe to be the best treatment for soldiers suffering from war neuroses. Afterwards, Ferenczi was asked by a delegation of medical students to give lectures at their university. Soon the students sent petitions to the Ministry of Education, asking that this new science and therapy be taught in their medical courses, even choosing Ferenczi as professor. On 30 March 1919, Freud's paper "On the teaching of psycho-analysis in universities?" (Freud, 1919j) was published in *Gyógyászat* a progressive medical review.

Shortly afterwards, two revolutions took place in Hungary. Student riots and demonstrations during the short Bolshevik Republic of Councils (21 March–6 August) had a happy outcome: Georg Lukacs, Minister of Education (1885–1971), created the world's first professorship of psychoanalysis (Moreau Ricaud, 1990). For three months Balint attended Ferenczi's lectures. At the end of the course, he went to Ferenczi's consulting room to have his student booklet autographed: "I … told Ferenczi what I did not like in his lectures. It was amusing. I was very young". Ferenczi took it well, sat for ten minutes and "tried to explain why he did this way or that" (Swerdloff, 1965, pp. 383–413). Did Balint, for the first time, meet a welcoming authority who accepted his criticism? It seems that his provocative transference to Ferenczi did not elicit anger, but a germ of debate, a confident mutuality between master and pupil.

But soon afterwards, anti-Semitism developed. Jewish students were attacked by a fascist group and Balint, along with Imre Hermann, took shelter in a laboratory. Balint began to specialise in biochemistry and bacteriology. Believing he had no future at the university, after marrying Alice, in 1921 they went to Berlin. He worked at IG Farben and started his doctorate. He also decided to train at Berlin Psychoanalytic Policlinic: "I wasn't very ill. I was a normal neurotic" (Swerdloff, 1965). He had a training analysis with Sachs, and a "control" for his first patient with Eitingon. An analyst at the Berlin Society, he also worked as a biochemist at the Charity Hospital and began to apply psychotherapy to patients suffering from psychosomatic diseases such as asthma, gastric ulcer, and obesity.

Ferenczi's influence developed

Dissatisfied with their training in Berlin (Dupont, 2016; Swerdloff, 1965, p. 388) the Balints returned to Budapest in 1924, and in 1925 had a son, János Sándor, named after Ferenczi! Michael also underwent a second analysis with Ferenczi, this time not a superficial training analysis but an authentic experience. He gave up his (non-psychoanalytic) scientific career, at which he excelled, and became a psychoanalyst and member of the Hungarian Psychoanalytic Association in 1926. Was his idealised transference to Ferenczi so strong as to push him to this decision? Or was he realistic enough to know that, given anti-Semitic laws and regulations (see Keve, Chapter Two), a research career would be impossible for him in Budapest? Following Ferenczi's lead, he gave lectures to physicians. Twenty years later, in London, he would create a special setting to train them. With his wife Alice, a child analyst, and his mother-in-law, Vilma Kovacs, they formed an active core group around Ferenczi, helping him in the administrative tasks of opening the long-awaited Psychoanalytic Institute. He was Ferenczi's assistant and later the institute's director.

Choice of England for his exile: Balint—"passeur"[1] of Ferenczi

In 1938 John Rickman came to Budapest to suggest emigration to the analysts there. Balint left Budapest in January 1939, settling first in Manchester and later, from December 1945, in London. Alice died suddenly of a burst aneurism in July 1939, followed by his mother-in-law. Michael became a member of the British Psychoanalytical Society after publishing "On transference and counter-transference", which he had written with Alice. He conducted three training analyses—Esther Bick, Betty Joseph, and Edna Oakshott—in the Ferenczian spirit in which he was trained, which included the first control being done by the training analyst (Dupont, 2015; Kovacs, 1936). He participated in the Controversial Discussions in London, defending Ferenczi's object-relations theory, and joined the Middle Group (Rayner, 1991).

In 1947, in London, he became a consultant at the Tavistock Institute and embarked on a plan to fulfil his secret goal: to publish Ferenczi's papers, Ferenczi's correspondence with Freud, Ferenczi's *Clinical Diary*, and to rehabilitate Ferenczi in the analytic community, following the banishment trauma to that community that had resulted from the falling-out between Ferenczi and Freud in 1932. Balint translated and published "Confusion of tongues" and a few other of Ferenczi's papers in the *IJP*, in 1949, and prepared the rest in various languages. Due to Anna Freud's refusal to publish the complete Freud-Ferenczi correspondence, and Balint's fear that the *Diary* would be misunderstood if it was isolated from the correspondence with Freud (Dupont & Brabant, Chapter Fourteen), Balint's goal was only achieved years after his death in 1970.

Ferenczi's heir: Theoretical advances

Balint brought his empirical-science mindset to psychoanalysis. As such, he was critical of Freudian theory on two points: libidinal stages and primary narcissism.

Following Ferenczi, Balint understood the contradiction between Freud's biological instinct theory and the object-relations viewpoint that grows from the practice of clinical psychoanalysis. Thus, he proposed a revision of the idea of libidinal stages (Balint, 1935), believing that the contradiction between these two theories could be solved if Ferenczi's concept of passive object love (which Balint saw as not totally passive) was accepted as present from the start of life.

Convinced by clinical facts that the object-relation exists from the beginning of life, Freud's idea of primary narcissism (speculative for Freud himself) also needed to be revised to include new observations.[2] Balint gradually elaborated a whole theory on the dynamic of regression, and ultimately replaced the concept of primary narcissism with the notion of primary love (Moreau Ricaud, 2005).

In "Psychosexual parallels to the fundamental law of biogenetics" (1930b), Balint introduced the notion of the "new beginning" that he had discovered in biology while working on Ferenczi's *Thalassa*.[3] To survive aggression, organisms revert to simpler forms of

---

1 Passeur: a person who helps somebody (a Jew) to pass to another country (to save him or her).

2 In the "Ferenczian issue" of the *IJP* (1949), for the sake of showing the empirical support for Ferenczi's position, Balint translated and published Endre Petö's "Infant and mother: Observations on object-relations in early intimacy" (1949).

3 In the preface of the Hungarian translation of *Thalassa*, Ferenczi expressed his gratitude to his student Michael Balint, who reviewed his book from the point of view of a modern biologist and drew his attention to some errors he had made in the original manuscript.

organisation; when the environment has improved, they resume their growth. He applied this idea to analytic treatment and regression. If the analyst accepts a period of regression in his patient, the patient can later resume his process of development (Balint, 1932).

Balint also adopted Ferenczi's idea that the person is inhibited by "educational errors" and constructs his character through mechanisms of defence that both protect himself and limit his possibility to love and to be happy in loving. Analytic treatment should not only free the patient from symptoms or heal the tendency to neurotic repetition, but give the patient flexibility, adaptability, and the possibility to love without anxiety. In *Primary Love and Psychoanalytic Technique* (1952), Balint postulated a first stage in psychic development, a primary pre-ambivalent stage, primary love (as opposed to Klein's primary sadism), characterised by a "harmonious relation to an undifferentiated environment" or by a "harmonious interpenetrating mix up" between the infant and his environment. The mother-infant bond brings gratification to both, who are interdependent and attuned to each other: what is good for one is good for the other (Moreau Ricaud, 2005). This stage is a "golden age" before the experience of trauma, and will leave vestiges—a topic to which I will return in my discussion of Balint's view of psychic trauma.

In his next book, *Thrills and Regressions* (1959), Balint studied the primitive and universal instinct of regression, a phenomenon where fear and pleasure ("thrill") get mixed up. Indeed, amusement parks, funfairs, merry-go-rounds, extreme sports, shows of tightrope walkers and acrobats are places where one can live intense feelings and vertigo in a relatively secure environment. The fantasy here is to find again this mythic love of the beginnings, where one was in harmony with the environment (in a flow with pre-objects and substances such as milk, air, odours, heat, contact, voice). In analytic treatment, regression might happen and frighten analysts. But analysts should not be so easily frightened of periods of regression; they must remain present and never drop the patient during these periods!

In this book, Balint talks about two types of primitive character defences that he discovered. Named after Greek roots, he called them "ocnophilia" and "philobatism". An "ocnophil" seeks to cling (*okneo*, to cling) to objects; space seems dangerous and solitude unbearable. A "philobat" (literally: "he who loves to walk on the border") fears objects and shuns them; he feels more comfortable in "friendly spaces" (Ferenczi's notion) and needs to stay on his own. These archaic configurations are different forms of regression.[4]

Balint's book *The Basic Fault* (1968) completed his development of this line of research. A *fault* is a notion discovered through his work with groups of doctors who complained of not being understood by their patients even when they provided clear explanations. In analytic treatment, too, some patients receive the analyst's interpretations not at an adult level, as useable information, but as an assault or a lack of respect, a narcissistic injury, and are unable to work with them analytically. In line with Ferenczi's final theory, this is a confusion of tongues between analyst and analysand.

Balint's patients complained of having a fault, or something missing in them (Lacan was influenced by Balint for his own theory "*du manque*"). The origin of this "basic fault" can be found in a significant "lack of 'fit'" (p. 22) between infants' psycho-physiologic and affective needs, and the care provided. This may happen either when infants have especially strong or "abnormal" congenital needs, or when they grow up in a dysfunctional or indifferent family; the result is that the child's developmental needs are not met. To prevent transference

4 In reviewing Balint's book, Winnicott (1954) simplified them as "the cautious" and the "foolhardy".

psychosis such as Ferenczi encountered with his famously difficult patient Elizabeth Severn, Balint came up with a differential diagnosis between "benign regression" (reversible and a therapeutic ally) and "malignant regression" (dangerous and potentially non-reversible) (Chap. 22). Using Rickman's conceptions of one-body, two-, three-, and multiple-body psychology, Balint proposed the new conception of three areas of the mind, reflecting different forms of object-relational experience and requiring different clinical techniques. The three-person relation is the classic oedipal relation involving psychic conflict; the technique here is the classical one: benevolent passivity and interpretations. The two-person relation is the basic fault situation, where only one person counts and the other must be present to meet his needs; here the technique is to create a secure climate, without interpretation. The analyst stays careful and non-intrusive, yet emotionally present; he carries the patient "not actively but like water carries the swimmer or the earth carries the walker" (p. 167). The analyst must not appear as "a separate, sharply contoured object" (p. 167), and must not fail. In the area of the one-person-relation, the patient is alone, without an external object, as found in the act of creation. The analyst has to evaluate the silence and the solitude, to reflect on the various possibilities of why the silence is happening, and to avoid disrupting the patient's creative process.

For Balint this area is also the zone for creating illness. He attempted to unify Freud's and Ferenczi's different theories of trauma in "Trauma and object relationship" (1969). For the first time the focus was put on "traumatogenic objects," that is, parents or others who have a parental relationship to the child. Sexual trauma is understood to have a triphasic structure: 1) there is a confident and loving relation between adult and child; 2) the adult does something exciting, painful, or frightening to the child. The child, sensitive to the adult's suffering, shows care and solicitude to him. A mutual, passionate relationship develops; 3) subsequently, the child tries to renew the passionate relationship, or to be comforted by the adult, who then rejects him or denies what had happened.

Balint added another type of trauma, a fright after an infant has fallen from a changing table: an ordinary situation, but interesting in its possible consequences: the child, *excessively* comforted by the guilty mother, who gives too much gratification, may shed light, in clinical work, on patients who are prone to accidents. Unlike Ferenczi, Balint did not extend psychoanalytic treatment to everyone. Ferenczi's failure with some patients whom he could not heal in spite of his *furor sanandi* led Balint, for very disturbed patients, to choose either psychotherapy, brief therapy, or focal therapy, to solve their presenting difficulties.

Ferenczi's influence never ceased

Even when Balint created his "training *cum* research group" for general-practitioner physicians at the Tavistock Institute (named Balint Group by his French followers), he came back to Ferenczi's care of doctors (Ferenczi at a certain time also delivered lectures to them, as Balint did, starting in 1926). In Budapest Balint had published two articles, one to initiate doctors into basic analytic concepts in order to enlighten and help them in their everyday practice (Balint, 1926), and the other to help them reflect on their own responsibility in neglecting the individual, human aspects of their patients in pursuit of an image of themselves as laboratory scientists; listening to the patient had been abandoned as the basis of the doctor-patient relation (Balint, 1930a). His wish to help doctors was not unrelated to the fact that his father was "a very good doctor but not a scientist" (Swerdloff, 1965, p. 384).

At the Tavistock Institute, collaborating with Enid Albu (later Enid Balint, his future third wife) and her casework seminar for social workers, he transformed the seminar by putting aside the reading of patients' records and using Freudian free associations to work on the cases. He later experimented with this method on volunteer doctors (Balint, 1957; Moreau Ricaud, 2005), creating a bridge between medicine and psychoanalysis. This approach was welcomed in France and the first *Société Médicale Balint* was created in 1967; it was then followed in England (Balint Society); later, an International Balint Federation (a non-governmental organisation, created in 1974) linked the Balint societies from all over the world. This method is now applied in other fields. Balint's success in this endeavour overshadowed his theoretical contributions to psychoanalysis in the world at large.

Perhaps a bit arrogant in his younger days, Michael Balint ultimately followed Freud's and Ferenczi's footsteps, but found his own path. As keeper of Ferenczi's flame, and in the spirit of his "*idéal de la Renaissance*" (Balint, 2000), Balint lived out his passion for research: "Analysis interests me most, I am an inveterate addict, and I can't help it. ... because it is so thrilling, so exciting, so exciting that nothing can compare with it" (Swerdloff, 1965, p. 409). He continued the work of his professor who later became his extraordinary psychoanalyst and friend, to whom, as he said with humour, the "transference (was) never resolved".

References

Balint, J. (2000). Balint comme père [Balint as a father]. In: M. Moreau Ricaud, *Michael Balint. Le Renouveau de l'Ecole de Budapest* [Michael Balint. The renewal of the Budapest School] (pp. 235–241). Ramonville St-Agne: Érès.

Balint, M. (1926). De la psychothérapie à l'intention du médecin généraliste [On psychotherapy for general practitioners]. In: M. Moreau Ricaud, *Michael Balint. Le Renouveau de l'Ecole de Budapest* [Michael Balint. The renewal of the Budapest School] (pp. 257–269). Ramonville St-Agne: Érès, 2000.

Balint, M. (1930a). The crisis of medical practice. *The American Journal of Psychoanalysis*, *62*: 7–15, 2002.

Balint, M. (1930b). Psychosexual parallels to the fundamental law of biogenetics. In: *Primary Love and Psychoanalytic Technique* (pp. 11–41). London: Hogarth, 1952.

Balint, M. (1932). Character analysis and new beginning. In: *Primary Love and Psychoanalytic Technique* (pp. 159–173). London: Hogarth, 1952.

Balint, M. (1935). Critical notes on the theory of the pregenital organizations of the libido. In: *Primary Love and Psychoanalytic Technique* (pp. 49–72). London: Hogarth, 1952.

Balint, M. (1952). *Primary Love and Psychoanalytic Technique*. London: Hogarth.

Balint, M. (1957). *The Doctor, His Patient and the Illness*. New York: International Universities Press.

Balint, M. (1959). *Thrills and Regressions*. London: Tavistock.

Balint, M. (1968). *The Basic Fault*. London: Tavistock.

Balint, M. (1969). Trauma and object relationship. *The International Journal of Psychoanalysis*, *50*: 429–435.

Dupont, J. (2016). *Au fil du temps*. Paris: Campagne Première.

Freud, S. (1919j). On the teaching of psycho-analysis in universities. *S. E.*, *17*: 169–173. London: Hogarth.

Kovács, V. (1936). Training and control-analysis. *International Journal of Psychoanalysis*, *17*: 346–354.

Moreau Ricaud, M. (1990). La psychanalyse à l'université: histoire de la première chaire Budapest (avril 1919- juillet 1919). In: *Psychanalyse à l'Université* (pp. 111–127). Paris: PUF.

Moreau Ricaud, M. (2000). *Michael Balint. Le Renouveau de l'Ecole de Budapest.* Ramonville St-Agne: Érès, 2007.

Moreau Ricaud, M. (2005). "Primary love", "Balint group", "benign and malignant regression". In: A. de Mijolla (ed.), *International Dictionary of Psychoanalysis* (2 Vols.). New York: Macmillan.

Moreau Ricaud, M. (2010) Un changement de nom chez un analyste hongrois. Le cas de Michael Balint. In: C. Masson & C. Wolkowicz (Eds.), *La force du nom* (pp. 407–420). Paris: Desclée De Brower.

Petö, E. (1949). Infant and mother. *International Journal of Psychoanalysis, 30*: 260–264.

Rayner, E. (1991). *The Independent Mind in British Psychoanalysis.* London: Free Association.

Swerdloff, B. (1965). An Interview with Michael Balint. *The American Journal of Psychoanalysis, 62*: 383–413.

Winnicott, D. W. (1954). Michael Balint. In: C. Winnicott, R. Shepherd & M. Davis (Eds.), *Psycho-Analytic Explorations*. Cambridge, MA: Harvard, 1989.

Chapter 26

Ferenczi and the Independents—Bowlby, Fairbairn, and Winnicott: Towards a third way in British psychoanalysis

Graham S. Clarke

Ferenczi's work on the benefits derived from an empathic or maternal patient-therapist relationship and the centrality of the mother-child relationship, on trauma, splitting of the self, and the reality of child abuse, was particularly influential on the generation of British analysts who came to analytic maturity in the 1940s. In this paper I will discuss the influence of Ferenczi's work on three prominent Independent analysts of the British Psychoanalytic Society (BPS)—Bowlby, Fairbairn, and Winnicott.

Introduction

Ferenczi's most famous paper was the "Confusion of the tongues between the adults and the child" which was presented at the twelfth IPA congress in 1932. In this paper Ferenczi discussed in detail the issues indicated above—clearly addressing the reality of childhood sexual abuse. The paper was published in German in 1932, but it is clear from the correspondence between Jones and Freud that they agreed that this paper would not be published in English in the *IJP*, of which Jones was then the editor (Clarke, 2014). However, the paper was published in English in the *IJP* in 1949 under the editorship of Willi Hoffer (1947–1959) under the influence of the previous editorial board, which also included John Rickman and Clifford M. Scott (1947–1948).

During the seventeen years between the German and English publications of this paper the world of psychoanalysis had gone through a number of profound shocks. Ferenczi died of pernicious anaemia in 1933 and Freud died in 1939. Because of the political unrest, anti-Semitism, and the impending threat of a Second World War, analysts from Vienna and Berlin came to England in the 1920s and 30s and brought with them disputes over theory and practice, in child analysis in particular, in the persons of Melanie Klein and Anna Freud.

After the death of Freud, and in the context of considerable conflict and distress within the BPS in the early 1940s, the Controversial Discussions took place (King & Steiner, 1992). These discussions were intended to address the splits that had developed within the BPS, but as Kohon comments:

> Since the Controversial Discussions had done very little to resolve the splits, the only solution was to devise ways of allowing the rival groups to coexist. What had started as a war between two women ended up with a "gentleman's agreement" signed by three women: Melanie Klein, Anna Freud and Sylvia Payne ... a Middle Group was created: the Society remained one, but divided into three separate groups with two training courses.
>
> (Kohon, 1986, pp. 44–45)

As Padel observes:

> The "middle group" (later the "Independents") was "institutionalized" (Hughes, p. 20 and p. 25) in the British Society in 1946, at the same time as the two groups which had formed by mutually antagonistic polarization within the Society. It was the original British Society, and so it only later became more tightly organized as a group—unlike the other two, which had been militant from their inception. This needs emphasis because of a current, erroneous way of speaking of the middle group as a later formation than the others.
>
> (Padel, 1990, p. 717)

Of the British Independents at that time three of the most influential were John Bowlby, Ronald Fairbairn, and Donald Winnicott (Padel, 1987, p. 272), each of whom was instrumental in developing a British object relations approach to psychoanalysis that was different from, but influenced by, Melanie Klein's object relations approach. This group of British object relations thinkers went on to influence developments in the USA of self-psychology and the interpersonal, relational, and intersubjective approaches to psychoanalysis.

However, the question of the wider influence of both the Independents and of Ferenczi was by no means guaranteed. Grey (1994) looks at the sorry tale of the " 'secret committee' for preserving doctrinal orthodoxy" (p. 104), founded in 1913, of which Ferenczi was a leading member and later became among "its best known victims". Ferenczi's ideas were considered heretical and rigorously excluded from American journals.

> An index published by the American Psychoanalytic Association in 1987 ... lists all of more than 6500 papers appearing in five journals, "the major psychoanalytic periodicals in English". ... no papers about Ferenczi appeared in these publications from the 1930s through the 1970s. Not until the 1970s did the ideas of Ferenczi or Klein or Balint or Fairbairn or Winnicott receive exposure in the American periodicals. From then until 1986 all five of these theorists merited only 9 papers.
>
> (Grey, 1994, pp. 104–105)

The *IJP* did publish work by and on the Independents and Ferenczi including the belated publication of the "Confusion of Tongues" paper, so the occlusion of Ferenczi's ideas must have other, more complex roots. This might be explained, in part, by some comments of Balint, who was Ferenczi's patient, his most important student, a close friend and literary executor who immigrated to Britain at the end of the 1930s:

> The historic event of the disagreement between Freud and Ferenczi acted as a trauma on the psychoanalytic world. ... the shock was highly disturbing and extremely painful. The first reaction to it was a frightened withdrawal. ... This is particularly true for the attitude of what may be called the 'classical' massive centre of psychoanalysis.
>
> (Balint, 1979, p. 152)

There is no doubt that the British object relations approach developed by the Independents was influenced by Ferenczi. This influence may have been direct through the reading of

Ferenczi's work or it may have occurred indirectly through the work of the Scottish psychiatrist and psychotherapist working at the Tavistock Clinic named Ian D. Suttie:

> Suttie ...was an early champion of Ferenczi's. Long prior to Balint's arrival in England in 1939 Suttie had been promoting and elaborating Ferenczi's ideas, even as Ferenczi's former analysand, Melanie Klein, was taking many of Ferenczi's ideas, and taking many British analysts, in different directions.
>
> (Shaw, 2003, p. 260)

Shaw's assertion that Suttie's influence was through his "highly popular discussion groups at the British Psychoanalytical Society" (p. 260) is wrong—as I have confirmed through contact with the Institute of Psychoanalysis. Shaw was probably thinking of the Tavistock Clinic, which as Cassullo says "provided the environment where ... Suttie was able to develop and communicate his views on therapeutic practice" (Cassullo, 2010, p. 20n).

Dorothy Heard (1988) in her informative introduction to Suttie's book *The Origins of Love and Hate* (1935) says that Suttie's wife Jane was the translator of most of Ferenczi's papers in his *Further Contributions*. Suttie's work was, like much of Ferenczi's work, only "rediscovered" in the 1980s.

Suttie died in 1935 at about the time his book was published and his work remained undeveloped. Suttie was never a member of the BPS, so references to him are absent from works devoted to the history and contributions of the Independents. Over the years there has been increasing interest in Suttie (e.g., Bacal, 1987; Cassullo, 2010; Clarke, 2011; Rudnytsky, 1992; Shaw, 2003) and his role as a bridge between Ferenczi and the later British object relations theorists like Fairbairn and Winnicott.

Bowlby has eloquently and economically expressed the powerful influence of Ferenczi on the later thinkers in his foreword to the reissued edition of Suttie's book. Bowlby cites Suttie in London, and Ferenczi, Hermann, Alice and Michael Balint in Budapest as seeing "the infant as striving from the first to relate to his mother, and his future mental health as turning on the success or failure of this first relationship. Thus was the object relations version of psychoanalysis born" (Bowlby, 1988, p. xvi). Along with Ian Suttie, Bowlby considers himself and Harry Guntrip also to be in this group.

> With the notable exception of Melanie Klein, all those named have held explicitly that most differences in individual development that are of consequence to mental health are to be traced either to differences in the way children are treated by their parents or else to separations from or losses of parent-figures to whom the children had become attached.
>
> (Bowlby, 1988, p. xvi)

It is important to note that of the three Independents considered here only one, Bowlby, seems to have been open about his sources, so that the influence of Ferenczi and Suttie on Fairbairn and Winnicott has had to be unearthed by researchers struck by the strong resonances between the earlier ideas and those of the later theorists and therapists.

Each of the three Independents under consideration might lay claim to having initiated the development of a third way for British psychoanalysis—John Bowlby with the development of attachment theory, Ronald Fairbairn with the development of a psychology of dynamic structure, and Donald Winnicott with a ludic approach to reality that has beguiled and enchanted many practitioners over the years. Each has a large following and together they have transformed the landscape of psychoanalysis in Britain and around the world.

There have been two books devoted to describing the history of the Independents and detailing the theoretical and practical approaches of the many different analysts who have been included in this group (Kohon, 1986; Rayner, 1991). The views expressed in these books on the origins and nature of the British object relations group are totally congruent with those of Bowlby quoted above. Kohon acknowledges that Ferenczi was perhaps the first analyst to recognise the importance of object relations in the analysis of regressed patients and that the deepest analyses include regression to primitive object relations:

> Ferenczi's concept of "early maternal deprivation", and his notion that object relations exist even in the deepest layers of the mind, were the theoretical background that allowed the ideas of Melanie Klein, Michael Balint, Ronald Fairbairn and Donald Winnicott, and others to develop. These authors concentrated their attention on the early development of the infant, rejecting the idea of an infant who does not relate to his objects from the very beginning.
>
> (Kohon, 1986, p. 21)

The importance of the earliest mother-child relationship is crucial to the Independent approach and the reality of early trauma and its endopsychic consequences are central for Bowlby (internal working models of mother), Fairbairn (dynamic endopsychic structures), and Winnicott (true and false selves).

> Fairbairn, Winnicott, Bowlby and Balint all unequivocally see the origins of much pathology in infantile traumata. These are often seen as arising from various forms of loss of real intimacy with parents—particularly with mother. ... [this] loss... constitutes a trauma.
>
> (Rayner, 1991, pp. 24–25)

Haynal stresses the importance of trauma, dissociation, and fragmentation and the direct influence of Ferenczi on the Independents.

> Ferenczi was, indeed, the precursor of all subsequent psychoanalytical ideas about the fragmentation of the self and of object relations, as one can find them again in the work of Fairbairn, Winnicott, and Guntrip (all probably influenced by Balint), Rickman (a friend of Balint's), and by the fact that Ian and Jane Suttie were familiar with Ferenczi's work.
>
> (Haynal, 2014, p. 101)

A third way

This brief review of the influences of Ferenczi's work on the Independent thinkers has discovered that this was often and in many ways mediated by Suttie, so that when the question of a third way between and beyond the Kleinian Scylla and the Freudian Charybdis is raised it is Suttie's name that is invoked by Brown (1961), Miller (2007), and Shaw (2003), who described Suttie's theory as "the most detailed English [sic] dynamic theory of personality" (Brown, 1961, p. 82). Miller who has made a detailed study of Scottish psychoanalysis (2007) refers to Suttie's views on our innate sociability:

> Suttie ... championed the primary sociability of the human animal. Unlike ... Reich, but like ... Gross and ... Fromm, and later R. D. Laing, Suttie asserted that Freud's psychopathology inverted the real causal nexus in human development, that is, that perversions and anti-social behavior were due to deformations of our innate sociability, rather than sociability deriving from a supposedly sexual source via sublimation.
>
> (Burston, 1996, p. 74, quoted in Miller, 2007, p. 670)

Miller has both developed and defended Suttie's approach and his role in the development of a Scottish psychoanalysis (2008a, 2008b). Shaw in his discussion of analytic love comments on Suttie:

> Both Fairbairn ... and Winnicott ... directly acknowledge Suttie's influence on their work, and Bacal (1987) notes that Suttie's ideas were seminal, significantly anticipating those of Fairbairn, Guntrip, Balint, Winnicott, Bowlby, Sullivan, and Kohut ... Anticipating Fairbairn's claim that the infant is object-seeking, Suttie's alternative to drive theory was "the conception of an innate need-for-companion-ship which is the infant's only way of self-preservation".
>
> (Miller, 2003, p. 260)

The development of a third way within British psychoanalysis will require a response to Gerson's (2009a, 2009b) robust critique of Suttie and a synthesis of the work of the British Independents that remains heir to the work of Ferenczi and Suttie.

Bowlby

Van der Horst and van der Veer (2010) provide an excellent and comprehensive description of Bowlby's early experience and influences including his relationship to Suttie, whom he never met (p. 36).

Bowlby (1969) says that attachment theory "was developed out of the object-relations tradition in psychoanalysis", but that it also draws on concepts from "evolution theory, ethology, control theory and cognitive psychology" resulting in a reformulation of psychoanalytic metapsychology ... compatible with modern biology and psychology and in conformity with ... natural science" (p. 120).

Bowlby adds that attachment theory emphasises:

> The primary status and biological function of intimate emotional bonds between individuals ... [and the] utilising of working models of the self and attachment figure in relationship with each other. The powerful influence on a child's development of the way he is treated by his parents, especially his mother-figure, and that present knowledge of infant and child development requires that a theory of development pathways should replace theories that invoke specific phases of development in which it is held a person may become fixated and/or to which he may regress.
>
> (Bowlby, 1969, p. 120)

Bacciagaluppi (1989, 1994a, 1994b), who has written extensively on Bowlby, suggests that Bowlby may be regarded as one of the strongest exponents of an alternative psychoanalytic approach initiated by Ferenczi. He suggests that Bowlby's most important contributions are to have placed psychoanalysis on to a firm evolutionary basis, and to have generated an enormous amount of empirical research. He believes that:

> The main traits he shares with Ferenczi are (1) the emphasis on the child's primary relatedness, (2) the stress on real-life traumatic events in psychopathology, (3) a great independence of mind, (4) the stress on a loving relationship in normal development. (5) A fifth important link between Ferenczi and Bowlby concerns the denial of trauma on the part of the environment and the dissociation of the traumatic experience on the part of the child.
>
> (Bacciagaluppi, 1994a, p. 100)

He suggests that this influence was mediated and that rather than the direct influence of Ferenczi there may have been some convergence of ideas:

> Due to Bowlby's association with Melanie Klein and the British Middle Group. As regards the specific issue of real-life experience, although Bowlby acknowledges Ferenczi's priority, he seems to have arrived at this concept independently.
>
> (Ibid.)

Bowlby draws attention to the importance of Suttie and in regard to the view that "object-seeking behaviour is exhibited from birth" he says:

> One of the most systematic presentations of this last view is advanced in *The Origins of Love and Hate*, the work of a British psychotherapist, Suttie, who, although much influenced by psychoanalysis, was not himself an analyst. Writing at the same time as the Hungarian School, Suttie and others of the pre-war Tavistock group postulated that 'the child is born with a mind and instincts adapted to infancy', of which 'a simple attachment-to-mother' is predominant. This need for mother is conceived as a primary 'need for company' and a dislike of isolation, and is independent of the bodily needs which mother commonly satisfies.
>
> (1969, p. 376)

Bowlby suggests that it was Suttie's criticism of Freud that led to his being ignored, although the fact that Suttie is closely linked with Ferenczi might well have played a part. It is worth reminding ourselves of the deep connections, albeit for the most part unacknowledged, of Suttie's influence on Winnicott and Bowlby (Cassullo, 2010) and, as I have argued, on Fairbairn (Clarke, 2011, p. 953). Rudnytsky (1992, p. 294) reaches similar conclusions. Significantly, in his 1989 paper Bacciagaluppi points to the similarities that exist between Bowlby's view of aggression and those of Fairbairn (1989, p. 125), and in another paper remarks on Main's acceptance that the internal working models of mother in attachment theory are like the endopsychic structures as described by Fairbairn (1994b, p. 469).

Bowlby's development of attachment theory has burgeoned during the subsequent years and it is the most scientifically well founded of the Independent's approaches and has strong contemporary links to neuropsychoanalysis and developmental psychology.

Fairbairn

I have looked in detail at Fairbairn's relations to Ferenczi (Clarke, 2014) and to Suttie's influence on Fairbairn (Clarke, 2011), based on the finding of heavily marked copies of Suttie's book (1935) and Ferenczi's *Contributions to Psycho-Analysis* in the Fairbairn archive jointly held by the University of Edinburgh and the National Library of Scotland (www.fairbairn.ac.uk).

It is on this basis that I believe the following features of Fairbairn's theory were influenced by Ferenczi: the importance of (a) the early mother child relationship, (b) the real experiences of the child as opposed to phantasy, (c) trauma and splitting, (d) the importance of an internal world that is a dynamic endopsychic structure of persons in relation, and (e) the real relationship between therapist and patient. Indeed, I would say that Fairbairn's account of the structure-generating period of early infant dependence is based upon a view of trauma that he finds in Ferenczi.

Borgogno (2014) suggests that Fairbairn's thoughts on dreams, which Fairbairn called "state of affairs" dreams, following a comment by one of his patients, herself a prolific dreamer (Fairbairn 1952, p. 99), might have derived from Ferenczi who used Silberer's term "autosymbolic" to describe dreams.

> In his conception of the dream as a place made up of the "constitutive parts of the personality," not all of which definitely come from the subject because some might be of primitive introjective and projective origin (by suggestion, contagion, mimetism), Ferenczi is particularly close to Fairbairn's 1944 idea of dreams as "snapshots or rather shorts (in the cinematographic sense) of situations existing in inner reality".
>
> (Borgogno, 2014, p. 77n)

As Frankel makes clear, there are also significant parallels between Ferenczi's idea of "identification with the aggressor" and Fairbairn's theory of the "moral defence", a point that is also made in Itzkowitz et al. (2015).

> I think Fairbairn ..., who struggled with the same clinical observation a decade after Ferenczi did, was closer to the mark in his discussion of what he called the "moral defense." Fairbairn believed that an abused child takes on the aggressor/parent's badness ... in order to exonerate the parent; however badly her parent treats her, she can see him as being loving and good because she is bad and deserves the abuse. ... Fairbairn believed, children need to feel that they love and are loved by a parent who is good ... They cannot feel that they are good or that there is hope of love and goodness if they see their parent as bad. ... Nothing in Fairbairn's explanations requires that the perpetrator feel guilty.
>
> (Frankel, 2002, p. 164)

I have drawn attention to a significant parallel with respect to psychic structure between Ferenczi (Elast) and Fairbairn (1963) concerning a distinction they both make between aspects of what Freud calls the superego (Clarke, 2014). Both distinguish between a positive ego-ideal and a punitive superego and the need to encourage the preconscious ego-ideal whilst ameliorating the destructive punitive unconscious superego/antilibidinal self.

Winnicott

While Freud is an assumed reference in Winnicott's work, the parallels with Ferenczi are striking, but almost totally unreferenced. There is one explicit reference to Ferenczi in Winnicott's paper on classification (1965), where he notes that in regard to the study of psychosis "Ferenczi … contributed significantly by looking at a failed analysis of a patient with character disorder not simply as a failure of selection but as a deficiency of psycho-analytic technique" (p. 125).

Winnicott himself acknowledged that he was often unsure of where his ideas and influences came from.

> It's quite possible for me to have got this original idea of mine about the antisocial tendency and hope, which has been extremely important to me in my clinical practice, from somewhere. I never know what I've got out of glancing at Ferenczi, for instance, or glancing at a footnote to Freud. (1967, p. 579)

In Winnicott's theory the importance of a sense of reality and the ability to play are pre-eminent and determine the degree to which a person might achieve a true self or have to work from within a false self based upon the responses to an impinging environment. The importance of the development from early dependence to qualified independence via transitional levels of confusion between self and other is an influential aspect of his theory and the potential space between self and other as a place of creativity is emphasised.

Borgogno (2014), in discussing Ferenczi's ideas on dreams, bemoans the fact that these ideas, and others, are often borrowed by later analysts, without appropriate acknowledgement, one of whom he identifies as Winnicott (p. 85). In his 2007 paper on Ferenczi and Winnicott, Borgogno aims to present "the close link between Ferenczi's and Winnicott's theoretical, clinical and therapeutic thought, indicating how this link has become something of a 'missing link' in the history of psychoanalytic ideas, an implication which we retain, in part, to this day" (2007, p. 221). Some of the parallels Borgogno sees between Ferenczi and Winnicott are that "instinct is not the main engine of growth" and "the intense children's yearning for 'being welcome' by a 'responsive' partner" (p. 227), and they are common to the other Independents too.

Borgogno (2007) goes on to consider the part that trauma played for Ferenczi and Winnicott, which is also true for Fairbairn and Bowlby.

> To them … trauma is not the result of phantasy, but a gradual accumulation of experiences that really occurred and that were "recorded in the flesh". These experiences, often not sufficiently integrated and metabolized, could only be grasped from their implications and "reactive scars"—the intense feelings of "annihilation", "apathy", "agony", "breakdown" and "catastrophe" which replaced trauma. Moreover … traumas were inevitably and repeatedly bound to resurface within analysis. "Regression is revision", highlights Winnicott in full harmony with Ferenczi who believes that repetition is the opportunity of retranscribing unassimilated real life events from a different angle: a revision in the unconscious expectation to find an emotional and cognitive situation in the analytical relationship "in contrast" … with the one experienced in one's childhood and adolescence, and to obtain and receive the answers which may "trigger a spark of hope" for a reliable environment and confidence in one's own resources.
>
> (pp. 228–229)

Borgogno concludes that for Ferenczi and Winnicott "what is most important for the development and for the analysis of the child and patient alike, is 'the pursuit of reality' and not the flight from or distortion of it … 'it is the relational context that makes things intelligible'" (p. 229).

Margaret Tonnesmann (2012) opens her excellent paper on early emotional development in Ferenczi's and Winnicott's theories by referencing Ferenczi's paper "Stages in the development of the sense of reality" (1913), a heavily marked copy of which can be found in Fairbairn's library at the National Library of Scotland (www.fairbairn.ac.uk). She describes her chapter as having tried to trace in Ferenczi's contributions to psychoanalysis the development of a one-body to a two-body psychology, which foreshadowed those object-relations theories that Winnicott and other British psychoanalysts have developed and that are practiced in particular by analysts of the Independent Group of psychoanalysis in the UK (p. 41). She raises the interesting proposition that had Ferenczi survived "for another fifteen years" he might have developed "his traumatogenic theory in similar directions to those of Balint or Winnicott or even Fairbairn" (p. 41).

Conclusion

There is no doubt that Ferenczi directly influenced the Independents. He also influenced them indirectly through the work of Suttie and the other Hungarian analysts, Imre Hermann and Michael and Alice Balint. There can also be little doubt that one of Ferenczi's analysands, Melanie Klein, was influential on the British Independents, even if this was more of a reaction to her theories than their positive acceptance. It is the shock wave from the Controversial Discussions that has still not been resolved, that opened up the potential space for a third way in psychoanalysis that has yet to be fully realised.

References

Bacal, H. A. (1987). British object-relations theorists and self psychology: Some critical reflections. *International Journal of Psychoanalysis, 68*: 81–98.

Bacciagaluppi, M. (1989). The role of aggressiveness in the work of John Bowlby. *Free Associations, 16*: 123–134.

Bacciagaluppi, M. (1994a). The influence of Ferenczi on Bowlby. *International Forum of Psychoanalysis, 3*: 97–101.

Bacciagaluppi, M. (1994b). The relevance of attachment research to psychoanalysis and analytic social psychology. *Journal of the American Academy of Psychoanalysis, 22*: 465–479.

Balint, M. (1979). *The Basic Fault: Therapeutic Aspects of Regression*. London: Tavistock.

Borgogno, F. (2007). Ferenczi and Winnicott: Searching for a "missing link" (of the soul). *The American Journal of Psychoanalysis, 67*: 221–234.

Borgogno, F. (2014). A "work in progress" between past, present and future: The dream in/of Sándor Ferenczi. *Psychoanalytic Inquiry, 34*: 80–97.

Bowlby, J. (1969). *Attachment and Loss: Volume I: Attachment*. London: Hogarth.

Bowlby, J. (1988). Foreword. In: I. D. Suttie, *The Origins of Love and Hate* (pp. xv-xviii). London: Free Association.

Brown, J. A. C. (1961). *Freud and the Post-Freudians*. London: Penguin.

Burston, D. (1996). Conflict and sociability in Hegel, Freud, and their followers: Tzvetan Todorov's "living alone together". *New Literary History, 27*: 73–81.

Cassullo, G. (2010). Back to the roots: The influence of Ian D. Suttie on British psychoanalysis. *American Imago, 67*: 5–22.

Clarke, G. S. (2011). Suttie's influence on Fairbairn's object relations theory. *Journal of the American Psychoanalytic Association, 59*: 939–959.

Clarke, G. S. (2014). Fairbairn and Ferenczi. In: G. S. Clarke & D. E. Scharff (Eds.), *Fairbairn and the Object Relations Tradition*. London: Karnac.
Fairbairn, W. R.D. (1952). *Psychoanalytic Studies of the Personality*. London: Routledge.
Fairbairn, W. R. D. (1963). Synopsis of an *Object-Relations Theory of the Personality. International Journal of Psychoanalysis, 44:* 224–225.
Ferenczi, S. (1913). Stages in the development of the sense of reality. In: *First Contributions to Psycho-Analysis*. London: Karnac.
Frankel, J. (2002). Identification and "traumatic aloneness": Reply to commentaries by Berman and Bonomi. *Psychoanalytic Dialogues, 12*: 159–170.
Gerson, G. (2009a). Culture and ideology in Ian Suttie's theory of mind. *History of Psychology, 12*: 19–40.
Gerson, G. (2009b). Ian Suttie's matriarchy: A feminist utopia? *Psychoanalysis, Culture and Society, 14*: 375–392.
Grey, A. (1994). Ferenczi and the Interpersonal school: A study of political climates in psychoanalysis. *International Forum of Psychoanalysis, 3*: 103–108.
Haynal, A. (2014). Trauma—revisited: Ferenczi and modern psychoanalysis. *Psychoanalytic Inquiry, 34*: 98–111.
Heard, D. (1988). Introduction. In: I. D. Suttie, *The Origins of Love and Hate*. London: Free Association, 1935.
Itzkowitz, S., Chefetz, R., Hainer, M., Hopenwasser, K., & Howell, E. (2015). Exploring dissociation and dissociative identity disorder: A roundtable discussion. *Psychoanalytic Perspectives, 12*: 39–79.
King, P., & Steiner, R. (1992). *The Freud/Klein Controversies in the British Psycho-Analytical Society, 1941–5*. London: Routledge.
Kohon, G. (1986). *The British School of Psychoanalysis: The Independent Tradition*. London: Free Association.
Miller, G. (2007). A wall of ideas: The "taboo on tenderness" in theory and culture. *New Literary History, 38*: 667–681.
Miller, G. (2008a). Scottish psychoanalysis: a rational religion. *Journal of the History of the Behavioural Sciences, 44*: 38–58.
Miller, G. (2008b). Why Scottish "personal relations theory" matters politically. *Scottish Affairs, 62*: 47–62.
Padel, J. (1987). Freudianism: Later developments. In: R. L. Gregory (Ed.), *Oxford Companion to the Mind* (pp. 270–274). Oxford: OUP.
Padel, J. (1990). *Reshaping the Psychoanalytic Domain*: *The Work of D. W. Winnicott, W. R. D. Fairbairn, and Melanie Klein*: By Judith Hughes. *International Journal of Psychoanalysis, 71*: 715–717.
Rayner, E. (1991). *The Independent Mind in British Psychoanalysis*. London: Free Association.
Rudnytsky, P. L. (1992). A psychoanalytic Weltanschauung. *Psychoanalytic Review, 79*: 289–305.
Shaw, D. (2003). On the therapeutic action of analytic love. *Contemporary Psychoanalysis, 39*: 251–278.
Suttie, I. D. (1935). *The Origins of Love and Hate*. London: Free Association.
Tonnesmann, M. (2012). Early emotional development: Ferenczi to Winnicott. In: J. Szekacs-Weisz & T. Keve (Eds.), *Ferenczi for Our Time: Theory and Practice* (pp. 29–42). London: Karnac.
van der Horst, F. C. P., van der Veer, R. (2010). The ontogeny of an idea: John Bowlby and contemporaries on mother–child separation. *History of Psychology, 13*: 25–45.
Winnicott, D. W. (1965). Classification: Is there a psycho-analytic contribution to psychiatric classification? In: *The Maturational Processes and the Facilitating Environment: Studies in the Theory of Emotional Development*. London: Hogarth.
Winnicott, D. W. (1967). D. W. W. on D. W. W. In: C. Winnicott, R. Shepherd & M. Davis (Eds.), *Psychoanalytic Explorations* (pp. 569–582). London: Karnac, 1989.

Chapter 27

Melanie Klein's development of, and divergence from, Sándor Ferenczi's ideas

Luis Minuchin

Sándor Ferenczi exerted a powerful influence on Melanie Klein, which I would divide into two types: the first is emotional, the second is scientific-conceptual, though they are closely linked to each other.

Emotional influence

The influence I call emotional is related to Klein's entire living experience in her analysis in Budapest with Ferenczi, especially in the personal and family circumstances she was going through. As Grosskurth (1986) documented in her biography—to which I will refer regarding Klein's personal information—when Klein began her analysis she was struggling with a deep depression, which worsened after her mother's death. Melanie's mother was a very authoritarian woman and influenced her powerfully. In addition, Klein's married life was not very satisfying. Even though she had never got along well with Mr Klein, she married him; most probably, Ferenczi influenced her divorce. The support he provided in relation to her son's death and during the whole grieving process—which she later outlined in her articles about grieving and its relation to manic depressive disorders (Klein, 1935, 1940)—was also significant.

For that reason, Ferenczi supported and encouraged her in her personal decisions, as well as in her scientific and intellectual development. He influenced her especially in regard to child analysis practice and theoretical-conceptual developments such as introjection, early transference, and archaic superego formation. Nevertheless, Klein gave all these matters an original twist. Klein's understanding of early superego formation, for example, is rather far from Ferenczi's idea of sphincter morality and/or of superego precursors, and she widened the concept of psychoanalytic symbolism. I will return to all these points below.

Returning to the emotional influence Ferenczi had on Klein, it was, to my mind, much more powerful than any particular conceptual legacy she could have received from him. It was he who had encouraged her to present her first scientific paper, in July 1919, with which she became a member of the Hungarian Psychoanalytical Society. That paper was also published the following year in the *Internationale Zeitschift fur Psychoanalyse* with the title "Der Familienroman *in statu nascendi*" ("The making of the family romance"), which was about her analysis of her own son, Erich, even though the real identity of the child was suppressed in later versions.

It was Ferenczi, I repeat, who encouraged her to analyse children, something which at the time was considered hardly possible, since psychoanalysis was based on words, while little children have limited language capacities. Klein realised that no words were necessary and that children's emotions and symbolic phantasies could be expressed through play—an insight that opened the door, with Ferenczi's support, to her analysing young children.

In her autobiography, Klein states:

> During this analysis with Ferenczi, he drew my attention to my great gift for understanding children and my interest in them, and he very much encouraged my idea of devoting myself, particularly child-analysis [sic]. I had, of course, three children of my own at that time.... I had not found ... that education ... could cover the whole understanding of personality and therefore have the influence one might wish it to have. I had always the feeling that behind was something with which I could not come to grips.
>
> (Klein, cit. in Grosskurth, 1986, p. 74)

Ferenczi also encouraged other colleagues to focus on child analysis, like Ada Schott and even Anna Freud. However, in Klein's case, it is possible that Ferenczi suggested her watching children carefully as a way of understanding her own problems (Grosskurth, 1986, p. 74).

Early precursors of the superego

Klein describes the idea of the early formation of the superego in her article "Early stages of the Oedipus conflict" (1928), where she outlines the idea of an archaic superego, prior to the one described by Freud and accepted by his disciples, including Ferenczi. She lays out not only the rise of the Oedipus complex, earlier than Freud had described, but also the existence of an unconscious guilt feeling in children, from the first year of life onwards. Guilt feelings are seen in clinical work with children not only because they feel guilty about something they have done but also for the "accidents" they suffer: that is, guilt feelings are prior to any external event, as Freud had already observed. According to Klein, though, such guilt feelings in children originate in a more archaic oedipal dynamic with their parents than Freud had thought, particularly in their wish to attack their parents during intercourse.

Klein observes that these guilt feelings play a significant role in learning sphincter control, and in the beginning of superego formation. It was her analyst, Ferenczi, who first explored this link, talking about sphincter morality in sexual behaviours (Ferenczi, 1913). Klein acknowledges this; but, while Ferenczi understood sphincter morality as the superego's physiological precursor, what she says is more psychological than physiological, and thus more psychoanalytic (Etchegoyen & Minuchin, 2014).

Klein focused on the consequences of the unconscious guilt feeling—not on the feelings themselves, but rather on their manifestations, such as the blows, falls, or wounds that children suffer, or the punishments they inflict upon themselves. For Freud's supporters, like Ferenczi, that was not the expression of an early superego but was connected to what they called "super-ego precursors" and would later on conceptualise as "biological dykes" of the erogenous zones. These dykes cannot be infringed without consequences: guilty feelings, shame, etc. Therefore, the discomfort the child feels does not come from the existence of an archaic superego but from the transgression of any of such dykes (Klein, 1928).

One can already see the analysand diverging from her former analyst. We should also emphasise that in her 1928 essay Klein gradually traces back the rise not only of the superego, but also of the Oedipus complex, until she sets out its beginning in the second half of the first year of life. Ferenczi did not support these concepts. Furthermore, in the same article Klein develops what we could call a stratification of superego formation in parallel with ego-development, along different phases and stages. So we can observe that, while Ferenczi (1913) described the stages in the development of an aspect of the ego, Klein (1928) considered that a similar and parallel development occurs in the superego. This is the conceptualisation of the development of the superego that, not making of it just the Oedipus complex's inheritor (as Freud believed), allows us to explore its multilayered structure by following its pre-oedipal formation. And according to Klein, who follows Abraham's model of the development of object relations in connection to the development of the libido (Abraham, 1924), the more archaic the super-ego layer is, the more sadistic it will be. As she writes:

> The child himself desires to destroy the libidinal object by biting, devouring and cutting it, which leads to anxiety, since awakening of the Oedipus tendencies is followed by introjection of the object, which then becomes one from which punishment is to be expected. The child then dreads a punishment corresponding to the offence: the superego becomes something which bites, devours and cuts.
>
> (1928, p. 168)

Summing up, Klein's theoretical lineage would be: Freud describes libidinal development in his *Three Essays on the Theory of Sexuality* (1905d); Ferenczi describes the ego development and structure in relation to the rise of the sense of reality (1913), as I will describe in more detail, below; while Abraham describes the type of object relation that is established in each developmental stage of the libido (1924). On her part, I would add, Klein gives her fundamental contribution to the genetic-evolutionary theory of psychoanalysis by developing a detailed conceptualisation of the superego formation.

Symbolism

Let us now deal with Ferenczi's influence on Klein as regards symbolism. Ferenczi dealt with symbolisation in the already mentioned "Stages in the development of the sense of reality" paper and in other papers of the same period. Broadening Freud's ideas, Ferenczi stated that symbols arise from an identification—during the "projection stage, of the development of the ego" (Ferenczi, 1913, p. 227)—between the objects of the external world and parts of the body: an object construction in which the child creates his own symbols. Basically, the mother's body is used for comparison, but it is not in fact "the object", as it will become for Klein. Ferenczi's idea is that the child compares his body or organs with external objects and, on the base of that identification, starts creating a symbolic chain that will eventually lead to more complex symbols. Ferenczi thus explains that basic symbols are very limited. What can be symbolised is linked to the child's organs (the complete anatomy or different body aspects), as well as consanguineous relations: family relationships.

Ernest Jones (1916) takes Ferenczi's ideas and he adds that it is the pleasure principle that makes that equation possible, because the individual compares, due to his own interest, a part of his own body with an external object. Jones then affirms that this symbolism will be the basis of all sublimations.

Klein enriches this theory by suggesting that symbolism may not just be a matter of comparing one object to another, but of partly *creating* the new object by an act of projection of the internal subjective world of the infant. And then she links this process to her theory of the development of the superego, which I have described above. She writes:

> Since the child desires to destroy the organs (penis, vagina, breast) which stand for the objects, he conceives a dread of the latter. This anxiety contributes to make him equate the organs in question with other things; owing to this equation these in their turn become objects of anxiety, and so he is impelled constantly to make other and new equations, which form the basis of his interests in the new objects and of symbolism.
>
> (1930, pp. 25–26)

This is an extension of what Jones affirmed in "The theory of symbolism" (1916): it is the pleasure principle that leads, for example, an individual to compare the penis with the arm and the arm with the machine, and so on. By interest or similarity (the penis would be similar to an arm for its shape), under the aegis of the pleasure principle, the mind shifts from one object to another, because it is more comfortable for the individual to think of the arm than the penis. As the signifying, or displacement, chain is too close, an individual may later begin to replace the arm with another external object, such as an umbrella, an airplane, and so on. In brief, the child compares some part of his own body to an external object (by similarity) and that comparison gives him a certain pleasure (Jones), but at the same time triggers anxiety (Klein). He will escape such anxiety and, somehow, will start searching for new objects to symbolise the initial object of thinking. So, for Klein it is anxiety that impels us to displace and create symbols (Segal, 1957).

People build their external realities based on their own phantasies. We not only reproduce, but perceive, the external world through a symbolic chain, rooted in our own desires. Consequently, we live in a symbolic world built upon our childish phantasies, and can never fully get to a veridical perception of reality. The world is therefore essentially a phantasy-construction of the baby. As soon as the baby's ego begins to work with symbols, the ego itself starts to grow up and it gradually develops a greater functioning richness and modes of expression.

Primitive psychic phenomena

Here we come to the core of the Kleinian contribution to psychoanalysis—her paper, "Notes on some schizoid mechanisms" (1946), in which she elaborates the concept of projective identification; but before doing that, she engages the later theories of her first analyst. Klein writes:

> Ferenczi in "Notes and Fragments," 1930, suggests that most likely every living organism reacts to unpleasant stimuli by fragmentation, which might be an expression of the death instinct. Possibly, complicated mechanisms (living organisms) are only kept as an entity through the impact of external conditions. When these conditions become unfavourable the organism falls to pieces.
>
> (1946, p. 238n)

But then she proposes that active splitting processes constitute, from an early stage, the principal defence of the ego to overcome the primary anxiety of being annihilated by a destructive force within, the death instinct. Or better, first the ego splits the object, along with the relationship with it, and then a corresponding split takes places in the ego itself.

Therefore, Klein emphasises the fragmenting pressure of the death instinct, while Ferenczi stresses the integrative pressure of the environment.

The distance between the two thinkers is well shown in Klein's (1925) re-reading of Ferenczi's and Abraham's discussion of tics. For Ferenczi, tics are symptomatic expressions that did not undergo symbolisation, that is, a primarily narcissistic expression; while for Klein they are already mentally associated with unconscious phantasies, thus being an object-relational symptom linked—as per Abraham—to the anal-sadistic stage.

In particular, on one side Klein agrees with Ferenczi's remark that tic is equal to masturbation, but on the other side she does not agree with him when, by qualifying it as a primarily narcissistic and thus psychotic symptom, he maintains that it is not accessible to therapeutic influence. She states instead that this is only true as long as the analysis has not succeeded in uncovering the object relations on which it is based.

Finally, Ferenczi's early interest in primitive psychic phenomena, namely introjection (Ferenczi, 1909), surely had an enduring influence on Freud and all psychoanalysts, but it proved to be particularly profitable for Melanie Klein. Yet, as discussed in other chapters, Ferenczi focused on the "identification with the aggressor" (what later Fairbairn called the "introjection of the bad object"); conversely, it was left to Klein to open the issue of the "introjection of the good object" (the "good breast") as a defence against persecutory anxieties and the basis for the early ego development and formation.

Concluding remarks

We know that Klein quoted Abraham more frequently than Ferenczi, although in her autobiographical notes she mentions her first analyst much more than in her works. In her notes she acknowledges: "There is much that I have to thank Ferenczi for. One thing that he conveyed to me, and strengthened in me, was the conviction in the existence of the unconscious and its importance for mental life. I also enjoyed being in touch with somebody who was a man of unusual gifts. He had a streak of genius" (Klein, in Grosskurth, 1986, p. 73).

Therefore, I would conclude by asserting my belief that—in the spirit of Klein's final book, *Envy and Gratitude*—gratitude is the feeling she kept for her first analyst, Sándor Ferenczi.

References

Abraham, K. (1924). A short study of the development of the libido, viewed in the light of mental Disorders. In: *Selected Papers on Psychoanalysis* (pp. 418–501). New York: Basic Books, 1953.

Etchegoyen, H., & Minuchin, L. (2014). *Melanie Klein. Seminarios de introducción a su obra* [Melanie Klein. Introductory seminars to her oeuvre]. Buenos Aires: Biebel.

Ferenczi, S. (1909). Introjection and transference. In: *First Contributions to Psycho-Analysis* (pp. 35–93). London: Hogarth, 1952.

Ferenczi, S. (1913). Stages in the development of the sense of reality. In: *First Contributions to Psycho-Analysis* (pp. 213–239). London: Hogarth, 1952.

Freud, S. (1905d). Three Essays on the Theory of Sexuality. *S. E.*, *7*: 130–243.

Grosskurth, P. (1986). *Melanie Klein: Her World and Her Work*. New York: Knopf.

Jones, E. (1916). The theory of symbolism. *British Journal of Psychology*, *9*: 181–229.

Klein, M. (1928). Early stages of the Oedipus complex. *International Journal of Psychoanalysis*, *9*: 167–180.

Klein, M. (1930). The importance of symbol-formation in the development of the ego. *International Journal of Psychoanalysis, 11*: 24–39.
Klein, M. (1925). Contribution to the psychogenesis of tics. In: *Contributions to Psycho-Analysis* (pp. 117–139). London, Hogarth, 1968.
Klein, M. (1935). A contribution to the psychogenesis of manic-depressive states. *International Journal of Psychoanalysis, 16*: 145–174.
Klein, M. (1940). Mourning and its relation to manic-depressive states. *International Journal of Psychoanalysis, 21*: 125–153.
Klein, M. (1946). Notes on some schizoid mechanisms. In: J. Mitchell (Ed.), *The Selected Melanie Klein* (pp. 175–200). London: Penguin, 1986.
Segal, H. (1957). Notes on symbol formation. *International Journal of Psychoanalysis, 38*: 391–397.

Chapter 28

Sándor Ferenczi and Jacques Lacan: Between orthodoxy and dissidence

Yves Lugrin

Ferenczi and Lacan: A good beginning

In 1932 Lacan (1901–1981) defended his thesis in medicine, and in 1939 he became a member of the Paris Psychoanalytical Society (SPP). At the end of 1952, the creation of a training institute aroused severe conflicts within the society. In June 1953, many analysts who were recalcitrant about what they saw as power games resigned from the SPP and founded the French Society of Psychoanalysis (SFP) of which Lacan soon became one of the leading figures. In July the IPA refused membership to those analysts who had resigned from the SPP: they probably did not envisage such extreme consequences.

It is within this turbulent context that Lacan turned to Ferenczi's works and life to seek the support he needed in order to legitimise his reading of Freud. By keeping this context in mind, we can understand some aspects, discussed below, of Lacan's relation to the leader of the Hungarian school of psychoanalysis.

Though Lacan had long been interested in Ferenczi, and had probably read his German publications, it was not until 1955 that he made mention of him, declaring "The elasticity of psycho-analytic technique" to be a "luminous article" (Lacan, 1955, p. 282). Nevertheless, in the 1950s he could not have had access to Ferenczi's complete works—which would be translated into French much later (1968–1974)—, nor to the *Diary*, or to Ferenczi's correspondence with Freud: both were published after Lacan's death. Thus Lacan could only have had a partial knowledge of Ferenczi's works.

Thus, Lacan owed his rediscovery of Ferenczi to Michael Balint, whom he considered a remarkable interlocutor; in his words: "One of the best trained analysts of the Ferenczian school of authenticity" (ibid., p. 288). Consequently, he became more interested in Balint's work than in Ferenczi's.

In 1952 Lacan's ideas caused a crisis within the SPP: he disputed didactic analysis and standard treatment, supported lay analysis, and advocated the fundamental role of speech and language in the unconscious life. His colleagues denounced him in 1953 for his technique of variable-length sessions and petitioned to have his status as a training analyst removed.

It should be noted that thirty years earlier, in 1932, Ferenczi had been questioned for his innovative conception of trauma and technical ideas. It is in fact the dissident Ferenczi whom Lacan rediscovers and praises, like a fellow explorer and like a brother, through his reading of Balint. The latter denounced the suggestive elements of the analytic training, in particular referring to the British Society (Oppenheim-Gluckman, 2015). In 1953 Lacan makes use of Balint's two papers on the training system (ibid.) as an endorsement for his own denunciation of the training in France.

These three characteristics of Lacan's relation to Ferenczi's work (namely, his limited knowledge of it, indirect reading through Balint, and focus on his immediate interest) lead me to affirm that Lacan was satisfied with obtaining what he needed in order to defend his cause. His position is simple: Ferenczi asks the right questions but fails to produce the right answers, those which Lacan himself intended to provide. His high praise of the Hungarian analyst is thus accompanied by a criticism that is both pertinent and misguided.

Lacan's applause for Ferenczi reached its peak in mid-July 1953, with the following words written to Balint: "Until soon, dear friend, you may be assured that I always conduct a significant part of my teaching in the spiritual legacy of Ferenczi" (Lacan to Balint, Lacan & Balint, 1953, p 119). In 1955, he still acknowledges Ferenczi as "the first-generation author who most relevantly raised the question of what is required of the analyst as a person, in particular as regards the end of the treatment" (Lacan, 1955, p. 282). In 1958 Lacan recalls that Ferenczi was the first analyst to open the kind of reflection that he himself intends to pursue: "The question of the analyst's being arose very early in the history of analysis. And it should come as no surprise that it was introduced by the analyst [Ferenczi] most tormented by the problem of analytic action" (Lacan, 1958, p. 512).

Lacan's critique of Balint (and Ferenczi)

At the end of his first seminar, held in 1953–1954, Lacan devotes three sessions to Balint, later grouped under the eloquent title "M. Balint's impasses". Balint fails because he lacks the (Lacanian) theory needed "for introducing the intersubjective relation"; therefore he finds himself "entangled in a dual relation, and denying it" (Lacan, 1953–1954, p. 205). The verdict, addressed to Ferenczi through Balint, is severe: "A failure of the theory which corresponds to this deviation in technique" (p. 230). Lacan then formulates the same critique even more harshly when he argues that Balint's work—and thus Ferenczi's—is based on a "mirage that is not even discussed: the completeness of the subject" (Lacan, 1966, p. 192). According to Lacan (1958), the two authors ignore the "lack of being" (p. 524) inherent to the condition of the speaking-being. Lacan denounces both Balint's axiom of primary love between the child and the mother and that of genital love to which the analysis should lead. To him, in fact, the demand for love is imaginary, and it can thus only be disappointed, since no object will ever fill it. Consequently, the end of the analysis does not consist in reaching a lost fulfillment, but in the assumption of a lack.

Lacan's critique can in turn be criticised, even deconstructed, because it hinges on a misunderstanding. Lacan ignores that Ferenczi, at the end of his investigations, is concerned less with the neurotic adult than with the traumatised child present in the adult on the couch. In other words, the critique would be justified if applied to the lived experience of neurosis, but when applied to the underlying experience of the trauma it loses its relevance because it does not distinguish between neurotic repression and post-traumatic narcissistic splitting. In addition, Lacan moves his critique from the point of view of his new theory of the symbolic and the intersubjective relation, which he himself would soon rework in order to promote his concept of the Real and the object a. Furthermore, when he undertakes his own profound revision of the Freudian notions of trauma and repetition, in 1964, he fails to mention that Ferenczi had already preceded him along this path. In conclusion, his reading is patently and arbitrarily selective.

Why does he end up speaking of Ferenczi in terms of "errors", "mirages", "theoretical sauce", "biological delirium", "extravagances", and "pyramids of heresy"? Could the reason be Balint's friendly relationship with Lagache, the other major figure of the SFP and Lacan's future rival? Yet there are two more events pertaining to political-institutional life that can help us understand why Lacan reached his harsh conclusions on Ferenczi.

Political convenience

The first event is Granoff's denouncement of the unfair fate reserved for Ferenczi. Granoff was not a student of Lacan, he was, rather, one of his best-trained peers. Passionate about the history of psychoanalysis, he read Ferenczi with a true interest and underlined that Freud and Ferenczi did not have in mind the same child. Freud referred to the oedipal child in conflict with the law of the father (as Lacan would say): that is, the child—speaking through the adult on the couch—with a polymorphic-pervert sexual predisposition. Ferenczi referred to the pre-oedipal child, that is, the child—crying through the adult on the couch—who has been precociously traumatised in his vital bond to the mother. Lacan refuses this distinction, and gets angry.

Granoff's denunciation arrived in 1958, when he presented "Ferenczi: False problem or real misunderstanding?" to the SFP. In the same year, Lacan presented his paper "The direction of the treatment and the principles of its power", in which he relegated Ferenczi to a bygone past. In opposition, Granoff observed that Ferenczi "has always and will always be the main character in psychoanalysis". And: "If Freud invented psychoanalysis, Ferenczi did analysis. And more ... he did analysis insofar as it is a living pulsation" (in Chertok & Stengers, 1989, p. 103). Thus, Granoff used Ferenczi to publicly manifest his dissociation from Lacan, whose name is not mentioned even once.

Thirty years after his death, we find Ferenczi at the heart of a conflict that will lead to the death of the SFP. Along with other analysts, Granoff would soon contribute to a second split within the French analytical movement, in 1963, becoming one of the main instigators of Lacan's removal from the list of training analysts. A year later, Lacan established his own analytic school, the Freudian School of Paris (EFP). The most faithful followers of Lacan would never forgive Granoff, whom they considered a traitor. From then on, Lacan lost any interest in Ferenczi. Yet, though he never retracted his previous criticisms, he also never denied his initial praise.

A second event contributed to Lacan's rejection of Ferenczi. Again, in October 1967 a new subversive initiative on the part of Lacan generated malaise within his brand new school—a malaise that would grow to the point of leading him to dissolve the school. The cause was the standard procedure for the nomination of the school analysts, previously the responsibility of the training analyst. According to Lacan, the analysis cannot be considered as a "training analysis", neither at its beginning, nor at its end. It is only in *après-coup* (ex post) that in the history of the analytic process the analysis can turn out as having been a training analysis. In these conditions, the function of the "training analyst" becomes a nonsense. Lacan gave the name of the "pass" to this new procedure of legitimising, authenticating, and of nominating a new analyst, who is considered—by two "passers" chosen from the candidate's analysands—capable of the transmission of the crucial concerns of psychoanalysis (Lacan, 1967).

After long and aggressive debates within the EFP, the proposition of the pass, which was revolutionary with respect to the established analytical order, wasn't approved by all of Lacan's oldest peers, many of whom were psychiatrists with significant clinical experience of psychosis. It should be noted here that at that date Lacan no longer held his seminars at the Hôpital Sainte-Anne; he lectured instead at the École Normale Supérieure to an audience mostly made up of intellectuals who had less clinical experience, or none at all. Two years later, in 1969, some of its senior, more experienced, clinicians left the EFP and established a new association on their own: The Fourth Group, the most famous being François Perrier, who, as Granoff before him, showed himself to be receptive to the work of Ferenczi. Lacan's most loyal followers could, once again, find a reason for rejecting Ferenczi, as if he was a guilty ally of Perrier, after having been Granoff's accomplice.

Let us note the paradoxical situation that this conflict gives rise to, but which could also be symptomatic of a contradiction present in Ferenczi's work. While it is in the name of the "orthodox Ferenczi" that some EFP members denounced the pass, Lacan had created this subversive initiative in the spirit of the "dissident Ferenczi", who was the first to declare, in 1932, "no special training analysis!" (Diary, p. 114).

Thus we see that Ferenczi is present at the outset of Lacan's teaching and writing, and, although he disappears for a long time, his shadow is cast over the dissidence between Lacan and psychoanalytic institutions. The departure of some of Lacan's most notable peers doesn't end the debate on the pass. Some viewed it as an improvement in psychoanalytic transmission, others rejected it on the grounds that the analyst might collude with the analysand. When, 1980, it became clear that the opposite positions could not be reconciled, Lacan dissolved his school. He died a year later.

Coming to today

These various historical points help explain why Ferenczi's work has been relegated to obscurity for a long time, shrouded by the confusion of the analytical languages that broke out first in France and later within the EFP. Fortunately, the climate improved after Lacan's death, and the polemical attitude gave way to a more clear-headed and balanced approach to Ferenczi's work.

In 2006 a conference titled "Ferenczi after Lacan" was held in Budapest, gathering many analysts from various different groups established after the dissolution of the EFP. Much to their surprise, many of them discovered that Ferenczi's work anticipates Lacan's on different crucial points, which are still to be fully discussed.

In 2013 Safouan (one of Lacan's oldest colleagues and one of the finest scholars of his work) published a book that underlined the kinship between Lacan and Ferenczi in the light of their dissidence with the IPA. Just like Lacan, however, Safouan limits the discussion to Ferenczi's active technique, leaving aside his final works on trauma.

In my opinion, within contemporary Lacanian circles, Patrick Guyomard is the foremost thinker about the relationship between Lacan and Ferenczi. He claims that, although Lacan corrects some of Ferenczi's weak theoretical hypotheses, the later clinical experimentations of Ferenczi elucidate and even justify some of Lacan's own advances. Likewise, in an article published in 2007, Guyomard draws attention to the neglected issue in Ferenczi's final works, concerning the devastating effects of trauma in early childhood.

This new reading also allows for the deconstruction of the misguided idea introduced by Lacan that Ferenczi ignores the effect of "lack of being" in neurosis: "The recognition of castration and of the lack of being is perfectly compatible with the aim of restoring the pre-traumatic relationship; the reliability of the analyst and the trust in the analytical process are not opposed to the notion of big Other, quite the opposite. Lastly, regression is not a journey to the limit of the ineffable, and transference too is also a novelty and a creation" (Guyomard, 2006, p. 104).

A new approach to Ferenczi, who is conceived as a nexus between Freud and Lacan, is arising today in the Society of Freudian Psychoanalysis. Under its publisher, six Ferenczian books recently appeared: Oppenheim-Gluckman (2010), Sabourin (2011), Lugrin (2012, 2017), Jimenez Avello (2013), Prado de Oliviera (2014), and Dupont (2015).

What will come of this new attitude within Lacanian circles is uncertain. Personally, I am convinced that, to quote the last sentence of my book (Lugrin, 2012), without the violence of Freud's desire, psychoanalysis would not exist; but without that of Ferenczi, would it still exist?

References

Chertok, L., & Stengers, I. (1989). *A Critique of Psychoanalytic Reason: Hypnosis as a Scientific Problem from Lavoisier to Lacan.* Stanford, CA: Stanford University Press.

Dupont, J. (2015). *Au fil du* temps. Paris: Campagne-Première.

Guyomard, P. (2006). Il n'y a que les mots qui different: Ferenczi, Lacan, la confusion de langues. In: *La sexualité infantile de la psychanalyse.* Paris: P.U.F., 2007.

Jimenez Avello, J. (2013). *L'île des rêves de Sándor Ferenczi, Rien que la pulsion de vie.* Paris: Campagne-Première.

Lacan, J. (1955). Variations on the standard treatment. In: *Écrits: The First Complete Edition in English.* New York: Norton, 2006.

Lacan, J. (1958). The direction of the treatment and the principles of its power. In: *Écrits: The First Complete Edition in English.* New York: Norton, 2006.

Lacan, J. (1953–1954). *The Seminar, Book I: Freud's papers on Technique.* New York: Norton.

Lacan, J. (1966). On the subject who is finally in question. In: *Écrits: The First Complete Edition in English.* New York: Norton, 2006.

Lacan, J. (1967). Proposition du 9 octobre 1967 sur le psychanalyste de l'Ecole. In: *Autres écrits.* Paris: Éditions du Seuil, 2001.

Lacan, J., & Balint, M. (1953). Lettre de Lacan à M. Balint. In: *La scission de 1953. Ornicar?, 7*: 119.

Lugrin, Y. (2012). *Impardonnable Ferenczi, Malaise dans la transmission.* Paris: Campagne-Première.

Lugrin Y. (2017). *Ferenczi sur le divan de Freud. Une analyse réussie?* Paris: Campagne-Première.

Oppenheim-Gluckman, H. (2010). *Lire Sándor Ferenczi, un disciple turbulent.* Paris: Campagne-Première.

Oppenheim-Gluckman, H. (2015). *Reading Michael Balint: A Pragmatic Clinician.* London: Routledge.

Prado de Oliviera, L.-E. (2014). *L'invention de la psychanalyse, Freud, Rank, Ferenczi.* Paris: Campagne-Première.

Sabourin, P. (2011). *Sándor Ferenczi, un pionnier de la clinique.* Paris: Campagne-Première.

Safouan, M. (2013). *La Psychanalyse.* Paris: Thierry Marchaisse.

Chapter 29

Mind your tongue! On Ferenczi's confusion of tongues, Laplanche's general theory of seduction, and other "misunderstandings"

Timo Storck

Seduction, fantasy, and seduction again

At first, Ferenczi wanted to title his 1932 talk at the Wiesbaden IPA Congress "Die Leidenschaften der Erwachsenen und deren Einfluss auf Charakter- und Sexualentwicklung der Kinder" ["The passions of adults and their influence on the sexual and character development of children"]. However, he ended up publishing it as "Sprachverwirrung zwischen den Erwachsenen und dem Kind (Die Sprache der Zärtlichkeit und der Leidenschaft)", which appeared in the 1949 English translation as "Confusion of tongues between the adults and the child (The language of tenderness and of passion)".

Putting emphasis on language (and confusion) in such a strong way seems surprising insofar as Ferenczi does not resort to an explicit theory of language. In what follows I will pursue this question further, linking Ferenczian thought to what would emerge as Laplanche's general theory of seduction (cf. Van Haute & Geyskens, 2004). In doing so, I will discuss the three pivotal terms in its title: passion, confusion, and language, sketching their influence on Laplanche.

To discuss the relevance of Ferenczi's seminal ideas, one should keep in mind some aspects of Freud's seduction theory. Seduction stands at the beginning of psychoanalytic theory formation: the hysterical patient is linked to the perverse father. Often mistakenly termed as an abandonment of seduction theory, it is its revision that initiated the development of the concept of unconscious fantasy. Both the "real" sexual trauma and the traumatic impact of the drive have their potential influence in the aetiology of the neuroses, albeit in different ways and with different consequences.

Thus, if Anna O, the first specimen patient of psychoanalysis, was convinced of having had a sexual relationship with her therapist, Freud's senior colleague Josef Breuer, and of expecting his child, then this was to be understood, according to Freud, as the effect of unconscious fantasy shaping the transference. This is not to say that incestuous seductions and sexual trauma are unmasked as mere fantasies—rather, seduction theory is expanded by the concept of unconscious fantasy. Accordingly, only from Freud's *Three Essays on the Theory of Sexuality* onwards can one assess the impact of sexual trauma from both poles of drive action, the endogenous and the exogenous (cf. Laplanche & Pontalis, 1967).

Passion

Against this backdrop, Ferenczi asks, in "Confusion of tongues", for a re-evaluation of the exogenous conditions of sexual trauma in terms of an abusive-seductive violation on the part of an adult. Passion is here meant to refer to the sexuality coming from the adult that violates the child's boundaries and transcends the child's capacities for psychic representation, or even destroys them. In other words, something belonging to the order of passion (and drive) is presented by the adult to the child as pertaining to the order of tenderness. This direction involves not merely a breach between the inner world of an innocent child and the adult, but also a breach between the pregenital pleasure of the child and the (pseudo?) genital pleasure of the adult. Ferenczi describes convincingly the effects of this "premature implantation of passionate adult eroticism and genitality" (Diary, p. 79): that is, he asserts that the feelings of guilt in the child do not rely on the fantasies of an active seduction towards the adult but rather stem from an introjection of the aggressor, a sort of borrowed guilt feeling, which is alien but which nonetheless feels like one's own (for details, see Frankel, Chapter Nineteen).

With this, Ferenczi lays the ground for some thoughts that, years later, became central to Laplanche's fundamental anthropological situation and general theory of seduction—universal situations that transcend cases of actual, abusive seduction in the usual sense, as in sexual trauma.

As early as 1968, Laplanche and Pontalis recognised Ferenczi's merit in having filled out "the myth [of seduction] with two essential ingredients: behind the facts, and through their mediation, it is a new language, that of passion, which is introduced by the adult into the infantile 'language' of tenderness. On the other hand, this language of passion is the language of desire, necessarily marked by prohibition, a language of guilt and hatred" (Laplanche & Pontalis, 1968, p. 5).

Laplanche will later come to view Ferenczi's confusion of tongues as "some sort of preface to the General Theory of Seduction" (Laplanche, 1987, p. 152).[1] Laplanche criticised Freud for the so-called abandonment of his seduction theory and argued for its theoretical expansion. Much like Ferenczi, Laplanche emphasised the generational differences in early seduction, while he considered incestuous aspects less pivotal. He praised Ferenczi for loosening his grip on "familial exclusiveness" and viewed it as a "matter of contingency" that "a child is commonly being raised by *parents*" (p. 157).

The original situation is one of a "confrontation between the child and the world of adults" (Laplanche, 1986b, p. 221). In Laplanche's view, the (bodily) interactions between adult and child are mediated by enigmatic messages that are implanted in the child by the adult's unconscious sexuality. This is not only the case for concrete abusive behaviour, but also for part of any "tender" interaction, because of the effects of the repressed, infantile sexuality on the part of the adult. By highlighting the infantile part of the adult's sexuality (instead of it being integrated in the primacy of genitality), Laplanche, after having transcended Freud's notion of seduction, now transcends Ferenczi's.

> It seems that Ferenczi at some point wanted to complete this ingenious model [which Freud presented with the idea of *Niederschrift*—inscription—in the *Outline of Psychoanalysis*] by his term of a "confusion of tongues". He marks the difference the whole movement originates from, the opposition of two languages. But he doesn't succeed in grasping that it is paramount to this difference that it isn't located between child and adult but inside the adult's language.
>
> (Laplanche, 1986a, p. 171*f*)

1 All translations from the German edition of Laplanche's work are by Timo Storck, except for Laplanche and Pontalis, 1968.

This is to say that it is not the quality of the relationship itself, but it is unavoidable that the adult, due to the nature of his own infantile sexuality, will implant enigmatic messages into the child, beyond his own conscious intention. There is "this relationship of the child to an adult who lets the child know something he himself does not know about" (Laplanche, 1986a, p. 173). Thus, an "exogenous" part of sexuality is part and parcel of the development of psychic life. There is always a blending of tender interactions with passionate, drive-related ones.

French psychoanalysts later built on this intuition of Laplanche's, eventually coming to develop notions such as "unconscious fantasy transmission from adult to infant" (Birksted-Breen et al., 2010, p. 771), and "censorship of the woman-as-lover", which takes the maternal function beyond Ferenczi's (and Winnicott's and Bion's, to name just two) vision of it: the mother is conceived not just as a passive recipient, but as an active stimulator of erogenic—and thus in a way vitalising—unconscious dilemmas (ibid.).

However, following a different theoretical track (from Lacan, passing through Winnicott), the idea of the "mirror-role" of the mother (Winnicott, 1967) was the basis on which French psychoanalyst André Green (1983) built the very influential notion of the "dead mother", echoing Ferenczi's concept of "terrorism of suffering", expressed in "Confusion of tongues" (Frankel, Chapter Nineteen).

Confusion

Here we come to "confusion". For Ferenczi, there are three sides to this confusion that results from any sexual assault. First, the child's inner world becomes fragmented, with unintegrated introjects and multiple dissociations profoundly shaping the child's psyche—Ferenczi's "autoplastic reactions" (see Bokanowski, Chapter Twenty). This results in "a mind which consists only of the Id and Super-Ego" (Conf, p. 163). The ego appears to be left out, or is lacking in coherence due to the consequences of boundary violations.

Yet there is also a confusion between tenderness and passion on the part of the adult (as Laplanche points out); these confused communications, including the adult's hidden passion, are nevertheless transmitted to the child; his needs for attachment can thus become sexualised, and sexuality can develop as a dysfunctional means to achieve closeness.

Again, Ferenczi's ideas about such a confusion had to be rediscovered in the conceptual field—a typically French one—of the *malentendu* (misunderstanding) between patient and analyst (e.g., André and Simpson, 2006). Recently, Haydée Faimberg developed this French tradition of investigation—to which the work of Laplanche gave a great impetus—concerning the narcissistic links and the alienating identifications transmitted between generations, by means of a sort of misunderstanding of the child's specificity by the parents. She described how the parents appropriate what is good in the child for themselves, and intrude what is bad in themselves into the child. The child's unconscious identifications with the "voice of the other" are at the basis of the process of identity construction of the subject. The creative-therapeutic part of Faimberg's idea is that a somewhat similar misunderstanding may affect the communications between the patient and the analyst during analysis. Faimberg suggests that the analyst should thus listen closely to the way the patient listens to the words of the analyst in order to discover such a frequent misunderstanding between the two of them—a misunderstanding that parallels a similar one that the patient experienced during infancy (Faimberg, 2005).

Tongues

"Tongues" is the third key term in Ferenczi's title. Tongues, in the English translation, is a *pars pro toto*, referring to language. There is a basic asymmetry between adult and child that spans two conceptual fields: generational differences and acquisition of language. Not by chance, the term *infans* is derived from the very young child's inability to actively use language. Consequently, infantile sexuality has to do with something outside of language. As Laplanche writes:

> The language of the adult is enigmatic, not due to confusion or total strangeness, nor due to polysemy (for in the latter case all messages would be enigmatic), but through a *one-sided excess* that introduces a *disequilibrium* into the interior of the message. Excess, *disequilibrium*, the need to translate, there is (to invoke Ferenczi's terms) an intrusion of the signifiers of "passion" into the language of "tenderness" common to both adult and infant.
>
> (Laplanche, 2002, quoted in Fletcher, 2007, p. 1253, italics added)

I want to repeat this, because it is a central point. Laplanche talks about the adult's implantation of enigmatic excitations, deriving from his own unconscious infantile sexuality—sexual fantasies that are infantile not only in their early origin, but because they remain outside of language, outside of symbolic representation. As such, they are beyond the adult's own grasp, rendering him unable to help the child make sense of the enigmatic messages being implanted—messages that the child feels the need to translate into psychic content, to grasp, but cannot. The child, therefore, is consistently confronted with the arduous task to "mind its tongue", to translate the enigmatic messages into psychic content—for Laplanche, this can but result in translations that never fully get the point, but nevertheless constitute the basic elements of psychic life.

Furthermore, the adult also installs another "foreign body" into the child: language itself. And indeed, both infantile sexuality and language play primary roles in structuring the growing child's subjective experience and psychic development. Both aspects of the adult's implantation into the child—an alien infantile sexuality and an alien language—point to the key pathogenic elements in Ferenczi's trauma theory.

Concluding

In concluding, it can be stated that Laplanche's emphasis on the inherently unsymbolisable nature of the adult's infantile fantasy (stemming from pregenital infantile sexuality), together with the inherent power imbalance, asymmetry, disequilibrium of the adult-child relationship, as a function of the child's lack of language competence, and of the generational difference more broadly, add a universality to an adult-child dynamic of implantation-intromission (or introjection) that Ferenczi had discussed in terms of child abuse.

Moreover, paralleling Eyal Rozmarin's words (2015), the common ground between Ferenczi and Laplanche, beyond their theoretical distinctions, is that they share a different vision of child development as compared to the "post-seduction theory of Freud" mainstream:

> They see the child not as the author of disturbing urges, that are then put in order by the adult intervention, but as the subject of alien desires that he must struggle to

> accommodate. For both Ferenczi and Laplanche, the child is the object of the adult's power and desire intermingled. It is not the child's but the adult's desire that emerges on the horizon.
>
> (Rozmarin, 2015, p. 267)

Ferenczi's "Confusion of tongues" was the first paper to create a Copernican revolution that shifted the focus of psychoanalytic inquiry from the desires of the child to the desire of the adult that raised that child, and discussed how the adult's desire is transmitted, or not, by way of passion, confusion, and language. A similar focus on the desire of the other characterised post-Freudian French psychoanalytic thinking, starting with Lacan's "mirror stage" (1949) and including Laplanche's general theory of seduction, as well as that of many other original French thinkers.

References

André, J., & Simpson, R. B. (2006). The misunderstanding (Le malentendu). *Psychoanalytic Quarterly, 75*: 557–581.

Birksted-Breen, D., Flanders, S., & Gibeault, A. (Eds.) (2010). *Reading French Psychoanalysis*. New York: Routledge.

Faimberg, H. (2005). *The Telescoping of Generations: Listening to the Narcissistic Links Between Generations*. London: Routledge.

Fletcher, J. (2007). Seduction and the vicissitudes of translation: The work of Jean Laplanche. *Psychoanalytic Quarterly, 76*: 1241–1291.

Green, A. (1983). *The Dead Mother*. London: Routledge, 1999.

Lacan, J. (1949). The mirror stage as formative of the function of the I as revealed in psychoanalytic experience. In: D. Birksted-Breen, S. Flanders & A. Gibeault (Eds.), *Reading French Psychoanalysis* (pp. 97–104). New York: Routledge, 2010.

Laplanche, J. (1986a). Trauma, Übersetzung, Übertragung und andere Über(Schwenglichkeiten). In: J. Laplanche, *Die allgemeine Verführungstheorie und andere Aufsätze* (pp. 148–176). Tübingen: Diskord, 1988.

Laplanche, J. (1986b). Von der eingeschränkten zur allgemeinen Verführungstheorie. In: J. Laplanche, *Die allgemeine Verführungstheorie und andere Aufsätze* (pp. 199–233). Tübingen: Diskord, 1988.

Laplanche, J. (1987). *Neue Grundlagen für die Psychoanalyse*. Gießen: Psychosozial, 2011.

Laplanche, J., & Pontalis, J. B. (1967). *The Language of Psychoanalysis*. London: Karnac, 1988.

Laplanche, J., & Pontalis, J. B. (1968). Fantasy and the origins of sexuality. *International Journal of Psychoanalysis, 49*: 1–18.

Rozmarin, E. (2015). A second confusion of tongues: Ferenczi, Laplanche, and social life. In: A. Harris & S. Kuchuck (Eds.), *The Legacy of Sandor Ferenczi* (pp. 264–273). London: Routledge.

Van Haute, P., & Geyskens, T. (2004). *Confusion of Tongues: The Primacy of Sexuality in Freud, Ferenczi, and Laplanche*. New York: Other Press.

Winnicott, D. W. (1967). Mirror-role of the mother and family in child development. In: *Playing and Reality* (pp. 111–118). London: Tavistock.

Chapter 30

The influence of Ferenczi on Interpersonal Psychoanalysis

Robert Prince

Establishing Ferenczi's impact on Interpersonal Psychoanalysis should hardly be challenging. The *Handbook of Interpersonal Psychoanalysis* (Lionells *et al.*, 1995) features Ferenczi's photograph, along with portraits of Sullivan, Thompson, Fromm, Fromm-Reichmann, and Horney—all in the firmament of the founders of interpersonal psychoanalysis. Ortmeyer (1995) includes him in his essay on the originators, noting that though he was "not one of the founders of the Interpersonal School; because of his theoretical and clinical influence on Interpersonalism, he merits being included in this chapter" (p. 25).

Ferenczi's deviation from Freudian principles, in fact, is credited with the development of a democratic interactional field for mutual examination. Thompson writes: "He was one of the pioneers bringing in a new era which stressed the importance of the analytic situation as a vital living experience" (1944, p. 250). Moses and McGarty refer to Ferenczi as a "forefather of Interpersonal thought" (1995, p. 663). Fiscalini (2004) calls him the "first coparticipant analyst" (2004, p. 45), whose efforts to develop a "true coparticipant base ... have born fruit in succeeding generations of analysts and led to the vast and momentous shift in psychoanalysis" that he calls the "interpersonal turn" (p. 48). For Fiscalini, Ferenczi foreshadowed the field theory that constitutes the philosophical underpinning of the interpersonal school. Wolstein (1989) also locates the origins of the interpersonal school in Ferenczi's experiments in clinical methods and further credits him with providing "American interpersonal relations with mainstream roots" (Wolstein, 1993, p. 177).

One or many interpersonal traditions?

An immediate caveat in establishing Ferenczi's impact is one of classification: Interpersonal psychoanalysis is hardly monolithic and some of Ferenczi's ideas were also sharply criticised by even those Interpersonalists who simultaneously seemed to resonate with him. Boundaries with other, later movements overlap with many significant convergences between traditions. Ferenczi, an original Freudian, became identified as a major dissident while the American interpersonal school grew in reaction to Freudian orthodoxy.

The Interpersonalists represent a disparate group struggling with their own connection to the Freudian heritage as well as their loyalties and conflicts with each other. The former, like Sullivan, distanced themselves as much as possible from Freudian language and signature concepts. The latter, like Ferenczi, had a complex emotional and political relationship with the Freudian heritage and though deviating in significant ways often used Freudian concepts and language as a touchstone. However, the meanings of key concepts such as transference and countertransference and ideas about gender and development underwent transformations.

While Ferenczi's dissidence inspired their own, they were not immune from fears of being associated with the criticisms of him; they had their own reservations, and they were not innocent of participation in the *todschweigen* (death by silence) of Ferenczi, described by Rachman (1999). Their approach developed from independent contributions that converged with Ferenczi's, but they rejected important aspects and elided what made them anxious in his work. As Interpersonalism continued to evolve, and was characterised in Mullahy's words by a "healthy eclecticism" (1948, p. xvii), there was an ongoing affinity, with the example set by Ferenczi, for continuous experimentation. Thus, as Ferenczi struggled between his standing not only at the center, but also at the forefront, of the psychoanalytic world, in his role as Freud's most brilliant pupil and as the major dissident, his core contributions were deeply resonant with the evolving European and American psychoanalysts who came to be identified with the interpersonal/culturalist school. Their relationships to the Freudian centre were also ambivalent, ambiguous, sometimes contentious, and ever unfolding.

Convergences

The list of Ferenczi's convergences with the Interpersonalist approaches is long.

1. Ferenczi's interest in difficult cases certainly attracted Americans who were based in psychiatric hospitals in the Washington area (Silver, Chapter Thirty-one).
2. First among Ferenczi's core ideas is the two-person nature of psychoanalysis and the mutuality of the analytic experience (Bass, Chapter Twenty-three). Wolstein credits "Ferenczi's direct involvement in the experiential field of therapy" (1993, p. 178) as basic to this resonance.
3. His explorations of transference as not spontaneous in the treatment, but created in and by the analytic situation, is a theme that echoes through the work of, for example, Edgar Levenson (1972, 1995) and Donnel Stern (2010), related to an emphasis on current dynamics, the interest in "what's going on around here" in the analytic relationship (Levenson, 1972).
4. Theoretically, Ferenczi's concern with the actual occurrences in the patient's life and the centrality of actual physical and sexual trauma as well as disturbed family relations in the aetiology of psychopathology, were important to interpersonal thinking, as was his recognition of the importance of the mother.
5. The rejection of the Freudian stereotype of the detached and objective analyst and the embrace of the analyst as a real person would be another common denominator. Thompson (1944) attributed to Ferenczi primacy in being among the first to recognise the importance of the real personality of the analyst and qualities such as warmth, courage, playfulness, sincerity, authenticity, and self-disclosure. Interpersonalists agreed that the analyst's participation is inevitable and wrestled with the intense affective involvement of the analyst, sometimes criticising Ferenczi's ideas without fully understanding that he himself regarded them as experimental.
6. They developed a central interest in countertransference and the reciprocity between patient and analyst, mutuality signified by an interest in the experience of both participants (Miller, 1991) and how it becomes known and shared within the relationship and evolves into the patient's need to heal the analyst.
7. Fiscalini (2004) credits Ferenczi as the first analyst to recognise the relationship as the mutative force in psychoanalysis, which led to Thompson and Fromm-Reichmann's

emphasis on the patient's need for a new interpersonal experience and the privileging of empathy.

8 The list would also include a conception of psychoanalysis as a learning experience located in a cultural context, elasticity of technique and experimentation, clinical flexibility, the creation of a relaxed therapeutic atmosphere and a safe place.

9 Sensitivity to power, concern for authority, attention to social issues including poverty and social class also became part of the interpersonal tradition.

Transmissions

While the reflections of Ferenczi in the mirror of the Interpersonalists are clear, the exact way in which these have been transmitted is both complicated and subtle. Levenson (1995) warns of committing the archaeological error of overlapping strata of meanings, confusing later concepts for similar earlier words. In many instances Ferenczi's influence is silent. For example, Silver (1996) traces a path to Ferenczi through Groddeck and Fromm-Reichmann by reviewing minutes of staff conferences at Chestnut Lodge, which clearly articulate his concepts without mentioning his name.

The literature before the publication of the *Diary* contains fewer direct citations of Ferenczi, while subsequent references are to more informal influence and metabolised concepts: phrases like the Ferenczian "tradition" or "manner" recur. Hirsch refers to Wolstein's ideas of mutual influence in the therapeutic dyad as being in "the spirit of Ferenczi" (1995, p. 657); Wittenberg describes Rioch as "absorbing and creatively expanding a lesson that had been taught ... by Ferenczi" (1995, p. 45); Boschan describes mutual analysis as "giving way to an attitude of mutually" (2011, p. 316). Thompson herself emphasises an affinity of ideas while denying direct influence, for example stating of herself: "I found Sullivan's and Ferenczi's approach more in keeping with my own ways of thinking than the classical Freudian methods" (1950, p. 5). She avers that Sullivan found Ferenczi's ideas compatible, but denies that he was influenced by them. However, Levenson describes Sullivan's influences "as coming second or third hand ... like a spider in the sense of a maestro of kinetics and connection" (1995, p. 126). Seventy-five years ago Thompson credited Ferenczi's primacy: "Today, other analysts—notably Fromm and Sullivan—have presented similar ideas, but I believe Ferenczi was quite alone in Europe around 1926 in this type of thinking" (1944, p. 247).

Despite demurrals, Thompson and Sullivan are outstanding conduits for Ferenczi's influence on Interpersonal psychoanalysis. Bacciagaluppi (1993) states that they represent one of two avenues, with Fromm representing the other. (It is relevant to note that Fromm became Thompson's third analyst.) There are discrepancies in the details of their initial contacts, as reported by Green (1978), Perry (1982), Shapiro (1993), Silver (1996), and Thompson herself (1944, 1950). Ferenczi spent 1926–1927 in New York and was an extremely popular speaker whose analytic hours quickly filled. He was charismatic, but also ostracised by many New York analysts because of his support for lay analysts. Sullivan knew of Ferenczi, according to Perry (1982), through reading his papers. But he also heard him lecture and succeeded in bringing him to Washington to speak despite the disapproval of William Alanson White. White was apparently either distrustful of the Europeans or wary of becoming embroiled in psychoanalytic politics, but also wrote privately to Jelliffe that he considered Ferenczi to be brilliant (Silver, 1996). Ferenczi delivered five lectures in Washington, for one of which Sullivan was a formal discussant, under the auspices of the Washington Psychoanalytic Association. Ferenczi, in 1926, while in America, also published a paper in an

American journal, *Mental Hygiene* (1926), that contained ideas that would become reflected in the Sullivanian condensation as "the one genus hypotheses", which is understood as the Interpersonal motto.

Sullivan, who had become enchanted with Thompson, insisted to her: "This was the only analyst he had any confidence in" (Perry, 1982, p. 202). Thompson wrote that Sullivan regarded Ferenczi as the most important of the European psychoanalysts, and he sent her to Budapest so "she could come and teach him what she had learned" (Perry, 1982, p. 200). She communicated with Sullivan, with whom she would be involved personally and professionally for the rest of both their lives. Sullivan had at least 300 hours of analysis with her and referred to her as his training analyst (Green, 1978). The arrangement may strike modern ears as odd, but it was not unheard of at the time for analyst and patient to also have a social relationship; complications often resulted.

The importance of personal and social relations on the development of the interpersonal school, from the beginning through to today, is easily "selectively unattended", but should not be underestimated. To begin with, many of Ferenczi's ideas were transmitted privately. Thompson writes: "Only his pupils, in private conversations, obtained an uncensored glimpse of Ferenczi's own thinking. This thinking deviated quite radically from that outlined in most of his published works" (1944, p. 247). Thompson later wrote more generally that techniques had been taught "chiefly by word of mouth through group and individual discussion. This makes it a difficult subject for the historian to pull together" (1950, p. 226).

Thompson became the first director of the William Alanson White Institute and served until her death in 1953. Many of her analysands went on to become leading Interpersonal psychoanalysts, not the least of whom was Benjamin Wolstein, who credits her as his most important influence (Hirsch, 2000). Wolstein himself went on to analyse many of today's leading Interpersonal analysts, who can thus be thought of as Ferenczi's analytic great-grandchildren.

Interpersonalists were also critical of Ferenczi, though not to the extent that classical analysts were. During Thompson's own analysis in Budapest, her boasts about sitting on "Papa" Ferenczi's lap, which were relayed to Freud through another American, Edith Jackson, hardly enhanced Ferenczi's reputation. Thompson (1944) subsequently charged Ferenczi, while having "sound" ideas, with taking "indulgence" (Relax) to an extreme. She warned that analysis "should not degenerate into mutual analysis" (Thompson, 1950, p. 187). Fromm-Reichmann (1950), referring to Ferenczi, cautioned about techniques that resulted in gratification for the analyst. Shapiro, in her critique of Thompson, charges that Thompson ignored Ferenczi's interest in sexual and physical abuse, his interest in nonverbal measures, and his appreciation of victims' helplessness.

The early Interpersonalists were also critical of his views on regression and helping patients relive early trauma. Rachman (1997), reviewing the curriculum at the White Institute through 1990, observes that Ferenczi was not listed on bibliographies. Wolstein (1993) recounts that what he heard in the 1950s were "only vague and half-stated rumors … about dangerously obscene efforts at mutual analysis, which only the mad Hungarian could think had therapeutic possibilities" (p. 180).

Wolstein's observations underscore how social relations have to be considered part of Ferenczi's impact. Ferenczi's struggles with Freud, culminating in his declining the presidency of the IPA and presenting the "Confusion of tongues" paper in 1932 (Prince, 2014), set a model for resisting conformity while aspiring to connection. The "polygamous analysis" described by Berman (2015), that is, that Ferenczi's analysands socialised with each other, a practice that seems to have silently and informally persisted over successive generations, was repeated among Interpersonalists beginning with Sullivan and Thompson, and certainly affected analytic discourse.

Similar to American politician Tip O'Neill's famous epigram about national politics, "All *psychoanalytic* politics is local", Horney found herself in an analogous situation to Ferenczi's in 1932 when he insisted on presenting "Confusion of tongues" at the Psychoanalytic Congress in Wiesbaden despite Freud's disapproval and displeasure. She, in 1941, persisted in her heretical teaching at the New York Psychoanalytic Institute and, demoted, resigned from it. Where Ferenczi, in his own way, remained loyal to Freud and the IPA, she and five others founded the interpersonally inflected Association for the Advancement of Psychoanalysis and their own institute. Their explanatory letter for their resignation "echoed Ferenczi's life long sentiments" (Galdi, 2015, p. 2). There was then a second schism, with Thompson leaving to form the William Alanson White Institute over the issue of lay analysis and in support of Fromm, who also shared Ferenczi's fate of being extruded from mainstream psychoanalysis. The trauma between Freud and Ferenczi, culminating in Ferenczi's Wiesbaden paper, was reenacted in New York in the context of the intense personal relations of the protagonists.

Concluding

In conclusion, if the question of Ferenczi's influence is easily answered, it may also be poorly framed. It implies a direct chain of causation rather than a field with many moving parts. Perhaps the better question is: How does Ferenczi fit in to the complex field of psychoanalytic theory, praxis, and importantly, personal relationships of which interpersonal psychoanalysis is a part. As Levenson writes: "Nothing … can be understood outside its time and place, its nexus of relationships" (1972, p. 8). Kurzweil (2012) examines the cultural circumstances and social context in which psychoanalysis is embedded, that influence interest and acceptance of the main themes in Ferenczi's work: love, mutuality, abstinence contrasted with gratification, scientism contrasted with an empathic method, sexual abuse, and identification with the aggressor. Thus Fromm, who had not been familiar with "Confusion of tongues", characterised it, when he finally read it in 1957, a quarter of a decade later, as "having extraordinary profundity and brilliance—in fact, one of the most valuable papers in the whole psychoanalytic literature" (cited in Bacciagaluppi, 1993, p. 187). Rachman (1997) locates the revival of interest in Ferenczi to the publication of the *Diary* and the shift in the centre of gravity of psychoanalysis from the Freudian heritage to relational frameworks. Controversy and conflict, along with recognition over his pioneering and groundbreaking contributions, are suggested by the words used to describe the current interest in him: "renaissance", "rekindling", "revival". These imply a rediscovery and assertion of his legacy, and reflect the Interpersonal principle that past and present are reciprocally embedded in each other.

Wolstein, probably like many others, did not discover Ferenczi until after being influenced by him. He writes: "I had never heard about the existence of Ferenczi's Diary … until its publication in 1988. Imagine my feelings of surprise, after all of those years of being told my ideas were outside the main currents of psychoanalysis, to learn that precursive ideas had already appeared in the historical center of psychoanalysis, unavailable to the psychoanalytic community though that historical record may have been kept" (Wolstein, 1993, p. 180). His comments bring to mind the struggle to find a secure base in the world of psychoanalysis while finding one's way on the path of one's own experience. Freud receives recognition as the father of psychoanalysis while Ferenczi is increasingly identified as its mother. And the role of the mother in the complexity and turmoil of a family life is to provide the security that allows separation and independence.

References

Bacciagaluppi, M. (1993). Ferenczi's influence on Fromm. In: L. Aron & A. Harris (Eds.), *The Legacy of Sándor Ferenczi* (pp. 189–198). Hillsdale, NJ: The Analytic Press.

Berman, E. (2015). On "polygamous analysis". *The American Journal of Psychoanalysis, 75*: 29–36.

Boschan, P. (2011). Transference and countertransference in Sándor Ferenczi's clinical diary. *American Journal of Psychoanalysis, 71*: 309–320.

Ferenczi, S. (1926). Freud's importance for the mental hygiene movement. *Mental Hygiene, 10*: 673–678.

Fiscalini, J. (2004). *Coparticipant Analysis: Toward a New Theory of Clinical Inquiry*. New York: Columbia University Press.

Fromm-Reichmann, F. (1950). *Principles of Intensive Psychotherapy*. Chicago: University of Chicago Press.

Galdi, G. (2015). Celebrating the 75th anniversary of the American Journal of Psychoanalysis. *The American Journal of Psychoanalysis, 75*: 1–2.

Green, M. R. (1978). Thompson and Sullivan. *Contemporary Psychoanalysis, 14*: 485–487.

Haynal, A. (2002). *Disappearing and Reviving: Sándor Ferenczi in the History of Psychoanalysis*. London: Karnac.

Hirsch, I. (1995). Therapeutic uses of countertransference. In: M. Lionells, J. Fiscalini, C. Mann, & D. Stern (Eds), *The Handbook of Interpersonal Psychoanalysis* (pp. 643–660). Hillsdale, NJ: The Analytic Press.

Hirsch, I. (2000). Interview with Benjamin Wolstein. *Contemporary Psychoanalysis, 36*: 187–232.

Kurzweil, E. (2012). Ferenczi in context. In: J. Szekacs-Weisz & T. Keve (Eds), *Ferenczi and His World: Rekindling the Spirit of the Budapest School* (pp. 55–67). London: Karnac.

Levenson, E. (1972). *The Fallacy of Understanding*. New York: Basic Books.

Levenson, E. (1995). *The Ambiguity of Change*. New York: Basic Books.

Lionells, M., Fiscalini, J., Mann, C., & Stern, D. (Eds.) (1995). *Handbook of Interpersonal Psychoanalysis*. Hillsdale, NJ: The Analytic Press.

Moses, I., & McGarty, M. (1995). Anonymity, self-disclosure, and expressive uses of analyst experience. In: M. Lionells, J. Fiscalini, C. Mann, & D. Stern (Eds), *The Handbook of Interpersonal Psychoanalysis* (pp. 661–675). Hillsdale, NJ: The Analytic Press.

Miller, I. (1991). Experiential psychoanalysis and the engagement of selves: Ferenczi's vision and the psychoanalytic present. *Journal of the American Academy of Psychoanalysis, 19*: 67–82.

Mullahy, P. (Ed.) (1948). *A Study of Interpersonal Relations: New Contributions in Psychiatry*. New York: Grove.

Ortmeyer, D. (1995). History of the founders of interpersonal psychoanalysis. In: M. Lionells, J. Fiscalini, C. Mann, & D. Stern (Eds), *The Handbook of Interpersonal Psychoanalysis* (pp. 11–27). Hillsdale, NJ: The Analytic Press.

Perry, H. (1982). *Psychiatrist of America: The Life of Harry Stack Sullivan*. Cambridge, MA: Harvard University Press.

Prince, R. (2014). Balancing belonging and self-realization in psychoanalysis: The example of Sándor Ferenczi. *Psychoanalytic Inquiry, 34*: 135–144.

Rachman, A. (1997). *Sándor Ferenczi: The Psychotherapist of Tenderness and Passion*. Northvale, NJ: Jason Aronson.

Rachman, A. (1999). Death by silence (todschweigen): The traditional method of silencing the dissident in psychoanalysis. In: R. Prince (Ed.), *The Death of Psychoanalysis* (pp. 153–164). Northvale, NJ: Jason Aronson.

Shapiro, S. (1993). Clara Thompson: Ferenczi's messenger with half a message. In: L. Aron & A. Harris (Eds.), *The Legacy of Sándor Ferenczi* (pp. 159–174). Hillsdale, NJ: The Analytic Press.

Silver, A.-L. (1996). Ferenczi's early impact on Washington, D.C. In: P. L. Rudnytsky, P. Giampieri-Deutsch, & A. Bokay (Eds.), *Ferenczi's Turn in Psychoanalysis* (pp. 89–106). New York: New York University Press.

Stern, D. B (2010). *Partners in Thought: Working with Unformulated Experience, Dissociation, and Enactment*. New York: Routledge.

Thompson, C. (1944). Ferenczi's contribution to psychoanalysis. *Psychiatry*, *7*: 245–252.

Thompson, C. (1950). *Psychoanalysis: Evolution and Development*. New York: Hermitage House.

Wittenberg, E. (1995). Introduction: Janet MacKenzie Rioch. In: D. Stern, C. Mann, S. Kantor, & G. Schlesinger (Eds.), *Pioneers of Interpersonal Psychoanalysis* (pp. 43–45). Hillsdale, NJ: Analytic Press.

Wolstein, B. (1989). Ferenczi, Freud, and the origins of American interpersonal relations. *Contemporary Psychoanalysis*, *25*: 672–685.

Wolstein, B. (1993). Sándor Ferenczi and American interpersonal relations: Historical and personal reflections. In: L. Aron & A. Harris (Eds.), *The Legacy of Sándor Ferenczi* (pp. 175–184). Hillsdale, NJ: The Analytic Press.

Chapter 31

Psychoanalysis and psychosis: Ferenczi's influence at Chestnut Lodge

Ann-Louise Silver

Introduction to Chestnut Lodge

For almost a century, Chestnut Lodge hospital was a leading institution for the psychoanalytic treatment and care of persons suffering from psychotic disorders. It opened in 1910 and had four medical directors during its existence: Ernest Bullard, then his son Dexter Sr, then the latter's oldest son Dexter Jr, and finally Wayne Fenton. It had six directors of psychotherapy: Frieda Fromm-Reichmann, Otto Will, Ping-Nie Pao, Robert Cohen, E. James Anthony, and Christopher Keats. Its staff had a lot of success in treating patients most other institutions considered incurable. They took care of the patients with empathy and understanding, resisting introduction of psychotropic medication for many years, and redefining the notion of analytic setting. The hospital was sold in 1997, with the plan that it be converted to condominiums. It burned to the ground in 2009.

Although Ferenczi never visited Chestnut Lodge, his ideas were planted and nurtured there by pioneers like Frieda Fromm-Reichmann and Harry Stack Sullivan, who were deeply immersed in his work. Never formally on the staff, Sullivan strongly influenced Lodge styles and attitudes. The 246 lectures-discussions he held there, attended by the entire medical staff, constituted the basis for his *Clinical Studies in Psychiatry* (1956). In 1943 Sullivan, Erich Fromm, Frieda Fromm-Reichmann, Clara Thompson, and Janet and David Rioch formed the New York branch of the Washington School of Psychiatry: namely, the William Alanson White Institute. Six years later, in 1949, the year of Sullivan's death, the tie between the Washington School of Psychiatry—informally connected to Chestnut Lodge—and the White Institute was broken. The Lodge and the Institute, nonetheless, shared a common clinical lineage as well as some common theoretical founding-fathers, such as Ferenczi and Groddeck.

Early psychoanalysis and the treatment of psychosis

Psychoanalysis was born in a neurologist's private office—a fact that played an important role in the attitude of psychoanalysis towards the treatment of psychosis. Freud acknowledged in 1910 that, due to his private-office setting, he did not have the opportunity to treat persons with psychosis, aside from extraordinary circumstances (Freud, 1911, p. 9). For this reason, it can rightly be said that what Freud knew about this came from two "advisers": Viktor Tausk, who worked in psychiatric hospitals in Vienna, Sarajevo, and Belgrade, wrote an important early psychoanalytic interpretation of schizophrenia (Tausk, 1933), and succumbed to a tragic destiny (see Roazen, 1973); and Carl Gustav Jung, who was writing about the topic before meeting Freud (Jung, 1909), and returned to it at the end of his life. It was Jung who turned Freud's attention to the book *Memoirs of My Nervous Illness* by Daniel Paul Schreber.[1] More importantly, through him Freud hoped to prepare an assault on a terrain of university psychiatry: if Emil Kraepelin and Eugen Bleuler, the most distinguished psychiatrists in the world, would support psychoanalysis, Freud's conquest would be complete, and Jung happened to be Bleuler's assistant at one of the most prestigious institutions for studying and treating psychosis, the Burghölzli in Zurich. Kraepelin was never truly attracted, but Bleuler was for a time very receptive towards psychoanalysis. Through the Burghölzli, a whole generation of psychiatrists made contact with Freudian theories and, eventually, with the psychoanalytic movement. Indeed, many of them would later define the evolution of dynamic psychiatry (for instance, Jung, Ferenczi, Abraham, Jones, Brill, Eitingon, Binswanger, Spielrein, Rorschach, Assagioli). Retrospectively, we could even say that without this unique academic, scientific, and logistical support psychoanalysis would not have become what it is today.

Bleuler, however, harboured strong doubts about the prominent role Freud assigned to sexuality.[2] As Falzeder observes: "Bleuler's break with the psychoanalytic movement is important because it represents a crucial and until now largely underestimated turning point" (1997, p. 181). Freud's break with Bleuler, however, radicalised the former's positions about the analytic treatment of psychosis and delayed the natural flow of psychoanalysis into that stream of dynamic psychotherapy of persons with psychosis, which was then springing from the Burghölzli. After this break, Chestnut Lodge was one of the first psychiatric institutions to try once again to apply psychoanalytic principles to the treatment of persons with psychosis. However, this required appropriating Ferenczi's revision of the mainstream psychoanalytic setting, his experiments in technique, and his development of the elasticity principle—"it is not the patient who should adapt to psychoanalysis, but the other way round!" (Koritar, Chapter Twenty-two).

From Ferenczi to Chestnut Lodge

Freud, being a fierce authority and protector of the centrality of the Oedipus complex, strongly resisted the relevance of treatment of psychosis as part of the psychoanalytic endeavour (1924a, 1924b). In his opinion, these patients were encapsulated in the state of "narcissistic neurosis" and therefore incapable of developing transference, which made psychoanalytic treatment impossible (Freud, 1914c).

In 1916 Ferenczi conformed to Freudian orthodoxy, as illustrated in two footnotes in his paper "Some clinical observations on paranoia and paraphrenia" (p. 244, n1), in regard to *not* taking a patient into analysis who seemed to show the usual strong resistance to change

1 Most probably, it was Otto Gross—a pupil of the Munich-based professor of psychiatry Emil Kraepelin—who attracted Jung's attention to the book during their mutual analysis at the Burghölzli. In fact, Gross was the first psychiatrist and psychoanalytic pioneer to discuss the case (1904). In the same work, Gross also challenged Kraepelin's diagnosis of *dementia praecox* and advanced his personal definition of *dementia sejunctiva*: a disease characterised by a splitting or a disintegration of conscience. Unlike many other Freudians, Ferenczi included, Gross acknowledged his debt to Pierre Janet. Yet by applying Janet's concepts to psychosis, he anticipated by almost ten years Bleuler's famous description of schizophrenia (*schizein*, like sejunction, meaning splitting, division).

2 A few years later, Bleuler took from Freud's work on the psychosis of Schreber the concept of autoerotism, but he elided the sexual element, settling on the term autism.

seen in most paranoid patients. He wrote (Ferenczi, 1916, p. 249, n1): "As it seemed to me to be quite without prospects I did not want him to go through an analysis", concluding: "This peculiarity of his I had already noticed in fact and had interpreted in the sense of transferred erotism; naturally I had taken care not to call his attention to it nor to explain the symptom to him" (p. 245, n1).

Yet, at the same time, Ferenczi was from the start more inclusive in attitude than Freud and had far greater experience treating severely disturbed patients. There was a saying, "You could take a sick horse to Ferenczi and he could cure it." Indeed, as a psychiatrist he was more familiar with psychosis and treated "a large number of psychotic patients" (Hornstein, 2000, p. 44). Additionally, when he founded the Hungarian Psychoanalytical Association, in 1911, he did so with the help of Istvan Hollos, who served as the secretary to the society and co-authored with Ferenczi the monograph *Psychoanalysis and the Psychic Disorder of General Paresis* (1925), but was also the medical director of the Budapest mental hospital in Nagy-Szeben; through him Ferenczi had extensive acquaintance with hospitalised psychotic patients.

In 1926, Ferenczi came to the United States and delivered lectures in both New York and Washington. Harry Stack Sullivan, who had already moved from Washington to New York, commented that of the European analysts with whose work he was acquainted, Ferenczi's ideas were the most like his own. Ferenczi pushed for equality, be it for homosexuals, women, or assistants at the hospital, and saw patients and doctors as co-equals. He stressed the role of early severe trauma as a central factor in the years-later emergence of psychosis. Ferenczi also treated Clara Thompson every summer from 1928 until his death in 1933. She sought him out at the urging of Sullivan, who was her friend and with whom she would go on to co-found the White Institute in New York City, a project of the Washington School of Psychiatry. In its early years, faculty members of the Washington School of Psychiatry and of the Washington Psychoanalytic Institute travelled every week to New York to teach and supervise, while analysts of the White Institute travelled south on the alternate weekends to teach in Washington: "Thompson, Sullivan, and Fromm-Reichmann traveled back and forth by train between the two cities on a weekly basis" beginning in the fall of 1943 (Perry, 1982, p. 390).

Sullivan would later become close lifelong friends with Fromm-Reichmann, and their influence on Chestnut Lodge would be tremendous. As noted, the Lodge opened in 1910, with Ernest Bullard as its first medical director. By 1935, he was ready to retire. His son, Dexter M. Bullard Sr, was in his training analysis with Ernest Hadley, and had noticed first hand, having grown up on the hospital's grounds, how much psychotic speech and neurotic dreams overlapped in their form and content. He thought psychoanalysis was thus relevant to treating psychosis and puzzled over how to actualise a plan to make his hospital specialise in psychoanalytic treatment of psychosis. Coincidentally, Fromm-Reichmann had emigrated to the United States that year, and her former husband, Erich Fromm, tried to help her find employment there. He called Bullard's analyst, Ernest Hadley, who then asked Bullard whether he could use a German-Jewish analyst at Chestnut Lodge. Bullard resisted at first, but then agreed to meet her, and often said it was "love at first sight" (Silver, 1989).

Yet applying psychoanalytic principles to hospitalised patients required flexibility: the setting had to be co-created, and much of the therapy revolved around the negotiation of its boundaries.

From Ferenczi to Fromm-Reichmann and Searles

Fromm-Reichmann had worked closely with Georg Groddeck, and knew Ferenczi through Groddeck's symposia held in Baden-Baden (Fromm-Reichmann, 1989, p. x). She had developed a pattern early in her career of volunteering to help the teachers from whom she especially wanted to learn, calling them "my victims" (Silver, 1989). For example, she volunteered during the First World War to be the administrator of the hospital unit Kurt Goldstein was assigned to run, which specialised in brain-injured soldiers (Hornstein, 2000). Her next "chosen victim" was Georg Groddeck. She volunteered to organise the symposia Groddeck held at his Baden-Baden sanatorium. She was regularly called upon to comment from a woman's perspective although other women were there as well, including Karen Horney, the first woman training and teaching analyst at the Berlin Psychoanalytic Institute, where Frieda had received her own training.

Among the features Fromm-Reichmann shared with Ferenczi were an optimistic attitude, his interest in the most severely disturbed patients, his openness about the therapist's affective response, as well as a zeal to cure (Hornstein, 2000, p. 282). In her later years she devoted all her time to working with patients. In looking for guidance, Fromm-Reichmann did not have many senior colleagues to turn to, but Ferenczi was one she could. She attended his supervisions whenever he visited Groddeck in Baden-Baden (Hornstein, 2000, p. 45).

In her classic *Principles of Intensive Psychotherapy*, Fromm-Reichmann refers to Freud thirty-two times, while to Ferenczi only three times. She refers mainly to Ferenczi's and Rank's idea of "re-lived experience" during the analysis (Ferenczi & Rank, 1925), but she criticises it, not so much on the grounds that, contrary to what they proposed, acting should be discouraged in favour of thinking (the classical critique of Ferenczi and Rank, based on Freud's highly abstract and mechanical "two principles of mental functioning"), but on the grounds that the analyst should not gain too much narcissistic reward from the infantile needs and dependency of the patient.

This notwithstanding, in order to find Ferenczi in this book, one must search the index for the words communications, contact, countertransference, dependency, dissociation, empathy, safety, hostility, reassurance, and above all, tenderness. Fromm-Reichmann echoes—without quoting him directly—what Scottish psychiatrist Ian Suttie, building on Ferenczi (see Clarke, Chapter Twenty-six), called the "taboo on tenderness", stating that often patients are more at ease in narrating their infantile attachments to their parents in terms of sexual contact than in terms of tender contact, the same being true about the transference. Then, just as did Suttie, she underlines that work with psychotic patients shows us how our culture is characterised by a "taboo on tenderness" more than by an "incest taboo". In fact, those patients did experience a symbiotic-incestuous bond to the parents in infancy (and maybe in adulthood), but this "close bond" was not really a bond of closeness: in other terms, it hid an underlying lack of parental tenderness (for many possible reasons). This kind of symbiotic-yet-not-tender-bond is typically re-enacted by psychotic patients with the psychiatric institution and the psychiatrist. Intensive analytic therapy with psychiatric patients should thus be based on the working-through of this kind of dependency bond.

In the collection of Fromm-Reichmann's selected papers (Bullard, 1959), again, Ferenczi is mentioned three times to Freud's thirty-nine. In discussing the roots of anxiety, listing the perspectives of Ferenczi and nine others with whom she agrees, Fromm-Reichmann emphasises: "it seems that the feeling of powerlessness, of helplessness in the presence of inner dangers which the individual cannot control constitutes in the last analysis the common background of all further elaborations on the theory of anxiety" (Bullard, 1959, p. 110). The final reference relates directly to the treatment of individuals suffering from psychosis, their trauma having occurred before development of language and communicated through gestures, not yet through words (Bullard, 1959, p. 117). Hornstein (2000, p. 46) also underlines how Fromm-Reichmann confessed having learned from Ferenczi that when one cannot understand a patient, one should try the technique of "duplicating, actually or in imagination" her bodily movements.

If Fromm-Reichmann shared anything with Ferenczi it was the emphasis on (particularly the negative) countertransference: "As Ferenczi and his disciples have pointed out at various times, we know now that, being unreal, it is a dangerous pretense to think that one of the two partners—the analyst—can remain a shapeless nonentity to the other—the patient—in the course of a therapeutic procedure whose very essence is an intimately interpersonal experience and whose aim is the patient's re-establishment of real contacts in a real world" (in Bullard, 1959, p. 52). This pillar of psychoanalytic treatment was later amplified at Chestnut Lodge, most thoroughly in the work of Harold Searles. Together with the Balints, Winnicott, Little, and Heimann in Britain, and Racker in Argentina, Searles wrote fundamental early papers on countertransference in the mid-twentieth century (1965, 1979). Besides quoting Ferenczi himself, Searles relied so much on the work of the British Independents that, together with Hans Loewald, Ralph Greenson, and others coming from different and often rival psychoanalytic "schools", he can be considered a kind of American Independent.

Fromm-Reichmann also wrote that "the schizophrenic is capable of developing strong relationships of love and hatred toward his analyst" (in Bullard, 1959, p. 121). To understand and work on it, however, psychoanalysts had to change their frame and setting, in line with Ferenczi's idea of elasticity. Here is just one example of the psychoanalytic work with persons with psychosis at the Chestnut Lodge:

> [A] very suspicious patient, after two days of fear and confusion ushering in a real panic, became stuporous for a month—mute, resistive to food, and retaining excretions. In spite of this rather unpromising picture, I sat with him for one hour every day. The only sign of contact he gave to me or anyone was to indicate by gestures that he wanted me to stay; all that he said on two different days during this period was: "Don't leave!"
>
> One morning after this I found him sitting naked and masturbating on the floor of his room, which was spotted with urine and sputum, talking for the first time, yet so softly that I could not understand him. I stepped closer to him but still could not hear him, so I sat down on the floor close to him, upon which he turned to me with genuine concern: "You can't do that for me, you too will get involved!" After that he pulled a blanket around himself saying, "Even though I have sunk as low as an animal, I still know how to behave in the presence of a lady." Then he talked for several hours about his history and his problems. (In Bullard, 1959, p. 123)

However, this unorthodox way of handling the psychoanalytic setting led to the ostracism of many important contributors to Chestnut Lodge legacy, as it had done with Ferenczi. I suspect that these scanty references to the name of Ferenczi, more than to his ideas, relate to his banishment from the history of psychoanalysis during that time, and thereby hide the full acknowledgment of his contributions to Fromm-Reichmann's career trajectory; in any case, they did not help. The critique that "this is not psychoanalysis" was always lurking around the corner. At a meeting of the American Psychoanalytic Association, Fromm-Reichmann rose to say that many developmental events took place before the Oedipus complex. Edward Bibring publicly questioned her: "What right do you have to call yourself a psychoanalyst?" Fromm-Reichmann returned to Chestnut Lodge clearly shaken (personal communication, Robert A. Cohen).[3]

Chestnut Lodge was closed in 2001, although not for reasons of doctrine but for financial reasons. Nowadays, mental-health care provided to persons with psychosis is moving towards a de-institutionalisation of "severe patients", territorial organisation of catchment areas, and home-based pharmacological treatments. However, in this new scenario the clinical experience gained in institutions such as the Chestnut Lodge, and indirectly from Sándor Ferenczi's experiments, is all the more precious in terms of showing psychoanalysts that it is possible to (net-)work with multi-professional teams, in flexible-inclusive settings, with the inner feeling that "it is psychoanalysis". What else could it be?

References

Bullard, D. (Ed.) (1959). *Psychoanalysis and Psychotherapy: Selected Papers of Frieda Fromm-Reichmann.* Chicago, IL: The University of Chicago Press.

Falzeder, E. (1997). The story of an ambivalent relationship: Sigmund Freud and Eugen Bleuler. In: *Psychoanalytic Filiations: Mapping the Psychoanalytic Movement* (pp. 177–196). London: Karnac, 2015.

Ferenczi, S. (1916). Some clinical observations on paranoia and paraphrenia. In: *Contributions to Psycho-Analysis.* Boston, MA: Richard G. Badger.

Ferenczi, S., & Rank, O. (1925). *The Development of Psychoanalysis.* New York, NY: Nervous and Mental Disease Publishing Co., Monograph No. 40.

Freud, S. (1911). Psychoanalytic notes on an autobiographical account of a case of paranoia (dementia paranoides). *S. E., 12*: 9–82. London: Hogarth.

Freud, S. (1914). On narcissism: An introduction. *S. E., 14*: 67–102. London: Hogarth.

Freud, S. (1924a). Neurosis and psychosis. *S. E., 19*: 147–154. London: Hogarth.

Freud, S. (1924b). The loss of reality in neurosis and psychosis. *S. E., 19*: 181–188. London: Hogarth.

Fromm-Reichmann, F. (1989). Reminiscences of Europe. In: A.-L. Silver (Ed.), *Psychoanalysis and Psychosis* (pp. 469–481). Madison, CT: International Universities Press.

Gross, O. (1904). On the disintegration of the conscious. In: *Otto Gross. Selected Works: 1901–1920* (pp. 71–76). New York: Mindpiece, 2012.

Hollos, S., & Ferenczi, S. (1925). *Psychoanalysis and the Psychic Disorder of General Paresis* (pp. 238–249). New York, NY: Nervous and Mental Disease Publishing Co.

Hornstein, G. (2000). *To Redeem One Person Is to Redeem the World: The Life of Frieda Fromm-Reichmann.* New York, NY: The Free Press.

3 This authoritarian attitude was still in place at the APsaA in the late 1980s when I applied for certification, the procedure necessary for application for becoming a training and supervising analyst. My rejection letter read, "While you may be very helpful to these admittedly disturbed patients, this is not psychoanalysis as we know it, and thus we are at a loss as to what to advise you regarding obtaining certification." This would have been crushing had I been reporting on work with psychotic patients. However, all four of my patients were neurotic professionals. No parameters were ever necessary. They never called between sessions, never even wondered about medications, and were never hospitalised. They were neurotic folk who could report their dreams and work on decoding them. The committee knew in advance they wouldn't accept me, and so they hadn't wasted their time in reading my reports. What right did I have, like Fromm-Reichmann, to call myself a psychoanalyst?

Jung, C. G. (1909). *The Psychology of Dementia Praecox (Authorized translation with an introduction by A. A. Brill* (Vol. 3). New York, NY: Nervous and Mental Disease Publishing Company. (German original published in 1907.)

Perry, H. S. (1982). *Psychiatrist of America: The Life of Harry Stack Sullivan.* Cambridge, MA: Belknap.

Roazen, P. (1973). *Brother Animal: The Story of Freud and Tausk.* Harmondsworth: Penguin.

Searles, H. (1965). *Collected Papers on Schizophrenia and Related Subjects.* New York, NY: International Universities Press.

Searles, H. (1979). *Countertransference and Related Subjects: Selected Papers.* New York, NY: International Universities Press.

Silver, A.-L. (1989). *Psychoanalysis and Psychosis.* Madison, CT: International Universities Press.

Sullivan, H. S. (1956). *Clinical Studies in Psychiatry.* New York, NY: W.W. Norton.

Tausk, V. (1933). On the origin of the "influencing machine" in schizophrenia. *The Psychoanalytic Quarterly, 2*: 519–566. (German original published in 1919.)

Chapter 32

Echoes of Ferenczi in psychoanalytic self psychology: Ancestor and bridge

Donna M. Orange

Like Winnicott and other early post-Freudian psychoanalysts, Heinz Kohut was clearly affected by the spirit and work of Sándor Ferenczi. Also like them, he rarely alluded to this influence. Though this contribution will speculate about the reasons for this omission, it will give more attention to the actual traces: the centrality of trauma, the restoration of compassion and generosity, the hermeneutics of trust. Ferenczi's impact on psychoanalytic practice remains most clearly visible in intersubjective variants of self psychology. The more visible heritage of Ferenczi in contemporary relational psychoanalysis (Bass, 2001; Harris & Aron, 1997; Frankel, 2002) may provide common ground for fruitful dialogue in post-Freudian psychoanalysis today.

Ferenczi's ambiguous presence in the work of Heinz Kohut

When Heinz Kohut arrived in Chicago in the early 1940s, a refugee from newly annexed Vienna, medical degree in hand, he quickly enrolled in the Chicago Institute of Psychoanalysis. Evidently an avid student, eager to do well in his new land (Kuriloff, 2014), he read thoroughly and deeply, including the work of Ferenczi available at that time. Charles Strozier's biography (Strozier, 2001) remarks that the young Kohut seemed uninterested in other "dissidents" like Jung and Rank, but read Ferenczi carefully. We can see what impressed Kohut, and where he gradually diverged from Ferenczi as his prominence grew, as he became "Mr Psychoanalysis". The ambivalence is worth watching.

Kohut's earliest published writings concern psychoanalytic understandings of the experiences of listening to music, and here we also find his first references to Ferenczi, suggesting a kinship. Reviewing a French book on the psychoanalysis of music (Kohut & Ornstein, 1978, vol. 1, p. 167), he criticised its author for ignoring important sources like Ferenczi's (1921, pp. 198–217) "classical description of the use of music in the course of psychoanalytic therapy" (p. 167). Two years later Ferenczi appears again in his writing in a more favourable review of fellow emigré Theodor Reik. Kohut translated Ferenczi (1909) from the German: "I wonder whether there are *tone* associations that are not determined by verbal contents … A rhythm that corresponds to an affective state is probably sufficient to produce the associated emergence of a tune without text" (Kohut, 1978, vol. 1, p. 187). Two pages later Kohut returned to Ferenczi, commenting on Reik's discussion of "Three Blind Mice". "This example seems to corroborate Ferenczi's conclusion that it is a *rhythm* corresponding to an affective state that determines the associative emergence of tune. The rhythm of the ditty becomes especially cheerful where the words are most threateningly close to the unconscious meaning …" (p. 189). So music seems to have formed the first connection.

The second we might call phenomenology. Passionately interested in the lived experience (*das Erlebnis*) of his patients, Ferenczi revised practice and theory each time he realised that the accepted view had reached a dead end. His patients taught him to hear their agonised insistence that they had not invented their pain or their memories of abuse. Both psychoanalytic theory, attributing their troubles to instinctive wishes and fantasies, and practice, shielding analysts from all implication in their patients' suffering, only increased this very suffering. Heinz Kohut, long before he developed what came to be called self psychology, insisted that psychoanalysis as a field of inquiry concerned data only available through introspection and empathy (Kohut, 1959),[1] implicitly prioritising, as had Ferenczi before him, experience over theory, so prominent in the education of psychoanalysts. Both men may have relied, without mentioning this reliance, on the senses embedded in the word experience. In Latin-based languages (*periculum*, danger) we can hear peril from which we may have escaped. Ex-perience suggests something about emergence—perhaps sadder and wiser—from extreme circumstances, about having learned from an escape. The experienced person has lost innocence, perhaps, in French (*expérience*), in Italian (*esperienza*), and in English. German, famously, gives us two words for experience: *Erlebnis*, lived (*das Leben*, life) experience or personally lived event, and *Erfahrung*, accumulated learning, even practical wisdom. In *Erfahrung* we hear both *fahren* (to travel) and *Gefahr* (danger), where the word resonates with the peril we hear in the Romance languages. Both danger and travel may remind us of Odysseus. All these linguistic hints lead us to contrast experience with abstract theorising, but make us hesitate to absolutise or reify. In his last months of life, Ferenczi (Diary, p. 93), used his *Clinical Diary* to accuse Freud of preferring theory development over caring for patients.

Both Ferenczi and Kohut, choosing to prioritise experience, faced tremendous opposition from those who grip their theories tightly. Neither chose the outsider path willingly, but found that responding to suffering people rejected as unanalysable by the psychoanalytic powers left them both outside. It is hard to say whether Ferenczi's fate—banishment even from publication after his death, slander by Jones as having become insane—led Kohut to mention him less and less, or whether Kohut's desire to be thought original played a larger role. We can see, however, reading Kohut's correspondence (Kohut & Cocks, 1994) with John Gedo, already before *The Analysis of the Self* (Kohut, 1971), that Kohut's view of Ferenczi and of his place in psychoanalytic history became increasingly complex and perhaps ambivalent:

> I think that you have found a balanced attitude toward his [Ferenczi's] flights of fancy and toward his later restlessness. That his gifts were second only to Freud, with that I will agree—yet, taking an overall view, I think that Abraham's early emphasis on the pre-oedipal stages of the libido were more truly original and independent of Freud

1 Later (Kohut, 1977) Kohut directly attributed this view to both Freud and Ferenczi. He provided his own English translation of Ferenczi: "[Freud] discovered that it is just as possible to obtain new knowledge through the scientific ordering of the data of introspection as through the utilization of the data of external perception gathered with the aid of observation and experiment." And later: "Thanks to psychoanalysis we are now able to undertake a systematic approach to a new group of data—a group of data that has been disregarded by the natural sciences. Psychoanalysis demonstrates the activity of inner forces that can only be perceived through introspection (Ferenczi, 1927)", in Kohut, 1977, p. 306, n14).

> than Ferenczi's early hunches about archaic ego mechanisms ... Nevertheless to me the "Stages of the Development of the Sense of Reality" is Ferenczi's greatest contribution...
> (p. 153, 26 October 1966)

Kohut's preference for this early essay, also mentioned by him elsewhere (Kohut, 1966), probably reflects his own developing sense of the child's gradual consolidation of a sense of self in the care of those mirroring others he would come to call selfobjects. Already Ferenczi provided, intertwined with drive theories, an alternative developmental account, according to which a child could learn self-trust instead of the adult-induced confusion he would later see in his patients. Kohut may have seen this paper as precursor to his own studies of healthy and pathological narcissism. But Kohut hated Ferenczi's later "flights of fancy" with their tendency to mix the biological and the psychological, writing: "Ferenczi's *Thalassa* is the outstanding example of overextending the introspective and empathic method" (Kohut, 1959, p. 478, n8).

Another difficulty came from Kohut's rejection of Franz Alexander's innovations: less frequent sessions, psychosomatics, and corrective emotional experience. When Kohut was asked to redesign the curriculum for the Chicago Institute after Alexander's departure in the early 1950s, believing it his task to restore orthodoxy, he made no place for Jung, Ferenczi, Klein, or any other dissidents. So the influences of Ferenczi and Alexander on his own developing thinking had to remain underground, perhaps less than conscious even for him. We do not know how much the taboo on Ferenczi, and how much his own disapproval, influenced his decisions before he became a dissident himself. Kohut did fear, even scorned, efforts to provide what patients had been missing in childhood:

> Analysts do not hold the simplistic view, for example, that people who suffer from early deprivations must now have them made up for by a belated therapeutic compensation. The image of the aging Ferenczi, allowing his patients to sit on his knees, trying to provide them with the love of which they had been deprived in their childhood, does not represent our ideal. We are aware of the complexity of the results of early deprivation; but we do not encourage the therapeutic re-emergence of childhood demands in order to give now what had been missing in the past so that their curbing and transformation can finally be achieved ... our leading ideal will not be passionate truth-finding softened by humanitarian considerations, but the empathic expansion of the self with the aid of scientifically trained cognition.
> (Kohut, 1975, pp. 339–340)[2]

Still, Ferenczi's fallibilistic spirit, rejecting all hypocrisy, insisting that the patient's point of view, the patient's anguish, the patient's accusations against the analyst, all be heard and find response, pervaded self psychology from before its own clear beginnings.

The second generation

Howard Bacal first recognised explicitly and extensively the Ferenczian spirit of self psychology, though others (Brothers, 1995; Hazan, 1999; Lee et al., 2008; Ornstein, A., &

2 If we ask, in the face of this disclaimer, why Kohut in fact treated his patients with kindness, we must ask the same of Freud, whose "recommendations" to others he often permitted himself to violate. Ferenczi's crime was to practice kindness and humility openly.

Ornstein, P. H., 2005; Teicholz, 1999) have also made this connection. He and Kenneth Newman (Bacal & Newman, 1990), in their context-establishing *British Object Relations: Bridges to Self Psychology,* helped all of us to realise that Kohut's ideas had not emerged in a vacuum, but rather formed part of a chorus of related alternatives to the classical, individualistic psychoanalysis in which most of us had been trained. "Ferenczi," they wrote, "turned his attention to the relational perspective in ways that were later reflected in theories of object relations, including self psychology" (p. 3). Thus, intentionally or not, they prepared many self psychologists to recognise our kinship with the relational psychoanalysis emerging in the United States at that very time, a movement similarly indebted to Ferenczi, whose work was then beginning to be published,[3] and British voices like Fairbairn, Guntrip, and Winnicott. "Ferenczi," according to Bacal and Newman, "was also the first analyst to emphasize that the patient's experience of the analytic process was significantly affected by the nature of the interaction between the particular analyst and his patient" (p. 3).

Next, developing his specificity and optimal responsiveness views of psychoanalytic treatment, upending Kohut's "optimal frustration", self psychologist Bacal (1998) once again highlighted his own indebtedness to Ferenczi and his analysand Michael Balint. Noting with them the psyche-shattering betrayals of trust that bring so many into treatment, confusing their tongues as they identify with the aggressor's view that the child wanted what replaced tenderness, Bacal remembered that Kohut had once remarked to him that "Ferenczi had the right idea" (p. 36). With Ernest Wolf (1988), Bacal emphasises Kohut's insistence on acknowledging the analyst's contribution to clinical misunderstandings and impasses. As Ferenczi, ever the fallibilist, insisted on admitting his failures to his patients, so Kohut, in practice, Bacal believes, worked in the same spirit. Bacal regards Ferenczi, with also perhaps Ian Suttie, Michael Balint, and Donald Winnicott, as the most important influences besides Kohut on his own view of the curative action of optimal responsiveness and specificity (Bacal, 2006). Ferenczi listened for the patient's *experience*, confounding the analyst's preconceived ideas.

Intersubjectivity and developmental studies

Turning now to recent contributors from intersubjective systems theory and from developmental theories, we can again see Ferenczian echoes and often direct influence. The outsized impact of baby-watchers like Louis Sander (Sander et al., 2008), Daniel Stern (1985; 2004), and Beatrice Beebe (Beebe & Lachman, 2001) on contemporary psychoanalysis means that we can believe Ferenczi when he writes of child analysis in the analysis of adults (ChildAn). More than ever, we know that our relational history, from our first moments, lives in us, wreaking havoc and creating possibilities. Ferenczi learned from clinical experience what developmentalists are now learning and testing in the lab. Psychoanalysts, as relationalists who have listened to Ferenczi and Kohut both, and even to Hans Loewald (2000), can watch the mother-infant interaction films and make the connections.

3 In his Kohut biography (Strozier, 2001), Charles Strozier writes: "The recent rediscovery of Ferenczi and understanding of his great significance in the early history of psychoanalysis are therefore results of the work of Kohut. Until the paradigm shifted, Ferenczi inevitably was left on the margins" (p. 417, n7). Reading the text (p. 142) to which this footnote refers, Strozier seems to mean that until Kohut had written his theory, no one could see Ferenczi's value. Given the European and interpersonalist contributions to "rediscovering" Ferenczi, I am exceedingly dubious about Strozier's claim.

Developmentalist and motivational systems theorist Joseph Lichtenberg (Lichtenberg et al., 1992; 2002; 2010) calls Ferenczi his psychoanalytic grandfather (Lichtenberg, 1997). Evident in Lichtenberg's creative, inquiring, and inclusive spirit, this influence makes Lichtenberg a continuing bridge-builder in relational psychoanalysis and self psychology, as well as a nurturer of the talents of others.

Intersubjective systems theorists, no longer calling ourselves self psychologists but rather psychoanalytic phenomenologists, have a complex relation with Ferenczi. I find only one mention by Bernard Brandchaft (1986), contrasting Kohut's analysis of impasses with Ferenczi's interest in enactments, even though Brandchaft's later "pathological accommodation" analysis could well be restated as a form of "confusion of the tongues", including detailed accounts of Ferenczi's version of identification with the aggressor. I do not know whether Brandchaft saw these connections. As for George Atwood (Atwood & Stolorow, 2016; Atwood, 2011), Ferenczi has long been his hero, inspiring his lifelong work with psychotics and his clinical work generally. Both he and Robert Stolorow find Ferenczi's return to the centrality of trauma a touchstone for their own clinical and theoretical thinking. My own work (Orange, 2010, 2011, 2014, 2015) has treasured Ferenczi for his recognition of the patient's trauma and suffering, for his courageous trust in the patient's attempts to get through to the analyst, for his fallibilism and clinical humility, so unusual in his analytic world, or even in our own. Compassion and care have made a return, and have an ancestral voice. Ferenczi has been the central inspiration for my "hermeneutics of trust" (2011).

In this moment, when the psychoanalytic world remains traumatically fractured by its history of exclusion, dating back to Freud and including Ferenczi's painful experience with him, perpetuated in "that's not psychoanalysis", and "you are not relational enough", our common ancestor Ferenczi might bring many of us, his grandchildren of many relational voices, together in his spirit of humble service to the other.

References

Atwood, G., & Stolorow, R. (2016). Walking the tightrope of emotional dwelling. *Psychoanalytic Dialogues*, *26*: 103–108.

Atwood, G. E. (2011). *The Abyss of Madness*. New York: Routledge.

Bacal, H. A. (1998). *Optimal Responsiveness: How Therapists Heal their Patients*. Northvale, NJ: Jason Aronson.

Bacal, H. (2006). Specificity theory: Conceptualizing a personal and professional quest for therapeutic possibility. *International Journal of Psychoanalytic Self Psychology*, *1*: 133–155.

Bacal, H. A., & Newman, K. M. (1990). *Theories of Object Relations: Bridges to Self Psychology*. New York: Columbia University Press.

Bass, A. (2001). It takes one to know one; or, Whose unconscious is it anyway? *Psychoanalytic Dialogues*, *11*: 683–702.

Beebe, B., & Lachmann, F. M. (2001). *Infant Research and Adult Treatment: A Dyadic Systems Approach*. Hillsdale, NJ: Analytic Press.

Brandchaft, B. (1986). British object relations theory and self psychology. *Progress in Self Psychology*, *2*: 245–272.

Brothers, D. (1995). *Falling Backwards: An Exploration of Trust and Self-experience*. New York: Norton.

Ferenczi, S. (1909). On the interpretation of tunes that come into one's head. In: *Final Contributions to the Problems and Methods of Psycho-Analysis* (pp. 175–176). New York: Brunner/Mazel.

Ferenczi, S. (1921). The further development of an active technique in psycho-analysis. In: *Further Contributions to the Theory and Technique of Psycho-Analysis* (pp. 198–217). London: Hogarth.
Frankel, J. (2002). Exploring Ferenczi's concept of identification with the aggressor. *Psychoanalytic Dialogues, 12*: 101–139.
Harris, A., & Aron, L. (1997). Ferenczi's semiotic theory: Previews of postmodernism. *Psychoanalytic Inquiry, 17*: 522–534.
Hazan, Y. (1999). From Ferenczi to Kohut: From confusion of tongues to self-object. *American Journal of Psychoanalysis, 59*: 333–343.
Kohut, H. (1959). Introspection, empathy, and psychoanalysis. *Journal of the American Psychoanalytic Association, 7*: 459–483.
Kohut, H. (1966). Forms and transformations of narcissism. *Journal of the American Psychoanalytic Association, 14*: 243–272.
Kohut, H. (1971). *The Analysis of the Self: A Systematic Approach to the Psychoanalytic Treatment of Narcissistic Personality Disorders*. New York: International Universities Press.
Kohut, H. (1975). The future of psychoanalysis. *Annual of Psychoanalysis, 3*: 325–340.
Kohut, H. (1977). *The Restoration of the Self*. New York: International Universities Press.
Kohut, H., & Cocks, G. (1994). *The Curve of Life: Correspondence of Heinz Kohut, 1923–1981*. Chicago: University of Chicago Press.
Kohut, H., & Ornstein, P. H. (1978). *The Search for the Self: Selected Writings of Heinz Kohut, 1950–1978*. New York: International Universities Press.
Kuriloff, E. A. (2014). *Contemporary Psychoanalysis and the Legacy of the Third Reich: History, Memory, Tradition*. New York: Routledge.
Lee, R. R., Rountree, A., & McMahon, S. (2008). *Five Kohutian Postulates: Psychotherapy Theory from an Empathic Perspective*. Lanham, MD: Jason Aronson.
Lichtenberg, J. D. (1997). On progenitors and why we choose them. *Psychoanalytic Inquiry, 17*: 498–504.
Lichtenberg, J. D., Lachmann, F. M., & Fosshage, J. L. (1992). *Self and Motivational Systems: Toward a Theory of Psychoanalytic Technique*. Hillsdale, NJ: Analytic Press.
Lichtenberg, J. D., Lachmann, F. M., & Fosshage, J. L. (2002). *A Spirit of Inquiry: Communication in Psychoanalysis*. Hillsdale, NJ: Analytic Press.
Lichtenberg, J. D., Lachmann, F. M., & Fosshage, J. L. (2010). *Psychoanalysis and Motivational Systems: A New Look*. New York: Routledge.
Loewald, H. W. (2000). *The Essential Loewald: Collected Papers and Monographs*. Hagerstown, MD: University Publishing Group.
Orange, D. (2010). Revisiting mutual recognition: responding to Ringstrom, Benjamin, and Slavin. *International Journal of Psychoanalytic Self Psychology, 5*: 293–306.
Orange, D. M. (2011). *The Suffering Stranger: Hermeneutics for Everyday Clinical Practice*. New York: Routledge.
Orange, D. (2014). *A Psychotherapy for the People: Toward a Progressive Psychoanalysis*, by Lewis Aron and Karen Starr: A book review essay. *International Journal of Psychoanalytic Self Psychology, 9*: 54–66.
Orange, D. (2015). A review of traumatic narcissism: Relational systems of subjugation. *International Journal of Psychoanalytic Self Psychology, 10*: 296–300.
Ornstein, A., & Ornstein, P. H. (2005). Conflict in contemporary clinical work: A self psychological perspective. *Psychoanalytic Quarterly, 74*: 219–251.
Sander, L. W., Amadei, G., & Bianchi, I. (2008). *Living Systems, Evolving Consciousness, and the Emerging Person: A Selection of Papers from the Life Work of Louis Sander*. New York: Analytic Press.
Stern, D. N. (1985). *The Interpersonal World of the Infant: A View from Psychoanalysis and Developmental Psychology*. New York: Basic Books.

Stern, D. N. (2004). *The Present Moment in Psychotherapy and Everyday Life*. New York: W. W. Norton.

Strozier, C. B. (2001). *Heinz Kohut: The Making of a Psychoanalyst*. New York: Farrar, Straus & Giroux.

Teicholz, J. G. (1999). *Kohut, Loewald, and the Postmoderns: A Comparative Study of Self and Relationship*. Hillsdale, NJ: Analytic Press.

Wolf, E. S. (1988). *Treating the Self: Elements of Clinical Self Psychology*. New York: Guilford Press.

Chapter 33

Ferenczi's contributions to relational psychoanalysis: The pursuit of mutuality

Madeleine Miller-Bottome and Jeremy D. Safran

> "Should it even occur, and it does occasionally to me, that experiencing another's and my own suffering brings a tear to my eye (and one should not conceal this emotion from the patient), then the tears of doctor and of patient mingle in a sublimated communion, which perhaps finds its analogy only in the mother-child relationship. And this is the healing agent, which like a kind of glue, binds together permanently the intellectually assembled fragments, surrounding even the personality thus repaired with a new aura of vitality and optimism."
>
> (Ferenczi, *Diary*, p. 65)

The publication of Ferenczi's *Diary* in English, in 1988, coincided in time with two seminal events in the development of the relational tradition. The first was the publication of Stephen Mitchell's first solo-authored book, *Relational Concepts in Psychoanalysis* (1988). The second was the establishment of the relational track within the New York University postdoctoral programme in psychotherapy and psychoanalysis. Both Lewis Aron and Adrienne Harris recall eagerly reading and discussing the *Diary* along with Stephen Mitchell during this period. They were struck by the multitude of ways in which Ferenczi's writing and descriptions of his clinical work had anticipated what were already becoming key themes in relational psychoanalysis: his emphasis on mutuality, his openness to looking at his own contributions rather than blaming the patient's resistance, including his open exploration of countertransference with his patients, his willingness to experiment and take risks, his call for naturalness and spontaneity, and many more. It was in this context that Aron and Harris, with Mitchell's enthusiastic encouragement, organised the 1991 Ferenczi Conference in New York (Aron, personal communication, September 2016). This conference was the first major international conference on Ferenczi, and also ultimately led to the publication of Aron and Harris' collection: *The Legacy of Sándor Ferenczi* (1993).

Since the publication of the *Diary* in English and the renewed interest in his legacy, there has been a growing appreciation of Ferenczi's influence on the development of major theoretical and technical developments in a broad range of psychoanalytic traditions (e.g., Haynal, 1989; Szekacs-Weisz & Keve, 2012). What is unique about Ferenczi's contributions to the development of relational psychoanalysis in particular was not only his influence on the critical role that mutuality came to play in the tradition, but that key thinkers such as Aron and Harris (1993), Aron (1996) and Bass (2015, and Chapter Twenty-three) took up the exploration of Ferenczi's legacy and were eager to reclaim him as an ancestor. In this chapter, we review a number of Ferenczi's clinical innovations and theoretical ideas that continue to resonate in the relational psychoanalytic tradition today. At the root of Ferenczi's ultimate vision for psychoanalysis was the conviction that psychoanalysis is a mutual endeavour involving equal participation and openness from patient and analyst (Aron, 1996). Although this principle was applied to varying degrees over the course of the entire body of work (with his experimentations in mutual analysis perhaps on the extreme end of the continuum), his interest in mutuality is one that unites all of his ideas and connects them to the present-day relational psychoanalytic framework. In the pages that follow, we explore the evolution of Ferenczi's thinking and its contributions to relational psychoanalysis with a focus on his commitment to mutuality as a unifying thread.

Experience and reliving

Ferenczi believed that at the heart of the analytic cure was a healing relationship with the analyst, and that the analyst's expression of empathy was in itself a critical component of successful treatment (Elast). Ferenczi was an early proponent of working with countertransference not as an interference to be analysed away, but as an experience to be scrutinised as communicating something vital about the patient and the interaction with the analyst (see Hirsch, Chapter Twenty-four). Introducing a line of thinking that has remained central to a relational psychoanalytic framework, Ferenczi focused on countertransference experiences as not just reactions to the patient (Wolstein, 1988), but as infused with the analyst's internal conflicts and dynamics, as is apparent in reading the *Diary*. Ferenczi was also concerned about the potential consequences on the patient of what he considered to be the pretense of an un-emotive, all-knowing analyst. This critique became an important element in his work on trauma (Ferenczi, 1933). Ferenczi felt strongly that the whole personality and subjectivity of the analyst influenced the therapeutic process as much as the patient's did, and that the contributions of the analyst should be acknowledged and explored (ibid.).

The focus of relational psychoanalysis on the importance of here-and-now experience can be traced back to Ferenczi and his collaboration with fellow Freud protégé, Otto Rank. Ferenczi and Rank (1924) re-examined the assumption that the analytic cure was achieved through interpretation and insight alone, considering instead the therapeutic action in exploring emotion and present experience. Both argued that experience, and specifically the *re*-experiencing of traumatic events from the patient's early relationships in the context of the analytic situation provides an essential opportunity for undergoing a new experience in the analytic relationship that functions as an active mechanism of change in its own right (Ferenczi & Rank, 1924; Ragen & Aron, 1993). Ferenczi and Rank's work was a clear precursor of later developments that have become central to the relational orientation: the concept and value of enactment (Jacobs, 1986), and more broadly the therapeutic value of non-interpretive interventions and the curative potential of implicit experience in the analytic relationship (Rachman, 2010; Stern et al., 1998).

Ferenczi's view of the analyst-patient relationship at the centre of the psychoanalytic cure extended to a reconsideration of transference and countertransference phenomena in radically relational terms. Ferenczi (Elast) suggested that resistance can be understood as a legitimate form of communication of the patient's needs in the interaction and sometimes even as a self-protective response provoked by a lack of empathy from the analyst (Aron, 1996, p. 186). Transference, when viewed in the same light, is not always a distorted projection emerging from the patient's psyche, but can be evoked by the analyst's particular communications and manner (Diary, p. 95). This line of thinking expanded the frame of analytic work to include the contributions of the analyst and sharpened the focus on patients' communications as reactions to the analyst as well as revelations of their own intrapsychic material. In this way, the co-creation (Hoffman, 1992) of transference-countertransference configurations, a concept central in relational thinking, was one that Ferenczi began to formulate early on.

Trauma

Ferenczi's focus on early traumatic experiences and their re-enactment within the therapeutic relationship culminated in his theory of trauma. In a significant departure from Freud, Ferenczi took seriously the validity of patients' accounts of sexual trauma and incest in families, considering them not as a product of patients' fantasies but as real, lived events with deleterious and lasting consequences for patients. Ferenczi developed a view that the external (interpersonal) realm of experience was just as important as the internal (intrapsychic), and he became an early proponent of a model of development in which the individual is fundamentally motivated towards achieving and maintaining intimate bonds with others. In his famed paper "Confusion of tongues", Ferenczi put forward recommendations for how to understand the re-emergence of traumatic experiences in the therapeutic interaction and made specific recommendations about how to work through this material effectively.

Three clinical principles emerged from his work in trauma that became important strains of thought in the consolidation of a relational psychoanalytic framework. First, the analyst inevitably participates actively, if unwittingly, in the recapitulation of the patient's traumatic experiences. Because of this, Ferenczi viewed the abstinent, neutral stance, or "restrained coolness" of the analyst as "professional hypocrisy" (Ferenczi, 1933, p. 226)—a disavowal of the analyst's feelings and their impact on the patient. Ferenczi came to feel strongly that such an attitude and its attendant withholding of the analyst's personal reactions and feelings inflicted on to the patient the same repression, denial, and inaccessibility by the parent at the time of the original trauma, and compounded the damaging effects of the trauma. Second, to work through this in a therapeutic fashion, Ferenczi advised analysts to communicate responsibility for their contributions to the traumatic re-enactment. By admitting fault (Ferenczi, 1933, p. 225) and discussing the analyst's contributions openly, the analyst takes the blame off the shoulders of the patient (blame which Ferenczi thought the child assumes the brunt of in the aftermath of the trauma). According to Ferenczi, the potential for repair lay in the restoration of trust that accrues in the act of the analyst communicating openly her missteps and contributions to a painful re-enactment in the relationship. Third, the analyst's emotional availability and communication of "sincere sympathy" (Ferenczi, 1933, p. 226) is key to responding to patients' disclosures of their traumas. This was in keeping with his explorations of analytic "tact" (the communication of a warm, trusting, and empathic attitude towards the patient) as an essential ingredient in responding to patients who are struggling to free associate (Ferenczi, 1920; Rachman, 2010). Conveying empathy via genuine affective responses was viewed by Ferenczi as both a precondition for the exploration of traumatic experiences and as offering a therapeutic experience in and of itself. Ferenczi felt that responding to patients' disclosures in an emotionally open fashion was healing for the patient in that it validated and made "real" the traumatic experience, the existence or importance of which was denied by the perpetrating family member originally (Diary, p. 24; see also Aron, 1996, p. 167). To Ferenczi, the ideal of the analyst as an objective, un-emotive "blank screen" was unattainable, or worse, a traumatic deception with significant consequences for the relationship.

Ferenczi's work on trauma helped develop a perspective on the nature of clinical psychoanalysis as an interpersonal and experientially focused enterprise that has all but been taken for granted in contemporary relational thought. In his work on trauma, Ferenczi was already moving away from a unilateral view of the analytic relationship to one in which the interaction and the material emerging from it reflects the inner workings of the analyst *as well as* the patient. Ferenczi was among the first to suggest that the patient may have unique insight into therapist's countertransference problems and that for the benefit of the treatment, patients should be encouraged to point out the ways in which the analyst is affecting the process (Diary; Ragen & Aron, 1993, p. 219). Ferenczi's idea that patient and therapist could collaborate in discovering the nature and roots of the interaction unfolding between them laid the groundwork for the practice of more mutual forms of analysis and has survived today as one of the guiding principles in contemporary relational work.

The thread that connects us

While Ferenczi's experiments with mutual analysis may have been a controversial mark on his legacy (see Bass, Chapter Twenty-three for a more in-depth review of this period in Ferenczi's work), his interest in the mutuality of psychoanalysis extended beyond the proposal of mutual analysis (Aron, 1996). Ferenczi was also interested in the shared experience of emotion between patient and analyst and the involvement of the analyst's subjectivity in exploring patients' internal states. Ferenczi wrote about the potency of feeling and reflecting back the suffering of the patient as a form of "sublimated communion" analogous to the mother-child relationship (Diary, p. 65). Ferenczi described a joint experiencing of feeling between patient and analyst that is achieved by the analyst "mirroring" the patient's experience with her own emotional expression. Ferenczi suggests that the "mingling" (Diary, p. 65) of subjective states between patient and analyst is the same modality through which attunement is communicated between mother and infant. Just as the mother attunes to her infant's internal states with her own affective responses, Ferenczi implied that the patient attains recognition of his experience through the communication of the analyst's own subjective state.

Ferenczi articulated an intersubjective view of the analytic relationship—what, over sixty years later, came to be referred to as a "shared dyadic state" or "moment of meeting" (Stern et al., 1998) between patient and analyst. This perspective, which has been embraced by relational psychoanalysis, sees a direct line from the nonverbal language of affective attunement shared between mother and infant to the patient-analyst dialogue (Stern et al., 1998). Ferenczi anticipated this development in his view of the analyst's subjectivity as the "thread that connects [the patient] to us" (Ferenczi, 1933, p. 226). He suggested in these lines and indeed throughout his work that the healing work of analysis is mutual and made possible by moments of shared experience.

Concluding thoughts

In the last thirty-five years, there has been a growing recognition of Ferenczi's role as arguably our most significant relational ancestor (Harris & Kuchuck, 2015). Taking stock of his many clinical ideas and contributions, it is easy to see why. Ferenczi maintained throughout his lifetime a belief in the healing power of the analyst's emotional availability and honesty. His experimentation with mutual analysis was a radical reconceptualisation of the assumed premises of the analytic situation and an implementation of treatment along more egalitarian lines. His suggestion that therapeutic impasses and troublesome resistance from the patient can be a response to the analyst's own deficiencies and conflicts paved the way for the relational orientation long before such a movement in psychoanalysis could even be imagined. Ferenczi's thinking about the analytic relationship evolved over time from spotlighting the analyst's contributions to the process to seeing the healing process of analysis as reciprocal and affecting patient and analyst in equal measure. Ferenczi's interest in mutuality both inspired and provided a meaningful origin narrative for the first generation of relational psychoanalysts, and, as his legacy continues to be mined, is likely to contribute towards future refinements in theory and practice.

References

Aron, L., & Harris, A. (Eds.) (1993). *The Legacy of Sándor Ferenczi*. Hillsdale, NJ: Analytic Press.

Aron, L. (1996). *A Meeting of Minds: Mutuality in Psychoanalysis*. Hillsdale, NJ: Analytic Press.

Bass, A. (2015). The dialogue of unconsciouses, mutual analysis and the uses of the self in contemporary relational psychoanalysis. *Psychoanalytic Dialogues, 25*: 2–17.

Ferenczi, S. (1920). The further development of the active therapy in psycho-analysis. In: *Further Contributions to the Theory and Techniques of Psycho-Analysis* (pp. 198–217). New York: Brunner/Mazel, 1980.

Ferenczi, S., & Rank, O. (1924). *The Development of Psycho-Analysis*. Madison, CT: International Universities Press.

Ferenczi, S. (1933). Confusion of tongues between the adults and the child—(The language of tenderness and of passion). *International Journal of Psychoanalysis, 30*: 225–230, 1949.

Haynal, A. (1989). *Controversies in Psychoanalytic Method: From Freud and Ferenczi to Michael Balint*. New York: New York University Press.

Harris, A., & Kuchuck, S. (Eds.) (2015). *The Legacy of Sandor Ferenczi*. New York: Routledge.

Hoffman, I. Z. (1992). Some practical implications of a social-constructivist view of the psychoanalytic situation. *Psychoanalytic Dialogues, 2*: 287–304.

Jacobs, T. (1986). On countertransference enactments. *Journal of the American Psycho-analytic Association, 34*: 289–307.

Mitchell, S. (1988). *Relational Concepts in Psychoanalysis: An Integration*. Cambridge, MA: Harvard University Press.

Rachman, A. (2010). The origins of a relational perspective in the ideas of Sándor Ferenczi and the Budapest School of Psycho-analysis. *Psychoanalytic Perspectives, 7*: 43–60.

Ragen, T., & Aron, L. (1993). Abandoned workings: Ferenczi's mutual analysis. In: L. Aron & A. Harris (Eds.), *The Legacy of Sándor Ferenczi* (pp. 217–226). Hillsdale, NJ: The Analytic Press.

Szekacs-Weisz, J., & Keve, T. (Eds.) (2012). *Ferenczi for Our Time*. London: Karnac.

Stern, D. N., Sander, L. W., Nahum, J. P., Harrison, A. M., Lyons-Ruth, K., Morgan, A. C., Bruschweiler-Stern, N., & Tronick, E. Z. (1998). Non-interpretive mechanisms in psychoanalytic therapy: the "something more" than interpretation. *International Journal of Psychoanalysis, 79*: 903–921.

Wolstein, B. (1988). *Essential Papers on Countertransference*. New York: New York University Press.

Chapter 34

The influence of Ferenczi's thinking on child psychoanalysis

Patrizia Arfelli and Massimo Vigna-Taglianti

In this chapter, we will examine the contribution that Sándor Ferenczi made to the evolution of child psychoanalysis, attempting to go well beyond the rather simplistic remark that he was Melanie Klein's analyst and that—as is well known—he explicitly encouraged her to explore the boundaries of her work with young disturbed patients.

Ferenczi never practised child analysis himself, and discussed the topic in only one article, with reference to adult psychoanalysis (1931); yet, in a paper titled "A Little Chanticleer" (1913), he described his diagnostic investigation, not therapy, of a five-year-old troubled little boy. In this early text, Ferenczi ascribed the child's cruel fantasies about roosters to the oedipal component (at that time Melanie Klein had not yet theorised the presence of pre-oedipal aggressive fantasies in children, and Ferenczi himself was still far from seeing symptoms like the boy's cruelty and aggressiveness as a result of identification with aggressor, in the sense in which Anna Freud (1936) discussed it: coping with the helplessness of trauma by becoming an aggressor), and was not able to understand that the child could not associate but needed to play. As we can see through his words, he missed the chance to discover that playing represents the main path of access to children's unconscious: "I got him to tell me the story about the cock. But he was already bored and wanted to get back to his toys. Direct psycho-analytic investigation was therefore impossible ... " (p. 244).

Nevertheless, his body of work was so lucid and exhaustive and his theoretical dialogue with Freud enjoyed so many subsequent expansions and revisions that it sparked specific repercussions on the various roots of the two main doctrinaire currents that initially characterised the birth of child psychoanalysis: on the one hand, the work of Anna Freud and, on the other, the theories of Melanie Klein.

We believe these repercussions mainly fall into two camps. The first, of a strictly theoretical-technical nature, regards how the setting of the child analysis is established, its specific object of observation, and the analyst's mental disposition at work with children. The second, of a broader metapsychological sweep, has to do with a theory about the genesis of children's mental pain and their psychopathology: for the first time since Freud revised his seduction theory, this theoretical point of view assigns a fundamental role to the primary environment and to the affective characteristics of the interpersonal relationship, both aspects that will be developed in an extraordinarily creative way, the first one mostly by Winnicott (1965, 1967) and the latter by both Winnicott and Bion (1962).

The Ferenczian matrix of child psychoanalysis: unconscious ways of communication and the analyst's mental attitude

In this section, we will explore the development of Ferenczi's theories in greater depth, in order to describe how his thinking encouraged the birth of child psychoanalysis and at the same time set out a line of such fertile theoretical-technical research that, even today, it points child analysts in a similar exploratory direction.

In short, following a historical perspective, we believe that the theoretical foundations at the heart of the child analyst's listening in the session (that is, her mental disposition) can already be found in Ferenczi's paper "On transitory symptom-construction during the analysis" (1912). Ferenczi here precedes others and is the first to place greater attention on the patient's *ways* of communication rather than on its *content*. Indeed, he maintains that the patient's ways of communicating are frequently pre- and para-verbal long before they are verbal: something that is particularly noticeable in child analysis. Ferenczi claims that these ways always express an acting in the transference of repressed impulses and thoughts. Melanie Klein would develop this concept to the extent of explicitly contesting Anna Freud's assumption that the transference could be strictly conceived only in terms of direct and immediate references to the analyst, inherent in the patient's material. In opposition to this, Klein (1932), taking her cue from these Ferenczian ideas, would theorise that children act out in the transference repetition profound unconscious fantasies and archaic modes of relating to their own original objects, personifying, in the play that unfolds in the session, specific aspects of their internal objects.

This shows that one of Ferenczi's main merits lies in having stimulated the Kleinian school to explore the functioning of children's primitive phantasies and how they are communicated—continuously and through different means of expression—in analysis, leading, as a result, to an understanding of the profound roots of the transference as the "total situation" (1985), as Betty Joseph theorised.

In addition, Ferenczi's insight concerning the importance of the therapist's capability to carry out a continuous emotional recognition of the analytic dialogue has been so profoundly influential that even today we can find traces of it in the majority of the developments in current psychoanalytic thinking.

The importance Ferenczi assigned to the nonverbal thus provides an opening towards the bodily communication typical of child analysis. Whoever works with children is well aware of the significance in the session of their motor activity and the bodily engagement they ask of the analyst, as well as the communicative value of their secretory and excretory activities. In fact, during analysis, tears, saliva, mucous, faeces, urine, and farts can all have the meaning of archaic, concrete, and regressive communications, or of acted-out attempts to express sometimes aggressiveness, sometimes a search for contact.

Another fundamental intuition appeared in the 1912 "On transitory symptom-construction during the analysis", that Freud would take up in his works on technique and that would have huge repercussions on today's child psychoanalysis: an authentic transformation in the patient's psychic functioning is possible only if the analytic couple affectively relive, in the transference-countertransference dynamics, psychic events that have not been portrayable up to that moment. In short, these are events whose pain can be "felt" but not "suffered" (Bion,

1970), because one never had the emotional experience of one's own pain. With regard to this, ahead of his time, Ferenczi affirms that the individual cannot reach any real conviction through rational cognition alone: in order to arrive at that certainty, it is necessary to have affectively lived the events, to have experienced them in one's own body.

This assertion is more thoroughly theorised in *The Development of Psycho-Analysis* (1924), a text he co-authored with Rank that proposes to fill the gap created between theory and practice when Freud gave up working on technique. The text refers to "Remembering, repeating and working-through" (Freud, 1914), but goes beyond it, underlining the need to attribute the main role to repeating instead of remembering, and to the present rather than the past. The path chosen by the patient's unconscious to reproduce and repeat what he is unable to remember (even whole dissociated passages of emotional life) necessarily passes through forms of primary nonverbal and gestural communication—in other words, through enactments. The reverberations in those who would become the theoretical-technical pillars of child psychoanalysis are all too clear: indeed, child analysis is based mainly on the action and on the enactment of an unconscious language that, even if it is not verbal, is nevertheless highly communicative.

On this point, while Melanie Klein considers symbolic playing to be the main path that leads to the child's primitive phantasies and to his inner world, Ferenczi's way of thinking places more emphasis on the compulsion to repeat inherent in the play itself as an attempt not only to turn into active what has been passively suffered (as Anna Freud (1936) subsequently theorised, with an ideal reference to the game with the reel (Freud, 1920)), but also to master an experience that has not been worked through, probing in the transference—via enactment—how the analyst's mind can, in its turn, tolerate, transform, and make it thinkable.

In this way Ferenczi laid the foundations and anticipated Winnicott's (1953) theorising on the intrinsic value of playing as a "creative potential space" in which internal and external realities can meet and come to some sort of compromise: a space for playing in which regressive aspects can emerge that are once more re-enacted before being experienced and worked through.

However, the most relevant legacy for child analysis left to us by Ferenczi's 1924 text concerns, in our opinion, the concept of analysis as an essentially emotional process rather than a cognitive one. Indeed, in Ferenczi's view, it was not enough simply to reactivate the trauma; it was necessary to relive it in the here and now, and emotionally work it through within the analytic couple, in order to make it representable. Getting to the deepest roots of child suffering consequently entails a transformative rather than a pedagogic analysis, which envisages the analyst's interpersonal commitment and affective participation. This last aspect has enjoyed particular theoretical and clinical confirmation in child analysis.

The analyst's interpersonal commitment and affective participation inevitably bring to mind the concept of psychoanalytic empathy, developed by Kohut (1959) and more recently by Bolognini (2002), although already well focalised in Ferenczi's 1928 paper "The elasticity of psychoanalytic technique". In this work, Ferenczi postulates that analytic technique implies something of an individual nature that can be ascribed to the subjective "personal equation", "a scarcely definable, individual factor" (Elast, p. 88) of the analyst, which must be fine-tuned by training analysis and that effectively translates into her capacity for empathy, which Ferenczi defines as psychological tact. In the relationship with the patient, tact is expressed as specific attention towards the object, with the analyst's conduct marked by authenticity and therefore renouncing any intellectualising and interpretative fanaticism. With regard to the technique of child analysis, this latter aspect in particular was undoubtedly a source of Anna Freud's (1970) recommendations concerning the potential iatrogenic damages resulting from a stubborn insistence on an immediate and profound interpretation of the unconscious material.

For Ferenczi, tact and empathy bring to mind an analyst who does not necessarily have such a keen and penetrating stance, but, on the contrary, who is more humble and above all *elastic*: that is to say, capable of communicating her interpretations as provisional proposals, recognising her own errors, and performing with plasticity and humility the role of an "Aunt Sally" (Elast, p. 93). The latter point allows the patient to have the analyst experience the patient's unpleasant feelings—via projective identification and role-reversal—in other words, those aspects of the self that he cannot yet represent, own, and think about.

In a later work, "Child analysis in the analysis of adults", Ferenczi further clarified the characteristics of the psychic environment that the analyst must be able to provide: patience, comprehension, and benevolence, but also an honest admission of the unpleasant countertransference feelings evoked in her by the patient's attacks in order to avoid damages deriving from falsity and hypocrisy as the analyst's professional illness. A mental attitude of this type is an indispensable characteristic in the clinical practice of child analysts, who we know have to be particularly responsive, capable of playing along and ready to bring into play that "willing suspension of disbelief" (Coleridge, quoted in Trilling, 1955) that will allow them to understand the unconscious communications of their little patients. Kindred to Bion's (1970) adaptation of Keats's concept of "negative capability", this particular aptitude must, however, complement the analyst's inevitably active—at times, stormy—participation in the child's play, making the psychic setting of the child therapist highly specific.

Transitional space, playing and enactment: the Ferenczian roots

Ferenczi's "Child analysis in the analysis of adults" refers, to some extent, precisely to the sphere of playing. In our opinion, it is not only a text about technique and a piece of research on the genesis of trauma and splitting, but it also includes: 1) the idea of analysis as a stage set on which to play out once again the individual drama (an idea taken up in Kahn, 1974); 2) a harbinger of the concept of transitional space; and 3), in embryonic form, a view of analysis as a sort of highly specialised playing (both points subsequently theorised in Winnicott, 1953).

Here, Ferenczi was the first to perceive that merely reactivating the infantile condition and reproducing the original trauma, acted out on the analytic stage, is not enough. He believed that a contemporary phase of re-elaboration is necessary to allow the patient to reach that recollection that today we would call the capacity to think and dream. Opening up the path for theoretical-technical developments in child and relational analysis, Ferenczi intuits the need to pass inevitably through what today we call the enactment, a fundamental precursor of a subsequent symbolic elaboration, both for the analyst and for the patient. Ferenczi therefore acknowledges that the adult patient has the right to behave as a "naughty (i.e. uncontrolled)" child, allowing the most archaic and dissociated components to slip on to the analytic stage, through Freud's *agieren* (ambiguously translated by Strachey as "to act") (1905), in order to transform deadly repetitiveness into new opportunities for psychic integration and symbolic narration (Sapisochin, 2015; Vigna-Taglianti, 2015).

Lastly, we would like to point out how this text by Ferenczi is imbued with an innovative idea of analysis (he explicitly talks of "play analysis") that anticipated Winnicott's theories on transitional space and on analysis as a form of highly specialised play that comes to life between two people, the patient and the analyst. This found resonance in Winnicott (1971), in his illustration of how he intends the playroom to be: certainly not an inert space, but an empathic environment capable of giving back to the patient his feelings, welcomed and understood in such a way that they can be further worked through mentally by the patient himself with the help of the analyst. This setting is seen, therefore, as a structure capable of actively adapting to suit the needs of the little patient, becoming in this sense a close relative of maternal holding in its significance of a sustaining containing environment.

Ferenczi's anticipation of the concepts of holding and containment (for example, his famous metaphor of the analyst as a "tender mother") and the birth of a line of thought that ascribes greater significance to the relationship than to the interpretation, provided generations of child analysts with valuable tools for both participating and interpreting: suffice it to think of the fundamental role of empathy in the analysis of children.

Ferenczi and child psychic suffering

Ferenczi's hypothesis that traumatic failures in the mother-child relationship generate profound psychic pain, both in the actual moment of the child's life and in the child frozen in the mental crypt of the suffering adult, is an undercurrent that runs through all the works we have already considered, and finds its culmination in "Confusion of tongues", which is focused on exogenous traumatic factors and on the phenomenon of identification with the aggressor (Frankel, Chapter Nineteen).

This conceptual guiding thread was already evident in Ferenczi's 1929 work, "The unwelcome child and his death instinct", in the whole *Diary*, and in "Child analysis in the analysis of adults". For example, in the last of these, Ferenczi formulates the hypothesis that the child's positive affective movements derive essentially from the relationship of tenderness with the mother and from this he deduces that behaviour lacking in tact and tenderness, suffered by the child at the hands of people within his environment, almost always generates "naughtiness, fits of passion and uncontrolled perversion" in him (Ferenczi, 1931, p. 473).

Ferenczi specifically singled out in "The unwelcome child" the parents' lack of tact and enthusiasm for the baby as factors that determine a deficit of such magnitude in the child's vital capacity as to be responsible for a psychic suffering so pervasive that it may lead to states ranging from suicidal tendencies to the total inability to give any meaning to life.

This Ferenczian concept innovatively considers the trauma above all as a *minus*, in other words, as the consequence of the fact that something that should have happened did not. This accounts for a new way of understanding the death instinct: as a "sliding" towards a state of psychic non-existence stemming from an early deficit of adequate maternal mirroring. The concepts of loss of vitality and psychic agony will be taken up again decades later by Winnicott (1974), who will reformulate them when describing the primitive breakdown and the absence of "realness".

Equally important is the fact that Ferenczi (most clearly in "Confusion of tongues") creates a fundamental connection linking the traumatic event, the denial of the child's subjective perception (the true traumatising agent), and his consequent narcissistic fragility. Ferenczi's contribution regarding the defensive mechanisms of self-narcissistic splitting (splitting into one brutally destroyed part sensitive to pain, and another that is omniscient but insensitive) and identification with the aggressor (introjection of the aggressor with resulting alienation of aspects of one's subjectivity) anticipates and opens the way for Kohut's exploration of the narcissistic deficit, understood as an arrest in the development of one part of the personality (Kohut, 1971).

To conclude this chapter, we would like to draw attention to the fact that in our clinical practice as child analysts, every day, in our small playroom, we come across wise-babies and wild-babies, secret crypts inhabited by deformed and undeveloped embryonic twins, mental agonies and psychic deaths—the gamut of consequences of childhood trauma that Ferenczi so compellingly described. We would not be able to recognise these clinical facts or these characters and we would not be able to attempt to transform their psychic pain were it not for the theoretical-technical tools conceived by Ferenczi and refined with much effort and commitment by subsequent generations of analysts.

References

Bion, W. R. (1962). The psycho-analytic study of thinking. *International Journal of Psychoanalysis, 43*: 306–310.

Bion, W. R. (1970). *Attention and Interpretation*. London: Tavistock.

Bolognini, S. (2002). *L'empatia psicoanalitica*. Turin: Bollati Boringhieri. (English translation: *Psychoanalytic Empathy*. London: Free Association, 2004.)

Ferenczi, S. (1912). On transitory symptom-construction during the analysis. In: *First Contributions to Psycho-Analysis*. Boston: R. G. Badger.

Ferenczi, S. (1913). A little chanticleer. In: *First Contributions to Psycho-Analysis*. Boston: R. G. Badger.

Ferenczi, S. (1924). *The Development of Psycho-Analysis*. New York and Washington: Nervous and Mental Disease Publishing Company, 1927.

Ferenczi S. (1931). Child analysis in the analysis of adults. *International Journal of Psychoanalysis, 12*: 468–482.

Freud, A. (1936). *The Ego and the Mechanisms of Defense*. New York: International Universities Press.

Freud, A. (1970). Child analysis as a subspeciality of psychoanalysis. In: *The Writings of Anna Freud, vol. 7* (pp. 204–222). New York: International Universities Press, 1971.

Freud, S. (1905). Fragment of an analysis of a case of hysteria. *S. E., 7*: 7–122. London: Hogarth.

Freud, S. (1914). Remembering, repeating and working-through. *S. E., 12*: 145–156. London: Hogarth.

Freud, S. (1920). Beyond the Pleasure Principle. *S. E., 18*: 1–64. London: Hogarth.

Joseph, B. (1985). Transference: The total situation. *International Journal of Psychoanalysis, 66*: 447–454.

Khan, M. (1974). *The Privacy of the Self*. London: Hogarth.

Klein, M. (1932). *The Psycho-Analysis of Children*. London: Hogarth.

Kohut, H. (1959). Introspection, empathy and psychoanalysis: an examination of the relationship between mode of observation and theory. *Journal of the American Psychoanalytic Association, 7*: 459–483.

Kohut, H. (1971). *The Analysis of the Self*. New York: International Universities Press.

Sapisochin, G. (2015). Playing: listening to the enacted dimension of the analytic process. In: G. Saragnano & C. Seulin (Eds.), *Playing and Reality Revisited*. London: Karnac.

Trilling, L. (1955). *Freud and the Crisis of Our Culture*. Boston: Beacon.

Vigna-Taglianti, M. (2015). Ruptures and reconnections: play as a thread for sewing up? In: G. Saragnano & C.Seulin (Eds.), *Playing and Reality Revisited*. London: Karnac.

Winnicott, D. W. (1953). Transitional objects and transitional phenomena. In: *Playing and Reality* (pp. 1–25). London: Tavistock, 1971.

Winnicott, D. W. (1965). *The Maturational Processes and the Facilitating Environment: Studies in the Theory of Emotional Development*. London: Hogarth.

Winnicott, D. W. (1967). Mirror-role of mother and family in child development. In: *Playing and Reality* (pp. 11–118). London: Tavistock, 1971.

Winnicott, D. W. (1971). *Playing and Reality*. London: Tavistock.

Winnicott, D. W. (1974). Fear of breakdown. *International Review of Psycho-Analysis, 1*: 103–107.

Part IV

Applications and Extensions

Introduction

Part IV explores applications and extensions of Ferenczi's ideas beyond individual patients and the consulting room. We start in the political realm, first with Eszter Salgó, a scholar of both international relations and psychoanalysis. Salgó informs us that Ferenczi understood that social structures reflect human nature, and that psychoanalysts, therefore, are well positioned to point the way toward a healthier social order. And he saw personal liberation through psychoanalytic treatment as a bulwark that could prevent authoritarianism from taking hold. Indeed, Ferenczi organized the Hungarian Psychoanalytical Society along democratic lines, in contrast—and perhaps implicitly as a criticism—of authoritarianism both within the psychoanalytic world and in the Hungarian government after the First World War.

Ferenc Erős continues the political theme, introducing us to Ferenczi the social critic, and to Ferenczi's analysis of society, which foreshadowed the Frankfurt School's later critique—notably, Ferenczi's elaboration of how violence is often disavowed, hidden behind hypocritical guises, in society as well as in the family and the consulting room. Erős presents two recently discovered political manuscripts by Ferenczi, in which Ferenczi proposed a society that supports self-liberation in place of "blind adoration of dogmas and authority", and advocated a "liberal socialism"—compatible with a psychoanalytic worldview and ethical sense—that finds a middle way between "ruthless capitalism ... [and] fanciful egalitarianism"—a model that anticipated the modern welfare state.

Clara Mucci brings Ferenczi's concepts about individual trauma and its treatment to the phenomenon of massive traumas like the Shoah and the unfortunately many similar events in recent human history. Mucci takes as her starting point Ferenczi's pioneering understanding of the traumatic response as a process of internalising actual violence. She then focuses on the role of an empathic witness to this violence, which Ferenczi understood to be crucial, describing how the lack of such a witness greatly compounds trauma's damage, while the presence of one is crucial in recovery. Mucci's key conclusions: survivors, especially of massive trauma, require "the reconstruction of a social community" that provides "recognition and acceptance", and an analyst who can be a "totally benevolent and committed" witness for someone whose capacity to carry within himself an internal witness has been destroyed.

Shifting away from the sociopolitical world to other arenas where Ferenczi's thinking has made important contributions, Julianna Vamos describes how Ferenczi's ideas inform her work with new families in a Paris maternity clinic. Starting from Ferenczi's writings about the damage that results from children not being truly welcome in their families, and about the importance of families adapting to their children, she reflects upon "what it could take to be not an unwelcomed child ... but a welcomed child in a contemporary western urban family." She elaborates how, relying largely on the work of Hungarian pediatrician Emmi Pikler to actualise Ferenczi's ideal of an "enlightening environment", she provides a "child-centred, warm-hearted accompaniment for parental education" that helps new parents become more attuned to their baby, especially the baby's movements and rhythms. This helps these parents trust and support both their baby's nascent autonomy and a dependency in the baby that does not turn into helplessness.

Steven Kuchuck examines Ferenczi's impact on clinical social work and education in the US. Mainly through his collaborators, students, and patients, but also directly during his stay in New York in 1926–1927, Ferenczi had a central, though underappreciated, influence on the development of clinical social work in its formative years. Ferenczi's approaches that are fundamental to clinical social work include the use of self, the social worker's emotional involvement and participation, exploring ways to shorten the length of treatment, trauma theory and the importance of the real environment, and working with disenfranchised populations. Regarding education, Ferenczi mainly addressed children's education by parents, placing parents' insight into their own childhoods as crucial in allowing them to be sensitive to their children. In regard to schools, Ferenczi was wary of practices that could encourage excessive repression.

Josette Garon expands upon Ferenczi's ideas about gender, sexuality, and the maternal. She examines Ferenczi's personal background as it shaped his attitudes in these areas; explores his theoretical speculations about the prehistoric origins and "biology of pleasure" and human sexuality, in his singular book, *Thalassa*; and elaborates the influence of his ideas about the maternal on his understanding of transference and the importance of a tender, mothering analytic stance. Garon shows us how Ferenczi equated the female and maternal with understanding, kindness, forgiveness, conciliation, and a tolerance for suffering, and also how he understood female homosexuality as normal—a reflection of the fact that the mother is the original love-object for women as well as men.

Finally, Aleksandar Dimitrijević investigates the validity of Ferenczi's mature clinical thinking by deriving testable hypotheses from Ferenczi's final paper, "Confusion of tongues", and examining what empirical psychological research has to say about these propositions. These hypotheses address the pathogenic impact of childhood trauma, and of parents' faulty emotional regulation, capacity for empathy, and degree of self-understanding; the accuracy of Ferenczi's descriptions of the results of childhood trauma; and whether helping professionals tend to have had traumatic childhoods. After a detailed examination of empirical research in these areas, Dimitrijević concludes that "all Ferenczi's clinical insights and intuitions were completely sound and many were confirmed by studies that employed the best methodology currently available", and advises greater mutual understanding between psychoanalysts and researchers.

Chapter 35

"Eat, bird, or die!" The contribution of Sándor Ferenczi's ideas to the critique of authoritarianism

Eszter Salgó

According to Herbert Marcuse "psychoanalytic categories do not have to be 'related' to social and political conditions—they are themselves social and political categories" (1970). José Brunner (2001) and Peter Homans (1989) are among those who offer political readings of Freud's writings. While the former puts to the fore Freud's tendency to opt for authoritarian solutions, the latter considers psychoanalysis as part of the modernisation process that swept across the West. I will neither endorse nor contest these arguments. The main purpose of this chapter is to provide a political reading of Sándor Ferenczi's psychoanalytic theory and practice and explore the many ways through which Freud's grand vizier expressed his refusal of all forms of authoritarianism and his call for a free and autonomous society. My argument is that the development of Ferenczi's new methods is intimately linked to his disappointment not only with the classic Freudian technique, but also with the increasingly authoritarian nature of the various political regimes that succeeded each other in Hungary.

In the late nineteenth and early twentieth centuries, in Central Europe, writers, artists, and intellectuals were deeply involved in discussions on political and social issues. Many of them were driven by a progressive spirit, by the quest to emancipate Hungarian society from its feudal remnants, to modernise and democratise all aspects of national life. Ferenczi was convinced that to understand social structures we needed to understand human nature. The same drives, survival, and pleasure impulses, "selfish" and "libidinal tendencies" (in other words, the *panem et circenses* principle), shape both individuals' feelings and behaviour and societies' development (1914). According to him, physicians, and particularly psychiatrists, could play an active role in turning society towards being more free and autonomous. In 1910, in his letter to Freud he highlights "the sociological significance of our analyses" where one can "investigate the real conditions in the various levels of society, cleansed of all hypocrisy and conventionalism, just as they are mirrored in the individual" (Fer/Fr, 22 March 1910, pp. 153–154). For the health of a society he attributes responsibility to children's caregivers—"if there is a place where war can be defeated, without a doubt, it is the children's room" (Kosztolányi, 1918)—and to political and social actors: "we may expect real progress only from the evolution of social organisations" (1914). He rejected the authoritarian rule of Franz Joseph, pointing out the senselessness of taking away from the individual more liberties than that which public interest demands. From his standpoint, the relaxation of parental authoritarianism would not entail the destruction of the social order. If, instead of imposing dogmas in an authoritarian manner, people were allowed to exercise freely their faculty of independent judgment, a new social order could arise, which would not necessarily be based on the interests of a few powerful individuals only (Ferenczi, 1914).

At the end of August 1918, Freud was harbouring the hope of establishing the centre of the international psychoanalytic movement in Budapest; and for this reason, he paved the way for Ferenczi's nomination to the presidency of the IPA. The arrival to power of the communist Béla Kun regime (21 March 1919) brought new nominations for Ferenczi: he became a university professor and was asked to give birth to a public clinic. While these were times in Hungary when it was getting more and more complicated to stay out of politics and/or to remain neutral, Ferenczi did his best to preserve his intellectual and moral liberty. As he wrote to Freud on 13 April 1919: "Ψα. is being courted on all sides; it is costing me an effort to defend myself against the solicitations. But yesterday I was unable to avoid a direct invitation to take over a section of a state hospital" (Fer/Fr). The decision of some members of the Hungarian Psychoanalytic Society to play an active political role in the new regime had contradictory effects on the movement (Fer/Fr, May 1919, p. 357):

> My fervent wish to legitimize Ψα. and my didactic intentions at the university has [sic] been brought to fruition all too stormily through the somewhat adventurous politics of Dr. Radó. I hope I will succeed in keeping Ψα. free of all political tendencies at all times ... The Hungarian Society is working less promptly since Radó has been inundated with state business.

A month later Ferenczi laments the emergence of a "small coalition" of regime-friendly psychoanalysts led by Radó and Révész, increasingly upset with him. The source of their anger is that "[b]oth are somewhat intoxicated by the grandiose personal successes that they have to register in the new era and are dissatisfied with my—for them all too temperate—manner" (Fer/Fr, June 1919). The fall of the Béla Kun government (31 July 1919) and the inauguration of the Horthy regime signified the end of Ferenczi's academic career—he was fired from the university and from the Hungarian Association of Medical Doctors and became more and more marginalised in the international movement, getting replaced as IPA president in 1920 by Ernest Jones. In the same year, the peace treaty following the end of the First World War deprived Hungary of sixty-seven per cent of its territory, generating what became known as Hungarian society's painful "Trianon trauma". The new right-wing government transformed this collective distress into a foundation myth (promising the resurrection of St Stephen's Great Hungary) as a means to legitimise its (authoritarian) power. Ferenczi described the violence inflicted on some segments of the population by the regime as follows:

> After the unbearable "Red terror," which lay heavy on one's spirit like a nightmare, we now have the White one... the ruthless clerical-anti-Semitic spirit seems to have eked out a victory. If everything does not deceive, we Hungarian Jews are now facing a period of brutal persecution of Jews. They will, I think, have cured us in a very short time of the illusion with which we were brought up, namely, that we are "Hungarians of Jewish faith". I picture Hungarian anti-Semitism—commensurate with the national character—to be more brutal than the petty-hateful type of the Austrians... Personally, one will have to take this trauma as an occasion to abandon certain prejudices brought along from the nursery and to come to terms with the bitter truth of being, as a Jew, really without a country.
>
> (Fer/Fr, 28 August 1919, pp. 365–366)

Notwithstanding the humiliations and the deepening sense of solitude, unlike other members of the Society who emigrated, Ferenczi did not follow Freud's advice to withdraw his libido from his country (Fr/Fer, 27 October 1918, pp. 304–305), and he remained in Hungary.

During the communist era it was impossible for Ferenczi to express openly his political views in articles or even in private letters. Censorship, he lamented, had a paralysing effect on him: "I ... curse the impediments which prevent me from talking everything out ... in these times" (Fer/Fr, 13 April 1919, pp. 346–347). On 23 May 1919, the "rare opportunity" of sending an "almost uncensored letter" generated excitement in him and prompted him "to write in the kind of detail in which I haven't been able to report to you in months" (Fer/Fr, 23 May 1919, pp. 355–358). Yet just a month later he gives voice again to his "longing for some freedom" (Fer/Fr, 29 June 1919, pp. 361–363).

Disenchanted after the negative experience of academic life and seeking also to provide an explanation (or self-justification), in an article published in 1922 in the *Nyugat* magazine, he unveils the hypocrisy of authoritarian regimes in supporting certain innovative and marginalised intellectual, cultural, or scientific groups, and their underlying political motivations. His ideal form of good government remains what he conceptualised in 1908 as "socialist individualism"—a political system that would respect and safeguard the natural differences between individuals, guarantee a balance between people's lust for independence and happiness on the one hand, and the necessary restrictions by society on the other, in other words, a political system that would reconcile individual liberty and social equality. In two manuscripts (probably written in 1920, identified and analysed by Ferenc Erős: see Erős, Chapter Thirty-six) Ferenczi highlights the reasons why psychoanalysis doesn't have much in common with the "partly paranoid partly infantile visions" of Marxism, communism, or anarchism and why it has more to do with Durkheim's theories (Erős, 2013). He draws a parallel between sublimation and social progress and emphasises that his policy proposals are "liberal socialism" and "political democracy"—models towards which the route leads through psychoanalysis (Erős, 2013).

From the beginning of the 1920s onwards, Ferenczi preferred to express his political views indirectly, rather than through open statements. His political views, his rejection of authoritarianism and quest for liberty, become visible in the way he reorganised the Hungarian Psychoanalytic Society and how he reinvented psychoanalytic technique. Psychoanalysis served as a tool through which the hidden and unutterable could be brought to light and put into words, through which personal and social traumas could be mourned. If the structure of the international psychoanalytic "movement", between 1910 and 1930, reflected the authoritarian atmosphere of the Austro-Hungarian Empire and of its successor states, as André Haynal claims (1988), we could argue that the Hungarian circle mirrored its members' refusal of their country's repressive atmosphere, and their adherence to liberal and democratic values. Ferenczi accomplished what he yearned for in the early 1910s: the group he created was devoid of a father figure endowed with dogmatic authority; what kept the members of the movement together in their refusal of the authoritative government was mother-type feelings. In the 1920s, psychoanalysis in Hungary assumed an inclusive, human, tolerant, and open character. Instead of replicating Freud's "secret societies", Ferenczi, thanks to his innovative and liberal personality, acted as a "plenary man" (Mészáros, 2008) and managed to transform the Society into a democratically functioning multidisciplinary workshop.

During the same period (from the early 1920s) Ferenczi "democratised" the technique of psychoanalysis. His new method (see Bass, Chapter Twenty-three and Koritar, Chapter Twenty-two), was based on multidirectional processes of interpersonal and intersubjective elements. His vision of countertransference redefined psychoanalysis as a system of interactive communication, a "relationship-based" process (Haynal, 2002), as a form of playing (Frankel, 2011). It is mainly, though, the elaboration and the use of his new technique and his trauma theory (see various chapters in Part III) that we can identify Ferenczi's symbolic acting-out of his intellectual and affective involvement in social and political issues. It is in this indirect and veiled manner that he attempted to communicate his refusal of the authoritarian and repressive power structures, his rejection of the Horthy regime based on hypocrisy and conformism, and to mourn the lost mother(land). Only in coded language could he express his eagerness to foster the emergence of a democratic system characterised by authenticity and freedom, where a "maternal" political elite would guarantee a "facilitating environment" in a Winnicottian sense, allowing Hungarians to work through their collective traumas and live a creative and, in the broadest sense, a playful life. It thus seems appropriate to depict Ferenczi's new way of thinking and working as part of his resistance to the loss of hope for democracy, as an attempt to respond both critically and constructively not just to an individual but also to a socio-historical sense of alienation.

Ferenczi's writings are of great relevance for political and social scientists (see also Salgó, 2014). He anticipated Donald Winnicott, for whom, in a truly democratic country, "there is a sufficient maturity in the emotional development of a sufficient proportion of the individuals that comprise it for there to exist an innate tendency towards the creation and recreation and maintenance of the democratic machinery" (1950), and Béla Hamvas, who pointed out that whether a situation evolves in the right or in the wrong direction depends on people's psychological maturity (1943). István Bibó (1942–43) perhaps drew on (Hungarian?) psychoanalytic theories when designing a parallel between a society's and an individual's reactions to traumatic situations. He might have had Ferenczi's trauma theories in mind when describing a society that is experiencing a "collective hysteria" as a paralysed society losing contact with itself, failing in its problem-solving function and rejecting the real world by conjuring up an illusory world, and generating omnipotent fantasies.

Jonathan Lear aptly proposed the following question: "Might it not be possible to expand our understanding of ethical life to take account of the fact that human beings live with unconscious motivations?" (1999).

Back in 1908 Ferenczi harboured a similar dilemma. At the Salzburg conference of the IPA he claimed that psychoanalysis could serve as a tool against authoritarian rule, that it could enhance in people an internal liberation, helping them get rid of the constraints posed by a restrictive upbringing based on hypocrisy and by a similarly repressive social milieu. In his interpretation, in political revolutions, coercive tools pass from one leadership to another. Only individuals' inner transformation represents a real revolution able to bring relief to people; only people liberated through psychoanalysis could prevent the return of authoritarianism (Edu) and lead to an era in which hypocrisy, the blind adulation of dogmas and authority and the absence of self-criticism, would belong to the past (1911). To deal with societies' discontents it is necessary to deal with people's individual malaise. For societies to progress, individuals must undergo an internal transformation. Ferenczi's thoughts resonate with those of Cornelius Castoriadis. For this Greek psychoanalyst and philosopher, in psychoanalysis, in pedagogy, and in politics the goal should be to enhance individuals' ability to live an autonomous and creative life, instead of calling for the emergence of a fear-less, hatred-less, utopian, and therefore necessarily authoritarian society. As Castoriadis outlines, one of the paradoxical aspects of the "impossibility" of politics is that there can be no democracy without democratic individuals (and vice versa) (1997).

We could conclude by suggesting that Sándor Ferenczi, using various tools, sought to convey the message that a) to understand politics we must understand human nature and focus our attention on individuals (and not only on institutions); b) we must recognise (and heal) the psychological and emotional damage that societies experiencing authoritarianism suffer(ed); c) the "violently excessive goodness", the "eat-bird-or-die policy" (Diary, p. 154) which forces people to introject the aggressor, to subordinate themselves like "mechanical, obedient automatons" (Conf, p. 163) to the political leadership's will and gratify their desires, should be resisted; d) hypocrisy favours the endurance (or return) of authoritarianism while authenticity and playfulness are conducive to democratic politics; and e) psychoanalysis represents a powerful tool to help people work through their traumas, to enhance individual transformation and build an autonomous society based on individual liberty and social equality. Not only do Ferenczi's thoughts help us better understand the causes and the effects of authoritarianism, they also represent a fruitful ground for political scientists and policy-makers to rethink the "model" of the democratisation process, reject the transition paradigm (the theory according to which countries leaving behind authoritarian rule move necessarily toward democracy), and adopt instead an interdisciplinary and individual-centred approach in the study of societies and political systems.

References

Bibó, I. (1942–43). Az európai egyensúlyról és békéről. In: I. Bibó (Ed.), *Válogatott tanulmányok*, vol. I. (pp. 295–633). Budapest: Magvető, 1986.

Brunner, J. (2001). *Freud and the Politics of Psychoanalysis*. New Brunswick: Transaction.

Castoriadis, C. (1997). Psychoanalysis and politics. In: D. A. Curtis (Ed.), *World in Fragments: Writings on Politics, Society, Psychoanalysis and the Imagination* (pp. 125–36). Stanford: Stanford University Press.

Erős, F. (2013). Két Ferenczi-kézirat. *Imago Budapest, 3–4*: 145–160.

Ferenczi, S. (1911). Az öntudatlan megismerése. *Szabadgondolat, 2*: 75–78.

Ferenczi, S. (1914). A pszichoanalízisről és annak jogi és társadalmi jelentőségéről. *Gyógyászat, 6*: 88–91.

Frankel, J. (2011). Ferenczi's concepts of identification with the aggressor and play as fundamental processes in the analytic relationship. In: A. B. Druck, C. Ellman, N. Freedman, & A. Thaler (Eds.), *A New Freudian Synthesis: Clinical Process in the Next Generation*. London: Karnac.

Hamvas, B. (1943). Az ősök útja és az istenek útja. In: B. Hamvas & A. Dúl (Eds.), *Hamvas Béla művei*, vol. 15 (pp. 165–262). Budapest: MEDIO Kiadó, 2007.

Haynal, A. (1988). *Technique at Issue*. London: Karnac.

Haynal, A. (2002). *Disappearing and Reviving*. London: Karnac.

Homans, P. (1989). *The Ability to Mourn: Disillusionment and the Social Origins of Psychoanalysis*. Chicago: University of Chicago Press.

Kosztolányi, D. (1918) Orvosi konzilium. Dr. Ferenczi Sándor idegorvos nyilatkozik a háború ésbéke kérdéséről az Esztendő olvasóközönségének. *Esztendő, I-4*: 5–16.

Lear, J. (1999). Happiness. The Tanner Lectures on human values. Clare Hall, Cambridge. 29–30 November. Online. Available: <http://tannerlectures.utah.edu/_documents/a-to-z/l/Lear%20Happiness.pdf> (Retrieved on 3 June 2016).

Marcuse, H. (1970). *Five Lectures: Psychoanalysis, Politics and Utopia*. Boston: Beacon.

Mészáros, J. (2008). *"Az Önök Bizottsága". Ferenczi Sándor, a budapesti iskola és a pszichoanalitikus emigráció*. Budapest: Akadémiai Kiadó.

Salgó, E. (2014). *Psychoanalytic Reflections on Politics: Fatherlands in Mothers' Hands*. London: Routledge.

Winnicott, D. W. (1950). Thoughts on the meaning of the word democracy. In: E. Trist & H. Murray (Eds.), *The Social Engagement of Social Science: A Tavistock Anthology* (pp. 546–557). London: Free Association, 1990.

Chapter 36

Against violence: Ferenczi and liberal socialism

Ferenc Erős

The violence of hypocrisy

Violence is one of the central themes in Ferenczi's work. Violence can be interpersonal, familial, therapeutic, or social: Ferenczi treats these different aspects simultaneously, since he regards each as inseparable from the others, in their structure as well as in their traumatogenic function. Violence is not a single act, but a series of events, which includes its antecedents as well as its consequences. One consequence of a violent act may be the complete annulment or concealment of the act itself. As Ferenczi describes this process in his emblematic article "Confusion of tongues":

> When the child recovers from such an attack [the trauma], he feels enormously confused, in fact, split – innocent and culpable at the same time – and his confidence in the testimony in his own senses is broken. Moreover, the harsh behaviour of the adult partner tormented and made angry by his remorse renders the child still more conscious of his own guilt and still more ashamed. Almost always the perpetrator behaves as though nothing had happened, and consoles himself with the thought: "Oh it is only a child, he does not know anything, he will forget it all." Not infrequently after such events, the seducer becomes over-moralistic or religious and endeavours to save the soul of the child by severity.
>
> (Conf, pp. 162–163)

In the same article Ferenczi also speaks about a "hypocrisy hitherto regarded as unavoidable", that is: professional hypocrisy (ibid.). Professional hypocrisy is a main concern for Ferenczi in the *Diary* too. For example, he writes: "Patients *feel* the hypocritical element in the analyst's behaviour" (*Diary*, p. 200), or "Hatred of patients is behind the hypocritical friendliness of the doctor toward the patients" (p. 201). He recognises a similar hypocrisy, an endeavour "to save the soul of the child by severity", on the part of the educators, teachers, and parents, too, who are "pregnant with rage that is disguised in benevolent behaviour" (p. 167). In the *Diary,* Ferenczi regards benevolence, "excessive goodness", as a manifestation of the overcompensated sadism of obsessional neurotics.

The negativity of "goodness," "fairness", or "benevolence" as masks concealing a trauma was also a topic for Erich Fromm, who in his essay on "The social determinants of psychoanalytic therapy", speaks about the apparent tolerance of the therapist, which is in fact a concealment of the "doctors' hidden sadism" (1935, pp. 160–161). Or, as Lacan puts it even more provocatively in his essay on the "mirror stage": "We place no trust in altruistic feeling, we who lay bare the aggressivity that underlies the activity of the philanthropist, the idealist, the pedagogue, and even the reformer" (1949, p. 103).

For Ferenczi, on a more general level, the whole society is, at least "under the prevalent regime", hypocritical (*Diary*, p. 200). The benevolent surface or skin hardly conceals the suffering, which we are all victims of, mostly through repressive and authoritarian child-rearing practices and "the passionate behaviour of adults" (ibid.). The consequence of all these is mysticism, religiosity, defences against sexual impulses, rigidity, and authoritarianism, as Wilhelm Reich, as well as Erich Fromm, Theodor Adorno, and other members of the Frankfurt school showed in the very next decade.

An active social reformer

It would be tempting to explain Ferenczi's later passionate rage against hypocrisy by his growing alienation from and his traumatic breach with Freud in the late 1920s. However, the critique of social and educational hypocrisy had been one of his main concerns since the beginning of his psychoanalytic career, that is, from 1908. Hypocrisy, in Hungarian, "*képmutatás*", literally "showing a picture" or "showing a face", was certainly an everyday experience for the citizens of the Austro-Hungarian monarchy. The hypocrisy in the world of the monarchy was perhaps best characterised by the Austrian writer Robert Musil, in his important novel *Man Without Qualities:*

> [This country] by its constitution ... was liberal, but its system of government was clerical. The system of government was clerical, but the general attitude to life was liberal. Before the law all citizens were equal, but not everyone, of course, was a citizen. There was a parliament, which made such vigorous use of its liberty that it was usually kept shut; but there was an emergency powers act by means of which it was possible to manage without parliament.
>
> (1930, p. 33)

Ferenczi focused on the *individual* side of this hypocrisy. As he wrote in his first psychoanalytic contribution, in the paper read at the first international congress of psychoanalysis in Salzburg, titled "Psychoanalysis and education": "Only when the hypocritical mysteriousness in sexual matters has ceased to exist, when everyone will know of the processes of his own body and mind – i.e. only with conscious cathexis – will sexual emotions be truly mastered and sublimated" (Edu, pp. 285–286). In his letter to Freud on 5 February 1910, Ferenczi affirmed: "Once society has gone beyond the infantile, then hitherto completely unimagined possibilities for social and political life are opened up. Just think what it would mean if one can tell everyone the truth, one's father, teacher, neighbour, and even the king. All fabricated, imposed authority will go to the devil" (Fer/Fr, p. 130).

The key concepts of these earlier works are the notions of "unnecessary compulsion" and "excessive repression". Repression in contemporary society, Ferenczi argues, demands not only a minimum of instinctual renunciation that the already sufficiently pressing external circumstances require, but also the subjugation of its members, the deprivation of their freedom, human dignity, and autonomy. "Excessive repression", speculates Ferenczi, sets free those instinctual forces that lead to religious superstitions, to the cult of authority, and to a rigid adherence to obsolete social forms. In "Psychoanalysis and education", he argues that

> liberation from unnecessary inner compulsion would be the first revolution to bring real relief to mankind, for political revolutions have achieved only that the external powers, i.e. the means of coercion, have changed hands, or that the number of the oppressed

> has risen or fallen. Only people liberated in this real sense will be able to bring about a radical change in education and prevent permanently the return of similar undesirable circumstances.
>
> (Edu, p. 283)

Ferenczi as a social critic had maintained a strong link to the progressivist and intellectual movements of his age, like the Galileo Circle and other groupings of young scholars and students in Budapest of the *fin-de-siècle* period; groups whose members had devoted themselves to the most diverse innovative, exciting ideas, reform plans, and revolutionary dreams. Ferenczi as a "reform-utopian" had drawn a vision of a future society in which natural strivings and desires would be treated not with negation and repression, but with a "sound government" that would replace hypocrisy and the blind adoration of dogmas and authority (1911). In an article on "Psychoanalysis and its judicial and sociological relevance", Ferenczi affirmed that "between anarchy and communism ..., between unrestrained individual license and social asceticism, there must be somewhere a reasonable individual-socialistic just milieu that cares also for individual welfare as well as for the interests of society, that cultivates the sublimation instead of the repression of instincts, thereby preparing a quiet path for progress assured from revolutions and reactions" (1913a, p. 433).

In Ferenczi's focus was, however, not only society as such, but the process of its reproduction, the child, the infantile on both onto- and phylogenetic levels. His fundamental essay "Stages in the development of the sense of reality" (1913b) described the structural trauma of the individual and the collective, the trauma of birth, the "same cruel game repeated with every new stage of development" (p. 80), the violent renunciation of omnipotence, the splitting of the ego through projection and introjection. Ferenczi, in this work, had already brought into connection "the great step in our individual repression, the latency period" with "the last and greatest catastrophe that befell our primitive ancestors ... with the misery of the ice age, which we still faithfully recapitulate in our individual life" (ibid.). This truly Lamarckian idea of the ice age was further elaborated during the First World War, and then in his work *Catastrophes in the History of Sexuality*, known also as *Thalassa,* and published in 1924.

In fact, shortly after the outbreak of the First World War, in an article published under the title "The ice-age of catastrophes", Ferenczi wrote:

> In peacetime, only through the complex examination of dreams, of neurotic symptoms, of artistic creations, of diverse religions can one demonstrate ... that the human psyche presents multiple layers, the culture is but a prettily decorated shop-window whilst at the back of the store, the more primitive merchandise is piled up? War had brutally wrested off this mask and has shown us man in his deepest, truest nature at the heart of man, the child, the savage, the primitive .... It is in this way that the catastrophes of the ice-age have forged long-ago in the first familial and religious society, the basis of all subsequent evolution. War has simply thrown us back into the ice-age, or rather, it has unveiled the deep imprints that it had left in the psychic universe of humanity.
>
> (Ferenczi, 1915, p. 125)

It was the Great War, indeed, that forcefully introduced Ferenczi, a military doctor between 1914 and 1918, into the reality of a series of massive social and collective violent events (for details, see Erős, 2015). At the end of the war, in the turbulent autumn of 1918, hundreds of medical students had petitioned the new revolutionary government of Count Mihály Károlyi to invite Ferenczi to teach psychoanalysis at Budapest University. The university, however, resisted, and Ferenczi's university assignment was realised only months later, by the new government of the Council's Republic led by Béla Kun. Ferenczi accepted the professorship from the communist regime as a kind of compensation for his earlier neglect by previous regimes. Although he sympathised with some of the government's plans for reforming public health and medical education, he was far from an enthusiastic supporter of Béla Kun's regime. In particular, he felt threatened by the new government's plans to nationalise the whole health system and to deprive doctors of their private praxis (for details see Erős, 2012; Erős & Giampieri, 1987).

After the defeat of the first Hungarian communist regime on 1 August 1919, Ferenczi was among those professors who were immediately dismissed from their positions. A year later, he was also excluded from the Budapest Royal Medical Association. After the traumata of the failure of revolutions and in the atmosphere of severe repressions, Ferenczi felt himself in a vacuum both politically and professionally.

In these circumstances, he became acquainted with Aurél Kolnai, who later became known in the West primarily as a political scientist and a conservative moral philosopher (1900–1973). Kolnai studied social sciences in Budapest and Vienna, was a member of the Galileo Circle, and was, for a short time, intellectually committed to psychoanalysis (although he became an ardent critic of it a few years later) (see also Kolnai's autobiography, 1999). In early 1920, he joined the Hungarian Psychoanalytic Society, and gave a lecture under the title "Psychoanalysis and sociology", which was also the title of the book he had published in the same year in Vienna at the International Psychoanalytic Publishing House (Kolnai, 1920). This work was basically a pamphlet directed against Russian Bolshevism and the recently failed revolutionary movements in Central Europe. Kolnai saw revolution as a mass psychological phenomenon, a manifestation of an oedipal revolt of the tribal brothers against the domination of the Father that only leads to an even more repressive domination of tyrannical leaders, "substitute fathers".[1]

Kolnai was particularly critical of what he called "anarcho-communism", and he advocated for "liberal socialism" as an antidote for anarchistic degenerations. His views were echoed by Ferenczi, especially in his two brief, recently discovered and published manuscripts entitled "Parallel between Marxism, communism and anarchism", and "Parallel between psychoanalysis and liberal socialism".[2]

Two unpublished manuscripts of Ferenczi's on liberal socialism

In Manuscript I, Ferenczi raises the issue of parallels between psychoanalysis and the Marxist idea of history. He comes to the conclusion that this parallel is unsatisfactory, since the goals of the two schools are basically different. He associates Marxism with "rigid dialectics", and

1 Freud's major work on mass psychology, *Group Psychology and the Analysis of Ego*, was published a year later, in 1921.

2 Both manuscripts belong to the Ferenczi legacy donated to the London Freud Museum by Judith Dupont. I would like to thank Stefan Marianski of the Freud Museum for his invaluable help in identifying the manuscripts. See more details and the full texts in Erős, 2014.

refuses its alleged economic determinism and the concept of "class struggle", arguing that for psychoanalysis *homo infans* rather than *homo oeconomicus* is the basic structure. He contrasts the Darwinian "selectionism" attributed to Marxism with a Lamarckian evolutionism. In fact, Ferenczi's critique is directed not only against Marxism, but also against a so-called "psychoanalytic mentality" that "is almost equivalent with an anarcho-communist mentality", which dreams of the elimination of all repressions, of the satisfaction of all desires, and envisages a "fatherless society" as the ultimate goal of psychoanalysis. Ferenczi contrasts this kind of "wild" mentality with "the healthy stock" of psychoanalysis whose aim is not the "liberation of instincts", but is rather "an instrument for the self-liberation of personality". Finally, Ferenczi acknowledges that "a certain historical innovative role, an experiment for a new, more deeply penetrating, more scientific approach to things", is common to both movements; however, "psychoanalysis rather joins to Durkheim and not to the Marxist sociology and politics, and, in concrete and actual questions joins to liberal socialism".

In Manuscript II, Ferenczi further elaborates his ideas about a possible parallel between psychoanalysis and liberal socialism. He argues that while the parallel with Marxism failed, "psychoanalysis and liberal socialism share the same worldview, the same ethical sense, and the same task in the service of the welfare of men". Psychoanalysis, he argues, cannot bring "salvation", but only works "on the self-salvation of the individual". Discussing some basic themes of liberal socialism, Ferenczi points out the discovery of the significance of land,

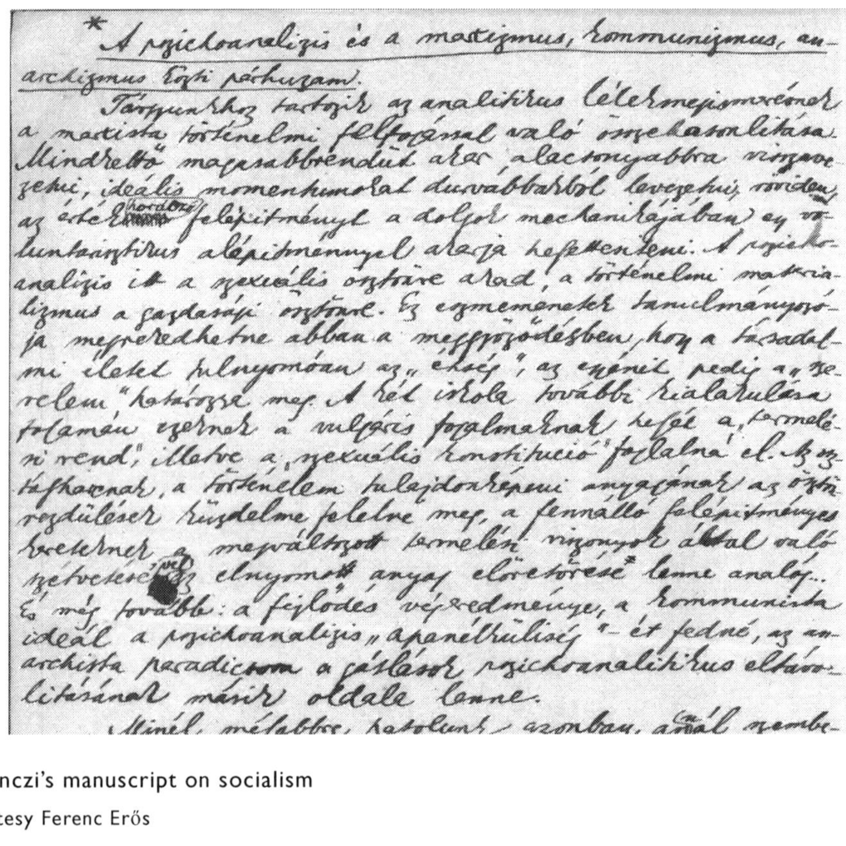

Ferenczi's manuscript on socialism

courtesy Ferenc Erős

attributing the main responsibility for all social diseases to two conditions. The first is an "antirational, rigid fixation to the land, which resists industrialism"; the second is "the treatment of land as a simple commodity". As for the fixation to the land, Ferenczi finds a psychoanalytic parallel for it in "land eroticism", and in "an incestuous fixation to the mother, which inhibits free consciousness and supports the primary despotism of the father." On the other hand, argues Ferenczi, "the treatment of land as a simple commodity would be equivalent with a helpless repression, which is incapable of higher developments."

The idea of liberal or individual socialism reappeared in an article entitled "Psychoanalysis and social politics" (Ferenczi, 1922). In this article, he expresses his hopes that "time will allow for the development of an 'individual-socialist' orientation which would take into account the natural differences between individuals, of their aspiration to independence and happiness, whilst acknowledging the need for communal life, and the restrictions, at times difficult to bear, which it imposes" (p. 211). In the article he affirms that even if he had accepted a professorial position during the communist government in 1919, he did not sympathise with the regime, since "psychoanalysis has refused to perceive any political party, be it individualistic or collectivistic, as the representative of true human nature" (p. 212).

In the 1920s, Ferenczi's main theoretical orientation turned towards his idea of the prehistoric catastrophes *preceding* the ice age of phylogenetic and ontogenetic traumata, the "thalassic regression". Shortly before his death, however, in the *Diary*, he returned to his earlier ideas on "individual collectivism". Even if there is no salvation for the individual faced with trauma, terror, and death, Ferenczi foresees improvements and progress for humanity, based on a "successful interaction of egoistic and universal tendencies" (Diary, p. 18). Elsewhere in the *Diary* he writes: "If one were not ashamed to indulge in prophecies, then one would expect from the future neither the triumph of one-sided ruthless capitalism nor that of fanciful egalitarianism, but rather a full recognition of the existence of purely selfish drives, which remain under control but must be partly satisfied in reality; the elimination of a great deal of neurotic, still passionate, one might even say violently excessive goodness (eat-bird-or-die policy) and, finally, perhaps the gradual unfolding of a naive good-heartedness" (p. 152).

This was, of course, a naive and utopian idea in the shadow of Stalinism and the threatening victory of Nazism in Germany in 1933, the year of Ferenczi's death (on Ferenczi's utopianism, see Berman, 2003). It can be regarded, as well, as an anticipation of the social policy of a modern welfare state, attempting to find a balance between "ruthless capitalism" and "fanciful egalitarianism".

References

Berman, E. (2003). Ferenczi, rescue and utopia. *American Imago*, *60*: 429–444.

Erős, F. (2012). Psychoanalysis behind iron curtains. In: L. Auested (Ed.), *Psychoanalysis and Politics: Exclusion and the Politics of Representation* (pp. 203–222). London: Karnac.

Erős, F. (2014). Freedom and authority in the *Clinical Diary*. *The American Journal of Psychoanalysis*, *74*: 367–380.

Erős, F. (2015). Torture or therapy? Uses of psychiatry and psychoanalysis in the First World War. Presented at the 2015 ASEEES convention, Philadelphia, 19 November 2015.

Erős, F. & Giampieri, S. P. (1987). The beginnings of the reception of psychoanalysis in Hungary 1900–1920. *Sigmund Freud House Bulletin*, *11*: 13–28.

Ferenczi, S. (1911). Az öntudatlan megismerése [The discovery of the unconscious]. *Szabadgondolat*, *1*: 75–78.

Ferenczi, S. (1913a). On psychoanalysis and its judicial and sociological relevance. In: *Further Contributions to the Technique of Psycho-Analysis* (pp. 424–435). London: Hogarth.

Ferenczi, S. (1913b). Stages in the development of the sense of reality. In: J. Borossa (Ed.), *Sándor Ferenczi: Selected Writings* (pp. 67–81). London: Penguin, 1999.

Ferenczi, S. (1915). The ice-age of catastrophes. In: J. Borossa (Ed.), *Sándor Ferenczi: Selected Writings* (pp. 125–126). London: Penguin, 1999.

Ferenczi, S. (1922). Psychoanalysis and social policy. In: J. Borossa (Ed.), *Sándor Ferenczi: Selected Writings* (pp. 210–213). London: Penguin, 1999.

Fromm, E. (1935). The social determinants of psychoanalytic therapy. *International Forum of Psychoanalysis, 9*: 149–165, 2000.

Kolnai, A. (1920). *Psychoanalyse und Soziologie.* Wien: Internationaler Psychoanalytischer Verlag [Engl. Trans. *Psychoanalysis and Sociology.* New York: Nabu, 2013].

Kolnai, A. (1999). *Political Memoirs*. Lanham, MD: Lexington.

Lacan, J. (1949). The mirror stage as formative of the function of the I as revealed in psychoanalytic experience. In: D. Birksted-Breen, S. Flanders, & A. Gibeault (Eds.), *Reading French Psychoanalysis* (pp. 97–104). New York: Routledge, 2010.

Musil, R. (1930). *The Man Without Qualities. Vol. 1*. London: Pan, 1979.

Chapter 37

From individual to massive social trauma

Clara Mucci

The reality of traumatisation and the consequences of violence and of identifying with the persecutor

After the Second World War and the atrocities that human beings endured and were responsible for in the twentieth century, the times were ready for a new understanding of the consequences of massive trauma. As Werner Bohleber observed at the 2007 IPA Berlin Congress, "the catastrophes and extreme experiences that people underwent and suffered in the twentieth century turned trauma into its hallmark" (2007, p. 330).

Following the illuminating work of Jay Frankel on trauma and the "identification with the aggressor" and on the "intimidation by the person of authority" (1998, 2002), I will trace here Ferenczi's fundamental contribution to the understanding of the impact violence has on individual subjectivity as well as on communities and groups, which I undertook at greater length in *Beyond Individual and Collective Trauma* (Mucci, 2013).

The entire question raised by Freud about trauma as something external, deriving from a real event that the psyche cannot bear, is resolved and clarified by Ferenczi's understanding of the progressive adjustments the psyche of the individual undergoes to adjust to the reality of abuse and violence. This forced adjustment becomes a fundamental identification that will have a bearing on future identifications and is even likely to have intergenerational consequences, as I will try to explain with the help of Ferenczi's *Diary*.

Ferenczi clearly describes a modification of the personality as a consequence of traumatisation, including the child's persistent belief that he must be bad and deserving the evil he receives, since he cannot believe that the adult, the parent, and the external world are so evil; in a word, the child needs to believe in a source of love from the outside, therefore the evil must be his own fault (cf. Fairbairn, 1943; Frankel, 2015):

> *Protection of the personality by loss of consciousness, compensating fantasies of happiness, splitting of the personality* … The child is helpless and confused, should she struggle to prevail over the will of an adult authority, the disbelief of her mother, etc. Naturally she cannot do that, *she is faced with the choice–Is it the whole world that is bad, or am I wrong?–and chooses the latter. Thereupon displacements and misinterpretation of sensations, which ultimately produce the above symptoms.*
>
> (Diary, p. 80, italics added)

Such a process supports the idea that the roots of internalised violence in the subject lie not in something like what Freud termed a "death instinct" or Thanatos (as counterposed to Eros, in *Beyond the Pleasure Principle*, 1920), a mostly innate instinct, but rather in an internalised experience of having suffered violence and received "evil" from the person who should, more than anybody else, take care of him. As a consequence, subjects are prone, through identification, to repeat the experience, either by inflicting active violence on an other or inflicting it on themselves in self-destructive behaviour, or through "finding" themselves victimised in repeated, similar circumstances. Ferenczi traces a sort of "soul murder" (Shengold, 1989), describing the experience of the child as "giving up the ghost", a sort of fainting, or "death" (Diary, p. 39), when he says: "Trauma is a process of dissolution that moves towards total dissolution, that is to say, death" (p. 130).

This is a turning point in understanding the presence and the repetition of violence in a cycle in which the traumatised subject finds himself re-enacting it and continuously releasing and playing out the traumatic core of victim and persecutor, while at the same time re-experiencing the traumatic and often dissociated memories. This might happen, I believe, at various levels, such as in couples, in families, in communities, in institutions, and on a larger societal scale: the subject plays out behaviours activated by emotions and/or impulses that have at their core a dissociated piece of reality (Ferenczi would have spoken of "fragmentation" (Diary, p. 38)), and acts out identifications with victim and/or persecutor. Present-day neurosciences have explained the reaction to traumatisation due to violent relationships as hyperarousal, on one hand, creating a stress response in the body and the mind, and dissociation, on the other, as a parasympathetic modality of response in which the nervous system disconnects form reality because it is overwhelmed (Schore, 2015). Dissociated memories, split from consciousness, are therefore stored in what we nowadays term implicit memory, rooted in the body and in the corporeal memory-self (Schore, 2015; Mucci, 2013, 2016b). Dissociated memories of violent content can haunt the survivor through the internalised partially conscious views of self and other, dysfunctional modalities of relation that are imprinted in the so-called IWM (internal working models), as Bowlby named them, that is, the representations of self and other based on relational experiences starting from birth (and probably before birth, in prenatal life).

This introjection of negative aspects of traumatic experiences reminds us of what Fonagy and Target (1996) have described as the "colonization of the self" by an insensitive or negative caregiver, and the "alien self" that results from this (p. 228, p. 229). This introjection is a very important source of future severe pathology and often takes the form of self-harm or destructive behavior of other kinds, and might even get externalised as criminal behavior. Most often this "alien self", created interpersonally in traumatic parental relationships or in other disturbing significant intersubjective experiences, needs to be "externalised" (Bateman & Fonagy, 2006), that is, acted out, as if it were not a part of the self, often through aggressive and anti-social behaviour with another; externalising these introjects in one's interactions with other people, perhaps including one's children, thus perpetuates the spread and the cycle of trauma.

These destructive introjects can be acted out in destructive behaviour against the self and especially one's body (through self-cutting, or other self-destructive behaviour like eating disorders, destructive sexual behaviour, or drug abuse or addiction—behaviours often seen in borderline disorders). Notably, a traumatic origin has been discovered in at least sixty per cent of the entire borderline population (Gabbard, 2014).

We can posit a continuum of traumatisation, by degree of severity. This continuum begins at a level that includes both severe neglect and lack of empathy. Allan Schore has described how severe neglect, which he has termed "early relational trauma", can have severe consequences for brain development and might even result in the impairment of the emotional capacity to put oneself in the other's mind through empathy and emotional responsiveness and sensitivity (Schore, 2015). Lack of empathy may create a neuropsychological basis for anti-social behaviour and a tendency to dehumanise the other (Schore, 2015). A second level of traumatisation stems from active violence and/or sexual exploitation of the child. The third, most devastating level of traumatisation, massive trauma, happens in the wake of events like the Shoah or other genocides and massive exterminations such as those that took place in Ruanda or the former Yugoslavia, as described in *Beyond Individual and Collective Trauma* (Mucci, 2013).

Responding to massive trauma and the cycle of intergenerational transmission

The internalisation of bad objects (which could be understood as another form of identification with the aggressor, resulting in internalising the evil into oneself) in massive trauma and in survivors has been understood and described profoundly by Laub and Lee:

> The victim, to ward off the horrors of objectlessness, internalises and identifies with the only object available to him: the perpetrator, a bad object... Failure of the empathic connection and the consequent loss of the internal good object produce feelings of absence and of rupture, a loss of representation, an inability to grasp and remember trauma, and a loss of coherence.
>
> (2003, p. 441)

The criminal acts of the offenders may be seen in relation to the internalised object relations, as an acting out of them (Welldon & Van Velsen, 1997). These internalised split identifications (split between victim and persecutor), and the dangerous levels of erasure and voids or empty spaces or black holes at the core of the traumatised psychological experience, need to be worked through and elaborated in precise steps in the therapy, if we want some kind of healing and reparation to take place (Mucci, 2013). This reparation goes back from the individual to past generations and therefore to society at large.

Ferenczi's understanding of traumatisation as "introjection" of negative parts, and his tracing the root of destructiveness in human beings back to a violent internalised relationship, indicates, then, a totally different route that psychoanalysis could have taken, a route closer to Pierre Janet's theory, and distinctly distant from both Freud's and Klein's theorisations of trauma, with their conceptualisations of death instincts and innate aggressiveness in both children and adults.

It is now generally accepted that the intergenerational transmission of trauma and violence is acted out, to start with, through the mechanisms of the attachment system, which gives a major intergenerational imprinting: not only does having a secure attachment mean having protection in dealing with future traumatic experiences, whether man-made or natural trauma, but a parent's disorganised and insecure attachment also predicts disorganised and/or insecure attachment in the child in up to eighty per cent of cases. Moreover, it should also be noted that dissociation in a child can also be triggered simply by the dissociative moments of the mother, without real maltreatment and abuse (Liotti, 1992). Therefore, support to the families and to the mothers or the caregivers is the first measure of protection against the repetition of the cycle of violence. The understanding of how trauma gets "injected" from parent to child, and is therefore carried intergenerationally, was clear to Ferenczi as early as 1932:

> I am indebted to several patients for the idea, recorded elsewhere, that adults forcibly inject their will, particularly psychic contents of an unpleasurable nature, into the childish personality. *These split-off, alien transplants vegetate in the other person during the whole of life ...*
>
> (Diary, p. 81, italics added)

After the extreme traumatisations at both individual and collective level during the twentieth century, several contemporary authors, beginning in the sixties and seventies, have worked on the "transposition" of trauma from one generation to the other (Kestenberg, 1989), about "cumulative trauma" (Grubrich-Simitis, 1981), "vicarious traumatization" (Kogan, 2007), or what has been called the "unconscious organizing principle for future generations" (Laub & Auerhahn, 1984).

The absence of a loving, welcoming, attentive, witnessing environment compounds individual trauma. Most specifically in "Confusion of tongues", Ferenczi says that children can get over almost anything if there is someone to listen, to comfort, to accept the child's experience; without this, the permanent damage occurs.

Extreme traumatisation such as the one faced in Europe during and after the Second World War, most pointedly the Shoah, has forced us to rewrite the very tenets of psychoanalytic metapsychology and how we understand what it means to be human and to be in an empathic and trustful relationship with others, and, therefore, our understanding of humanisation *vs.* dehumanisation.

It should also be kept in mind that the same mechanisms operating in individual minds (such as dissociation, identification with victim and persecutors, paranoid projections, splitting, denial) are active in groups and institutions in society at large, only reinforced by what we now know are the mechanisms applying to group psychology per se (see the famous Milgram experiment (Milgram, 1963)) with paranoid ideologies triggering social violence and perpetrating murder and extreme suffering or annihilation. The mechanisms of identification with the aggressor and the split core of victim and persecutor are therefore re-enacted to a massive criminal extent.

"Testimonial communities": How to go beyond trauma, and how to work with the victims of collective trauma

The traumatised patient, especially in the case of massive trauma and organised state violence, as happened in the Shoah, in Cambodia, various South American countries, or the Soviet Union among numerous examples, faces not only the radical split between victim and persecutor within, but a total annihilation of trust and hope, since atrocities of this kind erase the very possibility of keeping inside what Dori Laub has termed "the empathic dyad" with the rupture of an internalised (presumably) good object. As Belgian philosopher Jean Amery wrote:

> Anyone who has been tortured remains tortured ... Anyone who has suffered torture never again will be able to be at ease in the world, the abomination of the annihilation is

> never extinguished. Faith in humanity, already cracked by the first slap in the face, then demolished by torture, is never acquired again.
>
> (Quoted in Levi, 1988, p. 25)

Extreme isolation and a tendency to withdraw from any communal participation is usually strongly felt in survivors; they tend to connect to other survivors, the only ones who can understand their experience and their existential quest. As a survivor explains, in the Fortunoff Video Archive for Holocaust Testimonies at Yale University, why she married her husband, who had undergone the same experience of the extermination camp: "he was the only one who knew who I was, and I was the only who knew who he was".

Like extremely "unwelcome guests" (Unwel) to their family-state-social organisation, survivors introject the death instinct and the extreme rejection and violence they felt in their environment, carrying with them sometimes severe psychosomatic symptoms and active destructiveness and masochism in their lives. This extreme lack of social support and collective comfort and witnessing environment compounds individual trauma and makes massive trauma especially devastating.

This is why the reconstruction of a social community, and the gaining of some kind of faith, and belonging to a social group become fundamental for the healing of the survivor. Community creates a sort of solace, refuge, intimacy, protection, recognition, and acceptance of one's experience, and a way to cushion pain. The reconstruction of meaning, both in the sense of making sense of one's personal trajectory in life and within society's development, becomes constitutive and restitutive, and this might in turn imply, for the survivor, a new involvement in politics and society, a new "mission". Community and society at large need to contribute to the restoration of integrity, hope, and meaning for its inhabitants, and this seems totally consistent with Ferenczi's thought that, like society, the family needs to adjust and welcome the child and not vice versa.

As Ferenczi clearly stressed in his paper on "Relaxation and neocatharsis", and also repeated in his *Diary*, traumatised patients need accommodation, indulgence, care, and love.

In therapy with survivors, the recreation of a safe and holding environment is the first element to sooth the pain of the patient and help recreate hope and trust in oneself and in humanity. To this aim, the ethical and totally committed attitude of the therapist is of primary importance. Contrary to Freud's neutrality, which Ferenczi equates to "hypocrisy", the Hungarian analyst proposes a therapeutic attitude that is compassionate and empathic: the analyst needs to be a witness, totally benevolent and committed. Since the internal desperation of the survivor often involves an incapacity to communicate with others who do not share the same experience, and therefore he feels a total loneliness, to be in contact with an empathic listener who is totally committed, a "benevolent and helpful" companion (Diary, p. 24), and to integrate this benevolence and care (or even love) emotionally and cognitively into one's own self, is decisive. The stance of the therapist in Ferenczi's view, a totally committed and benevolent witness, makes it possible to bridge this gap of unreachable silence and unspeakable pain. To be able to speak about trauma, one needs to be in the company of another who has become a witness to one's experience of what would otherwise have no internal witness (since the internal object is dead in massive trauma (Laub, 2005).

In fact, the patient will not "remember" and restore parts of his own atrocious experience unless he is in the presence of another who is totally dedicated and empathically connected (Mucci, 2016a).

In Ferenczi's view the psychoanalytic process and treatment becomes a "testimonial process" (Mucci, 2013), a path towards recuperation of historical truth in society, a way to restore hope and therefore a practice towards healing, in the individual, as well as in society. To echo Dori Laub, I do believe that "what is needed for healing is the creation of a testimonial community" (Laub, 2005, p. 264).

References

Bateman, A., & Fonagy, P. (2006). *Mentalization-based Treatment: A Practical Guide*. Oxford: OUP.

Bohleber, W. (2007). Remembrance, trauma and collective memory: the battle for memory in psychoanalysis. *International Journal of Psychoanalysis*, *88*: 329–352.

Fairbairn, W. R. D. (1943). The repression and the return of bad objects (with special reference to the "war neuroses"). In: *Psychoanalytic Studies of the Personality* (pp. 59–81). New York: Tavistock/Routledge, 1952.

Freud, S. (1920). *Beyond the Pleasure Principle*. *S. E.*, *18*: 7–64. London: Hogarth.

Fonagy, P., & Target, M. (1996). Playing with reality: 1. Theory of mind and the normal development of psychic reality. *International Journal of Psychoanalysis*, *77*: 217–234.

Frankel, J. (1998). Ferenczi's trauma theory. *The American Journal of Psychoanalysis*, *58*: 41–61.

Frankel, J. (2002). Exploring Ferenczi's concept of identification with the aggressor: Its role in trauma, everyday life, and the therapeutic relationship. *Psychoanalytic Dialogues*, *12*: 101–139.

Frankel, J. (2015). The persistent sense of being bad: The moral dimension of identification with the aggressor. In: A. Harris & S. Kuchuck (Eds.), *The Legacy of Sandor Ferenczi* (pp. 204–222). New York: Routledge.

Grubrich-Simitis, I. (1981), Extreme traumatization as cumulative trauma: psychoanalytic investigation of the effects of concentration camp survivors and their children. *The Psychoanalytic Study of the Child*, *39*: 301–319.

Gabbard, G. (2014). *Psychodynamic Psychiatry in Clinical Practice*. Washington, DC: American Psychiatric Publishing.

Kestenberg, J. S. (1989). Transposition revisited. Clinical, therapeutic, and developmental considerations. In: P. Marcus & A. Rosenberg (Eds.), *Healing their Wounds: Psychotherapy with Holocaust Survivors and their Families* (pp. 67–82). New York: Praeger.

Kogan, I. (2007). *The Struggle Against Mourning*. Lanham, NY: Jason Aronson.

Laub, D. (2005). From speechlessness to narrative: The cases of holocaust historians and of psychiatrically hospitalized survivors. *Literature and Medicine*, *2*: 253–265.

Laub, D., & Auerhahn, N. C. (1984). Reverberations of genocide: its expression in the conscious and unconscious of post-Holocaust generations. In: S. S. Luel & P. Marcus (Eds.), *Psychoanalytic Reflections of the Holocaust* (pp. 151–167). New York: The Holocaust Awareness Institute, Center for Judaic studies, University of Denver, and KTAV Publishing House.

Laub, D., & Lee, S. (2003). Thanatos and massive psychic trauma: the impact of the death instinct on knowing, remembering, and forgetting. *Journal of the American Psychoanalytic Association*, *51*: 433–463.

Levi, P. (1988). *The Drowned and the Saved*. New York: Vintage.

Liotti, G. (1992). Disorganised/disoriented attachment in the etiology of the dissociative disorders. *Dissociation: Progress in the Dissociative Disorders*, *5*: 196–204.

Milgram, S. (1963). Behavioral study of obedience. *Journal of Abnormal and Social Psychology*, *67*: 371–378.

Mucci, C. (2013) *Beyond Individual and Collective Trauma: Intergenerational Transmission, Psychoanalytic Therapy and the Dynamics of Forgiveness*. London: Karnac.

Mucci, C. (2016a). Ferenczi's revolutionary therapeutic approach. *American Journal of Psychoanalysis*, *77*: 239–254.

Mucci, C. (2016b). Implicit memory, unrepressed unconscious and trauma theory. In: G. Craparo & C. Mucci (Eds.), *Unrepressed Unconscious, Implicit Memory, and Clinical Work* (pp. 99–128). London: Karnac.

Schore, A. N. (2015). *Affect Regulation and the Origin of the Self: The Neurobiology of Emotional Development*. London: Routledge.

Shengold, L. (1989). *Soul Murder: The Effects of Childhood Abuse and Deprivation*. New Haven, CT: Yale University Press.

Welldon, E. V., & Van Velsen, C. (1997). *A Practical Guide to Forensic Psychotherapy*. London: Jessica Kingsley.

Chapter 38

Hello Baby. In the footprints of Sándor Ferenczi: Welcoming a child into a contemporary family

Julianna Vamos

> It is Tuesday afternoon and Mrs H comes in for a postnatal consultation at the maternity clinic. We have seen each other five times before the birth of her daughter, and she comes back today to introduce her. The girl is one month old. Mrs H tells me how lost she was in the first few weeks after the birth, and recognises how helpful it was to decelerate in the last three months of her pregnancy. Slowing down permitted her to prepare the welcoming of her baby.
>
> I can see through Mrs H's smile how exhausted she is. She holds the baby up against her, vertically on her lap. The baby, Noémie, has eyes wide open and looks curious. After explaining to me in detail how things have been going, during a little silence I turn towards and address Noémie, saying how nice it is to see her and how interested she seems with her big eyes. I also say that I wonder why she is frowning so much. I go to sit next to them, feel Mrs H open up, so I suggest to her that she lay her daughter down on her back in a more horizontal position, so that she doesn't have to hold her head up. Noémie's little face relaxes, she looks up at her mother in a new exploring attitude. Her mother, surprised, says that they have never looked at each other in such a tender way. This is a moment of long, loving contemplation between mother and baby. "The first", says Mrs H, her voice revealing how moved she is by the deep connection she discovers with her daughter.

The progressive Parisian maternity clinic called "les Bluets" has a very well thought out pre- and postnatal parental facility. Parents can come for individual consultations as well as group meetings with me, a psychoanalyst. I am doing prevention work and the team helps me in creating the environment to allow new families to be born.

The extraordinary empathic observer and socially sensitive visionary Sándor Ferenczi, with a good measure of *bon sens* in the last six years of his life, put greater and greater emphasis on the early conditions that are needed to prevent certain psychopathologies and forms of narcissistic identity problems. Parallel to this, his elastic technique in his analytic work was experienced, and looked upon, both as a success and with severely critical eyes. The sincerity of the analyst in the analytical session, and the sincerity of the parents and caretakers, was questioned and reflected upon. It is the question of welcoming the baby into the world (the French word *accueil* communicates this more strongly) and of early care that I would like to pick up on, with some observations from my perinatal and follow-up clinical experience, and by developing some Ferenczian intuitions. I wish to propose, beyond some well-known elements of caregiving, an original proposition, and that is to reflect not upon what it takes to be an unwelcome child, as Ferenczi discussed (Avello, Chapter Seventeen), but a welcome child, in a contemporary western urban family.

In his 1927 article, "The adaptation of the family to the child" Ferenczi (1928) maintains that it is the family that should adapt to the baby and not the other way round. In this article, he also talks about the necessity for the parents to be able to understand *themselves* so they can learn to understand and attune to the baby. He clearly expressed how beneficial it is to the education of the child that the parents be enlightened by psychoanalytical discoveries (Arfelli & Vigna-Taglianti, Chapter Thirty-four).

In his *Diary* Ferenczi highlights the environmental factor. He refers to "the enlightening environment" (p. 210), an expression that, for me, shines a light on the importance of accepting the unconscious dimensions of being human, including one's infantile sexual drives. Contrary to Otto Rank, he doesn't consider birth to be a priori traumatic (Adapt, p. 64), and points out other fields that could be explored as sources of possible traumatism. For example, starting with his early papers, he emphasises that in the ordinary conditions of the traditional upbringing of his time, the question—still present in contemporary society—of weaning and toilet training could turn out to be traumatic. He thus recognised more subtle forms of environmental influence, long before other psychoanalysts did.

Ferenczi emphasised the idea that parents and caretakers should be attentive and take seriously the actions and reactions of the child, in the service of better "attuning" to them and eventually getting insights into their child's difficulties. Though he did not use this word, he was in tune with Daniel Stern's later reflections on attunement (Stern, 1985).

> So in my intervention with Noémie and her mother, attuned to the baby's facial expression, bodily tension and to the mother's state of mind, I suggested that mother move baby into another posture … so the baby doesn't have to cope with gravity and can find herself in a relaxed body that opens to another quality of communication. Little detail, important consequences.

Having worked for fifteen years in the maternity clinic "Les Bluets" I am privileged to have observed the changes in families, around families, and, through them, in society. In contemporary western society new forms of parenthood are appearing and give us a lot to think about. As Irène Théry (2016) points out, in France difficulties arise from the fact that society's institutions have not kept pace with technological changes in procreation and new family organisations, nor with the greater isolation of urban families. All manner of new family arrangements lead us to investigate what remains essential for the baby's psychically healthy development. The caring envelope surrounding new families is not a luxury but an absolute necessity, and has to be taken seriously. Beyond personal health, well-being, and the realisation of the child's potential, its impact on future society is crucial. My work guiding and supporting new families is my contribution.

Caregiving environment

The child-centred, warm-hearted accompaniment for parental education is based on an environment where babies can learn from experience in a world where clear landmarks, neither authoritarian nor too liberal, are present. Between the traditional, western, authoritarian parental attitude and that of the liberal, over-invested approach of the post-1968 generation, parents need a framework that nurtures the child's personal capacities. If the environmental dimension is adjusted, and if it's understood that the baby is a competent person from the earliest age onwards, adequate parenting lets the baby actively contribute to his own development.

Julia Kristeva, in "Motherhood today" (2005), beautifully describes the "passionate violence of the maternal experience". Mothers have to sublimate the intensity of the maternal drive, with its inevitable controlling and destructive elements. This allows the affect to "turn into tenderness, caretaking and benevolence". Winnicott's "good enough mother" can transform this passion to tenderness but also can position herself by differentiating her newborn from herself. The father and language development obviously also both play important parts.

For the past fifteen years I have offered bi-monthly groups for new parents and their babies, with the intention of accompanying them, in their baby's first development, with a certain "philosophy". As in my clinical individual therapies, in these groups the question remains, what sort of envelope can sustain, after a crucial period of fusion, mother-baby differentiation. The importance of transitional spaces and the parents' delicate "holding" can provide the preventive action Ferenczi talked about in his *Diary*. The integration of the work of Hungarian pediatrician Emmi Pikler (1979) on the baby's potential is a key element of my analytical support. What Ferenczi intuited as an enlightening environment, Pikler created in a concrete and emotional setting. Here, parents or caregivers can untangle the unconscious knots they have faced in their relationships with their own baby-selves, to a degree that allows them to generously provide time and space to the new babies, so they, in turn, can listen to their own "internal aspiration".

> Mrs H comes back with Noémie, two months old now, to the "Parents-Aise" group with seven other parents. (The group functions bi-monthly for parents who need guidance.) One mother with a three-week-old baby just falls apart, the baby seems to be devouring her, she cannot sleep enough, so she just cries and feels inadequate. Mrs H shares with the group her own struggles, which have become easier. Being there for each other and listening to each other, mothers can put their own experiences into perspective. Noémie is comfortable now in her mother's arms, she is even placed on my "*tapis de jeu*" and enjoys her own movements. Mother and baby are radiant. None of the babies cry in the circle of Parents-Aise, it holds and envelops them.

Encounter with Pikler's paradigm

Emmi Pikler's interactive observation focuses on the internal resources of the baby, and the permanent creation of an environment with its small, everyday details, that indirectly lets the potentialities come alive. She foresaw that a facilitating environment would sensitise parents and caretakers to baby's nascent autonomy, which, if respected and not impinged on, makes a major contribution to the baby's processes of subjectivisation. Such an environment allows the baby to take pleasure in discovering his own way to act, think, be, and do. This joy of doing it by oneself is the essential parameter, not to be confused with all kinds of "training for autonomy".

If the Pikler approach is an actualisation of the Ferenczian phrase "enough attention to the needs and internal aspirations of the child", she proposed a highly original dynamic relationship between two kinds of nurturing—nurturing in direct relation with the object, as most of the literature talks about, and nurturing indirectly, by leaving space for the baby's own activity.[1]

Pikler's fundamental conception is based on her discovery of the importance of the baby's self-initiated motor development, and on the understanding that it is principally during bodily care that the relationship is built and the child feels and lives the quality of the adult's investment.

The innate capacity of the infant to unfold his own motor development is Pikler's discovery, made through extensive systematic observation of babies. Respecting the infant's internal developmental rhythm gives freedom of movement, which prepares freedom that will later be a feature of the mental space. The adult's trust can be felt by the baby through this environment that reflects and meets his capacities.

Having integrated the Piklerian approach, one has a new conception, a different representation, of the child's development and caretaking. This conception is partly transmissible, and partly has to be discovered by an internal emotional experience, to be able to be in the presence of an active, competent, free baby, who has influence. The therapeutic atmosphere of the Pikler model is based upon giving up the idea of exercising power over children. The most subtle form of mistreatment involves the failure to take the child's basic expressions and needs into account. Pikler's approach asks the adult to choose her intervention carefully, without interfering in the baby's spontaneous developmental movement.

The enlightening environment

Being a parent is difficult, especially in the new constellations, which require the invention of one's own way of parenting. Getting input from various sources, parents can develop numerous contradictory attitudes towards their baby. Professional aid is not always accessible, nor even desirable. But community resources, specifically parent-infant groups, can provide a containing environment around the parents and become one of the solutions.

In my article "Free to move, free to be" (Vamos, 2015) I concluded with the idea that Ferenczi and Pikler deeply understood that the resources and resourcefulness of the infant can be preserved if, and only if, the environment is enlightening enough to allow the naturalness of growing to be preserved. Then, babies won't need to use unnecessary splitting, nor renounce their own rhythm and taste for activity, and the ever so essential need of the healthy (not "traumatic") self-organisation can be protected.

In this text I hope to make a further step. Proposing a certain psychoanalytically oriented support, parents and therapist can create space and time to observe, together, babies in their free activities. Being attentive to the progress and creativity of their baby's own movements and playing, parents can introject the resourceful, active, competent infant. The parents' representation of their baby's potential, needs, and desires becomes transformed. To be able to see the baby as competent in his own playful space can call for a different partnership with him. Dependency and autonomy can find their right dosage.

1 Among her collaborators who continued to develop her ideas, Anna Tardos, Éva Kàllo, Maria Vincze, Judit Falk, and Agnes Szànto should be mentioned.

Sharing with parents a deep interest in the child's free movement in a protected rigorous framework and in a group is like providing a "velvet carpet" to produce mother-baby differentiation. The narcissistic pleasure of mothering shifts away from being about providing constant proximal care and towards sharing the baby's joy in developing his own competence.

An enlightening environment in Ferenczi's footsteps starts with welcoming the child. But beyond this feeling and attitude, welcoming the infant involves special attention, active observation, and continual readjustment to baby's relational need as well as to his need for autonomy. I wish to pay attention here to this less developed area. Not abusing baby's natural benevolence, taking seriously his tempo, his expressions, his "reveries", is a way not to disqualify baby's experiences. In such a rhythm the child doesn't feel pushed toward a hurrying "traumatic progression" (Conf, p. 165) or to develop a "precocious maturity" (ibid.), as described by Ferenczi at the beginning of the 1930s. The infant's probable effective knowledge of adult sexuality doesn't take up all his available mental space. This stance of active observation and continual readjustment also helps the parents not to abuse, consciously or unconsciously, baby's vulnerability. The infant's self-organisation, under the influence of such an environment, may take a complicated road, but at least it is unlikely to be that of the overburdened "wise baby" (Martín Cabré, Chapter Eighteen).

This environment is constructed by discoveries from the clinical observations and psychoanalytical speculations of Ferenczi, from the paediatric psychoanalytical contribution of Winnicott's notions of health and care, and from Pikler's baby observation of emotional and educational care. Pikler's pragmatic contribution means dealing with time in slow motion, proposing organised space, and laying out materials in a special facilitating way. It can be seen as the research of the "ecological" human environment where the adults providing these qualities protect the natural resources of the baby. When in this way the adult finds another position of partnership, she preserves the dignity of the baby, who can figure out his own ways to move, to play, to grow.

"The child has to be induced, by means of an immense expenditure of love, tenderness and care," says Ferenczi, "*to forgive his parents* for having brought him into the world without any intention on his part" (Unwel, p. 105, italics added). But considering all the above-mentioned qualities of a providing environment, I would suggest that the question of blame is no longer relevant. As Ferenczi continues: in his analytical sessions he would provide to his adult patients "indulgence … to enjoy the *irresponsibility* of childhood…" (p. 106, italics added). Yes, childhood should be free from the responsibility for parental matters the baby takes upon himself. But I would also advance that in an adjusted environment and with adults' respectful attitude, happy, carefree (insouciant) childhood is not without responsibility. In the Piklerian environment the baby can enjoy exercising his little responsibility concerning his baby life—the small enjoyable autonomy he has from the beginning. It communicates parents' trust in his initiatives, resources, capacities, instead of teaching and training him.

The enlightening environment is a territory of sincerity. Sincerity in care for the baby allows him to experience his contributions on his own level, enjoy autonomy, and be dependent without that being distorted into helplessness.

In western societies, accelerating changes demand that so much must be understood and adapted to quickly. But the universal unchanging elements of the human baby's needs will remain. I have tried to show in this chapter how to understand, value, and respect baby's original autonomy, so his dependency is not turned into helplessness. With the right circumstances and support, parents can offer a haven where the child can feel welcomed.

References

Kristeva, J. (2005). Motherhood today. Link: http://www.kristeva.fr/motherhood.html
Pikler, E. (1979). *Se mouvoir en liberté dès le premier âge*. Toulouse: Eres.
Stern, D. (1985). *The Interpersonal World of the Infant*. New York: Basic Books.
Théry, I. (2016). *Mariage et filiation pour tous: Une métamorphose inachevée*. Paris: Seuil.
Vamos, J. (2015). Free to move, free to be. *The American Journal of Psychoanalysis*, *75*: 65–75.

Chapter 39

Sándor Ferenczi's impact on clinical social work and education

Steven Kuchuck

Introduction

Beginning in the 1920s during "the psychiatric deluge" (Woodroofe, 1971), Freudian psychoanalytic theory began to have a deep impact in the US, not only on the emerging field of social work, but on education as well. Although Freud's name was most closely linked to the prevailing theories that touched both social work and education, the ideas of Sándor Ferenczi and his closest colleagues also crossed the Atlantic. The aftermath of the First and Second World Wars, "shell shock", and the newly formed child guidance clinics exposed social workers to these teachings (Goldstein, 2002a). Many of them entered into treatment and supervision with the rapidly growing community of European psychoanalysts who immigrated to the United States and often worked in the child guidance clinics (Aiello, 1998). Although his name was barely uttered alongside Freud's except perhaps in apologetic whispers, Ferenczi already had a huge direct and indirect impact on some of the émigrés before their arrival. Those American social workers who travelled to Europe to study and be analysed were of course also exposed to Ferenczi's thinking.

Even prior to the translation and release of Ferenczi's previously embargoed *Diary*, his correspondence with Freud, and other of his writings, Ferenczi's work began to quietly infiltrate contemporary American psychoanalysis via his collaborators, students, and patients. But until this material became available, scholars have only had limited evidence to explain how his ideas were able to cross the barriers of language, geography, professional rank, and politics necessary for introduction and eventual integration into clinical social work as early as the mid-1920s and through to the mid-1930s. Citations for this evidence of Ferenczi's very early influence on the development of clinical social work are scant in the social work and psychoanalytic literatures. In English, they are almost non-existent before the late 1980s and early 1990s.

In this chapter, I will review this content and introduce new findings from previously unpublished primary source material to show that the earliest roots of clinical social work can be traced to Sándor Ferenczi. I will provide evidence to support the contention that early psychoanalytic theory—often directly handed down from Ferenczi—either launched or expanded core ideas about the social worker's use of self, the importance of working with disenfranchised populations, short-term therapy techniques, trauma theory, and other psychoanalytically informed practice interventions. Taking this into account, I will argue that psychoanalysis—and more specifically Ferenczi's work—helped to shape clinical social work during the formative decades of its evolution and further suggest that it continues to have an impact on the field, even though it is often disavowed due to the dominance of "evidence-based" and short-term models. Finally, I will explore Ferenczi's contributions to the field of education, specifically by looking at the ways in which he believed psychoanalytic ideas could support both teachers and parents in raising healthy children.

Theoretical background

There is a link between the feminine, caring role that social work has historically held and the early influences of Ferenczi on psychoanalysis (Horowitz, 1998). Freud was often described as a scientifically detached and distant observer, and was for all intents and purposes more interested in developing psychoanalytic theories than practice techniques. Ferenczi, on the other hand, was described by patients and colleagues as warm, engaged, maternal, and more emotionally invested in clinical work than the more paternalistic Freud. Ferenczi was deeply interested in treatment techniques—what worked or did not when sitting with each individual patient. This emphasis on clinical technique and emotional investment has always had special relevance for social workers, who were more often interested in building a profession that launched its work via caring (initially, primarily female) "friendly visitors" (Tannenbaum & Reisch, 2001) than through scientific detachment and theory building.

Ferenczi's emphasis on avoiding hierarchy in favour of mutuality, and employing authenticity and love as they emerge, are more consistent with clinical social work's approach to the nature of therapeutic action (Bodenheimer, 2010; Kuchuck, 2012, 2013, 2015; Vida, 2002). In his own writing and in collaboration with Otto Rank (1925), Ferenczi's then-revolutionary "active technique" spawned the first time-limited psychoanalytic model (Koritar, Chapter Twenty-two). This model and those derived from it are still in frequent use by social workers treating clients in agencies with long waiting lists and financial or theoretical structures that don't allow for longer-term treatments (Tosone, 1997). Even when not used as a short-term model, Ferenczi's active technique and the more participatory, directive stances it encourages are well-suited to social work clinicians, who are trained in and usually oriented towards person-in-environment, biopsychosocial, and co-participatory perspectives.

Ferenczi's impact on the evolution of psychoanalysis and clinical social work

As "the analyst of last resort" (Rachman, 2007, p. 79), Ferenczi was willing to work with more seriously troubled patients thought to be beyond psychoanalytic help. Typically, marginalised voices of people of colour, the economically challenged, lesbian, gay, bisexual, and transgendered people were also warmly welcomed into his practice and not pathologised in ways that society and psychoanalysis have tended towards (Gentile, 2016; Afuape & Hughes, 2015). These often oppressed and frequently economically challenged patients have always been the kinds of clients that social workers are most likely to encounter in agency practice. The theories and techniques already mentioned and yet to be noted were often developed by Ferenczi as a result of his work with these patients and therefore highly suited to clinical social workers (Borden, 2000; Danto, 2008; Goldstein, 2002b; Raines, 1996).

Ferenczi significantly influenced his patients who were also analysts. One of the most well-known was Clara Thompson, who went on to join Harry Stack Sullivan in forming the interpersonal school of psychoanalysis (Prince, Chapter Thirty), which had its own significant impact on clinical social work (Kanter, 2013). Thompson, "in turn, educated social workers in the 1940's and 1950's" (Danto, 2008, p. 716). Ferenczi also had a significant professional influence on his patient Michael Balint, one of the early founders of object-relations theory and an extender and translator of Ferenczi's work. Many believe that Ferenczi was therefore the father of contemporary and, more specifically, relational psychoanalysis (Harris, 2011; Rachman, 2010). Some social work educators and numerous social work psychoanalysts have incorporated elements of object relations and relational thinking in their work (Seinfeld, 1990, 1993, 1996, 2003; Siegel, 1995, 1997; Tosone, 2004, 2013). But due to their arrival on the scene well past the psychoanalytic golden age of clinical social work, the influence of these theories—at least until very recently—has been far less than Ferenczi's.

Due to his work with traumatised soldiers during the First World War (Hamburger, Chapter Ten), Ferenczi was among the earliest clinicians to identify shell shock, as it was called then. He developed specific therapeutic techniques for working with these soldiers (Harris, 2010) based on his growing understanding of dissociation, anxiety, and trauma, especially as these emerge via somatic symptoms that replicate battle and other physical and psychic injuries. In later years, Ferenczi worked with traumatised patients using what came to be his preferred "relaxation technique" (Koritar, Chapter Twenty-two), making space for a more fully realised human relationship through which patients could begin to make contact with previously dissociated memories and aspects of self, feel affects, and relive emotionally charged events. As will be discussed below, these techniques for working with trauma survivors informed early generations of psychoanalysts and social workers and are still relevant to and in use by clinical social workers, who have always worked with this population (Tosone, 1997, 2011; Goldstein et al., 2009).

Ferenczi and the social work literature

Due to the fact that much of Ferenczi's most important work was withheld from English translation until the late 1980s, awareness of his importance to the early development of clinical social work is much less widespread than it otherwise would be. Much more recently, social work scholars Jeffrey Seinfeld (1990, 1993, 1996, 2003), Herbert Strean (1977, 1993, 1994, 1998), Carol Tosone (1997), Danna Bodenheimer (2010), and others cited above, mention or even write extensively about his work.

Although this more recent literature is an important part of reviving interest in Ferenczian thinking in clinical social work, these publications occurred well after the field had moved past its primary theoretical identification with psychoanalysis. I would therefore argue that although social work practitioners might not have realised it until after the publication of his major work and correspondence, the profession has actually been learning from Ferenczi for close to one hundred years. Because his teachings, even if rarely cited at the time, were introduced so much earlier than many ever knew, they were absorbed into the mainstream psychodynamic core of clinical social work.

Ferenczi's earliest influence on American social workers

Social workers studying and practicing during the early decades of the twentieth century were exposed to Ferenczi's teachings in numerous ways. As previously mentioned, some of the psychoanalyst émigrés teaching at the child guidance clinics would have been directly or indirectly impacted by his work before coming to the United States. And some, like Caroline Newton and Grace Potter, both of whom were analysed in Vienna before returning to the United States, studied with Ferenczi, who mentions them in his correspondence with Freud (Fer/Fr, vol. 3, pp. 216, 268, 335). In addition to other contributions, Newton translated

Ferenczi's and Rank's (1925) book into English. Potter was one of the first female psychoanalysts to practice in New York City.

At the invitation of the New School for Social Research, Ferenczi taught a course in New York City and also received invitations to lecture in Washington, DC during an eight-month period between 1926 and 1927. During this visit, he supervised and treated a number of lay analysts, many of whom were, and/or worked closely with, social workers. As part of his stay and as detailed in his letter to Freud, Ferenczi gave a lecture to about one hundred psychiatric (clinical) social workers at Greenwich House, in New York City (Fer/Fr, vol. 3, p. 299). Although Ferenczi refers to his contact with lay analysts in New York numerous times, it is rare that he singles out social workers for specific mention. This letter therefore provides important documentation that Ferenczi taught (and, perhaps likely, supervised and treated) social workers during the formative years of clinical social work.

Esther and William Menaker, both social workers who studied at the Vienna Psychoanalytic Institute beginning in 1930, very likely didn't have direct contact with Ferenczi. But upon their return to New York City in 1935, they met Ferenczi's former patients and students Izette de Forrest and Clara Thompson. Along with de Forrest's niece Alice Lowell—also a former patient of Ferenczi's—the five formed a study group that exposed the Menakers to Ferenczi's work (Menaker, 1989). Some years later, Esther became interested in the work of Otto Rank, a close collaborator of Ferenczi's (Menaker, 1982). As part of her work at the Jewish Board of Guardians in the mid-1930s, and later as a faculty member at the National Psychological Association for Psychoanalysis—the first psychoanalytic institute to accept social workers—Esther and perhaps Bill would have likely taught Ferenczi's work to generations of social workers.

Rank (and Ferenczi) go to social work school

Prior to Rank's departure from Vienna and the rift that occurred in his friendship with Ferenczi, the two enjoyed a collaborative working relationship built upon their membership in Freud's Wednesday Society and a shared outlook on psychoanalytic theory and technique (Grosskurth, 1991). Rank and Ferenczi collaborated on their pioneering book, *The Development of Psychoanalysis* (1925), in the years just before Rank's break with Freud and Ferenczi. Following his professional break with Freud in 1926, Rank moved abroad and began teaching at the New York School of Social Work and at numerous social work and lay psychoanalytic organisations. Beginning in 1927, at the invitation of his former patient Jessie Taft and her life partner Virginia Robinson (founders of functional casework), Rank began to teach at the Pennsylvania School of Social Work. Over the course of more than a decade, Rank lectured to, supervised, and treated numerous social workers (Taft, 1958).

As a result of their early, close professional connection, one might expect that Rank's lectures would be coloured by Ferenczi's theoretical approaches as well. But I could find no mention of specific course content in the literature to either support or refute this assumption aside from course titles and brief descriptions (Taft, 1958), although Rank discusses Ferenczi's work in several English-language publications that social workers would likely have had access to (Rank, 1921, 1926, 1927, 1929). Fortunately, Rank's lecture notes are available for examination in the archives at Columbia University, and they tell a fascinating story (Personal Collection of Otto Rank, Otto Rank Association Records, Rare Book and Manuscript Library, Columbia University).

Rank lectured to his social work students on a number of topics written in conjunction with Ferenczi and/or addressed by Ferenczi in his own writing. Among others, these included the active technique—including the importance of re-experiencing affects connected with original trauma, the importance of working in the here and now, and the need for social workers to be more active than passive in their technique. As did Ferenczi, Rank emphasises the importance of feeling rather than merely intellectually knowing things, and discusses with his students the importance of offering the option of short-term therapy. Here is just a brief excerpt from Rank's notes for a lecture offered to his students in 1934, "The therapeutic application of psychoanalysis" as part of a larger course, "The practical bearing of psychoanalysis":

> This is not possible by merely communicating to the patient analytic knowledge. Therefore, an emotional re-experience is necessary. The analyst can only bring about a radical cure by first rousing the repressed conflicts before he can solve them … one cannot do without a certain amount of active intervention. (1934)

Very curiously, while this and numerous other lecture notes offer an example of Rank teaching his social work students Ferenczian theory, I could find no mention of Ferenczi by name in any of Rank's notes, save for two footnotes—one on Ferenczi's understanding of tics and one that describes Ferenczi unconsciously enacting the role of a patient's mother, thereby, according to Rank, restricting rather than freeing the patient from desiring the mother. Perhaps the paucity of explicit mention of Ferenczi in Rank's archived lectures after 1926 can be attributed to the chilling of Rank's relationship with his former collaborator and friend. Still, even these scant mentions of Ferenczi by name and certainly the teaching of his theories provide new and important evidence of yet another way in which Ferenczi's work reached clinical social workers in the early days of that profession.

Final thoughts on Ferenczi and social work

As previously mentioned, in recent decades clinical social work has been largely rejecting of psychoanalysis, even if it is still very much influenced by it. Short of these theoretical/financial sea-changes, the profession's problem has been with classical psychoanalysis's propensity to pathologise, blame the victim, and reduce complex biopsychosocial problems to intrapsychic dynamics. Additionally, the classical tendency—despite progress made by contemporary Freudians—to adhere to older notions of femininity, gender and sexual identity, and to exclude larger systemic factors in understanding psychological and social problems, has been a reason that many social workers have turned away from Freud. Now that Ferenczi's writings are available and his reputation restored, identifying his teachings on the importance of intrapsychic dynamics as well as social problems and the client-clinician relationship is a way that clinical social work can begin to more consciously and comfortably reclaim some of the psychoanalytic lessons it once declaratively valued.

Ferenczi on education

It is challenging to delineate the exact nature of Ferenczi's impact on education. His writing about the subject, and his influence within the field of education, while significant, pales in comparison to his influence on social work. We do know that Ferenczi addressed the subject of education to a group of pediatricians during a 1927 lecture in Britain. We also know that he was curious about how schools impacted the healthy development of their students and that his interest in education extended to and overlapped with his interest in parenting.

The two papers that tackle education most explicitly were written at different points in Ferenczi's career: "Psycho-analysis and education," first published in 1908; and his lecture

"The adaptation of the family to the child," delivered before a meeting of the British Psychiatric Society in 1927. Though written nearly twenty years apart, these two essays strike a consistent tone regarding Ferenczi's perspective on the value psychoanalysis had to offer education, and they also address his theories on healthy parenting and child development.

The crux of Ferenczi's perspective on what underlies a healthy education for a growing child relates directly to the psychological capacity and sensitivity of the child's parents. He argues that in order for parents to be sufficiently adapted to the introduction of a child into their lives, they must "first of all *understand themselves*" (Adapt, p. 62), a state of being that Ferenczi suggests can only be achieved when the parents both remember and understand their own childhoods. In his 1908 paper, Ferenczi explains that his thinking on this critical point was inspired by the writings of Adalbert Czerny, the Austrian physician broadly considered to be the co-founder of modern pediatrics. Ferenczi describes how Czerny criticised parents for insufficiently or falsely remembering their own childhoods, claiming that such a lack of memory prevented parents from parenting properly. Ferenczi argues that this "infantile amnesia" underlies the limits of progress in education, describing a "vicious circle" in which unconscious processes lead parents to raise their children in damaging ways, and where "education, in its turn, piles up unconscious complexes in the children" (Edu, p. 283). The solution to breaking the circle begins with "the enlightenment of grownups" through the incorporation of the teachings of Freud—an intervention that would benefit not only the education of their children, he argues, but also provide a "cure for mankind suffering from unnecessary repressions" (ibid.).

The arguments that follow from Ferenczi's central point further elucidate his conviction that when it comes to education, it is best to avoid giving children additional "unconscious complexes". For the most part, Ferenczi's positions relate more directly to what we would now consider parenting practices rather than school-based education, although he touches upon that topic as well. In "Adaptation", Ferenczi cautions against overly harsh training for children in cleanliness and toilet training, urging parents to be attuned to the feelings of the child and aware of the difficulties inherent in "training". In "Psycho-analysis and education", he discourages swaddling of newborns, arguing that children should be able to freely move about. Referencing Czerny again, he encourages "feeding at healthily proper intervals" (Edu, p. 284) and also breastfeeding, which he argues is a means through which a mother and child develop their emotional bond.

Ferenczi's direct commentary on education as practiced in a school setting is limited, but nonetheless consistent with the psychoanalytically informed positions he advocates in parenting. In "Adaptation", he cautions against co-education, arguing it could be dangerous for children because it would force them to repress passionate affects in ways that could lead to the development of neurotic symptoms. He also urged educators needing to punish their students to resist the strong temptation to retaliate in doing so. Then he makes reference to his visit to the Walden School (1914–1988), a progressive private school in Manhattan that integrated psychoanalytic principles into its pedagogical practice. At Walden, students called their teachers by their first names, competition was discouraged, and students were given great flexibility. What struck Ferenczi the most about the school was its approach to engaging parents, given that they emphasised the importance of parents understanding their children in order to help facilitate healthy development.

Looking forwards from his position in the early twentieth century, Ferenczi's primary hope for the future of education—and by extension, parenting practices—was that children would be educated and raised in ways that would minimise the dangers of "unnecessary repression" (Edu, p. 282) and that social institutions would be reformed accordingly. Parents and educators were equally responsible for a child's adequate development. Ferenczi felt that such a reformation would be critical to supporting the future health of civilisation.

Conclusion

Ferenczi left behind a powerful legacy even though, tragically, for much of the twentieth century his influence was underappreciated—or even unknown. His contributions to both early and contemporary clinical social work are palpable, even if rarely cited. In de-emphasising individual pathology to also focus on the role that family, societal factors, and larger environmental issues play in human suffering, Ferenczi presented ideas very much in line with social work's ongoing emphasis on person-in-environment and strengths-based perspectives. His instinct was to challenge a hierarchical power structure in favour of allowing patients and therapists as well as parents and children room to be themselves while being mindful of each other. This was in contrast to the stance of classical psychoanalysis, and is one, I would argue, that not only influenced social work and education but also numerous other disciplines and perspectives.

Note

1 Portions of this chapter were published previously in "From ghost to ancestor: Sándor Ferenczi's impact on clinical social work" in *The American Journal of Psychoanalysis,* June 2017, vol. 77, issue 2, pp. 146–162, and are reprinted here with the kind permission of the editor.

References

Afuape, T., & Hughes, G. (2015). *Liberation Practices: Towards Emotional Wellbeing Through Dialogue*. New York: Routledge.

Aiello, T. (1998). The influence of the psychoanalytic community of émigrés (1930–1950) on clinical social work with children. *Child and Adolescent Social Work Journal, 15*: 151–166.

Bodenheimer, D. (2010). Sándor Ferenczi: A life lived dyadically. *Psychoanalytic Social Work, 17*: 17–29.

Borden, W. (2000). The relational paradigm in contemporary psychoanalysis: toward a psychodynamically informed social work perspective. *Social Service Review, 74*: 352–379.

Danto, E. A. (2008). Same words, different meanings: notes toward a typology of postmodern social work education. *Social Work Education, 27*: 710–722.

Ferenczi, S., & Rank, O. (1925). *The Development of Psycho-Analysis* (C. Newton, Trans.). Eastford, CT: Martino Fine Books, 2012.

Gentile, J. (2016). *Feminine Law: Freud, Free Speech, and the Voice of Desire.* London: Karnac.

Goldstein, E. G. (2002a). *Object Relations Theory and Self Psychology in Social Work Practice.* New York: Free Press.

Goldstein, E. G. (2002b). Psychoanalysis and social work: Historical perspectives. *Psychoanalytic Social Work, 9*: 33–40.

Goldstein, E. G., Miehls, D., & Ringel, S. (2009). *Advanced Clinical Social Work Practice: Relational Principles and Techniques.* New York: Columbia University Press.

Grosskurth, P. (1991). *The Secret Ring: Freud's Inner Circle and the Politics of Psychoanalysis*. New York: Addison-Wesley.

Harris, A. (2010). Ferenczi's work on war neuroses. In: A. Harris & S. Kuchuck (Eds.), *The Legacy of Sándor Ferenczi* (pp. 127–133). London: Routledge.

Harris, A. E. (2011). The relational tradition: Landscape and canon. *Journal of the American Psychoanalytic Association, 59:* 701–735.

Horowitz, J. (1998). Contemporary psychoanalysis and social work theory. *Clinical Social Work Journal, 26*: 369–383.

Kanter, J. (2013). Helping, healing and interpreting: Sullivan, the Interpersonal School and clinical social work. *Journal of Social Work Practice, 27*: 273–287.

Kuchuck, S. (2012). Please (don't) want me: The therapeutic action of male sexual desire in the treatment of heterosexual men. *Contemporary Psychoanalysis, 48:* 544–562.

Kuchuck, S. (2013). Reflections on the therapeutic action of desire. *Studies in Gender and Sexuality, 14:* 133–139.

Kuchuck, S. (2015). On the therapeutic action of love and desire. In: A. Harris & S. Kuchuck (Eds.), *The Legacy of Sándor Ferenczi* (pp. 223–234). London: Routledge.

Menaker, E. (1982). *Otto Rank: A Rediscovered Legacy.* New York: Columbia University Press.

Menaker, E. (1989). *Appointment in Vienna: An American Psychoanalyst Recalls her Student Days in Pre-war Austria.* New York: St. Martin's Press.

Rachman, A. W. (2007). Sándor Ferenczi's contributions to the evolution of psychoanalysis. *Psychoanalytic Psychology, 24*: 74–96.

Rachman, A. W. (2010). The origins of a relational perspective in the ideas of Sándor Ferenczi and the Budapest School of psychoanalysis. *Psychoanalytic Perspectives, 7:* 43–60.

Raines, J. C. (1996). Self-disclosure in clinical social work. *Clinical Social Work Journal, 24*: 357–375.

Rank, O. (1921). Dream interpretation. *International Journal of Psychoanalysis, 2*: 106–110.

Rank, O. (1926). The genesis of genitality. *Psychoanalytic Review, 13:* 129–144.

Rank, O. (1927). Psychoanalytic problems. *Psychoanalytic Review, 14:* 1–19.

Rank, O. (1929). Beyond psychoanalysis. *Psychoanalytic Review, 16:* 1–11.

Rank, O. (1934). *The Therapeutic Action of Psychoanalysis.* Personal Collection of Otto Rank. Otto Rank Association Records. Rare Book and Manuscript Library. Columbia University, New York, NY.

Seinfeld, J. (1990). *The Bad Object.* Northvale, NJ: Jason Aronson.

Seinfeld, J. (1993). *Interpreting and Holding: The Paternal and Maternal Functions of the Psychotherapist.* Northvale, NJ: Jason Aronson.

Seinfeld, J. (1996). *Containing Terror, Rage & Despair: An Object Relations Approach to Psychotherapy.* Northvale, NJ: Jason Aronson.

Seinfeld, J. (2003). *A Primer on the Negative Therapeutic Reaction.* Northvale, NJ: Jason Aronson.

Siegel, J. (1995). *Repairing Intimacy: An Object Relations Approach to Couples Therapy.* Northvale, NJ: Jason Aronson.

Siegel, J. (1997). Applying countertransference theory to couples treatment. In: M. F. Solomon & J. P. Siegel (Eds.), *Countertransference in Couples Therapy* (pp. 3–22). New York: W. W. Norton.

Strean, H. S. (1977). A note on the treatment of the schizophrenic patient. *Psychoanalytic Review, 64:* 203–2010.

Strean, H. S. (1993). *Jokes: Their Purpose and Meaning.* Northvale, NJ: Jason Aronson.

Strean, H. S. (1994). *Psychotherapy with the Orthodox Jew.* Northvale, NJ: Jason Aronson.

Strean, H. S. (1998). *When Nothing Else Works: Innovative Interventions with Intractable Individuals.* Northvale, NJ: Jason Aronson.

Taft, J. (1958). *Otto Rank: A Biographical Study Based on Notebooks, Letters, Collected Writings, Therapeutic Achievements and Personal Associations.* New York: Julian Press.

Tannenbaum, N., & Reisch, M. (2001). From charitable volunteers to architects of social welfare: A brief history of social work. *Ongoing Magazine*, Fall 2001.

Tosone, C. (1997). Sándor Ferenczi: Forerunner of modern short-term psychotherapy. *Psychoanalytic Social Work, 4:* 23–41.

Tosone, C. (2004). Relational social work: Honoring the tradition. *Smith College Studies in Social Work, 74*: 475–487.

Tosone, C. (2011). The legacy of September 11: Shared trauma, therapeutic intimacy, and professional posttraumatic growth. *Traumatology, 17*: 25–29.

Tosone, C. (2013). On being a relational practitioner in an evidence-based world. *Journal of Social Work Practice, 27*: 249–257.

Vida, J. E. (2002). The role of love in the therapeutic action of psychoanalysis. *American Imago, 59:* 435–445.

Woodroofe, K. (1971). *From Charity to Social Work in England and the United States.* Toronto: University of Toronto Press.

Chapter 40

Gender, sexuality, and the maternal

Josette Garon

> "Let me ask you to picture the surface of the earth as still entirely enveloped in water. All plant and animal life still pursues its existence in an environment of sea-water. Geologic and atmospheric conditions are such that portions of the ocean bed become raised above the surface of the water. The animals and plants thus set upon dry land must either succumb or else adapt themselves to a land and air existence … As soon as the fish was stranded upon dry land and became an amphibian, the male developed special callosities on the thumb for holding fast to the female, and later, after it had been transformed into a reptile, evolved specific male sex organs, thus making provision that the fertilized ova safely reached the uterus of the female, there to develop."
>
> (Ferenczi, 1924, pp. 99–101)

Sándor Ferenczi's work shed new light on female psychology, femininity, and the maternal. In 1924, he published *Thalassa*, titled after a mythological divinity personifying the ocean—the Oceanic Mother. He conceptualised the origin of the human species and the development of sexuality in relation to the geological "catastrophe" of the sea drying up and adaptation to life on land. His argument links ontogenetic and phylogenetic evolution (the first recapitulating the second) to pre-genital instincts and the origins of both sexual life and primal trauma. This integration of biology and psychoanalysis, or "bioanalysis," as Ferenczi (1924, p. 102) termed it, provided a new and different perspective on symbolic repetition, even as it occurs in the course of an analytic session.

Ferenczi's contributions in this area can be traced to his personal life, his relation to his own mother, his complicated relationship with Gizella and her daughter Elma, his equally complicated relation to Freud, and the analysis of his patients.

Freud privileged the father in his work. After his father's death, he wrote *The Interpretation of Dreams*, followed by *Totem and Taboo* (the murder of the father of the primal horde) and finally *Moses and the Monotheism*, in which Moses is assassinated by his own people. In *Totem and Taboo* Freud constructed his own myth concerning the prehistory of mankind: the murder of the father of the primal horde. *Totem and Taboo* ends dramatically with a line from *Faust*: "In the beginning was the Deed" (Goethe, *Faust*, Part I, Scene 3) (Freud, 1912–1913, p. 161).

We could say that for Ferenczi "in the beginning was the Oceanic Mother and the geologic catastrophe". The inspiration for *Thalassa* can be traced to Ferenczi's many exchanges with Freud after the publication of Freud's *Three Essays on the Theory of Sexuality,* which Ferenczi translated into Hungarian in 1914. In Ferenczi's introduction to *Thalassa* he relates the genesis of this work to the period 1914–1923, starting during the war when he was chief doctor at the military garrison in Pàpa in Hungary. In 1915 Freud was elaborating his own phylogenetic speculation, finalised in *Overview of the Transference Neuroses* (1915), and sent a detailed abstract to Ferenczi (Fr/Fer, 12 July 12 1915, pp. 65–66). On 29 April 1916, Freud expressed his enthusiasm for Ferenczi's project (Fr/Fer, pp. 126–127). In 1919 Ferenczi presented his own theory to Freud and a few friends and was encouraged to go ahead with the publication of his work.

We can also trace back the roots of *Thalassa* to Ferenczi's childhood. Sándor, apparently his father's favourite child, was fifteen years old when his father died. His mother Rosa, whom Ferenczi later described in a letter to Groddeck as hyperactive, overwhelmed, and "too harsh", was unable to assure the needed "basic trust". This was Ferenczi's own childhood catastrophe: an early infantile trauma caused by deficiency of the primal object, what Winnicott would later call "environmental failure". This experience would have a major influence on his definition of trauma, according the same importance to the external reality of the object, the primary mother-infant relationship, as to the internal reality of the subject in its evolution. In the face of trauma, the helplessness and unpreparedness of the child makes it impossible for him to modify the environment. He therefore transforms himself in an autoplastic way, an autoplastic narcissistic split, acquiring the precocious maturity of the "wise baby" (Martín Cabre, Chapter Eighteen).

In *Thalassa,* Ferenczi constructed a mythical *phantasia* of the prehistory of humanity. He conceptualised the origin of the human species and the development of sexuality in relation to the primordial "catastrophe" of the sea drying up and adaptation to life on land, forcing many living creatures to adapt to sexual life outside the oceanic womb. He abandoned the traditional idea of developmental stages in favour of the revolutionary concept of *amphimixis*, or concomitance of different pleasures. Ferenczi argues that "Freud's entire sexual theory is a purely psychoanalytic one, the biological evidence for its correctness must be supplied subsequently by the physiologists" (1924, p. 10). He therefore invokes the scientific term of *amphimixis* that refers to male and female gametes fusion as an illustration of his "biology of pleasure", to point specifically to the fusion of two and more eroticisms or partial instincts in a higher unity, the genitality. He considers genitality in both its dimensions, ontogenetic and phylogenetic, in relation to the pregenital instincts on the one hand and the primeval traumas on the other hand. With this symbolic coherence of the universe, he emphasises the idea that the purpose of the whole of evolution, and especially the sex act, is an attempt to return to the mother's womb, a universal trend of maternal regression: "this thalassal regressive trend does not cease its activity even after birth, but manifests itself in various expressions of eroticism (especially those of coitus)" (1924, p. 56).

Ferenczi's bioanalytic conception of genital processes gives form to the Oedipus wish for sexual intercourse with the mother, adding a biological dimension to Freud's Oedipus complex: "The œdipus wish is precisely the psychological expression of an extremely general biological tendency which lures the organism to return to the state of rest enjoyed before birth" (1924, p. 19).

His thinking is beautifully summed up in the chapter "Male and female, psychoanalytic reflections on the 'theory of genitality', and on secondary and tertiary sex differences", where Ferenczi says:

> Genitality itself is apparently a retrogression to the original striving and its gratification, which is now attained *hallucinatorily, symbolically* and *in reality,* all three simultaneously. In reality it is only the germ cells which participate afresh in the bliss of the

> prenatal state; the genital organ itself adumbrates this striving symbolically in the form of its activity; while the rest of the body shares in the happiness of intrauterine state only, as in the case of sleep, in the form of hallucination.
>
> (1924, pp. 98–99, original italics)

Bioanalysis combined with psychoanalysis allows Ferenczi an understanding of sexual differentiation. The male, says Ferenczi, projects himself outward with his erect penis. The woman, overcome by this, develops more complexity, a finer differentiation and a better adaptation to complex situations:

> The male has imposed his will upon the female, and in so doing has spared himself the task of adaptation; he has remained the more primitive. The female on the other hand knew how to adapt herself not only to the difficulties in the environment but to the brutality of the male.
>
> (1924, p. 104)

Ferenczi insists on the humiliating fiasco inherent to the Oedipus complex: the mischievous revolt of the son against the father, for the purpose of obtaining possession of the mother and of women, ended in a complete fiasco; none of the sons was strong enough, as the father once had been, to impose his will on the whole clan, and a bad conscience forced them to long to return to, and to re-establish, the authority of the father and respect for the mother (1924, p. 104).

Ferenczi adds that aggressivity, even attenuated by this humiliation, remains a characteristic of the male psyche. As for the woman, she is characterised by kindness and modesty with beauty as her only weapon! Further on, he develops his ideas concerning the psychological consequences of these differences in both sexes:

> Woman is innately wiser and better than man; as offset to this, man has to keep his brutality in check by a more marked development of the intelligence and of the moral superego. Woman is a creature of finer feelings (moral) and of finer sensibility (æsthetic), and has more "common sense"; but man created, perhaps as a measure of protection against his own greater primitiveness, the strict rules of logic, ethics and aesthetics which woman in her awareness of an inner trustworthiness in all such things makes light of or disregards.
>
> (1924, p. 105)

Ferenczi nevertheless grants that in some instances the intelligence of the woman exceeds by far that of the average man. He links the tendency of some women to choose "masculine" activities, which Freud called the "masculinity complex", to the prehistory of human kind, to the phase of evolutionary struggle around sexual differentiation.

Ferenczi's views on gender, sexuality, and maternality also have a bearing on his way of differentiating types of suggestion and hypnosis: they are maternal when tender, kind, and caring, masculine when marked by authoritarianism and intimidation (Ferenczi, 1909). This distinction also reflects his conception of the dynamics of analytic process and of the different types of transference and countertransference. He contrasts fright and authority, or father-hypnosis, with seduction and benevolence, or mother-hypnosis, as the two means of rendering the other person tractable.

Freud and many others have reproached Ferenczi for being too much of a tender mothering analyst. Ferenczi was well aware of the universal aspiration to be reunited with the primal oceanic mother, and the importance of allowing the patient to recover with the analyst something of the loving mother he longs for (Howell, Chapter Twenty-one). Indeed, Ferenczi's relaxation technique (Koritar, Chapter Twenty-two) is explicitly based on his pioneering recognition that maternal love is crucially important for the child's development. But he also addressed the need, for himself and his patients, to address the negative transference, not disavowing his own hatred, violence, death wishes, and role in repeating the patient's original catastrophe.

Ferenczi's paper "Introjection and transference" (1909) already foreshadowed and contained in gestation all the richness and also the whole of the paradox with which Ferenczi was grappling all his life, both in his relation with Freud and in his work with traumatised patients. In this fascinating paper, his remarks on maternal and/or paternal hypnosis prefigure his different technical approaches and will evolve into his wish to heal by mothering on the one hand and, on the other hand, his more and more acute awareness of the inevitable murder that does in the end help the patient. In his *Diary*, on 8 March 1932, he puts forward the cutting edge of psychoanalysis: "In case B, I have finally come to realize that it is an unavoidable task for the analyst: although he may behave as he will, he may take kindness and relaxation as far as he possibly can, the time will come when he will have to repeat with his own hands the act of murder previously perpetrated against the patient. In contrast to the original murder, however, he is not allowed to deny his guilt" (p. 52).

In a letter to Georg Groddeck, Ferenczi wrote about the harsh effects of paternal hypnosis, the severity and coerciveness he experienced at the hands of both his mother and Freud (Fer/Grod, 25 December 1921, pp. 7–15). In this letter he refers to the Palermo incident, when in September 1910 he went to Sicily with Freud in order to work together on the question of paranoia. He felt pushed away and humiliated by a severe father who only wanted to dictate to him, and he reacted strongly. Ferenczi had very openly tried to discuss Freud's treatment of him (Bonomi, Chapter Five). Requesting from Freud the same openness and sincere acknowledgment, and asking for maternal comprehension and mutuality, he addressed his own issues of passivity, homosexuality, and negative transference, but Freud was not willing to openly address their conflict and Ferenczi's needs were stonewalled.

Ferenczi nevertheless continued to explore the avenues of mutuality, openness, and sincerity to the very end of his life (Miller-Bottome & Safran, Chapter Thirty-three), for himself and for his patients; especially with the help of his female patients. He modified his technique from active technique to relaxation and mutuality. In his 2 October 1932 note in the *Diary*, talking about his patient Elizabeth Severn, he recorded that "she finds my constant 'probing' painful, unnecessary, a device for keeping (and for torturing) patients" (p. 214). He developed his ideas on the necessary combination of techniques in a note entitled "Antihomosexuality as a consequence of the masculine 'protest'", a note most certainly, although subtly, addressed to Freud:

> An analyst who has developed an aggressive disposition may play the role of the strong father admirably. Another, who participates in all the patients' emotions, is admirably fitted to be a surrogate mother. A real analyst should have the capacity to play all these

> roles equally well. Active therapy was paternal-sadistic, purely passive therapy was maternal. Relaxed, natural behaviour, without a preconceived plan, may elicit now the one and then the other characteristic. Only the principal condition remains: the sincere acknowledgment to oneself of actual feelings.
>
> (Diary, pp. 91–92)

Ferenczi often equates female and maternal characteristics such as understanding and forgiveness, for example, in a wife's desire to understand and soothe as opposed to masculine self-assertion, as illustrated in his *Diary* note, "Femininity as an expression of the pain-alleviating principle faced with a case of impotence":

> The capacity for such adaptation to renunciation is perhaps explicable only if we assume the existence in nature of a second principle next to that of egoistical self-assertion, namely an appeasement-principle; that is, selfishness (infantility, masculinity) versus motherliness, that is to say kindness.
>
> (Diary, p. 146)

In his *Diary* Ferenczi elaborated further on the ideas put forward in "Male and female", linking them with the reality principle and also with the masochism necessary to the life instinct:

> I came to the realization, following a conscious lead by the patient, that in the female organism or psyche a specific principle of nature is embodied, which, in contrast to the egoism and self-assertion of the male, could be interpreted as the maternal willingness to suffer and capacity for suffering. According to this the capacity for suffering would be an expression of femininity, even though suffering, endurance, and toleration appear to occur in every sphere of nature, that is, to seem completely independent of sexuality. … The drives for self-assertion and conciliation together constitute existence, that is life in the whole universe. … The singular consequence of the acceptance of the instinctual in the "wish to conciliate" leads directly to the assertion that, for the substance or being in which this drive is or becomes strong or exclusively dominant, suffering is not merely something that can be endured, but something desirable or a source of satisfaction.
>
> (Diary, pp. 41–42)

Ferenczi gives the example of the pleasures of motherhood, which encompass toleration of the development of a parasitic being at the expense of one's own body, a masochism in the service of the life instinct as opposed to the selfish principle or sadism. He concludes this note with another reference to Freud's principles: "The drive for self-assertion may be seen as the basis for Freud's pleasure principle, the drive for conciliation as the basis of his reality principle" (Diary, p. 42).

For Ferenczi, female homosexuality represents an alternative answer to the woman's longing for primal bliss (a nostalgia, as noted, that is shared by both sexes). He therefore concludes that female homosexuality is "normal":

> It has been too little noted that female homosexuality is in fact a very normal thing, just as normal as male heterosexuality. Both man and woman have in the beginning the same female love-object (the mother). For both sexes, deep-reaching analysis leads

> to conflicts and disillusionments with the mother. ... Society does not appear to judge female homosexuality so harshly either. The girl's relationship with her mother is much more important than that with her father. Indeed, even acts of sexual aggression in early infancy, coming from the male side, had a traumatic effect mainly because they dislocated the relationship with the mother.
>
> (Diary, pp. 78–79)

What immediately follows is also interesting in so far as it sheds a light on Ferenczi's view of feminine passivity:

> In accordance with the hypothesis of a very close connection between anatomy and psyche, it may be presumed that vaginal eroticism, in the inner vagina that has never been touched, arises in fact quite late, and with it an increased interest in passivity. (p. 79)

In a later note, titled "*Normalis feminine homosexualitas*", Ferenczi adds:

> "Men don't understand", women say, and are (even in analysis) very reticent about their homosexual feelings. "Men think women can only love the possessors of penises". In reality, they continue to long for a mother and female friend, with whom they can talk about their heterosexual experiences – *without jealousy*.
>
> (pp. 124–125)

On 24 March 1924, the same year as *Thalassa,* Ferenczi wrote to Freud (Fer/Fr, p.132) that there was no doubt that the Oedipus conflict remained the specific element responsible for the genesis of neuroses, but also adding that the culturally generated neuroses originally owe their traumatic power to the unconscious identity of the Oedipus conflict and the conflict between the nostalgia for the maternal body and the fear of the maternal body. In accordance with Ferenczi's "reverse symbolism", as he calls it, we could say: longing for an oceanic bliss and terrified by a traumatic catastrophe, Ferenczi forcefully embodied with his patients the clinical implications of his views.

References

Ferenczi, S. (1909). Introjection and transference. In: *First Contributions to Psycho-Analysis* (pp. 35–93). London: Karnac.

Ferenczi, S. (1924). *Thalassa: A Theory of Genitality*. London: Karnac, 2005.

Freud, S. (1912–1913). *Totem and Taboo: Some Points of Agreement between the Mental Lives of Savages and Neurotics. S. E., 13*: 1–161.

Freud, S. (1915). *A Phylogenetic Fantasy: Overview of the Transference Neuroses.* Cambridge, MA: Harvard University Press, 1987.

Chapter 41

"Confusion of tongues" as a source of verifiable hypotheses

Aleksandar Dimitrijević

Much of the controversy related to Ferenczi's reputation in the world of psychoanalysis was connected to the accusations that he suffered from mental disorder in the final years of his life, so that his late papers were not only non-psychoanalytic, but also pointless products of a madman that do not deserve serious consideration by contemporary researchers (Bonomi, 1999).

I will test this assertion by reading "Confusion of tongues", Ferenczi's final paper and the best developed statement of his mature clinical thinking, with the aim of extracting from it several hypotheses that can be and indeed have been put to the test by empirical psychological research. From the rich material of this important paper, I have focused on Ferenczi's original ideas about development and formulated the following hypotheses:

1 Adults with mental disorders very frequently have histories of real childhood trauma;
2 Trauma can be one of the factors that leads to mental disorders;
3 Most attachment traumas are inflicted on children by adults with impaired emotional regulation;
4 Traumatised children show clear signs of paralysing fear, splitting, and fragmentation;
5a Children suffering the worst consequences of trauma have parents who cannot provide an empathic response;
5b Helpful parents understand themselves and their childhoods;
6 Helping professionals have significantly more traumatic childhood experiences than members of other professional groups.

In what follows, I will review the existing empirical evidence related to each of these hypotheses.

H1 – Adults with mental disorders very frequently have histories of real childhood trauma

In "Confusion of tongues" Ferenczi wrote that "trauma, especially the sexual trauma, as the pathogenic factor cannot be valued highly enough. Even children of very respectable, sincerely puritanical families, fall victim to real violence or rape much more often than one had dared to suppose" (Conf, p. 161). This idea alone was, probably, enough to lead to Freud's dismissal of the whole paper and even Ferenczi as a person and colleague. It was not, however, more familiar to mental health professionals of the day outside of psychoanalysis. Up to the 1980 edition, one of the internationally most widely used psychiatry textbooks, Kaplan's *Synopsis of Psychiatry*, relied on a 1955 study that claimed incest occurred in one out of a million American families (Ross, 1996, pp. 6–7).

Table 1 Percentage of different types of trauma in general population (adapted after Putnam et al., 2015)

	Women	*Men*	*Total*
Sample size	N=9367	N=7970	N=17337
Type of abuse			
Physical abuse	27	29.9	28.3
Sexual abuse	24.7	16	20.7
Emotional abuse	13.1	7.6	10.6

Recent epidemiological data reveal that the situation is completely different. Estimates for the whole of the US vary from approximately one million substantiated cases of child abuse and neglect each year (US Department of Health and Human Services, 2016), to 702,000 children (0.94% of the child population of 74,356,370) who were neglected or abused, 75% of whom were neglected, with 17% physically and 8.3% sexually abused, in 2014 (US Department of Health & Human Services, 2016, p. 22).

This is in accordance with findings relevant for Western Europe and Anglo-America that about 15% of children in non-clinical populations, and 82% of maltreated children (Lyons-Ruth & Jacobvitz, 1999, p. 526), are classified in the group of disorganised attachment based on systematic observation in laboratory settings (Van Ijzendoorn & Bakermans-Kranenburg, 1997, p. 136), and that this pattern is not only regularly connected to but is considered to be a consequence of attachment trauma (Solomon & George, 2011).

Over the last decade, many studies focused on adverse childhood experiences (ACE) were conducted in different countries. The reason was that it was found, first in children and then in adults as well, that the number of ACEs strongly correlated with various somatic diseases, especially if the number was above four. Not all ACEs, however, refer to gross traumatic experiences, some are about neglect or parental alcohol abuse, which are nowadays separated from trauma in the strict sense of the word, so that trauma is just a fraction of ACEs. Another limitation of the study is that most often students or adults are asked to remember their childhood, which is not the most reliable source of information. Despite this, one of these studies found the incidence of trauma to be above ten per cent. An ACEs study performed on a nationally representative sample of English adults (N=3,885) reported that the incidence was lower than in the US. Still, almost half of the participants (46.4%) had experienced at least one ACE, while 8.3% had suffered four or more. Expectedly, parameters of low life satisfaction and low mental well-being increased with the number of ACEs, and particularly with "growing up in a household affected by mental illness" and with "suffering sexual abuse" (Hughes et al., 2016).

H2 – Trauma can be one of the factors that leads to mental disorders

The underlying topic of the whole of "Confusion of tongues" is explicated in its first paragraph: "The exogenous origin of character formations and neuroses" (p. 156). There is ample reason to discuss this issue even today, because some psychoanalysts still hold that causes of mental disorders lie in largely endogenous inner fantasies and most psychiatrists look for them in brain anatomy or physiology and/or in behavioural genetics.

Table 2 Frequency of childhood trauma among adults with mental disorders (after Read et al., 2004)

	General Population	*Psychiatry Patients*
Physical abuse	3% of men/ 5% of women	30% of men/ 34–42% of women
Sexual molestation	3% of men/ 12% of women	18% of men/ 51% of women
Incest	7% of men/ 13–17% of women	62% of men/ 62% of women
Parental loss	No data	38% of patients with schizophrenia/ 17% of patients with bipolar affective disorder

Experimental studies that could discover causes are (still) ethically impossible to conduct, so I will review correlational studies that report on connections between trauma and mental disorder. Beforehand, it should be emphasised that research studies about this have repeatedly been published in highly respected journals like the *American Journal of Psychiatry*, the *British Journal of Psychiatry*, and *Schizophrenia Bulletin*, and all have reached the same conclusion. Likewise, it should be noted that despite longstanding doubts about their reliability, "patients' reports tend to be accurate when judged against the reports of siblings, are stable over long periods, are unaffected by current symptoms, and are therefore most likely valid" (Bentall et al., 2012).

Dealing with this issue, colleagues brought together by the *International Society for Psychological and Social Approaches to Psychosis* have reviewed more than forty research studies on trauma and psychosis published between 1984 and 2003. Clinical samples have ranged between seven and 321 subjects, and have included persons with schizophrenia, other psychoses, outpatient samples with at least 50% psychotic persons, child and adolescent inpatients. Based on data provided by authors, I have drawn a simple table to make the frequencies of trauma in the general population and among psychiatry patients easier to compare.

Methodologically more robust evidence comes from a meta-analysis that included 2048 patients from case studies, 41,803 patients followed into adulthood, and 35,546 patients from cross-section studies (all of these with corresponding control samples), which found that all types of studies showed significant correlations between childhood adversity and incidence of psychosis in adulthood (Varese et al., 2012). The risk for developing psychosis that came just from belonging to the population of traumatised was estimated at 33%.

Researchers have found various consequences of childhood trauma (Osofsky, 2011; Read et al., 2004, p. 223; Lieberman & Van Horn, 2011):

- greater likelihood of being given up for adoption by one's parents, child fatalities, developmental delays;
- poor attachment and socialisation, low self-esteem;
- distortions in sensory perception and meaning, constrictions in action, deficits in readiness to learn, attention, abstract reasoning, and executive function;
- HPA/cortisol dysregulation, smaller frontal lobe volume, asymmetry of left and right brain centres included in the cognitive processes of language production;
- more self-mutilation, higher symptom severity, more suicide attempts;
- earlier first psychiatric admissions;
- higher dosages of medication;
- longer and more frequent psychiatric hospitalisations and seclusions.

In another study, childhood rape was associated with later hallucinations, and being brought up in an institution with showing paranoid symptoms (Bentall et al., 2012).

Disorganised attachment among twelve-month-old infants, itself connected with or caused by traumatic experiences, is linked to various mental health-related phenomena, like controlling, pseudo-parental behaviour in preschool years, problems with adaptation to school, or aggressive behaviour in as many as 83% of seven-year-olds (Solomon & George, 1999, p. 294); a majority of these adolescents have problems like delinquency, addictions, and personality disorders, and about 80% of these adults will belong to the clinical population (Greenberg, 1999, p. 479); especially important here are dissociative phenomena and disorders.

The connection between the aforementioned ACEs and mental disorders was confirmed in many studies performed in various countries. So, for instance, in an American nationally representative sample of children investigated by child welfare authorities (N=912; still living in their homes), it turned out that 98.1% of them had at least one ACE and the average number of ACEs was 3.2. These scores were associated with poor early childhood mental health, chronic medical conditions, and problems with social development (Kerker et al., 2015). More than four ACEs were found in 58% of youths suffering from bipolar affective disorder type I and 57% of those suffering from catatonia, with around one in four exposed to severe abuse or neglect (Benarous et al., 2016), as well as in several types of mental disorders, like mood, anxiety, and substance abuse disorders (Putnam et al., 2013).

H3 – Most attachment traumas are inflicted on children by adults with impaired emotional regulation

Ferenczi proposed a very specific idea as to who were the adults that might traumatise children: "Play may assume erotic forms but remains, nevertheless, on the level of tenderness. It is not so, however, with pathological adults, especially if they have been disturbed in their balance and self-control by some misfortune or by the use of intoxicating drugs" (Conf, p. 161). What does research tell us about this?

It was already shown that disorganised attachment in children is caused by traumatic experiences. There is further evidence about the details of this connection. It was long known that parents' and children's attachment patterns correlate around .8, which is extremely high for correlations of psychological variables. One London-based study of ninety-six pregnant women showed that maternal attachment patterns correlated with children's—.75 when the babies were twelve months old, remaining high and significant ($p<.001$) even when they were five-years-old (Hesse, 1999, p. 407).

A meta-analysis with the sample of 854 parent-child dyads revealed the following correlations for individual corresponding patterns (Van Ijzendoorn & Bakermans-Kranenburg, 1997):

- Autonomous, secure $r = .47$
- Dismissing, avoidant $r = .45$
- Preoccupied, ambivalent $r = .42$
- Unresolved, disorganised $r = .53$

We see a great risk that disorganised attachment can develop in dyads with parent(s) who exhibit features of unresolved attachment: they were traumatised and could not overcome the problem; they cannot distance from their painful emotional experiences, differentiate past from the present; they have low scores on measures of reflective functioning; they frequently split off parts of their experiences, have low life-quality and have been diagnosed with addiction and/or personality disorders. It is their emotional turmoil that makes it impossible for them to be emotionally available to their growing children. On the one hand, we know that most disorganised children's parents are still suffering from an unresolved loss (Van Ijzendoorn & Bakermans-Kranenburg, 1997, p. 136) and that more than half of them have parents who had suffered significant loss(es) at least two years before the children's birth (Lyons-Ruth & Jacobvitz, 1999, pp. 528–529, p. 540). On the other hand, it was found that most mothers suffering from depression and schizophrenia, and about 80% of mothers with anxiety disorders, have insecurely attached children (Greenberg, 1999, p. 478).

H4 - Traumatised children show clear signs of paralysing fear, splitting, and fragmentation

One of the most admirable aspects of Ferenczi's late work is his capacity to imagine and describe the inner world of perpetrators and victims of trauma. In "Confusion of tongues" he writes that abused children "feel physically and morally helpless, their personalities are not sufficiently consolidated in order to be able to protest, even if only in thought, for the overpowering force and authority of the adult makes them dumb and can rob them of their senses. ... When the child recovers from such an attack, he feels enormously confused, in fact, split–innocent and culpable at the same time–and his confidence in the testimony of his own senses is broken" (p. 162).

Empirical evidence shows that trauma inhibits exploratory behaviour and heightens the need for attachment comfort. Especially if trauma occurs inside the attachment relationship, the traumatised child will defensively inhibit her capacity to mentalize, trying to avoid the insight that the parent, who is the source of security and comfort, may wish to hurt her (Fonagy et al., 1997, p. 253). In consequence of this, trauma will impede deeper procession of emotional experiences and interfere with the (further) development of mentalizing capacity, or can even destroy it (Fonagy et al., 2002). These children thus move toward parents, looking for comfort, and at the same time away from them in anguish, and are thus forced to create multiple models of caregivers and themselves (Liotti, 2004). This connection was confirmed in two longitudinal (infancy to late adolescence) studies (Lyons-Ruth, 2003; see also Fonagy & Bateman, 2008, pp. 140, 145), where it was noted that emotional unavailability might be a worse problem than traumatisation. To this I turn in the next section.

H5a – Children suffering the worst consequences of trauma have parents who cannot provide an empathic response

Ferenczi claimed that traumatised children additionally suffer from the lack of empathic understanding by other adults: "Usually the relation to a second adult—in the case quoted above, the mother—is not intimate enough for the child to find help there, timid attempts towards this end are refused by her as nonsensical" (Conf, p. 163). Not only was this confirmed in the field of attachment research, but its importance is emphasised even more strongly.

In frame-by-frame micro-analytic studies, it was found that if mothers react with smiling, surprise, withdrawal, or looking away to the signs of distress in their four-month-old infants this is predictive of later disorganised attachment; also, discrepancies between maternal facial and vocal emotional expressions are predictive of adult dissociation (Beebe et al., 2016).

Even closer to Ferenczi's clinical observations, we now know that mothers of securely attached children do not suffer from unintegrated trauma, but are not particularly helpful in extreme situations, while securely attached mothers who have experienced significant loss(es) were able to show the least frequency and intensity of frightening or frightful behaviour, and proved to be most helpful to their distressed or traumatised children (Coates, 1998). Because of this, a new etiological hypothesis was offered that claims mental disorders develop as a combination of: a) severe childhood trauma, and b) lack of a person who could provide the intersubjective foundation for mentalizing (Fonagy et al., 2002).[1] There is, however, a bright side to this as well.

H5b – Helpful parents understand themselves and their childhoods

Ferenczi devoted one paper solely to the topic of adaptation of the family to the newborn (Arfelli & Vigna-Taglianti, Chapter Thirty-four and Vamos, Chapter Thirty-eight), which should ideally be read together with his paper on unwelcome children (Avello, Chapter Seventeen). Specifically, Ferenczi believed that "lack of understanding of their own childhood proves to be the greatest hindrance to parents grasping the essential questions of education" (Adapt, p. 62). Ideas identical to his were put to the test over the last two decades.

Secure attachment in adults is defined precisely by the capacity to answer to the Adult Attachment Interview questions about childhood emotional experiences with coherent narratives and relative emotional distance. When, for instance, asked about childhood losses, these subjects are able to report details about actual events, and reflect on their emotional experience without being overwhelmed by these memories.

Research also explored how children's attachment can be improved. It turned out there was just one way. A meta-analysis of seventy studies with eighty-eight different interventions, including 7,636 parents and 1,503 children, found that there was a small but significant improvement only when programmes were focused on improving parental sensitivity (Bakermans-Kranenburg et al., 2003). No matter how much you might help children, this would not lead to improvements in children's attachment status if parents would not get help as well. But it was not just any type of help that would improve the situation: parents would have to become more focused on and accurate in observing and interpreting their children's nonverbally expressed wishes and needs.

H6 – Helping professionals have significantly more traumatic childhood experiences than other professionals

Ferenczi realised that traumatic experiences may induce in children what he called "terrorism of suffering": "The fear of the uninhibited, almost mad adult changes the child ... into a

1 It is impossible to trace possible lines of influence here. Although Peter Fonagy is fluent in Hungarian and his father, renowned linguist Ivan Fonagy, was analysed by an analyst from Ferenczi's circle, he quoted Ferenczi only infrequently and, to the best of my knowledge, has never assigned him a central position in the development of psychoanalysis.

psychiatrist and, in order to become one and to defend himself against dangers coming from people without self-control, he must know how to identify himself completely with them .... A mother complaining of her constant miseries can create a nurse for life out of her child, i.e. a real mother substitute, neglecting the true interests of the child" (Conf, p. 165).

My colleagues and I have compared about 500 psychology students from two university cities in Serbia with an equal number of their peers from the departments of philology, and natural and technical sciences (Dimitrijević et al., 2011). Using standardised questionnaires, we asked them to describe themselves in terms of attachment, empathy, and mentalization. For the purpose of this chapter I will simply mention that psychology students scored significantly higher on a measure of unresolved family traumatisation ($F(1.852) = 4.483$; $p = .035$); the result was particularly striking in the male subgroup.

This is just one piece of evidence adding support to the belief about "wounded healers", to use a Jungian archetypal image: helpers motivated to aid others by their own pain, having been shaped and oriented towards the profession by growing up with depressed mothers or ill siblings, so that containing the pain of the others becomes natural for them. Indeed, in one study no less than 75% of the interviewed psychotherapists told such autobiographical stories (after Rizq, 2009).

Conclusion

Although Ferenczi's late writings have at times been thought of as obscure and speculative, it appears that some of his key ideas are in fact very close to hypotheses that have been confirmed by contemporary empirical research. I have tried to illustrate this with several, mostly developmental, ideas from the "Confusion of tongues". It turned out that all Ferenczi's clinical insights and intuitions were completely sound and many were confirmed by studies that employed the best methodology currently available. Perhaps other parts of the paper, or many parts of the *Diary,* would turn out to be tougher challenges. Yet i believe that it would obviously be worthwhile to take up these challenges—psychoanalysts might learn to express their ideas in a more modest, communicable, and operationalised fashion and researchers might stop denying their psychoanalytic roots.

References

Bakermans-Kranenburg, M. J., van IJzendoorn, M. H., & Juffer, F. (2003). Less is more: Meta-analyses of sensitivity and attachment interventions in early childhood. *Psychological Bulletin, 129*: 195–215.

Beebe, B., Cohen, P., & Lachmann, F. (2016). *The Mother-Infant Interaction Picture Book.* New York: W.W. Norton.

Benarous, X., Mikita, N., Goodman, R., & Stringaris, A. (2016). Distinct relationships between social aptitude and dimensions of manic-like symptoms in youth. *European child & adolescent psychiatry, 25*: 831–842.

Bentall, R. P., Wickham, S., Shevlin, M., & Varese, F. (2012). Do specific early-life adversities lead to specific symptoms of psychosis? A study from the 2007 adult psychiatric morbidity survey. *Schizophrenia Bulletin, 38*: 734–740.

Bonomi, C. (1999). Flight into sanity: Jones's allegation of Ferenczi's mental deterioration reconsidered. *International Journal of Psychoanalysis, 80*: 507–542.

Coates, S. (1998). Having a mind of one's own and holding the other in mind: Commentary on paper by Peter Fonagy and Mary Target (1998). *Psychoanalytic Dialogues, 8*: 115–148.

Dimitrijević, A., Hanak, N., & Milojević, S. (2011). Psychological characteristics of future helping professionals: Empathy and attachment of psychology students. *Psihologija, 41*: 97–115. (In Serbian.)

Fonagy, P., & Bateman, A. (2008): Mentalization-based treatment of borderline personality disorder. In: E. L. Jurist, A. Slade & S. Bergner (Eds.), *Mind to Mind: Infant Research, Neuroscience, and Psychoanalysis* (pp. 139–166). New York: Other Press.

Fonagy, P., Gergely, G., Jurist, E. L., & Target, M. (2002). *Affect Regulation, Mentalization and the Development of the Self.* London: Karnac.

Fonagy, P., Target, M., Steele, M., Steele, H., Leigh, T., Levinson, A., & Kennedy, R. (1997). Morality, disruptive behavior, borderline personality disorder, crime, and their relationship to security of attachment. In: L. Atkinson & K. J. Zucker (Eds.), *Attachment and Psychopatology* (pp. 223–274). New York: Guilford.

Greenberg, M. T. (1999). Attachment and psychopathology in childhood. In: J. Cassidy & P. R. Shaver (Eds.), *Handbook of Attachment: Theory, Research and Clinical Applications* (pp. 469–496). New York: Guilford.

Hesse, E. (1999). Adult attachment interview: Historical and current perspectives. In: J. Cassidy, & P. R. Shaver (Eds.), *Handbook of Attachment: Theory, Research and Clinical Applications* (pp. 395–433). New York: Guilford.

Hughes, K., Lowey, H., Quigg, Z., & Bellis, M. A. (2016). Relationships between adverse childhood experiences and adult mental well-being: Results from an English national household survey. *BMCP Public Health, 16*: 222–233.

Kerker, B. D., Zhang, J., Nadeem, E., Stein, R. E., Hurlburt, M. S., Heneghan, A., Landwerk, J., & Horwitz, S. M. (2015). Adverse childhood experiences and mental health, chronic medical conditions, and development in young children. *Academic Pediatrics, 15*: 510–517.

Lieberman, A. F., & Van Horn, P. (2011). *Psychotherapy with Infants and Young Children: Repairing the Effects of Stress and Trauma on Early Attachment.* New York: Guilford.

Liotti, G. (2004). Trauma, dissociation, and disorganized attachment: Three strands of a single braid. *Psychotherapy: Theory, Research, Practice, Training, 41*: 472.

Lyons-Ruth, K. (2003). Dissociation and the parent–infant dialogue: A longitudinal perspective from attachment research. *Journal of the American Psychoanalytic Association, 51*: 883–911.

Lyons-Ruth, K., & Jacobvitz, D. (1999). Attachment disorganization: Unresolved loss, relational violence, and lapses in behavioral and attentional strategies. In: J. Cassidy & P. R. Shaver (Eds.), *Handbook of Attachment: Theory, Research and Clinical Applications* (pp. 520–554). New York: Guilford.

Osofsky, J. D. (Ed.) (2011). *Clinical Work with Traumatized Young Children.* New York: Guilford.

Putnam, K. T., Harris, W. W., & Putnam, F. W. (2013). Synergistic childhood adversities and complex adult psychopathology. *Journal of Traumatic Stress, 26*: 435–442.

Putnam, K. T., Harris, W. W., Putnam, F. W., Lieberman, A., & Amaya-Jackson, L. (2015). Opportunities to change the outcomes of traumatized children. Downloaded from CANarratives.org

Read, J., Mosher, L. R., & Bentall, R. P. (Eds.) (2004). *Models of Madness: Psychological, Social and Biological Approaches to Schizophrenia.* London: Routledge.

Rizq, R. (2009). Teaching and transformation: A psychoanalytic perspective on psychotherapeutic training. *British Journal of Psychotherapy, 25*: 363–380.

Ross, C. A. (1996). History, phenomenology, and epidemiology of dissociation. In: L. K. Michelson & W. J. Ray (Eds.), *Handbook of Dissociation. Theoretical, Empirical, and Clinical Perspectives* (pp. 3–24). New York: Plenum.

Solomon, J., & George, C. (1999). The measurement of attachment security in infancy. In: J. Cassidy & P. R. Shaver (Eds.), *Handbook of Attachment: Theory, Research and Clinical Applications* (pp. 287–316). New York: Guilford.

Solomon, J., & George, C. (Eds.) (2011). *Disorganized Attachment and Caregiving.* New York: Guilford.

US Department of Health & Human Services. (2016). *Child Maltreatment 2014.* Downloaded from: www.acf.hhs.gov/programs/cb/research-data-technology/statistics-research/child-maltreatment.

Van Ijzendoorn, M. H., & Bakermans-Kranenburg, M. J. (1997). Intergenerational transmission of attachment: A move to the contextual level. In: L. Atkinson & K. J. Zucker (Eds.), *Attachment and Psychopathology* (pp. 135–170). New York: Guilford.

Varese, F., Smeets, F., Drukker, M., Lieverse, R., Lataster, T., Viechtbauer, W., Read, J., van Os, J., & Bentall, R. P. (2012). Childhood adversities increase the risk of psychosis: A meta-analysis of patient-control, prospective and cross-sectional cohort studies. *Schizophrenia Bulletin, 38*: 661–671.

Epilogue

Closing Thoughts

André E. Haynal

Psychoanalysis, as it occurs in practice and in accompanying reflections, represents an original perspective for seeing human beings: a synthesis of psychological, biological, literary, and philosophical insights. Emerging from nineteenth-century concepts, today it endeavours to speak to the anxieties, worry, disillusionment, and hopelessness of contemporary post-modernity. This work of renewal was powerfully influenced, almost from the beginning, by a great figure: Sándor Ferenczi, a foundational inspiration of contemporary psychoanalysis.

As we saw at the beginning of this book, Ferenczi, before his arrival on the psychoanalytic scene, was part of a large family in Miskolc (Kapusi), a small town in northeast Hungary, close to the Tokaj vineyards. His parents' famous bookshop,[1] and later their printing company, along with their cultural agitation, very much impressed and inspired the child Ferenczi. The problems of his childhood, such as his difficult relationship with his mother, left their mark on Sándor's psychic evolution, notably through his later relationships with women, perhaps most especially with Gizella and Elma, in the "fateful quadrangle" that included Freud (Berman).

The following stage of his life takes us to bustling, exuberant, international Budapest, and its cultural explosion (Keve); to his epistolary communication with colleagues, particularly Freud (Falzeder); and to his active presence in the local media. While Freud's attitude to the press can be characterised by rejection and distance, Ferenczi was, unlike Freud, part of public life, being active in the popular press and giving interviews concerning many different topics (Friedrich). He had a vital role in the founding of the International Psychoanalytical Association and the Hungarian Psychoanalytical Society, despite complicated circumstances (Harmatta).

In a farsighted speech in 1911, Ferenczi proposed the establishment of a scientific organisation in order to foster the exchange of psychoanalytic ideas (Harmatta) and legitimise psychoanalysis as a science and a profession. With this, Ferenczi's immersion in the psychoanalytic movement acquired a new dimension. And later, Ferenczi was initiated into psychoanalysis in yet a new way, by three brief but concentrated installments of personal analysis with Freud, at a level of exceptional intensity even in today's norms, that is, a total of 131 hours, two sessions a day; this analysis would as much influence his future relationship with his master as it would his own private life (Berman). While Ferenczi's love for Freud, and his craving to be loved by him, were manifest even earlier, with Groddeck's help,

1 "The widowed Mrs. Ferenczi re-built the bookshop's display, lived through the First World War, the Soviet Republic, and [the] Trianon [peace treaty]. Her mental freshness hardly withered" (Kapusi).

in the 1920s and into the 1930s, Ferenczi reflected on the conflictual character of his relationship with Sigmund and the negative feelings and fantasies that Ferenczi could not broach in his own psychoanalysis, though Freud later defended himself from Ferenczi's reproach about this (Bonomi; Breger; Fortune). It was not only Ferenczi's own analysis, however, but mainly those of his patients that inspired his later experiments in technique and theoretical discoveries (Brennan). Unfortunately, a deteriorating, conflict-laden period in his relationship with Freud followed, coinciding with his own declining health (Hoffer).

In addition to these events, we see the influence of his relationships with the people he met over the course of his professional engagement, whether in the United States, Budapest, or elsewhere, and including those faithful ones who would surround him until his death (Bentinck van Schoonheten; Fortune; Moreau Ricaud).

Sometimes preceding Freud in his ingenuity (Cassullo), sometimes not even daring to assert himself when face-to-face with him (Breger), Sándor also profited from his contacts with other colleagues, despite the difficulties these relationships sometimes presented (Bentinck van Schoonheten). Great creative stimulation was gained from Otto Rank and Georg Groddeck (Fortune), allowing Ferenczi to crystallise critical points of what would become his legacy in his practice.

With this background laid out, we are better able to grasp the development of Ferenczi's ideas. "The extraordinary freshness of his themes for psychoanalysis itself is unparalleled in our field" (Borgogno).

The complexity of his *Clinical Diary* (Dupont & Brabant) imparts a scrupulously faithful image of his analytic work, a reflection of absolute sincerity that allows us to discern every essential detail. If, in the Freud-Ferenczi correspondence the protagonists pour out their hearts, in his *Diary*, Ferenczi reveals the most secret, fine, delicate, and delicious of his ideas. A document of great importance, comparable to that correspondence, it is a kind of message about what he saw as the central issue of psychopathology: trauma. Along with Rank, he recognised the importance of *reliving* the traumatic experiences on an emotional, rather than an intellectual, level, a true paradigm shift (Mészáros).

In this *Diary*, his patients, out of discretion, are rendered anonymous by abbreviations. Thanks to Brennan, Ferenczi's patients have since been identified, including those mentioned in the *Diary*. Among his patients were Ernest Jones, Melanie Klein, Michael and Alice Balint, Clara Thompson, John Rickman, David Eder, Elizabeth Severn, and Izette de Forest.

The early study of war neuroses (Hamburger) helped Ferenczi discover the defences involved in post-traumatic developments, which, in his later formulations, ranged from splitting, dissociation, fragmentation, denial, and projection (Bokanowski) to the most important piece of this defensive maneuver: the identification with the aggressor and its tragic consequence of enslavement (Frankel). The later-named dissociative identity disorder had already begun to cast its shadow on the work he inspired in later generations (Howell). At this point, we can follow Ferenczi's experimental approach to research, trying out different attitudes of the analyst and their respective influences on the course of the psychoanalytic cure (Koritar).

Ferenczi's (still) radical understanding of psychoanalysis as a "dialogue of unconsciouses", rather than a unidirectional solitary process in which one unconscious (the analyst's) "reads" and "interprets" the unconscious of another (the analysand), reminds us that each analysis carries the potential for deepening self-awareness and for working through new realms of psychic experience for *both* participants (Bass). We are also reminded that Ferenczi was the first to posit that the analytic relationship, in and of itself, can have mutative properties, and that the patient's sensitivity to the analyst's participation shows that there is no cause for an analyst-analysand hierarchy (Hirsch).

The concept of the "unwelcome child" allows us to reconsider the problem of the death instinct (Jiménez Avello). The potential for resilience appears with the image of the "wise baby", pointing to the survival value of narcissistic splitting, as a part of the self develops a protective capacity (Martín Cabré), even as the person's emotional life pays a heavy price. The Ferenczian-Severnian Orpha and Winnicott's later False Self take shape already.

These new perspectives on the subject of mutuality and the significance of trauma (Mészáros; Jiménez Avello), as well as the experiments for improving the analyst's clinical effectiveness, would mark a transformation from a "one-body psychoanalysis" approach to a relational process (Miller-Bottome & Safran; Prince).

It is here that we might mention Ferenczi's successors, that is, those in whose work and approach we hear echoes of Ferenczi himself. They were numerous and took remarkably different paths. Some of them, the most radical innovators, would even remove any reference to parts of Freud's texts and concepts (for example, drives); others, however, tried to preserve Freud's legacy *in toto*. It is interesting to note that a great portion of the influential British leaders, like Jones, Klein, Balint, and Rickman, among others, had been in direct contact with Ferenczi (Moreau Ricaud; Clarke). His student Michael Balint likewise influenced French psychoanalysis, Lacan especially (Lugrin), and also Laplanche (Storck) in his contributions to language-related approaches and seduction theories.

Ferenczi thus stands not only as a radical innovator, but as a restorer, an analyst who tried to re-establish the balance between the original ideas in psychoanalytic practice and theory. His essential ideas exerted a tremendous influence, sometimes not explicitly stated as such, on contemporary psychoanalytic traditions. The studies in this book may bring a nuanced observation about the multiplicity of Ferenczi's influence.

Contemporary psychoanalysis is organised into different groups in which Ferenczi's legacy is more or less apparent. His complex influence can be felt inside different organisational structures of the American Psychoanalytic Association (APsaA) and the IPA (for example, Kohut, presumably due to his links with the British) as well as outside of them. Many groups outside APsaA, including a significant portion of interpersonal and relational psychoanalysts (Prince; Miller-Bottome & Safran), the former of whom had great influence at Chestnut Lodge (Silver), are organised in an independent manner. Perhaps Ferenczi's independent spirit influenced this kind of evolution. The notable differences between these groups may reflect different aspects of Ferenczi's legacy. Perhaps the independence of these groups exhibits the influence of Ferenczi's ideas: in order to avoid fighting within a large organisation, which might be rigidified by power-hungry hierarchies that would threaten their members' freedom, interpersonal and relational psychoanalysts opted sometimes to develop into separate schools of closely aligned followers. Nevertheless, they are not necessarily cohesive groups. Sándor himself suffered enough from similar oppressive phenomena, even within the organisation (IPA) of which he was founder and for a time president (and then forgotten: even his name temporarily disappeared from the roster). Let us remember that, in a quasi-symbolic final act, Jones prevented the translation of Ferenczi's last great testimonial manifesto, which remained inaccessible in English for nearly two decades, even as this "grand finale" summarised the key points of his final considerations. The restoration of compassion and generosity, as well as the hermeneutics of trust (Orange), had thus to wait for several years before returning to the psychoanalytic scene.

Ferenczi's impact on the two traditions of child psychoanalysis—those of Anna Freud and Melanie Klein (Arfelli & Vigna-Taglianti)—is important, as Ferenczi was, in some way, the main inspiration of this kind of work. Over Melanie Klein, to whom Ferenczi provided a long analysis in Budapest in the 1910s, he had without a doubt a particular influence, notable in her use of the mechanisms of intro- and pro-jection and other relational defence mechanisms, and in her views on early transference and on the conditions of the birth and development of the superego (Minuchin).

Concerning the political trends of his time, Ferenczi believed that they represented an expression of the human psyche, and therefore that psychoanalysis could play a role in facilitating a collective metamorphosis through an analytically inspired scientific study (Salgó). Ferenczi's ideas can even shed light on present-day political problems, as I show in my book on *Fanaticism* (Haynal et al., 1983) and my recent autobiography (Haynal, 2017). Ferenczi's views imply close relationships between individual traumata and the external social reality in a given society. It was, in fact, war experiences and the problems of the traumatic neuroses caused by war and other upheavals that drove psychoanalysis beyond the pleasure principle. His recently discovered manuscripts from 1920 confirm for us his positive views on liberal socialism in the framework of a new "mass psychology" (Erős).

We owe to Ferenczi the understanding of trauma as a series of real-world events impacting the psyche of the subject, in contrast to a view of trauma as rooted mostly in the fantasy dimension. His concept of "identification with the aggressor" implies taking in not only the aggressiveness of the perpetrator (a fundamental tool in the repetition of violence), but also a split-off sense of guilt towards the aggressor (Mucci).

In scrutinising Ferenczi's influence over other types of professional activities, let us remember the importance of assisting, when necessary, young parents' efforts to adapt to their new situation (Vamos). For social workers, Ferenczi's active and relaxation techniques, his emphasis on empathy, relatedness, and other clinical approaches have proven particularly useful (Kuchuck) and, in any case, more so than sticking to strict neutrality. As one of the earliest advocates (with Alexander) of shorter-term psychoanalytic treatment via his active technique and, later, followed in this by Balint, Ferenczi's impact on short-term social intervention should also be remembered. As early as 1908, Ferenczi addressed the topic of education, a first in the psychoanalytic literature (Kuchuck). Garon explores Ferenczi's contributions to understanding female sexuality and the maternal.

Today, empirical psychological research allows us to test some of his theses, for instance, those arising from his trauma theory. Indeed, traumatised children show clear signs of paralysing fear, splitting, and fragmentation; those suffering the worst consequences of trauma are children of mothers who cannot provide sufficient specific help. By the way, it is interesting to note that helping professionals report significantly higher incidence of personal traumatic childhood experiences than other professionals (Dimitrijević).

In the section on the echoes that Ferenczi's oeuvre provoked among his successors, Brennan cites numerous North American analysands of Ferenczi, by whom Ferenczi himself was inspired and educated in return. Among Ferenczi's North American patients whom Brennan discusses, Clara Thompson became an important figure, as a founding mother of the Baltimore-Washington Psychoanalytic Society and the William Alanson White Institute, the latter being an important home of interpersonal psychoanalysis. Thompson is also famous for having been the analyst of Harry Stack Sullivan.

Ferenczi was thus open to different stimuli, and these influenced him in a complex manner. Towards the end of his life, he concentrated on the profound and unique importance of difficult events in one's life: traumas. Trauma is an event that overwhelms the subject, with the result that the memory and internal consequences prevent him from living in a fulfilling manner. Even Freud came back to the importance of trauma in his work on *Moses and Monotheism* (1939a), perhaps as a late echo of Ferenczi's intuition. The impact of trauma is particularly severe and damaging if it happens early, in the first years of life, while the child's abilities to respond are, as yet, insufficient, and he is not yet able to ward off the force of destructiveness ("Thanatos"), such as that of a hostile environment, the neglect of caring persons, bullying, or inadequate and hurtful remarks or gestures. Evidently, if shock occurs later, it is the equilibrium between the traumatising force and the state of the consolidation of the personality at that moment, as well as later (*Nachträglich 54*[2]), that is challenged. If the state of the person (self) is not ready for such an event, the unexpectedness and surprise intensify the impact of an array of traumatising factors. That is "Thanatos", in the sense that Ferenczi meant it (Jiménez Avello).

To mend this wound later by mobilising it is the task of the therapy. For Ferenczi, neither the trauma nor its repair, the psychoanalytic cure, happen in isolation, but involve two (or more) people, in certain cases requiring explicit mutuality. He even wrote that the clinical situation consists of: "two equally terrified children who compare their experiences and, because of their common fate, understand each other completely and instinctively try to comfort each other. Awareness of this shared fate allows the partner to appear as completely harmless, therefore as someone whom one can trust with confidence" (Diary, p. 56).

Little by little, and under the influence of Groddeck, his own illness, and the illnesses of his patients, Ferenczi became interested in the role of the body, of the somatic involvement in the inner life.

After having considered the ideas inspired and practiced by Freud, Ferenczi, and their circle—presented above in a longitudinal, diachronic manner—I propose here to study a sort of cross section, a synchronic perspective. In fact, this perspective reflects, in condensed form, the conflicting forces that arose and determined the subsequent development of psychoanalysis. Thus, in 1924, in my eyes the most important year in this history (Falzeder, 2005, pp. 249–270; Rudnytsky, 2002, p. 142), different insights emerged in the form of no less than four seminal books published that year. They lay out for us different views and present us with potential approaches that have diverse consequences.

The first text: *Thalassa: A Theory of Genitality*, by Ferenczi, was the outcome of a decade-long epistolary exchange with Freud. According to the hypothesis of Robert Kramer (2017), Otto Rank, the director of the "Verlag", would have very much encouraged a hesitant Ferenczi to draft his ideas expressed in *Thalassa* (Fer/Fr, 25 July 1923, p. 110; letter from Freud to Rank, 10 August 1923, in Lieberman & Kramer, 2012, pp. 165–166).

Ferenczi puts the mother at the center of human destiny, in contrast to Freud's preceding theories, of which the primary focus was conflict with the father in the oedipal complex. From this moment, the "pre-genital" dimension—thusly named by Rank—became increasingly important, and would, notably, pave the way for a series of important, innovative works.

Otto Rank's *The Trauma of Birth* (1924), which followed *Thalassa*, presented an expansion of the same theme of the maternal relationship, where the first separation from the mother would determine the later development of the child. Ferenczi writes to Freud that he recalls "the walk during which you shared with me the Rankian discovery (trauma of birth)

2 Can be translated by "in a deferred manner" or "postponed" or simply by "later".

for the first time. ... You accompanied your narration with the remark: ... this is the most significant advance since the discovery of psychoanalysis" (Fr/Fer, 24 March 1924, p. 131).

Fitting together all these new insights, born in clinical practice outside the hitherto established theoretical legacy, raises difficult questions. Therefore, Freud proposed, quite exceptionally, to award a prize to the authors who would elaborate new illuminations on this theme: "The questions to be discussed are how far the technique has influenced the theory and how far they assist or hinder each other at the present time" (Freud, 1919c, p. 270).

Ferenczi and Rank, for reasons of fairness, did not want to present material already discussed with Freud and they withdrew themselves from the competition, although they were the only ones to try to address this issue. Their reflections appear in a collaborative text under the title *Goals for the Development of Psychoanalysis* (1924). Ferenczi and Rank summarised what they considered to be questionable in the development of psychoanalytic practice up to that point, and tried to reorient psychoanalytic practice in the direction of greater freedom and openness to unexpected ideas and insights. According to their thinking, a true dialogue should develop in the cure between the analysand and the analyst, who becomes a partner rather than a mere shadowy passive mirror.

Thereafter, Freud was reluctant to continue to accept these innovations; eventually, he withdrew and distanced himself from them. He probably feared jeopardising the unity of his own inner circle, the "Secret Committee". In fact, after Rank's distancing, his relocation first to Paris and then to the United States, and the deterioration of his relationship with Ferenczi, the unity of this circle ultimately crumbled (Falzeder, 2015, p. 288). Abraham, Eitingon, Sachs, and Jones took on important roles in the leadership of the psychoanalytical movement, organisation, congresses, and journals. Abraham, moreover, published his book the same year (not long before his death, in 1925): *A Short Study of the Development of the Libido*. This work completes the theory of libido, and is the fourth of the influential books published in 1924.

At the same time, women—Anna Freud, Marie Bonaparte, Lou Andreas-Salomé, and Melanie Klein—became increasingly influential.

Some authors (Strachey, 1959; Jones, 1957, *passim*) consider Freud's work *Inhibitions, Symptoms and Anxiety*, published in 1926, as a kind of response to the four seminal books. In this book, however, there is no explicitly quoted consideration of Ferenczi's and Rank's ideas. Moreover, we know that Freud's volume was published by the "Verlag" without Rank (its director!) even knowing it, which deeply hurt him (Kramer, 2017). The confrontation of these five books ended without a comprehensive overview of the various questions, either in the committee or in any congress or publication. When Ferenczi eventually addressed them in his own way in 1933, in Wiesbaden, he did it in opposition to Freud. Rank's later work, emerging after 1926, was also largely ignored—and still is—by parts of the psychoanalytical establishment.

Theory and clinical practice remained in conflict. Freud had the tendency to sometimes forget that psychoanalysis had been conceived by a patient, and that "the merit of the physician lay in the very fact that he was always ready to accept his patient's guidance and to learn from her the new method of healing".[3] Freud himself wrote: "A chance observation showed her physician that she could be relieved of these clouded states of consciousness if she was

3 This description by Ferenczi was quoted by Balint, 1957, p. 238.

induced to express in words the *affective* phantasy by which she was at the moment dominated" (Freud, 1925d, italics added).

Surprisingly, already by 1906, Freud says that analysis was: "actually a '*healing through love*'"[4] (Fr/Ju, 6 December 1906). One year later, at the scientific meeting of the Vienna Psychoanalytic Society, on 1 October 1907 (Nunberg & Federn, 1962, p. 101), Freud repeats this same idea that "the treatment lies in the transference love". However, in the subsequent evolution of Freud's thinking and that of the psychoanalytic movement in the war-time emigration, the factor of "insight" takes prominence, leaving the emotional communication, empathy [*Einfühlung*], a bit on the side. It would become Ferenczi's concern to reintegrate this concept, as he would do for other views (like "seduction"), into the subsequent development of psychoanalytic thinking. Thus, as always, he attempts to reach a balance between new ideas and tradition in the psychoanalytic theory and practice, for the benefit of both the analyst and her analysands.

This balance is what we still sometimes miss today. Perhaps, following Ferenczi's (and Freud's!) path in this respect, continuing to seek a balance between innovation and parts of our valued heritage would be highly beneficial for a rejuvenation of psychoanalytic thinking and practice.

References

Abraham, K. (1924). A short study of the development of the libido. In: *Selected Papers*. London: Hogarth.

Balint, M. (1957). *Problems of Human Pleasure and Behaviour*. London: Hogarth.

Falzeder, E. (2005). 1924: Le traumatisme. In: A. Haynal, E. Falzeder & P. Roazen (Eds.), *Dans les secrets de la psychanalyse et de son histoire*. Paris: PUF.

Falzeder, E. (2015). *Psychoanalytic Filiations*. London: Karnac.

Ferenczi, S. (1924). *Thalassa: A Theory of Genitality*. New York: The Psychoanalytic Quarterly, repr. 1938.

Ferenczi, S., & Rank, O. (1924). *[Goals of] The Development of Psycho-analysis*. New York: Nervous and Mental Disease Publ. (repr. Madison, CT: International Universities Press).

Freud, S. (1919c). A note on psycho-analytic publications and prizes. *S. E., 17*: 267–270. London: Hogarth.

Freud, S. (1925d). An autobiographical study. *S. E., 20*: 3–74. London: Hogarth.

Freud, S. (1939a). *Moses and Monotheism*. *S. E., 23*: 1–138. London: Hogarth.

Haynal, A. (2017). *Encounters with the Irrational: My Story*. New York: IP Books.

Haynal, A., Molnar, M., & de Puymège, G. (1983). *Fanaticism: A Historical and Psychoanalytical Study*. New York: Schocken.

Jones, E. (1957). *Sigmund Freud. Life and Work, Vol. 3*. London: Hogarth.

Kramer, R. (2017). Personal communication.

Lieberman E. J., & Kramer R. (Eds.) (2012). *Inside Psychoanalysis. The Letters of Sigmund Freud & Otto Rank*. Baltimore: Johns Hopkins University Press.

Nunberg, H., & Federn, E. (Eds.) (1962). *Minutes of the Vienna Psycho-Analytic Society. Vol 1, 1906–1908*. New York: International Universities Press.

Rank, O. (1924). *The Trauma of Birth*. New York: Dover, 1994.

Rudnytsky, P. L. (2002). *Reading Psychoanalysis: Freud, Rank, Ferenczi, Groddeck*. New York: Cornell University Press.

Strachey, J. (1959). Introduction. In: S. Freud, *S. E., 20*: 83–86. London: Hogarth.

4 "*Eigentlich eine Heilung durch Liebe*".

Index

Abandonment 116, 126, 134, 137–138, 201–202
Abraham, Karl 12, 14, 26, 54, 59, 66
  Illness and death 63
  Presidency of the IPA 56, 58, 63, 106–107, 209, 244
Abraham, Nicolas 67
Acknowledging errors 157, 167, 175–176, 197, 235
Acting out 75, 155, 246, 257
Active technique 86–87, 91, 93, 153–154, 199, 269, 271, 279, 294
Adaptation 123, 125, 150, 235, 263, 273, 276–278, 280, 285, 287
Addiction 256, 285–286
Adler, Alfred 26, 28, 34, 49, 54–56, 60, 101
Adolescence 140–141, 187, 286
Adorno, Theodor 137, 249
Adverse Childhood Experiences (ACE) 283
Aggression 75, 109, 118, 134–137, 175, 185, 281
Alcoholism 22, 60, 90–91, 123
Alexander, Franz 222
Alien transplants 125, 127, 143, 258
Ambivalence 4, 32, 34, 36, 65, 119, 220
American Journal of Psychiatry 284
American Psychoanalytic Association 56, 60, 181, 217
Amery, Jean 258
Amphimixis 277
Anaclitic depression 123, 146
Analyst 4–5, 22, 26–27, 32–36, 41–42, 49, 63, 78–79, 84, 86–90, 98–99, 101, 104, 106, 110, 114, 116–117, 130–134, 138, 140–142, 144, 147, 151, 155–156, 159–163, 165–167, 171–172, 174–177, 183, 185, 191, 193–194, 196–199, 203, 206–207, 292–294, 296–297
  Abstinence 26, 138, 156, 210
  as a blank screen 156
  as mirror 26, 36, 86, 157, 203, 205, 208, 230, 236, 248, 296
  authority 25–27, 49, 116, 138, 166, 174, 214, 241, 245–246, 249–250, 255, 278, 286
Analytic action 197
Analytic relationship 4, 38, 50, 130–131, 160, 207, 228, 230–231, 292
  traumatizing aspects 4, 130–131, 228, 292
Anarchism 245, 251
Andreas-Salomé, Lou 49, 60, 296
Anna O. (Bertha Pappenheim) 201
Annihilation 187, 258
Anonymity 138, 161
Antisemitism 3
Anti-social behaviour 256–257
Anxiety 34, 42, 66, 86, 106, 119, 135, 142, 144–145, 176, 192–193, 216–217, 270, 285–286, 296
Anzieu, Didier 34
Archaic Super-ego 190–191
Aron, Lewis 30, 38, 166–167, 220, 227–230
Asch, Joseph Jefferson 89, 94
As-if personality 18, 31, 36, 45–46, 48, 50, 72, 89, 91, 93, 98, 116, 118–119, 125, 131–132, 135, 140–141, 143, 148–150, 165–166, 173, 184, 186, 191, 207, 227–228, 236, 245, 252, 255, 258, 285–286, 295
Association for the Advancement of Psychoanalysis 210
  Free Associations 156, 160, 178
Atomization 140–141
Attachment 167, 182, 184–185, 203, 216, 257, 282–288
  and relation to vulnerability to trauma 292
  anxious 207
  avoidant 285
  disorganized (Found only in reference)
  impact of parent's attachment status 184, 287
  secure 257, 285–287
  Status 184, 287
  theory 182, 184–185, 204–205, 257, 293–297
  trauma 292

Attacks on linking (Found only in reference)
Atwood, George 224
Authoritarianism 241, 243, 245–247, 249, 278
  and identification with the aggressor 236, 257–258
  traumatic impact 228, 292
  vs. democracy 245–247
  authoritarian child-rearing practices 249
Authority 25–27, 49, 54–55, 116, 135, 138, 166, 174, 208, 214, 241, 245–246, 249–250, 255, 278, 286
Autoerotism 214n2
Automatic writing 18–19
Autoplastic adaptation and defences 125, 203, 277
Autotomy 125, 130

Balint (Albu), Enid 178
Balint (Szekely-Kovacs), Alice 87, 94, 188, 292
Balint Groups 177
Balint, Michael 29, 36, 38, 45, 48, 51, 57, 86, 102, 116, 167, 171, 173, 178, 182–183, 188, 196, 223, 269, 292–293
  Thrills and Regressions 176
Baltimore-Washington Psychoanalytic Society 88, 294
Beebe, Beatrice 233, 287
Benedek, Therese 93
Benign regression 177
Bibó, István 246
Bibring, Edward 218
Bick, Esther 175
Binswanger, Ludwig 54, 59
Bion, Wilfried xxii
Biopsychosocial perspective 269, 272
Birth 7, 88, 122, 185, 232–233, 236, 244, 250, 256, 262–263, 277, 286, 294–295
Bleuler, Eugen 54, 59, 214
Bodenheimer, Danna 270
Bolshevism 74, 251
Borderline Personality Disorder (Found only in reference)
Borgogno, Franco xiii, xxviii–xxix
Boundaries 4, 13, 20, 46, 61, 202, 206, 215, 232
Bowlby, John 181–182
Brabant, Eva 5, 98
Brain development 257
Brandchaft, Bernard 224
Breger, Louis 3, 25
Brennan, B. William 5, 85
Breuer, Josef 201
Brill, Abraham 54
British Journal of Psychiatry 284
British Psychiatric Society 273
British Psychoanalytical Society 94, 173, 175, 182
Brody, Sandor 93
Brown, Anella 87–88, 183
Brunner, Jose 243
Budapest 3, 5, 9, 12–18, 20, 26, 42–43, 45, 56, 58–59, 107, 173–175, 177, 182, 190, 199, 209, 215, 243, 250–251, 291–292, 294
Bullard, Sr., Dexter 213, 215
Burghölzli hospital 54, 59, 91, 214
Burlingham, Dorothy 87, 91
Butte, Montana 90

Caregiving environment 263
Caretaker self 149–151
Caring envelope 263
Casonato, Marco 18, 22
Cassullo, Gabriele 18–22
Castoriadis, Cornelius 246
Castration 34, 86, 144, 199
Chestnut Lodge 172, 208, 213–218, 293
Chicago Institute of Psychoanalysis 220
Child 122–128, 147–151, 232–237, 262–266
  Abuse 27, 118–119, 137, 180, 204, 283
  Analysis 89, 99, 129, 149, 155, 172, 180, 190–191, 223, 232–236
  guidance clinics 268, 270
  neglect 283
  trauma, physical, behavioural, cognitive, and emotional consequences 124–125, 148–149, 150–151
Clark University 54, 59
Cognitive Theory 184, 187, 234, 284
Communism 74, 245, 250–251
Consciousness 19–20, 34, 65, 115, 131, 160, 253, 255–256, 296
Conspiracy of silence 134
Control Mastery theory 25
Controversial Discussions 180, 188
Co-participatory perspective 269
Coping 53, 120, 129, 232
Countertransference 165–168

Daly, Marcus 90
de Forest, Judy 91
de Forrest, Izette 271
Death instinct (Thanatos) 69, 99, 10, 117, 122–126, 128, 193–194, 236, 255, 259, 293
Defencelessness 118–119
Defences 88, 117–118, 125, 176, 249, 292
Degeneration Theory 21
Delinquency 285
Democracy 245–247
Dependency and autonomy of the baby 144
  Dependency vs. helplessness 143
  Parental attitudes toward 242
Depression 17, 50, 117, 123, 190, 286
Deprivation 126, 183, 222, 249

Deutsch, Felix 62
Deutsch, Helena 20
Devereux, George 20
Dialogue of unconsciouses 159–164, 166, 292
Differences between the sexes 278, 280
Disclosure 49, 157, 161, 207
Disociative Identity Disorder 149, 292
Displacement 193
Dissent in the psychoanalytic movement 54
Dissociation 69, 114, 117, 135–136, 149–151, 183, 185, 198, 216, 256–258, 270, 287, 292
  Impact of parent's dissociative state 147
Dubovitz, Margit 93
Dukes, Géza 93
Dupont, Judith 5, 32, 38, 48, 98–104
Durkheim, Emil 252
Dynamic endopsychic structures 183

Early maternal deprivation 183
Eating disorders 256
Eckstein, Emma 35
Economic theory of drives 153
Education 268–274
Ego 31, 54, 66–68, 74, 78, 99, 115, 117–118, 130, 141–143, 155, 186, 191–194, 203, 222, 250–251
Ego Psychology 67, 99
Eissler, Kurt 88, 109
Eitingon, Max 28, 5, 63
Elasticity 93, 144, 147, 153–158, 196, 208, 214, 217, 234
Ellenberger, Henri 20
Emotional regulation, impaired 242, 282, 285–286
Empathy 26–27, 103, 156, 208, 213, 216, 221, 228–229, 234–236, 242, 256–257, 288, 294, 297
Enactment 69, 165, 228–229, 234–235
Enigmatic messages 202–204
Environment 26, 124–127, 130, 136, 145, 148, 157, 167, 176, 182, 185, 187, 194, 232, 235–236, 242, 246, 258–259, 262–266, 269, 276–278, 295
  Enlightening 242, 263–266
  Facilitating 145, 246, 264
  Traumatic 125, 130
Epidemiology 283
Ethical and boundary issues in the analytic relationship 4, 46
Ethology xxvi, 184
Evacuation 143
Evidence-based psychotherapy 268
Evolution theory 184
Experience 4, 21, 26–27, 46, 65, 67, 69, 72, 76, 79, 86, 88, 93, 98, 101, 103–104, 113, 115–118, 150–151, 155–156, 159–160, 162–163, 165, 167, 174, 176–177, 184–185, 190, 197–199, 204, 206–207, 256–259, 262–263, 266, 272, 277, 287, 292
Experiments in technique xxiv, 214, 292
Exploratory behaviour 286
Expulsion 26, 136, 143
Extrojection 143

Failure of empathy 26, 28
Faimberg, Haydee 203
Fairbairn, Ronald 136, 171, 180–188, 194, 223, 255
  Moral defense 186
False self 141, 187, 293
Falzeder, Ernst 4, 48–51
Family relations 119, 207
Fantasy 8, 27–28, 32, 34–35, 116, 129, 137, 157, 162, 176, 201, 294
Father 8–9, 54–55, 102, 118, 126–127, 150, 171, 173, 177, 251, 253, 264, 270, 276
Fear 31, 35–36, 106, 108, 119, 130, 135, 137, 175–176, 217, 222, 281
Feldmann, Sandor 76
Felszeghy, Mrs. 93
Female psychology 276
Femininity 272, 276, 280
Ferenczi, Sandor 38–47, 72–76, 78–84, 196–200, 262–266
  Allegations of Ferenczi's mental illness 78
  And authenticity 196, 269
  And mutuality 269
  And the IPA 78, 196, 199
    Ferenczi's presidency 38–47
  As social reformer 249–251
  Capitalism vs egalitarianism 241, 253
  Childhood and adolescence 187
    Early sexual life 187
    Family 176
    Father, Bernat 177
      Death and burial 93
    Mother, Róza Eibenschütz 8, 10
      Death and burial 8–10
      Ferenczi's relationship with 8–9
    Schooling 8
    Sexual abuse during childhood 89, 115, 118–119
    Siblings 9–10, 284, 288
  Death 43, 45, 74, 76, 78, 82
  Empathy 208, 288
  Family name (Fraenkel) 6
  Fatal illness (pernicious anemia) 106, 108, 110
  Ferenczi's dreams 35
  Ferenczi's mental health during his final illness 9
  Ideas about parenting 120, 150, 264–265, 272–273

Ideas about societal dynamics 20
Relation of individual and group psychology 54, 258
Influence on education 206–211
Influence on social work 272
Caring attitude 263, 269, 278
Importance of work with disenfranchised populations 242, 268
Short-term therapy 268, 272
Trauma theory 115–120
Use of self 159–164
Jewish heritage 10
Jewishness 38, 215
Originality 63, 67, 113–114
Orthodoxy vs. dissidence and rebelliousness 196–200
Ferenczi as "enfant terrible" 49, 132, 173
Personal qualities 82, 142
Physical and psychosomatic expression and symptoms 78, 82, 117
Political opinions 58, 60, 68, 72, 74
On impatience and the appeal of irrationality 92, 122
On socialism 74, 241, 294
Professorship 174, 251
Progressive social ideals 42, 68, 74
Relationship with Gizella Palos 38–47
Relationship with, and treatment of, Elma Palos 38–47
Social and political attitudes/reformism 22
Authoritarianism vs. individual freedom 243–247
"Socialist individualism"/"liberal socialism" 245
Trauma theory 115–120
Time in New York, 1926–1927 168
University professorship 174, 251
University studies 8
Utopianism 253
Wartime service 85
Work as forensic specialist 85
Work with prostitutes 8, 18, 85
Ferenczi's *Oeuvres complètes* 102
Ferenczi on cynicism 76
Ferenczi's patients 85–95
Adam Empie 94
Alice Balint 87
Alice Lowell (patient B) 87, 90
Anjelika Bijur Frink (Mrs. G.) 90
Antal H 21
Carolyn Newton 94
Clara Thompson (patient Dm.) 94
Col. Claud Dangar Daly 94
Countess Harriot (Hattie) Sigray (patient S.I.) 90
Croatian musician 86
David Eder 94
Edward Kempf 94
Eleanor Morris Burnet 93
Elizabeth Severn (patient R.N.) 87–88, 90–91, 94
Elvin Morton Jellinek 91
Ernest Jones 86, 94
Estelle Maud Cole 94
Ethilda Budgett Meakin-Herford 94
Eugénie Sokolnicka 91
George S. Amsden 94
Grace Potter 94
Izette de Forest (patient Ett.) 87, 90, 94
John Rickman 86, 94
Joseph J. Asch 94
Lewis B. Hill 94
Little rooster man (Little chanticleer, Árpád) 86
Marjorie E. Franklin 94
Melanie Klein 86–87, 94
Michael Balint 86
Natalie Rogers (patient O.S.) 89–90
Roberta "Robbie" Nederhoed (patient N.D./N.H.D.) 89
Rosa K. 86
Rosetta Hurwitz 94
Ruth Gates 89, 91, 94
Theodore "Teddy" Miller (patient U.) 90
William Blumenthal (Joseph Ferdinand) 92
William S. Inman 94
Ferenczi's "prepsychoanalytic" papers
Consciousness and evolution 20
Feminine homosexuality 21
Love in science 21
On the coordinated and the assimilated mental diseases (dual diagnosis) 21
Paranoid dementia 21–22
Spiritism 19–20
Ferenczi's works
A little chanticleer 232
Adaptation of the family to the child 123, 263, 273
Child-analysis in the analysis of adults 89, 99, 155
Clinical Diary 98–104
As foundational document of twenty-first century psychoanalysis 101
Challenges for the reader 101
Publication history 102–103
Spirit 103–104
Confusion of tongues between adults and the child 125
Contra-indications to the active psycho-analytical technique 153
Elasticity of psychoanalytic technique 155, 234

Introjection and transference 18, 194, 279
Male and female, psychoanalytic reflections on the "Theory of Genitality", and on *secondary and tertiary sex differences* 277, 295
Notes and fragments xxix, xxx, 85, 124, 131, 193
On development of the sense of reality 68
On forced fantasies 154
On transitory symptom-construction during the analysis 233
Parallel between Marxism, communism and anarchism 251
Parallel between psychoanalysis and liberal socialism 251–252
Principle of relaxation and neocatharsis 89, 155
Psychoanalysis and education 249
Psychoanalysis and its judicial and sociological relevance 250
Psychoanalysis and social politics 253
Some clinical observations of paranoia and paraphrenia 214
Stages in the development of the sense of reality 123, 188, 192, 250
Thalassa 27, 75, 81–82, 175, 222, 242, 250, 276–277, 281, 295
The adaptation of the family to the child 123, 263, 273
The Development of Psychoanalysis 26, 60, 84, 155, 271, 296
The dream of the clever baby 94, 129
The ice-age of catastrophes 250
The unwelcome child and his death instinct 99, 117, 122–126, 236
First World War/Great War/World War I 3–4, 9, 12, 14–16, 32, 56, 61–62, 68, 73, 173, 216, 241, 244, 250, 270
Fliess, Wilhelm 26, 30
Fonagy, Ivan 287n1
Fonagy, Peter 287n1
Ford, Ora 89
Fortune, Christopher 5, 48, 78–84
Fortunoff Video Archive for Holocaust Testimonies 259
Fragmentation 117–118, 125, 130, 140–146, 151, 183, 193, 256, 282, 286, 292, 294
Frankel, Jay 114, 134–138, 255
Frankfurt school 249
Free School of Social Sciences 72
French Society of Psychoanalysis 196
Freud Archives 88
Freud Museum, London 16, 38, 100
Freud, Anna 38, 45, 102, 118, 123, 180, 191, 232, 234, 294, 296
Freud, Mathilde (Not found in the text)
Freud, Sigmund 15, 38–47
Authoritarian characteristics 46
Cancer 62
Death fantasies and anxiety 34
Fainting spells 34
Freud's cancer 62, 106
Freud's dreams 43
Freud's self-analysis 35–36
Obituary for Ferenczi 56, 67
Personal vulnerabilities 50, 118
Political attitudes and implications of his work 43, 116–117
Freud, Sophie 38, 62
Freud-Ferenczi 3, 38, 45–46, 56, 102, 175, 292
Correspondence 38, 45, 175, 292
And mind-body connection 3
As Ferenczi's personal analysis 30
Self-analysis 3, 18, 30–31, 34–35
Social reformism 22
Traumatic pathogenesis 99, 116–117
Ferenczi's conflict between independence and submission to Freud 79, 82
Ferenczi's "crown prince" fantasy 28, 34–35
Ferenczi's traumatic reactions to Freud 26, 31
Ferenczi's wish for mutuality 168
Final meetings 28
"Kissing technique" letter 106
Palermo incident 30–31, 279
Relationship 3, 46
And the IPA presidency 4, 56, 62
And Ferenczi's conflict regarding Elma and Gizella Palos 38–47
As doing Freud's "dirty work"/or as Freud's spokesman 13
Attitudes toward mutual transparency 98
Declining relations between Freud and Ferenczi in later years 38, 270
Ferenczi's "negative transference" 33–34
Ferenczi's analysis with 30, 38
Ferenczi's role 4, 230
Final meeting 28
Freud's pathologizing Ferenczi 50
Misunderstandings between them 201–205
Related to Freud's refusal to be analyzed by others 99, 101, 175
Trip to America 30, 79
Freudian school of Paris 198
Frigyes, Karthiny 13, 93
Fromm, Erich 50, 87, 213, 215, 248–249
Fromm-Reichman, Frieda 172, 206–209, 213, 215–218
Frustration 81, 115, 123, 153, 156–157, 223
Furor sanandi 114, 177

Galileo Circle 57, 250–251
Gates, Ruth 89, 91, 94

Gay, Peter 29
Gedo, John 221
Genital love 197
Genitality 202, 277
Genocide 257
Gestalt psychology 20
Giefer, Michael 48
Good-enough mother 79, 264
Granoff, Wladimir xxix, 198–199
Greenson, Ralph 217
Greenwich House 271
Groddeck, Georg 5, 8, 48–49, 51, 78–84, 216, 279, 292
  As a "wild analyst" 5, 78
  As Ferenczi's "analyst" and mutual-analysis partner 79
  Correspondence with Ferenczi 78–79, 82
  Criticism and concerns about Ferenczi 81
  Das Es (*The It*) 78, 82
  Ferenczi's Letter of Christmas 1921 78–82
  Friendship with Ferenczi 78–84
  Importance of the mother 79
  Mind-body relationship 79
  Role in fostering Ferenczi's autonomy and productivity 79
  Sanatorium 78, 81, 89
  Trauma 79, 82, 84
  Use of psychoanalysis to treat organic illness 78
Gross, Otto 214
Grosskurth, Phyllis 79, 190
Guilt 43, 98, 101, 119, 127, 136–137, 177, 186, 191, 199, 202, 248, 279, 294
Guntrip, Harry 182
Guyomard, Patrick 199
Gyógyásza (journal, *Therapy*) 18–19, 174

Hajdu, Lilly 14
Hall, G. Stanley 54, 59
Hallucinations 131, 135–136
Hamvas, Bela 246
Harris, Adrienne 166, 227
Harvard University (Found only in reference)
Hate 33, 65, 119, 127, 130, 145, 182, 185
Hatvany, Lajos 93
Haynal, Andre 18, 101, 183, 245, 291–297
Heilprin, Mihaly 6
Heimann, Paula 217
Heitzig School 91
Helplessness 117, 119, 130, 135, 137, 143–144, 209, 216, 232, 242, 266, 277
Hermann, Alice 182
Hermann, Imre 14, 174, 188
Hermeneutics of trust 220, 224, 293
Hevesy, George 16
Heywood, Charles K. 88
Hierarchy 137, 166–167, 269, 293
Hirsch, Irwin 114, 165–168
Hoffer, Willi 180
Hollós, István 58, 215
Holocaust (Shoah) 241, 258
Homans, Peter 243
Homosexuality 21, 41, 55, 60, 242, 279–280
Honesty 3–4, 20, 26, 49, 56, 117, 132, 230
Horace, Frink 90
Horney, Karen 206, 210, 216
Hostility 29, 33, 108, 161, 216
Humiliation 278
Humility (willingness to admit one's own limits) 3, 222, 224, 235
Hungarian Psychoanalytic Society 57, 93, 109, 244–245, 251
Hungarian revolution 12
Hungarian school of psychoanalysis 196
Hungary 12, 14–16, 58, 62, 72, 85, 91, 102, 174, 243–245, 277, 291
Hypochondria 129
Hypocrisy 114–117, 134, 138, 222, 229, 235, 243, 245–250, 259
  And authoritarianism 249
  vs authenticity and playfulness 247
Hysteria 18, 66, 88, 115, 149, 153, 246

Idealization 18, 22
Idealizing transference 18
Identification 134–138
  Alienating 143
Identification with the aggressor 134–138
  Stockholm syndrome 137
Ignotus, Hugo 13, 58, 93
Implicit memory 256
Imre, Kalman 13–14, 171, 174, 188
Incest 216, 229, 282
Independent and Rectified Rite of the Golden Dawn 89
Independent Psychoanalysts 14, 25, 27, 30, 48–49, 54, 56–57, 98
Infantile 21, 26, 66, 69, 91, 114–115, 124, 130, 132, 14, 143–145, 149, 154, 183, 202–204, 216, 235, 245, 249–250, 263, 273, 277
  amnesia 141, 145, 273
  sexuality 114, 154, 202–204
  trauma 69, 130, 143–144, 183, 277
Insight 5, 45, 50, 101, 106, 161, 163, 165, 191, 228, 230, 233, 242, 286, 297
Insight in parents 116, 136
Integration 235, 264, 258, 276
Integrity 118, 120, 259
Internal working models 183, 185, 256
Internalization 117, 130, 144, 165, 257
Internalized violence 255

International Journal of Psychoanalysis (Found only in reference)
International psychoanalytic movement 243
Authoritarianism in 243
International Psychoanalytic Publishing House 251
International Psychoanalytical Association (IPA) 4
Liberal and democratic values 245
Nuremberg Congress, 1909 53–54, 56
Salzburg Congress, 1910 18
Wiesbaden Congress, 1932 49, 56
International Society for Psychological and Social Approaches to Psychosis 284
Internationale Zeitschrift fuer Psychoanalyse 29
Interpersonal relationships 113
Interpersonal school of psychoanalysis 269
Interpretation 11, 26, 30, 36, 66, 69, 89, 101, 116–117, 129–131, 138, 147, 155, 160, 176–177, 213, 228, 234–236, 246
Interpretative approach 234
Intersubjectivity 25, 223–224
Interwar period (not found in the text)
Intrapsychic 20, 117–118, 150, 228–229, 272
Introjection 18, 93, 119, 135–136, 150, 158, 190, 192, 194, 202, 204, 236, 250, 256–257, 279
introjection of guilt 136
introjection of the bad object 194, 257
Introspection 163, 221

Jackson, Edith 209
James, Gerard 91
James, William 20
Janet, Pierre 18, 21, 114, 218
"psychical weakness" 21
Jewish Board of Guardians 271
Johns Hopkins University (Found only in reference)
Jones, Ernest 26, 29, 48, 54, 58–59, 86, 94, 192, 244, 292
Analysis with Ferenczi 42, 86, 87–89, 91, 93–94, 109, 174, 191
Biography of Sigmund Freud 6
Purported anti-semitism 15–16, 62, 174, 180, 244
Relationship with Ferenczi 296
Treatment of Ferenczi in his biography of Freud 13
Joseph, Betty 175, 233
Jozsef, Attila 9, 13
Judaism 15, 173
Jung, Carl Gustav 54, 59, 218
Jung, Emma (not found in the text)

Kallo, Eva 265n1
Kann, Loe 61
Klein, Melanie 24, 58, 86–87, 94, 180–183, 188, 190–194, 232–234, 292, 294, 296
Kohut, Heinz 137, 172, 220–222
Kolnai, Aurel 93, 251
Kosztolányi, Dezso (Dr Moviszter) 13, 93
Kovacs, Vilma 93, 174
Kraepelin, Emil 214
Kristeva, Julia 264
Krudy, Gyula 9

Laboratory of Applied Psychology at Yale University 92
Lacan, Jacques 24, 196–200
Law of the father 198
Mirror stage 205, 248
Lagache, Daniel 198
Laing, Ronald D. 184
Lamarck, Jean-Baptiste 250, 252
Language 8, 13, 29, 103, 122, 130, 142, 149, 175, 190, 201–202, 204–205, 230
Lantos, Barbara 93
Laplanche, Jean 144n1, 172, 201–205, 293
Fundamental Anthropological Situation 202
Laub, Dori 258, 260
Laurvik, John 43
Lay analysis 75, 172, 196, 210
Lear, Jonathan 246
Levenson, Edgar 207–208, 210
Levy, Kata 93
Levy, Lajos 58, 93, 108
Liberal socialism 248–253
Libidinal stages 175
Libido 68, 115, 192, 221, 244, 296
Lichtenberg, Joseph 224
Lieberman, Joseph 48n2, 284, 295
Little, Margaret (not found in the text)
Loewald, Hans 217, 223
Lomas, Peter 51
London Psychoanalytical Society (not found in the text)
Lorand, Sandor 85, 90, 93
Loss 17, 42, 61, 74, 101, 137, 141, 183, 236, 246, 255, 257, 284, 286–287
Lovacs, Sandor (not found in the text)
Love 4, 18, 21, 27–28, 61, 75, 81, 87–89, 93–94, 110, 117, 123, 130, 134, 145, 156, 166–168, 173, 175–176, 182, 184–186, 197, 210, 215, 217, 222, 242, 255, 259, 266, 269, 279–281, 291, 297
Lowell, Alice 87–88, 90, 271
Lowell, Fred (not found in the text)
Lukacs, Georg 14, 174

Mademoiselle X (Erzsebet Molnar) 75
Main, Mary (not found in the text)
Major, Henry 88
Makari, George 53
Malentendu 203
Malignant regression 177

Marai, Sandor 13
Marcuse, Herbert 243
Marianski, Stefan 251n2
Marxism 245, 251–252
Masochism 259, 280
Massive trauma 241, 255, 257–259
Masturbation 91, 194
Maternal 276–281
Mauthausen concentration camp 90
Mayer, Oscar de Lima 89
Medicine 57, 67, 78, 87, 173, 178, 196
Memory 8, 101, 115–116, 141, 157, 256, 273, 295
Menaker, Esther and Tom 271
Menaker, William 271
Mental disorders 118, 282–283, 285, 287
 Causes 287
Mental health clinics 9, 182, 218, 282, 285
Mentalization 288
Mester, Sandor 73
Meszaros, Judit 7, 57, 83, 113, 115–120
Metapsychology 20, 69, 125, 154–155, 184, 258
Meyer, Adolf 88
Middle Group 175, 180–181, 185
Milgram, Stanley 137, 258
Mimicry 124–125, 128
Mind-body relationship 79
Mirroring transference 81, 157, 222, 230, 236
Miskolc 6–11, 15, 291
Mitchell, Stephen 167, 227
Mitscherlich, Alexander and Margarete 102
Moirae 34n1
Moro reflex 66, 69
Moscow Group 56
Mother-infant relationship 120, 277
Mother-infant research 117
Mucci, Clara 241, 255–260
Mutual analysis 159–164
Mutuality 227–231

Narcissism 67, 68–69, 130, 142, 144–145, 150, 175, 222
Narcissistic neurosis 214
Narcissistic splitting 142, 197, 236, 293
National Psychological Association for Psychoanalysis 271
Natural sciences 221
Nazism 253
Necessary environmental conditions for infants 176, 285, 287
Nederhoed, William 89
Negative therapeutic reaction 154, 157
Neglect 36, 82, 99, 119, 123, 177, 199, 251, 256–257, 283, 285, 288, 295
Neocatharsis 26, 89, 106, 144, 147–148, 155, 157, 259
Neuropsychoanalysis 185
Neurotic 27, 35, 50, 62, 66, 68, 75, 89, 102, 115, 134, 141–142, 148, 150, 156, 174, 176, 197, 215
Neutrality 4, 26, 153, 156, 161, 259, 294
New School for Social Research 85, 93–94, 271
New York Psychoanalytic Society 20, 56
New York School of Social Work 271
Newton, Carolyn 94, 270
Nijinsky, Kyra 89–91
Nijinsky, Vaslav 89
Non-interpretive interventions 228
Non-verbal communication xxix

Oakshott, Edna 175
Object 15, 21, 36, 67–68, 117–118, 124, 127, 129–130, 150, 205, 223, 232, 234
Object relations 67–68, 79, 117, 144, 155, 165, 175, 181–184, 188, 192, 194, 223, 257, 269–270
Occult phenomena (telepathy, Spiritism, medianism, animism) 18, 20
Ocnophilia 176
Oedipus complex 191–192, 214, 218, 277–278
Omnipotence 21, 250
Onanism 153–154
Optimal frustration 223
Optimal responsiveness 223
Orange, Donna 172
Orpha 89, 113, 131, 136, 293

Palermo incident 30–31, 279
Palos, Géza 39, 43
Palos Laurvik, Elma 38–47
 Correspondence with Michael Balint 38, 45
 Illness and death 39, 43
 Marriage to John Laurvik 43
 Work for the American Foreign Service 43
Parente, Massimiliano 10
Parenting attitudes (Not found in the text)
Parents 8, 27, 31, 38, 89, 91, 113, 177, 182–183, 184, 191, 202–203, 21, 236, 242, 248, 262, 266, 269
Parents' trust in the baby 266
Paris Psychoanalytical Society 196
Passion 27, 125–126, 264
Passive object love 175
Patient 4, 20–21, 103, 114, 116–117, 151, 201, 203, 258–259, 269, 271–272, 279
Payne, Sylvia 180
Pedersen, Annelisa (not found in the text)
Pembroke Women's College at Brown University 88
Penis 35, 65, 86, 193, 278, 281
Pennsylvania School of Social Work 271
Pernicious anemia 28, 82, 107–109, 167
Perpetrator 116–119, 134, 186, 248, 257, 286, 294

Perrier, Francois 199
Personality disorders 285–286
Perversion 184, 236
Pfeifer, Zsigmond 93
Phenomenology 221
Philobatism 176
Philology 288
Phylogenesis 66–69, 250, 253, 276–277
Pikler, Emmi 241, 264
Play 8, 13, 82, 106, 136, 156, 172, 187, 191, 204, 264, 266, 274
Play-analysis 172
Pleasure principle 68, 119, 124, 150, 192–193, 280, 294
Polanyi, Karoly 14, 57
Polanyi, Mihaly 57
Polymorphous perversion 184, 236
Positivism 155
Post-traumatic Stress Disorder 69
Potter, Grace 94, 270
Pre-genital 276, 295
Premature termination 154
Pre-primal-trauma 145
Preventive pre- and post-natal intervention (not found in the text)
Primary love 175–176, 197
Primary narcissism 175
Primary process 135, 150
Primary sadism 176
Professional hypocrisy (hypocrisy of analysts) 116, 134, 138, 229, 248
Protector self-states 150
Psychic pain 135, 144, 236–237
Psychic phantom 67
Psychological enslavement 134–138
Psychological qualities of the physician 20
Psychology students 288
Psychosis 213–218
Psychosomatics 222
Psychotherapy 6, 20, 118, 127, 157, 174, 177, 213–214, 216, 227
Psychotropic medication 213
Putnam, James Jackson 60, 87

Quantifiable empirical research 185, 242

Rachman, Arnold 107, 207, 209
Racker, Heinrich 20, 217
Rado, Sandor 58, 107, 244
Rank, Otto 25, 59, 89, 108, 155, 228, 263, 269, 271, 292, 295
Rank Veltfort, Helene 48n2
Rape 140, 144, 282, 285
Regression 36, 66, 102–103, 114, 120, 147–148, 151, 209, 253, 277
Regression in the service of the ego 148
Reich, Wilhelm 249
Reik, Theodor 74, 220
Relational psychoanalysis 25, 168, 172, 220, 223–224, 227–231, 270
Relaxation technique 157, 165–167, 270, 279
Remembering 117, 234, 273
Repetition compulsion 66, 69, 155
Replacement child 117
Repression 115, 129, 136, 141–142, 155, 197, 229, 242, 249–250, 253, 273
Resistance 26, 32, 35, 43, 62, 78, 90, 119, 138, 147, 153, 155–157, 214, 227–228, 230, 246
Retraumatization 27, 116, 156
Revesz, Laszlo 93
Revesz-Rado, Erzsebet 93
Rickman, John 86, 94, 175, 180, 292
Robinson, Virginia 271
Roheim, Geza 93
Role of Jews within the psychoanalytic movement 14–15, 17
Rozmarin, Eyal 205
Rudnytsky, Peter 69, 91, 182, 185, 295

Sachs, Hans 59, 61, 174, 296
Sadism 176, 248, 280
Safouan, Moustafa 199
Sander, Louis 223
Schaechter, Miksa 18–19
Schizophrenia Bulletin 284
Schore, Allan 256
Schott, Ada 87, 93, 191
Schreber case 42
Schur, Max 34
Scientific materialism 19
Scientism 210
Scott, Clifford M. 180
Searles, Harold 217
Second World War 14, 40, 45, 109, 172, 180, 255, 258
Secret Committee 4, 49, 59–63, 181, 296
Seduction 201–205
Seinfeld, Jeffrey 270
Self 159–164, 220–224
Self Psychology 25, 157, 165, 167, 172, 181, 188, 220–224
Self-analysis, Ferenczi's 3, 30–31
Self-esteem 28, 119, 284
Selfobjects 222
Sense of reality 68, 123–124, 187–188, 192, 222, 250
Severn, Elizabeth 51, 79, 81, 87–88, 90–91, 94, 118, 131, 157, 161, 166, 177, 279, 292
Severn, Margaret 73n1
Sexuality 276–281
Shame 98, 119, 137, 191
Shapiro, Sue 88, 90, 208–209
Short-term dynamic psychotherapy 157
Sigray, Margit 90

Silver, Ann-Louise 213–218
Simmel, Ernst 66
Sincerity 3, 20, 27, 98–99, 134, 207, 262, 266, 279, 292
Smith, Ely Jeliffe 89
Smuts, Jan C. 20
Social equality 245, 247
Social work 268–274
Societe Medicale Balint 178
Society for Psychical Research in London 88–89
Society of Freudian Psychoanalysis 200
Sphincter morality 190–191
Spielrein, Sabina 54
Splits in the psychoanalytic movement 58
Splitting 140–146
Stalinism 253
Stanford Prison Experiment 137
Stanton, Martin 87
Stein, Fulop 59
Stekel, Wilhelm 28, 54–56, 60
Stern, Daniel 223
Stern, Donnel 207
Stolorow, Robert 224
Strean, Herbert 270
Stress response 256
  Hyperarousal 256
Strozier, Charles 220, 220n3
Subjectivity 4, 46, 86, 94, 162, 165–166, 228, 230, 236, 255
Sublimation 184, 245, 250
Suggestion (hypnosis and trance) 18, 20
Sullivan, Harry Stack 88, 165, 172, 213, 215, 269, 294
Super-ego 191–192, 203
Suttie, Ian D. 182, 216, 223
Suttie, Jane 183
Symbolism 92, 190, 192–193, 281
Symbolization 130, 144–145, 156, 192, 194
Szanto, Agnes 265n1
Szilegyi, Geza 39, 43, 50, 93

Tact 26, 229, 234–236
Taft, Jessie 271
Tardos, Anna 265n1
Tausk, Viktor 213
Tavistock Institute 175, 177–178
Technical parameter 154
Technique 153–158, 159–164
Teller, Edward 17
Tenderness 27, 117, 119, 122, 130, 134, 151, 156–157, 171, 201–204, 216, 223, 236, 264, 266, 285
Teratoma 148
Terrorism of suffering 114, 119, 134, 137, 144, 203, 287
The Hague congress 62, 78
Therapeutic process 160, 228
Thery, Irene 263
Thompson, Clara 87, 90–91, 94, 109, 166, 168, 172, 213, 215, 269, 271, 292, 294
Thompson, Joseph Cheesman 88
Tic 194
Time-limited psychotherapy 269
Toilet training 263, 273
Torok, Maria 67
Torture 258–259
  Consequences in survivors 259
Tosone, Carol 269–270
Training analysis 86, 94, 174, 198–199, 215, 234
Transference 18, 20, 31, 33–34, 46, 65, 69, 78–79, 117, 130, 140, 201, 206–207, 214, 216, 228, 233–234, 278–279, 294, 297
  And countertransference 20, 46, 102, 155–156, 159, 206, 228, 278
  As the total situation 233
Transition paradigm (in political theory) 247
Trauma 4–5, 27, 65–66, 102, 150–151, 201–202, 204, 209–210, 215, 217, 220, 224, 228, 229–230
  As cause of borderline disorders 256
  As unconscious organizing principle 258
  Continuum of severity 248
  Cumulative 258
  Cycle of (intergenerational transmission of, implantation of) 256
  Extreme 209
  Loneliness 259
  Loss of internal objects 233
  Loss of mental functions 66
  Massive (collective) 241, 255, 257–259
  Mitigating (healing) factors 172
    Empathic, holding environment 259
    Ethical attitude and commitment of therapist 259
    Reconstruction of meaning 259
    Social community 259
    Testimonial community 260
    Witnessing 258–259
  Restoration of historical truth 260
  Transgenerational 120
  Vicarious 258
Traumatic progression (precocious maturity) 113, 120, 131, 136, 266
Traumatogenic objects 177
Two-person psychology xxvii

Unconscious 3, 20, 32, 35, 86–87, 101, 113, 115, 117–119, 155, 159–160, 201–203, 258, 263–264, 273, 281, 292
  Communication 161
  Dialogue xxvi
  Fantasy 87, 201, 203
Unwelcome child 122–128

Urban families 263
Urbantschitsch, Rudolf 72

Vamos, Julianna 262–266
Vanderbilt, Gladys 90
Vass, Ilona 90
Verification of hypotheses 282–288
Victim 82, 118–119, 126, 136, 143, 216, 256–258, 272, 282
Victim-persecutor split 256–258
Vienna 3, 8–9, 12, 14–15, 18, 55–58, 106–107, 172, 180, 213, 220, 251, 270–271, 297
  Psychoanalytic Society and Institute 56–57
Vietnam War 67
Vincze, Maria 265n1
Viola Wertheim, Bernard 90
Violence 31, 41, 69, 118, 134, 248–253
  Cycle of 258
  Role of support in mitigating 251
  State-organized 253
Voice of the other 203
von Karman, Theodor 16
von Neumann, John 14, 17
von Osten and Krall experiments with "clever horses" 72

Waelder, Robert 108
Wagner-Jauregg, Julius 68
Waite, Arthur E. 89
Wallenberg, Raoul 45
War Neurosis (shell shock) 4, 66, 68
Washington Psychoanalytic Association 208
Weaning 145, 263
Wednesday Psychological Society 53
Welcoming babies in contemporary Western families 241
Wertheim family 90
White, William Alanson 88, 172, 208–210, 213, 294
Wigner, Eugene 17
William Alanson White Institute 88, 172, 209–210, 213, 294
Winnicott, Donald Woods 114, 120, 141, 145, 167, 171, 180–188, 203, 217, 220, 223, 232, 234–236, 246, 264, 266, 277, 293
  Democracy 246–247
  Facilitating Environment 145, 246
  Transitional Space 235
  True/False Self 181, 183, 187
Wise Baby 129–133
Wittels, Fritz 53
Wolstein, Benjamin 165, 206–210, 228
Worcester State Hospital 92
Working-through 21, 216, 234
World Health Organization 92

Zentralblatt für Psychoanalyse 55
Zimbardo, Philip 137

Made in the USA
Middletown, DE
28 July 2021

44939468R00190